UNIVERSITY LIBRARY
UNIVERSITY OF ILLINOIS AT URBANA-CHAMPAIGN

The person charging this material is responsible for its renewal or return to the library on or before the due date. The minimum fee for a lost item is **$125.00, $300.00** for bound journals.

Theft, mutilation, and underlining of books are reasons for disciplinary action and may result in dismissal from the University. *Please note: self-stick notes may result in torn pages and lift some inks.*

Renew via the Telephone Center at 217-333-8400, 846-262-1510 (toll-free) or circlib@uiuc.edu.
Renew online by choosing the **My Account** option at: **http://www.library.uiuc.edu/catalog/**

History of Music in Russia from Antiquity to 1800

Nikolai Findeizen (1868–1928).

History of Music
in Russia from
Antiquity to 1800

VOLUME 1
From Antiquity to the Beginning
of the Eighteenth Century

VOLUME 2
The Eighteenth Century

---

*This work was brought to publication with
the generous support of
Joseph Bloch.*

RUSSIAN MUSIC STUDIES
Malcolm Hamrick Brown, founding editor

History of Music in Russia from Antiquity to 1800

VOLUME I

From Antiquity to the Beginning
of the Eighteenth Century

Nikolai Findeizen

TRANSLATION BY
Samuel William Pring

EDITED AND ANNOTATED BY
Miloš Velimirović and Claudia R. Jensen

WITH THE ASSISTANCE OF
MALCOLM HAMRICK BROWN AND
DANIEL C. WAUGH

INDIANA UNIVERSITY PRESS
BLOOMINGTON AND INDIANAPOLIS

This book is a publication of

Indiana University Press
601 North Morton Street
Bloomington, IN 47404-3797 USA

http://iupress.indiana.edu

Telephone orders	800-842-6796
Fax orders	812-855-7931
Orders by e-mail	iuporder@indiana.edu

The paper used in this publication meets the minimum requirements of American National Standard for Information Sciences—Permanence of Paper for Printed Library Materials, ANSI Z39.48-1984.

Manufactured in the United States of America

Library of Congress Cataloging-in-Publication Data

Findeizen, N. F. (Nikolai Fedorovich), 1868–1928.
[Ocherki po istorii muzyki v Rossii. English]
History of music in Russia from antiquity to 1800 / Nikolai Findeizen ; translation by Samuel William Pring ; edited and annotated by Miloš Velimirović and Claudia R. Jensen with the assistance of Malcolm Hamrick Brown and Daniel C. Waugh.
v. cm. — (Russian music studies)
Includes bibliographical references and index.
Contents: Vol. 1. From antiquity to the beginning of the eighteenth century. Introduction. The predecessors of the Slavs ; Pagan Rus' ; Kievan Rus' ; Novgorod the Great ; The activities of the Skomorokhi in Russia ; Music and musical instruments in Russian miniatures, woodcuts, and glossaries ; A survey of old Russian folk instruments ; Music in ancient Moscow (fifteenth and sixteenth centuries) ; Music in the monastery. Chashi (toasts). Bell ringing. Sacred performances (sixteenth and seventeenth centuries) ; Music in court life in the seventeenth century ; A brief survey of singers, composers, and music theorists of the sixteenth and seventeenth centuries ; Music and theater in the age of Peter the Great — Vol. 2. The eighteenth century. Music and theater, 1730–1740 ; Music in court life during the reigns of Elizabeth Petrovna and Catherine II ; Music in Russia's domestic life during the second half of the eighteenth century ; The Russian horn band ; Music in Russian public life during the second half of the eighteenth century ; Musical creativity in Russia during the eighteenth century ; Literature about music, publishers and sellers of sheet music, instrument makers and merchants.
ISBN-13: 978-0-253-34825-8 (v. 1 : cloth : alk. paper)
ISBN-13: 978-0-253-34826-5 (v. 2 : cloth : alk. paper) 1. Music—Russia—History and criticism. I. Pring, Samuel William. II. Velimirović, Miloš. III. Jensen, Claudia Rae. IV. Title.
ML300.F413 2008
780.947—dc22

2006037057

1 2 3 4 5 13 12 11 10 09 08

Book layout and composition: Alcorn Publication Design

These volumes are dedicated, with our thanks, to Joseph Bloch
and to Elizabeth (from M.V.) and to Brad, Anna, and Becky (from C.R.J.)
for their support and patience throughout.

Contents

Editors' Introduction to Volume 1   xi

List of Abbreviations   xvii

Author's Preface   xxi

1. Introduction: The Predecessors of the Slavs   1
2. Pagan Rus'   15
3. Kievan Rus'   33
4. Novgorod the Great   79
5. The Activities of the *Skomorokhi* in Russia   113
6. Music and Musical Instruments in Russian Miniatures,
   Woodcuts, and Glossaries   137
7. A Survey of Old Russian Folk Instruments   163
8. Music in Ancient Moscow
   (Fifteenth and Sixteenth Centuries)   191
9. Music in the Monastery. *Chashi* (Toasts). Bell Ringing.
   Sacred Performances (Sixteenth and Seventeenth Centuries)   205
10. Music in Court Life in the Seventeenth Century   245
11. A Brief Survey of Singers, Composers, and Music Theorists
    of the Sixteenth and Seventeenth Centuries   259
12. Music and Theater in the Age of Peter the Great   267

Music Appendix   287

Notes   299

Volume 1 Bibliography   417

Index   453

Editors' Introduction to Volume 1

This work is a complete translation of Nikolai Findeizen's *Ocherki po istorii muzyki v Rossii* (1928), a pathbreaking work which, in its scope and command of primary sources, and in its curiosity and generosity of scholarly inquiry, has remained a cornerstone for all subsequent studies of Russian music. A project of this nature is a collaboration from the outset. Findeizen, throughout his voluminous, even legendary, notes offers gracious thanks to the many scholars who contributed to his work, and it is a pleasure for us, the joint editors of this volume, to do the same. We must acknowledge, first and foremost, the heroic work of the original translator, Samuel William Pring, whose efforts and solutions to the many difficulties in this text were truly inspiring; our later work was in the nature of a dialogue not only with Findeizen but also with Pring, who managed to retain the author's own voice and spirit in his translation. Our work was also made possible by the farsighted generosity, patience, and skill of an important group of people who realized the importance of Findeizen's and Pring's labors and who made it possible to bring them to light. Our deepest gratitude goes to Joseph Bloch, who not only understood the importance of Findeizen's work but was willing to grant the financial support necessary to publish this English translation. We owe him many thanks for his foresight and generosity, and we dedicate this edition to him. We owe Malcolm Brown, editor of the Russian Music Series at Indiana University Press, unending thanks for his advice, timely prodding, and boundless patience. He was willing to discuss any passage, to ponder every thicket of translation, and, quite simply, his efforts made this project possible. Daniel C. Waugh, of the University of Washington, contributed to almost every page of this work, and his efforts in identifying manuscripts and puzzling out chronicle references gave this edition the same kind of scholarly rigor he has demonstrated throughout his career; we offer him our profound thanks. Finally, the editors at Indiana University Press have also given us nothing but patience and encouragement in our work on this difficult and complex text, and our thanks go to Janet Rabinowitch and her predecessor, Jeffrey Ankrom, the most supportive and tolerant editors we can imagine. We also wish to thank Rita Bernhard for her thoughtful and insightful work as copyeditor on this enormous project.

Although the editorial responsibilities for this volume rest with us, many scholars have given generously of their time and expertise, and it is a pleasure to acknowledge their contributions. We have tested the patience and generosity of Gregory Myers time and time again; his work on the most difficult passages of this volume and his willingness to answer voluminous e-mail messages on details of medieval Russian syntax put us greatly in his debt. Elena Dubinets has spent countless hours pouring over the text, patiently explaining subtleties of grammar and pronunciation; the work would not have been possible without her help. Dan Newton, of the University of Washington, has also invested many hours in solving riddles of translation, rendering a sometimes dense Russian prose into lucid English with cheerfulness and the requisite patience. Many have shared their knowledge of Russian music and Russian culture in our work on this far-ranging text, and to Olga Dolskaya, of the Conservatory at the University of Kansas, Missouri, and to Galina Averina, our thanks can be expressed only inadequately for the time and advice they have so willingly given. Jack Haney, of the University of Washington, contributed greatly to our work on the medieval *bylina* texts, responding generously to multiple questions and confirmations, as did Geoffrey Schwartz, also of the University of Washington, who translated the Ukrainian texts in chapter 7. We also thank the University of Washington Department of Slavic Languages and the School of Music for their support of this project.

Findeizen's work covers an enormous range of topics, and we have benefited greatly from the specialized knowledge so readily shared by the scholarly community. Edward Williams shared his incomparable knowledge of Russian bells and bell ringing in a series of detailed, lucid communications, and his work clarified many passages in this text; Robert Karpiak, of the University of Waterloo, worked patiently with us on both volumes of Findeizen's text in explaining nuances of keyboard terminology, as did Wanda Griffiths; and Elizabeth Sander generously gave her time and expertise in chapter 12 of this volume, sharing her work on the Bergholz diary—all these scholars enriched this project greatly. Alexander Levitsky and Elizabeth Sander also contributed graciously to the translations of the *kant* texts in chapter 12. For many years Martha Lahana has been most generous in sharing her expertise and work on Artemon Matveev and on late-seventeenth-century Muscovite culture, and she supplied many important printed and manuscript sources, as well as cheerful expert advice. Our understanding of early Russian terminology and sources has been deepened by contributions from Irina Lozovaia in Moscow, who graciously and frequently responded to our queries, and from Nicolas Schidlovsky, who was equally generous with his time. Thomas Mathiesen, at Indiana University, clarified issues of the Greek and Latin terminology in the volume, and George-Julius Papadopoulos was endlessly patient in his explanations of Greek accents, his discovery of crucial etymologies, and his solid advice—we owe him our deepest thanks for his work on both volumes. Our scholarly net was cast far and wide, and we thank Henry Cooper, at Indiana University, for his willing explanations of early Russian vocabulary; Isolde Thyrêt, of Kent State University, and Vladimir Morosan, of Musica Russica Press, for their contributions to our bibliography; and Michael Biggins, the Slavic librarian at the University of Washington, for his bibliographic wizardry over the course of many years. Nina Polina advised us on questions of translation, and Ben Albritton on terminology relating to musical instruments.

Of course, the one figure conspicuously absent in our listing above is that of Nikolai Fyodorovich Findeizen (1868–1928), who was one of the towering figures in Russian and Soviet music and musicology. Although his full biography remains to be written, we wish to provide some background on Findeizen's labors on this book. He began his career as a writer early on, in his twenties, after a general education in music. It was to be a remarkably prolific career; the listings in the authoritative catalog *Kto pisal o muzyke* [Who wrote about music] lists more than three hundred works, large and small, scholarly and popular, written over the course of nearly forty years. One of his most important contributions was the establishment of the *Russkaia muzykal'naia gazeta* [Russian musical gazette], which he started in 1894 and which ran to 1918; this was the most significant musical journal of its time, covering concert life and modern composers, and also including historical studies, many of which Findeizen wrote himself. Findeizen was deeply involved with contemporary musical life and found a kindred spirit in the figure of the important music and art critic Vladimir Vasil'evich Stasov (1824–1906), whom he met shortly before starting his journal. From 1899 Findeizen was a corresponding member of the International Music Society, headquartered in Berlin, and in 1909, together with Aleksandr Il'ich Ziloti (1863–1945) and Stanislav Maksimovich Sonki (1853–1941), he founded a Society of Friends of Music, which he headed from 1911.

Findeizen's long labors on his *Ocherki* are outlined in a collection of his papers, now at the Glinka Museum as f. 87, nos. 1067 (a small diary), 1068 (a larger diary with entries beginning ca. 1920), and 1069 (drafts of letters), which Miloš Velimirović was able to examine in 1991. No. 1069 contains a draft of a letter from May 1924 addressed to Michel-Dimitri Calvocoressi (1877–1944), the well-known writer on music residing at the time in England, which gives a sense of the lengthy gestation period of the *Ocherki*. Findeizen writes: "In 1918 I completed a work conceived thirty years ago, going through a period of collecting materials and sources. That is the *History of Music in Russia in the 17th and 18th Centuries*. Then, in 1919, I was assigned to the chair of History of Music in Russia in the Archaeological Institute (now the Archaeological Division of the University). I teach a new course on musical archaeology, the earliest period of Old Russia (before the seventeenth century) and in the last two years a course on musical paleography (history of Russian chant notation)." Findeizen wonders about the possibility of having this book translated, estimating that it might comprise around 750 pages, which is just over the length of only one of the two volumes he eventually produced. He included a proposed list of chapters, which corresponds roughly to the content of the final volumes but which lacks some of the ethnographic elements he was to uncover in the course of his work at the Archaeological Institute, which he mentioned in his letter to Calvocoressi. Thus, as of 1924, the proposed book lacked chapters on the *skomorokhi* (itinerant entertainers) and on musical instruments in early Russia (chapters 5–7 in the final version), and differed in other, smaller details of organization and content.

Plans for an English-language version of the *Ocherki* were discussed almost immediately, and in June 1924 Findeizen writes that he had sent Calvocoressi two sample chapters for translation. On September 14, in a letter in which Findeizen enclosed a report for the *Monthly Musical Record*, he notes that he had taken his first English lesson. By October 1925 Findeizen already writes a letter in English, accompanying an article to the *Musical Times*.

Findeizen's links to the English musical press in the 1920s reveal early contacts with the original translator of the present edition, Samuel William Pring (1866–1954), an amateur musician and polymath whose passion for Russian music, little known in England at the time, led him to learn the language on his own in order to pursue his interest in the subject. By the 1920s Pring had already translated many works on Russian music for the British musical press, so naturally he would have known of, and been interested in, Findeizen's writings. Pring is associated with some of the earliest appearances of Findeizen's name in English-language sources. Findeizen first appeared in British music periodicals in 1925, when Calvocoressi reviewed his book on Dargomyzhskii in the *Musical Times* (vol. 66, p. 45). His name again appeared in the same journal in 1928, when the *Ocherki* was mentioned in a column titled "The Musician's Bookshelf" in a note signed "S.W.P." An obituary appeared in the journal that same year. Earlier the *Monthly Musical Record* had published an article by Findeizen, "The Early Days of Chamber Music in Russia" (no. 55 [1925]: 262–63 and 292–93); in it, Calvocoressi, the translator, noted that it was an excerpt from a longer article written for *Cobbett's Cyclopedia*. Indeed, Findeizen's article on Russian chamber music does appear in volume 2 of *Cobbett's Cyclopedic Survey of Chamber Music* (1930), where the editor added a short note: "The remainder of Mr. Findeisen's [*sic*] interesting article deals with the output of native composers during the period 1860–1920. These are treated in detail, under their own names in the *Cyclopedia*. It is with great regret that I have to add that our contributor died after an operation in September 1928." An examination of Cobbett's volumes would thus reveal more of Findeizen's English-language publications. Findeizen's works also appeared in the *Monthly Musical Record* in an article on Borodin in 1927 (vol. 57) and in a note about the Leningrad Philharmonic's upcoming season (vol. 28 [1928]), both translated by Pring. A brief notice of Findeizen's death appeared later that year.

In addition to his early efforts at making his work known in the English-language press, Findeizen also recorded his attempts and frustrations at getting his work published in Russia. According to one of his diaries (no. 1068), he had received proofs of the first fascicles of volume 1 from the Music Section of the State Publishing House in March 1927 after a delay of three months. He was apparently still continuing to work on the text, however, for in that same month he records his irritation at being unable to acquire photographs of the Kupriianov leaflets from the Academy of Sciences, although he had requested them three months earlier—it seems they had been temporarily misplaced! Typesetting began only in May, and in August 1927 Findeizen remarked that the first fascicle was "officially set" in type.

Just after this date the diaries reveal Findeizen's declining health. In October 1927 he writes that he felt ill and that for the first time in his life he is "tired of work." Eight days later, however, he delivered to the press the text of the second fascicle of the *Ocherki*. His health continued to decline, and his diaries include disconnected sentences: "tortured nerves," "went to rest," "Stukkel diabetics." He continued his work nevertheless. Findeizen noted that, in spite of "a lot of unpleasantness and troubles," he was still working, although he was forced to pay a proofreader to assist him. He continued his research on volume 2 at the same time, finally acquiring only in that year a copy of the Madonis *Symphonies* (1738) through the efforts of the distinguished Ukrainian folk music collector and scholar Kliment Vasil'evich Kvitka (1880–1953).

A copy of the first fascicle of the *Ocherki* was finally sent to the Censorship Office only in February 1928, at which time Findeizen remarked: "Already thirteen months spent on this fascicle and a lot of blood and nerves did it cost me!" He had two copies of the first fascicle delivered to the State Publishing House later that month, and evidently the presses started rolling at that time. He also received proofs of the second and part of the third fascicle that month, with the comment: "The press work is getting worse and worse."

His health continued to deteriorate. The diary entries end in March 1928, but, according to the obituary by Zinaida F. Savelova, Findeizen spent the summer of 1928 at the Tchaikovskii Museum at Klin, near Moscow, where he consulted with physicians who recommended an immediate operation. His condition was not thought to be life-threatening, yet he died soon after the surgery, on September 20, in Leningrad. According to the obituary, on that same day A. N. Iurovskii, who was in charge of the Music Section of the State Publishing House, received a telegram informing him of Findeizen's death; a few days later Iurovskii received a letter Findeizen had written on the eve of the operation in which he stated that, having finished the final editing of his *Ocherki*, he was about to undergo surgery. Although, he writes, the physicians had assured him that the operation was not a serious one, he was prepared for anything and thus wished to express his personal thanks to Iurovskii for the publication of his last work. The first volume and part of the second volume were published in 1928, and the remaining fascicles of the second volume in 1929. The work, then, was truly Findeizen's scholarly testament.

Our editorial procedures in this translation are fairly straightforward. All editorial emendations and corrections are enclosed in square brackets and the notes to each chapter begin with a brief essay providing updated information on bibliography and current scholarship. In a few cases, we have supplied corrected or additional references to page numbers, or full bibliographic references for Findeizen's notes; this kind of information is not indicated by square brackets. It has not been possible to verify all of Findeizen's page references and we have not attempted to do so systematically. We have generally followed Findeizen's footnote placement fairly closely in the translation, facilitating comparisons with the original volumes. Added footnotes are indicated by capital letters, thus note 1 is Findeizen's, note 1A is our addition. We have been able to identify most of Findeizen's sources, but for more information see the note to the bibliography.

Transliteration, always a difficult, even vexing, problem, follows the Library of Congress system, which we have generally adhered to rigorously. Our twin goals have been accuracy and consistency in rendering the complex terminology and references in Findeizen's text; a strict transliteration facilitates comparisons with other sources, whether in Russian or English, and allows for ready identification of bibliographic references in the many on-line databases now available. A few exceptions, of course, remain. The stressed *e*, when it is pronounced as *yo*, is indicated here for common Russian names, for example, Fyodor (instead of Fedor) or Pyotr (instead of Petr); names of Russian rulers are designated by their familiar Latin versions (Peter I, Catherine II, and so forth), and familiar cities and terms are treated in the same manner (Moscow instead of Moskva, kopeck instead of *kopeika*); and names of liturgical books and a few other proper names are transliterated in a somewhat simplified manner, thus Stikhirar instead of Stikhirar' or Igor instead of Igor'. Otherwise the Russian soft sign has been retained throughout and is indicated by an apostrophe (e.g., *sopel'*) requiring a softening of the previous consonant. The letters я and ю have been strictly rendered as ia and iu throughout, thus Iurii (instead of Yurii).

The comments we have supplied, in the form of *addenda et corrigenda*, by no means exhaust everything that might be added to Findeizen's original text. Although Findeizen's writing includes some unintended slips of the pen, the sheer volume and breadth of his work are indeed inspiring considering the time and circumstances under which he labored so valiantly—literally to his last breath—to see this work in print. It is only natural that modern research has uncovered data unknown to this indefatigable student and writer, and Findeizen himself would certainly have made some of the corrections and emendations we have supplied had he lived and had he had access to a broader spectrum of foreign source material (not to mention on-line databases and catalogs!). Yet anyone who reads this text, from the first page to the last, cannot but feel admiration for Findeizen's persistence and devotion, which are manifest on every page of this, his magnum opus. It is our hope that this volume will inspire others to become involved in the study of this extremely rich Russian musical heritage, which has too long been ignored by too many and viewed as outside the mainstream of European culture, undoubtedly owing to that invisible yet still powerful "linguistic Iron Curtain." This volume proves to the reader how wrong that attitude was and remains.

Miloš Velimirović
Claudia R. Jensen

Abbreviations

ADIT — *Arkhiv Direktsii Imperatorskikh teatrov* [Archive of the Directorate of Imperial Theaters]. St. Petersburg: Direktsiia Imperatorskikh teatrov, 1892.

AE — *Arkheograficheskii ezhegodnik* [Archaeographic annual]. 1958–.

BLDR — *Biblioteka literatury drevnei Rusi* [A library of the literature of ancient Rus']. Edited by D. S. Likhachev et al. 11 vols. to date. St. Petersburg: Nauka, 1997–.

BSovE — *Bol'shaia sovetskaia entsiklopediia* [Great Soviet encyclopedia]. 65 vols. Moscow: Sovetskaia entsiklopediia, 1926–47.

ChOIDR — *Chteniia v Imperatorskom obshchestve istorii i drevnostei rossiiskikh pri Moskovskom universitete* [Readings of the Imperial Society of Russian History and Antiquities at Moscow University]. 1846–1918.

ES-BE — *Entsiklopedicheskii slovar'* [Encyclopedic dictionary]. 82 vols. plus appendixes. Leipzig: F. A. Brokgauz; St. Petersburg: I. A. Efron, 1890–1904.

EU — *Encyclopedia of Ukraine.* 6 vols. Toronto: University of Toronto Press and Canadian Institute of Ukrainian Studies Press, 1984–2001.

GIM — Gosudarstvennyi istoricheskii muzei [State Historical Museum], Moscow.

GSE — *Great Soviet Encyclopedia* [English translation of *BSovE*, 3rd ed.]. 31 vols. plus index. New York: Macmillan, 1973–82. Each volume was translated immediately after the publication of the Russian original, so the articles appear in the order of the Russian alphabet.

IRM — *Istoriia russkoi muzyki* [History of Russian music]. Edited by Iu. V. Keldysh et al. Moscow: Muzyka; references to vols. 1 (1983), 2 (1984), 3 (1985), 4 (1986), and 5 (1988).

IRMNO — *Istoriia russkoi muzyki v notnykh obraztsakh* [A history of Russian music in musical examples]. Edited by S. L. Ginzburg. 2nd ed., vol. 1. Moscow: Muzyka, 1968; 1st ed., vol. 2. Moscow: Gosudarstvennoe muzykal'noe izdatel'stvo, 1949.

JAMS — *Journal of the American Musicological Society.*

LPC — *A Collection of Russian Folk Songs by Nikolai Lvov and Ivan Prach,* by

Margarita Mazo. Edited by Malcolm Hamrick Brown. Russian Music Studies 13. Ann Arbor: UMI Research Press, 1987.

MA   Mooser, R.-Aloys. *Annales de la musique et des musiciens en Russie au XVIIIe siècle.* 3 vols. Geneva: Mont-Blanc, [1948–51].

MO   Mooser, R.-Aloys. *Opéras, intermezzos, ballets, cantatas, oratorios joués en Russie durant le XVIIIe siècle.* Bâle: Bärenreiter, [1964].

ME   *Muzykal'naia entsiklopediia* [Musical encyclopedia]. 6 vols. Moscow: Sovetskaia entsiklopediia–Sovetskii kompozitor, 1973–82.

MERSH   *Modern Encyclopedia of Russian and Soviet History.* Edited by Joseph L. Wieczynski. 60 vols. to date. Gulf Breeze, Fla.: Academic International Press, 1976–.

MGG   *Die Musik in Geschichte und Gegenwart.* 14 vols. plus appendixes. Kassell, 1949–69.

Mosk. vedomosti   *Moskovskie vedomosti* [Moscow gazette; newspaper].

MP   *Muzykal'nyi Peterburg: Entsiklopedicheskii slovar'* [Musical Petersburg: An encyclopedic dictionary]. Edited by A. L. Porfir'eva. 7 vols. St. Petersburg: Kompozitor, 1996–.

MQ   *Musical Quarterly*

NG2   *New Grove Dictionary of Music and Musicians.* 2nd ed., 29 vols. New York: Grove's Dictionaries, 2001; available as Grove Music Online, ed. L. Macy, at www.grovemusic.com.

OLDP   *Obshchestvo liubitelei drevnei pis'mennosti* [Society of Friends of Old Literature].

PKNO   *Pamiatniki kul'tury. Novye otkrytiia* [Monuments of culture. New discoveries]. Annual publication since 1974, with some missed years. Leningrad/St. Petersburg and Moscow: various publishers.

PLDR   *Pamiatniki literatury drevnei Rusi* [Monuments of literature of ancient Rus']. Moscow: Khudozhestvennaia literatura, 1987–.

PRMI   *Pamiatniki russkogo muzykal'nogo iskusstva* [Monuments of Russian musical art]. 11 vols. 1972–.

PSRL   *Polnoe sobranie russkikh letopisei* [Complete collection of Russian chronicles]. 40 vols. to date. 1841 to the present, with various reprints and re-edited volumes.

PVL   *Povest' vremennykh let po lavrent'evskoi letopisi* [The tale of bygone years, according to the Laurentian manuscript]. Edited by D. S. Likhachev. 2nd ed. St. Petersburg: Nauka, 1996.

Quellen-Lexicon   *Quellen-Lexicon der Musiker und Musikgelehrten* by Robert Eitner. 10 vols. Leipzig:

RBS   *Russkii biograficheskii slovar'* [Russian biographical dictionary]. 25 vols. St. Petersburg, 1896–1918 [incomplete].

RGADA   Rossiiskii arkhiv drevnikh aktov [Russian Archive of Ancient Acts; formerly TsGADA], Moscow.

RGB   Rossiiskaia gosudarstvennaia biblioteka [Russian State Library; formerly GBL], Moscow.

RGIA   Rossiiskii gosudarstvennyi istoricheskii arkhiv [Russian State Historical Archive], St. Petersburg.

RIB   *Russkaia istoricheskaia biblioteka* [Russian historical library]. 39 vols. St. Petersburg/Petrograd/Leningrad: Arkheograficheskaia komissiia, 1872–1927.

RIII   Rossiiskii institut istorii iskusstv [Russian Institute of the History of Arts], St. Petersburg.

RMG   *Russkaia muzykal'naia gazeta* [Russian musical gazette].

RNB   Rossiiskaia natsional'naia biblioteka [Russian National Library; formerly GPB], St. Petersburg.

SKK   *Slovar' knizhnikov i knizhnosti drevnei Rusi*

Breitkopf and Härtel, 1900–1904.

[A dictionary of writers and writing in early Rus']. Leningrad: Nauka, 1987–2004.

SKSR   *Svodnyi katalog slavianorusskikh rukopisnykh knig, khraniashchikhsia v SSSR: XI–XIII vv.* [A collated catalog of Slavonic-Russian manuscript books preserved in the USSR: 11th–13th centuries]. Main editor, S. O. Shmidt. Moscow: Nauka, 1984.

SM   *Sovetskaia muzyka* [Soviet music]. Moscow, 1933–91; continued by *Muzykal'naia akademiia* [Musical academy], 1992–.

Spb. vedomosti   *Sanktpeterburgskie vedomosti* [St. Petersburg gazette; newspaper].

TODRL   *Trudy Otdela drevnerusskoi literatury Instituta russkoi literatury* [Works of the Division of Old Russian Literature at the Institute for Russian Literature]. Leningrad/St. Petersburg: Akademiia nauk, 1934–.

TsMB   Tsentral'naia muzykal'naia biblioteka [Central Music Library], St. Petersburg (formerly the Music Library of the Imperial Theaters).

Author's Preface

This book was written during the years of upheaval that Russia experienced from the time of the war in Europe [World War I]. It is the end result of collection and research on the history of Russian music that was begun forty years ago, and it was polished and written in two relatively lengthy periods. Originally the author limited himself to two important historical time frames: the Muscovite period in the history of Russian social life, beginning with the Time of Troubles in the seventeenth century, when foreign influences were clearly becoming palpable in Russian life; and the first century of the St. Petersburg period, that is, the eighteenth century. During this period we first witnessed the flowering and then the beginning of the decline of foreign influence and the birth of musical culture here, and I was able to investigate the development of musical life in Russia during this time with the greatest possible fullness and necessary detail. Thus, in 1918, the studies on the history of music in Russia in the seventeenth and eighteenth centuries were completed.

In 1919, shortly after an invitation to join the faculty of Russian music at the Archaeological Institute in Petrograd, I found it necessary to change the curriculum, creating two independent courses, on the musical archaeology and the musical paleography of Russia, and I undertook the collection and examination of a series of new written sources and artifacts. My work on that new archaeological and paleographical material enabled me to write a series of studies of the period preceding the Muscovite era, beginning with the earliest era, the pagan past.

The direction I took was conditioned in part by the circumstances surrounding my work on these studies, and was completely different from the common practice of what was then only the fledgling discipline of musicology here. The author set himself the following method as the foundation for the present, long-considered work: to rely, as far as possible, only on primary sources (manuscripts, printed materials, and artifacts of material culture) and, if these sources were lacking or unavailable, to turn to compilations only after carefully verifying them. In addition, in contrast to most well-known works on music history, I found it necessary to show the connection between the past events of Russian musical life and the development of social phenomena, a connection which usually escaped the notice of those working in the field of music history.

Foreign historians, because of the lack of material or their biased beliefs regarding Russian music, gave it only an incidental place, as a kind of unavoidable appendage, almost like exotic music that was hardly studied and of minor interest to the cultured public. Unfortunately our [Russian] writers on music also touched on the subject only in general terms, limiting themselves primarily to two contiguous periods: first, that of the amateur romance and opera and, second, the birth and development of the Russian national school. Until now, our literature on music consisted mainly of a cursory survey of the entire extensive preceding period covering only religious music, a survey sometimes founded on the compilation of completely unverified facts, repeated on faith. In the accompanying notes to this book, this sort of work is subjected to analysis.

Similarly it was necessary largely to preserve the complete texts, both musical and literary, of primary manuscript sources in order to present a complete picture of the musical life of early Russia. Consequently the connections between early Russian painting—primarily miniatures but also icons—and its ideological significance within the history of Russian music were clearly manifested.

During the work on this material, new to the historian, from the surviving sources, there turned out to be a preponderance of material about court music (from the end of the Moscow period up to the second half of the eighteenth century), which is explained by the significance and variety of the surviving primary material in this sphere. Along with this, however, despite that until this time the history of urban and peasant music, including folk songs, remained almost completely unexplored, in a few chapters of our essays it was possible to collect material that revealed the social function of the oldest representatives of folk music, the *skomorokhi*, and to identify their musical repertory, as well as to determine the makeup, and give a brief history, of early Russian folk musical instruments. In the last quarter of the eighteenth century, moreover, there appeared a real interest and return to folk music, which manifested itself in the compilation, and even the appearance in print, of a series of sources, a few of which remained unknown to our scholars, and information about other sources appeared in print without verification.

Such material, collected and reworked in Russian literature on music, reveals ever more clearly, for almost the first time, the divergence between the music of folk and public life and the music connected with the court. This split runs through these essays as a scarlet thread, particularly in the second half of the eighteenth century, when the divide became fixed and when our own artistic works began to emerge.

One may find printed materials on the history of music in Russia more readily in scholarly works wholly unrelated to the musical literature, for example, by scholars such as F. I. Buslaev, P. P. Pekarskii, V. N. Peretts, A. N. Pypin, I. P. Sakharov, I. I. Sreznevskii, V. M. Undol'skii, and many others. Only a few of our music commentators have, in fact, worked with primary sources and have strengthened the concept of the necessity of more precise and deliberate work on the historical sources of our musical past. Writers taking this approach include V. F. Odoevskii, D. V. Razumovskii, S. V. Smolenskii, V. V. Stasov, S. K. Bulich, V. M. Metallov, A. S. Famintsyn, A. V. Preobrazhenskii, N. I. Privalov, and others.

This book most likely will show that a great deal of such outstanding source material exists, and it is the author's ultimate goal to aid later scholars in finding, organizing, and investigating these resources.

N. Findeizen

History of Music
in Russia from
Antiquity to 1800

VOLUME I

From Antiquity to the Beginning
of the Eighteenth Century

1. Introduction: The Predecessors of the Slavs

One can speak of the historical or ethnographical relics of a people, including the relics of their musical culture, only after they have begun to manifest an individual national character that reveals features unique to themselves and distinct from those of kindred or neighboring peoples and tribes. This applies, of course, to all the surviving artifacts of a people's creative culture, including literature (oral or written), music (folk or ritual), and musical instruments.

Indications of a national character become evident only when a people have emerged from the cradle of their primordial, ancestral existence and the first flickerings of their own cultural character become manifest. A people's earliest cultural expressions, however, tend to be grafted onto established traditions borrowed from neighbor nations who have more vigorous and advanced cultures. The cultural practices and *Weltanschauung* of such neighbors, facilitated by political and commercial relations, make a powerful impression on any newly budding culture. The relations of ancient Rus' with Greece, the West, and the Mongol East, for example, could not but influence the development of the social and cultural life of the ancient Slavs. Distinctively Slavic national traits developed and manifested themselves gradually. They can be discerned with some difficulty among the artifacts of primitive Slavic culture and emerge more certainly only during later periods of development.

As students of Russian music history, we should first shed some light on the relics of the musical culture of the predecessors of the Slavs preserved on Russian territory, and only then examine what ancient Rus' contributed, after she became a nation with distinctive national traits.

The earliest settlers of the territories later occupied by the Slavs hold no interest for us; they belonged to tribal peoples alien to the Aryan race of which the Slavs are a branch. "The stone implements found in Europe," says the archaeologist Schleicher, "could not have belonged to Indo-Europeans, because the latter had knowledge of metal before settling in Europe, and it is impossible to imagine that a people would forget how to use metal over the course of time. Consequently, these stone implements must be ascribed to the most ancient inhabitants of the territories which were only later occupied by Indo-European peoples." Another archaeologist, Professor Antonovich, has concluded as well that our country, with the exception of the Black Sea littoral, did not experience a Bronze Age as such, because it would have been concurrent with the widespread use of stone and iron tools.[1]

Although we shall not take account of the earliest primitive occupants of the countryside, we can hardly disregard later colonists who arrived here years before the appearance of the Slavic tribes proper and the founding of the Russian state. Our history must consider our forerunners, because the Slavic people who arrived later undoubtedly had many points of contact with their immediate predecessors and inherited many of their customs. Even a general acquaintance with the musical artifacts of Scytho-Sarmatian, Scytho-Greek, or purely Hellenic origin that were left behind, both in the interior of our country and in the Greek settlements along the coast of the Black Sea, convinces us that those distant forerunners of the nation of Rus' also left traces in the social and cultural lives of their Slavic successors.

We shall not concern ourselves with the generally known facts about the Scytho-Sarmatians and the other tribes—the Massagetae, Sacae, Skolots, and Sarmatians—who succeeded one another during the prolonged period before the Slavs settled the territory now known as Russia and whose names we know only from surviving written records bequeathed to us from other, more cultured peoples.[1A] Around the third century AD, the Scythians were driven out by tribes who then occupied the territory under their own names and who were displaced in turn by the Goths, the Manty, the Alans, the Roxolani, the Iazygians, and others. For us, it is important only to mention that we have firsthand records about these prehistoric predecessors of the Slavs from writers who represent the high culture of Greece and Rome.

These records, although fragmentary, possess undeniable historical importance. The Greeks scorned the distant Scythians as a barbaric people and referred to them accordingly, visualizing their land in wildly arbitrary terms. The famous lyric poet Anacreon (563–478 BC) says in one of his Bacchic odes:[1B]

> Nu, druz'ia, ne budem bol'she
> S takim shumom i oran'em
> Podrazhat' popoike skifskoi,
> Za vinom, a budem tikho
> Pit' pod zvuki slavnykh gimnov.
>
> So, my friends, let us no longer,
> With such clamor and tumult,
> Imitate the carousings of the Scythians
> While drinking, but let us sedately
> Drink to the strains of illustrious hymns.

Classical Greek writers pictured remote Scythia as a cold and barren wasteland populated by warlike inhabitants, and this image was based somewhat on fact. It was not only in war that the Greeks came to know the Scythians, for in the fifth and fourth centuries BC Scythian archers, probably mercenaries or prisoners of war, served as police in Athens and possibly also in other Greek cities. In Aristophanes' comedy, *Thesmoforiazousai*, a satire of Euripides staged in 410 BC, a Scythian appears as a comic character who speaks broken and corrupt Greek (just as in Russian plays we introduce the comic German or Englishman).[2] The testimony of Greek writers is more valuable, of course, as they could judge Scythians from personal contact with them. The grammarian and Sophist Julius Pollux, who lived much later, in the reign of Emperor Commodus (second century AD), relates in his *Onomasticon* [Lexicon] the very valuable information that the Scythians invented the pentachord, that is, a type of five-stringed harp or, more probably, kithara, whose strings were of "cured straps" (i.e., gut strings), with a goat's hoof serving as a plectrum. Furthermore, the same writer says that the Scythians (including especially the Androphagi, the Melanchlaeni, and the Arimaspians) "made flute-like instruments from the bones of eagles and kites." Both these reports demonstrate that the Scythians in that period were not a savage people and had long since abandoned a nomadic existence. The invention of a multi-stringed musical instrument and the use of gut strings indicate a certain degree of culture unknown to primitive nomadic tribes (see fig. 1).[3]

That the Scythians had wind instruments made from the bones of eagles and kites, as Julius Pollux says, also shows that they had progressed from the primitive reed pipe to more complex instruments of the flute type.[3A] Plutarch, who died about AD 120, tells us in his *Opera moralia* [Moral dissertations] of the music of the Hyperboreans, who lived in the Caucasus and were neighbors of the Scythians: "It is said," he writes, "that in ancient times sacred objects from the land of the Hyperboreans were sent to Delos, with flutes, reed-pipes, and kitharas." Thus, at the beginning of the new era, the oldest predecessors of the Slavs evidently had highly cultured types of musical instruments.

It is quite likely that some of the musical instruments were produced here as a result of contacts with more cultured neighbors, although, as we have seen, Julius Pollux ascribes to the Scythians themselves the invention of the pentachord. In this connection the story of Anacharsis, a highly educated youth of ancient Scythia, is quite interesting. Many Greek writers tell his story, including Plutarch, Herodotus, and Maximus of Tyre (a philosopher of the second century AD). Anacharsis was a Scythian of royal birth and seems to have been a contemporary of Solon; he therefore apparently lived at the end of the fifth and the beginning of the fourth centuries BC.[4]

FIG. 1. A Scythian playing a lyre-like instrument; fragment of a gold plate discovered in Sakhnovka (Kiev province).

For his own education, Anacharsis undertook a journey through Greece, where he astonished everyone by his wisdom and, at the same time, by the simplicity of his character and manners. He not only became a celebrity but his name was added to those of the seven sages—the greatest praise conceivable. In his *Septem sapientium convivium* [Banquet of the seven wise men], Plutarch writes: "Ardal, turning to Anacharsis, asked, 'Are there any female flute players among the Scythians?' The latter at once replied that there were not even any reeds. Ardal asked again, 'But, of course, the Scythians have gods?' 'Certainly,' Anacharsis answered, 'but gods understanding human speech; not like the Greeks, who think they speak better than the Scythians and nevertheless suppose that the gods listen with greater pleasure to instruments of bone and wood.'"

Anacharsis's reply evidently shows that, in his time, flute playing was not widespread or was not accepted in Scythian high society, particularly at religious rituals, whereas it is well known that flute players of both sexes gradually acquired great importance in Greece in religious ceremonies as well as in public games.[5]

From the same sources we learn that the semi-mythical Amazons were the Scythians' near neighbors. According to Herodotus and Strabo, the Amazons inhabited the shores of the Palus Maeotis (the Tauride Straits) and allowed no men in their land; for the propagation of their race, they visited their neighbors who lived near the Caucasus. Martianus Capella, a Latin author of the first half of the fifth century AD, says in the chapter on harmony in his satire *De nuptiis Philologiae et Mercurii* [On the marriage of Philology and Mercury], that the playing of the kithara attracted the Hyperborean swans, and that the Amazons performed their military exercises to the sounds of the reed pipes.[5A] He also relates an anecdote about one of the Amazons who, having presented herself to Alexander of Macedon with a desire to become pregnant, was given a flute player and returned home delighted with so great a gift.[6]

Such is the fragmentary information supplied by the ancient writers concerning the musical instruments of the Scythians and their nearest neighbors. We shall now acquaint ourselves with the relics of the musical culture of the Black Sea littoral or, as it is referred to in the scientific nomenclature, the Cimmerian Bosphorus.

Archaeological excavations from the second half of the nineteenth century have shown that almost from the seventh century BC this coast had a succession of wealthy Greek colonies with a flourishing social life. The ancient cities of Olbia, Cherson, Panticapaeum, and Phanagoria may be cited as examples. Excavations in these cities and in the neighboring tumuli have unearthed a mass of artistic relics indicating how prolonged the Greek influence was and how deeply into southern Russia it extended: to the area of Kiev and even to the basin of the Western Dvina and later to more northern localities. It can hardly be doubted that this influence, and the international ties arising from it, conditioned the subsequent relations between Byzantium and the Slavic tribes that also settled in these localities.

Among the most interesting remains of the southern shore's musical culture are the frescoes of the Panticapaeum catacomb, discovered in 1841 by the Odessa archaeologist A. Ashik, who described and illustrated them in *The Antiquities of Kerch*.[7] For us, as for every archaeologist, Ashik's book is especially valuable for its preservation of a now vanished monument of Byzantine culture in southern Russia.[8] Before the discovery, archaeologists had not suspected the existence of this catacomb, hewn out of the rock. The fresco paintings in the first of the catacombs to be discovered proved that the inhabitants of Panticapaeum observed the funeral customs of the motherland, Greece, and that their social life was marked by the splendor and refinement common to other cultured peoples of antiquity.

The fresco (fig. 2) represents the funeral procession of a notable citizen and, evidently, domestic scenes connected with that event. In this, as in the other frescoes of the catacombs, watercolor is used on pale gray plaster, and there are two rows of illustrations. Above the paintings, at the top of the wall, is a cornice in the Ionian style, about six inches wide, colored yellow and green; at the base is a red plinth about nine and one-half inches wide. In the middle of the wall is an arched doorway, and on both sides of the door are two rows of paintings, the lower row depicting scenes from the funeral procession and the upper row containing several groups of people. All the figures wear Greek attire; the men wear the chlamys, the women the chiton underneath the peplum, and the servants, short tunics. The first group on the left side, consisting of three figures (two women and a man), has no musical interest, but the three men in the second group introduce us to the instrumentalists of ancient Panticapaeum. The first musician, nude except for a green loincloth, blows a trumpet and turns toward a figure wearing a sleeveless chiton, girt about the waist, who plays a flute with five pipes (Ashik calls it a *svirel'*). The third musician, in a chiton without a girdle, also blows a trumpet and turns toward the door. Evidently the three musicians constituted an organized ensemble. The two trumpeters hold their instruments differently and stand in different positions: the player on the left has his trumpet in his left hand with the bell raised in the manner of Roman buccinists, whereas the other man's instrument is inclined slightly downward. The remaining figures in the upper row are not related to our study of music.

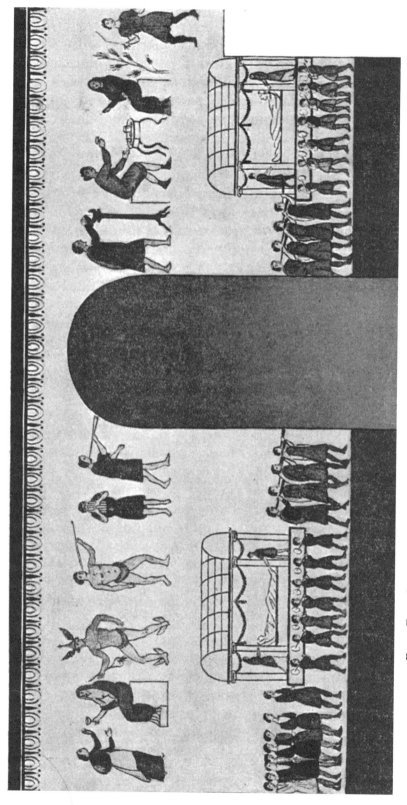

FIG. 2. Funeral ceremony with the participation of musicians; fresco from Panticapaeum, fourth century BC.

The lower portion of the fresco depicts two stages of the funeral procession. In the center we see the catafalque with the male corpse shrouded in white, lying under a cloth canopy supported by columns and adorned with garlands. At its head stands a woman who is dressed similarly to the woman holding a goblet, depicted in the first group of the upper row on the right. At the foot of the corpse is a youth in a sleeveless yellow chiton. The canopied catafalque is carried on the shoulders of youths wearing girdled white chitons. In the group on the left, the catafalque is preceded by four trumpeters. Both groups (to the left and to the right of the door) represent the same funeral procession and depict the groups of trumpeters with the same number of players. On the left side they precede the catafalque in the procession, and on the right they appear to face the catafalque, presumably about to enter the catacombs. Here, in fact, they seem to be sounding the farewell fanfare before the interment. The simultaneous appearance of four musicians indicates the existence of organized ensembles of wind players in the Cimmerian Bosphorus.

Ashik describes the remaining section of the Kerch fresco in detail. Without fixing the exact date of the construction of the catacomb, he ascribes it to the time of the archon Leucon, that is, in the second half of the fourth century BC. In another survey Ashik also describes some earlier finds in the central part of a stone kurgan (tumulus) discovered in 1830 about four miles from Kerch.[9] Here, while sifting the earth, archaeologists came across a small metal bell and some fragments of beech wood. Although the wood was much damaged, it was possible to conjecture that these were the remains of a wind instrument, probably a flute. Many of the fragments were covered with carved designs of remarkable workmanship, and the figures inscribed on them were depicted wearing Greek costumes.

Among the antiquities of the Cimmerian Bosphorus preserved in the Hermitage Museum, the Moscow Historical Museum, and in the museums of several large southern cities (Odessa, Kherson, and Kiev), one can find many early artistic artifacts with depictions of musical instruments or portrayals of religious and social scenes in which music played an obligatory role. Some of these artifacts were reproduced and described in detail in issues of the *Report of the Imperial Archaeological Commission,* primarily from the point of view of their artistic, historical, or social significance. These artifacts, however, offer extremely rich source material, hitherto uninvestigated, for the history of the musical art of ancient Greece and, to some extent, Rome, as well as the development of musical instruments in general. They also provide primary documentary evidence of the social life of these provinces from the fifth century BC to beyond the beginning of our era, that is, to the period of the later development of Greek art, which coincided with the expansion of the Greek colonies on the Black Sea coast. These relics interest us precisely because they testify to the flourishing state of these areas inhabited by the predecessors of the Slavs.

From the numerous treasures of this kind, found in the burial sites excavated on the Black Sea littoral in the second half of the nineteenth century and preserved in the Hermitage Museum, we shall select a few of historical and cultural interest. On two vases of the fifth century BC (figs. 3 and 4) we find scenes of a musical competition between kithara players painted in red on a black background. Figure 3 shows a bearded kitharist with a typical seven-string kithara; he has not yet begun his performance. Holding his instrument in his hands, he gazes fixedly at a goddess running toward him from his left side with a bowl in each hand. In accordance with the custom of Greek musicians, the competitor is about to pour a libation to propitiate the gods so that they may grant him success. From the other side, a second Nike approaches with a ribbon in her hands. The presence of the goddesses seems to predict success for the performer.

FIG. 3. A kithara player with a seven-string kithara, from a vase at the Hermitage; fifth century BC.

The drawing on a second vase (fig. 4) depicts the actual trial of a contestant, who stands on the thymele, the small dais generally used for musical or oratorical performances.[10] He plays on a large seven-stringed kithara, his head raised as if accompanying himself in song. The wide strip of checkered material hanging down beneath the kithara probably serves as a cover for the instrument, in place of a case. Three male figures surround

FIG. 4. The trial of a kithara player, from a vase at the Hermitage; fifth century BC.

the player. The most important, of course, is seated on a chair beside the performer; he is a bearded, bald man wearing a slender wreath on his head and holding a staff. He is undoubtedly the judge of the contest, and the youth and the bearded man wearing chitons

FIG. 5. A woman with a trigonon;
terra-cotta statuette from Kerch.

who are standing on either side and carrying long canes are his assistants, the so-called *rabdukhi*.[11]

Terra-cotta statuettes in the Hermitage tell us of other ancient Greek musical instruments in general use in the Crimean peninsula. One of them (fig. 5), found on Mount Mithridates near Kerch, is of a woman playing a trigonon, a multi-string triangular instrument similar to an Egyptian hand-held harp. Similar instruments made their appearance at a much later period, when Greek art was declining; they were undoubtedly of Eastern origin. The woman of the Hermitage statuette, which preserves traces of color, has lowered her dress to her hips. She wears a round amulet at her breasts, on her head a narrow diadem, and she stands beside a short column on which her instrument is resting. The trigonon is shaped like a triangular frame, open on one side across which the strings are stretched. The method of playing the instrument is clearly evident. Its shape is reminiscent to a certain extent of the later Slavic triangular *gusli*, although the latter had a sound board. There is no suggestion whatsoever, of course, that the Slavs borrowed or were influenced by the trigonon.

Another terra-cotta statuette (fig. 6) of rougher workmanship, found in Kerch in 1853, represents a horned, pointy-eared grotesque performing on panpipes. Creatures of this kind were called *nanoi* and were usually distinguished by bodily deformities. They played an important role in the wealthy houses of a later (Roman) period. This figure was undoubtedly influenced by the usual representation of the god Pan and therefore plays his favorite instrument.

Archaeological investigations have brought to light many similar works of art depicting various musical instruments used by the ancient inhabitants of the Black Sea coast. Relics of the classical Greek period were unearthed not only in these purely Greek settlements; in Kursk province, for instance, a glass saucer used in the Bacchic rite was discovered.[12]

A musical instrument of another kind, belonging to a later period but still before the Christian era, was found in a tumulus roughly five miles from Simferopol. It is evidently a hunting horn or a war horn with a silver mount (fig. 7), which probably belonged to an important person or to a warrior. It might have served as an attribute of dignity or rank, like the oliphants of the Middle Ages.[13]

Several other items, in addition to the horn, were found among the ashes in this grave: iron spears or darts, and an axe with a wooden handle encircled by a strip of gold. On the right side of the site was a gold snake ring; on the left, a silver ring with a seal. The tomb also contained a small vase of black lacquer, clay pitchers, and an amphora. The horn resembles the Slavic hunting horns discovered in the Chernigov tumulus and belonging to a far later period (ninth and tenth centuries AD). We discuss them in due course.

Both the written evidence and the archaeological excavations of the oldest settlements on the Black Sea coast thus offer convincing proof that various musical instruments were in general use in these areas among the Slavs' predecessors. These instruments also include small metal bells (hitherto unmentioned) found in gravesites. Their purpose has not yet been fully established. They have been dug up everywhere in Russia, singly, in pairs, or several together when fastened to girdles, for instance, as is still the custom among Siberian shamans. Some of the most interesting examples appeared on the bronze ornaments in the famous Aleksandropol tumulus (in the Ekaterinoslav district), discovered in the early 1850s.[14] Here, in addition to small bells and bronze discs, were rattles, a bronze trident, griffons, and so on. The lower end of the trident has a socket, evidently for the staff. A bird is placed at each point of the trident, and a little ring is threaded through the beaks of the two outer birds; from two other links a small bronze bell is hung. The same site also contained five plates of sheet silver shaped in the form of branches, which served for attachment to another object. Little metallic discs, which sound like a tambourine when shaken, were hung at the ends of the branches. With them were also found metal pendants with crude half-length figures of various animals, pierced around the edges, evidently for the attachment of small bells and metallic jingles to create a rustling sound. No fewer than 60 of these animals were found, some of them broken, together with 18 small copper bells, 318 concave copper discs, more than 500 bronze discs stamped with a rosette, and 244 little bronze bells. Most of these archaeological finds are reproduced in the album cited in note 14 above, *The Antiquities of the Scythia of Herodotus*.

The purpose of all these objects—the trident, the griffon, the (silver) plate in the shape of a branch, and the animal heads with bells and jingles—can only be surmised. Apparently they formed a part of the funeral chariot, richly decorated on its body and the front axle shaft, which was demolished on the spot prior to the burial. Originally they might also have served as cult objects, like the magic bells of contemporary shamans.

Immediately after the Aleksandropol discovery, forty-two small bronze bells were found in a grave at Chertomlytsk, about thirteen miles from Nikopol.[15] Some of them had the remains of the tongues and chains by which they were suspended to the plates, and there were two others with incisions (figs. 8 and 9).[16]

FIG. 6. *Nanoi* playing the panpipes; statuette from Kerch.

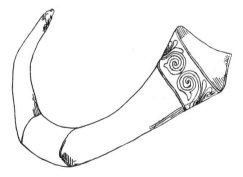

FIG. 7. A horn from the second to the first centuries BC discovered near Simferopol.

FIG. 8. Ancient bells discovered in a grave at Chertomlytsk.

FIG. 9. Ancient bell discovered in a grave at Chertomlytsk.

FIG. 10. A Siberian bell.

As we have stated, similar small bells and others of different shapes have been found throughout Russia, from the southern coast to Siberia (see the Siberian bell, fig. 10,[17] and the bells in the Roman bas-relief, fig. 11). Their purpose remains unclear.

Meanwhile, the oldest legends and artifacts of the ancient cult reveal the symbolism of similar finds in tombs. It is well known that biblical high priests had small bells at the hems of their pallia. At the consecration and purification of sacrifices, and also during prayers, the priests of Persephone in Athens rang a bell. In the remote past the Romans erected altars beside a sacred tree on which bells were hung (fig. 11).

Similarly, also in ancient times, a house was sprinkled with lustral water to the sound of bells in order to purify it or to expel evil spirits. Thus bells, great and small, have from the remote past been a symbol of purification, preservation from and exorcism of evil spirits, and an obligatory accompaniment to all kinds of prayers and religious ceremonies, including funeral rites. Their use for these purposes survives to this day in the attributes and "actions" of shamans and in the religious cults of many of our contemporary non-Christian and semi-barbarian tribes.

If we turn our attention from the Slavs' southern predecessors to the peoples inhabiting the more northerly districts of present-day Russia, we find equally interesting accounts in Arabic literary documents.[18] For our purposes here the most interesting of these Arabic travel writings is the well-known account by Ibn Fadlan, from the third decade of the tenth century. Despite the fact that almost every historian of the ancient Slavs has quoted from and commented extensively on these memoirs, the Muslim author's account of the funeral customs of the Volga Bulgars has a direct bearing on the elucidation of their successors' singing practices there.

FIG. 11. An ancient Roman bas-relief.

Ahmad Ibn Fadlan was sent by the Caliph Mukdashir as a member of the ambassadorial expedition to the Volga Bulgars, who were recent converts to Islam. His story, reproduced here in an abbreviated form, tells of events occurring in AD 922.

Soon after the emissary's arrival, a Bulgar notable died and the maidens of his harem were asked if any of them was willing to die with him. One volunteered. Then two other maidens were charged with keeping an eye on the volunteer and were not to leave her unattended for a single moment. They also set to work preparing funeral garments. Every day the victim drank and sang, celebrating and rejoicing. For the funeral they built a boat in which the body of the deceased was to be burned. On the day of the funeral, the vessel was drawn to the shore and surrounded with "wooden images in the likeness of giants"—probably idols. Along with the body, they placed on board pitchers filled with strong drink, fruit, and a musical instrument. Some French and Russian translators of the Arabic text call the instrument a lute, but the academician A. Kotliarevskii, in his treatise *On the Funeral Customs of the Pagan Slavs,* even suggests a balalaika (?).[18A] In any event, it was a stringed instrument, reminding the Arab of his native lute with its oval body. Ibn Fadlan describes further in the minutest detail the ceremonies preceding the lifting of the maiden onto the ship, where she was ready to consecrate herself to the flames. She was placed under the guard of an old woman who was called the angel of death and who took an active part in the closing scene; in the end she killed the maiden. But before this, several men came to the ship with shields and staves and offered the maiden a cup of strong liquor. She sang over it and drank, thereby bidding farewell to her companions. Then they gave her another cup over which she sang again, this time a song of some length. Ibn Fadlan even offers an Arabic translation of the girl's death song, which is approximately as follows: "Yonder I see my father and mother. Yonder sit all my dead kinfolk. Yonder, too, is my lord; he sits in paradise, and paradise is so beautiful, so green! Beside him are all his warriors and his children. He calls me, lead me to him."

This was probably a ceremonial song, one that was memorized, not improvised under the influence of the drinks and the funeral solemnities. The old woman (the angel of death) urged the girl to empty the cup and enter the pavilion erected on the boat on which her lord lay. Ibn Fadlan saw the girl falter; she wanted to go in and she pushed her head forward, and the old woman seized her by the head and drew her into the pavilion and went in with her. At this time the men began to beat on their shields with their staves in order to drown out the victim's cries, which might prevent other maidens afterward from "dying with their lords." Then six men went into the pavilion and, together with the old woman, killed the victim by strangling her and thrusting a broad-bladed dagger between her ribs, after which the ship with the dead bodies of the man and victim was burned.

The geographer Omar Ibn Dasta, one of the Arab writers closest to Ibn Fadlan, has left a more detailed description of many tribes that inhabited the vast spaces of Russia in his *Book of Precious Treasures,* also from the first half of the tenth century. He calls the Volga Bulgars an agricultural people, and says that most of them were of the Mohammedan faith and that "in their villages there were mosques and elementary schools, with muezzins and imams."[18B]

Putting all this information together, one concludes that culture had begun to penetrate the eastern portion of ancient Russia. While immolation on the funeral pyre was an admittedly heathen ceremony, the diffusion of Islam indicates a transition to other forms of social life. The establishment of elementary schools implies the first steps in education: literacy and writing. Instrumental music (especially the lute, so popular with Arabs) and vocal music (one has only to think of the chanting of the muezzins, so richly embellished with melismata, from the minarets) also played a significant role in Arabic culture in the early Middle Ages. When one keeps all this in mind, it must be admitted that in those far-off days, the territories beyond the Volga were not peopled by primitive savages. Their folk songs were evidently quite rich and varied. In the case of the sacrificial maiden, we have ceremonial songs that included hymns, which she sang almost ceaselessly and at great length. This is confirmed by Ibn Fadlan's statement that throughout the preparations of funeral rites, which lasted for several days, the sacrificial victim drank and sang daily as if being merry and rejoicing in the ritual; of course, we have no idea of the nature and context of these songs. On the final day she sang repeatedly on the funeral boat itself, first bidding farewell to her friends and then starting a song of such length that the old angel of death urged her to make an end of it.

We do not know, of course, what form these various ceremonial songs—expressing joy, bidding farewell, and preparing for death—might have taken so very long ago, but it may well be that in the songs of present-day inhabitants of the Volga region, we see remnants of these ritual songs, survivors from those far-off days.[19]

Arab writers have left reports not only about the Bulgars and other peoples inhabiting the vast spaces of Russia but also about the Slavs. These reports take us to the nearest center of Slavic public life, Kiev, and at the same time tell us something about the musical instruments of ancient Russia. A learned traveler from Baghdad, Abul Hasan Ibn Husein, known in Arabic literature under the name Al-Masudi, reports on the Slavs in one of his chronicles from the first half of the tenth century: "They are divided into many peoples, some of them Christians, some of them pagan sun worshipers. . . . Most of their tribes are pagans, who burn their dead and worship them. They have many towns, also churches where bells are hung, which they strike with a hammer, just as the Christians at home (that is, among the Arabs) beat a board with a wooden mallet."[20]

Ibn Dasta, mentioned above, writes in his *Book of Precious Treasures:*

> The land of the Badjaks is ten days' march from the land of the Slavs. On the edge of the Slav frontier is the town of Kuiab . . . All of them venerate idols. Their main crop is millet. At planting time they take millet seed in a ladle and raise it heavenward, saying: "Lord, thou who hast hitherto furnished us with food, give it to us now in abundance" . . . They have various kinds of lutes, *gusli*, and *svireli*. The *svireli* are two cubits long and their lute has eight strings.

The translation of the passage above is by Garkavi; we shall in due time look at other Arab reports about the Slavs.[20A]

In discussing the information given by Al-Masudi and Ibn Dasta, however, one must take into account the incorrect musical terminology employed by their Russian translators, out of ignorance or scanty knowledge of the structure of musical instruments in general. Both works are from around AD 925 or thereabouts, some sixty years before the official conversion of Rus' to Christianity. The Slavs are pagans, but Christians are to be found among them. They have churches or shrines with bells—more probably *bila*—which are struck with hammers (see fig. 12). From the Arab writers' accounts it is not clear whether the temples (or churches) were Christian or pagan; the shrines probably belonged to both.[21] At the time, pagan temples, shrines, or special places for prayers were undoubtedly found everywhere.[22]

The western pagan Slavs, for example, had very large temples. The Arab author calls the capital city of the Slavs Kuiab, that is, Kiev. The city was situated near the borders of the various eastern tribes: the Khazars, Pechenegs, Bulgars, and Polovtsians, who were then masters of the Crimea and the estuaries and great stretches of the Dnieper, the Don, and the Volga Rivers.

The pagan Slavs had various musical instruments: *svireli* (about twenty-eight inches long), the *gusli,* and an eight-string instrument the Russian translators called a lute, by analogy to the Arabic text. The lute, of course, was a very popular instrument among the Arabs, but it did not exist among the Slavs; they may, however, have had an instrument which suggested the lute to the Arab author. It might have been the ancient Russian *gudok,* whose oval shape does resemble a small lute. But the *gudok* could not have eight strings, and it was played with a bow. Old drawings of the instrument show

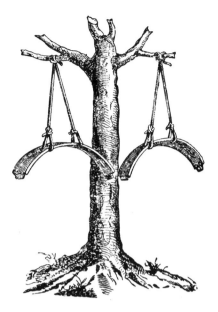

FIG. 12. Ancient oriental *bila.*

them with three strings. Much later the *bandura* was introduced to Ukraine, probably from Poland. Although the *bandura* is a lute-shaped instrument with an oval, but flat, body, there is no record of its existence in ancient Slavic life. It may be that the Arabic original (which may easily be interpreted variously) has been read incorrectly, and that Ibn Dasta's indication of the number of strings refers to the *gusli,* which at that period may well have been an eight-string instrument.

D. A. Khvol'son adds to Ibn Dasta's comments on the musical instruments of the Slavs:

Many ancient writers mention the propensity of the ancient Slavs for dancing, singing, and music in general. More detailed information on their musical instruments is found . . . only in Ibn Dasta. Theophylact and Ibn Fadlan make no mention of any instrument but the *gusli.*[22A] It would be interesting to investigate the musical instruments of the Western non-Slavic peoples, to see if they had instruments similar to those of the Slavs. If they did not, it would suggest that the ancient Slavs themselves made them, from which it may be inferred that they had some artistic culture.

Ibn Dasta's Russian translator is correct in assuming that the ancient Slavs knew something of art. Their musical instruments were certainly not imported; the *gusli* and the *svireli* were entirely indigenous, although similar instruments would probably be found among all the peoples and tribes inhabiting Europe at that time. In northern Europe, during the Bronze Age, huge metal lurs of excellent finish and sonority were produced (nineteen examples of these trumpets are preserved in the Copenhagen Museum), and complicated harplike instruments, though of very crude and antiquated native workmanship, are encountered even among the primitive savage tribes. [The lur is a prehistoric bronze trumpet or horn, generally S-shaped and found mostly in Nordic countries.] In this case, then, it is utterly impossible to assume that the ancient Slavs, with their social structure and their highly developed, varied, and splendidly decorative religious ceremonies, were incapable of making their own musical instruments, whether their neighbors had similar instruments or not.

Ibn Dasta has also supplied valuable and interesting information concerning the offering of millet seed in a ladle at sowing time. The activity indicates an ancient religious ceremony connected with people's lives and doubtless accompanied by songs and perhaps dances. The appeal to the divinity dwelling on high, when the supplicants offer the sacrificial millet, suggests the *khorovody* [round dances], not otherwise known at such an early period. They have survived from older ceremonial games in which two sets of players stepped forward opposite each other singing as follows [the phrase "did Lado" in the text below is a variant of a traditional refrain associated with spring songs]:

> A my proso seiali, seiali!
> Oi, did Lado, seiali, seiali!
>
> Ah, we have sown the millet, we have sown it!
> Oh, *did Lado,* we have sown it, we have sown it!

The refrain and the song itself, both known to this day, have come down to us in later variants in which the text has been altered to suit changes in social conditions, and the refrain probably does not retain its original purity. Nevertheless, the basis of this song, as ritual and an invocation of the divinity, and the general outline of the melody, which has not lost its amazing clarity, vigor, expressiveness, and simplicity, certainly belong to the remote past.

2. Pagan Rus'

Although we have inherited from pagan Rus' very few material artifacts that reflect musical practice at the time, far more has come down to us in ancient written documents, as well as in the still vibrant echoes of the past that live on in the folk traditions and songs of people today. The latter, from the musical point of view, remains for now only raw material that has not yet been carefully examined and subjected to scientific analysis, except for attempts to work out theories about the melodic and rhythmic nature of these songs.

Bells and jangles, which have been found everywhere in excavations of ancient graves and burial mounds, are not the only material relics that have survived from Russia's pagan past. An interpretation of their significance and function was presented in the previous chapter, which also included pictures. Metal objects survive much longer when buried, of course, than do those made of wood, which disintegrate over time, decayed by the soil's natural processes. D. Samokvasov's discovery in 1873 of a pair of very large ibex horns with silver mounts in a Chernigov tumulus is therefore particularly valuable (fig. 13).[23]

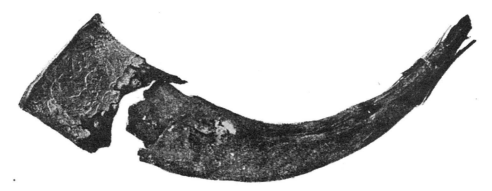

Fig. 13. An ibex horn (tenth century), discovered in a Chernigov tumulus.

They are evidently the hunting horns of a prince, and they correspond to the ivory oliphants appearing in a later (Muscovite) period. The carving on one of the horns depicts a northern barbarian with a bow, hunting a bird, and it also depicts griffins, dragons, birds, and so forth; the other horn has Eastern-style ornamentation. Unfortunately both specimens found in the well-known Chernigov tumulus, the so-called Black Grave, were broken, and parts of them were missing. The horn shown in figure 13 was chipped near the mouthpiece and the mounts were incomplete.

The construction of the Black Grave has been ascribed to the second half of the tenth century; Metropolitan Neofit was installed in Chernigov in AD 992, and all the inhabitants were certainly baptized at that time, so the raising of a pagan tumulus at a date later than this is not possible. Early in the nineteenth century another tumulus was excavated at Chernigov at a distance of four hundred paces from the Black Grave. The two are similar in shape and content. The second was the tumulus of "Princess Chorna" (the "Black" Princess?). Found inside were the mountings of a large horn, which were made of pure silver, chased and nielloed, revealing efficient and delicate workmanship. The narrow end near the mouthpiece is finished in the form of an eagle's head.[24] Enormous ibex horns similar to these may thus have been used by pagan Slavs of the ninth and the beginning of the tenth centuries. Archaeologists recognize the horns that were discovered as being of local Kievan workmanship, indicating that the ancient Russians possessed the art of engraving on metal, although they may have copied Eastern originals. It is also acknowledged that musical instruments with similar artistic ornamentation, giving them value in themselves, may have been in common use in those days among the upper classes of Slav society. We have seen a prototype in the hunting horn of the Simferopol tumulus (see fig. 7). Similar large—and very loud—horns [*truby*] were used for hunting and in military campaigns, and were also attributes of ruling princes and army commanders in the West. Consider, for example, the renowned horn or oliphant of Roland, one of Charlemagne's paladins, and, much later, the beautifully carved ivory horn of Tsar Aleksei Mikhailovich, and the still more splendid early-eighteenth-century horns of the age of Peter the Great, now in the Music History Museum.[25] Their existence at such an early period in the history of the Slavs shows that the upper classes of those days were acquainted with the customs of the West and with Greek culture, and also that the Slavs possessed not only home-produced folk musical instruments but also those of more artistic workmanship.

The existence of musical instruments and the indisputable beginnings of culture among the ancient Slavic tribes are confirmed by documents describing the Slavs' religious and social life. In his *History of Russian Life from the Most Ancient Times,* I. Zabelin writes:

> Taken together, the early legends of our Russian land as recorded in our chronicles lead to one conclusion: that life in Rus' improved on the whole from the influx of northern peoples. Moreover, tradition points to the beginning of historical events in the Il'men region, in its principal town, already called the "new town" [Novgorod], therefore the successor of some old town or of an older period of life that had entirely vanished from popular memory. Of this ancient time the chronicler has recorded the single fact that the Slavs who arrived at Lake Il'men were known as Slovenes and that they built a town they called "Nov-gorod."[25A]

Meanwhile, leaving aside for the moment a discussion of Novgorodian culture (the most important from a national point of view, following the destruction of the Great Principality of Kiev), let us turn now to the scanty information provided in the chronicles, since it corroborates the beginnings of an organized state life in the Il'men region and the founding of Novgorod on the site of, or near, a former town, which had existed there from prehistory. This "New Town" [or "fort"] was established by the Slavs, who had already appeared on the horizon of history.

We find information unknown to the Russian chronicler in the testimony of contemporaries of the ancient Slavs, from the western, as well as the eastern and southern regions. Historical investigation continually illuminates the significance of the cradle of the Slavic tribes in Central Europe: in the North on the Baltic coast (the Baltic and Polabian Slavs) and in the South in the Carpathian district. The ancient Wends and after them the Pomeranians, the Liutsin, and other tribes are all blood brothers of one and the same Slavic populace.

Even in the fifth century we have interesting evidence supplied by the Greek historians Theophylact, Anastasius, and Theophanes concerning the maritime or, more correctly, the Baltic Slavs, whose social life differed vastly from that of their neighbors. Some Russian investigators are rather skeptical about this information, but it is undoubtedly of historical value and has even been accepted by [the great Russian historian] Karamzin. Here is what these Greek historians have to say on the subject. At the time of the war with the Khagan [Khan] of Khazaria, at the end of the sixth century,

> the Greeks captured three foreigners who had kitharas (i.e., *gusli*) instead of weapons. The emperor asked: "Who are they?" "We are Slavs," the foreigners replied, "and we live at the farthest end of the Western Ocean (the Baltic Sea). The Khan of the Avars sent gifts to our elders and asked for troops to fight against the Greeks. The elders accepted the gifts but dispatched us to the Khan with the excuse that the great distance prevented them from helping. We ourselves were fifteen months on the journey. The Khan, disrespecting the sanctity of the calling of ambassador, would not let us return to our native land. Hearing of the wealth and the kindliness of the Greeks, we took advantage of the opportunity to go to Thrace. We do not know how to use weapons and only play the *gusli*. There is no iron in our country; ignorant of war and loving music, we live a quiet and peaceful life." The emperor, marveling at their gentle nature, their great stature, and their strength, entertained the ambassadors and provided them with the means of returning to their native land.

Karamzin ends his quotation with the remark that "the unanimity of the Byzantine historians in their accounts of this occurrence seems to confirm its truth, which is also corroborated by the conditions then prevailing in the North, where the Slavs could live peaceful lives, for, at the end of the sixth century, the Germans had departed to the South and the domination of the Huns had been overthrown."[25B]

This quotation, by the way, provoked an unfounded attack by S. Gedeonov in his book *The Varangians and Rus'*, in which he refers contemptuously to an "idyllic world" created by some of our scholars "where the sword is replaced by bagpipes."[25C] The Greek historians make no mention of the bagpipe, and the sending of the three innocuous *gusli* players to the warlike Khan (which might have been simply a diplomatic ruse) and their speech, after their escape to Greece, does not by any means imply that the whole tribe of the Baltic Slavs consisted at that time only of *gusli* players. The passage simply indicates their unwillingness to submit themselves to the military adventures of a far-off Khan, and also shows that the peaceful, mostly agricultural, northern Slavs had a great liking for music in general (and undoubtedly for folk song), and that the *gusli* was their native musical instrument. At any rate, the evidence from Greek sources that the Slavs had, as long ago as the sixth century, definite musical instruments fully agrees with the statements Arab writers made at a much later date that they had met with similar instruments among the Slavs of the southwestern portion of present-day Russia.

The testimony of the same contemporaries concerning the religious cult of the Slavs convinces us that they had pagan temples in Gniezno, Vilnius, Arkona, Novgorod, Kiev, and other places. The most accurate information has come down to us from the practices of the Baltic Slavs. In the town of Arkona, on the lofty summit of a promontory on the island of Ruegen, was the temple of the sun god Sviatovid or Svetovid, one of the principal deities of Slavic mythology, known by different names in different tribes: Volos, Khors, Dazh'bog,

Svarozhich, Radegast, Iarovit, and Iarilo.[26] It was not without reason that the tenth-century Arab writer Al-Masudi called the Slavs sun worshipers. Like the Greek sun god, Apollo the Kitharodos, the bard of the [epic medieval poem] *Slovo o polku Igoreve* [The lay of the host of Igor] calls Volos-Veles the ancestor of the prophetic singer Boian: "Or would you sing, wizard Boian, grandson of Veles."[26A]

The most famous temple to this god was at the Baltic site of Arkona, although there were temples to Sviatovid at other places. Offerings flowed into the Arkona temple from all parts of the Slavic littoral. The temple received not only tribute, but one-third of any war booty, and it even had its own military guard—thus the status of this pagan temple, its riches and, consequently, its magnificence. The annual feast of Sviatovid was celebrated with great ceremony with a service after the harvest, and songs and dances, concluding with a banquet for all. Masses of people from all neighboring Slavic territories attended the feast. In the Arkona temple, decorated with a huge idol of Sviatovid, horns sounded during the religious rituals. A description of the Arkona temple appears in the *Danish History* by Saxo Grammaticus (AD 1208).[26B]

After Sviatovid-Iarilo, the deities most respected by the Slavs were Perun (god of thunder and lightning) and Stribog (god of the wind). A temple was also dedicated to the Slavic Perun (equivalent to the Roman god Jupiter, the Scandinavian Thor, and the Hindu Adiwaraga Perunal, one of the incarnations of Vishnu), and idols representing him were located there. It is noteworthy that an idol was considered not merely the representation of a god but also his dwelling place. The chroniclers record that when the idols were destroyed after the introduction of Christianity, "in Novgorod they threw the idol into the Volkhov, and in [the idol] of Perun there was a devil that began to cry out, "Oh, woe is me!" and floating downstream he threw his club at the bridge." Saxo Grammaticus describes the destruction of the temple of Sviatovid in Arkona, declaring that, "when the idol fell to the ground, his spirit ran out of the temple in the form of a black wild beast."[26C] Volume 1 of the Moscow Archaeological Society's *Antiquities* contains a reproduction of the Lithuanian idol Perkun (or Perkunas, i.e., Perun), to whom oak groves and special temples were consecrated and sacrifices offered.[27] The high priest Kreve-Kreveite wore a representation of Perkun on his vestments. Friday was dedicated to Perkun and sacrifices were offered to him on that day. An echo of this old belief is preserved in "Il'inskaia piatnitsa" [Elijah's Friday], which in popular memory is blended with the story of the prophet Elijah.

Stribog, god of the wind, was also zealously worshiped by the Slavs. In the twelfth-century *Lay of the Host of Igor*, we have a poetic comparison associated with Stribog, idols of whom were also to be found in the temples:[27A]

> These winds, the grandsons of Stribog,
> blow from the sea like arrows,
> onto the brave warriors of Igor.

In Ukraine, popular memory has long preserved a prayer-song: "Blow, blow upon the land with the breath of thy holy spirit, Oh Lord!"[28]

Folk songs, similarly, have long preserved the names of the ancient Slavic goddess of love, Lada, and her sons, Dido and Lel'. When a pagan Slav married, he offered a sacrifice to this goddess. Lada was remembered on Trinity Sunday, when garlands were woven and used to foretell the marriage prospects of young girls. Lada's name was encountered until very recently in the folk songs of various locales, although the people have certainly long since forgotten the original reason for invoking Lada and Dido-Lado. Lel', in his turn, was the Slavic Cupid. Tacitus stated that the Sarmatians and Wends had idols of Lel'. Al-Masudi, in his accounts of the temples and shrines of the pagan Slavs, says that in one of them the principal idol was faced by another representing a woman or a girl.

In any case, the idols were the main adornment of the temple and the central place for prayer assemblies. The chronicles note the placement (and later destruction) of the idols: "In the time of Igor an idol stood on the mound," and "Vladimir then began to reign alone in Kiev, and he set up idols on the hills outside the castle with the hall: one of Perun, made of wood with a head of silver and a mustache of gold, and others of Khors, Dazh'bog, Stribog, Simar'gl, and Mokosh'"—that is, already a whole family of the gods of Slavic mythology.[29] "When Dobrynia came to Novgorod, he set up an idol beside the river Volkhov." Slavic idols were everywhere, according to the testimony of Arab and other foreign writers contemporary with pagan Russia ([twelfth-century historian] Helmhold, Thietmar, Adam of Bremen, Saxo Grammaticus, and so on). In AD 990, according to the Gustinskaia Chronicle, Vladimir destroyed the idol of Volos at Rostov, but despite the general baptism of the Slavs, the worship of idols continued in many places, probably largely in secret. It is known that there was a second destruction of an image of Veles, by St. Abraham, in Rostov in the twelfth century.

Along with these principal divinities, the Slavs worshiped Rod and the Rozhanitsy, and belief in these gods lasted longer and extended more deeply than for other pagan figures. This is borne out by the evidence of the *Domostroi* [a sixteenth-century guide to domestic management], the Troitskii Anthology, and other literary documents of the sixteenth century; in the anthology we find this reproach: "And you sing songs to the devilish Rod and the Rozhanitsy."[29A] N. I. Kostomarov identifies Rod with fate (including the destiny of human beings); the Greek word ειμαρμένη [fate, destiny] is translated by the Russian word *rozhdenie* [birth]. In this sense, the word *rod* was always used in the singular, and consequently, according to the ancient belief, one fate existed for all. The Rozhanitsy, on the other hand, were always referred to using the plural (old midwives who assisted at birth of babies made porridge for the "gathering of the Rozhanitsy"), which seems to indicate that everyone was supposed to have his own individual Rozhanitsa.[30] From the *Slovo Khristoliubtsa* [The discourse of the lover of Christ], we gather that the cult of Rod and the Rozhanitsy was still alive in the sixteenth century, when it was accompanied by various entertainments such as dancing, music, songs, and bonfires: "It is not proper for Christians to play demonic games; dancing, playing music, demonic songs, and sacrifices to the idols, or praying to fire and fairies and to Mokosh' and Simiregl and Perun and to Rod and the Rozhanitsy and to all those who are like them."[31]

We also see the survival of old pagan practices in the Russian Church. In the *Voproshanie Kirika* [Kirik's inquiry], addressed to the Novgorod bishop Nifont in the twelfth century, we read: "And they steal bread and cheese and honey [or mead] for Rod and the Rozhanitsy. They say it is strictly forbidden everywhere; woe to those who drink to the Rozhanitsy."[32] F. Buslaev sees here an allusion to the so-called *tropari* [hymns] to Rod and the Rozhanitsy which were used in ancient times at feasts.[33] These, perhaps, became the toasts to the Virgin, a rite established in Church regulations already in the eleventh century by the Holy Feodosii Pecherskii [of the Caves Monastery in Kiev].[34] They consisted of singing the appropriate *tropar'* at mealtimes, when toasts to the Virgin were drunk. This is supported by the *Slovo* [Discourse] of St. Gregory: "contrived in the sense that the first heathens, that is, pagans, worshiped idols and made sacrifices to them, that they now do the same," in the well-known Paisii collection of the fourteenth-fifteenth centuries:

See this damned foul service, which was created by the unclean tongue of the pagan Greeks—sacrifices to a sophisticated Devil, devised by the sorcery of the shadowy demon and mocker of holy things. With evil store, the malicious believers have changed to true vanity. The Greek lovers, who worship and bow to idols, make certain contrivances: the beats of the drum [*buben*], the whistling of the *svirel'*, the dances of Satan, the foreign *slon'nitsa*,[35] and the music of the *gusli* in honor of Rod, Osiris's cursed spawn, for his mother who gave birth to him created a god of him; and sacrifices to him beget mighty curses . . . It is the same thing, word for word, that when you begin to make sacrifices to Rod and the Rozhanitsy, it is as before their god Perun . . . Even now in distant lands they pray to him, to their cursed gods Perun, and to Khors, Mokosh, and Vil, and they make sacrifices in secret . . . From the table the invocations to Rod and the Rozhanitsy are a great fascination to the baptized believer, an abuse to holy baptism, and incurs an affront to God.

This source shows how long the Slavs preserved their ancient pagan practices in their domestic life at the fringes of the state; the author has a curious reference to the mythology of the Slavs and its origins in ancient peoples, for example Ozirida from Osiris. This is a literary opinion, of course, not a historical fact.[36]

On an equal footing with the invisible divinities of pagan mythology, personified by idols and stone images, the Slavs also worshiped the manifestations of nature: woods, groves, and individual trees; hills and stones; rivers and lakes; and so on. All these were the dwelling places of the gods, and traces of belief in them may be preserved best in folk songs, legends, sayings, and certain daily rituals. *Bel-goriuch' kamen'* [the white-glowing stone] is still mentioned in many popular rites, legends, and proverbs. Karamzin spoke of the Korochun stone.[37] On the *kon'-kamen'* [horse stone] on the island of Konevets in Lake Ladoga, a horse was offered as a sacrifice even in the fifteenth century. Another horse stone is to be found in the Efremov district of Tula province on the shore of Krasivyi Mech where, even in the last century, the rite of plowing accompanied by singing was observed at the time of cattle plagues.[37A] The survival of a similar pagan belief might have been observed not so long ago in the Volga regions, where it took the form of a stone hung on a pole in the villages or in the cattle sheds. Here the stone full of holes was regarded as a hen god [*kurinyi bog*].

Where and how were the religious rites of pagan Russia performed? I. I. Sreznevskii answers these questions in his study, mentioned above, as follows: "The terrestrial gods were worshiped wherever there was a consciousness of their presence and wherever they dwelt. The worship of celestial gods took place in special temples, before idols and under the open sky, or beneath a canopy of branches which sheltered the simple altars; this continued until the Slavs learned how to build temples." Even before the summoning of the Varangians, there were undoubtedly temples in Russia, not only pagan but Christian as well, and certainly also in Kiev. Prince Igor, the son of Riurik, confirmed an agreement with the Greeks in the year AD 945 by taking an oath with the pagan part of his army in the temple of Perun, swearing with his arms and gold, and placing his shields at the feet of the idol, in addition to placing rings and swords there as well. The Christian members of his army swore with a cross in the Church of St. Elijah in the Podol district in Kiev.

In the same way "sanctuaries for service to the water gods were on the shores of consecrated lakes, on the banks of rivers and streams, and at springs to which the people flocked for the performances of the sacred ceremonies."[38] In *An Essay in Compiling a Glossary of the Russian Language of the Simple Folk,* we find an interesting reference to the fact that, in Pskov, there was a saying as late as the eighteenth century: "Go to the Ipanis and drown yourself in it! You forgot God, venerated the earth, and poured yourself out to the water (i.e., offered a prayer)."[39] The author of the *Glossary* added that it was well known that the river presently called the Bug [Bog-reka or God-river] was formerly called the Gipanis and was held in the highest esteem by the ancient Slavs; they approached its banks with holy awe and drew water from it very cautiously, perhaps fearing that they might defile the sacred stream. The Bug was known as the Bog-reka at least until the end of the seventeenth century.[40]

Another elemental power, fire, long retained an important place in the Slavic singing tradition as an object of adoration, exorcism, and magic power. (The Slovaks from the Tatra Mountains believed that fire gave birth to the sun, the moon, and the stars.) The *khoro-vody* and songs sung on St. John's Night, when worshipers jumped across the flames of a crumbling bonfire (a symbol of purification by fire), remained in popular use until the most recent times of Christianity.

Al-Masudi, the Arab traveler mentioned previously on more than one occasion, has left some interesting information about the religious practices of the pagan Slavs: "There were sacred buildings in the land of the Slavs. One was on a high hill. This building was famous for its architecture: the placing of the stones of various kinds and colors; for the sounds spreading from the top of the building; and, finally, for the effect produced upon people when these sounds reached their ears."[40A]

The participation of a choir in the pagan Slavs' worship singing is thus confirmed by a contemporary witness; this is in addition to remnants of evidence in folk poetry, not always discernible in our time. I. I. Sreznevskii saw in Al-Masudi's statement a confirmation that "sung prayers, probably by a choir under the cupola, formed a part of the temple services." This would seem to suggest that in pagan Russia there existed fully trained singers, super-vised by the priestly caste, since a choir of simple people would not be placed under the cupola nor would it make an impression on the worshipers. And it is this impression that Al-Masudi mentions, that special effect created by singing from on high "when these sounds reached [the people's] ears." Sreznevskii also stated that "it should come as no surprise that the sung prayers inside the temple were accompanied by the sounds of instruments, as was the case in open-air ritual chants. This is the more probable because among the treasures preserved in temples were musical horns, as the biography of St. Otto indicates. At any rate, the chanting was a rightful part of the pagan religion of the Slavs."[41]

Remnants of these liturgical songs could have been preserved in the ritual folk songs transcribed in the course of the nineteenth and early twentieth centuries. A people which has gradually rejected its pagan concepts and, ultimately, learned to fear paganism still may have retained unconsciously in collective memory, and even in daily life, much that came from those remote times. This makes it possible to piece together what remains of pagan song-creations that have come down to us or, more accurately, the songs that have come down to the not-so-distant past, yet to a period when the words and music could be writ-ten down; this allows us to reconstruct a fuller and more complete picture of the Russian people's musical past.

The originality, artistic beauty, and variety of the pagan Slavs' ceremonial and folk songs may be judged from those fundamental characteristics preserved in folk memory, notwithstanding the Tatar yoke and foreign influences of every kind, ecclesiastical and governmental edicts and prohibitions, revolutions, the spread of industry and factories, and the like. Folk song, especially Slavic folk song, survived all these obstacles and misfortunes, and retained much of the richness and beauty of its melodies and the original and often ingenious rhythms, so different from those of other European peoples of Aryan descent. They survive perhaps not always in their pristine purity but in a far from mutilated form.

These songs could only be beautiful and original. But when and under what circumstances were they sung?

First of all, on the lap of Nature, since Nature herself, and her elements, were deified by the people. As we have said, throughout the long period of paganism, the people experienced the whole world as inhabited by spirits, good and evil, who dwelled in the forests, the waters, the stones, the fire, and everywhere, in both the natural world and domestic surroundings. The various spirits protected man or bore him malice and set traps for him. All these dwelling places of deified magical powers thus called for prayers, exorcisms, and songs, and their memory had to be preserved in folk song. Indeed, the Sun-Iarilo; river and lake; hills and stones; the protected forests and individual trees which must not be felled; and the sacred fire—all these offered the superstitious pagan opportunities and settings for worship and religious ceremonies, not just the officially designated temples and places for prayer. Aside from the recognized priests and sorcerers and the official caste of participants in religious rites,[42] no doubt the people themselves were directly involved. They took part in prayers and adorations, and sang various songs that might be religious but perhaps not strictly ritual.

In his study of the festivals of the Russian populace, I. Snegirev states: "In addressing their deities, the worshipers expressed their devotion by prostrating themselves and making obeisance. In Russian sacrificial songs at the time of the *Koliada* festival, the supplicants sat on benches around the fire with the aged priest in the middle."[43] One of these epic scenes is exactly preserved and portrayed in an old *koliada* song, first published by Sreznevskii in 1817 and later in a more complete form by I. P. Sakharov in his *Songs of the Russian People:*[43A]

> Za rekoiu, za bystroiu,
>   Oi koliodka! oi koliodka!
> Lesa stoiat dremuchie,
> Vo tekh lesakh ogni goriat,
> Ogni goriat velikie.
> Vokrug ognei skam'i stoiat,
> Skam'i stoiat dubovyia,
> Na tekh skam'iakh dobry molodtsy,
> Dobry molodtsy, krasny devitsy,
> Poiut pesni koliodushki.
>   Oi koliodka! oi koliodka!
> V sredine ikh starik sidit,
> On tochit svoi bulatnyi nozh.
> Kotel kipit goriuchii,
> Vozle kotla kozel stoit;
> Khotiat kozla zarezati.
>   Oi koliodka! oi koliodka!
> Ty, bratets Ivanushko,
> Ty vydi, ty vyprygni:
> Ia rad by vyprygnul,

Goriuch kamen'
K kotlu tianet,
Zhelty peski
Serdtse vysosali.
    Oi koliodka! oi koliodka!

Across the river, the rapid river,
    Oi, koliodka! oi, koliodka!
Stand the dense forests,
In those forests fires burn,
Great fires are burning.
Round the fires the benches stand,
Stand the oaken benches.
On those benches good lads,
Good lads and pretty maidens,
They sing the koliodushka songs.
    Oi, koliodka! oi, koliodka!
In their midst sits an old man,
He whets his knife of steel.
The boiling cauldron bubbles,
Beside the cauldron stands a goat.
They are about to slaughter the goat.
    Oi, koliodka! oi, koliodka!
You, little brother Ivanushka,
Come out, you, and skip about.
I would gladly have skipped.
The glowing stone
Draws near to the cauldron,
The yellow sands
Have sucked out the heart.
    Oi, koliodka! oi, koliodka!

In spite of its incompleteness and the deficiencies of the text (its tune, unfortunately, was not recorded), this song undoubtedly portrays a vivid picture of the ritual sacrifice.

The divinations and rites connected with water were equally poetic and picturesque. A Byzantine author of the tenth century, Leo the Deacon, testifies that Sviatoslav's warriors immersed infants and roosters in the streams of the Danube at the burial of those fallen in battle. An echo of the epic and picturesque past lingered as late as the nineteenth century in the custom of weaving garlands for the purposes of divination on St. John's Eve, or *khorovody* on the day of the *rusaliia*, Trinity Sunday. I. I. Sreznevskii, in his *Sanctuaries and Rituals,* has established the fact that services for deities were also held beneath a lone, ancient, hollow tree (oak, linden, walnut, and so forth), where a sanctuary was probably partitioned off by spears or curtained by fabrics thrown over the branches. Or perhaps the services might take place near a bush or in a grove that no one was allowed to enter except the officiating priests who performed the prayers, the sacrifices, or the divinations. Near the town of Shuia is a village called Dunilovo, whose name the old inhabitants derived from the word *dub* [oak tree] and who also called their village Dubnilovo. According to a local tradition, the village was built on a site formerly occupied by an oak forest (until recently there were many oaks on the River Teza) in which there was once an idol to Dubnilo.[44] Not long ago at Sazhino, a hamlet near Rostov, a sacred birch was hung with many colored streamers, frills, and crosses suspended by ribbons, to which the populace prayed as to an icon. Ancient documents describe a superstition of the Mordva from Murom, where "small hollow trees, their branches draped with streamers, are worshiped."[45] According to Sreznevskii, the song "Pod lipoiu stol stoit" [Beneath the linden stands a table], sung at *semik*, undoubtedly suggests a sacrificial rite of some kind. [*Semik* is a spring fertility holiday occurring on the seventh Thursday after Easter.] This song was first transcribed by I. Prach [in the eighteenth century] and was admirably utilized by Rimskii-Korsakov in his opera, *Snegurochka* [The snow maiden]; its text and music have probably preserved certain fundamental traits of ancient paganism.[46] Here are the opening lines:

> Ai, vo pole lipin'ka,
> Pod lipoiu bel shater;
> V tom shatre stol stoit,
> Za tem stolom devitsa.

> Ai, in the field [stands] a little linden tree,
> Beneath the linden tree, a white tent;
> In that tent, a table stands,
> By that table, a maiden.

In the time of Peter the Great the chanting of prayers before an oak tree was still forbidden by ecclesiastical statute, but even at a later period the people maintained a reverence for the old trees and the old practices, which cannot but recall the pagan rituals in natural settings.[46A] Although some of the songs may have been disfigured in certain respects by later accretions, they nevertheless preserved hints of their pagan past. Examples of these songs may be found in collections like that of Ivan Prach mentioned earlier, as well as in those of later collectors of the bygone heritage of Russian folk song. The following may be one example:

> Oi na gore, gore, na vysokoi, na krutoi,
> Oi Dido, oi Lado, na vysokoi, na krutoi,
> Na vysokoi, na krutoi stoial zelenyi dubok.

> Oi, on the mountain, the steep and lofty mountain,
> Oi Dido, oi Lado, on the steep and lofty [mountain],
> On the steep and lofty [mountain] stood a green oak.

This song includes a later amorous development in the narrative text, but with the obligatory refrain, the invocation of "Dido-Lado" (see musical example 2.1). Another version, perhaps one less altered by the passage of time, is in musical example 2.2. According to Prach, both versions of the song were transformed into dance songs [*pliasovye*] during his lifetime.

The text of the first verse of the song in musical example 2.2 has no relationship to the second verse ("Kak u starogo muzha zhena molodaia" [When an old man has a young wife]), but the first verse perhaps preserves traces of an even older, analogous song:

EXAMPLE 2.1. "Oi, na gore" [Oi, on the mountain] (from L'vov and Prach, *Russkie narodnye pesni*, 26 [no. 16; LPC, fac. 93–94]).

Oi na gore, gore, na vysokoi, na krutoi,
Oi Dido, oi Lado, na vysokoi, na krutoi,
Na vysokoi, na krutoi.

Oi, on the mountain, the steep and lofty mountain,
Oi Dido, oi Lado, on the steep and lofty [mountain],
On the steep and lofty [mountain].

EXAMPLE 2.2. "Ai, na gore" [Ai, on the mountain] (from L'vov and Prach, *Russkie narodnye pesni*, 27 [no. 17; LPC, fac. 95–96]).

Ai, na gore dub, dub,
Ai, na gore dub, dub,
Chto bela bereza,
Chto bela bereza.

Ai, on the mountain an oak, an oak,
Ai, on the mountain an oak, an oak,
And a white birch tree,
And a white birch tree.

Ai na gore dub, dub
Chto bela bereza.

Mezhdu duba i berezy
Reka protekala.

Reka glubokaia
Voda studenaia.

Nel'zia vodu piti,
Nel'zia pocherpnuti.

Ai on the mountain an oak, an oak
And a white birch tree.

Between the oak and the birch
A river flowed.

The river was deep
The water was bitterly cold.

One should not drink the water,
One should not draw it up.

The tune of this latter song, with a rhythmic structure of 2 + 2 and 3 + 3 bars [labeled in musical example 2.2 above], undoubtedly reveals traits of an ancient past.

In the next two songs from Ufa province, written down by N. E. Pal'chikov, there also is a feeling of later accretions of a lyrical character in the text.[47] Their flowing, festive tunes do not quite harmonize with the latter (except for the beginning, which has remained untouched), and possibly they have preserved features of the same remote pagan times; see musical examples 2.3 and 2.4.

Russian Lyric Folk Songs, compiled by N. M. Lopatin and V. P. Prokunin (Moscow, 1889), is a valuable ethnographic collection, representing the first attempt to systematize the tunes of similar songs and to cite their parallels.[47A] In this collection one finds some old, distinctive songs referring to mountains and the white-glowing stone, which, as we know, were objects of worship and of a superstitious cult. It should be noted in this connection that the collection includes variants of the song "Gory" [Mountains] from five widely separated provinces of central Russia, although the words in every case are almost identical, with only minor differences. The five areas are Riazan province, Kasimov district (musical example 2.5); Tambov province, Morshanskii district; Novgorod province, Valdai district (musical example 2.6); Tula province, Bogoroditskii district; and Orel province, Eletskii district. The text may also be found in songbooks containing texts only, such as that by

EXAMPLE 2.3. "Oi, ty roshcha" [Oi, you tiny grove] (from Pal'chikov, *Krest'ianskie pesni,* no. 52).

Oi, ty roshcha, ty moia,
Eroshcha,
Roshchitsa berezovaia
Ekh ty berezovaia.
Ah, da nichego-to v roshche ne rodilosia.

Oi, you tiny grove, my tiny grove,
My tiny birch grove
Ekh, you tiny birch grove.
Akh, yea, nothing flourished in the grove.

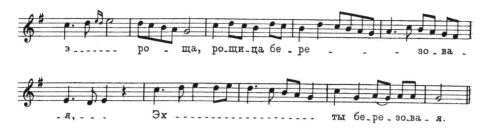

Ах да ничего-то в роще не родилося...

EXAMPLE 2.4. "Ty, dubrovushka" [You, tiny oak grove] (from Pal'chikov, *Krest'ianskie pesni*, no. 69).

> Ty dubrovushka, ty zelenaia, ekh!
> Eshche chem ty dubrova izukrashena.
> Ali kustikom, ali prutichkom. Ekh!
> Posered' dubravy est' polianochka,
> Na poliane stoit syr vysokii dub. Ekh!
> Na dubu sidit mlad iasen sokol.
>
> You, little green oak grove, ah!
> How else are you beautiful?
> Either with a small shrub or with a twig, ah!
> In the midst of the oak grove is a little meadow,
> In the meadow stands a single tall oak tree, ah!
> On the oak sits a young, fine falcon.

Chulkov (in the 1770s), Sakharov (in the 1830s), and in the *Noveishii polnyi i vseobshchii pesennik* [The latest complete and general songbook, 1818]; thus the song has preserved its ancient characteristics:[47B]

> Akh vy, gory, gory moi, da gory krutye!
> Nichego vy, gory, ne porodili,
> Porodili gory odin chast rakitov kust.
> (or: Porodili gory odin bel-goriuch kamen'.)

Ah you mountains, my mountains, yea craggy ones!
You, mountains, yield no fruit,
You have brought forth only the *rakita* [broom] bush.
(or: You have borne only the white-glowing stone.)

Regarding the musical and poetic characteristics of this song, the editors of the collection remark: "A certain mysteriousness, calm severity, and solemnity, inherent in our oldest songs, stands out prominently in the song 'Gory,' not only in singing but in the reading of the text itself, with the preservation of all the repetitions and the layout of the words. Whenever we heard the people sing it, they always gave it a solemnity and even a sort of sternness absent from their performance of any other songs."[48] This quality of mysterious awe and solemn severity perceived both in the melody and in the performance style can surely be ascribed to the prayerful character of this and similar songs, a character understandable from the perspective of the people's ancient religious beliefs. This is confirmed by the editors' observation about this particular song: "Collating all the variants presented here, which were transcribed in different parts of Russia, it became evident that almost everywhere the text of this song was the same and the singing was identical. The number of bars and the tune in each variant differed, but the character of the song and the principal transitions were rarely altered. The minor mode prevails in all of them, and there is always a descending scale characteristic of and inherent in this song."[49]

The prayers chanted to the luminous divinity—the sun—are equally solemn but brighter and more joyous. Exultation, confidence, and a suggestion of hope are heard in the refrain of the South Russian *koliadki* [carols]:

Slaven es', gei, slaven es',
Nash' milyi bozhe, na vysokosti!

You are glorious, ah! you are glorious,
Our dear god in the highest!

Setting aside the most popular Slavic folk song, and probably one of the oldest, "Slava Bogu na nebe" [Glory to God in heaven],[50] the next two songs from the Mel'gunov collection and the Filippov and Rimskii-Korsakov collection have apparently preserved examples of similar vocal appeals to Iarilo, the sun god.[51] In the first example, the original text of the *khorovod* song, "Vzoidi, vzoidi, solntse" [Arise, arise, oh sun], has added to it an entire game from everyday life, as suggested in the lyric refrain, "Ai, leshun'ki, liuli" (undoubtedly, like the tune, of very early origin). It is presented in musical example 2.7 in its original form, without N. S. Klenovskii's piano accompaniment.[51A]

A similar song was preserved by T. I. Filippov, as notated and harmonized by Rimskii-Korsakov; it was sung on the Volga, according to the collectors, but was also known in many other places. Although the song's principal theme is associated with the fate of bandits (it was probably an example of the bandit song), nevertheless its opening words, like the beginning of "Vzoidi, vzoidi, solntse," suggest ancient sun worship, as did the opening line of the preceding song (recorded by Mel'gunov), which has nothing in common with the bandit song of the Filippov and Rimskii-Korsakov collection (see musical example 2.8):

Ty vzoidi, vzoidi, solntse krasnoe!
Nad goroiu ty vzoidi, nad vysokoiu,
Nad dubravoiu ty vzoidi, nad zelenoiu.

EXAMPLE 2.5. "Gory" [Mountains], Riazan province, Kasimov district (from Lopatin and Prokunin, *Sbornik russkikh narodnykh liricheskikh pesen*, no. 1).

Gory, vy moi, nichevo vy, gory,
Nichevo ne porodili,
Oi! ne porodili gory nichevo

Oi! da nichevo!
Nichevo vy gory,

Nichevo ne porodili, nichevo!
Porodili, gory, porodili
Bel goriuchii, bel goriuch kamen'.

You, my mountains,
Have yielded nothing,
Oi, you have yielded nothing, mountains,

Oi! nothing,
Nothing, you mountains,

You mountains have yielded nothing!
You have brought forth, mountains, brought forth
The white-glowing stone.

EXAMPLE 2.6. "Gory" [Mountains], Novgorod province, Valdai district (from Lopatin and Prokunin, *Sbornik russkikh narodnykh liricheskikh pesen*, no. 4).

Uzh vy, gorochki, gory,
Gory, vy Valdai, vy Valdaiskie!

Vy Valdaiskie, po prozvan'iu gorochki gory Zimogo, Zimogorskie!
Zimogorskie, sporodili gorochki odin bel goriu bel goriuch kamen'!

Oh you hills, you mountains,
You Valdai mountains!

You are called the mountains and hills of winter!
You brought forth only the white-glowing stone!

Arise, arise, red sun,
Arise over the mountain, the lofty mountain,
Arise over the oak grove, over the green one.

We can find echoes of the ritual and religious songs of the ancient Slavic pagan cult in many similar songs. These songs are distinguished by the peculiar beauty of their tunes and by their original rhythmic structure, related to their text or, more correctly, to fragments of their text. At the same time, while seeking traces of antiquity in our folk songs, we must keep in mind the conditions under which these religious songs were originally sung, not only in sanctuaries and sacred buildings but also in natural surroundings, sometimes beautiful, sometimes stern and awesome.[52] These conditions in themselves added, on the one hand, beauty and picturesqueness, and, on the other, solemnity and even somberness to the religious music of the pagan Slavs.

EXAMPLE 2.7. "Vzoidi, vzoidi, solntse" [Arise, arise, oh sun] (from Mel'gunov, *Russkie pesni*, no. 6).

Vzoidi, vzoidi solntse, ne nizko vzoidi vysoko,
Ai liushenki, liuli, ne nizko vzoidi vysoko.

Arise, arise, oh sun, arise not low but high,
Ai, *liushenki, liuli*, arise not low but high.

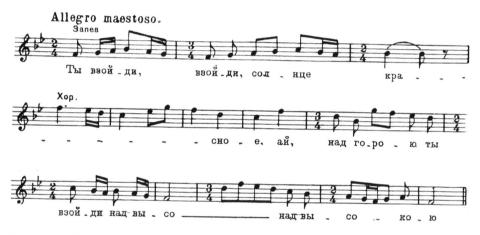

EXAMPLE 2.8. "Ty, vzoidi, vzoidi, solntse krasnoe" [Arise, arise red sun] (from Filippov and Rimskii-Korsakov, *40 narodnykh pesen*, no. 13).

Ty vzoidi, vzoidi, solntse krasnoe, ai,
Nad goroiu ty vzoidi, nad vysokoiu.

Arise, arise, red sun,
Arise over the mountain, the lofty mountain.

3. Kievan Rus'

1. Kiev as the center of governmental life. Relations with Byzantium. A fresco in the Cathedral of St. Sophia in Kiev

In the very earliest period of their existence as a state, the Slavic peoples already occupied locales in Eastern Europe, including a number of cities mentioned in the early histories. In the North, in addition to Novgorod, the cities of Pskov, Rostov, Beloozero, Smolensk, and Murom all took part in the summoning of the Varangians; in the South we encounter, in addition to Kiev, cities such as Chernigov, Pereiaslavl, Liubech, and others. Riurik, the first of the princes to be called in, founded the town of Ladoga. The very fact that these [foreign] princes were [voluntarily] invited rules out the notion that the ancient Slavs lived a primitive and savage existence or had an immature mode of life. The existence of cities, temples, and musical instruments (such as the artistically decorated ibex horns found in Chernigov, fig. 13) demonstrate that they had the beginnings of a culture in the ninth century AD.

The musicality of the Slavs, acknowledged in foreign countries as well, is undoubtedly proven by the fact that they were employed as professional musicians at the magnificent Byzantine court. Emperor Constantine Porphyrogenitus, in the tenth century, ordered that "on the day of the public games, there should be an official organizer to appoint everyone to his duty and to see to it that the Slavic musicians, who are used for playing on instruments, come to the theater."[53]

In this respect, the rapid growth and political importance of Kiev, soon to be recognized as the "mother of Russian cities," furnishes the best evidence that the Slavs were prepared for a new and responsible political life.

Askol'd and Dir, Varangian knights-errant who had probably arrived with Riurik in AD 862, soon parted from him and his brothers, and within two years they were masters of Kiev; in 882 they were killed there on Prince Oleg's orders. From then on Kiev became the residence of the Russian princes, and during the reigns of Igor Riurikovich (d. 945), his widow Olga, baptized as Helen (d. 969), Sviatoslav (d. 972), Vladimir (d. 1015), and Iaroslav the Wise (d. 1054), the city flourished and gradually extended its borders.

We usually associate those ancient times of the earliest Kievan princes with dreary internal strife, military campaigns, and plundering by roving bands of princely militia [*druzhina*], and the peoples' silent subjugation. We obtain a livelier and more varied picture of that period, however, from the chronicles and other documents, from the poetic tradition and songs (*byliny*), from the evidence of contemporary foreign travelers, and from other documentation, even though this evidence is fragmentary and at times obscure and in need of elucidation. Some of the most detailed pictures of the Slavs' social life were the results of their contacts with the more cultured peoples of the West and the South.

Pushkin's poetic genius has given us a series of such pictures in his "Poem of Oleg the Wise." There was a reason why the people labeled Oleg "the Wise": the Slavic prince was both their priest and their judge. The Laurentian Chronicle mentions that Prince Vladimir personally offered sacrifices to the gods.[53A] The "Tsargrad armor" [from Tsar-City or Constantinople] formed a part of the rich tribute Oleg acquired when he attacked Constantinople. The contact between the ancient Slavic world and Greek culture thus continued even after the decay and destruction of the Greek colonies on the Black Sea coast. The concluding verses of Pushkin's ballad give a vivid picture of the life of the ancient Slavs:

> The rounded, foaming bays sparkle
> At the sad solemn feast for the dead Oleg;
> Prince Igor and Olga sit on the hill,
> At the shore, the militia feasts,
> The warriors recall the days gone by
> And the battles in which they fought together.

This is a picture of a memorial feast. According to descriptions of funeral customs for the early princes, we know that the body was burned with solemn ceremonies, songs, and dances. Among the western Slavs a special dance was performed at the grave. It was known as the *dynia,* and the verb derived from it—*dynit'* [to dance in honor of the dead]—passed into Russian practice. The feasts and dances were, of course, accompanied by songs and instrumental tunes.

With respect to the particular influence of Byzantium on the customs at the Kievan court, a very interesting historical document describes the ceremonies arranged in Constantinople for foreign ambassadors and notable guests. Princess Olga had an opportunity to participate in similar ceremonies, when she visited Constantinople with her suite in September 957 during the reign of Emperor Constantine Porphyrogenitus, that is, twelve years after Olga's husband died and more than twenty-one years before Russia's official conversion to Christianity.

The marvels of Byzantium displayed at the ceremonial receptions in the *triclinium* of the Magnaura (the throne room of the Imperial Court at Constantinople) amazed foreign visitors, and for good reason. Their astonishment found expression even in our chronicles. Thus the Nikonian Chronicle mentions several of these marvels the Russians witnessed, making use of information from Byzantine sources:[54] "The [Byzantine] Emperor Michael [d. 867] exhausted the entire state treasury with his playmates. He wasted it not only on golden griffins [*gripsos*][55] but also on a golden poplar made with great craftsmanship—otherwise to say, a tree on which all manner of golden birds sat and sang their songs as if they were alive. And those who listened to it were greatly impressed, marveling at this new invention."

The Langobard historian [Bishop] Liutprand (d. 972), a contemporary of Princess Olga who was twice in Constantinople as an envoy, describes in detail the ceremony at the emperor's reception in part 6 of his *Antapodosis,* on which Russian scholars such as Ainalov and Zabelin rely. Liutprand describes the events as follows: "The ambassador, on entering the circle of persons standing at the sides of the throne, prostrated himself at the sound of the organs [*organy*], and then arose to the sound of percussion instruments [*udarnye organy*] and took up the position previously indicated to him."[55A] Princess Olga's procession at her reception by the emperor also must have been accompanied by the sound of organs, as it was a public ceremony. The throne on which the emperor received her was of pure gold studded with precious stones. Seated on it here and there were golden birds that burst into harmonious song at suitable moments. Other adornments included effigies of lions, which could roar as loudly as the kings of the jungle. Finally, near the throne were two trees (the chronicle says poplars) made of pure gold with golden birds singing on the branches, each bird in its characteristic voice. Several organs stood behind a curtain at the back of the throne: one of gold, enameled and with precious stones, another also of gold, and a third of silver. All these artistic and mechanical marvels were constructed in the first half of the ninth century for Emperor Theophilus, who enjoyed the service of a clever mechanic and jeweler named Leo.[56] The sounds of the organs, the songs of the birds, the roar of the lions, and the movements of the animals and of the throne itself (by means of a special mechanism, it could be raised almost to the ceiling with the emperor seated on it!)—no doubt all this was intended not only to astonish but also to terrify the foreign barbarian. Liutprand asserts, in fact, that to people unfamiliar with the "devices" employed at the emperor's receptions, much seemed marvelous and terrifying. Still more interesting is that echoes of such "devices" may even be found in Russian *byliny*, but more of this in its proper place.

The proceedings at the reception of the Russian Grand Princess by Emperor Constantine were as follows:[56A] when the *logothet* (a functionary corresponding to the Imperial Chancellor), placed the usual questions according to the established ritual, the lions began to roar, the birds on the throne and in the golden tree struck up a harmonious song, and the wild animals on the steps of the throne raised themselves on their footstools. While this was going on, the protonotary of the *dromos* brought in the gifts. Shortly afterward the organs began to play, the lions and birds became silent, and the animals sank back into their places. When the gifts had been inspected, the foreigner, at a sign from the *logothet*, bowed and withdrew, and during his progress to the exit, his procession was again accompanied by the roaring of the lions, the songs of the birds, and the sounds of the organs, and the wild animals raised up as before. As soon as the guest had passed behind the curtain, the organs stopped playing, the birds ceased their singing, and the animals resumed their places. The unexpectedness and effectiveness of all this undoubtedly aroused surprise, even terror, in the unprepared spectator. The mechanical structure of these devices is unknown, but they were likely set in motion by special levers at the sides of the throne like the levers or stops on a mechanical organ which are also used to create varied and complex timbres.

Accompanied by the sounds of *organy*, Princess Olga returned from the Magnaura into another hall, where the *kamelavkii* stood, and then into the portico of Augustus, where she seated herself.[56B] After the reception the emperor retired to the inner rooms of the palace, and a second reception by the empress took place immediately, as follows: A dais covered with purple cloths stood in the Hall of Justinian, and on it sat the great throne of the emperor Theophilus, with a simple royal armchair by its side. At a lower level behind the curtains stood the two silver organs from the two sides of the Hippodrome, and pneumatic organs stood in front of the curtains. On the same day and in the same Hall of Justinian, a grand banquet was given, which was attended by the *apostoliti* and the *aposophiti* (the choirs of the Churches of the Apostles and of St. Sophia) and they sang imperial songs; there was also entertainment, and buffoons and mimes performed. Meanwhile, another banquet was being held in the Golden Palace at the same time in honor of the envoys.[57]

Detailed data are preserved about the musico-theatrical portion of Princess Olga's reception. Here is what transpired: As soon as the emperor and the rest of the company were seated at the table, troupes of actors and dancers came in with their masters of ceremonies (directors). The proceedings began with a triumphal hymn sung by the chorus, after which the prefect of the table gave a sign with his right hand, by alternately spreading his fingers out like rays and then clenching them. A dance was started, with dancers circling the table three times. The dancers then retired to the lower end of the table, where they remained in a specific order. Next the singers came forward again, first the soloists and then the chorus, and every phrase was sung three times.

This was a festive hymn, a *mnogoletie* [or *polychronion,* a hymn for the long life of the emperor and his family], a type of hymn which later became part of church and court practice in ancient Rus'.[57A] Similar songs and spectacles continued throughout the banquet. Each course was accompanied by a new dance or a new song. The masters of ceremonies wore colored costumes—green and red, with short white sleeves—which varied with every change in the program. Changes of costume on ceremonial and festive occasions by the court functionaries was a recognized custom at the Byzantine court.[58]

Mimes, musicians, and acrobats took part in the entertainment provided at the banquet, supervised by special managers known as the *domestiki* of the spectacle and the *arkhontes* of the spectacle. Liutprand, who was sent to Byzantium by Emperor Berengar II in AD 946, described some of these entertainments, but especially interesting for us is that all of this recalls scenes depicted in one of the eleventh-century frescoes that adorn the interior of the Cathedral of St. Sophia in Kiev.

> The amusements I saw there (writes Liutprand), would take long to describe, but it would not be out of place to mention one of them which amazed me. A man entered, balancing a pole of some twenty-four or more paces long on his forehead without using his hands; at the top there was a cup and on the man's forehead, a double cup. Two boys were brought in, naked except for their foot gear. They climbed the pole and sat on it as though it were flat on the ground. Then, when the first one came down, the second, who remained there, performed various tricks by himself to my still greater astonishment . . . Remaining atop the pole, he preserved his balance magnificently, and after completing his act came down to the ground without any harm . . . The emperor noticed my astonishment. Turning to me, he asked, through an interpreter: "Who surprised you more, the boy who performed so confidently that the pole did not move, or the man who supported it so skillfully that neither the weight of the boys nor their movements wearied him in the least?" I replied that I did not know, whereupon he said with a hearty laugh that neither did he.[59]

The fresco in the Cathedral of St. Sophia, mentioned above (see fig. 14), includes an acrobat supporting a tall pole with a boy climbing it and a [cup-like] vessel on the top. Acrobatic feats of this kind were evidently in vogue at that time. According to D. V. Ainalov, a pillar with two boys climbing up appears in a miniature from the Gelatskii Monastery. This feat subsequently became a popular amusement in our country at folk carnivals.[59A]

Like Oleg, who returned from the Constantinople expedition laden with booty (amassed by plunder or received in the form of tribute), Princess Olga brought back splendid gifts and at the same time an abundant store of memories of things seen and heard. "Journeys of this kind," as Ainalov justly remarks, "must have had an enormous importance for Rus' at that time, especially for their cultural consequences. The magnificence of Constantinople, its enchanting palaces, the statues in the squares, the churches and sanctuaries, and, lastly, its various artifices, were well known to contemporary Rus'."[59B]

In one of our *byliny* describing the adventures of the heroic Kievan knights of the Vladimir cycle, we find echoes of the impressions made by the cunning devices seen in Constantinople by Princess Olga and her suite and by other travelers who came as ambassadors or as learned foreigners. The Greeks, of course, went to war with Oleg and Igor and other Slavic princes, and also negotiated peace treaties with them; Russian merchants had for a long time traded with Byzantium and may have heard there of the marvels of the Byzantine Imperial court.

The *bylina* in question concerns the foreign knight Diuk [Duke] Stepanovich. It includes an obscure episode hitherto unexplained by our scholars. When Diuk Stepanovich arrayed himself in the costly apparel sent to him by his mother, the widow Mamel'fa Timofeevna from the famous town of Galich, the Kievan prince Vladimir was frightened:[59C]

> On his [Diuk's] mighty shoulders was a fur coat of black sable,
> of black sable from abroad,
> Under the green velvet
> and woven into the silken buttonholes
> were God's little singing birds,
> and on the buttons were molded
> fierce serpents and wild beasts.
> When he pulled a cord through the buttonholes
> suddenly the birds began to sing,
> striking up a heavenly song
> and amazing the crowd,
> when he pulled a cord through the buttonholes.
> When he jingled the buttons against each other
> the beasts cried out with a roar
> and the fierce serpents begin to glide over the buttons,
> hissing at the tops of their voices.
> Everyone was horrified, all fell into a pit,
> but the others, when they fell to the ground, fainted straightaway.

This episode echoes impressions from Constantinople, some of which go back to Olga's visit: the organ playing, the lions and other animals which could rise up and roar, the birds singing in the trees. These marvels leaped and crawled from the buttonholes and buttons of the foreign knight's magic cloak; this is how the folk imagination, apparently, wittily transformed the accounts of the workings of the clever Constantinopolitan entertainments, which seemed so mysterious to the uninitiated. The buttonholes served as a substitute for the trees with mechanical birds, and the buttons may recall the registers and knobs that set in motion the complicated mechanisms in the Imperial Palace.

The famous fresco of St. Sophia is one of the oldest artistic monuments in Kiev. Not only does it show Byzantine influence, but it must have been created about the mid-eleventh century by Byzantine masters, or at least after Byzantine models, soon after Rus' converted to Christianity.

The history of Prince Vladimir's acceptance of the Greek faith is well known. It is interesting to learn, however, that his envoys, having "tested" the merits of various creeds, were captivated most by the church singing of the Greeks. After listening to the magnificent liturgical service, they admitted that they did not know if they were on earth or in heaven. It is also noteworthy that soon after the adoption of Christianity in 988, the principal church in Kiev was built and consecrated to St. Sophia, the same as the magnificent Cathedral of St. Sophia in Constantinople, the pride of Byzantium.

Vladimir, who had hitherto been a fanatical pagan and had set up idols in Kiev, became an equally ardent Christian after his conversion and began destroying the pagan idols along with the musical instruments and other appurtenances of the pagan cult. In this respect, the Eastern Slavs present a peculiar phenomenon. Either on their own initiative or acting under orders, they destroyed, smashed, or burned artistic and cultural treasures that they no longer needed, and did this so thoroughly that often no substantial traces of the treasures' former greatness remained. That is why our past can only be conjectured, and to some extent re-created, from no more than the fragmentary evidence of contemporaries and written records, whereas in the West it is not rare to find valuable relics and documentation of ancient culture, including music.

The scenes accompanying the compulsory baptism of the people and the destruction of the accessories of pagan life near and dear to them were no doubt lively and picturesque. Removed from their pedestals, the overthrown idols were broken up and sunk in the Dnieper River. The weeping people wailed, "Come to the surface, our Lord God, come to the surface." [The Russian word *vydybai* literally means "to swim out."] About four miles below the Podol district [in Kiev], the waves of the Dnieper carried some idols ashore at a place called Vydybichi, and on that spot the Vydubitskii Monastery was later built. Christian churches and monasteries were often erected on the sites of former pagan temples and sanctuaries, and people in daily life introduced Christian names instead of the pagan designations of the past. Near the present-day Church of the Presentation of the Virgin, there was once a pasture on which stood a temple of Volos, the protector of domestic animals. After the conversion, a church dedicated to St. Blasius, to whom people prayed during cattle plagues, was built there; the church was destroyed by fire in 1651. The prophet Elijah was the reincarnation of Perun, the god of thunder, and John the Baptist was identified with Kupala. On St. John's Night the people long preserved the memory of Kupala in the ritual and sacred fires, songs, and other ceremonies.

At the time of Russia's conversion, Kiev was a major commercial center and a fortified city. One of Vladimir's contemporaries, Bishop Thietmar of Merseburg (d. 1018), describes Kitava (Kiev) as enormously powerful and the capital of the state, with almost four hundred churches and eight markets.[59D] These figures may have been exaggerated, but foreigners agreed in their amazement at Kiev's greatness and splendor. Adam of Bremen, an eleventh-century writer, in his *Church History*,[60] speaks of Khive (Kiev) as a rival of Constantinople, the most distinguished ornament of Greece.[61] Russian historians have shown that during the reign of Iaroslav I (1015–1054), the city of Kiev grew to three times its former size, and its wealth and magnificence also increased. Prince Vladimir built the Church of the Tithe [the Desiatinnaia Church] and probably a number of smaller churches as well. His son, Prince Iaroslav, built the Cathedral of St. Sophia (1037), a princely palace, monasteries, and other buildings. The eleventh century may truly be called the golden age in the growth of Slavic Kiev.

In Vladimir's time the church choir was certainly instituted and properly organized, and doubtless sang in the principal church, the Church of the Holy Virgin, which was popularly known as the Desiatinnaia, because the Grand Prince devoted a tenth part [*desiatina*] of his income toward its upkeep.[62] According to the Gustinskaia Chronicle, Vladimir brought with him from Kherson the first metropolitan, bishop, and priest as well as singers, probably of Bulgar origin. The chronicle also tells us that his Christian wife, the Greek princess Anna, was accompanied to Kiev by a group of Greek ecclesiastics attached to her household and known as the empress's group [*tsaritsynyi*]. All these clerics from Byzantium and Kherson were musically trained and could, in turn, teach the new methods of singing to Prince Vladimir's local, recently Christianized, singers. There may even have been some Christian singers in Kiev already, since quite a few Christians could be counted among the prince's bodyguards and among the foreign artisans and traders, and they held divine services in accordance with the Christian rite. Shortly after the completion of the

Cathedral of St. Sophia in Kiev (1051), three more Greek singers were summoned to the city by Prince Iaroslav the Wise, and [the chronicler] Nestor claims that they taught the Slavs to sing *demestvennoe penie* [a special, elaborate type of singing]. Further, according to the Laurentian Chronicle, there was a house of *domestiki,* that is, court singers, near the prince's chambers in the immediate neighborhood of the Church of the Tithe: "There was another [palace] outside the city, where the palace of the *domestiki* [*dvor demestikov*] is now, behind the Church of the Holy Virgin."[62A]

We now resume the examination of the well-known fresco in the Cathedral of St. Sophia in Kiev. The staircase leading to the choir has wall decorations, and, in the past, these stairs apparently connected the church with the princely palace, since it is difficult otherwise to account for the secular nature of the paintings, which depict scenes associated with music and the theater.

Since their discovery and subsequent publication in V. A. Prokhorov's *Christian and Russian Antiquities,* several attempts have been made to explain the nature of these frescoes.[62B] Some scholars have assumed that they represent performances of Russian buffoons [*skomorokhi*] in the days of the Grand Prince, but the latest investigations by D. V. Ainalov and N. P. Kondakov have undoubtedly established not only their Byzantine origin but also their meaning. Professor Ainalov has studied these pictures in connection with literary documents of the same period, and Kondakov has analyzed their artistic execution. "These paintings," Ainalov says, "were probably executed by order of the prince. There can be no doubt, however, that the artists were not Russian but Byzantine, since many details in their compositions indicate not a Russian, but an entirely different life and environment."

The scene of the fresco of most interest here (fig. 14), "represents a series of performances by *skomorokhi.* We see two athletes preparing for a contest; dancers leading a *khorovod,* a type of round dance (we ought to add musicians, because, in the fresco, it is they who form a sort of *khorovod*); musicians playing a harp, a *truba,* a *dombra,* and a flute—in a word, the diversions so strongly opposed by the Church, and which can be found, for example, in St. Nifont's *Life,* which lists instruments and their evil roles: "Some were performing on *gusli,* others sounded instruments [*organnyia glasy poiushche*], and some sounded pipes from across the sea," or "some were beating *bubny* [tambourines or small drums], while others were blowing bagpipes and *sopeli* [wooden flutes]."[62C]

The fresco's Byzantine origin is established beyond any doubt by its subject matter, its style, and the character of its ornamentation. Its connection with Russian life is only indirect and is easily explained by our ancestors borrowing from Byzantine culture and also by the similarity of Christmas celebrations in most European countries. Hunting, jolly songs, and dances were the favorite diversions of the Kievan princes. Vladimir Monomakh is eloquent in his account of his hunting exploits, and the *Life* of Feodosii Pecherskii describes the festivities in the Prince's *terem* [a chamber or tower chamber]: "Many were performing before the prince, others were singing with the sound of instruments . . . and so all were playing and making merry as is the custom before the prince."[63]

In part 4 of *Russian Antiquities,* N. P. Kondakov gives an even fuller account of the Kiev fresco:

> The subject matter of the frieze of the fresco is a theatrical scene in the strict sense of the term: in the palace, on a stage specially built for the purpose (part of it is cut away in the fresco), musicians, clowns, and acrobats perform. All are dressed like actors, since in Byzantium even musicians were recruited from among the actors.

In accordance with an ancient Byzantine custom (mentioned by Constantine in the chapter on Gothic games), the musicians form a *khorovod* (comprising, one must suppose, a large number of people with *truby, sopeli, bubny,* and *bandury*—a harpist-kitharist in our scene is seated by himself); inside the *khorovod* are two dancers, one of whom has a kerchief in his left hand. An actor raises a curtain covering the entrance in order to admit a fresh "turn," a clown and a harlequin. On the right, a boy climbs a pole which an acrobat supports on his girdle, an act described by Liutprand, who, as we know, saw it at the Byzantine court. It is evident that we have before us the customary performance at festivals (especially around Christmas), at wedding ceremonies and birthdays, at receptions of ambassadors, and at banquets. The oriental allusions of this scene will remain obscure until the history of these theatrical forms is explained in detail and documentation is assembled concerning the itinerant troupes of actors in the period after the fall of Rome and the abolition of public games in Syria and Alexandria . . . Therefore we shall merely call attention in this scene to the oriental tunic cut high at the hips and the turbans of various shapes.[64]

The composition of the fresco is thus Byzantine, while the scenes of *skomorokh* performances represent histrionic traditions imported into Greece from the East. It is noteworthy, from our point of view, that the musical instruments depicted in the fresco are by no means Greek. Although the frescoes are of Byzantine origin and the scenes they depict were performed at the Byzantine court, and may also have been imitated and included in the repertory of the festivities at the court of ancient Kiev, the actors and their instruments were not necessarily Byzantine; the actors may well have been itinerant musicians from abroad, so popular at the time, who traveled from city to city. In addition to the costumes and the "acts," the musical instruments in the hands of the *skomorokhi* also convince us of this. Ainalov labels these instruments as harp, *truby, dombra,* and flute. But although the flute was widely known in Greece at the period of that nation's decline and was constantly encountered in the West, the Greeks had no harps, no trumpets such as these, and, of course, no *dombry*. Kondakov decided that the instruments in the fresco are *sopeli* (?) and *bandury,* and calls the harpist a kitharist, but this opinion is quite arbitrary. The Greeks had no *sopeli;* the ordinary little *sopeli* or *sopelki* were quite unlike the cultured Greek flute (aulos); *bandury* were unknown in Greece; and, in its form and construction, the Greek kithara is a stringed instrument of a precise and established type.[64A]

The stringed instrument with an oval body and a long fingerboard, which the musician standing above the seated harpist in the fresco is plucking, decidedly resembles a type of Asiatic *tanbur*. The early-tenth-century Arab writer Al-Farabi [probably Al-Masudi], by now well known to us, who lived some 100 to 125 years before the fresco was painted, describes two kinds of *tanburs: the tanbur* of Khorassan used by the Persians, and the *tanbur* of Baghdad, unique to the Arabs.[64B] Both might have been derived from an older, Syrian, source, which reached the Bulgars and then the Slavs through southern peoples. Villoteau[65] and Fétis[66] mention old and newer types of Bulgarian *tanbura* (fig. 15) which are analogous to the instrument depicted in the Kiev fresco.[67] From ancient Egypt a similar lute-shaped instrument found its way to Phoenicia and the coast of Asia Minor, whose inhabitants were strongly influenced by the art and literature of the Syrians during the first thousand years of our era. From there it crossed to Persia and to the Arabs, to the Caucasus and the Slavic peoples of the Balkan Peninsula, and to locales bordering on the Black Sea, including southern Russia. Villoteau, who studied the musical instruments of ancient Egypt and

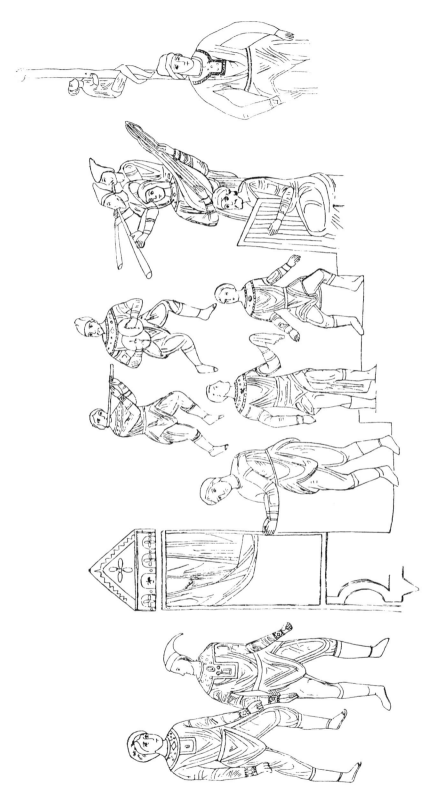

FIG. 14. Fresco on the staircase of the Cathedral of St. Sophia, Kiev; eleventh century.

the East, mentions the interesting fact that the *tanbur* was not found among the Greeks and the Jews; it was unknown in their ordinary life and made its appearance only when introduced by foreign performers from the East, whose ethnic provenance Kondakov was probably correct in identifying from the costumes of the musicians in the Kiev fresco.

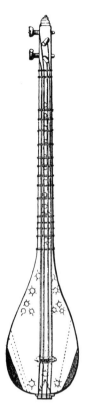

The harp in the fresco also has nothing in common with the Greek kithara. Rather, it is a trapezoidal harp-psaltery, without a resonance box, with which, for example, our *gusli* is equipped. Instruments of this type originated in the East and spread from there to Central Europe. The Egyptian and Assyro-Babylonian rectangular and trapezoidal harps were adopted in a modified and reduced form (the psaltery) by the Jews in Asia Minor and were subsequently brought to Europe. The trapezoidal ten-string harp of the Kiev fresco also appears in medieval miniatures depicting David the Psalmist, such as the miniature of the ninth-century codex in Paris, Bibliothèque nationale, no. 1118.[68] It is not found, however, in relics of Greek art illustrating indigenous traditions. Evidently the harp under discussion was associated with Syrian actors, who borrowed it from the daily life of Semitic peoples of Asia Minor.

There is no doubt about the other instruments in the fresco. In the upper row we have performers on the transverse flute (*Querflöte, flûte traversière*), metal cymbals, and two *skomorokhi* playing *truby*. The first of these instruments was common almost everywhere in ancient and medieval times in the East, in Greece, and in Rome, and it is therefore natural to find it in the hands of expert Syrian performers. Metal cymbals of this size seem to have been almost exclusively an Oriental instrument; in the later Middle Ages they were imported into the European orchestra from so-called Janissary [Turkish] music. Similar straight trumpets, not quite of the usual shape, possibly formed part of the equipment of the guild of Syrian itinerant players, such as those wearing caps in the St. Sophia fresco.

FIG. 15. Bulgarian *tanbur.*

There is another curious scene in the fresco: a sort of screen beside which stands an actor, and, according to Kondakov, "[he] raises a curtain covering the entryway to admit the next act, a clown and harlequin." Some figures can be seen behind the screen. This entryway resembles the facade of the screen in the much later *skomorokh* puppet theater (of Petrushka), and, even though the full extent of Byzantine theatrical entertainments has not yet been investigated, one might suppose that a structure like this with a folding curtain may have led to the idea of constructing a primitive puppet theater. [See the remarks preceding the notes to chapter 3 for current thinking about the interpretation of this portion of the fresco.]

The material we have acquired and discussed relating to the oldest period of the Kievan Principality convinces us, first of all, that the Slavs of those times were by no means a savage and uncivilized people. On the contrary, the elements of high culture were fully evident, if only in the rapid growth of the commercial and social activities of Kiev, the "mother of Russian cities." This fascinating pagan cult, whose musical and artistic side has only recently been revealed, had already experienced a complete and fully developed phase. In the earliest pagan times, we find priest-singers,[69] and apparently special temple music in which, according to Al-Masudi, a trained choir took part. The people also joined in the general singing. In addition to bells and *bila,* musical instruments (trumpets and horns) were used in the pagan temples.

Court life, or rather the life of the prince, was not confined to feasting, fighting, and hunting (for which huge horns of artistic quality, such as the Chernigov ibex horns, were designed). Later we examine the musical instruments used for these purposes, based on written records and on their representation in miniature paintings. In the prince's domestic life, we constantly come across secular songs and musical instruments (*gusli, sopeli, bubny,* and *truby*). The Slavic princes and their envoys visited Byzantium, observed its culture, and brought back with them specimens of the beautiful and artistic possessions used in the Greeks' everyday life. Christianity introduced a new current into the lives of the court and the people. Byzantine builders began to construct churches in Kiev (the Cathedral of St. Sophia and its frescoes, and, before that, the Church of the Tithe). Hence from the southern Slavs came new methods of church singing and musical notation. In the twelfth century and earlier Kiev was filled with foreigners, who introduced their own distinct culture. It is curious that at the time of the violent attack on Kiev on 1 January 1204 by the Polovtsians and their ally, Prince Riurik Rostislavich, the stoutest resistance came from the foreign merchants, who defended themselves so manfully in the stone churches of the capital city that the enemy had to be content with nothing more than their possessions. These merchants, of course, introduced into local life (more receptive in the South than in the sterner North) their own customs and musical instruments. More than seventy-five years earlier a great fire had destroyed the whole of the Jewish Street in Kiev. Not long before this, Jews had started to appear, and there was even a Jewish gate, which means that they had a synagogue and traditional festivals, and also explains the noteworthy music-historical detail frequently encountered in *byliny:*

> The songs come from Constantinople,
> And others come from Jerusalem,
> And the little refrains from beyond the Blue Sea,
> The Blue Sea of Vedenets,
> From beyond that verdant shore.
> (*bylina* about Solovei Budimirovich)[69A]

The knights and singers at court might have heard such songs and refrains from the Jews and other foreigners who had settled in Kiev.

2. Old Slavic musical instruments according to manuscripts, poems, and art objects[69B]

Most of the evidence of Russia's domestic musical practice in the period of its emergence as an organized state comes from literary references and allusions that survive in folk song. We shall first consider evidence relating chiefly to musical instruments, and then examine what has survived in the form of notated music for the Church.

We learn a great deal about the military and domestic practices of the ancient Slavs from the oldest manuscripts and the numerous miniatures illustrating them. These documents include narrative chronicles like the Hypatian, Novgorod, and others; the Manasses Chronicle (Vatican copy of the fourteenth century); and the illuminated Radziwill or

Königsberg Chronicle (fifteenth-century copy), among others; the renowned Khludov Psalter (thirteenth century); the richly illustrated Cosmas Indicopleustes (which came to us in a later, Novgorod copy of the sixteenth century); certain literary creations like the *Slovo o polku Igoreve* [The lay of the host of Igor], which has come down to us in a copy from the end of the eighteenth century but which scholars most recently ascribed to the twelfth century (the date of Igor's return from captivity), and the *Skazanie o Mamaevom poboishche* [The tale of Mamai's bloody battle], also an illustrated manuscript of which we have a sixteenth-century copy; as well as other sources. Apart from these, musical and archaeological data can be found in other artistic monuments of ancient Rus', for example, in the frescoes and sculptures of the twelfth-century Cathedral of St. Dmitrii [in Vladimir], from icons (such as the icon of the Miraculous Intervention of the Icon of the Sign of the Mother of God on the iconostasis of the Cathedral of the Sign in Novgorod), and so on.

The chronicler of Prince Sviatoslav Igorevich's Bulgarian campaign (in the 960s) says that "they go rank by rank, beating the *bubny* and the *truby*."[69C] The Hypatian Chronicle under the year 1151 says that "with *truby* blaring, the regiments began to sing along [*dospevati*]." The Suzdal Chronicle, mentioning the disputes of 1216 between Novgorod and the city of Vladimir, states that the Novgorodians had 60 *truby* in the field, and Iaroslav "had 17 banners and 40 *truby* and *bubny*."[69D] The Nikonian Chronicle under the year 1219 records that "Prince Sviatoslav Vsevolodovich ordered his subjects to arm themselves and unfurl the banners . . . and beat the *bubny* and the *truby* and the *surny*."[69E] In *The Tale of Mamai's Bloody Battle* one reads: "The sounds of *truby* were heard on both sides. The Tatar trumpets grew silent, while those of the Russians became louder" as if announcing Dmitrii Donskoi's victory over Mamai.[69F] Finally, the poetic *Lay of the Host of Igor* repeatedly mentions trumpets as an appurtenance of the Slavic army:[69G]

> Glory rings in Kiev,
> trumpets blare in Novgorod

Or Vsevolod, the wild Aurochs, says to his elder brother:

> Saddle, brother, your swift horses
> for mine are ready,
> saddled ahead at Kursk.
> And these, my men of Kursk
> are hardened fighters,
> swaddled to the blare of trumpets.

Truby, bubny, and *surny* thus formed a part of the basic, essential equipment of the Russian army in those ancient times. Illustrations of some of these instruments appear in miniatures and other artistic documents of the Slavs.

In one of the miniatures of the Vatican copy of the Manasses Chronicle (fig. 16),[70] two scenes of Sviatoslav's Bulgarian campaign are depicted: the upper part of the miniature, with the heading "Russian captivity," apparently represents a foraging expedition in the neighborhood of a town; the lower section, titled "Going to Dorostel'," represents an attack on the fortress of that name. In both portions of the miniature we see trumpeters [*trubachi*] on horseback among the armed cavalry. In the lower illustration the trumpeter's pose suggests that he is sounding a summons to an attack.

FIG. 16. A miniature from the Manasses Chronicle; fourteenth century.

One of the oldest Russian written documents, the well-known Khludov Psalter, contains a miniature (on fol. 270v) depicting the Jews crossing the Red Sea (fig. 17): Moses striking the sea with his rod for the second time and the destruction of Pharaoh's army (the heads of the drowning soldiers are visible); Aaron standing with uplifted arms with

FIG. 17. The Jews cross the Red Sea. A miniature from the Khludov Psalter; thirteenth century.

the prophetess Miriam standing beside him holding *kimvaly* (*bubny*) in both hands;[70A] and behind them three men blowing trumpets (two are straight with wide bells, and the third is a curved horn similar to the Hebrew *shofar*).

The Russian miniaturists nearly always depicted the breath issuing from the instruments, in this case emulating Western models (see fig. 18).[71] The inscription, unclear in the copy, beside the main group of people reads: "The children of Israel crossing on dry ground." An explanation appears in the inscription next to the angel, who is spreading a sort of tissue over the water (the Red Sea): "I lead into daylight with a cloud." According to Archimandrite Amfilokhii, the miniatures of this Psalter were the work of a Russian artist and were copied from Greek models.[72]

Similar trumpets with both large and narrow bells are preserved in the tale of Dmitrii Donskoi's victory over Mamai (*The Tale of Mamai's Bloody Battle*, 1380), in later illuminated manuscripts of the sixteenth century, giving us a whole series of representations of military metal trumpets, although of a much later period. This source was published by the Society of Friends of Old Literature in St. Petersburg in 1907, based on the Undol'skii copy, with a preface by S. K. Shambinago. The manuscript contains many miniatures, although other sources include

FIG. 18. Miniature from the *Hortus deliciarum;* Strasbourg University Library, twelfth century.

even more (see the Uvarov Collection, no. 492 from the seventeenth century, now in the Moscow Historical Museum [GIM 1831] and [GIM] 2596 from the eighteenth century, and in the Rumiantsev Museum in Moscow [RGB] 3123 from the seventeenth century).[73] The Friends of Old Literature edition reproduces the following miniatures:

1. fol. 21 (no. 21). Princes Dmitrii Ivanovich (Donskoi) and Vladimir on horseback facing each other on "a high place." Dmitrii is pointing to the troops standing below; in two detachments we find thirteen straight trumpets; three trumpeters playing on them are visible [see fig. 19]. According to S. K. Shambinago, similar straight trumpets are also represented in the Uvarov copy;
2. fol. 40v (no. 44). A cavalry troop with Prince Dmitrii Donskoi at its head with a banner depicting the image of the Savior-Not-Made-with-Human-Hands [Nerukotvornyi Spas] and five mounted trumpeters;
3. fol. 41v (no. 45). A detachment of Tatar horsemen with a banner and eight trumpets, one of which is curved;
4. fol. 53 (no. 59). Prince Vladimir's detachment of horsemen with two captured Tatar banners and another one with the image of the Savior-Not-Made-with-Human-Hands and a large painted trumpet with a wide bell;
5. fol. 57v (no. 66). A similar large straight trumpet in a cavalry detachment accompanying both princes on the battlefield. Dmitrii Ivanovich weeps at the sight of so many killed. The lower part of the miniature is lost;
6. fol. 59 (no. 68). Kulikovo Field after the battle with Mamai. In the lower part of the miniature are the two dead Russian knights, Osliabia and Peresvet. The prince's division is on one of the mounds, behind which are raised three regular straight trumpets and one enormous decorated one [fig. 20].

Two of these miniatures are reproduced here (the first and sixth, see figs. 19 and 20), illustrating the large number of brass trumpets in the Russian army, in both infantry and cavalry units. These miniatures also demonstrate the variety and sizes of military trumpets: plain and decorated ones, probably designating the importance of the duty assigned to the military units. In addition to these six miniatures, Shambinago mentions others representing musicians with trumpets which were not included in that publication (e.g., p. 90, miniature 76, "The troops, with the princes, attack Peresvet" in the Uvarov copy, where "at the head of the troops the trumpeters sound; the prince ordered them to play at that place").

Earlier illustrations of trumpets may be seen in the fresco of the Cathedral of St. Dmitrii in the city of Vladimir, built by Prince Vsevolod in the twelfth century, and on the Novgorod icon of the Miraculous Intervention, where the battle itself is also painted. The latter is mentioned later in examining documents of Novgorod's musical culture.

The illuminated Radziwill (or Königsberg) Chronicle, which is a fifteenth-century copy of an older original and which, according to N. P. Kondakov, may have been copied in the Suzdal area, contains no less than ten miniatures depicting scenes of military and social life in the twelfth and thirteenth centuries in which trumpeters appear frequently. A complete photo-offset edition of this manuscript was published in St. Petersburg in 1902 by the Society of Friends of Old Literature (no. 118 in their series), from which two illustrations are reproduced here. The first, on folio 207v (see fig. 21), is a kind of addition to the previous image, representing the toasts at the conclusion of a peace treaty between Vladimir Glebovich (Pereiaslavskii) and the Polovtsians in 1185. For this occasion, apparently,

FIG. 20. Miniature from *The Tale of Mamai's Bloody Battle*; manuscript from the sixteenth century.

FIG. 19. Miniature from *The Tale of Mamai's Bloody Battle*; manuscript from the sixteenth century.

FIG. 21. Miniature from the Radziwill Chronicle, fol. 207v.

two trumpeters are practicing on their instruments, which are now of a different shape: instead of straight trumpets, both players hold medieval curved trumpets (like cornets).

A different scene is depicted on the miniature on folio 243v (fig. 22), where in the year 1200 Prince Vsevolod Georgievich, grandson of Vladimir Monomakh, is meeting the citizens of the city of Vladimir, who pay obeisance to him, while two trumpeters on the tower play on their instruments. One has a straight trumpet and the other a horn-like curved one.

Other miniatures of interest in the Radziwill Chronicle depict a trumpeter on foot following the cavalry as they proceed toward Chernigov (fol. 169); a trumpeter playing in honor of Prince Vsevolod, to whom a cup is offered (fol. 169v); a trumpeter playing on a straight trumpet (fol. 196v); a trumpeter playing during a march by the Viatichians (fol. 203); apparently a city guard on a tower playing a straight trumpet during the attack on Riazan (fol. 227v); and two miniatures with trumpeters on horseback (one of them has a curved trumpet) during and after the battle with the Polovtsians (fol. 234v).

FIG. 22. Miniature from the Radziwill Chronicle, fol. 243v.

Similar miniatures depicting military musical instruments can, of course, be found in other manuscripts as well. Here we shall examine data about the nonmilitary, folk instruments of the Slavs. The most popular and most beloved of these instruments was the *gusli*. But the instrument had two kinds of associations. The very term *gusli* was revered as a musical instrument of the biblical tsar-psalmist and *gusli* player David, who was often represented with the *gusli* as his attribute. But the very same *gusli* in the hands of the common people, or rather in the hands of their professional entertainers, the *skomorokhi*, was an instrument disowned and condemned by the clergy, who did allow representations of the *gusli* to appear in the written documents of their ecclesiastical and ceremonial literature. The name *gusli* is an accepted term for a multi-stringed instrument with a large, hollow sound box (resonator). The word *gusli* is a plural form and its singular (*gusl'*, *giasl'*) is seldom found in ancient literature. Often the term *gusli* is used not as the name of a particular musical instrument but in a symbolic manner: "The Lord's *gusli* thou shalt tune with the hand of the Holy Spirit" (Putiatina Mineia, eleventh century, fol. 3, from the Public Library [RNB]).[73A]

In the Russian Primary Chronicle under the year 1015 there is a reference to Sviatopolk the Impious, which reads, "This Prince loves to drink wine to the sound of the *gusli* with his young counselors." In the same chronicle, describing the feasts at the court of Sviatoslav Iaroslavich (d. 1076), reference is made to *skomorokhi*, some of whom "were performing on *gusli*, others sounded instruments [*organnyia glasy poiushche*], and some sounded pipes from across the sea, and thus all were playing and making merry as is the custom before the prince." This extremely interesting testimony suggests not only the existence of a court cappella (not unlike those at the Poteshnaia palata in the seventeenth century) but also of a performance of instrumental and vocal music even of foreign origin, a point confirmed by our *byliny*.[73B]

The same chronicle contains other curious bits of information, with some ascribed to specific dates. The following entry appears under the year 1068: "The devil . . . alienates us from God by all manner of craft, through trumpets and *skomorokhi*, *gusli* and pagan festivals [*rusal'i*]," which documents the presence (and the rejection by the clergy) of the *skomorokhi*, *gusli* playing, and folk songs and customs.[73C] Although the clergy revered King David's *gusli* in the context of the Bible, they also placed it figuratively in the hands of the devil as a seducer of the people. Again in the same chronicle, under the year 1074, there appears a listing of a whole arsenal of musical instruments by means of which evil spirits, inspired by the devil ("the oldest of the demons") tried to tempt the Blessed Isaakii Pecherskii [a monk in the Monastery of the Caves in Kiev]: "Take up the *sopeli*, the *bubny*, and the *gusli* and play and make Isaakii listen. And they struck up with the *sopeli*, the *gusli*, and the *bubny* and began to make sport of him."[73D]

Thus we find that the principal instruments of the *skomorokhi* were the *gusli*, *sopeli*, and *bubny*. The latter instruments appear to have been in general use in the army, where instead of the *sopel'* they used the *surna* [a shawm-like instrument]. Performance on the *gusli* was often called *gudenie*, from the verb *gudet'* [to hum, buzz, or drone]. The expression "v gusli gudut'" [they play on the *gusli*] appears in the *Pouchenie* [Sermon] of Kirill of Turov. See also the *Life* of Andrei Iur'evich, chapters 36, 141, and elsewhere, where phrases such as "derzhashe gusli i gudiashe" [holding the *gusli* and playing on the *gusli*] appear.[73E] The term "guslenoe khudozhestvo" [the art of playing on the *gusli* or the *gusli* art], used by the translator of Cosmas Indicopleustes, differed completely from folk musicianship because it admitted elements foreign to folk songs but which were natural in an instrumental performance allowing for free improvisation.[73F] Not without reason was it stated in the *Zadonshchina* that "the texts with *gusli* music are distinctly different from songs [*ot pesen*]."[73G]

Surviving fragments of ancient *byliny* have preserved descriptions of *gusli* playing by medieval heroes, some of whom were specialists in that art. Later we shall acquaint ourselves with the most renowned of these, the Novgorod merchant Sadko. The following is an extract from a *bylina* about one of the most ancient Kievan heroes, Vol'ga Vseslav'evich, in which there is a vivid depiction of a banquet at Prince Vladimir's court:[74]

> Dobryniushka would set out to roam the open plain,
> Would drop in on Vladimir's splendid feast,
> And at the feast would play the *gusli*.
>> Ah, t'would happen on some day at noon,
>> The prince's table would be half-cleared,
>> And all 'round it drunk and happy,
>> Vladimir himself glowing with pleasure.
>> Then into the princely chambers
>> Would come the young Dobryniushka Nikitich . . .
>> . . . . . .
>
>> 'Twas not the golden trumpet that would sound,
>> Neither the silver *sapovochka* [a wind instrument]
>> That would play,
> But Father-Prince Vladimir himself who would exclaim,
> Who would call out in a loud voice:
> "Hark, my servants, my faithful servants
> Pour out a cup of green wine [vodka],
> Pour out a cup of strong beer,
> Pour out a cup of sweet mead,
> Mix all three together
> And take the cup to the good young fellow,
> To the young Dobryniushka Nikitich."
> . . . .
> Dobrynia would take the cup in one hand
> And drink it down in one draught
> And Vladimir himself would praise him on the deed.
>> And Prince Vladimir would say,
>> "Hark, young Dobryniushka Nikitich
> Take your vibrant *gusli*,
> Pluck its golden strings,
> And play us something mournful, something tender,
> Then play us something merry."
>> Then would Dobrynia take in his fine hands
> His clear-toned, vibrant *gusli*,
> He would pluck the golden strings
> And play a melancholy Jewish verse,
> Melancholy, yea, and tender.
> All at the feast would grow pensive,
> Pensive as they listened.
> Then Dobrynia would play something jolly,
> A dance tune from Jerusalem,
> Another dance tune from Constantinople,

And a third from the capital city of Kiev,
Which would lead everyone to merry-making.
Or so the playing seemed to Vladimir.

Another hero of the Vladimir circle, the young Solovei [nightingale] Budimirovich, was also, like the older Dobrynia, a master of the *gusli.*[75]

He [Solovei Budimirovich] plays on the vibrant *gusli*
Reaching from string to string
He sings songs to their melodies
To the clear-sounding strings.
The songs come from Constantinople
And others from Jerusalem,
And the little refrains from beyond the blue sea,
From beyond the blue sea of Vedenets,
From beyond that green shore.
Entertaining his mother
The young Ul'iana Vasil'evna,
Calming his brave companions.

Both of these *byliny*, along with their numerous variants, describe similar ways of playing the instrument. The very name *gusli* is described as *iarovchatye* or *iavorchatye*. The latter probably refers to the material from which the instrument was made in the past, the *iavor* tree (the sycamore maple, Acer pseudoplatanus) or the white maple [*belyi klen*]; this tree produces a light-colored timber with fine, lustrous graining especially suitable for the resonating box of the *gusli*. The designation *iarovchatyi* [bright, clear], however, may also derive from the strong, clear sound produced by the metal strings (which were gilded and highly resonant).

The *bylina* about Vol'ga Vseslav'evich recounts a whole series of domestic scenes: a ceremonial feast with the traditional wine cup in various shapes (the prototype of the Petrine goblet in the shape of a great eagle), a *gusli* player's varied musical interludes, and so on.[75A] Among the collection of folk wind instruments already mentioned, this *bylina* also refers to the (gilded) metallic trumpet and the *sapovochka*. But most interesting for us are the various "tunes" played on the *gusli* by the performers, including Solovei himself: "a melancholy Jewish verse," a jolly "dance tune from Jerusalem," "another from Constantinople," and "a third from the capital city of Kiev." To these tunes Solovei Budimirovich adds refrains from "beyond the blue sea of Vedenets" (Venice). All these details show that the repertory of the *gusli* players was by no means monotonous or limited to playing accompaniments, a kind of Slavic refrain, as it were, for the celebratory songs (*byliny*) ("a third from the capital city of Kiev"). The repertory was quite varied and we know what and how it might imitate other music: pilgrims to holy places brought back new, strange, and wonderful melodies, and the contacts with Byzantium, the East, and the West (political and trade relations, not to mention the work and trade of foreigners in Kiev), and the presence of a Jewish settlement in Kiev undoubtedly exercised strong influences on local life and were assimilated by the specialists in musical matters, the *skomorokhi*.

In one of the *byliny* describing Dobrynia's varied adventures, we find, for example, details of how he wound up at the court of a Kievan prince dressed as a *skomorokh.*[76]

Dobrynia Nikitich spoke:
"He [Alyosha Popovich] swore brotherhood with me:
If you are going to be at the feast in Kiev,
Bring my *skomorokh* attire,
And bring my clear-toned *gusli*,
And place them all in another room on the table."

And in this *bylina* Dobrynia, arriving at the Prince's feast,

Tightened his silken bowstrings,
His golden threads,
And began to wander over the strings;
Began to sing snatches of song, accompanying [them]
He played [a tune] from Constantinople,
And in his song [*vyigrysh*] he recounted all that had taken place in Kiev.

Other documents tell us more about the *gusli*, its shape and the number of strings it had. The oldest of these documents, the twelfth-century *Lay of the Host of Igor*, which we examine a little later, contains the following detail:[76A]

But Boian's ten falcons, brothers,
attacked no flock of swans.
His own magic fingers struck,
and the live strings
pulsed glory to the princes.

It may be assumed that the *gusli* had ten strings in the twelfth century. Unfortunately older artistic monuments, not of Novgorodian origin, give us no idea of the shape of the Slavic *gusli*. At any rate, I am not aware of any. The Church of the Intercession near Vladimir contains (or did contain) an old sculptural representation (twelfth century?) of King David holding in his left hand a *gusli*-like stringed instrument (fig. 23). This illustration is reproduced from the first volume of the *Proceedings of the First Archaeological Congress in Moscow,* where it is stated that similar figures appear on the west and south walls of the church (the example reproduced here was from the north wall).[76B]

The king's Byzantine dress and the traditional representation of the *psalterium* indicate that the statue was the work of a foreign master, and hence it is useless to look here for the Slavic *gusli*. The stringed instruments depicted in the Khludov Psalter

Fig. 23. A sculpture of King David from the Church of the Intercession near Vladimir; twelfth century.

(mentioned previously) are even less akin to the Slavic *gusli*.[76C] An illuminated miniature from the Khludov Psalter, which depicts King David "taking up" or "composing" the Psalter, is particularly interesting, because the instruments shown in it are completely different from Slavic instruments. In the center of the picture, which is titled "King David taking up [or composing] the Psalter," King David holds in his left hand a three-string *organistrum* [hurdy-gurdy], and in his right hand, the instrument's crank. Next to him, a bit lower, is Solomon with a five- or six-string psaltery, and on either side are youths playing a horn [*rog*], a wooden wind instrument, and a *crwth*, and beating small drums [*timpany*] and cymbals. Beneath are two groups of youths. The leaders of the group to the left are playing on a similar psaltery and a bowed *crwth* (although the outlines of both instruments are analogous); in the group on the right we have *bubny* and a hand-held horn. Like the setting and costumes of this outstanding miniature, the instruments are not Slavic but are borrowed from Western models. It is sufficient to compare this miniature with one of King David playing a bowed *crwth* in an eleventh-century miniature from the Bibliothèque nationale in Paris (manuscript no. 1118 from the Abbey of St. Martial in Limoges), and with a bas-relief from the same period from the St. Martin-de-Boscherville Abbey near Rouen. King David holds a bowed *crwth* (fig. 24) which is analogous to the *crwth* held by the youth in the group at the lower left in the Khludov Psalter and can be found in later miniatures in Slavic manuscripts. King David in the Khludov Psalter holds in his hands a medieval *organistrum*

(the prototype of the future European *Leyer* [or hurdy-gurdy] and the Ukrainian *lira*), which appears in fig. 25, reproducing a fragment of the Boscherville bas-relief of AD 1160.[77]

Illustrations of the Slavic *gusli* can be found only in Novgorodian manuscripts of a later date, since it was in Novgorod that *gusli* playing was developed in connection with the local *skomorokhi*. This is reflected in artistic monuments in which, along with the instruments that emulate foreign models, one may also find representations of genuine Russian folk *gusli*.

In the Kievan era, as we have already learned from the *byliny*, the *gusli* was not used only by the *skomorokhi*. Far more important for us are written documents attesting to the presence at the princely courts of more serious musicians and poet-rhapsodists. One of the earliest such representatives was Boian, often mentioned by the bard of the *Lay of the Host of Igor*, who may have lived in the early twelfth century, since, according to later documents, Boian mentions in his poems Vseslav Polotskii, who died in 1101. The word *slovo* [word] in the title *Slovo o polku Igoreve* must be understood to mean a poem, just as it does in the *Slovo o Zadonshchine*. N. S. Tikhonravov correctly interprets the term *starye slovesa* [old words] as old poems or heroic antiquities.

FIG. 24. King David playing a *crwth*. Miniature from an eleventh-century manuscript from Paris, Bibliothèque national.

FIG. 25. *Organistrum* players. A fragment from a bas-relief at Saint Martin-de-Boscherville, twelfth century.

Our scholars adhere to two contradictory viewpoints regarding the *Lay of the Host of Igor:* one group sees it not as a musical but as an exclusively literary document, denying the authorship of a bard-singer (this group includes Prince Viazemskii, A. I. Sobolevskii, V. N. Peretts, A. I. Liashchenko, and others); the other group sees the *Lay* as a poem which was sung [intoned] at the princely court in Kiev and which probably came into existence in this manner. Supporters of this opinion include not only Karamzin (who translated fragments of "Boianova pesnopeniia" [Boian's songs] in the original dactylic verse) but also such sophisticated students of Slavic antiquities as E. Barsov, N. Bitsyn, F. I. Buslaev, N. S. Tikhonravov, academicians I. I. Sreznevskii and F. E. Korsh, and also the Kievan scholar Iu. Tikhovskii. Korsh, in his edition of the poem (St. Petersburg, 1909), even provided a series of musical motifs to which certain verses might be set! He did not set his melodies to any texts, however, so it remains unclear to which verses his improvised tunes might apply (they are, by the way, entirely Russian in character). Korsh makes the interesting statement that 4/4 time is observed "apparently everywhere" in the poem.[77A]

Barsov, who ascribes the *Lay of the Host of Igor* to documents originating in Chernigov, declares in one of his studies of the poem that "so far [1878] no one has doubted the actual existence of Boian as a composer of songs in the days of Iaroslav and Oleg." He also points out that the "existence is clearly obvious of such 'tellers of tales about the armies'; history knows of more than a few peoples, among whom in their earliest times were professional bards endowed with the gift of poetical narration and who sang about the heroic exploits of their princes and their armies.... Our chronicle even introduces a *gudok* player named Or, a singer of Polovtsian songs."[78] Another scholar and translator of the *Lay of the Host of Igor,* N. Bitsyn, conjectures that the *Lay* was recited by a singer in a princely assembly hall before a large audience. It was delivered in a sing-song fashion, and the singer had learned where to raise and where to lower his voice. The musical cadence of its splendid verses has even now, after all these years, not lost its charm. The lilt of the tones in the *Lay* can be heard in the very poetry itself.[79]

All this convinces us more and more that the *Lay of the Host of Igor* is our most precious monument to the rhapsodic art of courtly *gusli* players/singers, a conviction not contradicted by even the most recent analyses of its details (especially by Liashchenko). Comparing it to another monument to the artistry of the rhapsodists, the *Zadonshchina,* I. I. Sreznevskii states, among other points:[80] "It is not possible to represent the *Lay of the Host of Igor* purely as a book ... and it is even more difficult to claim that it was not recited or sung, just as stories and verses, *byliny,* and legends are still being sung." The actual version of the *Lay of the Host of Igor* that has come down to us is not the complete poem as it must have been sung in its original form. There *is* no poem as such, which does not mean that there never was one. The fragments that have survived, says Sreznevskii, show themselves to be the remnants of ancient verses preserved in memory by the bard: "you would have sung this song to Igor, the grandson of Oleg," then he cites four lines of verse from the song:[80A]

> No storm has carried the falcons
> across the wide steppe;
> flocks of daws race
> toward the great Don.

Then the bard proclaims again: "Or would you sing, wizard Boian, grandson of Veles," and again cites a song of a distinctive structure:

> Horses neigh beyond the Sula;
> glory rings in Kiev;
> trumpets blare in Novgorod;
> banners stand in Putivl!

And at the end of the *Lay*, the singer cites two more lines of verse by Boian:

> Woe is the head without the shoulders,
> the body without a head.[81]

Not only in the *Lay of the Host of Igor* and the *Zadonshchina* do we find fragments of poetic similes taken almost verbatim from the repertory of ancient bards or perhaps from folk poetry. F. Buslaev points out in his *Historical Reader* that the author of the Volyn Chronicle (according to the Hypatian manuscript) was familiar with folk poetry, and indeed, when referring to the beginning of Roman Galitskii's reign, under the entry for 1201, the author describes Roman's wisdom and power entirely in the spirit of our bard rhapsodists: "He swooped down upon the pagans like a lion, raged like a lynx, laid waste like a crocodile, crossed their land like an eagle, was as brave as an aurochs."[81A] Indeed, according to the voice of the bard in the *Lay*, whenever the visionary Boian[81B]

> . . . wished to create a song,
> he would course through the tree in thought—
> as a grey wolf
> along the ground,
> as a dusky eagle
> beneath the clouds.

The use of similes was apparently a favorite method of our old rhapsodists, and from them the practice found its way into songs and *byliny*, and also into the literary language: "The sun dispersed for him the darkness of the way," "There shall be a great thundering and the Mighty Don shall rain arrows," and many others.[82] Such highly poetic images as these can scarcely have been meaningless to the humble mind of the ancient Russian scribe:[82A]

> We were not born to be offended,
> neither by the falcon, nor by the hawk,
> nor by the black crow, that pagan dog Mamai.

Or in *byliny:*

> The scoundrel flees like a black crow
> Beware (says Dobrynia's mother) that black crow, the scoundrel!

In a later tale from the *Zadonshchina* about the Grand Prince Dmitrii Ivanovich, one hears echoes of the old refrains of the Kievan bards:[82B]

> O skylark, bird of summer
> fine days' delight!
> Fly up beneath the blue heavens,
> glance toward the powerful city of Moscow
> sing out glory to the Grand Prince Dmitrii Ivanovich.

After all this, can it be maintained that the *Lay of the Host of Igor,* the *Zadonshchina,* and other fragments of our ancient literature were the creations of a humble, prosaic language, a language that shunned genuine poetry and which sometimes dismayed us by its scholasticism and its intolerance of any artistic creative work that exceeded the prescribed limits?

Korsh, in his previously mentioned work, has justly remarked that the *bylina*-like character of the *Lay of the Host of Igor* is realized chiefly when it is recited. At the same time the text often contains superfluous poetic feet or syllables which are not found in the *bylina;* they occur at the beginning or end of a verse and sometimes at both, for example:[82C]

> O Boian, nightingale of a former time,
> if you were to sing
> the glory of these campaigns, flitting as a nightingale
> through the tree of thought
> flying through the mind in clouds,
> weaving glories together
> at both ends of this time,
> loping along the path of Troian
> through the steppes toward the mountains
> you would have sung this song to Igor,
> the grandson of Oleg.

The additional poetic feet are italicized as found in Korsh's text.[83] They can be understood if the poem is accepted not as a purely literary document but as having the character of a *bylina,* as something to be sung. In a vocal performance these additional syllables are filled up naturally by recitative-like phrases such as we find in later records of northern *byliny* (in the collection of Kirsha Danilov, for example, in the *bylina* about Vas'ka Buslaev) and in those from southern Russia (Ukrainian *dumy* and historical songs).[83A]

Songs of praise were customary, and Boian, glorified in the *Lay of the Host of Igor,* was one of their creators and singers. Boian's fame outlived him, and the author of the later literary monument, the *Zadonshchina* (about the victory over Mamai in 1380), emulates the *Lay of the Host of Igor* in some sections, and recalls in its introduction the legendary Boian the *gusli* player:[83B]

> From there we shall mount upon the hills of Kiev
> Before anyone else we shall sing praises
> To the visionary Boian in the city of Kiev
> The dazzling player on the *gusli*
> This Boian was like a magician

Strumming with his golden fingers the living strings
Singing praises to the Russian princes
To the first one, to Prince Riurik
To Igor Riurikovich and Sviatoslav Iaroslavich
To Iaroslav Volodimerovich
Praising them in songs and words on the *gusli*.

And the poet of *Zadonshchina* adds: "I sing songs of praise with the poetry of the *gusli* to the Russian Lord, Lord Dmitrii Ivanovich."[84]

The poet of the *Lay of the Host of Igor* calls the visionary Boian the "grandson of Veles."[84A] The god Veles in Slavic mythology was, like Apollo, god of the sun, and in the imagination of the *Lay's* poet, Veles, like Apollo the Kitharodos, was the patron of the art of music. Boian should not be viewed as a mythical figure. The existence of eminent singers and professional *gusli* players in princely service, apart from the vast body of second-rate *skomorokhi,* is almost certain. Traces of such outstanding musicians and a confirmation of their existence can be found in some ancient documents as well as in *byliny.* An entry in the Hypatian Chronicle under the year 1201 explains that, at the death of Vladimir Monomakh, his brother "had left with Syr'chan a single *gusli* player, that very same Or [Orevi], and Syr'chan sent him to the Obez land to say: 'Vladimir is dead. Come back, Brother, come back home. Beseech him in my words, sing him [Otrok] songs of the Polovtsians; if he doesn't want to return, give him this grass, called *evshan,* to smell.'"[85] This passage implies that players at court were familiar not only with Slavic but with foreign (Polovtsian) melodies and songs, and that they were close to the prince and even carried out diplomatic missions. In the same Hypatian Chronicle, under the year 1243, there is a reference to a well-known singer, Mitus, who previously had not wanted to serve Prince Daniil Volynskii. At the time of the civil war between the Riazan and Volyn princes, the major-domo of the Volyn prince Andrei, "not being able to capture [Prince Konstantin of Riazan], captured instead a gentleman [. . .] and his servant. . . . the renowned singer Mitus—who for a long time from pride did not want to serve Prince Daniil—were persecuted and taken prisoner."[86]

There were undoubtedly quite a few of these "nightingales of bygone days." Their names are forgotten or have not yet been discovered, but their existence is certain. Their duties were the same as those of the much later Ukrainian *kobzary* and *lirniki:* to sing of bygone days and to praise and glorify their princes and their ancestors. [The *kobza* and the *lira* are stringed folk instruments; see chapter 7.] The references above show this clearly; the author of the *Zadonshchina,* mentioning Boian or the use of characteristic melodic formulas [*popevki*], says that "Boian used to place his skillful fingers on the living strings and sing glory to the Russian princes."[86A]

These poems also influenced the texts of the chronicles, spurring the use of similes, as in the example praising the memory of Prince Roman in the Hypatian Chronicle (1201), where the chronicler characterizes the prince as follows: "He swooped down upon the pagans like a lion, raged like a lynx, laid waste like a crocodile, crossed their land like an eagle, was as brave as an aurochs."[86B] All this is obviously taken from a song of praise.

The same Hypatian Chronicle, under the year 1252, in speaking of the war with the Yatviagians, tells us that "Prince Daniil came to Vin'za and crossed the river Narov and [Daniil and Vasilko] freed many Christians from imprisonment and they sang them a song of praise." We thus understand that Daniil freed them, and therefore they sang him a song of praise. Similarly, in an entry for 1242, the Voskresenskaia Chronicle tells about a song in praise of Prince Aleksandr [Nevskii], hailed on his return after his victory over the Germans at Pskov, and even gives the song itself: "Ever helpful God, to the meek David, to defeat the foreigners and to return to the true prince with our Christian arms, to free the city of Pskov from foreigners at the hand of the Great Prince Aleksandr Iaroslavich."[86C]

Even in a rather late document (a manuscript from the sixteenth century, formerly in the library of the Volokolamsk Monastery, and later in the Moscow Divinity School, no. 157–521, fol. 31) we read: "placing experienced fingers on the living strings and we sing a peaceful and merry song."[86D] All these are poetic relics of the days when eminent singer-poets and *gusli* players lived and sang at the princely courts, when their works were heard by princes, their retinue, and their guests. We find their echoes, preserved in varying states in the sources, in poetic fragments interspersed in some dry, bookish chronicle presentation, or scattered through the old *byliny* which are still preserved, at times amazingly so, in the memory of people who live in remote areas untouched by modern cultural developments.

3. Ancient church chant in Russia, its notation and manuscript sources[86E]

Rus' not only accepted Orthodox Christianity from Byzantium but also the singing practices and musical notation indispensable for performing the religious ritual. We already know about the first Greek and Bulgarian singer-clerics who arrived in Kievan Rus' to introduce the repertory of chants and, undoubtedly, brought with them examples of the notated chant books. These singers became the first teachers and *domestiki* [probably a kind of director] of Slavic church choirs, at least in Kiev and Rostov, which is noted in the chronicles and also in the *Stepennaia kniga* [The book of degrees]. Metropolitan Mikhail went from Kiev to the Rostov area where, in the words of the chronicle, "he baptized countless numbers of people, built many churches, ordained priests and deacons, organized a *klyros,* and established the rules."[86F] Soon, however, local Russians became masters of singing as well, among them the well-known Stefan, from Kiev, a pupil of Feodosii Pecherskii, who was himself an authority on singing. Stefan was also Feodosii's alternate as abbot of the Kievan Monastery of the Caves (ca. 1047). Other well-known musicians were Kirik, the *domestik* of St. Anthony's in Novgorod (first half of the twelfth century), and Luke, the *domestik* in Vladimir (twelfth century), whose singers the chronicler calls "Luke's offspring."[86G]

The Russians, and Slavs in general, had no musical notation of their own at the time, and the notation that made its appearance with the introduction of Christianity was undoubtedly of Greek or Greco-Bulgarian origin. This is corroborated by the oldest Slavic notated books, gospels with musical signs for cantillation (or solemn reading) of the sacred texts. According to our well-known paleographers A. I. Sobolevskii and N. M. Karinskii, the few extant complete copies of such documents were copied from Old Bulgarian or Old Church Slavonic originals, which are roughly the same. As for the musical notation, as we shall see, it was entirely analogous to contemporary Byzantine chant notation.

3a. Ekphonetic notation

The earliest of these sources are the well-known Ostromir Gospel and two parchment folios from a contemporary *aprakos* gospel known as the Kupriianov leaflets.[86H] Both are in the Russian Public Library [RNB],[87] and both were written in the eleventh century, that is, within a century after Rus' officially converted to Christianity. The notation found in both is ekphonetic notation as prescribed for cantillation, although the notation in the Ostromir Gospel appears to have been used more or less nonchalantly or in groupings, not systematically.[88] The notation in the Ostromir Gospel remains unresearched by our musicologists, although already in 1865 A. F. Bychkov had drawn attention to it, and N. M. Karinskii mentioned it later in his *Reader of the Old Church Slavonic and Russian Languages*.[89] This remarkable primary source has not been studied from the musicological point of view, even though it was published twice in photo-lithographic editions by I. K. Savinov in 1883 and 1889.[89A] On the other hand, the ekphonetic signs found in the two Kupriianov leaflets aroused scholars' interest from the time they were acquired by the Public Library in 1865, when D. V. Razumovskii made an attempt to interpret them. They were also reproduced, but neither exactly nor fully, by I. I. Sreznevskii in his *Old Slavic Monuments of Uncial Writing*,[90] as well as by F. V. Kaminskii, although quite inaccurately, incompletely, and without any explanations, in his recent study of this document.[91]

As we have stated, both sources contain similar notation of the ekphonetic type. The Kupriianov leaflets (fig. 26) present a fairly complete system of about twelve signs, insofar as one may judge from the present state of this valuable historical document; the fragment consists of some 160 lines of text and the ekphonetic signs appear in 92 lines. In the whole of the Ostromir Gospel, only two of the signs are to be found anywhere.

The ekphonetic signs in these documents are of considerable interest for both music and paleography. They are not limited to the two sources above but can be encountered and followed up in much later manuscripts, yet they have so far attracted little attention. In the former Synodal Archive there is, among other items, a manuscript of the four gospels, dated 1519, also containing ekphonetic notation.[92] It thus appears that these signs were used for at least five or six hundred years, from the eleventh to the sixteenth century. Consequently, even if the earliest records of ekphonetic notation have been destroyed by the forces of historical circumstances or, more accurately, by some misfortune, it is nevertheless quite likely that our libraries could still provide documents of a later date containing these signs, to which, for some reason, archivists have paid such scant attention.

There were three types of ekphonetic signs: those used in the same line as the text [*strochnye*], those used below the text [*podstrochnye*], and those used above the text [*nadstrochnye*]. According to the most recent studies by Abbé Thibaut and K. I. Papadopulo-Keramevs [Papadopoulos-Kerameus], the ekphonetic signs found in the Russian sources reproduce those encountered in earlier as well as in contemporaneous Greek manuscripts with ekphonetic notation (from the fifth to the twelfth century). But even more important for us is that a number of these ekphonetic signs were later incorporated into our oldest neumatic notation (*znamennaia notatsiia*). Table 3.1 contains a comparative listing of Russian ekphonetic signs with their names (which were first established by D. V. Razumovskii in 1865), based on the two eleventh-century documents and the 1519 Gospel, and the Greek signs.[93]

A comparison of the manuscripts illustrated in figure 26 (from the Kupriianov leaflets, an eleventh-century [Russian] gospel) and figure 27 (a Greek parchment gospel from the tenth century belonging to the Cathedral of the Dormition of the Virgin, in Moscow, fol. 29) reveals that the signs used in the Russian and Greek sources are identical and that the Russians borrowed the signs from Greek models, which they must have consulted for translation.[93A] The text is for Sunday of the Holy Fathers, and includes signs above and below the line ([the signs] *paraklitikē, apostrophos, kathistē, kremastē,* and *bareia*). The signs in table 3.1 had the following meaning for singing (or, more correctly, for solemn recitation):

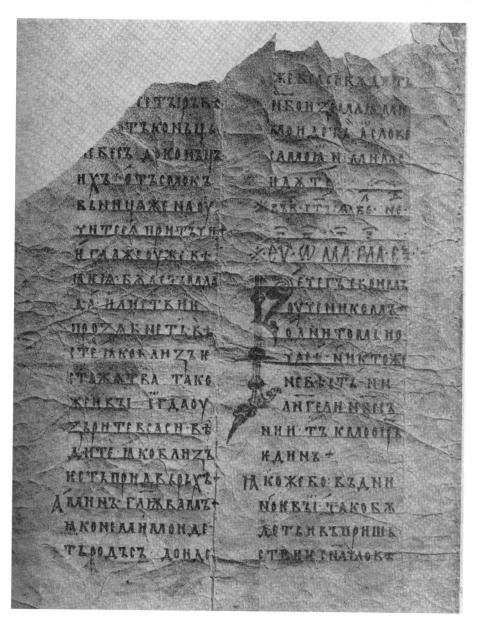

FIG. 26. Ekphonetic notation from the Kupriianov leaflets; eleventh century.

Signs written in the same line as the text [see Table 3.1]

1. The *krest*, or in the nomenclature of the later musical notation, the *kryzh* [both terms mean cross], indicated a brief rest in the reading of the text. In later neumatic notation, the *kryzh* was consequently placed at the end of a musical composition or, if added to another sign, indicated either a rest or a slowing down. The length of the pause in gospel readings depended on the reader; it was necessary to take a breath and to conform to the general tempo of the reading;

Fig. 27. Fragment from a tenth-century Greek parchment manuscript with ekphonetic notation belonging to the Moscow Cathedral of the Dormition (no. 1, fol. 29).

TABLE 3.1. Ekphonetic signs

	№№	Наим. по Разумовскому.	Еванг. л. XI (ркп. Публ. б. F. I, 57).	Слав. еванг. XVI в. (Арх. Синода, № 24).	Греческие евангелия XI — XII.	Наим. по J. Thibaut.
Строчные.	1	Крест (Крыж).				Téleia.
	2	Апостроф.		—		Hypocrisis.
Подстрочные.	3	Скоба.				Kathisté.
	4	Подвысь				Apostrophos.
Надстрочные.	5	Параклит.				Paraklétiké.
	6	Крюк.				Krémasté.
	7	Крюк светлый.		—		Не обозначен
	8	Стрела.				Oxeia.
	9	Апли.				Кентэмата (по Керамевсу)
	10	Палка.				Bareia.
	11	Двойная палка		—		Dipli bareia.
	12	Полустатья.		—		Не отмечено.

2. The *apostrof* [apostrophe] was placed between two syllables or words of text and indicated a descent in pitch in the tones linking them.

Signs written beneath the line of text

These were written under one or several words:

3. The *skoba* [staple] indicated that the word under which it was placed was pronounced on one tone but with a pause on each syllable;

4. The *podvys'* [rise] required a raising of the voice on the given syllable.

Signs written above the line of text

In ekphonetic notation, these signs resemble later signs of *kriukovaia* notation, the so-called *kriuki* [hooked] notation:

5. The *paraklit* was the most frequently used sign in the old Byzantine notation and its successor, the Russian *znamennaia* notation; it was always placed at the beginning of a reading or after a pause (+), and was therefore the initial note and one of the fundamental signs of the *kriukovaia* notation. In reading and singing, the duration of the *paraklit* corresponded to a half note;[94]

6. The simple *kriuk* (*kriuk prostoi* [*kriuk* means hook]) corresponded to a half note and indicated a lowering in pitch;

7. The *kriuk svetlyi* [literally, bright *kriuk*] indicated a rising pitch. Both these ekphonetic signs are also encountered in Latin neumes, where they were called *podatus* and *porrectus;* they were to be the basic neumes in the future *kriukovaia* notation;

8. The *strela* [arrow] indicated the lowering of pitch in recitation;

9. The *apli* indicated that the duration of a note was to be extended;

10. The *palka* [stroke or, literally, stick] indicated the duration of a half note;

11. The *dvoinaia palka* [double *palka*] indicated two quarter notes, as follows: (♩♩).

12. The *polustat'ia* [half a *stat'ia*] required a lengthening of the duration in reading equal to a whole note.

The *strela*, *palka*, and *stat'ia* were included among the signs of *kriukovaia* notation [see below on this stage of notation].

Of all these signs whose values we currently know, only the first two listed here are in the Ostromir Gospel, that is the *krest* (or *kryzh*) and the *apostrof*. They may be found in the following places in the manuscript:

1. fols. 1–16, both signs; the *krest* (+) is found no fewer than 250 times, and the three descending *apostrofy* (₹) some 79 times. They break off at the reading of chapter 8 of the Gospel of St. John, and the one and a half pages of fol. 17 are not notated. In the remaining folios, one finds only a single *krest* (+);

2. fols. 54–55, Gospel of St. John;

3. fol. 169v, where two *kryzh* signs seem to have been added later, and with no particular plan;

4. fols. 176v–179, the full reading of chapter 186 of the Gospel of St. John; the *krest* (+) is to be found thirty-eight times; and

5. fols. 211–211v, the full text of chapter 18 (59) of the Gospel of St. Luke; the cross (+) is found thirteen times.[94A]

The recitation of the gospel in church was not, strictly speaking, a musical art, but the notational signs accompanying the gospel text and indicating specific inflections of the voice (the raising and lowering of pitch, lengthening and pausing, a kind of cadencing at important points) were essentially musical and constituted the special ekphonetic notation. A number of these signs, as we know, became prototypes for the notational signs that developed later in Russian liturgical chant.

What was the character of the Russian Slavs' oldest church music, what musical notation or notations were used for this vocal art, and what written records remain?

The *Stepennaia kniga* contains, among other things, an account of the arrival in Russia, during the reign of Iaroslav the Wise in 1053, of three Greek singers "with their families" who laid the foundation of Orthodox Church singing in Russia. This bit of information, which has been interpreted in various ways by our scholars, must be supplemented with other data from the Hypatian and Pereiaslavl Chronicles, which record under the year 6645 (AD 1137) that in the reign of Prince Mstislav, "the eunuch Manuel was consecrated as a bishop of Smolensk, and was an expert singer who had come from the Greeks with several others." We also know that in 988, Princess Anna brought with her an "empress's choir" and that some four or five years later, in Rostov, Metropolitan Mikhail established a body of clerics [*krylos*] made up of Bulgars. Thus on several occasions skilled and devout singers, together with their families or with other singers ("s rody svoimi" and "sam tretii"), came to the newly Christianized Rus', and our church chant developed from them.[94B]

Chapter 6 of the *Stepennaia kniga* (the second "degree"), titled "Godly chanting from the Greeks," discusses the first period of Russian church-musical practice: "not only did God graciously permit that He be praised in Russia with words, but with godly song that embellished the church ritual. Thanks to the faith of the Christ-loving Iaroslav there came to him from Tsargrad [Constantinople] three God-inspired singers with their families.

From them originated in the Russian land angel-like singing, wonderful *osmoglasie* [singing according to the eight modes], and especially tripartite sweet-singing and the most beautiful *demestvennyi* singing to the praise and glory of God," and so forth.[95]

Our music researchers have accepted this "testimony" of the *Stepennaia kniga* as if it were a historical document, differing only in some details of interpretation. Stepan Vasil'evich Smolenskii has justly pointed out that "this annotation [in the *Stepennaia kniga*] was made some three hundred years after the event ... and the juxtaposition of the account in the *Stepennaia kniga* to contemporary evidence of undoubted authenticity cannot help but undermine considerably the testimony contained in the *Stepennaia kniga*."[96] But even he discerns in the text of the *Stepennaia kniga* references to two manners of singing and two subgroups in each, including even "penie na podobny" [this refers to the use of melody patterns]. Other scholars (Metallov, Preobrazhenskii, and Papadopulo-Keramevs) accept the statement in the *Stepennaia kniga* concerning the three ways of chanting, as if—during the embryonic period of our development!—they had all been established in Rus' from the very beginning; their division is as follows: (1) the angel-like octomodality; (2) the sweet three-part concord (including here *kondakarnoe* singing, and explaining it with some alleged three-part presentation, namely, a text, in the midst of which were the so-called *martirii*,[97] a tune, which was notated above the text, and an upper line, which had expressive markings); and (3) the *demestvennoe* singing, which had its own distinctive musical notation. [*Kondakari* are books containing special hymns called *kondaki*.][97A]

While acknowledging that the *Stepennaia kniga* is an intriguing literary monument of the second half of the sixteenth century,[98] soon after its publication in 1775 scholars called into serious question the reliability of its testimony concerning events related to the distant past.[99] All the same, a hundred years after Shcherbatov, Schlözer, Kalaidovich, and other scholars challenged the "fables" described in the *Stepennaia kniga*, our musical researchers have nevertheless accepted its testimony, even regarding the earliest period of Russian church singing and, moreover, taking the descriptions quite literally!

The notion of having three independent genres of liturgical singing at that remote period, a time when musical culture in Europe was generally lackluster and scholastic, seems absolutely bewildering. It would be more reasonable to explain the testimony of the *Stepennaia kniga* as an ornate exposition of the state of church singing at the time the document was written in the sixteenth century, even though it attributes these events to the era of Iaroslav the Wise. This, at least, would not contradict the historical facts. The disagreements among the scholars come from the rhetorical term "trisostavnoe sladkoglasovanie" [literally, "tripartite sweet-voicing"]. This concept was probably incomprehensible to early singers of minimal training but was likely completely understandable by the end of the sixteenth century, when the first efforts at three-part settings are found preserved in the old musical manuscripts. In this respect, an original attempt by V. V. Stasov in 1865 to explain the origin of this term has been disregarded by our later scholars.[100]

Relying on the likelihood that by the time the *Stepennaia kniga* was written in the sixteenth century, all traces of the church music practices of the tenth, eleventh, and twelfth centuries would have been forgotten, Stasov suggests that a simple translation of a Latin term was made, a term that existed at the time the *Stepennaia kniga* was compiled. A treatise on music by Sebastianus de Felstin (or Felstein), *Opusculum musices noviter congestum per honorandum Sebastianum Felstinensem artium baccalarium pro institutione adolescentum in cantu simplici seu Gregoriano* [A little work on music, newly collected by the Honorable Sebastian de Felstin, B.A., for the instruction of the young in plain or Gregorian chant], appeared in two editions in Kraków in 1534 and 1539; in it the author, using the florid scholastic language of the period, calls vocal music, among other things, tripartite: "Musica est scientia canendi modum indicans. . . . Quam musicam tripartitam esse Boetius . . . libro primo ca. 2 ostendit, Mundanam scilicet, Instrumentalem, ac Humanam." [Music is a science that shows the manner of singing. . . . Boethius, in book 1, chapter 2, indicates that music is tripartite, namely, universal, instrumental, and human.][101] Stasov asks whether the word *tripartitam* in this text is equivalent to the Russian *trisostavnoe*. Should this term, then, not simply be accepted as a translation of a word in general use in Europe at that time? It might have come to us from the West through Poland together with other ornate and scholastic expressions which occur in Russian translations of that period, and which, when incomprehensible to the translators, sometimes remained as Latin, Polish, or other foreign words simply spelled out using Russian letters. "The author of the *Stepennaia kniga*, finding it necessary to discuss the introduction of Greek music into Russia, naturally found it appropriate to signal the importance of the event in a special, flowery language, and to apply to the music an epithet more widespread and more widely used by more educated peoples."[102]

The history of Russian church chant can be divided into three main periods:
1. The old *istinnorechie* or *pravorechie* singing, which lasted for about four centuries (from the eleventh through the fourteenth centuries);
2. The *razdel'norechie* singing, from the fifteenth to the mid-seventeenth century;
3. The new *istinnorechie* singing, which began in the second half of the seventeenth century and may be considered as having ended in modern times.

We shall see, however, that these periods do not coincide exactly with the periodization of the development of Russian musical notation.

In the musical manuscripts and literary documents of the first period, the text represented the true and correct word [*istinnaia rech'*], that is, it was written as it was pronounced at that time. The semi-vowels, such as ъ, ь, and ŭ had separate neumes written above them, and they were sung just as vowels are sung today. For example, the word *днесъ* [today] had three neumes above it, one over each of the semi-vowels: *дьньсъ*. The following illustration is taken from a twelfth-century Lenten Triod in the library of the Moscow Synodal Typography [RGADA; a Triod, or Triodion, is a liturgical book containing Propers for Lent]:[102A]

Fɪɢ. 27ᴀ. Notation in a twelfth-century Triod (*istinnorechie*) [RGADA, f. 381, no. 148].

Scholars of Old Slavonic find in this example clear proof that, in at least parts of the early Russian language, syllables with mute letters [semi-vowels] had *length* in singing, as A. Potebnia comments, "with a graphic representation of the babbling which can be heard today in some country churches."[103] This comment refers to instances in which a series of semi-vowels appeared in succession in some words, for example *отъ зъьлъхъъ* (*отъ зълъхъ*) or *дъьъьньсъьь* (*дьньсъ*). In the Nizhnii Novgorod [or Blagoveshchenskii] Kondakar of the twelfth century (Russian Public Library [RNB], Q.ɪɪ.I.32, fol. 103), the word *Gospod'* [Lord] is notated with *kondakarian* neumes as shown in figure 27b.

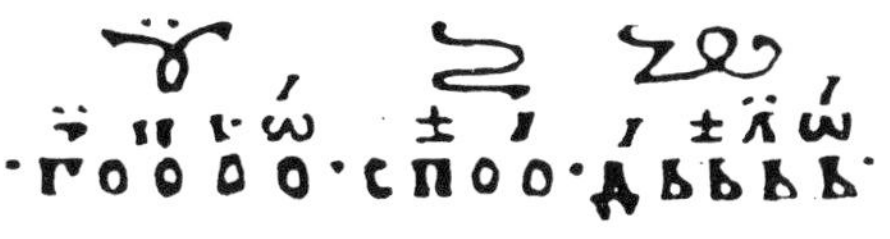

FIG. 27B. Notation over semi-vowels in the
twelfth-century Blagoveshchenskii Kondakar
from Nizhnii Novgorod [RNB, Q.ii.I.32)].

A Stikhirar [an early type of Slavic manuscript containing specific kinds of hymns called *stikhiry*] of the fourteenth to the fifteenth centuries prompted A. Vostokov to assert that "these letters [the semi-vowels] were in the past pronounced audibly and had duration in singing, like the otherwise mute *e* in French."[104]

In the fifteenth century the semi-vowels in the Slavonic liturgical chant texts underwent a change and were substituted by vowels. The change was owing to the difficulty of enunciating the semi-vowels and of singing the notational signs above them; to preserve the integrity of the tune and its notation, the text of the hymns began to be sacrificed. At first this substitution of some sounds for others does not seem to have made their pronunciation unrecognizable, although the vowels *o* and *e* which replaced the ъ [hard sign] and the ь [soft sign] were noticeably shorter in comparison with the pronunciation of the original vowels *o* and *e*. In *byliny*, songs, and even everyday speech it was possible, and perhaps still is, to encounter this peculiarity of the ancient language, which was in keeping with the general character of the pronunciation. In this regard, Potebnia, writing in the 1870s, declares:

> The ancient mute sounds are by no means so remote from us as some people think. No one will convince me that I have not distinctly heard in contemporary songs the syllables of an articulated or plosive *t*, that is, *t* plus a hard sign, as in the phrase, *za resho-t"-kami* [a colloquial phrase meaning behind bars, i.e., in jail] and a sibilant *z*, that is, *z* plus a soft sign, as in the phrase *za zhele-z'-nymi* [another colloquial phrase meaning behind the iron (bars), in jail]. By the same token, I would not believe anyone who says that it is now impossible to hear the name of the city of Kursk, a monosyllable, pronounced as if it were two syllables, Kuresk. And we are separated by some five hundred years from the fourteenth century.[105]

Interpolations such as this are even more easily understood in singing, when the accentuation of the tune coincides with the accentuation of the text. It must be pointed out, however, that in *razdel'norechie* singing, the rhythmic accents of the tune hardly coincide with the sounds associated earlier with semi-vowels in the text.

In singing practice the difference in pronunciation between the vowels *o* and *e* and the derivatives from the semi-vowels seems soon to have disappeared. The texts in the chant books lost their individuality and were smoothed out, a typical feature of *razdel'norechie* singing which was finally to lead to the complete distortion of the liturgical text. [In figure 27c, the same text appears in the old *istinnorechie* on the left and *razdel'norechie* on the right.][105A]

The syllable *khomo*, which constantly occurs in *razdel'norechie* singing, gave it yet another name, *khomovoe* singing, a term used until recent times to designate the chanting of the Old Believers. [*Khomoniia* or *khomovoe* singing refers to the practice of transforming semi-vowels into fully sounding vowels both between consonants and after the final consonant; see the passage on the right in figure 27c.]

Старое истинноречие.	Раздельноречие.
Съгрѣшихомъ, безъзаконовахомъ, не оправдихомъ предъ тобою, ни съблюдихомъ, ни сътворихомъ, якоже заповѣда намъ, но не предажъ насъ до конъца отъчьскыи Боже.	Согрѣшихомо и беззаконовахомо, не оправдихомо передо тобою, ни соблюдихомо, ни сотворихомо, якоже заповѣда намо, но не преда иже насо до конеца отеческыи Боже.

FIG. 27C. A comparison of *istinnorechie* and *razdel'norechie* [from Razumovskii, *Tserkovnoe penie v Rossii* (Church singing in Russia)].

By the end of the second period in the history of the Russian Church in the mid-seventeenth century, the Divine Liturgy, already adulterated by *khomovoe* singing, was further undermined and corrupted as a consequence of a practice in which the exceedingly lengthy service, with its obligatory texts that could not be omitted or abridged, was shortened by breaking it up into sections performed simultaneously by different voices. While one was reading the lesson, another sang, and a third chanted responses or acclamations.[106] The resulting "great discord" led to a reexamination of the entire sacred ritual, as well as of all the liturgical chant books, and in 1667 the Moscow Church Council issued a decree stating that the chanting must be sung "on the word" ("peti na rech'"). This initiated the third period, of the new *istinnorechie*, and led to the secession of the Old Believers (known as *raskol'niki*) from the official state church. The Old Believers retained in their liturgical practice, along with other older rites, the songbooks of the *razdel'norechie* period and its *khomoniia*.[107]

The example shown in figure 27d from a liturgical piece shows the same text in the three different stages [I. the old *istinnorechie;* II. the *razdel'norechie;* and III. the new *istinnorechie*]:[108]

I. Старое истинно- речие.	II. Раздельно- речие.	III. Новое истинно- речие.
Четвероконьцьный миръ дьньсь освящаєтьься четвероконьчьноумоу възвышаємоу твоємоу крьстоу. [108]	Четвероконеченый миро денесе освящатеся четвероконечену возвышаему твоему кресту.	Четвероконечный мiръ днесь освящается четвероконечному возвышаему твоему кресту.

FIG. 27D. A comparison of the old *istinnorechie*, the *razdel'norechie*, and the new *istinnorechie*.

Some thirty-two manuscripts are preserved from the first period of Russian church chant, not including the Ostromir Gospel, the two pages of the so-called Kupriianov parchment leaflets (two gospels on parchment), and the so-called Putiatina Mineia (a parchment manuscript in the Russian State Public Library [RNB, Sof. 202], which includes an example of the oldest neumatic notation, a *stikhira* for the Feast of the Dormition of the Virgin, on folio 135; the remainder of the manuscript contains no additional musical notation). Among these surviving manuscripts are five Kondakari from the eleventh to the twelfth centuries; fourteen Stikhirari from the twelfth to the fourteenth centuries; five Irmologii from the twelfth to the fourteenth centuries; six Triodi for Lent and the period from Easter to Pentecost from the twelfth to the thirteenth centuries; and two festal Minei from the thirteenth century. [A Mineia is a book containing the Proper of the Saints; the Irmologii is a liturgical book containing *irmosy*, hymns sung at Matins.][109]

Most of the surviving musical manuscripts of the first period are believed to have originated in Novgorod. This is explained not only by the superior education of the upper classes in that city but also by the province's distance from the Tatar devastations which destroyed nearly all the cultural treasures of Russia's central and southern cities.

The most recent scholarly work on these musical manuscripts confirms that our earliest musical notation is of Byzantine origin, and that the musical manuscripts themselves mainly represent copies of Byzantine and South Slavic models. This is quite understandable from a historical point of view. When accepting the new religion from Byzantium, the Slavs also accepted its ritual, including the musical portion of the church services (the melodies and singing practices) and its musical notation. Original Russian tunes could appear only in the appropriate circumstances, especially with the introduction of services and chants honoring the memory of Russian saints.[110] Such chants were likely created by Russian singers [*raspevshchiki*], but just as likely following Byzantine or Bulgarian models.

In some of the earliest notated musical manuscripts we encounter signs from the *kondakarian* notation, which is the one most closely connected with Byzantine notation. (See, for example, the three Stikhirari from the twelfth century [listed in n. 109]: GIM, Sin. 589; RGADA, f. 381, no. 152; and RNB, Sof. 384.) Other manuscripts of the same period have bilingual texts, that is, Russian (Old Church Slavonic) and Greek, as may be seen in a twelfth-century Stikhirar, from which a fragment was reproduced by D. Razumovskii:[110A]

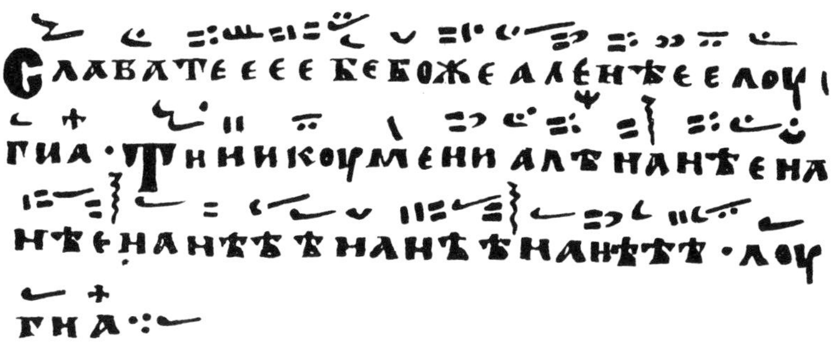

FIG. 27E. Bilingual texts (Old Church Slavonic and Greek) in a twelfth-century Stikhirar [from Razumovskii, *Tserkovnoe penie v Rossii* (Church singing in Russia)].

The text, in Slavic, is "Slava tebe bozhe alelugiia" [Praise Thee, Lord, alleluia] and in Greek [written in Cyrillic] "Ti ikoumeni alelugiia" [Over the entire earth, alleluia]. Some vowels and syllables are repeated to preserve the continuity of the tune. In addition to parallel texts—Slavonic and Greek—one often encounters in the old musical manuscripts quite lengthy melismatic ornaments, or even fragments of a tune, chanted to various syllables from Byzantine chant (*aneanes, nenagia, neanees*), which were eventually russified in Russian chant practice under the designation *ananeiki*,[111] or *ipe, khavoua, khivoua*, and the like; sometimes only single letters from these words appeared in the chant books. Their meaning, for Russian singers, was completely forgotten and lost, and they were possibly incomprehensible even to those who lived at the time the chant books were written.

The presence of Greek text and terminology in musical manuscripts with *znamennaia* and *kondakarnaia* notations may be explained by the fact that for a long time after the conversion, church chants were probably performed both in Slavonic and in Greek. This custom may have been maintained by the earliest priests in Rus', who were of Greek origin and could scarcely have had much knowledge of the language of the Slavs. At any rate, written documents tell us that even in the mid-thirteenth century in the city of Rostov the Great, during the reign of Peter of Rostov, the celebrants in the *kliros* on the left side of the altar in the Church of the Mother of God chanted in Greek ("levyi lik grecheski poiakhu"), whereas those on the right chanted in Slavonic. This testimony presumably means that both groups chanted the same melody but that the texts were sung simultaneously in two languages.[112] To this day some exclamations are in Greek, such as [the following, all written in Cyrillic]: "Kyrie eleison" [Lord have mercy], "Is polla eti despota" [Live for many years, despot], "Aksios" [It is meet], and others, which are still used in the service, survivals of the old ritual in the Greek language.

As indicated above, manuscripts of the earliest *istinnorechie* period contained two independent types of musical notation: *kondakarnaia* and *znamennaia. Kondakarnaia* notation was later completely abandoned and forgotten, and scholars even believe that the key to its understanding is lost. The second type of notation had greater vitality, and, as it developed, it served as a basis for the *kriukovaia* [hooked] *znamennaia* notation. This notation survived the period of Tatar domination and was eventually replaced by the five-line staff of Kievan notation (although not fully, for the old notation survives to this day in the religious practice of the Old Believers). Some of the earliest manuscripts contain both types of musical notation. One of the oldest of these is a church Tipikon with a notated Kondakar from the late eleventh or early twelfth centuries, from the library of the Moscow Synodal Typography, containing both *kondakarnaia* and the earliest layer of the *znamennaia* notation.[113] [A Tipikon contains instructions for the celebration of various liturgical services.]

3b. Kondakarnaia notation

The finest specimen of this notation appears in the twelfth-century Blagoveshchenskii Kondakar from the city of Nizhnii Novgorod;[114] the manuscript is now in the Russian State Public Library and contains mainly *kondaki* for the feasts of the Lord, the Virgin, and the saints.[115] In some places, the Greek text is written in Slavonic characters and includes numerous interpolations of syllables from Byzantine chant (*ananeiki, khi-khi,* and so forth). This is seen in figure 28, which reproduces folio 113v from this source, containing the ending of the alleluia with a Greek *ananeika*. The following line, "I povedaitesia bogou," is written in *kondakarnaia* notation and is followed by the beginning of the *kondak* for the Resurrection of Christ, in Mode 5, which is interrupted by the interpolated syllables mentioned above. It is evident from figure 28 that there are two rows of musical signs above the text: those in the upper row, large but fewer in number, resemble letters of the Greek alphabet, whereas the signs in the lower row are smaller but almost continuous. They closely resemble the signs used in *znamennaia* notation, and even an inexperienced eye will notice that they represent the melody to which the text is chanted.

Kondakarnaia [or *kondakarian*] notation was also borrowed from the musical practice of the Byzantine Church. Some of its signs resemble those of ekphonetic notation, from which they were undoubtedly developed and which was also of Byzantine origin. It is impossible, of course, to arrive at a definite conclusion about this extinct notation or to decipher all the signs arranged in the upper and lower rows above the text until some complete document of this notation has been researched and published.[116] In any case, our three oldest musical notations—ekphonetic, *kondakarnaia,* and *znamennaia*—clearly have some signs in common (table 3.2):

TABLE 3.2. Table of neumes

✝	.	.	.	.	крыж
➢:	.	,	.	.	будущий голубчик борзый
\\	.	.	.	.	двойная палка
⌣	.	.	.	.	крюк
⌐	.	.	.	.	стрела
ờ	.	.	.	.	чашка в крюк. нотации
ɛ	.	.	.	.	параклит.

kryzh [cross]
the sign later called *golubchik borzyi* [literally, swift dove, typical of the
    colorful names frequently given to Russian neumes]
dvoinaia palka [double stroke]
kriuk [hook]
strela [arrow]
chashka [cup] in *kriukovaia* notation
paraklit [from the Greek *parakletos,* an intercessor, referring to the Holy
    Spirit; the sign in Byzantine notation is called *paraklitikē*]

It is equally certain that a comparison of folio 113v of the Blagoveshchenskii Kondakar (see fig. 28) with any sample of the old *znamennaia* notation (fig. 29) will show that the signs in the lower line of the *kondakarnaia* notation have much in common with the oldest signs of the *znamennaia* notation.

    In any case, on the basis of fragments of *kondakarnaia* manuscripts published thus far, Smolenskii and other scholars make the following assumptions:[117] (1) the signs in the upper row in *kondakarnaia* notation had some sort of expressive significance and signaled the precentor to give a particular shading in performance, and the similar upper-row signs in Byzantine chants served the same purpose; and (2) the lower row of signs represented the actual tune.

    The results of future research and study of the *kondakarnaia* manuscripts are difficult to predict at this time. Previous conjectures as to the meaning of the upper-row signs may prove to be neither exhaustive nor accurate. If only five pages of a document such as the Blagoveshchenskii Kondakar alone could yield more than sixty different signs in the upper row (while at the same time the lower row provides barely forty distinct signs of its own), can it still be said that these upper-row signs are concerned only with "expressive" significance? On the other hand, we find in the upper rows some signs similar to those in the lower row, sometimes even combined with them (♪ , ϟ), and in the lower row there are signs written one on top of the other (ώ, ѿ). This arrangement suggests the possibility of singing in two or even three parts. Finally, if a series of *kondakarnaia* signs corresponds to signs in *znamennaia* notation, it is impossible to consider *kondakarnaia* notation as being completely isolated and totally forgotten. Many signs of the old *znamennaia* notation of the fourteenth century have also gone out of use and are incomprehensible now. The complexity of the *kondakarnaia* notation in two rows simply tells us that it was not only of Byzantine origin but that the singing it described was performed only by well-trained and experienced singers, possibly exclusively Greeks from Byzantium. It would seem that after the reorganization of our church chant at the beginning of the fourteenth century, the

FIG. 28. The twelfth-century Blagoveshchenskii Kondakar from Nizhnii
Novgorod (RNB, Q.n.I.32, fol. 113v).

kondakarnaia tunes were rewritten using ordinary signs, especially as some of these signs
were identical to those in the (by now) abandoned *kondakarnaia* system. Thus even in our
own time, in the most recent documents with *kriukovaia* notation (still in use by the Old
Believers) and even transposed into Kievan square [staff] notation, singers still perform the
ancient *kondakarnaia* tunes without being aware of it.

3c. Znamennaia notation

The parchment Mineia, organized by months, from the eleventh century is probably the earliest surviving Slavonic *znamennaia* setting of a liturgical text. This manuscript
belonged to the Cathedral of St. Sophia in Novgorod and is presently held in the manuscript division of the Public Library. The manuscript contains liturgical texts, and only on
folio 135 is there the single example of the oldest type of *znamennaia* notation, above the
text of the *stikhira* for the Feast of the Dormition of the Virgin.[118] These signs are identical

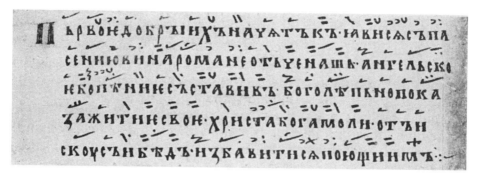

FIG. 29. The oldest type of neumatic notation, from a parchment Mineia;
twelfth century (GIM, Sin. 168).

to signs found in other musical manuscripts from the twelfth to the fourteenth century, listed above. An example of this notation is from a parchment twelfth-century Mineia in GIM, Sin. 168, fol. 13v, illustrating the notation above the text of a *stikhira* for the Feast of St. Romanos (see fig. 29).[118A]

The manuscripts we have listed have preserved the shapes of the oldest notational signs but not their meaning or their names. S. V. Smolenskii, having analyzed one musical source, the notated Irmologii of the thirteenth century from the Resurrection [New Jerusalem] Monastery, counted more than ninety different signs in this manuscript alone. Only a few of these signs correspond to those of later centuries, and the others remain undeciphered, as most of them went out of use and their musical meaning has been lost.[119] As far as we know, not a single manual or theoretical treatise on this notation from the period has been discovered. The earliest theoretical documents of this type are the notational ABCs [*azbuki*] of the fifteenth century containing "an explanation of how the signs are inscribed" ("Tolkovanie nadpisaniiu znamen"), that is, a listing of their names and shapes. The texts do not give any technical or musical explanation of the signs, this information apparently being obtained by oral tradition and transmission through practice over the years. These ABCs or rudiments of notation do establish an accurate listing of their names. One of the oldest such *azbuki* can be found in a mid-fifteenth-century Irmologii from the library of the Trinity–St. Sergius Lavra (RNB, Tr. 408–1345, fols. 161–161v), fully reproduced here (figs. 30a and 30b). [A *lavra* is a large, high-ranking monastery; the Trinity–St. Sergius Lavra is near Moscow.]

A comparison with the twelfth-century Mineia (see fig. 29) shows that the signs are similar in both manuscripts (the one from the twelfth century, the other from the fifteenth) and that only their character has been somewhat altered. In the *azbuka* from the fifteenth century the cursive writing has become rather elongated. Here follows a full listing of the neumes of this fifteenth-century Mineia *azbuka*, beginning in the middle of folio 161 (figs. 30a and 30b):

(1) *paraklit*; (2) *zmiitsa*; (3) *polkulizmy*; (4) *golubets'*; (5) *stopitsa*; (6) *stopitsa s ochkom*; (7) *stopitsa s dvema ochki*; (8) *chashka*; (9) *chashka polnaia*; (10) *kriuk*; (11) *kriuk' svetlyi*; (12) *skameika*; (13) *strela*; (14) *strela svetlaia*; (15) *strela gromnaia*; (16) *strela povodnaia*; (17) *strela poezdnaia*; (18) *statiia*; (19) *statiia svetlaia*; (20) *palka*; (21) *palka vzdernutaia*; (22) *palka svetlaia*; (23) *kulizma*; (24) *mrachnaia fita*; (25) *fita svetlaia*; (26) *kryzh'*; (27) *dva v chelnu*; (28) *fita zelnaia*; (29) *pauk*; (30) *pauk velikyi*; (31) *zakrytaia (stat'ia)*; (32) *cheliustka*; (33) *khamila*; (34) *slozhitiia*; (35) *triaska*; (36) *duda*; (37) *nemka s streloiu*; (38) *strela so oblachkom*; (39) *kriuk s potchashiem*; (40) *sorochiia noga*;

(41) *kliuch'*; (42) *mechik'*; (43) *osoka*; (44) *rozhek*; (45) *derbitsa*; (46) *kobyla*; (47) *pereveska*; (48) *dvocholnaia* (*dvuchelnaia fita*); (49) *gromoglasnaia* (*fita*); (50) *trestrelnaia* (*fita*); (51) *strela mrachnaia*.

In other *azbuki* contemporary with this fifteenth-century Irmologii, the signs vary in number, yet their shapes and names are similar. In the "Explanation of the writing of the signs" (GIM, Pev. sobr. 139) there are sixty-three signs;[120] in the chapter "And here are the names of signs" [A se imena znameniem] in the fifteenth-century manuscript RNB, Kir.-Bel. 9/1086, only forty-three signs are listed. The signs are not presented systematically in any of these alphabets. Systematization took place only later, in the seventeenth century, during the period of the final use and full development of *znamennaia* notation. At that time the notation received a different, more sharply defined and angular (hook-like) shape, fully justifying the newly established terminology in singing practice from about the end of the sixteenth century: the designation of *kriuki* [hooks], and therefore *kriukovaia* notation.

The musical meaning of the signs and the later *kriuki* was vague, acquired mainly by years of study and practice. The signs indicating pitch and duration were relative. The terms

FIG. 30A. Listing of neumes (*azbuka*), fifteenth century. From an Irmologii from the Trinity–St. Sergius Lavra (RNB, Tr. 408–1345, fol. 161).

prostoi [simple], *svetlyi* [bright], and *mrachnyi* [dark] denoted the pitch or, rather, the particular range [*soglasie*] within the overall scale. This scale, transcribed onto the five-line staff of Kievan notation which is preserved in church music practice to the most recent times, was divided into the four ranges of three tones in each, shown in musical example 3.1.

The sign indicating the lowest range was called *prostoi* [simple]; an added dot over the sign indicated the *mrachnyi* [dark] range; two dots indicated the *svetlyi* [bright]; and three dots, the *tresvetlyi* [very bright] ranges (see table 3.3).

The basis of Orthodox Church singing was rooted in the Byzantine system of the Octoechos [in Russian, *osmoglasie*], consisting of eight modes, of which four are deemed principal (or authentic) and four derived or supplementary (plagal). The beginnings of the Octoechos system in Christian musical practice (which borrowed this system from the ancient Greek modes) date from about the third or fourth centuries AD. As is well known, John of Damascus (d. 760) established the Octoechos as a well-developed system and determined the full cycle of chants for the services. Eight cycles of these chants were scheduled in pairs (authentic and plagal), and the tunes within a pair were related and often had identical melodic gestures (the pairing of modes was as follows: modes I and V; II and

FIG. 30B. Conclusion of the listing of neumes in RNB, Tr. 408–1345, fol. 161v.

EXAMPLE 3.1. The *soglasiia*

TABLE 3.3. Notation of the four *soglasiia* (*prostoi, mrachnyi, svetlyi,* and *tresvetlyi*)

	prostoi	mrachnyi	svetlyi	tresvetlyi
крюк				
стрела				
статья				—
подчашие				

VI; III and VII; and IV and VIII). Together they constituted the Octoechos or *osmoglasie* (the singers often abbreviating the term to *oktai, okhtai, oktaik,* and the like) containing the complete repertory of church chants in all eight modes.

The theoretical foundations of the Octoechos have not yet been fully elucidated in the Eastern Church, whereas in the West, the foundations were developed into a complete system of church scales by Glareanus in the sixteenth century.[120A] The ranges of our system of eight modes are represented in table 3.4.[121]

TABLE 3.4. The Octoechos

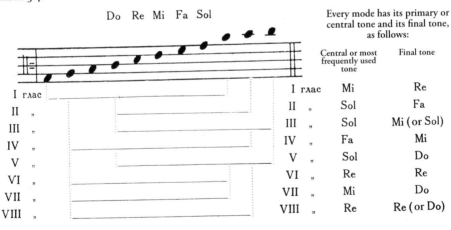

	Central or most frequently used tone	Final tone
I глас	Mi	Re
II „	Sol	Fa
III „	Sol	Mi (or Sol)
IV „	Fa	Mi
V „	Sol	Do
VI „	Re	Re
VII „	Mi	Do
VIII „	Re	Re (or Do)

Every mode has its primary or central tone and its final tone, as follows:

The current understanding of the structure of the Octoechos was reached in the eighteenth century and has meanwhile remained unchanged. This understanding was based, of course, on earlier singing practices that had survived to that period. The Octoechos was less strictly observed in the sixteenth and seventeenth centuries, as a consequence of favorite tunes from one mode being transposed to a different one, as well as by the incorporation of newly invented melodic turns [*popevki*]. This resulted in the weakening and gradual abandonment of the age-old theoretical foundations of the Octoechos. All the same, one can demonstrate convincing continuity in the transmission of *znamennyi* chant from Byzantium, by means of parallel analysis of the ancient tunes and their melodic patterns and modal system. All chants, as is well known, have indications of the mode in which they are to be performed. A comparison of the oldest and the more recent Church Slavonic musical manuscripts with contemporaneous Byzantine manuscripts confirms that the Slavic sources contain the same modal indications found in the Byzantine manuscript sources. This corroborates that in addition to borrowing Byzantine melodies, the theory of the Octoechos itself was also borrowed.[122] Thus *znamennaia* notation was essentially a Byzantine musical notation, at first only slightly altered to adapt to singing the Slavonic texts. As A. V. Preobrazhenskii's most recent investigations prove, this notation was borrowed to transcribe the original Byzantine melodies and not the Slavonic tunes, which, of course, did not yet exist in that early period. The latter made their appearance, as far as we know, only after the canonization of the first Russian saints. These new tunes were formed within the church singing practice, also based on the preexisting models used in the Eastern Church.

4. Novgorod the Great

The Novgorodian *byliny*. The *gusli* and other musical instruments. Bells and bell ringing. The melodic formulae [*raspevy*] and the singers of Novgorod.

In the ancient capital of Kiev, despite the prodigality of the court and of the prince's retinue, there was an increasing tendency to preach asceticism and abstention from worldly songs, dances, and musical games. In this connection, one need only recall the chronicle accounts or stories of the life of Feodosii Pecherskii [of the Caves Monastery in Kiev]. But it was very different in the freedom-loving city of Novgorod the Great.

Novgorod, one of the oldest cities of ancient Rus', took the initiative in the invitation to the Varangian princes. Relations between the Slavic tribes had been altered considerably after the transfer of the Grand Prince's capital to Kiev. In spite of this, the Laurentian Chronicle, when referring to the reign of Vsevolod Iur'evich of Suzdal (d. 1212), who extended his influence to Novgorod and Pskov, remarks: "And Novgorod the Great is the senior principality in the whole of Russia."[122A] The political and social life of Great Novgorod had long differed considerably from that of the other principalities and appanages of Rus'. This lasted until 1478, when Novgorod was incorporated into the Muscovite realm and its old social structure was finally destroyed. A system of elective government had been introduced in Novgorod in the mid-twelfth century which included even ecclesiastical authorities, who had influence in political matters. Both geographical and historical circumstances preserved Novgorod's ancient social foundations and fostered its further development at a time when Lower Russia was devastated by civil wars and invasions by Tatars and others, culminating in the Mongol domination. Novgorod was *Velikii* [Great] not only in name, but in reality. From the twelfth century, and perhaps even earlier, Novgorod established active trade relations with the West, and from the thirteenth century it was a member of the mighty Hanseatic League. Novgorod's possessions extended from the Arctic Ocean to the Urals. The foundations of its social and political life, trade and government by popular election (the *veche*), promoted prosperity among the people and secured for them a freer, more comfortable existence.

These factors also conditioned the development of Novgorod's artistic creativity and were reflected in the monuments of its musical culture. The earliest echoes of Novgorod's freedom-loving, commercial society are in its *byliny,* which are quite different from the earlier Kievan or later Muscovite types. The exploits of the Kievan heroic knights are unknown in the Novgorodian *byliny.* Novgorod's tales have their own local heroes, not fictitious characters but real historical figures, although their deeds were embellished by the popular imagination. To Novgorod also belongs the honor of the creation and preservation of the oldest remnants of Slavic musical notation, including the Ostromir Gospel and music books with the forgotten *kondakarnaia* notation, as well as the icons, frescoes, and especially miniature paintings which have preserved for us images of the oldest Russian musical instruments.

The Novgorodian *byliny,* notably, are contemporaneous with the establishment of the popular assembly; there is no trace in them of earlier events. In this context we must mention Pyotr Bezsonov's observation that the tales of Sadko, the wealthy merchant of Novgorod, are known only in the North, in Siberia, and in the Arkhangel'sk and Olonetsk regions, that is, in the areas populated by Novgorodian emigrants. They are not known in Central Russia. Furthermore, the heroes and other characters in the Novgorodian *byliny* and tales are either people with a talent for music (Vas'ka Buslaev and the rich merchant Sadko) or even professional *skomorokhi*, as in the tale of the merchant Terent'ishche. Whereas the Kievan *byliny* produced their wandering bards—serious, morose, and mysterious pilgrims—the Novgorodian *byliny* created the *skomorokh,* a blend of professional wandering minstrel, instrumentalist, and clown who appeared both at public gatherings and in private homes.[122B]

> In the glorious Great New City [Nov-gorod]
> Buslai lived for ninety years,
> Ninety years and nary a tooth in his head.

Thus from the very beginning of this Novgorodian *bylina* there is another spirit, the spirit of jesting and laughter. The singer of the *bylina* adds:

> Buslai lived to a ripe old age
> He'd had his day and passed away.
> . . . .
> And left behind a Mother bereft,
> the mother, Mamel'fa Timofeevna,
> and a dear little one,
> a charming lad, a much-loved child,
> Buslai's son, the young Vasilii.
> At the age of seven his mother dear
> sent Vasen'ka to learn to read
> and write with quill, to master
> learning as a skill. And so
> he learned to write with ease,
> then off to study how to sing
> the sacred songs in church.
> He mastered them with equal ease,
> and sang them best of all the rest.
> Throughout the whole of Novgorod
> None could match Vasilii Buslaev.

Buslaev's subsequent exploits are not directly related to the Novgorodian *byliny* which interest us, but we might mention Vasilii's banquets; the admission of confederates into his band; the battle he arranged on the bridge over the river Volkhov, which ended in a victory for the Novgorodian knight; and the intervention by his mother, carried out in a unique way, entirely in the *skomorokh* tradition:

> The old woman ran up to Vasilii,
> She flew at him from behind
> And fell upon his mighty shoulders.

All these details bear the imprint of a distinctly localized genre, as did the earlier tales about throwing the idol-statuette of Perun from the bridge into the river Volkhov. They recall ancient Novgorodian games (boxing matches) and the dispensation of justice on the Volkhov Bridge. We encounter yet another curious episode among the tales of Buslaev's exploits: when the men of Novgorod, during their fight with Vas'ka Buslaev, saw that "disaster was inevitable," they fled to the Monastery of St. Cyril and offered rich gifts to old Andronishche, Vasilii's godfather, so that he might appease his godson:

> Straight away, old man Andronishche
> lifts onto his mighty shoulders
> the monastery's brass bell.
> T'is not a large bell—but ninety *pudy* [about 3,510 lbs!]—
> then off to the river Volkhov, to that very Volkhov Bridge.
> He braces himself on the bell's clapper,
> Behold, the brush-cord road sags beneath the weight.

And in answer to his godfather's calming words:

> Vasilii strikes at once the bell
> with the axle of a cart.

Then Vasilii takes the axle and thrashes the Novgorodians:

> The brazen metal boomed and shuddered,
> as mighty old Andronishche
> dumped out upon the barren ground,
> without the time to make a sound.
> Vasilii glimpsed beneath the bell,
> the old man's brow bereft and bare
> of eyes and even eyelids now.[122C]

The introduction into a battle of the huge monastery bell is a popular embellishment involving specifically local color. Novgorod was so famous for its bells and its distinctive bell ringing that the singer of Buslaev's exploits found it necessary to include a bell in his story of the fight.

The hero of the Novgorodian *bylina* actually existed, although he may not have accomplished all the feats credited to him. The Nikonian Chronicle, under the year 1171, records that "in this year, the *posadnik* Vaska Buslaevich died." [A *posadnik* is an elected city official.][122D] The *bylina* also mentions him with the same diminutive form of the name [Vas'ka for Vasilii] which, as Bezsonov says, "suits the audacious, roguish fellow, the darling of the people." That his death was worth recording in the chronicle alongside great events indicates his importance in Novgorod, and explains his inclusion in the *byliny* along with Sadko, the favorite hero of the surviving Novgorodian tales.[123]

Sources preserve the opening of a *bylina* that is apparently incomplete, or forgotten and not recorded in full, on "The Death of Vasilii Buslaev":

> The ship flies across the blue sea, how it flies
> To Novgorod the ship races, how it races;
> On the ship Vasiliushka paces
> And teases the strings of the *gusli:*

> "Ah, little *gusli, gusli,* my *gusel'chiki*
> Play for me, *gusli,* for me . . .
> For the good lad Vasilii, the merchant's little son.[124]

This fragment gives us a new detail in Vasilii Buslaev's biography: his ability to play the *gusli.* Although this detail does not appear in more widespread variants of this *bylina* cycle, it nevertheless reinforces the general character of the Novgorod freemen and the free city itself, in which the *gusli* was truly a beloved and popular musical instrument. This detail only rounds out Buslaev's appearance as a celebrated singer, daredevil, and mischief maker, who naturally plays the *gusli.*

Another hero of the epic Novgorodian *byliny* is Sadko, who is noted in the folk tradition specifically as a professional *gusliar* [*gusli* player] and singer.

> In Novgorod the Great
> lived Sadko, a merry young fellow.
> He didn't possess a golden purse,
> but only a vibrant *gusli.*
> Sadko played at banquets,
> amusing merchants and townsfolk.
> Once upon a time,
> a whole day passed and nobody invited Sadko to a feast.

They did not call for him on the second day, and then on the third day:

> Then Sadko became bored
> And walked to Lake Il'men,
> And he sat on a white-glowing stone
> And began to strum his clear-toned *gusli,*
> And he played from morning to night.[125]

After various adventures in Novgorod, in another *bylina* the merchant-*gusliar* Sadko, now rich, had to descend from his ship to the submarine kingdom:

> Sadko quickly donned his finery
> And took his clear-toned *gusli*
> with the gilded strings so fine
> And carried his precious chess set
> with its golden board.

And with these items he descends into the sea. Although he became a rich merchant, Sadko was a professional singer and *gusli* player, and only by means of his profession, talent, and wit had he acquired riches and high standing in Novgorod. Sadko was also a historical figure, a contemporary of Vasilii Buslaev. He is often mentioned in Novgorodian chronicles, the rather inconsistent chronological statements of which were double-checked and clarified by Bezsonov in the fifth volume of *Songs Collected by P. V. Kireevskii.* The chronicles give Sadko's name as S"dko Sytinits' or Sotko Sytinich', and other variants. The Novgorod III Chronicle and the Pskov I Chronicle both record that, "in the year 1167 Sotko Sytinich' laid the foundation of a stone church of the holy martyrs Boris and Gleb in Okolotka."[125A]

The *byliny* also mention this event but confuse the Church of Sts. Boris and Gleb with the Cathedral of St. Sophia: "Sadko went and built the Lord's church, the Cathedral of Sophia the Wise." Some *byliny* ascribe to Sadko the building of two other churches in Novgorod, St. Stephen the Archdeacon and St. Nicholas of Mozhaisk. The latter helps to explain the *bylina* mentioned above that recounts the manifestation of Nicholas of Mozhaisk to Sadko in the submarine kingdom.[125B]

The lives and activities of both these Novgorodian folk heroes thus coincide. Both lived in the mid-twelfth century; the *posadnik* Vaska Buslaev died in 1171, and some four years earlier Sadko built the Church of Sts. Boris and Gleb in Novgorod. Both were folk singers and *gusli* players, and Sadko was also a *skomorokh* and earned his living as a professional entertainer. Buslaev became a *posadnik* and Sadko is mentioned (in the Novgorod II Chronicle) as a *sotnik* [a leader of a troop of soldiers], probably because the title sounds similar to his name.[125C] Both *bylina* heroes attained glory and position thanks to their artistic talents, and both were representatives of the Novgorodian freemen, within which they could grow and develop their talents.

We have called Sadko a professional *skomorokh*. The Kievan *byliny* we have discussed earlier mention another heroic knight, a historical figure who disguised himself as a *skomorokh* and who posed as one when circumstances led him to take up the *gusli* and play. It is curious that this Kievan hero, born a *skomorokh*, was from Novgorod: Dobrynia Nikitich, Prince Vladimir's uncle and one of his knights and advisers. In an entry for the year 980 the Laurentian Chronicle calls Dobrynia Nikitich a Novgorodian *posadnik*: "When Dobrynia came to Novgorod, he set up an idol beside the river Volkhov, and the people of Novgorod offered sacrifice to it as if to God himself."[125D] After Kiev's conversion to Christianity, Dobrynia was again zealous in his efforts in Novgorod but this time with different aims. According to the *Stepennaia kniga*, together with the Kievan metropolitan Mikhail and six bishops, "Dobrynia, Vladimir's uncle, arriving in Great Novgorod, smashed all the idols and destroyed the temples . . . the idol of Perun was cut to pieces and thrown to the ground," and so forth.[125E] Dobrynia may have known the Novgorodian customs or he may have learned the Kievan court amusements; in any case, the *byliny* frequently have this hero of the Kievan cycle change into *skomorokh* attire and play musical instruments. Apparently he was so much at home in that role that even "his own mother" could not recognize him.

In one of the Dobrynia *byliny*, a fragment of which was cited earlier, the text states that the knight, arriving at a princely feast:

> Tightened his silken strings,
> his cords of gold,
> and began to wander across the strings;
> singing along with them a song
> played in Tsar-grad [Constantinople],
> bringing it all to Kiev.[126]

Dobrynia was thus a skilled *gusli* player and knew a variety of tunes, as did Sadko and other *gusli* players. In some of the variants of the Sadko *byliny* we learn:

> Sadko plays in Novgorod
> a tune [*vyigrysh'*] brought from Tsar-grad.[127]

We find a similar detail in the *bylina* about Solovei Budimirovich:

> He plays dances [*tontsy*] from Novgorod,
> and others from Jerusalem,
> and little refrains [*pripevki*] from beyond the blue sea.[128]

or:

> They play games from Tsar-grad
> and melodious tunes [*napevki*] from Jerusalem.[129]

These variants in the *byliny* show that the *gusli* players had a wide-ranging repertory, that their tunes and refrains were not limited to local melodies but were borrowed or created under the influence of the foreign songs and instrumental music they heard in Kiev and Novgorod.

The steady trade and political relationships of the southern Kievan Principality with Byzantium, the East, and with the western Slavonic and Germanic tribes, the residence in Novgorod and its territories of foreign merchants, servants, and craftsmen of various guilds, and the journeys of Russian pilgrims to Jerusalem and to the Italian city of Bari, where the relics of St. Nicholas the Miracle-worker (especially venerated in Russia) were buried—all these elements profoundly influenced not only the quality of urban life and commercial interchange but also enriched and embellished artistic creation. Since, in old Russian painting and church architecture, including that of Novgorod, the presence of foreign masters and of Western, Southern, and Eastern artistic fashions and prototypes has now been positively established, perhaps it will not be long before we are able to confirm the general links between these foreign influences and old Slavonic song as well. At any rate, some details in our *byliny*, which until now have been insufficiently studied or viewed as incomprehensible and ambiguous, would seem to make such a statement possible.

The *byliny* treat the three heroes whose musical activities we have examined—Dobrynia Nikitich, Vas'ka Buslaev, and Sadko—very seriously and without any hint of disdain. We should mention yet another Novgorodian *bylina* that includes among its characters the city's ubiquitous *skomorokhi:* the tale of the merchant Terent'ishche. This tale is also rich in local details, depicting scenes from old Novgorod's domestic life, with *skomorokhi* playing the leading roles. The trivial, domestic subject matter of the Terent'ishche story is presented fittingly in a shorter and less elaborate form of *bylina*, popularly known as the *starina* [tale]. The very sound in Russian of the name of its hero inevitably evokes associations with things formidable, terrible or clumsy, or awkward and decrepit (as Bezsonov has shrewdly observed), thus it well suits the aged, cuckhold husband.

> In the capital city of Novgorod
> In Iur'evskaia Street,
> In the Terent'ev Quarter,
> There lived a rich merchant
> By the name of Terent'ishche.[130]

The poem describes the splendors of Terent'ishche's house. His young wife, tired of her husband, feigns illness and orders him out of the house: "Get out, go and fetch the doctors." The old man had scarcely departed before the wife's young lover appears in the bedroom.

Terent'ishche encounters a group of *skomorokhi* at the Church of the Exaltation of the Cross, by the bridge near the crossroads. *Skomorokhi* can be gracious and attentive to anyone worth their while, but they recognize the miserly old Terentii, from whom they have never managed to get anything. This time, however, old Terent'ishche tells them of his troubles and then promises:

> To him who can cure
> My young wife
> Avdot'ia Ivanovna
> I shall pay a hundred rubles.

The merry fellows soon figure out what is going on with Avdot'ia. Taking Terent'ishche's money, they buy what they need, along with a sack, then put the old man into the sack and set off to his house. At first the young wife hesitates to admit them, but glad to hear that the heartbroken old man is wallowing around on the ground by the bridge, she invites the *skomorokhi* to come in and enjoy themselves.

> Sit down on the benches,
> Play the *gusli,*
> And sing a little song,
> About the rich merchant,
> About the old rapscallion,
> Terent'ishche by name!
> May he stay away for ages!

So the merry *skomorokhi:*

> Sit down on the bench
> And play the *gusli*
> They sing a little song:
> "Listen here, you old fool,
> Muffled in fur around your shoulders,
> Listen well, Merchant Terentii,
> To what they are saying about you!"[131]

The denouement of this Novgorodian story is well known: the *skomorokhi* expose the wife's infidelity, she gets punished, and the husband rewards the *skomorokhi* with another hundred rubles. The *skomorokhi* themselves undoubtedly created and composed this pure *skomorokh* tale. Its subject is unlikely to have been inspired by popular Italian tales or others, although the situation on which it is based might be found anywhere. My search through more than a hundred novels by Boccaccio, Sacchetti, and other popular writers of the time has uncovered nothing reminiscent of the Novgorodian tale of Terent'ishche.

In this story the *skomorokhi* make their appearance as genuine representatives of their profession, giving us a chance to evaluate their way of life. The tale's jovial mockery and its jocular, satirical tone distinguish it from the more serious, narrative style of the Sadko and Vas'ka Buslaev *byliny,* but all these epic Novgorodian songs do have one feature in common: their heroes and characters are *skomorokhi* or singers belonging to the profession. They all play the *gusli,* and all are freemen of Novgorod.

The musical side of these songs is interesting from the viewpoint of their melodic variants. Although very few melodies have come down to us, surviving only in copies from the mid-eighteenth century at the earliest, they nevertheless reveal some striking features.

The oldest and most complete cycle of Novgorodian *byliny* is in Kirsha Danilov's famous collection. This collection is the earliest of its type, and includes folk texts and tunes, although there are some errors and, most important, they are not presented as songs, that is, not for vocal performance.[132] He gives what are more accurately called *naigryshi* [dance tunes] from the Novgorodian *stariny:* one on Vasilii Buslaev; two different *bylina* fragments about Sadko; and one about the Merchant Terent'ishche. There are also notated *byliny* about Buslaev and the Merchant Terent'ishche in the first volume of A. Grigor'ev's *The Arkhangel'sk Byliny,* and A. V. Markov has written down another song about Sadko.[133] In all, we are aware of seven tunes known so far from the extensive cycle of Novgorodian *byliny.* In addition to the earliest written record by Kirsha Danilov, these texts were published in collections by Gil'ferding, Kireevskii, Rybnikov, and others. The tunes were not recorded in the province of Novgorod but in either a remote district of Siberia (as in the Kirsha Danilov collection) or in the equally far-off White Sea region (by Grigor'ev and Markov). It is curious that there is no trace of any *byliny* in the special collection of Novgorodian songs assembled on the spot by E. Linyova and published by the Academy of Sciences.[134] This is because the original settlers of the Novgorod district were deported wholesale or fled in the fifteenth and sixteenth centuries, and a new population resettled their lands. The emigrants took their stories and songs with them to the far North or into the depths of Siberia. The *skomorokhi,* as we shall learn, persecuted by the clergy and the government and eventually dying out in places remote from the centers of government, transmitted their repertory from generation to generation by oral tradition. Fragments of this tradition thus found new life in later melodies, many of them no doubt corrupted, far from Novgorod's former greatness and secretly preserved in folk memory on the shores of the White Sea and in Siberia. Here are the tunes of the Novgorodian *byliny* that have come down to us, beginning with musical example 4.1. In this example, the form is more original than most of the others in Danilov's collection, consisting of the structure A (repeated) + B + A + C (the close). In the B section, the repetition on a single note has a recitative-like narrative effect, which is seldom, if ever, encountered in other examples from this collection.

EXAMPLE 4.1. "Vasil'ia Buslaeva" (from Kirsha Danilov)[135]

V slavnom velikom Nove grade
A i zhil Buslai do devianosto let;
S novym gorodom zhil ne perechilsia
So muzhiki novogorotskimi
po perek slovechka ne govarival.

In the famous Great New City [Novgorod]
Buslai lived to be ninety years old;
He had no quarrel with Novgorod
Or with the men of Novgorod
And no cross words did he utter.

A melody of a *starina* about Vasilii Buslaevich (from *The Arkhangel'sk Byliny,* 1:655) has been preserved on a phonograph recording by A. Grigor'ev. The singer was Timofei Shibanov, an eighty-year-old peasant who, according to Grigor'ev, sang out of tune. Consequently the music as taken down from the phonograph record is probably not accurate. Grigor'ev explains the additional signs over the musical notes as follows: / means the note should be slightly sharper than as printed; \ means slightly flatter; ⌣ means of shorter duration. The sign ⌣ over the rests at the end of lines 6 and 8 apparently indicates a shorter pause. It is nevertheless a well-proportioned tune: motif A is repeated two more times after its first appearance in line 2, recurring again in lines 7 and 9, and motif B is also repeated (in lines 5 and 8). The text and music are reproduced here according to Grigor'ev in musical example 4.2.

EXAMPLE 4.2. "Zhil byl Buslavei divenosto let" [Thus lived Buslavei ninety years]
(from Grigor'ev, *Arkhangel'skie byliny*).

Zhil byl Buslavei divenosto let.
I ostavalas' u Buslav'ia liubima sem(i)ia,
Liubima sem'ia da moloda zhona,
I moloda zhona, molody Vasilii (i) syn(y) Buslav'evich.
On(y) stavilsia Vasil'ia let (semi, shesti);
Stal on na ulitsi pokhazhivat',
S malyma ribiatami poigryvat':
Kogo za ruku khvatit, ruku vydernet,
Za nogu khvatit, nogu vydernet.

Thus lived Buslavei ninety years.
And left behind his beloved family,
His beloved family and young wife.
Yes, his young wife, young son Vasilii Buslaevich.
He left Vasilii, aged seven or six;
He began to walk along outside,
To play games with the little children;
When he catches a hand, he yanks on it,
When he catches a leg, he yanks on it.

A feature of the vigorous, entirely Russian dance tune in musical example 4.3 is the triple repetition of the melodic phrase marked *a*, slightly varied each time. In musical example 4.4, in spite of the sextuple (Italian) rhythm, foreign to the Russian people, the style is peculiar in the repetition of its melodic details: each of the passages marked *a* and *b* (the melodic cadence) is repeated twice.

EXAMPLE 4.3. "Sadko bogatoi gost'" [Sadko the wealthy merchant] (from Kirsha Danilov, III).

> Po slavnoi matushke Volge reke
> a gulial Sadko molodets tut dvenadtsat' let
> ni kakoi nad soboi pryt'i skorbi Sadko ne vidal.

> Along the glorious river, the glorious Mother Volga,
> Sadko, the good fellow, wandered for twelve years,
> Without a care to slow him down.

EXAMPLE 4.4. "Sadkov korabl' stal na more" [Sadko's ship put to sea] (from Kirsha Danilov, 144).

> Kak po moriu moriu sinemu
> begut po begut tridtsat' korablei
> edin sokol korabl' samovo Sadko.

> As they race over the sea, the blue sea,
> As thirty ships race over the sea,
> But one, like a falcon, belongs to Sadko himself.

The tune of the following Sadko *bylina* (musical example 4.5) recorded in the Arkhangel'sk province in the North is of a very different character (it is published in Markov's *The White Sea Byliny*). This *bylina* is made up of repetitions of the same four bars, slightly varied by the singer.[136]

EXAMPLE 4.5. "A kak khvalittse Sotko" [How Sadko boasts] (from Markov).

A kak khvalittse Sotko, da pokhvalittse Sotko
voini gradi tovary vse povykupit'
da na cherliany na karab'li povystavit'.
Da poshol Sotko da na dvenadtseti korablei,
Da po per'voi den' tovary vse povykupil,
Da na cherliany na karab'li povystavil.

[Summary of text] How Sadko boasts and praises himself, buying up all the goods in other towns and displaying them on his crimson ship. He went off on twelve ships, and on the first day he bought up all the goods and displayed them on his crimson ships.

The song in musical example 4.7, "Terentii muzh" [The man Terentii], recorded by A. Grigor'ev (*The Arkhangel'sk byliny*, 1:656), is cited here with an obvious repetition (slightly varied) of a basic two-bar melodic motif. (In the penultimate line of the song, Grigor'ev added a note saying that the performer apparently made a wrong turn; this point is marked in the score with an asterisk.)

The tunes of these Novgorodian *byliny* and tales differ from the more leisurely and serious motifs of the pilgrims and folk singers of the Kievan *byliny*. The basic element of the tune is repeated throughout and sometimes embellished with fresh details or slightly varied,

EXAMPLE 4.6. "Gostia Terent'ishcha" [Terent'ishche the merchant] (from Kirsha Danilov, 6).

V stol'nom Novogorode bylo v ulitse vo Iur'evskoi
v slobode bylo Terent'evskoi
A i zhil byl bogatoi gost'
A po imeni Terent'ishche.
U nego dvor na tseloi verste, a krugom dvora zheleznyi tyn,
Na tytyninke po makovke.

In the capital of Novgorod, in Iur'ev Street
In the Terent'ev Quarter
There lived a rich merchant
By the name of Terent'ishche.
His home is a whole *verst* wide, and round the home is an iron fence,
And on each fence post a crown-top.

as in all the examples cited above. The tunes of the Terent'ishche *starina* are shorter than the longer and more developed motifs of the Sadko and Vas'ka Buslaev *byliny*. They are more like the later *chastushki* [humorous, topical folk verse], usually with a brief two-bar phrase with an added introduction or conclusion, for example, the tunes in the Danilov and Grigor'ev collections. Furthermore, compared to the Sadko and Buslaev melodies, they demand a fast tempo, full of movement and life. They were easily and conveniently performed with the simplest musical accompaniment, requiring only two chords. These tunes may be viewed as typical examples, surviving to this day, of the remnants of the old *skomorokh* song repertory. Curiously the old peasant Timofei Shibanov, the informant of "The man Terentii" which Grigor'ev notated in the Arkhangel'sk province [musical example 4.7], used the term *stariny* for the two *byliny* he sang (including the Vas'ka Buslaev example), whereas he called the one about Terentii a *peregudka* and sang it to "a faster tune."[137]

EXAMPLE 4.7. "Terentii muzh" [The man Terentii] (from Grigor'ev, *Arkhangel'skie byliny*).

Zhil byl Terentii muzh.
U Terent'ia zhona moloda
Prasof'ia Ivanovna
Da ona s utra bol'nia i trudna,
Pod vecher neduzhna vsia:
Da na nedug po seredki rozlivaettse
Da vyshe grudi podnimaitstse.
Govoril Terentii muzh
Da Prasof'i Ivanovny
"Da uzh ty goi esi Terentii muzh!
Da ty poidi po Novu gorodu,
Da ty krichitko vo vsiu golovu,
Nazhivai sibe masterov
Da khitrykh mudryikh dokhturev;
Da ne znaiut li moei to zhony posobit'
Da Prosko(f'i) (I)vanovny?"
A na stretila skomorokhi, liudi vezhlivye,
Da skomorokhi otsesl(iv)yia.

[Summary of text] There lived the man Terentii and he had a young wife, Praskof'ia Ivanovna. From morning she is ill and cannot get up, and in the evening she is ill; the ailment floods around her middle and rises in her chest. Terentii, the husband of Praskof'ia Ivanovna, said, "Hey! Terentii, go into Novgorod and shout as loudly as you can and get the masters, the wise and learned physicians, to see if they know how to help my wife, Praskof'ia Ivanovna." And he came across some *skomorokhi*, polite folks.

In addition to the tunes cited here, the third volume of Grigor'ev's collection of
byliny and historical songs from Arkhangel'sk contains three notated *byliny* about Vasilii
Buslaevich with less interesting tunes (volume 3 was published in 1910; see pages 657, 677,
and 678).

So far we have discussed *byliny* about Sadko, Vasilii Buslaev, and the *skomorokh* origins
of Dobrynia Nikitich, as well as the special *skomorokh starina* on the merchant Terent'ishche,
and all of them point to the *gusli* as the most popular, indispensable musical instrument of
the Novgorodian singers and *skomorokhi*. But information about the Novgorodian *gusli* has
been preserved not only in orally transmitted folk poetry but in extremely valuable written
documents as well.

In some 1170 examples of Russian folk ornaments in V. V. Stasov's well-known *Slavic
and Oriental Ornament,* one finds only five drawings associated with music.[137A] All of them
are of Novgorodian provenance, and of these five, four depict the Novgorodian *gusli*. The
old Novgorodian manuscripts thus present unquestionable documentation of musical
instruments. All of these are initials in liturgical books drawn by Novgorodian masters.
There are representations of the *gusli* in two Novgorodian psalters presently in the Tolstoi
and Frolov collections of the Public Library [RNB; figs. 31a and 31b], in a euchologion [*sluzhebnik*] in the same library [fig. 31c], and in the gospel-*aprakos* dated 1358 in the Moscow
Synodal Library [GIM; fig. 32], inside the illuminated initials for the letters *T* and *D*.[137B]
The drawings depict two types of instruments, one with a triangular body (in the two psalters, figs. 31a and 31b), and one with a somewhat larger, oval body in the fourteenth-century
euchologion. The illuminations also show that the instrument was held and played with
both hands.

FIG. 31A. Illuminated initial
T in a thirteenth-century
Novgorodian psalter
(RNB, F. II.I.1, fol. 67v).

FIG. 31B. Illuminated initial
D in a fourteenth-century
Novgorodian psalter (RNB,
Frolov. 3, fol. 14v).

FIG. 31C. Illuminated initial
D in a fourteenth-century
Novgorodian *sluzhebnik*
(RNB, O. II.I.7, fol. 29v).

In these three examples the player sits while playing, which seems to have been the method generally depicted in drawings. If the drawings in figure 31 confirm the descriptions in our *byliny* of contemporary performance practice, however, the illustration in figure 32, which Stasov took from the 1358 manuscript, is of particular interest as it represents a player who is dancing while playing. The impression from such a performance must have been so sensational that the artist added a short inscription above in cinnabar ink: "gudi gorazdo" [plays well]. The costume (dark blue caftan, red morocco boots), the head-dress, the dancing, and the added inscription strongly suggest that here we have a picture of a singing, playing, and dancing *skomorokh*! It is possible, of course, that the players in figures 31a–c also represent *skomorokhi*. The fifth example in Stasov's book is discussed later.

The miniatures by the Novgorodian masters, found in a variety of manuscripts, give us images of other musical instruments in addition to the *gusli*. One such manuscript is the well-known *Kniga glagolemaia Kozma Indikoplov* [Book called Cosmas Indicopleustes], which is preserved in several copies.[138] Figures 33 and 34 are taken from a manuscript in the Moscow Synodal Library ([GIM] no. 997, from the sixteenth century) or, more correctly, cited from the second volume of F. Buslaev's *Historical Studies of Russian Folk Literature and Art,* which reproduces and describes fairly fully many miniatures from this precious document of old Russian art. In the first of these, figure 33, King David is shown "feeding his sheep and playing the *gusli*" (fol. 1248); our fragment is taken from a large and complex composition titled "And Then David Vanquished the Devil."[138A] King David wears the skin of a wild beast and is seated on a mound playing an oval *gusli,* its lower part arched or bow-shaped, a form which does not appear in earlier illustrations. Sheep graze at his feet.

FIG. 32. Initial from an *aprakos* Gospel of 1358 (GIM, Sin. 69, fol. 60).

Figure 34 is a fragment from another miniature showing King David surrounded by clerics of the Jerusalem temple who are playing a variety of musical instruments mentioned in the Psalms.[139] The instruments are depicted according to the contemporary artist's understanding and knowledge, and include tambourines [*bubny*], organs(!), and *sopeli*. But for us the most interesting one is the representation of David seated on a throne with an oval *gusli* in his arms, one similar to the instrument depicted in the preceding miniature. This is, most likely, the only instrument the artist took from real life, that is, he depicted the *gusli* he had seen in Novgorod, whereas most of the other instruments he copied from available foreign depictions. This is the only way to explain the appearance in the Novgorodian miniatures of musical instruments that were totally foreign to the Slavs (rubebs, organs, and others). These instruments appear in medieval Western miniatures from which they were copied in Russian literary sources. [A rubeb, or rabab, is a bowed lute or fiddle.] These images are examined later, along with the 1594 Godunov Psalter and other sources.

The initials and miniatures from the Novgorodian psalters and the fourteenth-century euchologion familiarize us with the Novgorodian *gusli* and with other musical instruments which were used in depicting the biblical King-Psalmist but not employed in Russian practice. In some examples we find representations of trumpets and bells, which did, however, play important roles in Novgorod's public life. Thus figure 35 is a fragment from the well-known Icon of the Miraculous Intervention (fifteenth century) from the iconostasis of the

FIG. 33. King David with a *gusli.* From the Koz'ma Indikoplov text in the Makarii Chet'ia Mineia (GIM, Sin. 997).

FIG. 34. King David with a *gusli.* From the Koz'ma Indikoplov text in the Makarii Chet'ia Mineia (GIM, Sin. 997).

Cathedral of the Sign in Novgorod, depicting the city's salvation from an attack by the city of Suzdal. Among the assailants are four trumpeters on foot with straight trumpets that have widened bells at the end. This icon is unquestionably the work of a Novgorodian master (it includes, among other things, a fifteenth-century plan of the city), and it is unlikely that the artist would have copied trumpets that were not from Novgorod.[140]

Another well-known icon, The Vision of Sexton Tarasii (sixteenth century), in the Cathedral of the Transfiguration at the Khutyn Monastery near Novgorod, mentioned earlier, contains two representations of local watchmen playing straight trumpets similar to those depicted in the Icon of the Miraculous Intervention.[141] The first image (fig. 36a) shows two watchmen: one, leaning on his halberd, has his trumpet pointing down, and the other, standing near the church, holds his halberd in his left hand and points his trumpet upward. Both watchmen are depicted standing near the walled Kremlin. The second drawing (fig. 36b) represents a watchman in the Slavic End [district] of Novgorod. He apparently blows into the horn, not from a roof, as one scholar of this document supposed, but standing on a little hill located behind the tower and not clearly delineated in the drawing taken from the icon. He is standing in the same pose as the watchman on the right in figure 36a, but his straight trumpet seems to have a sort of double bell, probably as a result of an error in copying. Street watchmen of this kind were posted throughout the city, as ordered by agents of Prince Vasilii Ivanovich, in order to prevent and suppress robberies and murders, and they also sounded their trumpets to warn citizens of fires and other public dangers.

In an earlier document, the Novgorod gospel of the fourteenth century (parchment manuscript in the Library of the Academy of Sciences [BAN]), a vignette of a similar watchman is reproduced in Stasov's *Slavic and Oriental Ornament*.[142] The Novgorod watchman, resting his left hand on a broad ax of an unusual form [or a tri-cross?], plays a trumpet he holds in his right hand. The instrument is short and straight but with a wider bell and finger holes, which suggests that it was made of wood (fig. 37). Ignoring the clothing and hats, it is apparent that the attitude and manner of playing the trumpet are represented in a similar way both in the fourteenth-century Novgorodian icon and in the sixteenth-century miniature.

Watchmen with trumpets were common in many Western cities in the Middle Ages, and their depiction in the Novgorodian documents shows that this custom also existed in Russian cities. The mid-fourteenth-century seal of the English city of Rochester shows a figure resembling the Novgorodian watchman standing on the city wall with a trumpet in his hand. Wagner's *Die Meistersinger*, whose subject and libretto were based on accurate historical data from medieval Nuremberg, introduces a night watchman announcing the "all is well" and playing a long straight trumpet. In addition to the Novgorod watchmen, we referred to other Russian trumpet players

FIG. 35. Fragment from the Icon of the Miraculous Intervention with a plan of Novgorod (fifteenth century), on which there is a depiction of the battle between Novgorod and Suzdal in 1169.

in watchtowers in figures 21 and 22, from the earlier Königsberg manuscript.

The Novgorodian watchmen's trumpets were undoubtedly taken from military practice. As elsewhere in early Russia, such trumpets were long used by the armies of Novgorod. Military trumpets are depicted in the Icon of the Miraculous Intervention, as noted above, and they are also mentioned in the Novgorod IV Chronicle, in the entry for 1216, describing the dispute between Novgorod and the city of Vladimir: "Iurii had seventeen banners and forty trumpets and as many drums."[142A] The military use of trumpets has already been discussed, and here it suffices to mention that this instrument is also used in Novgorod's secular practice, and to note the sources in which this practice is illustrated.

The miniatures and other representations of musical instruments we have examined are also interesting because they reveal the distinctive treatment instruments received at the hands of ecclesiastical and secular authorities. This should be understood in connection with a peculiar phenomenon in Novgorodian society.

We have already had occasion to remark (and shall do so again later) that when Christianity was introduced, the Russian clergy adopted an entirely hostile attitude toward folk song and the instruments associated with its practice. Ecclesiastical authorities always condemned the "voices of *gusli*" or "organ voices" and other "twitterings" from overseas. As

FIG. 36A. Fragment from the Novgorod icon of The Vision of Sexton Tarasii
(sixteenth century).

FIG. 36B. Fragment from the Novgorod icon of The Vision of Sexton Tarasii
(sixteenth century).

we read in one early sermon: "To take up the *sopel'*, to delight in the *gusli* and singing, frolicking and dancing, is to honor the dark demon."[142B] This hatred of the *skomorokhi* and, indeed, of any kind of musical performance passed from the clergy to the civil authorities; still, this did not prevent both individuals, including the tsar himself, from including *skomorokhi* among their servants or court staff. Nevertheless, as we shall see, the authorities, at the initiative of the clergy, would eventually not only banish or exile the *skomorokhi* but would also take decisive and far-reaching police action to destroy their musical instruments. Yet, at the same time, the clerics allowed their own books to contain illustrations of these hated instruments of Hellenic paganism and Satanic pleasures!

The fact remains that, in the miniatures and initials adorning liturgical and instructional books, there are whole groups of saints playing the *gusli* as well as various organs, trumpets, *sopeli, bubny,* and bowed instruments, including even the Western rubeb (see fig. 43, one of the miniatures from the Godunov Psalter of 1594)—in other words, all the instruments so harshly condemned by the clergy. They are not depicted negatively, in the hands of sinners and servants of hell, but instead are used to glorify God or as adornments of King David the Psalmist. The

FIG. 37. Miniature from a fourteenth-century *aprakos* Gospel (BAN 34.5.20, fol. 113v).

illuminated letters of Novgorod *gusli* players shown above in figures 31 and 32 would seem to contradict even more strongly the clergy's stern disapproval, especially the last of these, which depicts a *skomorokh* dancing and playing, along with the inscription "plays well," found in the 1358 Gospel, a manuscript written at the time of Aleksei, Metropolitan of Novgorod.

This last illustration, together with details of the Novgorodian icon of the Vision of Sexton Tarasii, gives us new impetus to study these artistic works by Russian masters in their relationship to everyday life. When we remember the deep veneration of icons and the importance of church books and other edifying works in ancient Rus', the images from daily life depicted in them, especially of the *skomorokhi,* who were apostates from the Church, inevitably arouse our interest in further investigation. This new and, in our view, crucial thread in the history of Russian art appeared probably for the first time in Novgorod, a free city, little affected by convention and tradition.

Novgorod is celebrated in the extant archaeological sources of music history not only for its *gusli* players and *skomorokhi* but also for its bell ringing, its chanting (that is, its singers [*raspevshchiki*]), and its church music books. The bells of the Cathedral of St. Sophia and the eleventh-century Monastery of St. George, one of the oldest in the Novgorod area, are mentioned by even the most recent investigators. Novgorod's belfries, incidentally, are equally famous, as are those of its "younger brother," the city of Pskov. True, in Novgorod, most of the extant bells belong to a later date, which suggests that the oldest ones were recast or, more probably, removed from Novgorod when it lost its autonomy. At any rate, the oldest and biggest bells are of historical interest, as are some of the local bell towers:

> The old alarm bell of the Cathedral of the Sign has been preserved; it has a doleful sonority and was rung to warn of fires. It weighs 120 *pudy* [4,320 lbs.] and is situated in a separate belfry by the south wall of the cathedral, an octagonal tower with a tented roof of sheet-iron;
>
> One of the oldest bells in the Antoniev Monastery was cast in 1573 by order of Tsar Ivan Vasil'evich. It weighs 165 *pudy* [5,940 lbs.];
>
> A bell in the Church of the Archangel Michael has the following inscription from the sixteenth century: "From the Christian, Christ-loving Tsar and

Sovereign Grand Prince Feodor Ivanovich of all Russia and the Devout Tsaritsa and Grand Princess Irina";

The Church of the Transfiguration of the Savior on the Nereditsa River, with its small belfry and three bells, has one dated 1609;

The octahedral belfry of the Church of St. Dmitrii, with its six stairwells and tented roof, has nine bells, three of which are dated 1627, 1667, and 1735, respectively;

There are two interesting bells in the old Church of Boris and Gleb and the old Mechinskaia Church (formerly the Convent of the Resurrection). One has a Latin inscription, "Gloria in excelsis Deo Anno 1636," from which it may be assumed that the bell was ordered or brought from abroad. The other, dated 1669, bears the inscription "M. Kordt Kleiman me fecit";

The belfry of the Cathedral of St. George contains a small bell brought from Holland and dated 1671, and a bell in the belfry of the Church of St. Theodore Stratilates is inscribed near the cannons: "Soli Deo Gloria. Anno 1680. Gloria in excelsis. Deo fundebat H. O. J. M. J. A. C."

We thus see that, in addition to bells of local or Russian origin, Novgorod's churches were ornamented with other bells brought from abroad or perhaps cast on the spot by foreign masters, for example, such as the foundryman Kordt Kleiman did at the Convent of the Resurrection.

The most famous were the bells and bell ringing of the Cathedral of St. Sophia and the Monastery of St. George, and the latter possesses what, at a later time, was probably the largest of all the Novgorodian bells. The belfry, built in the mid-nineteenth century after plans by the architect Rossi, is 175 feet high and has sixteen bells, the largest of which is called "The Unburning Bush," with a representation of St. Theoctist and weighing 2,100 *pudy* [75,600 lbs.]. The *voskresnyi krestovyi* bell weighs 1,140 *pudy* [41,040 lbs.]; the *polieleinyi* bell, nicknamed George, weighs 523 *pudy* [18,828 lbs.]; and the *vsednevnyi* bell, nicknamed Gabriel, weighs 267 *pudy* [9,612 lbs.]. There are also several smaller bells. [The *polieleinyi* bell is the third largest in a Russian bell tower, after the *prazdnichnii* (festal) and the *voskresnyi* (Sunday, or, literally, Resurrection) bell; the *vsednevnyi* (*povsednevnyi*), or daily, bell, mentioned below, is fourth in size.][142C]

The belfry of the Cathedral of St. Sophia was built in 1436 with five arches under one roof; the bells are hung in the arches. The largest was cast in Aleksei Mikhailovich's reign and weighs 1,614 *pudy* [58,104 lbs.]. The *povsednevnyi* bell was cast in the reign of Fyodor Alekseevich. Novgorod's populace took great pride in the sounds of the cathedral bells even in more recent times. One can find the complete repertory, if one might use that term, of the famous cathedral's bell-ringing practices in its Chinovnik [the Ordinal, containing the Pontifical Book of Offices, with instructions for all the prayers and ceremonies in accordance with local custom]. Although this is a later document from the seventeenth century, it undoubtedly preserved many regulations from an older liturgical practice. That these regulations were, in fact, written down at this time demonstrates that Novgorod's liturgical and musical-artistic practices ranked quite highly even after the city's loss of autonomy, and that Novgorod's practices were acknowledged as worthy models even in Moscow, the center of government. Here follow some examples of bell-ringing regulations, based on excerpts from the seventeenth-century Chinovnik (1689) that belonged to the Riazan archbishopric, published by A. Golubtsov:[143]

Month of September. On the first of the month, beginning of the *indikt* [a fifteen-year liturgical cycle starting on September 1], that is of the New Year . . . *Blagovest* for Vespers [is struck] at the beginning of the ninth hour of the day on the large bell, but *trezvon* [an elaborate collective sounding of the bells] is rung on all [the bells] . . . For Prime, *blagovest* is struck on the large bell after the fourth hour of the day. Following Matins at the beginning of the first hour of the day, they strike *blagovest* at the cathedral on the large bell and alternately on the [or on a] middle-sized and small bell, as customary for the call to worship on Sunday. And at that time the ringers create a place for the prelate opposite the Church of Praises for the Mother of God, and the sextons [*kliuchari*] above the ringers carefully watch him [the prelate]. And at half past the third hour of the day, they ring all the bells for a sufficient length of time, and at that point the *kliuchari* place shrouds appropriate to the feast day over the graves, and, with the ringing, the hierarchs move toward the prelate into the sacral cell ["v krestovuiu kel'iu"].[143A]

To clarify this citation it may be necessary to add that in the past, when New Year's Day was celebrated on 1 September, there was a special rite of welcoming the year (*letoprovodstvo*), for which the bell ringers built a place for the metropolitan, as described above. The New Year's ceremony is laid out in the Chinovnik, listing the *stikhiry* and other chants and the lessons to be read, and so forth. More details on this appear in our examination of other church "acts" practiced in old Russia. On holidays (for example, 3 and 20 September) the Chinovnik prescribes "*trezvon* with all [the bells] except the largest one" or "*trezvon* with all [the bells] except the large ones." On 25 September the Chinovnik prescribes "*blagovest* for the All-Night Vigil at the fifth hour, and sound all the St. Sophia bells during the church singing."[143B]

On 24 December, after Royal Hours, "the celebrant then goes from his cell to the cathedral with the hierarchs. And when they are opposite the Church of the Epiphany, at that time *blagovest* sounds and they ring five bells as a single *zvon*."

On 16 January "at Vespers *blagovest* sounds at the ninth hour, and the *voskresnyi* and the *polieleinyi* bells sound at the beginning of the eighth hour."

On the Feast of the Annunciation, on 25 March, "during the period before the feast *blagovest* sounds using the Makar'evskii bell at the beginning of the fifth hour, the hours are struck with that bell. *Trezvon* with all bells."[144]

The Chinovnik prescribes a whole series of similar gradations in bell ringing at St. Sophia. From this we learn the entire complement of bells (not by name, unfortunately, since only the large bells were given nicknames). In the seventeenth century the cathedral had large, middle-sized, and small bells, a daily [*vsednevnyi*] bell, *polieleinyi* and *sennye* bells, and others [see note 143B, above, on the term *sennye*]. Among the large bells, of course, was the Makar'evskii bell of 250 *pudy*, which was rung, as mentioned above, in connection with the Feast of the Annunciation. This bell was cast in the sixteenth century at the time of Archbishop Makarii, who, as we shall see below, is mentioned in the chronicles.

We have seen that the folk *bylina* about Vasilii Buslaev preserves an echo of Novgorod's famous bells and bell ringing. It is curious, however, that in addition to bells, Novgorod's religious practice also included the *bilo* and *klepalo* [suspended strips of heavy, resonant metal] which had been used in churches before bells were cast. Like the ancient Slavic *bila* (see chap. 1, fig. 12, above), the Novgorodian instruments were of cast-iron or metal, either straight (for the hand-held *klepalo*) or curved. The larger specimens were suspended on a pillar near the church and struck with an iron or wooden mallet. Sometimes they took the form of a narrow, arched board more than fourteen feet long.[145]

Novgorod's bells were cast by foundrymen not only from Novgorod but also from Pskov or Moscow (who were sometimes commissioned, according to extant documentation), as well as by foreign masters. Here is a list of Novgorodian bell foundrymen of the sixteenth and seventeenth centuries, including details on some of the bells they cast:[145A]

1. Il'ia (Ileika), 1545;
2. Ivan "from Gorodishche," 1554–66 (bells of the Cathedral of the Sign and the Churches of St. Philip and of the Ascension);
3. Filipp "from Gorodishche," 1557 (together with Ivan, listed above, cast the bell of the Church of St. Philip);
4. Mitia, stepson of the first Ivan, 1566 (assisted in casting the bell of the Church of the Ascension);
5. Dmitrii Kononov, 1568 (bells of the Churches of St. Nicholas the Miracle-worker and Sts. Peter and Paul);
6. Timofei, "the Novgorodian," 1597 (bell of the Church of the Transfiguration of the Savior on the Nereditsa River);
7. Ermolai Vasil'ev, the "resident master at St. Sophia's" (1651–59; cast, among others, a bell weighing 1,614 *pudy* [58,104 lbs.] for the cathedral);
8. Iakov Leont'ev, 1677;
9. Ivan Matveev, 1697 (three bells at the Church of St. Elijah; he may have come from Pskov).

To these must be added the names of bell foundrymen from Pskov who also cast bells for Novgorod churches:

1. Andreev, "the Pskovian," son of Mikhail, 1532 (the *vsednevnyi* bell of the Khutyn Monastery);
2. Tikhon Andreev, "the Pskovian," 1545 (*krasnyi* bell for the Vyzhitskii Monastery [*krasnyi* (beautiful) is a nickname for a bell with an especially pleasing sound]);
3. Koz'ma Vasil'ev, 1552.
4. Koz'ma Mikhailov, 1552, Koz'ma Vasil'ev's co-foundryman;
5. Vasilii Ivanov, 1599 (the *polieleinyi* bell of 200 *pudy* [7,200 lbs.] for the Khutyn Monastery).

The following Muscovite founders, who also worked in Novgorod, should be added to the list:

1–2. Vlasko and Iushko Poberezhkov, 1558 (bell for the Church of the Forty Martyrs);
3. Ian D'iachkov, 1558 (bell for the Church of the Forty Martyrs);
4–5. Afanasii Pankrat'ev and Iakim Ivanov, 1599 (the *polieleinyi* bell of the Khutyn Monastery);
6. Dmitrii Matveev, 1627 (large bell of the Vyzhitskii Monastery);
7–9. Vasilii, Iakov, and Fyodor Leont'ev, 1677 (*vsednevnyi* bell of the Cathedral of St. Sophia);
10. Ivan Matveev, 1697 (three bells at the Church of St. Elijah).[146]

In connection with the Novgorodian *bila* and bells and their foundrymen, we should also mention two miniatures, one illustrating the use of *bila* and the other the repair of bells.

Both miniatures are related to Novgorod, although the second was made in Moscow for a Muscovite event. The first is in an illuminated manuscript of the life of St. George belonging to the Trinity-St. Sergius Lavra. It depicts monks leaving a monastery, two of them holding straight *bila* in their hands. Above the miniature the inscription states: "They arose for the saint's day, and the blessed one ordered the *bilo* struck and the brotherhood to descend" (fig. 38).[147]

The other miniature is taken from the so-called *Tsarstvennaia kniga* [Tsar's book], a sixteenth-century manuscript (Moscow [GIM] Sin. 149, fol. 296). F. Buslaev published and discussed some of the miniatures of this precious and historic artistic document in the second volume of his *Historical Studies of Russian Folk Literature and Art*. The *Tsarstvennaia kniga* contains a narrative of the last days of Vasilii Ivanovich's reign and the first half of Ivan the Terrible's. According to Buslaev, the miniatures were the work of Novgorodian masters who were invited to Moscow for this purpose. The only miniature of interest here is the one depicting the repair and rehanging of a bell.

Under the year 1547 (7055) we read a paragraph headed "On bells,"

FIG. 38. A miniature from the Life of St. George (from the manuscript collection of the Trinity–St. Sergius Monastery, fol. 173v.

stating: "That spring, on 3 June, as the call to Vespers began, the bell's ears [cannons] broke off and the bell fell from the wooden bell tower and did not break. And the tsar ordered that new ears be made for the bell, of iron, and after making a big fire, they added new ears to the bell and placed it in the wooden belfry by St. John's and the bell sounded as before."[148]

This is the subject of the second miniature (fig. 39), which illustrates the repair of the bell. In the foreground we see the furnace and its bellows and the craftsmen with their hammers; they are engaged in attaching the cannons to the bell. In the next scene the bell is raised in the wooden belfry and sounds as it did before. In these and other illustrations we have examined, the Novgorodian artists did not always reproduce traditional types and models but, as we have seen, they often tried to express what they saw around them in real-life situations.

The earliest references to bells in Novgorod date back to the eleventh century, that is, there were bells in Novgorod already in the first century after the conversion. In the Chronicle under the year 1066, we read that Vseslav, Prince of Polotsk, having captured Novgorod, "took away the bells and candelabras." In the biography of the Blessed Anthony of Rome, there is a story of the time when, in the year 1106, he miraculously arrived in Novgorod at night, at the time when they started ringing the bells for Prime, and he heard the bells resounding through the city. We do not know whether there were bell foundrymen at that time in Russia. On his arrival from Rome, Anthony brought with him a small bell of 1 *pud* 10 *funty* [about 45 lbs.].[148A] We do know that there are a few foreign bells preserved in Novgorod from a later period. Bells were highly valued, and the chroniclers had good reason for their continual references to the casting of new bells and the recasting, repair, or loss of old ones. They also mention the melting of bells as a result of church fires: "and from the fire the copper, like a resin, spread out [*polzushche*]."

Apparently there were no local foundrymen in Novgorod at first. As late as 1342 a chronicler recorded that "the Novgorod bishop Vasilii had a craftsman named Boris brought from Moscow to cast a great bell for St. Sophia's."[148B] Later, in the sixteenth and seventeenth centuries, we find the names of the Novgorodian foundrymen listed above.

In 1530, on the same night and at the very hour of the birth of Ivan the Terrible, who was later completely to destroy the city of Novgorod, Archbishop Makarii ordered the casting of a 250-*pud* [9000-lb.] bell for the Cathedral of St. Sophia, the *Blagovestnik* bell. The chronicler recorded in 1530: "and in Novgorod and in the entire Novgorod region, there is not [a bell] of such magnitude; it blasts like an awesome trumpet."[148C] Over the next

Fig. 39. A sixteenth-century miniature from the Tsar's Book (GIM, Sin. 149, fol. 296); preparing new cannons for the bell and sounding the bell after hanging it in the wooden belfry. From F. I. Buslaev, *Historical Studies of Russian Folk Literature and Art,* 2:311.

twelve years, with the blessing of the same archbishop (the future metropolitan), more bells were cast for the Khutyn and other monasteries. On one of the bells, which is preserved to this day, the foundryman Andreev of Pskov, son of Mikhail, is named. Four bells from this period have been preserved in Novgorod, and from the second half of the sixteenth century five bells have survived. In 1554 Archbishop Pimen had another great bell, a *blagovestnik,* cast for St. Sophia's, "in order that God and the Blessed Virgin might deliver Orthodox Christians from mortal pestilences and unmerited death; the bell was cast by Master Ivan." Nevertheless, this bell did not gladden the ears of Novgorod for long. Sixteen years later, in 1570, it was transferred by order of Ivan the Terrible to the Aleksandrovskaia sloboda [near Moscow], where two years later, Master Ivan Afanas'ev cast another bell which was sent to Novgorod in exchange for the first.

Still earlier, in 1478, the Muscovite prince Ivan Vasil'evich (Ivan the Terrible's grandfather) abolished Novgorod's franchise and carried its assembly bell away to Moscow. It was recast in 1673 and became Moscow's alarm bell; ultimately it was sent to the Karelian Monastery of St. Nicholas in 1681 because on one occasion its chiming at midnight terrified Tsar Fyodor Alekseevich! The Pskov assembly bell was removed to Moscow in 1510 by order of Vasilii Ivanovich, Ivan the Terrible's father. Such was the fate of some of Novgorod's and Pskov's historic bells.[149]

To conclude our survey of Novgorod's musical and cultural antiquities, we must also take a look at the written musical documents and the musicians who cultivated the art of church singing there, documents that were appropriated and then passed into the legacy of the Muscovite state.

The question of special Novgorodian melodies and composers has so far remained unexplored. But we have proof of their existence through the names of several *raspevshchiki* [singers who created or elaborated the chant melodies] and theorists of Novgorodian origin, among them the inventor of the cinnabar signs, I. A. Shaidurov [or Shaidur]. Additional proof exists through direct references to Novgorodian melodies in the St. Sophia Chinovnik mentioned above. The Chinovnik often gives instructions such as the following, for 7 and 14 September, 4 October, and 27 July: "During the liturgy the choir on the right sings the *demestvennyi* chant and the choir on the left sings the one in parts from Novgorod ["strochnaia novgorodtskaia"]." On special days the memory of local miracle-workers was celebrated (Savva Visherskii on 1 October; Archbishop Jonas on 5 November; Palladii on 27 October; Archbishop John on 1 December; Bishop Nifont on 18 April; the *iurodivyi* [holy fool] Nikolai Kochanov on 27 July), or local icons (for example, the *streteniia* icon of the Vladimir Mother of God on 15 September; the Icon of the Miraculous Intervention on 27 November, and others).[149A] On such occasions the Chinovnik prescribes that "the singers perform the Novgorod ordo [Obikhod]" or that "for Vespers, the All-Night Vigil, Matins, and for the liturgy, the singers perform according to Novgorod usage ["novgorodtskoi ves' obikhod"] . . . and for the vestment and during the action [*deistvo*] the singers perform Novgorodian tunes in parts ["strochnaia novgorodtskaia"]."[150] Thus, at the beginning of the seventeenth century, Novgorodian melodies existed on equal terms with other Russian types (from Moscow, Rostov, Kiev, and other places) and included the whole cycle of services for the church year.

In addition to these literary documents, we also have the names of local composers and singers of church music. One of the earliest is the Novgorodian precentor Kirik, in the twelfth century, a monk of the Antoniev Monastery. The *Works of the Society of Russian History and Antiquities* published his "Uchenie, im zhe vedati cheloveku chisla vsekh let" [A teaching on how a person can calculate all the calendar years], in which the following inscription is recorded for the year 1136: "I wrote to Great Novgorod, I the sinful and lowly monk of the Antonov [Monastery], Kirik the deacon and *domestik* of the Church of the Holy Virgin."[151] This text shows that he was a choir master [*regent-raspevshchik*] at the Church of the Holy Virgin at St. Sophia, and that he was a well-educated man.

Novgorodian manuscripts are generally among the oldest existing sources of church music, despite the frequent and destructive fires from which the chroniclers recorded that there was "not enough time to rescue icons or books." Even so, aside from the eleventh-century Ostromir Gospel, no fewer than nine *znamennye* manuscripts and two Kondakari of Novgorodian origin survive from the earliest times to the fifteenth century. In the city of Novgorod itself, apparently only two musical manuscripts survived, seventeenth-century manuscripts with *kriukovaia* [hooked] notation in the Church of the Archangel Michael and the Church of St. Theodore Stratilates near the Cathedral of St. Sophia. This low rate of survival resulted from the fact that during Nikon's patriarchate, in the mid-seventeenth century, ecclesiastical authorities in Moscow ordered many old manuscripts from monasteries and churches throughout Russia to be sent to Moscow to be corrected. They were not returned but remained in Moscow, where they formed the rich collections of old Russian documents in the Moscow Synodal Library (formerly the Patriarchal Library [now in GIM]) and the Synodal Typography Library [now in RGADA].[152]

All these monuments of early Russian church music were, of course, anonymous, and the names of singers and copyists have not come down to us. Only toward the end of the sixteenth century in the history of Russian church music do we find the names of some of the prominent Novgorod artists in this sphere.

First we must mention the famous brothers Vasilii and Savva Rogov, from Karelia. Vasilii (whose monastic name was Varlaam) is considered to be one of the creators of the three-line [*troestrochnoe*] or three-part [*trekhgolosnoe*] singing. In 1587 he was elevated to the rank of Archbishop of Rostov, and two years later, when the Moscow patriarchate was founded, he became Metropolitan of Rostov.[153] Both brothers were renowned singers and *raspevshchiki* and apparently served (Vasilii only for a short time, of course) in Moscow in the Aleksandrovskaia sloboda during Ivan the Terrible's reign. Valuable information concerning the Rogovs and other Novgorodian singers is given in the preface to a seventeenth-century notated Stikhirar:

> And we, elders, as we grew up and were educated in this seventh millennium [from the creation of the world], with our own ears we have heard of the old masters: I am speaking of Feodor the Priest, called Khristianin [the Christian], who had become famous here in the ruling city of Moscow and was artful in the singing of *znamennyi* chant; many learned from him, and his compositions are famous to this day. From his students who are known to us we have heard that he, Khristianin, would tell them about the old masters of Novgorod the Great: Savva Rogov and his brother Vasilii, whose monastic name was Varlaam, Karelians by birth, and that later Varlaam was Metropolitan in the city of Rostov; he was a pious and wise man and was artful in *znamennyi* singing and composed *troestrochnyi* and *demestvennyi* hymns as well. His brother Savva had students—the aforementioned priest Khristianin, Ivan Nos [the Nose], and Stefan, called Golysh [the Pauper]. Ivan Nos and Khristianin lived in the reign of the pious Tsar and Great Prince of All-Russia, Ivan Vasil'evich [the Terrible, reigned 1533–84], whom they served in his beloved Aleksandrov Sloboda; Stefan Golysh, on the other hand, was not there, but went from city to city and taught in the Usol'e land [near the Ural mountains], and while in the employ of the [merchants] Stroganovs, he taught Ivan, called Lukoshko, whose monastic name was Isaia; and the master Stefan Golysh composed many *znamennyi* hymns. After him his student Isaia disseminated *znamennyi* singing extensively and perfected it. And from those same students of Khristianin we heard what he had told them concerning the Gospel Stikhira: that a certain wise and pious deacon in Tver' had set them to chant, while the Psalter was set to chant in Novgorod the Great . . . by a famous monk named Markel, called Bezborodyi [the Beardless] . . . He also composed a very artful *kanon* to [Saint] Nikita, Archbishop of Novgorod. The Triodia were set to chant and interpreted by Ivan Nos while he lived in Tsar Ivan Vasil'evich's suburb; and he

also set to chant the *stikhira* to many saints and the megalynaria [*velichaniia*]. The same Ivan set to chant the stavrotheotokia [*krestobogorodichny*] and the *theotokia* from the Menaion.[154]

A school of later Novgorodian composers was thus established, although some of its members were transferred to Moscow and its realms. One can thus trace three generations of this school, as shown in table 4.1.

TABLE 4.1. The genealogy of Novgorodian singers

	I. Savva and Vasilii (Metropolitan Varlaam) Rogov		
	Savva's pupils:		
II. Markel Bezborodyi (active in Novgorod; his teacher unknown)	1. Fyodor Kristianin (in Moscow and at the Aleksandrovskaia sloboda; he had many pupils, not mentioned by the author of the "Predislovie")	2. Ivan Nos	3. Stefan Golysh (in Usol'e; he taught Ivan Lukoshko and Faddei Nikitin)
III. I. A. Shaidur (in Moscow, his teacher unknown)			

On the basis of this document, whose author was apparently contemporary to the third generation of Novgorodian singers, we gather that the Rogov brothers, recognized as masters and *raspevshchiki* from Novgorod in the mid-sixteenth century (for Vasilii could have been elevated to the rank of archbishop in 1587 at an advanced age), were later the models for a whole school of church music composers in Moscow. It follows, then, that in early Novgorod singing and the mastery of church music were on a very high level. We can add a few more names of comparable masters active in the second and third generations, as summarized below.

For the period of approximately the last quarter of the sixteenth century and the beginning of the seventeenth, we have mentioned three pupils of Savva Rogov: Fyodor Kristianin [or Krest'ianin] and Ivan Nos (both were with Ivan the Terrible in the Aleksandrovskaia sloboda, and Fyodor became a well-known teacher in Moscow), and Stefan Golysh (who was active in Usol'e in connection with the Stroganov family, where he created the Usol'e singing [*usol'skii raspev*]). To this Novgorod group, we should add the names of two more singers who may also have been known to the Rogov school. Of these, Markel Bezborodyi, a famous composer and monk from Novgorod and later also the abbot of the nearby Khutyn Monastery, fully notated the Psalter in *kriukovaia* notation; the title [in summary] reads: "Psalter and a whole cycle of chants honoring men and women venerated in Russia as new miracle-workers, the cycle consisting of hymns and processionals and *stikhiry* covering the church year from September to the end of August" (i.e., the entire church year). In seventeenth-century manuscripts notated using *kriuki* one also encounters a special alleluia called "Radilova" [by Radilov], apparently by a Novgorodian *raspevshchik* from the end of the sixteenth or the beginning of the seventeenth century. That chant was performed annually during the liturgy on Sunday of the Holy Fathers.[155]

The celebrated Semyon Fyodorov Babin, a singer for the Archbishop of Novgorod, belongs to the third generation of singers who were active in the city in the middle and second half of the seventeenth century.[155A] I have in my possession a notated Oktoechos dated 1672 containing a chant, "Sviatyi Bozhe" [Holy God], labeled "Opekalov's"; one might add this name to the list of seventeenth-century Novgorodian singers (or Muscovite, but of Novgorodian origin).[155B]

Along with the Rogovs, we should mention the musical activities of another Novgorodian master, probably a somewhat younger contemporary: Ivan Akimovich Shaidurov [or Shaidur, the usage most common in current scholarship], a distinguished music theorist from the end of the sixteenth century, author of the *Skazanie o pometakh, ezhe pishutsia v penii pod znamenem* [A treatise on additional signs as these are written in chant underneath the neumes]. With the gradual increase in the number of neumes utilized in singing practice, the existing designations for pitch proved to be incomplete and, for the younger singers, unclear or difficult to understand. In the second half of the sixteenth century, older, more experienced leaders and teachers at singing schools began to introduce new signs written with red ink [*kinovarnye pometki*], in addition to signs in black ink. This seemed more convenient both for teaching and in practice, for one could indicate more accurately the pitch of any given neume with these new signs. Similar letter-signs were known long ago in Western neumatic notation. Already in the eleventh century the [Swabian] monk Hermannus Contractus established additional letters with the following designations: *e—equaliter* (unison); *s—semitonus* (half step); *t—tonus* (whole step); *ts—tonus cum semitonus* (minor third), and so on.[155C] It is not known if Russian singers were acquainted with Western singing practice. It is true that the additional signs in the West designated duration, whereas the added Russian signs indicated a neume's pitch and expressive character, but the principle of using letters is undoubtedly the same. The heterogeneity and variety of similar efforts, along with the growing number and complexity of signs, necessitated a reform and the establishment of a precise notational system. The Novgorod master I. A. Shaidur succeeded in this by introducing the cinnabar marks into a clear, comprehensible system, and integrating this system definitively into the *kriukovaia* notational practice. These signs were comprehensive and were used everywhere, and came to be called "Shaidur signs" [*shaidurovskie pomety*].[156] They consisted of the first letters of words used in singing pedagogy, written in Cyrillic. The signs designated the pitch of separate neumes and were written in red ink next to the neumes written in black. The additional signs with their literal and musical meanings are illustrated in musical example 4.8.

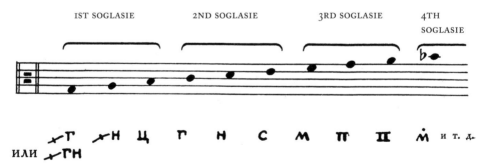

EXAMPLE 4.8. The *soglasiia*.

These signs had these meanings:

✗Γ or ✗ΓΗ - **g**orazdo **n**izko [very low]   FIRST
                                                               TRICHORD

✗Η   - **n**izko ([low] often written
               without the cross)

Ц   - designated the third sound in the
               low trichord

The same letters without the cross:

С   - **s**rednim glasom ([middle voice] in   SECOND
               cursive replaced by a dot .)   TRICHORD

М   - **m**rachno [dark]   THIRD
П   - **p**ovyshe mrachno [one step   TRICHORD
               above 'dark']

Ц   - **v**ysoko [high; written with an old
               form of the letter *V*]

The same letters with dots above them designate the   FOURTH
                                                             TRICHORD

Only one additional sign was added to each of the old signs. In later practice these additions came to be called degree signs [*stepennye pomety*], as they indicated the pitch [or degree; *stepen'*] of the sign, that is, they determined its place in the trichord. In addition to these, there were a few additional signs, called indicational [*ukazatel'nye*] signs, which indicated the manner of performance, and also octoechal [*osmoglasnye* or *glasovye*] signs, which designated the mode in which the chant was to be sung. The latter are understandable on their own, but the indicational signs, also written in red ink, were as follows:

—   horizontal line, top part of letter *T*
⌐   or, rarely, the truncated letter *T*;
             these signs signified **t**ikho [softly] and to be sung slowly

β   the distorted first letter of the word **b**orzo (to sing quickly);
             indicated an acceleration of the performance

З   **z**evok [literally, yawn]; to perform by throwing back or throwing out
             the voice; from the first letter of the word [*zevok*], added to the right of
             some signs and signifying the addition of two rising notes of shorter
             value. Thus the term "throwing back the voice" ["glasom zakinuti"]

ƛо   **l**omati [to break], from the word *lom* [literally, scrap or fragment]
             designated the interval of a third

«   this is the old cursive shape of the letter *K*, in words such as *kachati*
             (rolling the voice) or *kupno* (together); thus the sign is called *kachkaia* or

kupnaia [*pometa*]. In the first meaning, it was placed next to single neumes; in the second meaning, it was placed next to complex neumes

ρ   from the word *ravno* [alike]; it was usually represented by a vertical line | signifying that the neume following it was on the same pitch as the preceding neume

ч   *udarka*, from the word *udariaiu* [I hit, or I stress]; it signified a faster descent from a higher to a lower pitch

The cinnabar signs are encountered in most *kriukovye* manuscripts from the seventeenth century, especially from the second half of the century, when they were, so to speak, legislated by the special commission assembled in Moscow. The commission was headed by the famous elder Aleksandr Mezenets, former censor of the Moscow Synodal Typography and author of the well-known treatise "Izveshchenie o soglasneishikh pometakh" [Report on the most harmonious notational signs], which was published under the title *Azbuka znamennogo peniia* [Alphabet of *znamennoe* singing]. It is significant that this Muscovite chant theorist also lived for some time in Novgorod, and he may even have gone through his own schooling in chant there.

On the basis of the manuscripts and historical documents we have examined, we can state authoritatively that Novgorod was one of a few Russian cities to manifest, preserve, and develop its own individuality and distinctive national characteristics. These were manifest in the *byliny* epics, the emergence and flowering of Novgorod's *skomorokh* culture, and the wide dissemination of that purely Slavic folk instrument, the *gusli*. All bespoke an affirmation of life, joyfulness, freedom, and a thirst for adventure. This spirit was reflected in the miniature paintings by local artists and in the songs created by Novgorodians. While Kiev had its Greek and Bulgarian teachers and the rigid discipline of Feodosii Pecherskii, Novgorod gradually developed its own Russian musical notation and its own school of church singing.

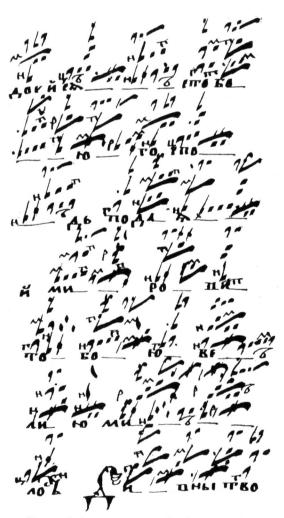

FIG. 40. A three-part score in *kriukovaia* notation.

Just as the Kievan principality was devastated by the Tatars (who, even earlier, had been aided by kindred Russian princes), so Novgorod's freedom and independence were gradually destroyed by attacks from Moscow. As is well known, Ivan the Terrible, especially after the conquest of 1570, deported Novgorodians from their native lands and replaced them with new inhabitants, to whom the free spirit of Novgorod was alien. The despoliation of the city had begun long before, during the reign of Ivan III (Ivan the Terrible's grandfather), who repeatedly feasted with the city's inhabitants, then plundered them. The St. Sophia Chronicle assembles curious data about Ivan III's arrival in Novgorod in 1476, listing the dates of all his banquets and the rich gifts offered to him by local authorities. In less than six weeks Ivan feasted at seventeen banquets, and each time he was presented with gifts of gold, silver, and the like.[156A] This listing tells us not only of the constant banquets held for the Muscovite prince and the richness of the obligatory gifts but also gives us reason to assume that participating at the banquets of Novgorod were *gusli* players and *skomorokhi*, who are not mentioned in the chronicle, of course, but who undoubtedly entertained the revelers. Thus, in the Novgorod II Chronicle, we read about an unusual requisition by Ivan III's grandson, Ivan the Terrible, in 1571: "At this time in Novgorod and in all cities and districts, they seized the merry folk [*veselye liudi*] for the sovereign," and even further, on 21 September 1571, we read that "Subbota (a clerk or scribe) departed with *skomorokhi* from Novgorod to Moscow, carrying bears on carts along with them."[157]

The Novgorod land registers [*pistsovye knigi*] indicate that in the 1580s the *skomorokhi* and their merry companions were not the only ones to disappear; these documents often mention "an empty abode, which had been the dwelling of a singer at St. Sophia's" or "owned by a singer."[158] The registers do not mention the reasons for the vacant dwellings, nor is anything said about the deaths of the occupants or their departures from Novgorod to "unknown destinations," as in other instances. It is reasonable to suppose that they were requisitioned, removed, or simply deported from Novgorod. Moreover, the same sort of thing can also be said about the best Novgorod bell ringers; the registers speak only of "the empty abode of the bell ringer at St. Sophia's, Mosorga Leont'ev, on Ostrovka at the Volkhova River," or "the vacant dwelling . . . of the St. Sophia bell ringer Trofimka, near Kamennyi Gorod on the way to the bridge," and so forth. The registers do not explain the disappearance of the most renowned bell ringers from the belfry of Novgorod's St. Sophia Cathedral.

Thus we see that, just as Novgorod had been dispossessed of her radically freedom-loving population, so she was also dispossessed of her *skomorokhi*, who were taken away to Moscow, and her bell ringers and singers, who were probably removed to Moscow as well. The renowned Novgorod masters Fyodor Kristianin and Ivan Nos appeared in Moscow and in the Aleksandrovskaia sloboda during the time of Ivan the Terrible. They were followed, voluntarily or not, by other singing masters, theorists, and singers—led by Ivan Shaidur—to Moscow, the powerful seat of government. And there is little to say about the plunder of bells and Moscow's requisition of musical manuscripts. So it was that the old songs of Novgorod were scattered to the hinterlands, to which, as we shall see, the "merry folk" finally fled as well. The Novgorod singing school, however, was transferred to Moscow, and lay the groundwork there for a new and autonomous school.

5. The Activities of the *Skomorokhi* in Russia

Based on our examination of sources documenting Kievan and Novgorodian musical culture, especially the *byliny* and the Novgorodian miniatures, we have seen that the *skomorokhi* were representatives of the musical profession from very early on.[159] One of the earliest appearances of the word *skomorokh* occurs in the Nestor Chronicle, under the year 1068: "By these and other similar customs the devil deceives us, and he alienated us from God by all manner of craft, through trumpets and *skomorokhi*, through *gusli* and *rusali*. For we behold the playgrounds stamped on by a great multitude, who jostle one another while they do shameful acts invented by the devil. The churches still stand" (empty).[160]

It is interesting to compare this to later references, which reinforce Nestor's comments from the eleventh century, in which the *skomorokhi* are listed along with trumpets and folk songs and games (*rusal'nye*) as accomplices of the devil, seducing and deflecting the Slavic residents from the Church. We have evidence from as early as the twelfth century that masks were one of the attributes of the *skomorokhi,* as recorded by Archbishop Luke [of Novgorod]: "It is unseemly, brothers, to wear masks [*moskoloudstvo*] or to say shameful words."[161] In the thirteenth century the Pereiaslavl-Suzdal chronicler mentions a special *skomorokh* costume, stating that the Latins wore a short coat and tight trousers, as our *skomorokhi* did; the chronicler says that they began to wear shirts rather than blouses, exposing themselves and wearing short jackets, with other shameless things like the *skomorokhi*.[162] This supports information from one of the Dobrynia *byliny* and from an illuminated initial or headpiece in a Novgorodian Gospel from 1358 [see chap. 4, fig. 32]. We know from Metropolitan Kirill's council decrees in 1274 that *skomorokhi* participated in public festivals and celebratory songs and games, saying that they "maintained the devilish customs of the thrice-cursed Greeks, staging on godly holidays shameful devilish acts with whistles and shouts, gathering in shameless drunkenness."[163]

In its censure of the *skomorokhi*, a Riazan nomocanon from 1284 reveals their repertory and the musical instruments they used.[164] [A nomocanon, or *kormchaia kniga,* is a collection of church canons; it also includes some civil law.] "In their performances in wagons or alone, or in their shameful song performances, or [the performances of the] *svirets* player, the *gusli* player, the *goudets* player, the dancer, or the tavern [performers] . . . [they should be] expelled [from the church]." This document thus lists performers on wind instruments (*svirets, svirelnik*), on stringed instruments (*goudets*), and on a bowed instrument (a *smychek* is a musician who uses a bow to play an instrument); the *gudok,* an old Slavic bowed instrument which later vanished from folk usage, almost surely belonged to this last category.

In addition to the Riazan nomocanon from 1284 and Metropolitan Kirill's somewhat earlier instructions from 1274, we read the following in a didactic article from an anthology of 1300: "and if you are at home when they are playing pagan games [*rousaliia*] and there are *skomorokhi* and there is drinking . . . or there are idolatrous games, then you should stay home."[165] Finally, in two documents from the fourteenth and fifteenth centuries we find listings of the repertory of the early Russian layman's "sinful entertainments." The volume known as the *Zlataia chep'* [The golden chain] from the Trinity–St. Sergius Lavra dates from before 1400, and, according to Buslaev, it is an original Russian compilation and not a translation from Greek, where there are other works entitled *The Golden Chain*.[166] This document includes a long list of "evil deeds" that true Christians should avoid: "These things are evil and nasty: . . . the wearing of blasphemous amulets, devilish song, dancing, *bubny, sopeli, gusli, piskove* [pipes], disorderly games, and pagan games ["igran'ia negodnyia, rusal'ia"]." The chronographer John Malalas warns against "creating *skomorokh* and puppet performances and all kinds of equestrian and gymnastic performances."[167]

Early Russian written sources from the eleventh century thus use the term *skomorokh* to mean an entertainer, a professional musician, and a participant in folk dances and traditional singing (*rusaliia*); we even have descriptions of the *skomorokh* dress, which was apparently similar to that of his Western confreres, and of wearing masks and the full scope of his activities. Finally, we have the precious reference in the fifteenth-century Malalas chronograph to "*skomorokh* and puppet" games, informing us of a new element in the varied *skomorokh* activities of the time, the puppet theater, which ultimately became the popular *petrushka*.[168]

The earliest documents and surviving *byliny* show us that *skomorokhi* generally appeared with the *gusli*. Other instruments and activities appear later on, gradually becoming part of their professional activities: playing the *bubny, sopeli,* trumpets, and the *gudok,* dancing solo, and then together with costumed entertainers or live bears, and finally the puppet theater. Later documents from the sixteenth and seventeenth centuries tell us that the long-standing professional *skomorokh* activities gave way, on the one hand, to the theater proper (with its comic and burlesque interludes), and, on the other, to the puppet theater with a more serious repertory and to the *petrushka* (although in the long run it returned to a trivial program, substituting the Italian barrel-organ for the old folk musical instruments).

First and foremost, however, the early Russian *skomorokhi* were the professional representatives of folk song and composition, and it is in that sense that we must understand Dobrynia's buffoonery and Vasilii Buslaev's and Sadko's *gusli* playing and adventures. Their participation in the people's domestic and religious life shows that the *skomorokhi* were descendants of those who took part in much older pagan rites, forgotten and never written down. The *skomorokhi* participate in memorial services and weddings,[169] in Whitsunday games (*rusaliia*), and at *Kupalo* [St. John's Eve] and other folk festivals. References to these activities appear not only in the documents we have cited but in many fragments from folk songs compiled by various scholars such as Beliaev, Famintsyn, and others. A sixteenth-century document, the *Stoglav* of 1551, records a custom popular at that time, one that had lasted for six centuries. [*Stoglav,* or *One Hundred Chapters,* refers to the statutes of the Church Council held in 1551 in Moscow.] It says that "on Trinity Saturday [*Troitskaia subbota*] men and women of the villages gather at the cemeteries and wail at the grave with loud cries, but when the *skomorokhi* and musicians ["gudnitsy i pregudnitsy"] begin to play, they cease weeping and start to dance, clapping their hands and singing Satanic songs." The council decreed that the priests should forbid and prohibit "the *skomorokhi* and *gusli* players and all such mockery" and devilish games during the commemoration of the dead.[169A]

Even one hundred years later, in the seventeenth century, by order of the tsar, a memorandum was sent to Siberia (and probably to other places as well), stating that,

> in Siberia, in Tobol'sk, and in other Siberian towns and districts, laypeople of all ranks and their wives and children do not go to churches on Sundays and other feasts of the Lord when holy chants are sung, but instead there is an increase of drunkenness and all kinds of disorderly devilish acts, of mockery and *skomoro-shestvo* with all kinds of devilish games . . .; that in the cities and districts . . .

people assemble . . . in the early morning and at night to practice witchcraft . . . and lead bears and dance with dogs . . .; that they indulge in licentious capering and dancing and sing diabolical songs . . .; that even at weddings there are disgraceful people and blasphemies and *skomorokhi* with all kinds of Satanic dances. [It is ordered that] all people should avoid excessive drinking . . . and should not invite the *skomorokhi* with their *domry, gusli,* bagpipes, and all kinds of games. [And even more decisively] when *domry, surny, gudki, gusli,* and masks and when all such honking instruments turn up, they should be taken out and broken and these diabolical playthings should be burned; those people who refuse to desist from all impious practices should be beaten with rods.[170]

I. Beliaev gives an interesting analogy to earlier *skomorokh* practice at funeral rites, supporting the idea that these activities must be understood as survivals of earlier, forgotten pagan practices. Beliaev says that in this situation,

the *skomorokhi* dared to appear at memorial services based on the ancient memory of some sort of generally accepted funeral rite, with dances and games. There is no doubt that, on the basis of this tradition, the public accepted them at grave sites and did not consider it improper to enjoy their dances and games. In fact, Cosma of Prague tells us that, in 1092, the Slavs, specifically the Czechs, offered sacrifices to the gods in groves, over springs of water, and in forests, particularly in places where they usually buried their dead. This took place on the third and fourth Sundays after Easter. After funerals they went to the crossroads and engaged in curious games in order to appease the spirits of the departed: they sang lamentations and ran about wearing masks. These funeral rites (more solemn in the eleventh century when paganism had a more immediate and serious significance for the populace) were performed in the sixteenth century, but their old meaning had been lost and the participation of *skomorokhi* simply made them comical.[171]

There is also no doubt that the ceaseless preaching of the high-ranking church hierarchy, together with police measures taken on behalf of the secular administration, led to a gradual decline in appreciating the *skomorokhi* as participants in ceremonies contrary to church practice, and led ultimately to their waning and their final extinction. The people recalled the original *skomorokhi* only in sayings, for example, in the nineteenth-century expression: "Everyone dances, but not like a *skomorokh*!"[172] The *skomorokh* of that saying is far removed from the *bylina* character Sadko, the Novgorodian *gusli* player and *skomorokh*.

Fifteenth- and sixteenth-century documents supply interesting and quite detailed information concerning the distribution and settlement of *skomorokhi* in the former province of Novgorod and in Muscovite Russia. This material appears in old land registers or cadastres [*pistsovye knigi*] and census books [*perepisnye knigi*] and unfortunately, with few exceptions, it has not yet been collected or studied.[173] In later documents *skomorokhi* and people associated with them are mentioned more and more rarely and by chance, their names often occurring only in edicts issued against them. They disappear completely in the second half of the seventeenth century.

The following study illustrates the distribution of *skomorokhi* in the sixteenth and seventeenth centuries, so that we may evaluate their activities in Novgorod and in Muscovite Russia.[174] In that period Novgorod and Moscow were, so to speak, the two centers of *skomorokh* life, but whereas Novgorod was shrinking, Muscovite Russia was expanding.

The Novgorodian land registers for the end of the fifteenth and first half of the sixteenth centuries testify to the state of *skomorokh* activities in that province.

According to land registers for the 1580s, there were relatively few *skomorokhi* in Novgorod itself. Some of them had died during the "pestilences" of the 1560s, and others were impoverished or vanished after Ivan the Terrible's devastation of the city in 1570. Thus, on Rostkina Street, one finds the "deserted taxable site of Mikhalko the furrier and Vorobei Skomorokh; Mikhalko died in 1571 and Vorobei goes [begging] from house to house," or "Tret'iatko Skomorokh and Grisha, impoverished and departed in 1572." Some were handed over to the state, for example, on Variazhskaia Street the "deserted taxable house of Lobanovskii the Jester [*veselyi*]; and Lobanko was taken into the tsar's jesters in 1569." According to these land registers, the few *skomorokhi* who remained, along with jesters, bear tamers, and those who played stringed instruments, lived out their lives primarily in the Zagorodnyi or Goroncharskii Ends [neighborhoods] of Novgorod, and specifically in Rostkinaia and Ianevaia Streets, in the Legoshchinskii Field, and in the back alleys of Dobryna and Variazhskaia Streets.[175] Other documents contain data about the resettlement of *skomorokhi* in most of the *piatiny* [the five districts that comprised the territory of old Novgorod].

In twelve parishes of the Derevskaia *piatina* there were no fewer than six villages named Skomorokhov or Skomorokhovo, and at least thirteen villages in which settled individual *skomorokhi* lived.[176] In the Deman'skii *prisud* [judicial district], in the little town of Demon and in two other parishes, there were two hamlets named Skomorokhov and three others in which individual *skomorokhi* lived.[177] In two *pogosty* (Naliuchsk and Ustiansk) of the Kursk *prisud*, there was a hamlet called Roga in which a *skomorokh* lived and a hamlet called Skomorokhovo. [A *pogost* is a small settlement as well as a rural district built around such a settlement.][178] *Skomorokhi* lived in two *desiatki* (Zhabenskii and Brodskii) of the Morevskaia *volost'* [a small rural district].[179] Vasko Skomorokh's house was located in the *volost'* of Buets, in the hamlet "na Kamenom" [on the stone].[180]

The home of Levonik Skomorokh was in the Kholmsk *pogost*.[181] Vaulka Skomorokh and his brother, Logonik, lived in the Dmitrevsko–Gorodenskii *pogost*.[182] In the Votskaia *piatina*, in the town and *uezd* [district or county] of Kopor'e, were the houses of Mikitka Skomorokh, Bobrok Skomorokh, and Iurka Skomorokh.[183] Marko Palkin Skomorokh lived in the town of Oreshka.[183A]

Ostash Skomorokh and Pribytka Skomorokh had houses in the *pogost* of Egorevskii Radshinsk.[184] In the Kuivoshskii *pogost* there was a hamlet called Riamuevo-Skomorokhovo, where the house of Selivanko Borisov was located; Selivanko "sowed four baskets of rye and harvested thirty haystacks and his income was half a barrel [about fifty gallons] of beer and a third part of bread."[185]

In the Shelonskaia *piatina* in the Ruchaiskii (or Rucheevskii) and Voskresenskii *pogosty*, there were hamlets and clearings named Skomorokhovo; individual *skomorokhi* had houses in a hamlet in the Kotorskii *pogost* and in three hamlets in the Pazherovitskii *pogosty*. In Vyshgorod there was a village called Skomorokhovo.[186] In the Bezhetskaia *piatina* there was a Skomorokhov *pogost*, and in the quarter of Mirogozhska Dubrova, the hamlet Skomoroshikha.[187]

This information is from land registers for the years 1495, 1498, 1500, 1539, 1545, 1552–53, and 1576. These documents list many representatives of the profession simply as *skomorokhi*, but from the mid-sixteenth century on we find some new aspects of the profession, especially in cities. For example, lists from four towns in Karelia in 1500 include nineteen *skomorokhi* (seven in Ladoga, six in Korela, five in Iama, and one in Kopor'ia). At the end of the sixteenth century, however, the Novgorod census registers list other representatives of the profession, such as *gusli* and *domra* players and singers who lived in various towns.[188] The statistical evidence from the Novgorod census books thus supports the evidence cited earlier from the Novgorod II Chronicle, which stated that, in 1571, the merry men [*veselye liudi*] were assembled "from all towns and districts" and sent to Moscow on many carts. These *skomorokhi* were, undoubtedly, more or less free representatives of their profession, that is freemen who lived settled lives in towns or hamlets, where they tilled the land with other peasants and were obliged to pay taxes (or else the records note specifically that "they do not plough" or "he does not plough"). For example, Vasko Skomorokh and Thatianko Zinovov lived in the Semenovskii *pogost* of the Derevskaia *piatina*, in the hamlet of Stavtsovo, where "they sowed three baskets of rye and harvested twenty haystacks."

The *skomorokhi* of the Muscovite state may be divided into two groups: the free, taxable members of the profession, and the domestic *skomorokhi* associated with powerful boyars and landowners. The latter included not only the *skomorokhi* associated with Princes I. I. Shuiskii and D. M. Pozharskii in the town of Shuia (in 1633 they presented a petition to Tsar Mikhail Fyodorovich) but also those listed as living on the estates of powerful landowners (in service to the Arsen'evs and to Prince Andrei Golitsyn in Tula, for example). There might be a separate, third group: those who kept shops in large trading centers, probably selling folk instruments. In Serpukhov, for instance, the *domra* player Fedka Vasilev had a shop, and another *skomorokh*, Plokhoi Trufanov, had part of a shop.

We now turn to the statistical data about *skomorokh* activities in towns of the Muscovite state. According to the *sotnia* book of 1552 [a *sotnia*, literally a group of one hundred, was a military or territorial unit], five *skomorokhi* lived in the town of Serpukhov: Borisko and Mitka Ivanov, who lived with the *skomorokhi* Ivashka Mikhalev and Fedka Ivanov, and Plokhoi Trufanov; two *gusli* players (Stepanko Vasilev and Vasko Sergeev); and the *domra* player Fedka Vasilev.

The 1540–41 census book of the town of Toropets lists one *gusli* player and six *skomorokhi*.[189] The *sotnia* book for the town of Ustiuzhna for 1597 lists one *skomorokh* among the tradesmen. In the chronicles there is a reference under the year 1490 to a *skomorokh* bathhouse [*skomorosh'ia movnitsa*] in Ustiug.[190]

The land register for Kolomna for 1577 mentions nine *skomorokhi* and one horn player [*rozhechnik*]. The Mozhaisk land register for 1595–99 lists two *dudka* players and one fiddler [*strunnik*].[190A] In the *pripravochnye* books from Tula for 1588, three *skomorokhi*, one *gudok* player, and one person who played a stringed instrument are mentioned. [A *pripravochnaia kniga* is another listing of populated areas and lands for tax purposes.][190B]

Kazan's sixteenth-century land register includes among the town's tradesmen a fiddler [*smychnik*], two *domra* players, four horn players, and a singer. The Sviiazhsk land register mentions two *gusli* players, and the land registers for Tver and its districts and old counties contain fairly detailed information concerning the *skomorokhi* settled in this area (the former principality of Tver) and their social status, as listed below.

In the city district, the land registers of the village of Shcherbinin mention the little settlement of Skomoroshino: "in it are thirteen houses; three are inhabited by *skomorokhi* (in one of the houses there is a widow, in another a bear trainer); they all plough the land." In the Kushalinskaia district, "in the Dorogobuzhskii patrimony of the Great Prince," there was a hamlet of two houses called Skomorokhovo.

Apparently the profession was represented in the greatest numbers in the Mikulinskaia quarter and *volost'* of the Tver *uezd* (the former possessions of the Princes Mikulinskii, which later came into the hands of the ruling [princely] court). For Prince Mikulinskii there remained, among others, the hamlet of Skomorokhovo (one house, two people); for A. Spiachev, the little village of Chiudovo with six peasants' houses, one of them occupied by Palka, a *skomorokh* who had no arable land; and in the same quarter there were two other hamlets named Skomorokhovo. A *smychnik* who had no arable land lived in the village of Gorodishche on the river Shosha (Mikulinskii *uezd*); in a *pogost* on the river Zhidovina there was a hamlet called Skomorokhovo, where a small craftsman lived without arable land (he probably made the musical instruments associated with his profession). There was also a plot of uncultivated land called Selishche Skomorokhovo.

In the Shesk *uezd* of the former principality of Tver, near the Monastery of St. Savva, was the hamlet of Gusel'nikovo and the *pogost* of Domernikov (deserted). [The names of these places refer to the *gusli* and the *domra*.] In the Shezsk *stan* [a rural administrative unit] on the Volga, in the village of Sukharino among the non-landowning houses, there was a house belonging to *domerniki* [*domra* players]. In the county of Uzkaia-Ugol, where the land belonged to children of "Tver boyars," there were two hamlets called Skomorokhovo.

In the Polotsk *povet* [district or township] in the Nevederskaia district there was a Skomorokhov parish; earlier it had been a plot of land called Skomorokhov with one house. In this same county, on the small Sviblitsa River, there was a plot of land called Skomorokhov-Vekshin. In the Viazemskii *uezd*, in the *stan* of Seraia Storona, were the hamlets of Dudkovo and Skomorokhovo (two houses) and another plot of land "that used to be the hamlet of Skomoroshkovo."[191]

According to the land registers from Tula for 1587–89, in the city itself "on Bol'shaia Street, to the left of the alley next to the Church of the Archangel, the house of Prince Andrei Golitsyn, and in it the *dvornik* [caretaker], a *skomorokh*; . . . the house of the widow Ovdot'ia Grigor'eva Karpov and her son Bogdan and in it, a *dvornik*, a *skomorokh*; . . . at the Water Gate, to the left, the house of the widow Maria Arsen'eva, wife of Fyodor . . . and in it, the *dvornik*, a *skomorokh*; . . . Farther, by the Odoevskii Gate at the Church of the Transfiguration of the Savior on the Rzhevets . . . and in the confines of the church, the house of the priest, another house of the *proskurnitsa* [the woman who baked the communion bread], a few cells, in one a merchant selling butter, a cell with a *gudok* player, one with a fiddler [*strunnik*], and seven cells in which the poor live." Apparently, then, two representatives of the *skomorokh* profession lived next to the church in cells that were rented out.

In the Kolodenskii *stan* of the Tula *uezd* in the Ivanovskii estate belonging to Bibikov, there was a plot of land called Menshkoe Skomoroshino on the river Moshina (six houses).[192]

In seventeenth-century land registers from Nizhnii Novgorod, for 1621–29, one finds the following: "Streletskaia suburb, the hut of Ondriushka *skomorokh*, on church land, a poor man; the hut of Ondriushka the Jester [*Veselyi*] on church land; the hut of jester Seryozhka Deviatyi on church land, a poor man . . . At Piatnitsa at the monastery, on monastery land, the hut of jester Smirka Ivanov . . . On the bank of the Volga the hut of the *strelets* [musketeer] Zakharko Skomorokh, not taxable." The same land registers mention near the Annunciation Monastery "on the Petushkov" a "soap maker Ivan the *domra* player, four fathoms [?], rent one ruble"; on Bol'shaia Street, by the Monastery of the Conception, the "small house of Avtamonka the Jester, son of Boris Treska," and, finally, near Il'inska Street there was a Domracheev Alley, undoubtedly named after the many *domra* players who lived there.[193]

Documents from the years 1617, 1655, 1658, and 1668 mention *skomorokh* breweries in the Kholmogorsk diocese;[194] a Skomorokh plot of land in the Novotorzhskii *uezd*; and a Skomorokh field and hamlet in the Starorusskii *uezd*.[195] In the Iaroslav *guberniia* [another administrative land unit] and district there is a village which to this day has preserved its old name, Skomorokhovo.[196]

The old folk saying, "the *skomorokh* from Presnia was strumming his songs," apparently refers to the settlement, or pale, in which the Muscovite *skomorokhi* lived, as well as the way they interpreted their repertory of songs.[196A]

New features of *skomorokh* life in old Russia emerge from these occasional, fragmentary, and, of course, incomplete data, including their widespread settlements and the decline of their profession. The settled *skomorokhi* had their own shops (in Serpukhov); one was a soap maker and paid quitrent (Nizhnii Novgorod), and one even manufactured salt (Kholmogory). There were *skomorokhi* who paid taxes and others who were labeled as poor (and probably paid no taxes), and there were domestic *skomorokhi* associated with prominent boyars. The earlier *skomorokhi* were not only called merry men or jesters [*vese-lye*], for example, in Nizhnii Novgorod, but began to be subdivided by their specializations: bear tamers who had dancing bears (in Tver; as we know, Ivan the Terrible requisitioned bear tamers from Novgorod); *gusli, domra,* and *gudok* players; *smychniki* [referring to bowed instruments]; those who played stringed instruments [*strunniki*]; singers; horn players; and so forth. Apparently *domra* or *gudok* players were considered *strunniki*; *smychniki* played the *gudok,* a bowed instrument. In the categories listed above, one does not yet find the "theatrical section" of the *skomorokh* profession, that is, the puppet theater or *petrushka,* mentioned in written documents from the fifteenth century. A seventeenth-century illustration of a puppet performance is preserved in Adam Olearius's well-known *Travels.*

The illustrations in Olearius's work are of great historical value, in spite of their sketchiness and lack of precision, understandable when making a quick drawing, especially when undertaken by a foreigner for whom the nature and appearances of Russian life were indeed strange.[197] The book nevertheless preserved many facts and scenes from old Russian life, and two of the drawings illustrate nearly the complete repertory of contemporary *skomorokh* activities, and are accompanied by a written description of what Olearius had observed. There is nothing of the sort in Russian documents of that time. The first of these pictures (fig. 41) was sketched in Ladoga, where, according to the land registers from 1500, seven *skomorokhi* were registered. The drawing shows an entertainment for the Holstein envoys of Olearius's party by local *skomorokhi.* Two are dancing, and two are playing musical instruments. In describing his visit to Ladoga, Olearius writes:

> Here we first heard Russian music. At midday of the 23rd [of July, 1634], while we were at table, two Russians with a lute and a fiddle came to entertain the ambassadors. They played and sang about the Great Lord and Tsar, Mikhail Feodorovich. Observing that we liked their performance, they added some amusing dances and demonstrated various styles of dancing practiced by both women and men. Unlike the Germans, the Russians do not join hands while dancing, but each one dances by himself. Their dances consist chiefly of movements of the hands, feet, shoulders, and hips. The dancers, particularly the women, hold varicolored, embroidered handkerchiefs, which they wave about while dancing although they themselves remain in place almost all the time.[198]

The Ladoga *skomorokhi* thus praised the tsar to the accompaniment of instruments. One of them played the bowed *gudok,* which Olearius called a violin. The other instrument, which he called a lute (*Laute*) is difficult to identify owing to the vagueness of the drawing in his book. Russians were not familiar with the lute, a multi-stringed instrument popular

FIG. 41. *Skomorokhi* in Ladoga, from Olearius, *Travels* (seventeenth century).

in the West at that time. Famintsyn assumed it was a *domra*, but the instrument's large body does not support this assumption. It was possibly a special form of the oval *gusli* used by local *skomorokh* performers. Olearius's drawing of the dance unquestionably represents an attempt to present a Russian women's dance, but his general observations apply to other dance forms, the *trepak* for instance.[198A]

The second drawing from Olearius's *Travels*, appended to the chapter describing Russian manners and customs, depicts a *skomorokh* show (fig. 42). In the center foreground is a *petrushka*, which, according to D. A. Rovinskii, shows how Petrushka bought horses from gypsies (a gypsy is thrust out to the right, in the center the long-nosed Petrushka is lifting the horse's tail, and on the left is probably Petrushka's bride).[199] Two *skomorokhi* appear to the right of this illustration, one with a *gudok* and the other playing a large *gusli*; in the background, on the left, is a *skomorokh* with a dancing bear. Olearius, in a detailed description of how Russians indulge in carnal pleasure and licentiousness, states:

> Tavern musicians often sing of such loathsome things, too [here Olearius is discussing "lusts of the flesh and fornication"], in the open streets, while some show them to young people in puppet shows. Their dancing-bear impresarios have comedians with them, who, among other things, arrange farces employing puppets. These comedians tie a blanket around their bodies and spread it above their heads, thus creating a portable theater or stage with which they can run about the streets, and on top of which they can give puppet shows.[200]

FIG. 42. *Skomorokh* performances (puppet theater, dancing bear, playing the *gusli* and the *gudok*), from Olearius, *Travels* (seventeenth century).

The *skomorokhi* ("tavern musicians") appear again in Olearius as singing folk songs (indecent ones this time) and staging shows with bears or puppets. The primitive stage made with a blanket later gave way to screens on which puppet shows were presented in the streets. In his description Olearius speaks of the "shameless dances" of the Russian *skomorokhi* with which they entertained the Danish ambassador Jakob.[201]

Documents from the fifteenth to the seventeenth centuries record other characteristics of *skomorokh* life. In the charter issued by the Dmitrov Prince Iurii Vasil'evich to the Trinity–St. Sergius Monastery on 14 January 1470, it was ordained that in the pagan [*inobozhskie*] villages of the monastery, "*skomorokhi* cannot play even in those villages. And if someone acts contrary to my charter . . . they will be punished by me."[202]

Grand Prince Vasilii Ivanovich's charter [*ustavnaia gramota*] of 9 April 1506, issued to the Marinina third part of the Artemonov *stan*, states, among other things: "*Skomorokhi* are not allowed to perform in the district."[203]

The charter of the Dmitrov Prince Iurii Ivanovich of 29 July 1509 to the trappers and the head of the Kamenskii *stan* stated that *skomorokhi* were not allowed to force themselves upon the public, they could play only if invited, and if they tried to force their show, they were to be expelled without a fine.[204]

Similar statements appear in Grand Prince Vasilii Ivanovich's charter to the Kas'iano-Uchemskii Monastery, dated 1 July 1522, on freeing the monastery and the villages in the Uglitskii district from taxes: "beggars if they are traveling through these villages are not to beg and *skomorokhi* are not to play; and if beggars, traveling through, are begging and *skomorokhi* are playing, then I order you to take [them] and give surety and to bring them before you, [that is] before [the authority of] the Grand Prince."²⁰⁵ Grand Prince Ivan Vasil'evich's charter to Onega (4 June 1536) included the following forbidden items: "And the judicial head and other appointed officials are not to attend a feast or celebration uninvited . . . and the *skomorokhi* there (in Onega) are not to force their performance in the *volost'*; and if some among them do force their performance in the *volost'*, the elders and the authorities of the *volost'* are to expel them from the *volost'*, and they will not be fined."²⁰⁶

The same proscription appears in another charter by the same Muscovite prince, dated 20 April 1544, to the Andreevskii villagers in the Zvenigorod district: "And the *skomorokhi* there in that settlement and in villages cannot force their performances . . . and if in my settlement and in the villages in this settlement the *skomorokhi* do force their performance . . . I shall order the *poselskii* of that settlement to give surety and stand before my court official in Dmitrov, whomever I have appointed to Dmitrov."²⁰⁷ "And the *skomorokhi* among you should not force their performances," reads another charter of 1 January 1548, from Prince Vladimir Andreevich of Staritsa to the Trinity–St. Sergius Monastery.²⁰⁸ In his charter of 28 February 1554 to the peasants of the villages of Afanas'evskii and Vasil'evskii in the Moscow district, Ivan the Terrible wrote: "and the *skomorokhi* among you in these villages and towns should not be allowed to play."²⁰⁹

All these charters are of interest as documenting the spread of *skomorokhi* in the Muscovite state in the sixteenth century. They forbid *skomorokhi* from forcing their performances on the populace but apparently permit them to perform when invited. Infringements of this regulation were either left unpunished ("and there should be no fine") or involved banishment from the district, or offenders might be arrested and brought before the grand prince, apparently for more severe treatment. In this, the *skomorokhi* are equated with beggars.

Ecclesiastical authorities adopted a much more rigorous attitude toward the *skomorokhi*, whom they classified with robbers, thieves, and sorcerers, as can be seen from a judgment of the Trinity–St. Sergius monastic council of 31 October 1555, which excludes harmful people from receiving refuge in the Prisetsk district: "Do not allow [the peasants] in the district to take in *skomorokhi* or sorcerers or fortune tellers or thieves or robbers; and if anyone takes in or if the head in his district has a *skomorokh* . . . there should be a fine of 10 rubles, and the *skomorokh* or the sorcerer or the fortune teller, having been beaten and stripped of his possessions, is to be expelled from the district by force; and wandering *skomorokhi* should not be allowed into the district."²⁰⁹ᴬ

This attitude is confirmed by another document, from the first half of the seventeenth century, which comes from the *skomorokhi* themselves and is thus a unique source. It is a petition from 1633 by the domestic *skomorokhi* associated with Princes Shuiskii and Pozharskii, as follows:

> To the Lord Tsar and Great Prince Mikhail Feodorovich, Tsar of all Russia, we, the *skomorokhi* of Prince Shuiskii, petition: Pavlushka Zarubin son of Kondrat'e, Vtoryshka Mikhailov, Konashka Domentiev and [the *skomorokhi*] of Prince Dmitrii Mikhailovich Pozharskii: Fed'ka Chechotka, son of Stepan of your lordship's village of Dunilovo; we were ordered to Ondrei Kriukov, Mikhailov's son, and his people. In this year, Lord, of 1633, on 25 May, we, Lord, arrived at your Lordship's village of Dunilovo on our business and on our way Ondrei appeared, and this Ondrei summoned us to his home and shut us up in a bathhouse and, from us, orphans, took seven rubles from Pavlushka and twenty-five rubles from Fed'ka and five from Artiushkin. Merciful Lord, Tsar, and Great Prince of all Russia

Mikhail Feodorovich, please accept your orphans' petition. Lord Tsar, please be merciful.[210]

This petition recounts not only the detention, beating, and robbery of *skomorokhi* but also reveals that they were men of some means: Pavlushka Zarubin had seven rubles stolen from him, and Fed'ka Chechotka a full twenty-five rubles, by no means small sums at the time. ("Artiushkin's" five rubles apparently belonged to an unnamed member of their company of *skomorokhi*, one Artemon, who did not go with them to Dunilovo.) Probably this was a small troupe of singers.

Many such troupes could be found in old Russia. The former type of *skomorokh*—a singer and *gusli* player—had dwindled away. In the time of Ivan the Terrible, the *skomorokhi* had become comic actors and their numbers grew enormously in the Muscovite state. The Novgorod *skomorokhi* had not been carted off to Moscow in vain. When Ivan IV, creator of the *oprichnina,* mocked the highest representatives of the Church, it was *skomorokh* buffoonery pure and simple. [The period of the *oprichnina* refers to the violent phase in Ivan IV's reign from 1565 to 1572 in which portions of the country were ruled as the tsar's personal territory.] Andrei Kurbskii was justified in accusing the tsar of collecting "*skomorokhi* who played the *dudka* and sang ungodly songs."[210A] Ivan's orgies in the Aleksandrovskaia sloboda were accompanied by *skomorokh* games and often by masked players. Their audacity, somewhat restrained during the reigns of Fyodor [Ivanovich, son of Ivan IV, r. 1584–98] and [Boris] Godunov [r. 1598–1605], came into full flower with the beginning of the Time of Troubles. Certainly companies of itinerant *skomorokhi* could be found among the wandering gangs of transients, robbers, and murderers going by the name of Cossacks.[211] The *skomorokhi* were at liberty during the Time of Troubles, but there was a new and distinct lowering of their moral standards, which led to their suppression and often their compulsory migration to remote parts of the state, where the surviving members of the profession lived out their remaining days.

Metropolitan Joseph, who lived at the time of the Stoglav Council [1551], was distressed at the increased numbers of *skomorokhi* even at court, and he implored Ivan the Terrible "in the name of God to get rid of them wherever they might be in your state." The tsar agreed with the clergy's requests but still continued with his own *skomorokh* activities. But once the minimum of order had been restored in the state [after the Time of Troubles], the authorities began to deal with the *skomorokhi* more seriously. In 1636 the Patriarch of Moscow wrote: "They do things contrary to and abuse the Lord's feasts . . . instead of a spiritual celebration they cultivate games and devilish blasphemies, bringing bear tamers and *skomorokhi* onto the streets and markets and at crossroads playing satanic games, beating *bubny,* and howling into *surny,* clapping their hands and dancing and doing other indecent things."[212] At the same time Tsar Mikhail Fyodorovich sternly forbade "indecent blasphemies, bear tamers, and *skomorokhi* on the streets and in the markets" under pain of "ecclesiastical punishment." And the son of the first Romanov, the "Most serene" Tsar Aleksei Mikhailovich [r. 1645–76], issued orders for the suppression of *skomorokhi* of every type (excluding, of course, those attached to the court). One recalls Aleksei Mikhailovich's 1649 decree to the governor of Verkhotur'e, in Siberia (cited above), with its references to "godless *skomorokhi* with their *domry* and *gusli*," which orders the *skomorokhi* to report to the governor for punishment, where they were fined and beaten, and says that "when *domry, surny, gudki, gusli,* and masks and when all such honking instruments turn up, they should be taken out and broken and these diabolical playthings should be burned." This order may be juxtaposed to the raid on musical instruments in Moscow reported by the

Holsteiner Adam Olearius, which also apparently took place in 1649. In light of these events it would seem that the relatively free (or, more accurately, the officially permitted) residence of *skomorokhi* in the state came to an end around 1649–50. After that time they were expelled and suppressed by decisive measures. Over the course of the next decades one encounters documents attesting to measures taken against the *skomorokhi,* that is, attesting to their existence; the appellation *skomorokh* itself, however, disappears from the registers. One of the last documents connected with the persecution and complete destruction of *skomorokh* practices is from Metropolitan Iona of Rostov in 1657, forbidding *skomorokhi* and bear tamers from plying their trade in the districts of Ustiug and Sol'vychegodsk. This is a fascinating document, drawn from the standpoint of everyday, ordinary life, and showing the decisive steps taken toward the eradication of the *skomorokhi.* I cite it here almost in its entirety, as it is unique among what must have been a series of such documents, no longer surviving:

> In the year 1657 on the 23rd day of October, with the blessing and at the order of the Great Lord and His Holiness Iona, Metropolitan of Rostov and Iaroslav, the clerk in the Metropolitan's office, Matvei Lobanov, [was ordered] to travel to the Ustiug district, in Dvina, and to all its *stani* and *volosti,* and to the Sol'vychegodsk *posad* [urban settlement] and to the Usol'sk district and to its *volosti* and *pogosty,* to priests and deacons for this reason: in this year of 1657 on 21 October, the order of Iona, Metropolitan of Rostov and Iaroslav to Archpriest Vladimir and all brethren in the Ustiug *posad* and district with the strict order that there shall no longer be *skomorokhi* or bear leaders allowed, that they shall no longer play on *gusli, domry, surny,* and bagpipes, or play devilish games and sing satanic songs, and no longer entice laypeople; and should such people appear and not obey this holy ordinance, and bear leaders start coming by and *skomorokhi* begin playing the *gusli* and the *domra* and the *surna* and the bagpipes, and playing devilish games and singing satanic songs, and they entice laypeople and laypeople start letting the *skomorokhi* and bear tamers and their bears into their homes and this becomes known to His Holiness, he shall punish these people and *skomorokhi* and bear leaders without any mercy by excommunicating them from the Lord's church; and send the ordinance to Ustiug and to Sol'vychegodsk and to all the villages and *pogosty* of Ustiug and Usol'sk to all the priests and deacons as written above about *skomorokhi* and bear tamers and the strict orders taken against them so that such people are no longer allowed; and this order is to be read in the Ustiug *posad* and in church by each priest and deacon and the crier shall announce it for many days in a row.[213]

The *skomorokhi* were thus decisively destroyed in Muscovy in connection with the government edicts of 1649–50. The orders, threatening harsh punishment and excommunication, were copied and distributed in churches located not only in the settlement but in all the remote *stany, volosti,* and *pogosty* of the area where, probably, *skomorokhi* had sought refuge after being persecuted in the central areas of the state.[214]

The subsequent fate and the multifaceted changes of the profession extend beyond the scope of this study. We are concerned here with another question: Have any traces of the musical side of the *skomorokh* heritage been preserved? And, if so, to what extent and where should one look for them? Until this subject has been more thoroughly studied, we can answer only hypothetically; here is only a beginning.

In examining the musical motifs of the Novgorodian *skomorokh* tales, we have seen that their tunes were short and resembled the later *chastushki* rather than the [longer] motifs characteristic of the heroic knightly *byliny* and ritual folk songs. They were in two-bar units or, less frequently, four-bar units, with a varied tune, sometimes slowing down, probably to coincide with the performer's miming gestures and movements. In addition to these songs, which were preserved in the memories of the narrator-singers of the *byliny,* one must seek out remnants of the *skomorokh* repertory in ancient folk songs, those often concerning everyday life and with no connection whatsoever to the *skomorokh* profession.

The musical examples in this chapter are from A. Grigor'ev's study of Arkhangel'sk *byliny,* and contain a series of songs that were undoubtedly part of the *skomorokh* repertory.[215] [Musical example 5.1 is from Pochezer'e, sung by a peasant there.] In musical example 5.2, I have taken the liberty of marking the rhythm as a mixed 3/8 and 2/8, as it actually sounds in the transmission of the tune, instead of the complex and not always correct meters of 8/8 and 7/8, as indicated in the Grigor'ev collection; these meters were probably suggested by I. S. Tezavrovskii, who transcribed the music from the phonograph record.

EXAMPLE 5.1. "Nebylitsa" [An invented tale] (from the peasant Katerina Pashkova in
Pochezer'e; Grigor'ev, *Arkhangel'skie byliny,* 672).

> Le da tsiudo le da netsiudole?
> Da na pets'nem stolbu da tut pevun sidit,
> Da tut pevun sidit da kukarekaet,
> Kukarekaet da starinu poet,
> Da starinu poet: "Da starika svezhu,
> Da starika svezhu so starukhoiu."

> What wonder of wonders?
> There on a stove chimney, there is a rooster,

The rooster sits and cock-a-doodle-doos,
Cock-a-doodle-doos and sings a tale,
Sings a tale of olden times; "Tie the old man up,
The old man with an old woman."

EXAMPLE 5.2. Another "Nebylitsa v litsiakh" [Invented tale] (from the peasant Maria Krivopolenova in Shotogorka; Grigor'ev, *Arkhangel'skie byliny*).

Nebylitsia v litsiakh, nebyval'shenka,
Nebyval'shenka da ne slykhal'shenka:
Ishsha syn na materi snopy vozil,
Kak snopy vozil da fse konopliany;
Kak stara mati da v koreniu byla;
Malada zhona da v pristiazhi byla.

A folk tale in verses, n'er'a'happening,
N'er'a'happening, never heard of;
A son went and carried sheaves for his mother,
Carried sheaves, all sheaves of hemp;
As the old mother stood among these roots,
A young woman was in traces.

EXAMPLE 5.3. "Vdova i tri docheri" [The widow and three daughters] (from the peasant Ekaterina Pashkova in Pochezer'e; Grigor'ev, *Arkhangel'skie byliny*, 673).

Tprundy tprundai, Zdunai, nai, nai!
Shcho u tetushki, shcho bylo u vdovushki,
Tut bylo tri docheri
Tprundy tprundai, Zdunai, nai, nai!
Dve to docheri, dve byli liubimye.
Tprundy tprundai, Zdunai, nai, nai!

Drum, drum, tiddly bom bom bom!
Auntie, the widow, had three daughters,
Drum, drum, tiddly bom bom bom!
Two daughters, two daughters were the favorites,
Drum, drum, tiddly bom bom bom!

In musical example 5.3 the rhythm is more complex, consisting of variations of the periods *a* + *b* (the second part of *b* is repeated, and marked *c*) + *a* + *b* + *a*. The *a* period is the introduction and refrain, and the *b* period is the actual song; they are quite similar melodically. The refrain "zdunai-nai" is common in Russian folk songs (an example of this in a *skomorokh* song is cited later), and the rhyming exclamation "Tprundy-tprun-dai" may be an imitation of the balalaika, the *domra,* or some other stringed instrument. According to the collector, the final two bars of musical example 5.4 slowed down. The tune is an unchanging two-bar phrase without any variations except as required by the text, for example in the last line, where it becomes slightly broadened out (4/4 instead of 3/4). [Musical examples 5.5 and 5.6 are both from Shotogorka.]

EXAMPLE 5.4. "Puteshestvie Vavily so skomorokhami" [Vavilo's journey with the *skomorokhi*] (from Maria Krivopolenova in Shotogorka; Grigor'ev, *Arkhangel'skie byliny*, 686).

U chesnoi vdovy da u Nenily
A u ei bylo tsiado Vavilo,
A poekhal Vavilushko na nivu,
On vet' nivushki svoei orati,
Ishsha belaiu pshanitsy zasevati.

The honorable widow Nenila
Had a child Vavilo,
Little Vavilo went into the field,
He wanted to plough,
Trying to sow seeds of white wheat.

EXAMPLE 5.5. "Kostriuk" (from Maria Krivopolenova in Shotogorka;
Grigor'ev, *Arkhangel'skie byliny,* 682)[216]

Vo Taulii vo gorode,
Da vo Taulii v khoroshome
Da poizvolil nash tsar (i) gosudar'
Da tsar' Ivan(y) Vasil'evich,
Poizvolil zhanitese,
Ne u nas(y), ne u nas na Rusi
Da ne u nas(y) v kamennoi Moskve,
U tsaria v(y) Bal(i)shoi orde . . .

"A . . . da ne detiam by, ne vnuchiatam,
Da ne vnuchiatam, ne pavnuchiatam."

In the city of Tauliia, the good city of Tauliia,
Our Tsar and Lord Ivan Vasil'evich deigned to marry;
Not from among us in Russia and not in Moscow, stone-walled Moscow,
But [he married from the family] of the Great Horde's Tsar . . .
(the last two lines are nonsense words listing generations: children,
grandchildren, and so forth)

EXAMPLE 5.6. "Usishcha grabiat bogatogo krest'ianina" [Usishcha (and his gang) rob the rich
peasant] (from Maria Krivopolenova in Shotogorka; Grigor'ev, *Arkhangel'skie byliny,* 687)[216A]

Ishche za rekoi rekoi, bylo chetyre dvora,
Da chetyre dvora da iz vorot(y) v vorota,
Ishsha zhil takoi krest'ianin:
On solodune rostil, za vsegda pivo varil;
On i denekh ne kuet, da den'gi vzaimy daet.

Nakormil da zhivotom nas nadelil.
"Ush my dvor(y) tvo(i) znaem, opiat' zaidem."

Oh beyond the river, beyond the river there were four households,
Four households from door to door;
And there lived a peasant, he grew malt
And was always brewing beer;
He doesn't mint coins, but gives money out on loan.

He filled our bellies, that peasant.
"We know where you live and we'll be back."

All these *skomorokh* songs were recorded either in Siberia or in the Far North, and I have found similar pieces in collections of Great Russian songs. No. 36 in N. Abramychev's *Collection of Russian Folk Songs* is a widely known *nebylitsa* like those from the Arkhangel'sk province.[216B] Musical example 5.7, an old ballad of Foma and Eryoma, is typical of the *skomorokh* type, and its heroes also appear in popular woodcuts and stories. The song was recorded in the town of Elabug. Abramychev's harmonization is preserved here in the piano accompaniment of simple, syncopated chords, such as might be played *pizzicato* on a stringed folk instrument.

EXAMPLE 5.7. "A Erema zhil na gorke" [Eryoma lived on a little hill] (from the town of Elebug; Abramychev, *Sbornik russkikh narodnykh pesen*)

A Erema zhil na gorke, a Foma to pod goroi,
A Erema nosil lapti, a Foma to sapogi.
Erema poshel v gorod, Foma-to na bazar.
Erema kupil loshad', Foma-to solovka.
Erema kupil sokhu, Foma-to boronu.
Erema zapriagat', Foma pesniu zatiagat',
Eremina ne tianet, Fomina-to ne vezet.
"Akh, ty, brat li moi Foma, neudacha nam byla.
Ne luchshe li, Foma, po dorogam nam stoiat'
Da obozy razbivat'?"

Erema sel na gorku, Foma-to za penek,
Za Eremushku zadeli, Fomu vytashchili.
"Okh, ty, brat li moi Foma, neudacha nam byla.
Akh, ne luchshe li, Foma, po ozeram nam khodit',
Belu rybitsu lovit'?
Erema da Foma, kupili lodku bezo dna.
Erema utonul, i Fomu potianul.
Erema sel na dno, i Foma s nim zaodno.
Eremu skhoronili, a Fomu-to pogrebli.

Eryoma lived on a little hill and Foma at the foot of the mountain;
Eryoma wore bast shoes and Foma wore boots;
Eryoma went to the city and Foma to the bazaar;
Eryoma bought a horse and Foma a nightingale;
Eryoma bought a plough and Foma a harrow;
Eryoma to put on a harness and Foma to draw out a song;
Eryoma doesn't haul and Foma doesn't pull [draw];
"Ah, my brother Foma, things are bad for us!
Wouldn't it be better, Foma, if we hung about the roads and smashed up carts?"
Eryoma sat on a hillock and Foma behind a stump;
Eryomushka was knocked down and Foma was pulled out:
"Ah, my brother Foma, things are bad for us!
Wouldn't it be better, Foma, to go to the lakes and fish for white fish?"
Eryoma and Foma bought a boat without a bottom;
Eryoma drowned and pulled Foma down;
Eryoma sat on the bottom and Foma did the same;
Eryoma was buried and Foma got a funeral.

Naturally the adventures of Foma and Eryomka did not require a more colorful tune, as the audiences for whom such songs were performed were unsophisticated. The tune itself is the two-bar phrase stated twice in the first period, and slightly varied and transposed a third lower, again stated twice, in the second. Both the motif and the text of the song may have been a later formulation, but the heroes' names came from an old folk woodcut and the character of the tune is undoubtedly from the *skomorokhi*.[216C]

A very interesting *khorovod* song is no. 31 in the *Forty Folk Songs* collected by T. I. Filippov and harmonized by N. A. Rimskii-Korsakov; it is shown here in musical example 5.8.[217]

What kind of popular *khorovod* song is this? All the elements of the *skomorokhi* are present in this song: the short, lively, four-bar refrain with the text "Ai, Dunai, moi Dunai" (reminiscent of the refrain in the song about the widow and her three daughters, from Arkhangel'sk province [see example 5.3]), and the whole content and jocular treatment of the subject, especially as narrated by the singer himself. People may simply have taken it over and used it in a *khorovod* because of its colorful motif and cheerful, merry refrain. But it is also possible that T. I. Filippov (who became a state official but never lost his love of folk songs), recalling the songs he had long before heard and memorized and had then performed throughout the 1840s in Moscow, might easily have forgotten some of the details of the original performances by the time he was singing them for Rimskii-Korsakov

EXAMPLE 5.8. "U vorot, vorot batiushkinykh" [By the gates, by my father's gates]
(from Filippov and Rimskii-Korsakov, *40 narodnykh pesen*, no. 31)

U vorot, vorot, vorot, vorot batiushkinykh.
Ai, Dunai, moi Dunai, veselyi Dunai.[218]
Vorot batiushkinykh, novykh matushkinykh,
Razygralisia rebiata, raspoteshilisia;
Odnomu li molodtsu khudo mozhetsia,
Khudo mozhetsia, nezdorovitsia,
Nezdorovitsia, guliat' khochetsia,
Ia ukradusia, naguliaiusia,
Ia sapozhki na nozhki, smur kaftanchik na plecho,
Smur kaftanchik na plecho, chernu shliapu na ukho,
Ia gudochik pod polu, pod pravuiu storonu
Ia udariu vo strunu, strunu serebrenuiu;
Vy poslushaite, rebiata, chto struna-to govorit.
Chto struna-to govorit, nam zhenit'sia velit,
Nam zhenit'sia velit, staru babu vziat';
Staru babu vziat', na pechi v uglu derzhat',
Kiselem ee kormit', molokom ee poit';
S kiselia-to vesela, s moloka-to moloda.

By the gates, by my father's gates;
Hey, Danube, my Danube, jolly Danube (refrain after each verse);
My father's gates, new ones of mother's;
There the children played, they amused themselves.
One of the fellows doesn't feel right, doesn't feel well, feels like walking;
I shall steal away, walk around,
Boots on feet, fur caftan on shoulder, black cap over an ear;
I'll play the *gudok* and on the right side
I shall strike the string, the silver string;
You listen, boys, to what the string says;
It says that I should get married;
Take an old woman, keep her atop the stove in the corner,
Feed her with custard and quench her thirst with milk;
She shall be merry when eating custard, and the milk shall make her young.

for the latter to transcribe. This seems all the more likely as the song collection does not indicate clearly where or under what circumstances each song was performed, an important consideration ignored by most of our earlier musical ethnographers. This song may certainly be regarded as an ancient folk song, perhaps one of the best in the repertory of the *skomorokhi*.

The song entitled "Bychok" [Fish (or bullhead)], transcribed by N. Pal'chikov in Ufa province, probably belongs to the later "balalaika period" and should be classified with the unexacting *skomorokh* fairy tales, similar to those found in collections from Arkhangel'sk and Viatka provinces, discussed above; "Bychok" is shown in musical example 5.9.[219]

EXAMPLE 5.9. "Bychok" [Fish (or bullhead)] (from Pal'chikov, *Krest'ianskie pesni*, no. 125)

Eshche gdezhe eto vidano
Eshche gdezhe eto slykhano.
Chtoby kurochka bychka rodila,
Porosenochek iaichko snes.
Chtoby v seredu to maslenitsa,
A v chetverg uzh razgovlen'itse.
Chtob bezrukii-to klet' obokral,
Golopuzomu za pazukhu naklal,
A slepoi-to podsmatrival,
A glukhoi-to podslushival,
Bez"iazykii karaul zakrichal,
A beznogii v pogon' pobezhal.

Whither has yet that been seen?
Whither has yet that been heard?
That a hen would give birth to a bull-head fish;
That a piglet would lay an egg;
That *Maslenitsa* would fall on Wednesday
And on Thursday break the fast;
That an armless man would steal a cage
And hide it in bare-belly's bosom;
The blind man would stare
As the deaf man eavesdrops;
The tongueless guard scream,
And the legless run in pursuit.

We may only be sure that the tunes of the *skomorokh* songs quoted above do not represent the actual song repertory of the sixteenth and seventeenth centuries but rather are reinterpretations and variants of melodies that have been passed down through successive generations—generations which lived through a series of momentous events and circumstances that led to major changes in their daily lives and, of course, to the loss or reinterpretation of their past musical heritage. But whatever the case, the similarity of their musical makeup is convincing. They are all short, fast, and with rhythmically simple tunes (a two- or three-bar phrase, very seldom a four-bar unit), repeated with slight variations and sometimes without any at all. This is quite understandable: the listener had to be given a simple, easily grasped motif (usually of a dance type) with a text (always of an anecdotal, even nonsensical sort) to seize his attention and make him laugh and allow him to continue to enjoy himself, encouraging him, holding his attention with gesticulations and mimicry that at times were probably quite unceremonious, unseemly, and even vulgar. The accompaniment for this type of *skomorokh* song was necessarily primitive—strummed chords on some sort of stringed instrument or an *ondulé* on a bowed *gudok,* creating a nasal-sounding drone or harmonic pedal.

In terms of their geographical distribution, the remnants of these *skomorokh* songs and tales, primarily from Novgorod, were preserved mainly in the repertory and memory of singers in remote parts of the country: the White Sea area (as recorded in the collections of Grigor'ev and Markov) and Siberia (in the Kirsha Danilov collection). We know the reasons for this. As a result of governmental repression, some of the *skomorokhi* undoubtedly fled to distant regions far from the center of government, where it was possible to sing and play *skomorokh* songs to their heart's content, without prohibitions, and to pass these songs along to future generations. At the same time, others among them, yielding to the influence and spirit of the times, "legitimized" themselves and probably intermingled with Peter the Great's "assembly of jokesters," that hard-drinking fraternity of *skomorokh*-like merrymakers. After all, one of Peter's Muscovite predecessors, a century and a half earlier, had engaged in similar buffooneries.

6. Music and Musical Instruments in Russian Miniatures, Woodcuts, and Glossaries

Part 1

We currently do not have a history of the development of Slavic folk instruments, nor do we know the complete range of musical instruments used by the people of Muscovite Russia and earlier. Although many works and written evidence concerning musical instruments have come to light, this evidence has often been erroneously taken as historical fact, which accounts for the variety and uncertainty frequently found in describing and documenting a specific instrument.

We have seen in previous chapters that many manuscripts and artistic works include references to, even illustrations of, all kinds of musical instruments. It is sufficient here to recapitulate only briefly sources such as the Khludov Psalter of the twelfth to the thirteenth centuries; the Novgorod psalters, gospels, and the service book of the fourteenth century; the icons of The Miraculous Apparition of the Virgin and The Vision of Sexton Tarasii of the fifteenth and sixteenth centuries; the Book of Cosmas Indicopleustes and the *Tsarstvennaia kniga* of the sixteenth century; and, finally, chronicles such as the Manasses chronicle of the fourteenth century, the Radziwill chronicle of the fifteenth century, and the sixteenth-century *Tale of Mamai's Bloody Battle.* All these sources contain illustrations and vignettes of music or musical instruments, as do many other chronicles, historical documents, and literary works. The considerable literature of the ancient *azbukovniki* [alphabetic glossaries] of the fifteenth to the seventeenth centuries belongs to this last category. These "interpretive dictionaries" have remained completely uninvestigated from the point of view of their music-historical content. Finally, there is the vast body of materials in woodcut illustrations, the *lubochnye kartiny.* [A *lubok* is a woodcut broadside which became popular in Russia in the late seventeenth century.]

One of the richest and most valuable of these historical documents is the Godunov Psalter of 1594, presented to the Ipat'ev Monastery in Kostroma by Tsar Boris. In 1897 copies of these illustrations were made for the Music History Museum of the former Court Orchestra in St. Petersburg [see n. 25]. We shall examine two miniatures from this late-sixteenth-century artistic document, keeping in mind that the originals are in color.

The first (fig. 43) depicts a heavenly gathering in the form of an ensemble of people playing the oval *gusli.* The second miniature (fig. 44) is a complex composition similar in its subject matter and composition to the miniatures in Cosmas Indicopleustes and the Makarii Mineia of the sixteenth century: King David composing the psalter [see chapter 4]. Beneath the throne is a large organ with twenty pipes and an organist sitting at the keyboard; on the other side of the instrument a person is working two sets of bellows.

This work is just as complex as the Novgorodian miniature in the Cosmas Indicopleustes manuscript in the Makarii Mineia, which we discussed earlier, in GIM, Sin. 997, fol. 1248v (and with variants in other manuscript copies; see figs. 45 and 46). Buslaev published a clearer and more careful reproduction of that miniature, depicting "David's choir" or, more correctly, the subject of "the creation of the Psalter," in the second volume of his *History of Folk Art* (325). In the center of the upper half of the miniature King David plays the Slavonic *gusli.* On either side are the choirs [*liki*] of Moses and Solomon, with scrolls in

FIG. 43. "The righteous rejoice in the Lord" (from the Godunov Psalter of 1594, fol. 128v). In the center on the throne is the Lord Sabaoth, beneath, the Prophets rejoice, and on the sides sit the righteous, all playing *gusli.*

their hands, and at the foot of the throne are musicians. Those on the left side are playing trumpets, and those on the right are beating small drums [or tambourines; *bubny*]. In the lower center portion of the miniature there are two organs, with their organists seated before them and servants pumping the bellows (with the inscription "and they sing to organs and *sopeli*"). Over the first organ, however, the word *tsymbaly* is written, and over the second the word *kimvaly*. Apparently the artist had no clear idea about the correct representation of these instruments. To the sides of the central figures are choirs of the biblical instrumental ensembles of the Jerusalem Temple, led by Kore, Asaf, Afam, Iil't, Idufiml, and so forth.[219A] Almost all of them play straight or small curved horns ("they sing to *sopeli*") or *bubny*.

It is worthwhile to compare this miniature to its variant in Cosmas Indicopleustes, as published by the Society of Friends of Old Literature (fig. 45). Although these illustrations share the same subject matter, inscriptions, and overall design, the details are simplified in figure 45 and the musical instruments are placed in the hands of some of the "choristers." At the sides of the steps to the throne, instead of groups of players there are only two: one playing the *rubeb* (the bow is missing in his right hand) and the other playing an instrument similar to the bagpipe with a rounded bladder or body. This instrument was called a *Platerspiel* in the thirteenth century; a fully developed model appears in the miniature of a manuscript in the library of the St. Blasien Monastery [see fig. 47].[220] "Kore's choir" [in the highest of the three boxes on the right side of figure 45] has one figure blowing a horn while another holds a small clapping board [*bil'tse*]. In "Asaf's choir" [middle group on the left] instead of horns there is a large drum [*buben*] and a bowed rubeb. The organs with their players and servants recall the preceding miniature, but one should note that the drawing of the pipes of the upper organ resemble the trumpets in the illustrations of the *Tale of Mamai's Bloody Battle*.

All the miniatures cited above from the Godunov Psalter and the two redactions of Cosmas Indicopleustes fully support my contention that the *gusli*, in all possible variants of the King David representations or in the hands of "singing choirs" of saints and prophets, were the only musical instruments the artists depicted from direct experience in Novgorod or Moscow. All other musical instruments, whether stringed rubebs and *crwths*, or the *Platerspiel*, organs, and even trumpets, were drawn using conventional foreign models, since neither the Novgorodian nor the Muscovite masters could have seen the original instruments. One might find instruments similar to those depicted in the Khludov Psalter miniatures in drawings and sculptures in works from the National Library in Paris and at Saint Martin-de-Boscherville [see chap. 3, figs. 24 and 25, above]; similarly, illustrations of the rubeb, the *crwth*, and the organ in similar sources were undoubtedly well known and used as models by Russian miniaturists of much later periods. One need only to compare the Russian representations of organs and organists to illustrations in manuscript no. 17403 in the Munich State Library or in the St. Elizabeth prayer book in the Cividale Museum to be convinced of their similarities to Russian miniatures (see figs. 48 and 49, both from the thirteenth century).[221]

Most of the illustrations of musical instruments in miniatures from literary and other early Russian artistic sources were thus based on Western models, since harps, psalteries, lutes, rubebs, *crwths*, and organs were not found in Russian musical practice. Even the wind instruments often designated in these sources as pipes or reed pipes [*svireli, sopeli*] have nothing in common with these instruments but are, in fact, Western trumpets, horns, and small horns [*truby, roga, rozhki*]. The only native Russian or Slavic instrument is the *gusli*,

FIG. 44. King David composes the Psalter (from the Godunov Psalter of 1594, fol. 590). In the center is David on his throne, playing the *gusli;* to the left and right are choruses, holding scrolls with passages from the Psalter; underneath are two groups of trumpeters. Below to the left they are playing *bubny* and to the right are musicians playing bowed instruments (similar to *crwths*), lutes, and *gusli.*

FIG. 45. A miniature from the *Koz'ma Indikoplov* text, from RGADA,
Obolenskii collection, no. 159 (sixteenth century).

Fig. 46. King David composes the Psalter. Novgorodian miniature from the sixteenth century (from the *Koz'ma Indikoplov* text in the Makarii Chet'ia Mineia; GIM, Sin. 997, fol. 1248v).

Fig. 47. A fragment from a miniature from the library of St. Blasien, thirteenth century, showing a performer on the *Platerspiel.*	Fig. 48. A miniature from the thirteenth century (Munich, Staatsbibliothek, no. 17403); on the right a servant works the bellows, on the left the organist's hands at the organ stops.	Fig. 49. A miniature from the thirteenth-century manuscript of the prayer book of St. Elizabeth (Cividale Museum). The organist holds the organ stops (or registers) in his hands.

unless we include the balalaika, which is mentioned casually in a much later document, no longer extant. We have not come across the *gudok, domra,* or *volynka,* or authentic folk instruments such as the *dudka, sopel',* or *svirel'.* That these instruments appeared in church literature at the same time as the clergy rejected and condemned them is an issue we consider at a later point.

Part 2

The old *azbukovniki,* a type of interpretive dictionary or glossary, include a great deal of interesting material for an investigation into Russian folk instruments and attitudes toward them as well as for a more general consideration of the art of music itself. These documents circulated widely in early times and provided the most complete explanations possible of terms and subjects that appeared in contemporary literary or religious manuscripts, although these definitions are sometimes quite unintelligible. For the most part, these terms were borrowed and translated from Greek, Eastern, or Western languages. Words incomprehensible to the translator were often simply transcribed into Cyrillic, and the reading [or spelling] of a given word was not always accurate. At any rate, these alphabets, often titled something like *Skazanie o neudob' poznavaemykh rechakh* [An explanation of difficult words], must be recognized as valuable and unique dictionaries containing early Russian musical terminology.[222] To convey as full a picture of these sources as possible, I have collated terms in parallel columns from four of these dictionaries from the sixteenth and seventeenth centuries [see Table 6.1]. The sources are the following:

1. Manuscript dated 1596, in the Pogodin Collection, no. 1642 of the Public Library [RNB] titled: *Kniga glagolemaia Alfavit inostrannykh rechei* [A book called an alphabet of foreign words];[222A]
2. An alphabet published by I. Sakharov in the second volume of his *Tales of the Russian People,* based on a manuscript from the end of the sixteenth century;[222B]
3. *Leksykon slovenoros'kyi* [Slavonic-Russian lexicon] compiled by Kir Pamva Berynda, published in 1627 in Kiev and republished by Sakharov in his book listed above;[222C]
4. Manuscript from the end of the seventeenth century in the Solovetskii collection of

the Public Library [RNB], no. 18, titled *Alfavit rechei inostrannykh* [Alphabet of foreign words].[222D]

Most of the definitions are self-evident, but a few require additional clarifications or may be expanded by means of other manuscript sources. Judging from some of the explanations, it appears that the compilers of these volumes, like the miniaturists, did not always understand the musical instruments they were describing. This is true especially of the explanations by the Kievan Pamva Berynda, although one might think he would have had more accurate information because of Kiev's contacts with the culturally advanced Poland; he apparently used Polish sources.

Some of the terms, although not necessarily having a direct relationship to musical instruments, may be useful in clarifying the terminology associated with old Russian musical notation or sources: *akafismato, alliluiia, voks', demestnik, kafisi, krikela, okhtaik, prosodiia* (explanations of this word contain many signs of the ekphonetic notation used in early times to designate solemn recitations), *pesn' stepennaia, stavros* (a Greek term which turned into a Slavicized Latin term), *kryzh* in *kriukovaia* notation, *Tipokar', Triod'*, and so forth. The following terms require additional explanation or clarification:

> *Arfaliutnia*—none of the documents interprets this term correctly. This is not the *gusli*, the violin, or the *skreben'ki* but probably rather the bass lute or archlute, widely used in Western Europe and Poland in the sixteenth and seventeenth centuries.
>
> *Bilo*—there is no definition of this term as *klepalo* [*semantron*]; it is described instead as a key for tuning and a plectrum.
>
> *Buskinarum, buskini*—a poorly transcribed but correct description of the ancient Roman *buccina*.
>
> *Volotsuga*—an accurate description of an itinerant *skomorokh*.[222E] To such ancient folk terminology relating to both singers and instruments, one should add definitions of words such as *veselo, zhart, pigoly, pipeli, piskanie, pishchal', rusaliia, sopets*, and so forth. [See Table 6.1 for definitions of these terms.]
>
> *Vrutka*—the definition as "any kind of trumpet" [or, more generally, pipe] was taken from an added Polish inscription.
>
> *Gafra* (instead of *garfa*)—the *Alphabet* in the Solovetskii collection, in addition to the definition as a musical instrument, also suggests the idea of angelic verse ["stikh angel'skii"].
>
> *Gimny* [hymns]—explained variously in the glossary in the Pogodin collection as "devilish songs," by Berynda as "verses of chanted texts," and under the word *pesn'* [song] as a "song in praise of God, which praises God" (p. 86). The Pogodin glossary generally takes a rather inimical attitude toward all Greek musico-theatrical productions: *karmoniia (recte: garmoniia* [harmony]) as "devilish songs"; *komediia* as "plays, in which the mindless Greeks staged feasts after death, dancing senselessly and playing and ribaldry in a debauched way"; *thimilicheskaia peniia* as songs "created at devilish Greek games." In the same manuscript, one encounters equally curious interpretations of the names of some of the Greek deities, not cited in the chart, for example:

> > *Artemida*—there was a woman among the Greeks having that name, a witch and a sorceress and an insatiable fornicator. The senseless Greeks had her as a goddess. (fol. 10v)

TABLE 6.1. A comparison of musical terms found in the *azbukovniki* (alphabetic glossaries)

Kniga glagolemaia Alfavit [RNB, Pogod. 1642; internal date 1596, date of manuscript, 17th century]	Azbukovnik publ. by Sakharov [GIM, Uvar. 310 (2088) and 311 (2094)]; 16th century	Leksykon slovenoros'kyi by Berynda (first published in 1627)	Alfavit rechei inostrannykh [RNB, Sol. 18], 17th century
Akarteri, a tone, to wait for it (fol. 8)			
Akafismato, not sitting in church [a stational hymn]	**Akafismatos**, not sitting		
Akafisto, not sitting (fol. 4v)	**Akafist**, not sitting (p. 142)		
Akomipsalum, I still sing (fol. 18v)			
Alliluiia, praise to God, in the Grammars it is explained that "all" is come, "il" is God, and "ouiia" is to sing out, to sing (fol. 11)			
Arthaliutnia, *gusli* or *skreben'ki* [a stringed instrument; see Findeizen's comments] (fol. 6v)			**Arfaliutnia**, *gusli* or violin (fol. 51)
			Bilo, a mallet with which strings are stretched, or a plectrum [*piorko*] with which one strums the strings (fol. 93v)
		Briatsalo, briazkal'tse, to strike something, such as a *klepalo*, a zither [*tsitra*], organ pipes [*fistula*], *tsimbaly*, or a harp [see Roizman, *Organ*, 42] (p. 21)	
Buski narum, a military trumpet; a *buskini* trumpet (fol. 26)	**Buskinarum**, trumpet; *buskine*, a military trumpet (p. 148)		
Veselo, a wedding; with merriment at a wedding (fol. 29)			
Vikanie, exclamation in church hymns (fol. 31)			
Volotsuga, a fool [jester] who wanders everywhere (fol. 32v)			
Voks', voice (fol. 33v)			
Voksom, with, by means of, the voice (fol. 34)			
Vrutka, any kind of trumpet (fol. 34)			
			Gafra, *gusli*, violin, angelic verse

Kniga glagolemaia Alfavit [RNB, Pogod. 1642; internal date 1596, date of manuscript, 17th century]	Azbukovnik publ. by Sakharov [GIM, Uvar. 310 (2088) and 311 (2094)]; 16th century	Leksykon slovenoros'kyi by Berynda (first published in 1627)	Alfavit rechei inostrannykh [RNB, Sol. 18], 17th century
Gimny, devilish songs (fol. 38)		**Gimny**, hymns, with verses of chanted texts (p. 31)	
Gudenie, playing the *gusli*, or the *domra*, or the *lyra*, or similar instruments (fol. 41)		**Gudenie**, playing, blowing [on an instrument], a player, harpist, or *tsitarist* [zither player] (p. 31)	**Gudenie**, that is, playing on the *gusli*, the *domra*, the *gudok*, or the *tsymbaly*
			Gudenie, piping, playing, or playing on the pipes (fol. 153v)
Gudets, a player on the *gusli* and *domra* (fol. 40v)			**Gudets'**, a player on the *gusli* and the *gudok* and the *domra*; that is, one who learns how to interpret a thought, transfiguration (fol. 153)
			Gudets, harpist, *tsytarist*
		Gusli, violin (p. 31)	
		Gusl', harp, *tsitra* (p. 31)	**Gusl'**, harp, *tsytra*
Demestnik, a singer of *stikhi* [verses] (fol. 42v)		**Demestik**, *protopsaltes*, a leader, director, or master of singing (p. 32)	**Demestik**, Latin; [Greek] *protopsaltes*, that is, first singer; in Greek, a leader, director, or master of singing, that is, a chanter of verses [*stikhi*]
Domestnik, a chanter of church singing (fol. 46)			**Domestik**, a chanter of church singing (fol. 164)
		Difthong, two-voiced [dual vowel] (p. 33)	
	Epimifaus, a Greek who turned to musical secrets (p. 157)	**Epinikion**, a song of victory (p. 36)	
Zhart, blasphemy (fol. 59)	**Zhart**, blasphemy (p. 158)		
Zviniaiu, I strike (fol. 62)		**Zvonets**, bell [chime] (p. 40)	
		Zvuk, trumpet voice [sound of a trumpet; various synonyms follow: *dzvienk*, *briank*, *br"men'e*, *briazk*, *golos*] (p. 40)	
Znak, a sign, indicating something, naming something (fol. 60v)			

Kniga glagolemaia Alfavit [RNB, Pogod. 1642; internal date 1596, date of manuscript, 17th century]	Azbukovnik publ. by Sakharov [GIM, Uvar. 310 (2088) and 311 (2094)]; 16th century	Leksykon slovenoros'kyi by Berynda (first published in 1627)	Alfavit rechei inostrannykh [RNB, Sol. 18], 17th century
		Igralishche, a place of entertainment, where there are horse races and fights and comedies [plays] (p. 42)	
		Irmoloi, a Greek [service] book that contains *irmosy* (p. 45)	
		Irmos, a model by means of which one sings and hears *tropari*, that is, verses (p. 45)	
Kambaniia, carillon (fol. 74v)	**Kambany**, bells (p. 163)		
Kanban, bell (fol. 74v)			
Karmonii [*garmoniia*— N.F.], devilish songs (fol. 75v)	**Karmonia, garmoniia,** senseless singing (p. 163)		
Kafisi, seated/sitting			
Kathismo, seated [stational hymn] (fol. 75v)			
Keleouma, a song sung when grapes are harvested (fol. 77v)	**Keleuma**, a song sung when grapes are harvested (p. 164)		
	Kimval, voice (p. 164)		
Kiniry, *lyri* (fol. 81v)		**Kinira**, *tsitara*, harp; one sounds the *kinira* and on the harp, one strikes (p. 49)	
	Kodoni, little bells which the Jewish priests had on the bottoms of their vestments (p. 165)		
Komediia, plays, in which the mindless Greeks staged feasts after death, dancing senselessly and playing and ribaldry in a debauched way (fol. 85v)	**Komediia**, according to the devil [?!—N.F.] (p. 165)		
		Kontroversiia, see *penie* (p. 51)	
Korpus, horn (fol. 85v)			
Krikela, ring (fol. 80)			
Kryzh, (Latin) cross [used in Western Slavic groups]			

Kniga glagolemaia Alfavit [RNB, Pogod. 1642; internal date 1596, date of manuscript, 17th century]	*Azbukovnik* publ. by Sakharov [GIM, Uvar. 310 (2088) and 311 (2094)]; 16th century	*Leksykon slovenoros'kyi* by Berynda (first published in 1627)	*Alfavit rechei inostrannykh* [RNB, Sol. 18], 17th century
		Lik, loud singing or shouting, or a dance (p. 53)	
		Likovanie, dancing, a dance which is played (p. 53)	
		Likovstvuiu, celebratory dancing (p. 53)	
		Likovstvovanie, dancing or a celebratory dance (p. 53)	
		Likuiu, I dance (p. 53)	
		Lira, violin [*skripitsa*] (p. 65)	**Lira**, violin [*skripitsa*] (fol. 280v)
	Mathematiiskiia knigi, repudiated books, of which there are four: arithmetic, music, geometry, astronomy (p. 170)		
	Miga, *sopel'* (p. 171)		
Mimi, *skomorokhi* (fol. 97v)			
Mim, *skomorokh* (fol. 97v)	**Mim**, *skomorokh* (p. 171)		
Muza, *sopel'* (fol. 100)	**Muza**, *sopel'* (p. 171)		**Muza**, *sopel'* (fol. 306)
Musikiiskim, with an organ, with a vessel [instrument] (fol. 100)	**Muzykiiskii organ**, the melodious organ (p. 172)		
Musikiia, playing on the *gusli*, *domry*, and *lyri*, and *tsinbaly*, and on other [instruments] with strings; all that is called music, and musical organs (fol. 100)	**Musikiia**, playing, or playing the *gusli* or the *kinary*, called the lyre, and the *doliar* [sic; probably *domra*—N.F.], and all types of instruments: trumpets, *svireli*, which are called *pigoli*, *pesnevets*, called the psaltery, *sambikiia*, which are pipes [*tsevnitsy*], *kiniry*, which are lyres, *timpany*, and *kimvaly* (p. 172)	**Musika**, singing, or making music with the voice or playing; the fourth of the seven liberal arts (p. 59)	**Musika**, singers or vocalists [vocal players] who sing or play, from the seven liberal arts, the seventh science of the book of philosophies
		Musikii, a singer or player (p. 59)	**Musikii**, a singer or player

Kniga glagolemaia Alfavit [RNB, Pogod. 1642; internal date 1596, date of manuscript, 17th century]	Azbukovnik publ. by Sakharov [GIM, Uvar. 310 (2088) and 311 (2094)]; 16th century	Leksykon slovenoros'kyi by Berynda (first published in 1627)	Alfavit rechei inostrannykh [RNB, Sol. 18], 17th century
	Musikiia, songs are written in it and devilish tunes, sung by the Latins to the musical organ, that is, playing on tuneful instruments (p. 172)		**Musikiia**, Daniel 3:18 [3:7 or 10], that is, playing the *gusli*; Maksim Grek, ch. 12, and on the lyre, and the *tsymbaly*, and the *domry*. All of these are types of musical instruments, which are vessels of a performing construction, to which belong types of musical instruments called trumpets, and *svireli* (Daniel 3), and *tsevnitsy* 487, 613, and those called organs, that is, those which release from themselves a voice 330 (fol. 306) [the meaning of these numbers is unclear].
	Musikiiskii organ, the melodious organ (p. 172)		
Okhtaik, *osmoglasnik* [Octoechos] (fol. 107v)		**Oktoikh**, *osmoglasnik* [Octoechos], Greek *Paraklitiki* [Parakletike], a [service] book (p. 69)	
Organ, a vessel [instrument] and also the human body; the soul lives within the body as if in a container (fol. 108)	**Organ**, in Scripture it is called a sounding vessel, for example, a trumpet, *svirel'*, horn, *timpany*, or *kimvaly* (p. 175)	**Organ**, instrument, implement, *gusli*; see *lira* (p. 70)	
	Organ, the human body; the body is the vessel of the soul (p. 175)		
Orthei, a *gusli* player; a Thracian (fol. 108)	**Orfeovytreby**, Orfei was a *gusli* player, a Thracian. This Thracian performance was an imaginary mystery, called festivals and rites (p. 175)		
		Paraklit, called comforter (p. 73)	
Paizopez, I play [Greek] (fol. 115v)			
Paizopekso, I leap [Greek] (fol. 115v)			
Psalin, they sing [Greek]	**Psalmo**, I sing (p. 180)		
Psalmos, song [Psalm; Greek] (fol. 115v)	**Psalmos**, singing, song (p. 180)	**Psalom**, song, tune, played on an instrument or sung [a chanted song] (p. 85)	

Kniga glagolemaia Alfavit [RNB, Pogod. 1642; internal date 1596, date of manuscript, 17th century]	*Azbukovnik* publ. by Sakharov [GIM, Uvar. 310 (2088) and 311 (2094)]; 16th century	*Leksykon slovenoros'kyi* by Berynda (first published in 1627)	*Alfavit rechei inostrannykh* [RNB, Sol. 18], 17th century
Psaltyr', among the Jews, this was a vessel [instrument] like the depiction here, like a *domra* with ten strings; held aloft, this instrument, which is a psaltery, that is, *pesnevets*, was played by stroking [strumming] while accompanying a song. David, the king and prophet, compiled the following book, guided by the Holy Spirit, and called by the name of Psalter (fols. 113–113v)	**Psaltir'**, the Jews made a wooden vessel [instrument], on it were ten strings, this vessel was called a psaltery by the Greeks, and by the Slavs, *pesnevets* (p. 180)	**Psaltir**, intellect, wisdom, valor, or song, harp (p. 85)	
Pigoly, *svireli* (fol. 119v)			
Pipely, small *surenki* (fol. 119v)			
Piskanie, playing trumpets and *svireli* (fol. 121)			
Piskakhom, played [piped] (fol. 120)			
	Pishchal', *svirel'* (p. 177)	**Pishchal'**, flute, pipes [*pishchalka, piska, pishchki*] (p. 74)	**Pishchal'**, *svirel'* (fol. 177)
		Pliasalishche, place of [wild] performing, games, revelry	
		Pozorishche, a place where one sees [lewd] entertainments (p. 76)	
		Pozorishche podvigov, a place where there are . . . dances and customs [?] (p. 76)	
Protopsalt, principal singer (fol. 121v)	**Protopsalt**, principal singer (p. 180)		
Prosodiia, *prosodiia* means literary strength of the letter; for example [a long series of references to names of chant neumes follows]			
		Penie, hymn, singing (p. 86)	

Kniga glagolemaia Alfavit [RNB, Pogod. 1642; internal date 1596, date of manuscript, 17th century]	*Azbukovnik* publ. by Sakharov [GIM, Uvar. 310 (2088) and 311 (2094)]; 16th century	*Leksykon slovenoros'kyi* by Berynda (first published in 1627)	*Alfavit rechei inostrannykh* [RNB, Sol. 18], 17th century
	Pesnitsa, *tsevnitsa* [reed flute] (p. 181)		**Pesnivitsa**, Daniel 3, i.e., *gusli* and *domry* (fol. 375v)
		Pesnopenie, a hymn to God, singing a hymn (p. 86)	
		Pesn', pesn'ka, also a song in praise of God, which praises God (p. 86)	
Pesn' stepennaia, a high [ascending] song sung by virtuous people as they are ascending a ladder to God (fol. 126v)		**Pesn' stepennaia**, a high song, ascending to it (p. 86)	**Pesn' stepennaia**, i.e., ascending [step] song, which is sung on the ladder going to heaven (fol. 375v)
Rod musikiin, an instrumental [vessel] construction (fol. 129v)			
Rusaliia, which are for players, wild games, and ugliness (fol. 129v)	**Rusaliia**, games, *skomorokh* games (p. 182)		
Sambikiia, *tsevnitsa* [pipes; Greek] (fol. 133)			
		Svirel', a little pipe [*pishchalka*], insignificant music, like a flute, Muscovite and Greek, in general a shepherd's pipe; see *sopl'* (p. 92)	**Svirel'**, a little pipe [*pishchalka*], insignificant music, like a flute, Muscovite and Greek, in general a shepherd's pipe; see *sopl'* (fol. 375v)
		Sveriaiu, I play a *svistelka* [flute, whistle] (p. 92)	**Sveriaiu**, I play a *svistelka* [flute, whistle] (fol. 421v)
	Skripitsa, *gusli* (p. 184)		**Skrypitsa**, *gusli* or *lira* (fol. 421)
		Sopl', [a list of instruments:] *sopel'*, *pishchalka*, *fletnia*, *fuiara*, *duda*, *surma*, *zholomeika*, pipes [*festula*] for the organ or regal (p. 96)	**Sopl'**, [a list of instruments:] *sopel'*, *pishchalka*, *fletnia*, *fuiara*, *duda*, *surma*, *zholomeika*, pipes [*festula*] for the organ or regal (fol. 413v)
		Sopl' pastyrskii, a shepherd's *fuiara* [from Polish *fujara*, a pipe—N.F.] (p. 96)	**Sopl' pastyrskii**, a shepherd's pipe [*fuiara*] (fol. 413v)
		Sopets, player, flute player [*pishchalnik*], horn player [*surmach, kornetista*] (p. 96)	**Sopets**, player, flute player [*pishchalnik*], horn player [*surnach', kornetista*] (fol. 409v)
Soptsy, *skomorokhi* (fol. 137)			**Soptsy**, i.e., *skomorokhi* or one who plays the trumpet (fol. 409v)
Sosviri, play [or blow] (fol. 138)			**Sosviri**, play [blow] the *svirel'* (fol. 409v)
Stavros, Cross (fol. 130)			

Kniga glagolemaia Alfavit [RNB, Pogod. 1642; internal date 1596, date of manuscript, 17th century]	Azbukovnik publ. by Sakharov [GIM, Uvar. 310 (2088) and 311 (2094)]; 16th century	Leksykon slovenoros'kyi by Berynda (first published in 1627)	Alfavit rechei inostrannykh [RNB, Sol. 18], 17th century
Tanets, dance (fol. 141)			
Tantsovanie, dancing (fol. 141)			
Teatrum, shamefulness (fol. 143)			
Timpan, voice (fol. 144v)	**Timpan**, voice (p. 187)	**Timpan**, small drum [*buben*] (p. 103)	
Tipokar', *ustavshchik* [singing leader, *domestik*] (fol. 143v)			
Tragediia, a play [*igrishcha*] or pity and sorrow (fol. 142)			
Triod', the Book of the Three Odes, three-fold song [Triodion] (fol. 143v)		**Triodion**, three-fold song; *tri*, three; *odi*, song (p. 106)	
Thamiliia, Greek games [*igrishcha*] (fol. 151v)			
Thilompiia, Song of Songs (fol. 152v)			
Thimilicheskaia peniia, [songs] at games created at devilish Greek games (fol. 152v)			
Khalmoni [*garmoniia*—N.F.], a musical sounding [*gudenie*] (fol. 156v)			
Khoros, dance (fol. 158)			
		Tsevnitsa, [names of instruments:] *svistelka*, *fletnia*, *shalamai* [chalumeau?] (p. 114)	

Afrodita—there was a woman among the Greeks, insatiable fornicator, sorceress, and witch. The senseless Greeks had her as a goddess, and because of that it is said that things [*dela*] associated with Aphrodite are fornication matters. (f. 18v)

Dionis—imaginary god of the Greeks, fornicator and drunkard he was, and was later butchered by those of the netherworld. (f. 45v)

Zeves—is a star . . . The Greeks viewed as god a man named Zeves, who was a sorcerer and magician; he dreamed that he could transform himself into animals and all kinds of vile creatures, even doing foul deeds like fornicating with dead women. He begat Dionysius,

Heracles, Apollo, Artemis, and others, and from them he named dancers and players on musical instruments, and all these the senseless Greeks named as gods. (f. 61v)

Gudenie—in addition to an understandable explanation of each sound and each sounding [e.g., by an instrument], the definition testifies to the existence of the *domra* and *lira* in sixteenth-century musical practice, and of the *domra, gudok,* and *tsimbaly* in the seventeenth century.

Gudets'—in addition to the definition as an instrumentalist, the seventeenth-century Solovetskii manuscript interprets this word as "creating a thought, transfiguration."

Gusli, gusl'—in two documents this term refers to a stringed instrument in general (harp, small violin, zither [*tsitra*]) and not specifically to the Slavic and Russian musical instrument known to us from the miniatures.

Kinira—the term is also explained as a stringed instrument in general, and in the 1596 manuscript even as a form of the lyre, but it could hardly refer to the Little Russian *lira* (*rylia*) which came from the Western European *Leyer* and which had nothing in common with classical Greek lyres.

Musikiia (and *musika*)—a term which brought forth the greatest variety and even contradictory explanations: (1) as a term corresponding to our understanding of music in general in all four sources; (2) as a term designating the fourth volume of "philosophical" sciences (in glossaries of the seventeenth century). In the *Skazanie o 7 svobodnykh mudrostiakh* [An explanation of the seven liberal arts], the fourth subject [literally, the fourth wisdom, *chetvertaia mudrost'*] is called *musika* (this source is in [GIM] Chud. 298, from the late seventeenth century);[223] and (3) "devilish tunes, sung by the Latins to the musical organs," in other words, the reference is specifically to the hymns and chorales of the Western church, accompanied by organs or instrumental music (see the sixteenth-century *azbukovnik* published by Sakharov). The 1654 *Alphabet* ([GIM] Sin. 353) gives the following detailed explanation of this term:

> As to what *musikiia* is. *Musikiia,* playing, that is, the sounding of *gusli* and *kiniry,* or lyres [see Findeizen's comments above], and *domry,* and similar things. These are all types of music and all types of playing. The types of music, in addition to the above-named [instruments], are trumpets, *svireli,* also called *pigoli,* and *pipeli.* Added to this is the psaltery and the *sambikiia,* which is a *tsevnitsa* [a pipe], and *kiniry,* which are lyres, and other similar [instruments], as is written in Psalm 108, [with] timpani, strings, and cymbals [*kimvaly*], and with such the Jews meant to submit offerings to God. We the Orthodox Christian multitudes and the New Israel and sons of True Light do not do it, and do not accept such music. As those were foretelling the image of forthcoming blessing, they offered to God the services of the Psalter of the senses, yet we, exclaiming through [the Psalter of] purified reason, do it through thoughts. They by the *gusli,* we with kind thoughts, and so on as is written in Psalm 108.[224]

This explanation clearly depicts the artistic meaning of details in most of the miniatures in the Khludov Psalter and in the variants of Cosmas Indicopleustes, representing David "creating" the Psalter and surrounded by choruses of musicians, the precentors of the Temple in Jerusalem: "with such [music] the Jews meant to submit an offering." The Synodal Alphabet labels such details "[the Psalter] of the senses," against which is juxtaposed "[the Psalter] of purified reason."

Organ—this word not only refers to the musical instrument, but it also symbolizes "the human body; the soul lives within a body as if in a container" (*Alphabet* of 1596). The term *psaltyr'* has similar and even more widespread meanings.

Psaltyr'—not only a musical instrument used "by Jews . . . to sing songs" (1596 *Alphabet*), but it also symbolizes "intellect, wisdom, valor" (Berynda). The glossaries of 1596 and of the late seventeenth century give a detailed description ("made of wood, has ten strings"), and the 1596 glossary includes an illustration, rare in these works.

Svirel' and *sopl'*—in both seventeenth-century glossaries these terms are explained on the basis of a single Polish source from which many explanations in other old Russian glossaries were probably borrowed. The Russian compilers did not always have a clear understanding of these unfamiliar words, and a discovery of such Polish original sources would unquestionably clarify many misunderstandings. The comparison of the *svirel'* and *sopl'* to the stringed lute, an unrelated instrument, is obviously the result of a misreading and poor transcription into Russian of the word *fletnia* [flute; written in Latin letters]. The *svirel'* and *sopl'* are both flute-like wind instruments.

Skripitsa—glossaries of the sixteenth and seventeenth centuries show that this is another term demonstrating that the Russian commentators had no understanding of the instrument. It was not yet known in Russian domestic or public life (apparently the first violins in Moscow appeared only at the beginning of the eighteenth century), and the compilers obviously got the idea from their sources that it was supposed to be a stringed instrument, thus their comparisons with the *gusli* and the Little Russian *lira*.[224A]

Khalmoniia—in the 1596 manuscript this is described only as a musical sounding (*gudenie*); apparently borrowing this from some foreign source, the compiler of the glossary preserved the term *harmonie* [in Latin letters] but substituted the letter *l* for the *r* in the original [i.e., *kharmoniia* became *khalmoniia*].

Some of these definitions, as we have seen, convey different meanings for terms designating musical instruments. For example, in the late-seventeenth-century Solovetskii manuscript, the term *gudets* is described as a "player on the *gusli* and the *gudok* and the *domra*, that is, one who learns how to interpret a thought; transfiguration." The same kind of definition appears for the term *organ*. One of the most curious glossaries of this kind is the manuscript in the Solovetskii Library, no. 276 [RNB], containing a work mentioned above, the *Interpretation of Incomprehensible Words, Starting First with the Psalter, Made Beautiful with the Gusli*.[224B] This document gives some unusual interpretations: "Psalter—

mind; *gusli*—thoughts; strings—fingers; organ—good thought when directed to God; *tim-pan*—voice; trumpet—throat; *stepenna*—an elevated song to God" (fol. 464v).

Interpretations like these explain why many different musical instruments appear in illustrations in religious literature, even though these instruments are rejected and even condemned by religious authorities. In most cases the illustrations ought to be understood as symbols. This explains the appearance in Russian gospels and psalters of representations of foreign instruments—organs, *timpany*, trumpets, stringed *crwth*, rubeb—and, of course, the *gusli*. They were necessary to express certain religious thoughts and concepts. Of course, the miniaturists selected for that purpose the best available Western models, and thus the Godunov Psalter, for example, includes Western organs and courtly minstrels with lutes and *crwths*, which are totally foreign to us. These representations were not meant to be taken literally.

The attribution of symbolic meaning to musical objects and to the very concept of music was characteristic of the upper strata of Russian society, especially the clergy, which was also true in the West in antiquity and the Middle Ages. The Kostroma Society for Church History owned a nineteenth-century allegorical painting on canvas in the shape of a cross, with the caption: "Music is necessary for all Christians" (item no. 710 in that collection). At the top an eagle was depicted with the inscription *alto;* at the bottom was a hand holding a cross, with the inscription *bass;* on the right side were two clasped hands and two lamps, with the inscription *discant;* and, on the left, was a man's face encircled by a halo depicting four hands and four feet, with the inscription *tenor.*[225]

In addition to the *azbukovniki* containing references to mostly foreign musical instruments, some interesting pictorial material appears in Karion Istomin's illustrated *Bukvar'* [Alphabet] from the end of the seventeenth century.[226] The compiler, the Moscow master and hieromonk Karion Istomin, made this work for Peter's son, Tsarevich Aleksei, in 1692, and two years later it was engraved by Leontii Bunin, a master at the Silver Workshop [Serebrianaia palata].[227] The *Alphabet* was made up of forty-three sheets engraved with Slavic, Greek, and Latin letters. Illustrating each letter were drawings of people, scenes, and a variety of objects from domestic life or society beginning with that letter, and the introductory illustration was described through appropriate verses. Some of Istomin's illustrations supplement the glossaries; the musical instruments represented in the *Alphabet* are apparently contemporary Russian instruments.

The most interesting in this respect is the symbolic representation of the psalter in the context of an entire instrumental ensemble (fig. 50, from fol. 33). This is an illustration of the Slavonic [Greek] letter *psi* and the two main terms starting with that letter: *psalter* and *psalms.* The word *psalms* is represented by a book with musical notation (actually, two books; the second is placed between the violinist and the *gusli* player as if it were for use by one of the musicians). The book is written in Kievan staff notation, which by that time had replaced the older *kriuki* notation in liturgical practice. The instrumental ensemble is headed by a *gusli* player, a youth seated in an armchair resembling a throne with a foot-stool, exactly as King David is depicted in miniatures. Beside him stands a performer playing a straight trumpet, apparently made of wood. The musicians sitting around him play a violin and a Little Russian *bandura* (*kobza*). In spite of the primitive quality of the drawing, because of Bunin's poor engraving, their Little Russian nationality can hardly be doubted. The inscription above this ensemble is similar to explanations given in the glossaries: "Psalter, that is, music, sweet singing."

Of the remaining illustrations in the *Alphabet*, it is sufficient to mention the drawings for the letters *Zh* [Ж], *Z* [З], and *O*. For the first letter, a *zhenikh* [suitor] is represented by

FIG. 50. From Karion Istomin's *Alphabet* (1694).

a trumpet with a large bell between his legs [fig. 51]. The second illustration [for the letter Z] shows a kneeling trumpeter playing on a *zmeevik*, a curved horn reminiscent of the medieval serpent [fig. 51A]; the same instrument is repeated for the letters *A* and *K*. The third letter shows a large organ (with the inscription "organy") with its keyboard and a row of pipes above a square case [fig. 52]. These last two images may have been copied from models existing at the time in Moscow.

FIG. 51. Illustration of the letter
Ж with a straight trumpet. From
Karion Istomin's *Alphabet* (1694).

FIG. 51A. Illustration of the letter З
with a curved horn. From Karion
Istomin's *Alphabet* (1694).

FIG. 52. The organ. From Karion Istomin's *Alphabet* (1694).

Part 3

In addition to these illustrations, old folk woodcuts [*lubki, lubochnye kartinki*] provide a more complete collection of musical instruments. In D. A. Rovinskii's well-known publication, one finds a series of scenes, most of them humorous, containing representations of various musical instruments. Some of the instruments are undoubtedly of folk origin, but most are copied from foreign originals, for example, in the series of seventeenth- and eighteenth-century woodcuts appearing in Rovinskii's printed collection.[228] In the second volume of the posthumous edition of *Russian Folk Drawings* ([listed in n. 228] p. 392, no. 280), there is an eighteenth-century composition depicting singing and dancing; the dancing buffoons are copied from the *polichinelles* of the famous French engraver Jacques Callot (d. 1635). One of the dancers is a Polichinelle with a lute, a woman dancing and playing on a *lira* (*Leyer*). A bowing Pantalone turns to her with a request: "Please, play the *ryle*." On the left is a group of peasant dancers in front of a seated musician with a pipe [*dudochka*], saying, "First, gentlemen, I'll play a dance for you." The picture is a crude composition, copied from several foreign models.

A picture of a complete vocal-instrumental ensemble headed by a dancing buffoon reveals more careful workmanship (fig. 53).[228A] Here we also see a foreign *Leyer* and a pipe player [*dudochnik*]; a girl standing next to them is holding a music book. The costumes, faces, instruments, and setting suggest a foreign original. The following engraved text appears:

> A. Hold the book lower
> So that I can see it closer;
> I'll play the *ryla*
> And I'll sing from the book.
>
> B. I'll hold the book in my hand as best I can
> And that I can understand;
> And I'll start singing with you.

C. Do what your mother wants;
You are playing the *ryla* from the notes;
I won't move far away from you,
I'll take up the *dudochka*
And hope that our music
Will be good and loud.

D. I've danced with a lot of folks
But I've never seen such music.
What a comfort it is
To have such fine playing on the *ryla*.
I don't want to stop,
I'm happy to dance forever.

The *lira* (*Drehleier, vielle,* hurdy-gurdy), which reached Little Russia and White Russia from the West, here has the name *rylia* or *ryle;* we encounter it again in the description of Russian folk instruments [in chapter 7].

Foreign buffoons, *polichinelles,* and Hanswursts, russianized as the *skomorokhi* Foma and Eryoma, Vavilo and Danilo, Savos'ka and Paramoshka, and other similar merrymakers, were almost always provided with foreign musical instruments and were copies of foreign jesters; only a few of them, such as the musicians in "The Parable of the Wealthy and Wretched Lazarus," were crudely russianized. In the folk woodcut of Foma and Eryoma (fig. 54) in which Eryoma tells his friend to play an old song, Foma has a small lute-like instrument, and the picture itself is undoubtedly a copy of a foreign original. The wood-cut of Savos'ka and Paramoshka (fig. 55) is also derived from a foreign source. Savos'ka plays a four-string *gudok*–rubeb and Paramoshka, who is riding a goat, accompanies him with castanet-like shakers (rather like the Russian *lozhki* [spoons]). Neither they nor any of the characters depicted in figures 57 and 58 can be taken for Russian buffoons.[228B]

The viol-playing musicians in the edifying woodcut "The Parable of the Wealthy and Wretched Lazarus" (fig. 56), although somewhat russianized, were certainly copied from foreign illustrations.[228C] The woodcut depicts two musicians entertaining the Prodigal Son, playing on viols of a rather fantastic form and construction. The complex series of twenty-four woodcuts illustrating "The Story of *Semik* and of *Maslenitsa*" is somewhat closer to real life.[228D] One of these pictures shows *skomorokhi,* who "ride on the backs of pigs with various

FIG. 53. Music-making, from an eighteenth-century woodcut.

types of music [*muzyka*] and with *gudoks*" in the Carnival procession (fig. 59). They are preceded by a *skomorokh* playing a *gudok* resembling the common folk type (unlike foreign instruments, it has no F-holes); the other characters in the picture are playing *dudki* and a *volynka*. All the characters in this fragment have instruments in their hands, and the instruments resemble those of the Russian folk type rather than foreign types. The very manner in which the first *skomorokh* holds the *gudok*—vertically—recalls the scene in Adam Olearius's *Travels* of playing and dancing *skomorokhi* in Ladoga (cf. fig. 42).

The dancing bear and goat in an eighteenth-century woodcut (fig. 60) hold two folk instruments, the *dudka* and the spoons. The text reads: "Bear delights in music for his own amusement. And Bear put on his hat and played the *dudka*, and Goat, in a blue sarafan with ornaments and little bells and [playing the] spoons, jumps and dances up and down." This scene is interesting because of the subject matter, namely, a performance by *skomorokhi*.

One of the wittiest woodcuts, well known in numerous editions and translations as "The Mice Bury the Cat," is fully Russian in subject and composition. Rovinskii, in his *Russian Folk Drawings* and in the accompanying pictorial volumes, has carefully studied various versions of this eighteenth-century print (some more detailed, others less so), which was frequently reprinted in *lubok* collections to the end of the nineteenth century. He justly speculates that it was created by the Old Believers on the death of the much-hated Peter the Great. The inscription over the cat's body, "The Cat of Kazan, the mind of Astrakhan, the intellect of Siberia," parodies the imperial title, "Tsar of Kazan, Tsar of Astrakhan," and so on. The burial of the cat is accompanied by mice, some of whom are joyously playing and beating on a variety of instruments. In the top row on the right, the text reads: (1) "Jolly Vavilko [*sic:* Vaviko], who plays the *volynka* and sings tunes,

FIG. 54. Foma and Eryoma, from an eighteenth-century woodcut.

FIG. 55. The jesters Savos'ka and Paramoshka, from an eighteenth-century woodcut.

says prayers for the cat"; and (2) "The *sur-nach* Chiurilko plays the *surna* but does not know the key." In the second row on the left, a mouse beats a large side drum. These same instruments can be found in other versions of this woodcut.[228E]

In summarizing our survey of the old miniatures, the explanations in the glossaries, and the woodcuts, we reach the conclusion that only a few of the musical instruments they depicted or described can be accepted as genuinely Russian (the *gusli, gudok, surna, dudka, baraban-buben,* and *lozhki*). Most of the others were copied from Western models and were, in fact, unknown in Russian folk life. Furthermore, many representations of these instruments had a merely symbolic significance.

FIG. 56. Musicians playing viols, from the woodcut "The Parable of the Wealthy and Wretched Lazarus."

FIG. 57. A fragment from the woodcut "The Banquet of the Pious and the Profane."

FIG. 58. A fragment from the woodcut "The Little Old Man Plays the Little *Gudok.*"

ПЕРГД ЪНЄЮ СКАЧУТЬ НА СВИ
НЬАХ Ъ ВЄРХАМИ СРАЗНЫМ·
МУ ЗЫКИ ИГУДКАМИ

FIG. 59. *Skomorokh* musicians in the eighteenth-
century woodcut "Semik and Maslenitsa."

FIG. 60. "Bear and Goat Entertain Themselves"
from an eighteenth-century woodcut.

7. A Survey of Old Russian Folk Instruments

We learn from the earliest written records that there were various types of musical instruments in this period, including some of rather complex construction. These instruments range from the ten-string *gusli* mentioned in the *Lay of the Host of Igor* (twelfth century) to the very simple instruments that must have existed in general usage. To avoid repetition, I refer in this chapter to documents and passages introduced earlier without quoting them again. I also bypass the question of the origins and borrowings of Russian folk instruments, since that question transcends the limits of this volume. For us it is sufficient to stress that the Slavs had a talent for music and that, in the remote past, they used wind and stringed instruments, in addition to percussion instruments, which are the least complex in their construction.

Many terms were used to designate a musical performance or musicians themselves: *briazdati, briaznuti, briatsati,* or *udariati* [verbs meaning clash, jingle, clang, and strike]. In an interpretive psalter of the eleventh century, for example, the text reads: "those striking the spiritual *gusli*." In the teachings of Ephrem the Syrian (manuscript in the Academy of Sciences, dated 1377), the text reads: "and my *gusli* you strike, saying . . ." In the Mineia of 1096, we read "play, strike the *briatsalo* [small drums]," and in the Russian Primary Chronicle for the year 1074: "Take *sopeli*, drums, and *gusli* and strike them, so that Isakii can dance."[228F] These are the earliest, and general, references to musical performances. At the same time the performer—*igrets*—was known as *igr'nik, igr'ts', igrets'*. For example, in the Efrem nomocanon of the eleventh century: "Players [*igr'nitsi*], heretics or Greeks" and in the Novgorod nomocanon of 1280: "player and choral singer."[228G] There were other terms long used in religious literature to designate music, musicians, and musical performance. The terms *gudenie* (or *guzhenie*), *gudets,* and *gud'ba* refer specifically to stringed instruments. For example, "it is not proper for Christians to play devilish games, that is, dancing, playing [*gudba*], and secular songs" according to a sixteenth-century discourse, or "let us praise the vatic Boian, skilled player in the town of Kiev," from the *Zadonshchina.*[229] The musician of the ancient past was thus called an *igrets* or a *gudets* [player], and playing musical instruments in general, but especially stringed instruments, was known as *briatsanie, udarianie, gudenie,* and *gud'ba*. Wind instruments also had their special vocabulary: *pipelovat'* meant to play the *pipel'* (*svirel'*); *piskat'* also meant to play the *svirel'*. An example of this usage is in the *Thirteen Orations* of Gregory of Nazianzus (in an eleventh-century manuscript in the Public Library [RNB]): "Tell me, O miracle-worker, is it good to dance or play on the pipe?"[229A]

These passages reveal the earliest names of folk instruments, although they do not always specify a particular instrument. A single instrument could be designated by several names, and over time each of the terms came to mean a separate instrument. There is a similar sense of uncertainty and confusion regarding the names of medieval Western instruments as well. The *dudka, rozhok,* and *svirel'* undoubtedly existed long ago; we think of them today as different forms of wind instruments, but in manuscripts of the eleventh to the sixteenth centuries the terms *pipel', pishchal',* or *sopel'* are used interchangeably. I. I. Sreznevskii and other scholars say that, in most instances, these terms indicate the *svirel'*.

The simplest wind instrument was the wooden or reed *dudka-svistelka,* also called *posvistel'* in very early times, as in the text of the Novgorod IV Chronicle, under the year

1343, describing the Pskov troops: "They, having come from Oreshok at noon, struck trumpets, drums [*bubny*], and pipes [*v posvisteli*]." The Nikonian Chronicle from the same year says: "Trumpeting on the trumpets and striking the drums and the pipes" ["v sopeli i v posvisteli"].[229B] Thus the Nikonian Chronicle in the mid-fourteenth century distinguishes between the *dudka-posvistel'* and the *sopel'*, but it is still difficult to establish the difference between them. One of them may have been straight [like a modern recorder] while the other resembled the transverse flute. Along with the *dudka*, horns [*roga*] were used in general practice. At first, in accordance with their name, these instruments were made from animal horns. We know in antiquity of the *turii rog*, made from the long horn of an aurochs; when the aurochs died out, horns were made of wood yet retained their ancient [curved] shape. Even today, in the far corners of the Olonets region, one may find wooden shepherds' horns, shaped like natural horns but made of wood and bound with birch bark. N. I. Privalov's *The Musical Wind Instruments of the Russian People* contains an illustration of an Olonets horn belonging to the ethnographic division of the Russian Museum (fig. 61) and also gives its tuning, as shown in musical example 7.1.[229C]

FIG. 61. A wooden horn from Olonets.

The five-note pattern illustrated in musical example 7.1 conforms exactly to the ancient scale of the Karelo-Finnish melodies for epic poems, the *Kalevala*, and also to the pitches of the natural scale to which the Finnish five-string *kantele* was tuned. Thus we find that the late survivals of this native musical instrument preserve the same tuning pattern used in remote antiquity.

EXAMPLE 7.1. Tuning of the *rog*

In more recent times the old horns and their smaller derivatives (*rozhki*) have, of course, undergone changes and become more widely distributed. Matthew Guthrie, in his *Dissertations sur les antiquités de Russie*, has a drawing of a Siberian horn bound with birch bark from the end of the eighteenth century (fig. 62), which recalls the curved horn in Istomin's *Alphabet* (see fig. 51a).[230] According to Guthrie, this horn was used by local shepherds and consisted of two sections bound together with birch bark; it had no finger holes.

The modern metal trumpets used by the Russian army from the seventeenth century on undoubtedly influenced this form of the wooden shepherds' horn, for we see various examples

FIG. 62. A Siberian horn (from Guthrie, eighteenth century).

FIG. 63. A Karelian trumpet [*truba*] from the late nineteenth century.

of wooden trumpets in popular use, replacing the straight shepherds' horn. Privalov, in *The Musical Wind Instruments of the Russian People,* reproduces examples from the ethnographic division of the Russian Museum, the Music History Museum [see n. 25], and private collections [figs. 63 and 64]. They were widely used in Karelia (Olonets province) and in central areas of Russia (in Nizhegorodskii province); a similar horn was brought to me in 1925 from this area. This wooden horn, shaped like a French horn, was tuned as shown in musical example 7.2.

Small wooden horns [*rozhki*] with finger holes have different ranges, spanning diatonically up to 1½ or 2 octaves, starting from the octave below middle C; larger instruments produce tones an octave lower.[231] To date, only three forms of horns can be distinguished:

FIG. 64. A Karelian trumpet [*truba*] from the late nineteenth century.

EXAMPLE 7.2. Tuning of a wooden horn

1. natural horns (including the aurochs horns of the tenth century from the Chernigov tumulus);[232]
2. wooden horns (so-called shepherds' horns) without finger holes;
3. small wooden horns with finger holes.

There is some uncertainty about the names of other wooden folk wind instruments mentioned in old manuscripts and in modern publications. We encounter the terms *pishchal', svirel', sopel', sapovka (sapovochka),* and *tsevnitsa* and, according to some investigators, all of them correspond to ancient Greek panpipes.

Guthrie defines them as follows: the single pipe he (correctly) calls the *dudka* [fig. 65]; the two-pipe *dudka* he calls *zhaleika* [fig. 66]; and the multi-pipe instrument he terms the *svirelka* [fig. 67]. N. I. Privalov has more accurately established the names of the last two as the *svirel'* (with paired pipes) and *tsevnitsa* (with multiple pipes).[233]

The *zhaleika* [fig. 68] is a separate wooden wind instrument with a reed, which was and probably still is made in Tambov, Smolensk, and Orel provinces from the bark of elder or willow trees. The reed gives the instrument its mournful sound, which may have led to its name [*zhalkii* means pitiful, sad]. Others believe that the name *zhaleika* is derived from the willow, which usually grows on *zhal'niki,* the old name for tombs and cemeteries. Privalov says that the *zhaleika* is widely used in Orel and Riazan provinces.

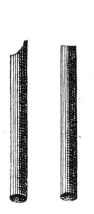

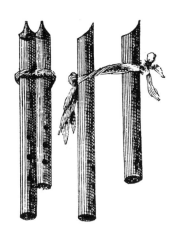

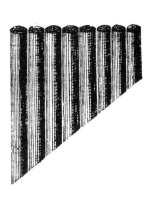

FIG. 65. The *dudka* (from Guthrie, eighteenth century).

FIG. 66. The *zhaleika* (from Guthrie, eighteenth century).

FIG. 67. The *svirelka* (from Guthrie, eighteenth century).

FIG. 68. Playing the *zhaleika* (the double *dudka;* from Guthrie, eighteenth century).

Let us return to the *svirel'* (double flute), which is found almost everywhere in Russian folk practice up to recent times, and which V. V. Andreev incorporated into his Great Russian orchestra in the late nineteenth century. This instrument is mentioned in the oldest manuscripts. A person who played the instrument was called a *svirets'* (*svir'ts'*) or *svirel'nik,* and the verbs *sviriat'* or *svirevat'* indicate the actual playing itself. A Riazan nomocanon of 1284 states: "whether a *svirel'* player or a stringed instrument player [*goudets*] or one bowing an instrument or a dancer . . . [all] to be excommunicated." A thirteenth-century document, the sermons of the monk Grigorii, asserts: "Do not allow *gusli* players and *svirel'* players in your home for entertainment."[233A] An earlier document, a twelfth-century manuscript known as the *Zlatostrui* [a term usually designating sermons of St. John Chrysostom] tells us that *svireli* were played using a thin reed.[233B] Surviving *svireli* show that the tuning depended on the size of the instrument and on the spacing and number of finger holes. Guthrie's *svireli* (he called them *zhaleiki*) had three holes; instruments from Smolensk province (where later, improved types of these double *dudki* began to be made) have three finger holes, two on one side and one on the other. My own collection contains a pair of wooden *dudki* without mouthpieces, the longer one having four finger holes and the shorter only two. Other variants probably exist as well. In any case, in playing the *svirel',* the performer holds the longer pipe (or *dudka*) in his left hand and the shorter pipe in his right hand. Both produce four notes within the range of a fourth, and by over-blowing, an octave higher. On the Smolensk *svireli*, for example, the longer pipe produces the pitches as shown in musical example 7.3, or an octave higher, and the short pipe plays the pitches shown in musical example 7.4, or an octave higher.

EXAMPLE 7.3. Notes produced on the longer pipe of a *svirel'*

EXAMPLE 7.4. Notes produced on the shorter pipe of a *svirel'*

N. I. Privalov quotes the following example of the folk song "Nauchit' li te, Vaniusha" [Shall I teach thee, Vaniusha], shown in musical example 7.5, played on the improved type of *svirel'*.

EXAMPLE 7.5. "Nauchit' li te, Vaniusha" [Shall I teach thee, Vaniusha] (from Privalov)

We encounter the term *tsevnitsa* in the oldest manuscripts.[234] From this old Slavonic term are derived the Russian *tsevka* and *tsavka*, the Polish *kavka*, the Ukrainian *kuvitsa*, and *kuvichka* in Kursk province. Privalov explains this series of etymological transformations. In the last quarter of the nineteenth century a descendant of the old Slavic *tsevnitsa* was used in folk practice in Kursk province as a partner in a duet of two wind instruments. The Kursk *kuvichka* is a *tsevnitsa* with five pipes (fig. 69). Its reed pipes are graduated in length, and their lower ends are stopped. They are not fastened together; the player arranges them according to their pitches (there is an interval of one tone between each pipe) and, holding them to her lips [as in fig. 69], she blows into them, moving the *kuvichka* rapidly back and forth in time with a dance song played on several *dudki*. In Kursk province this ensemble accompanied the spring *khorovody*, in which the musicians are placed in the center of the ring.[235]

The *volynka* [bagpipe; fig. 70] is another woodwind instrument

FIG. 69. A duet with the *dudka* and *kuvichka*, in Kursk province, 1860s.

that has been in popular use from early times to the present, and that we have already seen in folk woodcuts. We find it in the hands of professional musicians in the woodcut titled "The Banquet of the Pious and the Profane," where it is used to entertain at the feast of the impious; we see it used by one of the *skomorokhi* in "*Semik* and *Maslenitsa*" (fig. 71, and see fig. 59); and we see it carried by the mouse Merry Churilko in "The Mice Bury the Cat."[235A] The artists who made the woodcuts undoubtedly depicted contemporary instruments. In an earlier, sixteenth-century illustration from Cosmas Indicopleustes, we saw an instrument akin to the *volynka* but of a more primitive construction, using two pipes and a bladder. This instrument, shown above in figure 45, was copied from the primitive German *Platerspiel* of the thirteenth century. I do not know of other, earlier Russian illustrations of the *volynka*. It is not clear when the *volynka* first appeared in Russia. Judging from written evidence, woodcuts, and certain popular sayings and proverbs, one might suggest that the *volynka* was a popular folk instrument used by the *skomorokhi* and their successors in the sixteenth century and throughout the seventeenth and eighteenth centuries.[235B] It can be found in many places: Great Russia and White Russia; Volhynia (according to the Academy of Sciences' *Dictionary of the Russian Language*, the *volynka* originated in Volhynia);[236] Moldavia (where it is called *koza* [she-goat]); the Caucasus (known there as *bliadzestviri*, after Bliadze, the local "inventor" of the *volynka*);[237] among the Chuvashes (*chuvashkii puzyr'* [bladder or bubble] as a primitive form of the *volynka*); and, of course, in Poland. The earliest specimens of the Polish bagpipe, for which the goatskin was used, including even the head and the horns (as in the *Platerspiel* type),[238] was known long ago in Germany as the *polnischer Bock* [Polish goat].[239]

FIG. 70. A Russian folk bag-pipe of the eighteenth century (from Guthrie).

Players on this instrument were known as *volynochniki* or *volynshchiki*. The body of the instrument itself was made of goat or calf skin, tightly sewn like a wineskin, fitted with a full-size *dudka*, a mouthpiece on top of the securely sewn windbag to keep it inflated, and underneath, one or two chanter pipes with holes to be fingered by the piper.[240] To be more precise, in performance, either one or both of the chanter pipes produced a continuous drone bass, like a pedal point or organ point, while the piper played the melody on the *dudka* with the finger holes. Polyphony, therefore, was the unique characteristic of the *volynka*. Another folk instrument involving the principle of a drone bass was the stringed *lira* or *relia*.

The tuning of the bagpipe varied from place to place. Mendel's music dictionary gives the following tunings of bagpipe-type instruments in medieval Germany, and these tunings can obviously be taken as examples of the pitches produced by the Russian *volynki*, or at least as suggesting the approximate musical possibilities and pitch relationships of the instrument's chanter pipes (see musical examples 7.6a–d).[241]

Among the wind instruments used in armies from ancient times, one finds *truby* [trumpets] and *surny* [shawm-like instruments], although, as we know from woodcuts, *surny* were also often used by *skomorokhi*. The *surna* (or more rarely *sur'ma* and sometimes in the plural, *surenki*) came to us long ago from the East (the Persian *zurna* was included in the Caucasian folk orchestra). The instrument had a harsh, nasal tone, and was usually made of elm wood (Ulmus pamila). The reed mouthpiece was fitted into a small brass tube which passed through a brass ring and was inserted into the wooden tube of the *surna*, which had seven finger holes on one side and one on the other. The larger *surny* were bell-shaped at the end, but smaller instruments with egg-shaped bells have also been found. Performers were called *surnachi* or *surenshchiki*. One of the first references to the *surna* as a military instrument appears in the early thirteenth century, and it was undoubtedly used in a military capacity even earlier. The Nikonian Chronicle under the year 1219 says that, from afar, the troops "beat the drums [*bubny*] and the trumpets and the *surny*"; another reference from the St. Sofia Annals, under the year 1551, says that "the ruler himself in great joy ordered military *surny* to play ["v surny igrati v ratnyia"] and to blow the trumpets."[241A] But by the mid-seventeenth century, in addition to military *surny*, we find these instruments used at the Moscow court together with trumpets and kettledrums [*litavry*]. At that time the court, as a result of exposure to Western customs, introduced the use of fanfares and musical receptions in general, with the object of making official ceremonies more imposing. Consequently the court maintained

FIG. 71. *Skomorokhi* playing the *gudok* and the bagpipes (from the woodcut "Semik and Maslenitsa," eighteenth century).

a sizable musical establishment, as we learn from Kotoshikhin's treatise *On Russia*, in which he writes: "At the Imperial Court they play on trumpets and *surenki* and beat kettledrums [*litavry*] . . . And in the tsar's residence there will be in all about one hundred trumpeters, drummers, and *surenki* players." Contemporary chronicles report that "the Sovereign paid the trumpeters and *surna* players a Novgorodian golden coin."[242]

We have already seen many illustrations of trumpets in miniatures, icons, frescoes, woodcuts, and so forth. They were used by the army, by town watchmen (see the Radziwill Chronicle and the Novgorod icon of *The Vision of Sexton Tarasii*), and by the *skomorokhi*. Like the *surna*, the trumpet was used at court, as we have seen from Kotoshikhin's book.

EXAMPLE 7.6, A–D. Bagpipe tunings (after Mendel)

In an eleventh-century source, we find references to trumpets in the hands of watchmen at fortresses and probably in cities.[243] The chronicles and other sources cited above show that the trumpet was an indispensable instrument in the military; chroniclers gauged the size of the army by the number of trumpets (the Suzdal Chronicle, under the year 1216, states: "he had seventeen banners, and forty trumpets and drums").[243A] The trumpet player was known as a *trubach, trubachei*,[244] or *trub'nik* (thus the adjective *trub'nichii*), although already in the seventeenth century the word *trubnik* had another meaning. Sometimes in official documents it signified a plumber or someone employed on waterworks, or a fireman who used a hose or a pipe, but not a musician.[245] In the court bureaucracy, however, the term *trubnik* sometimes meant not only a trumpeter but also the musical profession as a whole and everything associated with it. For example, in an inventory of Tsar Boris Godunov's armory from 1589, the *nabaty* [a large drum], *litavry* [kettledrums], *nakry* [another type of drum; see below], and trumpets are designated as "trumpeter's things" [*trubnicha rukhliad'*].[246] The trumpet, a familiar wind instrument, has a long cylindrical or conical body with openings at both ends, the narrower end being the mouthpiece and the wider end, the bell. It has no finger holes, but produces a series of overtones, up to the sixteenth partial, including several chromatic notes; the ability to obtain these notes depends on both the length of the instrument and the player's skill.

The stringed instruments used in Russian folk practice are confined to the *gusli, gudok, domra*, and balalaika. In Little Russia we also come across the *bandura* (*kobza*), the *lira* (*rylia*), the *tsimbaly*, and the *skripki* (fiddles); in White Russia we find the same instruments except, apparently, the *bandura*. Among the Russians, the *gusli*, mentioned in the oldest manuscripts, is recognized as a serious instrument, pleasing to God, which is why medieval miniaturists usually depicted King David the Psalmist with a *gusli* in his hands. The other stringed instruments, in contrast, were attributes of the *skomorokhi* and were condemned by the clergy. Of course, in the hands of *skomorokhi*, even the *gusli* came in for criticism. Stringed instruments were known in ancient times. In the *Lay of the Host of Igor*, Boian's "own magic fingers struck, and the live strings pulsed," and a twelfth-century *Zlatostrui* mentions "the strings of the *gusli*."[246A] Sometimes the term was applied to playing on any kind of stringed instrument: "Bang the drum, sound the *sopel'*, and play the strings" ["gudut struny"] reads the letter of Abbot Pamfilii to the regent of Pskov in 1505.[246B] At the same time a stringed instrument (probably the *gudok* and related instruments) was called a *smyk* and its player a *smychek* [or *smych'k*; the word refers to a bow].[247]

The simplest types of stringed folk instruments were, of course, the *gudok* and the *domra*. The first of these, the *gudok*, was an ancient Russian three-string, bowed instrument, usually with an oval, pear-shaped wooden body. In one of his illustrations, however, Olearius shows a *gudok* shaped like a violin, with indented sides, and N. I. Privalov, in his book on the instrument, mentions an eighteenth-century miniature depicting a *gudok* with a rounded body.[248] The woodcuts reproduced in figures 55 and 57–59 preserve the instrument's various forms, mostly copied from foreign specimens. The happy exception is evidently the instrument in the hands of a *skomorokh* in the drawing "*Semik* and *Maslenitsa*" (fig. 71) and in the illustrations from Adam Olearius's *Travels*, which provide the oldest pictures of the Russian *gudok* used by *skomorokhi* in the mid-seventeenth century. Figures 72–74 provide additional examples of the instrument; they are taken from a portrait of one of the last *gudok* players, the Pskov peasant Stepan, drawn by Privalov and mentioned in his study of the *gudok* (fig. 72); from Guthrie from the late eighteenth century (fig. 73); and from a miniature from P. Ovchinnikov's manuscript anthology (fig. 74).

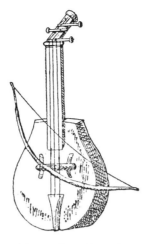

FIG. 74. The *gudok* in a fragment from an eighteenth-
century miniature, from
a manuscript anthology
from the collection of P. A.
Ovchinnikov.

FIG. 72. A *gudok* from Pskov
(nineteenth century).

FIG. 73. An eighteenth-
century *gudok* (from Guthrie).

All these illustrations confirm the instrument's primitive construction, its generally oval shape, and the required use of a bow. The tuning of the instrument remains to be investigated, and the date of its appearance in Russia is also unknown. Privalov assumes that it came to Russia in the fourteenth or fifteenth century, at a time when a few other Eastern instruments, such as the *domra, surna,* and *smyki,* found their way into Russia.[249] The *gudok* is first mentioned in written documents of the seventeenth century, but the verb *gudet'* and its derivatives *gudets, pregudnik,* and *pregudnitsa* (meaning a *skomorokh*-musician) existed earlier. For example, a sixteenth-century text from the Stoglav reads: "but when the *skomorokhi* and musicians ["gudtsy i pregudnitsy"] begin to play . . ."[249A] Even the name of the instrument itself existed earlier. A number of examples from fourteenth- and fifteenth-century documents are collected by I. I. Sreznevskii, for example: "Drinking wine [to the sounds of] the *gusli* and *skomorokh* musicians [*pregudnitsy*] and remaining ignorant of God's works."[250]

In early times, *gudok* players were on the staff of the court Poteshnaia palata, or Hall of Entertainment, and one of the last references to them in that capacity is found in documents from the final years of the reign of Peter the Great.[251] The *gudok* remained in folk usage up to the nineteenth century, and by that time it was widely known in Little Russia and in the lower [down-river] provinces. In these areas, along with the *volynka,* balalaika, and *dudka,* it accompanied the songs and dances of the *khorovod.* According to Professor D. V. Razumovskii, the highest string of the instrument was used to play a melody, and the other two strings, tuned a fifth lower, served as accompaniment. The *volynka* was used in a similar way.[252]

The word *gudok* is rarely encountered in the old glossaries, but this, of course, cannot be taken as evidence that this primitive musical instrument was not in general use, but rather that the writers and miniaturists did not consider it worthy of mention or reproduction.

On the other hand, a more complex stringed instrument, the *domra,* is mentioned in old documents such as the 1654 *Alphabet* in the Moscow Synodal Library: "As to what *musikiia* is: *Musikiia,* playing, that is, the sounding of *gusli* and *kiniry,* or lyres, and *domry,* and similar things."[252A] According to A. S. Famintsyn, we borrowed the *domra* from Asiatic peoples and it appears in russified form from the Arabic *tanbura* (instruments of a similar shape are the *dombur, dunbure, dumbra, dombra, domr,* and *domra*).[253] It was already known in the sixteenth century, judging from the description of a lute-like *pandura* made for the Veronese Alessandro Guagnini (d. 1614), a former Polish governor in Vitebsk.[253A] Adam Olearius, in describing Ivan the Terrible's mockery of Archbishop Pimen of Novgorod (1570), states, among other things, that Ivan ordered a *volynka* and other musical instruments to be hung on the deposed prelate as attributes of the *skomorokhi.*

No accurate description of the *domra* has come down to us. The instrument (almost like a tambourine) held by one of the Ladoga *skomorokhi* drawn by Olearius in his *Travels* (1634) has been accepted by Famintsyn and other scholars as a *domra,* although it is somewhat different from the ordinary *domra* used in folk practice in the nineteenth century and perhaps even to this day, for the instrument in the drawing is too large, has no fingerboard, and is played in a different manner [see fig. 41]. The reproduction of a two-string balalaika with a rounded body in Guthrie's book from 1795 (fig. 75) is much closer to our idea of a *domra.* The fingerboard has six pairs of frets, probably made of string. There are eleven round sound holes on the soundboard of the instrument, in addition to the bridge. Guthrie explains that this balalaika is a very old copy of the Russian two-string guitar.

FIG. 75. A two-string bala-laika in the form of a *domra,* late eighteenth century (from Guthrie).

FIG. 76. A three-string *domra* from Viatka province, nineteenth century.

Three-string *domry* were in widespread use in Viatka province until the end of the nineteenth century (fig. 76). They have a rather long body, a circle truncated at the bottom. Three primitive wooden pegs are inserted perpendicularly into the back of the neck, and there are seven sound holes on the soundboard: a large one in the middle and six smaller ones around it. The fingerboard has six gut frets, and the strings are also made of gut. The tuning of a Viatka *domra* in my possession is as follows: B below middle C; E (a fourth higher); and A (another fourth higher). V. V. Andreev has adopted this tuning in his improved *domra* for his Great Russian folk orchestra.

The balalaika is apparently a variant of its forerunner, the *domra,* but it is plucked with the finger or fingernail, whereas the *domra* was played with a plectrum (*piorko* in the nomenclature of the seventeenth-century *Alphabet;* see the word *bilo*).[253B] The balalaika's triangular shape seems to have become established in the eighteenth century, although judging from the drawing in Guthrie's book, round or oval instruments were also found in this period. A Kirghiz instrument, the *dumbra,* illustrates a form similarly diverse, with both oval and triangular types.[254] Triangular forms of the *domra* similar to the balalaika are also to be found among the Buriats and the Kalmucks.[255] In the eighteenth century the bala-laika seems to have supplanted the *domra* as an instrument in widespread use. It was adopted by wandering musicians who played in courtyards and public houses—the successors of the *skomorokhi*. It even began to be represented on icons in this context, for example, in the Church of the Archangel Michael in Korsun (in Simbirsk province), there was an icon from the mid-eighteenth century depicting the deeds of John the Baptist. It included an illustra-tion of an actual banquet in which a musician with a balalaika, personifying seduction, is shown.[256] We find the instrument represented in pictures of folk life from the beginning of the eighteenth century, for example, in the woodcut depicting a love scene in the presence of a lad holding a balalaika under his arm [fig. 77] or in one of the variants of the famous woodcut "The Mice Bury the Cat" [fig. 78].[257] It is also at this time that the term appears in historical documents. Balalaika players are mentioned as participants in Peter the Great's celebration of the mock wedding of the prince-pope in 1715.[258]

FIG. 77. A two-string balalaika, from an eighteenth-century woodcut.

FIG. 78. A mouse playing a two-string balalaika (from the eighteenth-century woodcut "The Mice Bury the Cat").

Although there were virtuoso performers on the balalaika and the instrument has remained in general use to the most recent times, it was not held in as much esteem in folk practice as was the *gusli* among the Great Russians or the *bandura* among the Little Russians. It is evident from the proverb "the balalaika is prose, the *gusli*, poetry" that, in comparing the two instruments, people somewhat derisively viewed the balalaika as a sort of antithesis to the more serious and elegant *gusli*.[258A] Nevertheless, because of the simplicity of its construction, the balalaika was widely used even in the southern parts of Russia, in Little Russia. The folk balalaika of the late nineteenth century varied in shape, tuning, and the number of strings. It was usually triangular [see fig. 79], but in some areas the instrument might have an oval body (in Voronezh province, for instance).[259] As a rule, the first two strings of the three-string balalaika were tuned in unison, and the third string could be tuned either a third, a fourth, or a fifth higher, as in musical examples 7.7 and 7.8. The *razlad* was tuned differently (a fourth and a fifth, or two fourths), as in musical examples 7.9 and 7.10.[259A] The four-string balalaika of Poltava province [fig. 79a] used at the end of the nineteenth century by a local player, Anton Kokar', was tuned as shown in musical example 7.11.

EXAMPLE 7.7. Normal balalaika tuning

EXAMPLE 7.8. Normal balalaika tuning

EXAMPLE 7.9. Alternative balalaika tuning

EXAMPLE 7.10. Alternative balalaika tuning

EXAMPLE 7.11. Tuning of a four-string balalaika

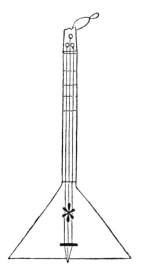

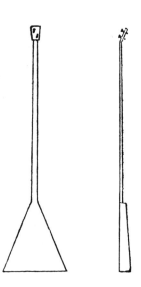

FIG. 79. The normal folk balalaika, with three strings.

FIG. 79A. A four-string balalaika from Poltava province (in Findeizen's collection).

FIG. 79B. A two-string balalaika from Arkhangel'sk province.

In the Dashkov Ethnographic Museum in Moscow, there is a two-string balalaika from Arkhangel'sk province [fig. 79b].²⁵⁹ᴮ It has a flat back and narrow sides; apparently the two strings were tuned at the interval of a fourth or a fifth, but this is not definitely known. On most of the surviving instruments, there are strings (or visible traces of them) wound around the fingerboard to serve as frets. The balalaika was made of ordinary wood (investigators do not state of what kind). According to Rovinskii, in *Russian Folk Drawings* (vol. 4, 262 n.), "in its simplest form, the balalaika consists of four small triangular boards glued together with the addition of a fretted fingerboard." Instruments from Arkhangel'sk have two small, parallel triangular boards with sides glued on. In *Dead Souls* Gogol told the tale of a balalaika made from so-called gourds, Moldavian pumpkins.[260] A consideration of V. V. Andreev's later, modernized balalaika is beyond the scope of this work.[261]

The most respected folk instrument in early times was the *gusli,* the most complex and the most refined of the Russian folk instruments. It is true that, like the other instruments, the *gusli* was censured in religious writings from the eleventh century on, but in such instances one hears the voices of ascetic extremists; thus the passage in the *Life of St. Feodosii:* "enticing us from God . . . with *gusli, sopeli,* and all kinds of games [or playing]."[261A] The term *gusli* and all the derivatives from the root verb *gusti* (*giasti, gudet'*) generally referred not to the *gusli* itself but to any instrument or instrumental performance associated with the *skomorokhi,* rebels in the eyes of the Church. From the miniatures and illuminated initials we have surveyed, we see that despite the clergy's negative attitude toward the *gusli,* the instrument was nevertheless permitted to appear in illustrations in religious books. The representation of King David is inconceivable without the *gusli,* which, as we have pointed out earlier, were modeled on real instruments in actual use, whereas other instruments were either copied or imagined from foreign models.

In most of the miniatures, the *gusli* symbolized some religious concept, but its portrayal in everyday surroundings in the fourteenth-century illuminated initials in Novgorodian psalters, missals, and gospels had no particular symbolic value; the same was true, for example, in the depiction of the watchman with a trumpet in the vignette from the fourteenth-century *aprakos* gospel (see fig. 37). And since these were religious books, the *gusli* must not only have enjoyed popularity but also respect in ancient times, comparable to the piano in our day. The instrument was played at court (for example, by the bard of the *Lay of the Host of Igor,* who played for the Kievan prince), a custom observed from the remote past until the time of the last of the *gusli* players, Fyodor Trutovskii, during the reign of Catherine the Great. The *gusli* apparently occupied an important place in the domestic life of the highest society, and it was not mentioned only in folk songs and *byliny.* One of the earliest Russian literary works is the well-known *Devgenievo deianie* [The deeds of Devgenii], a translation and elaboration of a Greek original [*Digenis akritas*]. Recent scholarly opinion places the first Russian version in the Kievan period in the twelfth to the thirteenth century, and the work reflects the tastes of that time, showing that the *gusli* was the favorite musical instrument in that milieu. The hero of the story, Devgenii, setting out to visit his sweetheart, Stratigovna, dresses himself in magnificent attire, takes his *gusli,* and goes to Stratig's court, where he plays the *gusli* and sings songs in honor of his beloved.[262] Musical accomplishments probably formed part of a young man's private education in those days.

In his historical essay *The Gusli, a Russian Folk Musical Instrument,* A. S. Famintsyn discusses in detail the relationship between the ancient Russian *gusli* and the Finnish *kantele.* He believes that the Finns borrowed their instrument from the Novgorodian *gusli,* and not the other way around. Karelia, which has preserved to this day its favorite native instrument, the *kantele,* was in early times part of Novgorodian territory. The five-string *kantele* (the oldest type, recorded in the Finnish national *byliny,* the *Kalevala*) was undoubtedly similar to the Novgorodian *gusli,* which originally also had five strings corresponding to the pentatonic scale of ancient Russian folk songs.[263] From Novgorod, the *gusli* found its way into the Kievan principality and became widely known in other Russian lands. The original type of Novgorodian *gusli,* completely analogous to the Finno-Karelian *kantele,* existed until recent times. In his *Dissertations,* Guthrie has a sketch of these five-string *gusli,* which existed in folk usage at the end of the eighteenth century [fig. 80].

Evidently the tuning of this type of *gusli* coincided with the tunings Boieldieu reported to the French scholar Fétis in the early nineteenth century [see n. 263, above]. The shape and tuning of this Great Russian *gusli* fully agree with that of the Karelo-Finnish *kantele*.

A most interesting correlation between tune, rhythm, and instrumental accompaniment characterized the ancient Finnish epic: the songs were in a five-beat measure, accompanied by a five-string instrument, the *kantele*, whose tuning duplicated the melodic content of

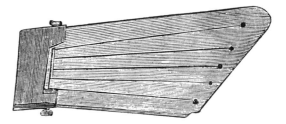

FIG. 80. A five-string *gusli* from the eighteenth century (from Guthrie).

the vocal line [fig. 81].[264] There may be a similar analogy in the case of the ancient *gusli*, for the oldest Russian folk songs use a five-note scale, and a five-beat rhythmic pattern is one of the characteristics of these songs.[265]

FIG. 81. A five-string *kantele* (Stockholm).

As noted in previous illustrations and manuscript references, the number of strings on the *gusli* gradually increased and its tuning was thus altered. In the twelfth-century *Lay of the Host of Igor*, the prophetic Boian plays on a ten-string instrument; later, in the fourteenth century, Novgorodian miniatures depict *gusli* with five and eleven strings (see fig. 31). Over time, the *gusli* was not restricted to any single type, either in terms of its shape or in the number of strings. In his book, Famintsyn describes one of the older types of this instrument, a seven-string *gusli* belonging to the Conservatory. It came from the Luzhskii district of old Novgorod province, and Famintsyn dates it to the middle, even to the first half, of the eighteenth century. A reproduction was made for its previous owner, the ninety-five-year-old peasant Trofim Anan'ev. The seven metal strings of the copy were tuned as shown in musical example 7.12.

Professor Marenich's description of the old *gusli* player's performance is quoted in Famintsyn's book: with the fingers of the left hand, the performer covered the strings not needed at the moment, while with the right hand or, rather,

EXAMPLE 7.12. Tuning of a seven-string *gusli* (from Famintsyn)

with the plectrum (the ancient *bil'tse*, the *piorko* of the glossaries) he played the remaining strings.[265A] Trofim Anan'ev was already advanced in years when he learned how to play, and the result was something like the transcription in musical example 7.13.

Instead of using the plectrum, Anan'ev put his thumb and first two fingers of his right hand together and glided them up and down across the strings at the upper end of the instrument, strumming them with his fingernails and producing the chords shown in the example. Sometimes he struck the strings with the fleshy part of his fingers. He did

EXAMPLE 7.13. Transcription of a performance on the *gusli* by Trofim Anan'ev (from Famintsyn)

not always touch the lower string, E♭ (the pedal, or as the *gusli* player called it, the *podgoloska* [literally, the under voice], but this note sounded continuously, "mitigating the sequence of pure fifths, which seemed harsh to our ears, and imparting a unique harmonic vagueness." Anan'ev always played his chords very softly and delicately.

The shape of the *gusli* varied. Guthrie's type was four-sided and to a certain degree resembled Anan'ev's, although the latter was of a more complex construction; this four-sided type was the earliest. In the Novgorodian miniatures we also find triangular and oval *gusli*. A triangular *gusli* is clearly shown in the four-teenth-century Novgorodian initials of the letters *D* and *T* (see fig. 31). The oval type appears in a twelfth-century euchologion and in the Makarii Mineia of the sixteenth century. Olearius's *Travels* contains an illustration depicting a twenty-six-string Chuvash

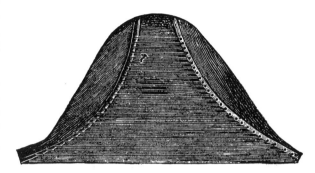

FIG. 82. A twenty-six-string *gusli* from Nizhnii Novgorod.

gusli, which, until recently, could be found in Nizhegorod province (fig. 82; and see fig. 42). The popular name for the triangular *gusli* was *zvonchatie* [ringing like a bell, clear-toned], from the metallic, resounding strings. Fyodor Artamonov and Osip Smolenskii (both d. 1918) were the last performers on this instrument. The *gusli zvonchaty* was included in the Great Russian orchestra of folk instruments.

The *gusli* gradually became the favorite musical instrument of Russian society. This was partly the result of improvements introduced in the first half of the eighteenth century, when the instrument assumed the form of a square case on legs. Its sonority was more powerful and attractive than that of the small, old-fashioned clavichord (not yet furnished with jacks and pedals), and the *gusli* thus became widely used in Russia and fashionable in society, following the example of the St. Petersburg court. The academician Jacob von Stählin described the so-called table *gusli* (on legs) as follows:

> The *gusli* or the horizontal harp, in construction, shape, and size is very much like the ordinary clavichord, except that it is not provided with tangents ([small metal blades] which were used at that time instead of hammers). The copper strings (stretched as in the ordinary clavichord and attached to iron pegs) are sometimes tuned in semitones, and are played with the fingers of both hands, touching or plucking them ...The sound of the *gusli* is very agreeable and full and at a distance it resembles the registers of a stopped organ pipe. As a consequence, the *gusli* is used in many nobles' houses for table-music, and produces the same effect as an ensemble of three or four instruments; it surpasses the best harpsichord in that it produces a more sustained and sonorous tone.[266]

The horizontal or standing *gusli* was thus played in the same way as the harp: striking and running over the strings with the fingers instead of using a plectrum and simultaneously damping the non-resonating strings. The table *gusli* became the favorite instrument of the Russian clergy and was often called the priest's *gusli* [*popovskie gusli*]. A drawing of this type of *gusli* "played by a cleric" appears in Famintsyn's book (115). With improvements to the clavichord and the piano, and with their widespread popularity, this type of *gusli* also fell out of fashion. One of the last of the *gusli* virtuosi was A. M. Vodovozov (d. 1910), who played on an instrument made in 1821.[267] Later we examine stringed instruments used in Ukraine and White Russia.

Moving to the family of percussion instruments used in Great Russian practice, we must first discuss the *buben* or *bubny* [plural form], one of the oldest Russian folk instruments of this type. It seems to have been the predecessor of the later *baraban* [a large drum], which was apparently adopted by the Russian or, more correctly, the Muscovite army toward the end of the sixteenth or the beginning of the seventeenth century, when Muscovite regiments were reorganized along Western lines and strengthened by the importation of foreign military instructors. At any rate, the *buben* was used both by the Russian *skomorokhi* and in the Slavic armies in early times, and it was even a distinguishing attribute of high-ranking leaders. It must therefore be recognized that its shape and construction were not uniform in this early period but encompassed various types of percussion instruments. The present-day *buben,* as used in symphony orchestras and military bands or by singers and in gypsy choruses, is a wooden or metal hoop several inches in diameter, over which a piece of calfskin or ass's skin is stretched; the underside is hollow. There are holes in the sides of the hoop into which metal discs threaded on iron pins are inserted to rattle when shaken. Sometimes little bells are fastened to the inside rims of the hoops. This type of *buben* was apparently developed at a later date, probably not before the eighteenth century. In ancient times the *buben* seems to have been made of small brass bowls with a skin stretched across the opening ("on it a calfskin covering," according to a description of Tsar Boris Godunov's armaments). It was beaten with a leather thong or with a short stick to which a ball of wood or leather called a *voshchaga* was fastened with a thick strap. In cavalry regiments the *bubny* were attached to the saddles. Commanders of small detachments had *bubny* of this sort, which were beaten during an attack on the enemy. Similar smaller *bubny* were called *briatsalo* in early times. We find the phrase "Play, strike the *briatsalo*" in the September Mineia from the year 1096.[267A]

In addition to the ordinary *bubny*, the Russian army at that time had others that were unusually large, and these seem to have been called *nabaty* and were, in fact, huge kettle-drums [*litavry*]. They were carried on four horses harnessed together and were played by eight drummers. As soon as "they began to beat those large and small *bubny* and blow their trumpets, while the warriors raised a stentorian shout, such an extraordinary uproar was produced that the enemy was easily thrown into confusion."[268] According to Viskovatyi, the *nabat* came to us from the Tatars;[269] in Arabic, the term *naubet* means beating the drum in surrender. *Nabaty* were used in the princely militias, each of which had its own instrument. "The Prince ordered [them] in the field to beat the *nabaty*, gathering the people," we read in the St. Sofia Annals from 1553. Boris Godunov's *nabaty* are described as follows: "Turkish *nabat,* decorated with colors; another decorated *nabat* ["nabat kadnoi pisan klintsy"], on it a calfskin covering."[270] In the old Russian army, small *bubny* occupied the position later filled by the *baraban* (large drum), as seen in the following chronicle references showing the numbers of these instruments in contemporary armies. The Troitskaia Chronicle under the year 1216 records: "Prince Iurii had thirteen banners and sixty trumpets and *bubny;* they said that Iaroslav had seventeen banners and forty trumpets and drums."[270A] The fifteenth-century *Tale of the Zadonshchina* mentions *bubny* as percussive musical instruments used by the army: "they are beating the *bubny* at Kolomna." But in subsequent military usage, apparently, the name of this percussion instrument (that is, a small cuplike shape with a brass bowl and skin stretched over it) was again changed. The ancient *briatsalo*, which had been changed to *buben*, began to be called a *tulumbas*, and it appears with this name in an inventory of Boris Godunov's equestrian equipment from the end of the sixteenth century: "Big Turkish steel *tulumbas*, gilded, engraved on the opening."[270B] The new name for the *buben* also came from the East.

It is difficult to determine the shape and size of the *buben* in the hands of court or independent *skomorokhi*, or as used by other representatives of some free profession. It is possible that in *skomorokh* use, the instrument did not change its name or shape, remaining a hoop covered with skin and embellished with jingles. This type of *buben* closely resembled the round, ceremonial *buben* of the shamans, without, of course, their exorcising purposes. We may assume that this was the type of *buben* in the hands of the impure powers tempting the Blessed Feodosii of the Kievan Monastery of the Caves in the eleventh century (in the Russian Primary Chronicle under the year 1074): "Said one of the demons . . . take the *sopeli, bubny,* and *gusli* and strike them so that Isakii can dance" [see chapter 3 above]. The instrument is mentioned as being in the hands of *skomorokhi* and women of easy morals in medieval times.[270C] In later folk woodcuts, however, for example, in the well-known early eighteenth-century woodcut "The Mice Bury the Cat," the term *buben* sometimes designates a [large] *baraban.*

The *baraban* had, by that time, been fully accepted in military practice and, because it was a percussion instrument, the populace may have called it a *buben* from force of habit. The old type of folk kettledrums, the *nakry*, which also came from the East (the Persian term is *nakare*), were similar to the *baraban* and are the same as the old *briatsalo*, except that they appear in pairs and are struck by small sticks. They are mentioned in written documents from the fifteenth century on, when they had apparently become accepted in daily life, especially at court.

In the armies it was "truby i bubny" [trumpets and drums] (in the seventeenth century, oboes and *barabany*); at court, "nakry i surny"; and trumpets, borrowed from Western court practices, were added in the seventeenth century. The Nikonian Chronicle seems to be the first to record the use of *nakry*, under the year 1453: "The Turks let out their terrible cry [prayer, *skvernaia molitva*] and began playing the *surny* and beating the *nakry* and *barabany*."[270D] In a document from about the same time, the *Khozhdenie za tri moria Afanasiia Nikitina* [The travels of Afanasii Nikitin beyond three seas] from 1466–72, there is a description of entertainments at the Persian court:[271] "One hundred camels with *nagary*, and 300 trumpeters, and 300 dancers . . . every night his palace is guarded by one hundred men in armor, twenty trumpeters, ten drummers [*10 nagar*], and ten large *bubny*,[272] each of which is played by two people." The Eastern custom was imitated in Muscovite court practice. In the St. Sofia Annals under 1553 we read, "and it was ordered to beat the *nabaty* and many *nakry*, and to play the *surny*," and in the inventory of Boris Godunov's armory we find, "seven *nakry*, big and small." Even in 1700, in the expense accounts of the tsar's palace, we see a "List of Orders by the Great Palace to the trumpeters, *nakry* players, and *surna* players."[273]

As indicated earlier, in the seventeenth century *bubny, nabaty, tulumbasy,* and *nakry* were replaced by *barabany* and *litavry*, which were introduced into military units and were then adopted by the court orchestra. One of the oldest examples, a military kettledrum dating from about 1720, is in the Music History Museum.[274] At the same time, *barabanshchiki* [drummers] appeared in the Russian army and in civilian life. There were about twenty of them in the regiments, for example, in the Olonets Dragoon Regiment in 1713.[275] The monasteries apparently employed drummers as watchmen; one of them, Ivashka Trofimov, was sent to Moscow by the Monastery of the Iversk Mother of God in Valdai in 1669.[276] From the *skomorokhi*, the *baraban* found its way into folk practice. As late as the nineteenth century in the villages of Kazan province, there was a curious instrumental combination made up of a couple of wandering musicians, one of whom played a clay wind instrument and the other a primitive wooden *baraban;* a skin was stretched across the latter, and it was beaten with crude wooden drumsticks. These musicians were quite popular and were known as *kokshaiskie* (from the village of Kokshaisk in the Tsarevokokshaisk district of Kazan province).[277]

The exact form of the old Russian percussion instrument known as *vargan* is unknown. It was probably not the same as the small metal instrument well known in folk practice today or, until recently, under various names, all of which indicate the same general type and construction: the Great Russians call it *dyrdla* or *drdla;* the Ukrainians and Bessarabians call it *dryba;* the Iakuts, *komos* or *khomuz;* the Cheremisses and Chuvashes, *kabash* or *kabas* [cf.

FIG. 83. The *vargan* (Jew's harp).

Jew's harp]. It is a small U-shaped piece of metal held in the mouth or pressed against the teeth; between the frame is a flat metal tongue (fig. 83). A jarring, tinkling sound is produced on striking this metal tongue, the pitch varying according to the shape of the mouth, which serves as a resonator.[278] It is doubtful that this is the same instrument as the old *vargan* mentioned in chronicles and written documents from the fifteenth century on, since the *vargan* of the chronicles presupposes a noisy percussion instrument, terrifying to the enemy, like the ancient Egyptian and Roman sistrum.[278A] The contemporary *vargan*, on the contrary, has a feeble sound. The old Russian *Tale of Mamai* states: "They beat the *vargany* loudly."[279] In 1453 the Nikonian Chronicle reads "they began playing the *surny* and beating the *nakry* and *barabany*," and later, under the year 1536, "many Lithuanians were killed and their standards and *vargany* captured." All this evidence suggests a type of military instrument as yet unknown to us.[279A]

Later percussion instruments include *lozhki* [spoons], which take the place of the Spanish and Italian castanets. We come across them for the first time in eighteenth-century woodcuts ("The Jesters Savos'ka and Paramoshka" and "The Bear and the Goat"; see figs. 55 and 60), and also in Guthrie's book (fig. 84). They were ordinary wooden spoons with long handles to which several rows of little jingle-bells were fastened. The bowls of the spoons were clapped together, or, with the *lozhki* held above the head, the bells were shaken. The bells were later discarded, and the *lozhki* were introduced into Andreev's Great Russian folk orchestra. In this context, two pair of *lozhki* are used, like castanets; sometimes the handles of a larger pair are thrust into the player's boot tops and he strikes them with the *lozhki* he holds in his hand. Some virtuosi obtain an interesting effect by pressing the bowl of the spoon against the mouth, which serves as a resonator; with skillful movements of the tongue when they strike the empty spoon, the performers are able to produce notes of varying pitch. *Lozhki* were and still are employed to enhance and embellish the performance of instrumental music, and they have a stimulating, even captivating, effect on the listener.[280]

The folk instruments used by the peoples of Ukraine and White Russia constitute a separate group. They were rarely, if ever, found in Great Russia, except for the improved *bandura* which was fashionable even at court in the eighteenth century; later, in the hands of expert players, a more highly developed form, the *torban,* entertained the patrons of

restaurants and taverns until the mid-nineteenth century.

The simplest type of the Ukrainian
bandura was the *kobza*. Its players were
called *kobzary,* a name they retained even
when, under the influence of the *pandura,*
the instrument was improved and began
to be known as the *bandura.* According
to D. I. Evarnitskii and other Ukrainian
researchers, the Cossacks borrowed the
kobza from Central Asia, retaining a name
closely resembling the Eastern original (in
Turkic it is called *kabyz, kobyz,* or *koboz;*
the Tatar word *kobyz* is the general term
for a musical instrument).

FIG. 84. Spoons [*lozhki*] with bells, from the
eighteenth century (from Guthrie).

We do not know the form of the Ukrainian *kobza* in the earliest times. Evarnitskii
describes it as "a well-known musical instrument, rounded, pot-bellied, about forty-two
inches long, with a small circle in the middle; it had many metal strings and an elaborate
fingerboard decorated with mother-of-pearl."[281] This description does not correspond to the
kobyz still to be found among the tribes of Central Asia and the Trans-Volga Turks. Their
kobyz remains even now a primitive bowed instrument of rough workmanship and finish,
and usually has only two horsehair strings. The body is hollowed out in the form of a ladle
with a long handle/fingerboard, and little resembles the simplest type of lute-shaped *kobza*
with a rounded body, which is a plucked instrument.[282] The Cossacks may have brought
back the word *kobza* from their raids as a general name for a musical instrument, but more
likely they borrowed the shape and construction of the *kobza* itself from their neighbors,
the more cultured Poles under whose influence, we know for certain, the *kobza-bandura*
would soon be perfected.

Be that as it may, for a long time the *kobza* was the most popular and widely used
instrument among the Zaporozhian Cossacks. They loved to dance to it, according to
Evarnitskii, and nobody could compete with them when the music continued throughout
the day. As one of the Cossack songs says:

> Hrai, hrai! Ot zakynu zaraz nohy azh za spynu
> Shchob svyt zdyvuvavsia, iakyi kozak vdavsia.

> Play, play, kick your legs behind your back
> So that the world might admire what a Cossack is like![283]

The modern *bandura* (fig. 85) has been described by N. V. Lisenko, the well-known
Ukrainian composer and folk song collector. He states that it is made from a single piece
of linden and has a flat, oval body. The upper surface of the instrument, called the *verkhniak*
(lacking in the *kobyz*) has sound holes in the form of a star or a circle (called the *golosniki*);
between these holes and the small curved band, usually of metal (*pristrunnik*), to which the
strings are attached, is a wooden bridge (*kobilka*) on which the strings rest. The wide fingerboard (*ruchka*) ends in a small head [or pegbox] into which the pegs (*kilochki*) are screwed.
The upper oval is called the *spidniak.* The number of strings varies. There can be four or six
long ones (*bunti*) stretched along the fingerboard to the pegs, and from six to thirteen, or

even more, short strings called *pristrunki*. In the days of the famous Ukrainian *kobza* player Ostap Veresai (d. 1890), the tuning of the *bandura,* according to Lisenko, was done as illustrated in musical example 7.14.[284] The player is seated when playing, and runs his right hand across the strings; there is a small metal thimble on his index finger.

This lute-shaped instrument retained the name *bandura* in Ukraine, even in its latest, Western-influenced development. Its head was extended by the addition of a second, smaller, head, an extension of the fingerboard which made it look like the Western archlute

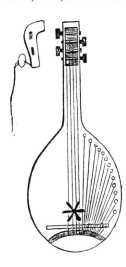

(the *arfaliutnia* of the old glossaries) or theorbo; in Poland, it was called a *pandura,* in Ukraine, a *panskaia bandura* [Polish *bandura*], and in Great Russia, a *torban.* Figure 86 shows how the instrument was constructed, with its long, egg-shaped body. Musical example 7.15 shows the tuning of the more elaborate urban *torban.*[285] The number of strings and their tuning undoubtedly varied depending on the ability of the performer, who retuned them in other major and minor scales.

The history of the *kobza-bandura* and of other Ukrainian musical instruments has not yet been sufficiently elucidated. Among the Slavonic groups, the Little Russians are probably the most devoted to singing and the most musical, in the purely Italian sense. In spite of their almost continuous political subordination, they have preserved their love of liberty and a highly developed love for their native land in the broad sense of the term, not just the boundaries of their own district or province. In this they surpass the Great Russians and White Russians, and they have preserved a certain individuality in their musical creativity, unlike their western and northern neighbors.

FIG. 85. The Ukrainian *bandura.*

Although alien to the Ukrainian spirit, the eighteenth-century historian A. Rigel'man has done justice to their musicality and its varied manifestations in their national life. "These people love music and other kinds of gaiety," he wrote. "Nearly all of them dance in

EXAMPLE 7.14. Tuning of a *bandura* [the lower notes, in bass clef, are produced by the *bunti;* the higher notes, in treble clef, are produced by the *pristrunki*]

the Polish manner and still more in their own Circassian way. They have many good musicians. They mostly play the violin, double bass, *tsimbaly, gusli, bandura,* lute, and trumpet; in the villages they also have the violin, the *kobza* (a sort of *bandura*), and the *dudka;* and in Lithuania, the *volynka.* They lead trained bears through the towns to the sound of the trumpet. All Ukrainians are good singers and have a strong inclination for various forms of knowledge."[286]

Fig. 86. The Polish *bandura.*

The same author draws a picture of the heedless debauchery of the Cossacks of the Zaporozhian Sich on their return laden with booty. "The Cossacks . . . assembled in a gang, seized everything they came across . . . then returned from a successful raid. On their return to the Sich, they divided the booty and celebrated the occasion like conquerors, with no small rejoicing, walking about the streets, shouting and proclaiming their bravery; behind them they carried in buckets and kettles honey, wine, and a concoction of wine and honey. Some were followed by an enormous band of musicians and schoolboys singing . . . Others

Example 7.15. Tuning of a *torban* (the strings attached to the smaller head (*malaia golovnia*) are wrapped with wire; those attached to the large head (*bol'shaia golovnia*) are of gut; and the *pristrunki* are made of metal)

drank to such excess that they were heavily in debt for liquor, music, and singers."[287] Gogol's *Taras Bulba* has familiarized us with this picture.

The *kobza-bandura* was the Cossacks' favorite musical instrument. The essential part this instrument played in their social life, along with *gorilka* (corn brandy), is illustrated in the extremely popular oil painting, "The Cossack Mamai" (fig. 87), which one might have found in a landowner's manor or in a peasant's hut. Many copies of this picture are now in museum collections in Kiev, Ekaterinoslav, Odessa, Kherson, and other cities. All these are copies or variants of the original, skillful and witty pictures of the adventures of the popular national hero, Mamai, the Cossack bandit.

FIG. 87. A typical image of the Ukrainian "Cossack Mamai," with a *kobza*.

In these pictures the Cossack Mamai is portrayed as a favorite type among Ukrainians. The original Mamai, a historical figure of the first half of the eighteenth century, was a Zaporozhian Cossack, a highwayman executed around 1750. After his death another Cossack, Andrei Kharchenko, took the name Mamai and continued to fight the Cossacks' natural enemies. He, in his turn, seems to have been executed around 1758. Mamai is not a surname but a nickname, meaning a wanderer, a free son of the steppe who retained a Cossack's freedom of action. The Ukrainian expression "to go or stumble on Mamai" means "to follow your nose, to be free." Mamai's closest friends (always depicted in paintings, as were the enemies he pursued) were his horse, his tobacco pipe, and his *bandura* (he calls them his *druzhina virnaia,* that is, his wife). At his death Mamai considers how to dispose of his beloved *bandura:*

> My golden, ornate *bandura,*
> My faithful companion
> Where should I hide you:
> Should I lay you in a grave,
> Should I drown you,
> Should I set you free as ashes in the wind?
> The wind strums your golden strings,
> It will play and sing for you,

And folks will remember the poor Cossack.
(Communicated by D. I. Evarnitskii)

One of the earliest Mamai paintings is in the Kiev Museum. The most important element of the painting is the inscription, describing in detail the significance of this Mamai and his attributes. Since the topic of Mamai has not been investigated and the numerous paintings depicting him have not been described, cited here is a long inscription on a large Mamai painting in the Kherson Museum:

> Hey, my golden *bandura*! If a young woman would dance to your music, not one *chumak* [traveling merchant] would shun his bag of money, because when I played, not one person danced. And having awaited this wedding, not one Cossack cried. A Cossack is not a true Cossack and does not wear a *sorochka* [Cossack shirt] if he does not drink, does not fight the enemy, and does not roam. Look and look, but you will not guess . . . Everyone wants to know my name, but no one can guess. Only one girl guessed it, the one who gave me a good horse. And if you name me, I will allow everything, but if you call me a merchant, I will scold you for it. Oh, when I was young, what strength I had! While fighting the Poles, my hand did not weaken and I overcame the enemy. I will not be sad to die in the steppe. I will only be sad that there is no one to bury me: the Jew shuns me and the Pole approaches only as if he were seizing a beast in the ravine.[288]

An interesting eighteenth-century *bandura* is preserved in the Music History Museum (Inventory no. 1127). It shows how highly this instrument was valued by the free Cossacks and their *baiany* [minstrels], the *kobza* players and singers who composed lyrical and historical songs and *dumy* [also a type of song or ballad]. This old instrument belonged at one time to the famous Poltava *bandura* player Mikhail Kravchenko, who appeared at the Twelfth Archaeological Congress, held in Kharkov in 1902. His *bandura* had a carving on its head representing the head of a Cossack with a forelock—a Mamai of the usual type. On the back of the instrument is the following inscription: "This *bandura* was made in 1740 by Mark Garasymovych Nydbailo, and repaired by his grandson Pavlo Pytrovich Nydbailo in 1805 on 1 October, and came into the hands of the *kobzar* Mykhail Stypanovich Kravchenko." This is one of the oldest surviving specimens of a Russian folk instrument.

A detailed account of the development of the *bandura* in Ukrainian folk composition is beyond the scope of this study. For us it is only important to note its appearance in Moscow and then in St. Petersburg at the end of the seventeenth and the beginning of the eighteenth century at court and in fashionable society. The illustration from Karion Istomin's primer engraved in 1694 for the young Tsarevich Aleksei Petrovich (see fig. 50) is interesting because it shows an ensemble of musical instruments undoubtedly used in Ukraine in the last quarter of the seventeenth century and known at the same time in Muscovy. The performers and their attire are typically Little Russian, as is the *bandura-kobza* of the simplest shape (without the *pristrunki*), and the violin, which had not yet come into general use in Muscovite society. Contemporary evidence shows that society was well acquainted with these musicians. The secretary of the Holstein embassy, F. W. von Bergholz, mentions in his diary the *bandura* players belonging to Prince Kantemir of Wallachia, Princess Cherkasskaia, and the Duchess of Mecklenburg. Of Prince Kantemir's musician, he writes (1721): "While preparations were being made for supper (in Prince Kantemir's house) we listened to a blind Cossack playing a *bandura* (*pandur*), an instrument resembling a lute but smaller and with fewer strings. He sang many apparently rather indecent songs, accompanying himself on the *bandura,* and the result was not bad."[289]

At an appropriate place we shall become more closely acquainted with the diary of the Kammerjunker Bergholz and with the court *banduristy* of the eighteenth century. The *bandura* was used by Cossacks, Little Russian singers, and poor blind singers, mainly for accompaniment but very often, given the virtuosity of the performers and their ability to improvise, for instrumental riffs of a programmatic or illustrative character in the performance of *dumy* and historical songs.[290]

In later times, with the development of the utilitarian side of life and the diminution and even disappearance of its poetic element, the *bandura* gave way to the less sonorous Little Russian *lira,* which requires no virtuosity on the part of the performer. This is the instrument of the professional blind beggar. P. Kulish, in his *Notes on Southern Rus'* (1856), mentions a professional singer who abandoned the *kobza* for the *lira,* because the latter had a fuller sound and was more suitable for use at weddings, where the noise is continuous.[290A]

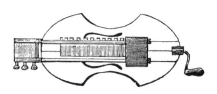

FIG. 88. A Ukrainian *lira.*

The Ukrainian *lira* was known earlier as *lyria, rylia, ryle,* and sometimes *rel',* a name derived from its turning handle, or *rel'* (fig. 88). The instrument originated in the West where, in the latter part of the Middle Ages, it was called a *Leyer* [hurdy-gurdy]; in the ninth century it was known as the *organistrum,* which had the same mechanical structure. The existence of the *lira* in old Moscow is confirmed by the diary of a Pole named Maszkiewicz, which contains a reference to playing the *lira* there in 1605–6, during the reign of the so-called First False Dmitrii.[290B] Further confirmation appears in the alphabetic glossaries, where the *lira* was identified as the biblical *kinnor.*

The instrument appears in old folk woodcuts, where it was depicted with a large wooden body with broad sides, shaped like a violin and with F-shaped sound holes on the front. A small covered box is affixed on top of the soundboard and through it pass three or more stout gut strings, wound on pegs. The two outside strings sound continuously as a drone accompaniment for the tune, which is played on the middle string. On top of the box, through which the middle string runs, there are about eleven push-button keys that change the pitch of the string. The sound is produced by the friction of a wheel with ridges (sometimes without ridges) on a shaft handle, which has a crank to the side opposite the peg box. The Western European *Leyer* or hurdy-gurdy was similarly constructed and was also used

FIG. 89. A blind Ukrainian *lira* player.

by itinerant musicians and children begging for alms [fig. 89]. In Ukraine and in White Russia the professional *lira* players who accompanied the performance of songs and ballads formed independent guilds and even had their own training schools.[291]

The most complex musical instrument in Ukraine is the *tsimbaly* [cimbalom or dulcimer], unquestionably also of foreign origin.[291A] It takes the form of a wooden box (body) with a series of metal strings which are struck with two hammers. There are examples of *tsimbaly* in ethnographic museums in St. Petersburg. This instrument, which originally came from the East, was apparently brought to Europe by gypsies and passed from them to the Jews, Little Russians, White Russians, and other Slavic peoples. The tuning of the Russian *tsimbaly* has not been established. It seems to have come into popular use at a later date and can still be found in Ukraine and White Russia.[292]

The remaining instruments used in Ukraine, the violin and the *gusli*, require no explanation. The violin arrived here from Poland and was soon simplified, as it began to be made from common and less durable material and its features became cruder, as we have seen in Istomin's *Alphabet* [see fig. 50] and in other pictures of folk life. The *gusli*, on the other hand, appears to have been imported from Russia and, most important, at a time when the instrument had been improved and was fashionable. These instruments completed the Cossacks' musical ensemble, as described by Rigel'man and other Ukrainian writers.

White Russian folk instruments —*liry*, violins, *tsimbaly*, *volynki*, and so forth—have been studied even less than Ukrainian instruments, which they closely resemble. It would be most interesting, of course, to elucidate their significance in everyday social practice. We know that the White Russian *lira* was the instrument of the professional blind beggars, who used it to accompany their singing and who formed their own guilds. Figure 90, a fragment from an engraving by Mate, shows one of these mendicants from the Kholmsk region and gives an idea of the instrument's primitive construction and method of playing it.[293]

FIG. 90. A blind Belorussian *lira* player.

Data concerning other professional musicians from White Russia are presented by the well-known ethnographer P. V. Shein.[294] He tells us that in the past, in Belorussia, they used the violin and preferably the *duda* (*volynka*) for dances. Without the *duda*, gaiety was not so gay and one's feet did not move as fast. As one White Russian song goes:[294A]

> Oi bez dudy, bez dudy,
> Khodziuts' nozhki nia tudy,

A iak dudku potsuiuts'
Sami nogi tantsuiuts'.

Oh, if there is no *duda*,
Feet won't move anywhere.
But when they hear the *duda*
Feet dance on their own.

The *duda* players were highly esteemed by the populace. There were many of them, and in some places, Minsk province, for example, old inhabitants testify that they formed close corporations, like the *lira* players. But by the 1880s, according to Shein, a *duda* player in White Russia was as rare as a *kobza* player in Little Russia. They had been supplanted by fiddlers known locally as *skomorokhi*, who were indispensable at folk festivities. Shein also published the texts of three songs by *duda* players from Minsk, Novogrudok, and the Slonimsk district of Grodno province, as well as the tune of another old number, which Rimskii-Korsakov recorded from Shein (see musical example 7.16):[295]

EXAMPLE 7.16. "Byli u bats'ki tri syny" [The old man had three sons]
    Byli u bats'ki tri syny [chorus] Ukhia!
    Use ony da Vasili, Ukhia!

    The old man had three sons, hey!
    All of them and Vasilii too, hey!

The White Russian "*skomorokh*" folk musicians are generally known as *muzyka*, and for the last forty or fifty years have looked upon the violin, which superceded the *duda*, as their instrument. A violinist-*skomorokh* answered the first call to appear at a festivity without any preliminary bargaining, for he was confident that his art would be sufficiently rewarded. When playing for dances, these later White Russian *skomorokhi* also supplied a tuneful vocal accompaniment by singing short songs. These songs often consisted of only four verses, or even just two, and at times their subject matter was far from proper, but they were distinguished by humor and were connected to everyday life. White Russians called these little songs *pripevki* and the audience, captivated by the violinist's animation and the general mood of gaiety, freely repeated after the *muzyka* a refrain that pleased them. Shein has included a number of these Belorussian *pripevki* in his collection.[296]

Returning to the Great Russian musical instruments we have discussed, we must emphasize that most of them disappeared from folk life as a result of actions by ecclesiastical and civil authorities. This is confirmed by police actions in the mid-seventeenth century. According to Olearius, in about 1649 there was a house-to-house collection of all musical instruments in Moscow. The instruments were loaded into five carts, taken to the

Moscow River, and burned.[296A] This was in Moscow, and in the same year Tsar Aleksei Mikhailovich issued stern edicts to provincial officials, such as the following, to the bailiff of the Verkhotur'e district in Siberia: "And when *domry, surny, gudki, gusli,* and masks and when all such honking, devilish instruments turn up, they should be taken out and broken and these diabolical playthings should be burned."[296B] In the face of such measures, it is no wonder that no seventeenth-century folk instruments have come down to us.

8. Music in Ancient Moscow (Fifteenth and Sixteenth Centuries)

W e have few definite facts and sources concerning music at court and in Muscovite society for the whole early period during which the Muscovite state began to take shape and grow, gradually absorbing the appanage principalities and free cities. The written documents we have examined concerning church-musical practice are, to a certain degree, an exception to this statement. Other kinds of documents have not yet been studied to the extent that we might determine their original setting; an example is the *Zadonshchina*, which sings praises to Dmitrii Donskoi's exploits (see the miniatures discussed previously). Surviving copies of this work testify to the undoubted influence of, and even borrowings from, the *Lay of the Host of Igor.* The *Zadonshchina*, for example, preserves the memory of "the eloquent boyar and expert singer in Kiev," that is, the bard of the *Igor Tale.*[296C] Although in general the *Zadonshchina* is undoubtedly a literary document, some details show characteristics of folk song, for example, in the following lines:[296D]

> O skylark, bird of summer,
> fine days' delight!
> Fly up beneath the blue heavens,
> glance toward the strong town of Moscow,
> sing out glory to Grand Prince Dmitrii Ivanovich
> and his brother, Prince Volodimer Andreevich.

or:

> O nightingale, bird of summer,
> If only you, nightingale,
> could glorify with your song the Great Prince.

or, finally, borrowed from the bard of the Igor tale:[296E]

> What noise is that I hear, what trample,
> before the early rays of dawn?
> Prince Volodimer
> Is reforming his troops.

The *Zadonshchina* was originally an ode in praise of Mamai's conqueror and the times of the first Muscovite princes, and it was later reworked in literary form by "old Sofronii" of Riazan. Textual details such as those above suggest that it may have been performed before a princely court, like the Kievan *Lay of the Host of Igor,* which it certainly imitates.[297]

The oldest copy of this poem is dated 1470, from the time of Ivan III, a period pregnant with events pointing to a new direction in the court and social life of the consolidated Muscovite state. These new directions include the summoning of foreign experts to Moscow in 1490, among them an organist, the Augustinian friar Johann [or Giovanni] Salvatore, who in Moscow was renamed Ivan Spasitel' [a literal translation of the name]. This is significant, for it indicates that despite all the teachings by ecclesiastical figures, foreign wiles had long before penetrated the princely palaces. The appearance of an organist in Moscow coincided with other important events. The Muscovite court was reorganized on new and more sumptuous lines borrowed from abroad, including the establishment of a special cappella for the grand prince, leading to the institution of the sovereign singers.

The new foreign trends manifested during Ivan III's reign resulted from circumstances that were quite important in early Muscovite life. Contacts with foreign governments from the West as well as the East, whether political, mercantile, or even as a result of religious pilgrimages, found a quick response in the Muscovite state. In this period Moscow opened relationships with Italy, the German Empire (or, more correctly, Austria), and Denmark; in the South and East with Khiva, Bukhara, and Turkey; and even the Iverian (Georgian) ruler Aleksandr asked for Ivan III's protection. In the 1470s Afanasii Nikitin of Tver made his famous trip to India, which, as we have seen, left its traces on Muscovite court life. It was also at this time that the construction of magnificent buildings in Moscow was begun. These buildings, including the Cathedral of the Dormition, were built by the renowned Aristotle Fioravanti from Bologna, who was brought to Russia by the Muscovite ambassador to Venice, Semyon Tolbuzin, the first Russian emissary sent abroad.

An immediate consequence of these relations with the West was Ivan III's marriage to the Greek princess Sofia Paleologue, who lived in Venice and was regarded as the heir to the Byzantine emperors. She arrived in Moscow in November 1472, when the wedding took place.

Around this time the notion began to take hold in Moscow that Byzantium, which had been subjugated by the Turks, was to be restored and reincarnated in Russia. At the same time, however, older Muscovites became firmly convinced that, from that time on, the long-cherished Russian way of life was altered. During the reign of Sofia's son, Vasilii, a Russian man named Bersen told Maxim the Greek: "Since the mother of our great sovereign [Vasilii] arrived here, our country got mixed up." He also added: "The Grand Prince has changed our customs."[297A]

Undoubtedly the ceremony and pomp of the Byzantine emperors' court life was more or less taken over by the Muscovite court. An ivory throne with carvings in the Greek style, for example, appeared in the princely palaces; it was decorated with images of Apollo playing his lyre, a boy with a small ivory horn, a hunting scene in which one of the hunters blows a horn, and the expulsion, at spear point, of a musician holding another Greek lyre.[298] Afterward, a special type of regalia called *barmy* [a robe decorated with precious stones] was executed for the court. Among its decorative elements was a scene showing King David playing a harp and several musicians with Western European instruments: zither, lute, a bowed rebab, three kinds of trumpets, small kettledrums, and a tambourine.[299] But for us the arrival of the organist Johann Salvatore in Moscow in 1490 is of the greatest interest. Sofia's brother brought him from Rome as one of several foreign experts.[300] Englishman Jerome Horsey's *Travels* informs us that the appearance of a Western musical instrument in Moscow was not a unique event. Horsey was sent to Moscow with gifts from the English queen Elizabeth in 1586, almost one hundred years later, during the reign of Ivan the Terrible's son, Fyodor Ivanovich. "The Emporis his sister," writes Horsey,[301] "invited to behold the same [the gifts], admired especially at the organes and virgenalls, all gilt and enambled, never seinge nor heeringe the like before, woundered and delighted at the lowd and musicall sound therof. Thousands of people resorted and steyed aboutt the pallace to heer the same. My men that plaied upon them much made of and admitted into such presence often wher myself could not com."[302] Music flourished in England during

Queen Elizabeth's reign, as is well known. We know of a series of prominent composers who created a local school and who compiled the famous collection known as the Fitzwilliam Virginal Book (mistakenly credited to the initiative of the queen herself) in 1625. This collection contains 416 pieces for the virginal (a small spinet with quills) by John Bull, William Byrd, Thomas Morley, T. Philips, John Dowland, and others. Some of their compositions were apparently played at Fyodor Ivanovich's court in Moscow.[302A]

Organs played an important role in the court ceremonies of the Byzantine emperors, and we notice also that the arrival of foreign organs at the Muscovite court was soon reflected in the work of Russian miniaturists. In the Novgorod miniatures we have seen, the Mineia and the so-called Godunov Psalter of 1594, one finds a whole series of similar illustrations whose appearance is now explained [by the presence of organs at court].

Afanasii Nikitin's account of his Indian travels, which he undertook shortly after the Greek tsarevna [Sofia] moved to Moscow, is of some interest. Afanasii, a native of the city of Tver, described his "sinful adventures across three seas" during the reign of Mikhail Borisovich, the last Grand Duke of Tver (r. 1461–85). He journeyed by way of the Volga and visited the countries beyond the Derbent, the Indian, and the Black Seas, as they were then called. This is how he describes his stay in the East:

> Bidar is the capital city of Beserman Hindustan. The city is large . . . The land is populous and the farmers are very poor, but the nobles have great power and are wealthy. They carry the nobles on a silver chair and, ahead, the horses lead in golden harnesses, as many as twenty horses, and, behind, there are three hundred riders and, on foot, five hundred soldiers, ten trumpeters, ten drummers [*nagarniki*], and ten *svirel'* players. When the sultan goes for an outing with his mother and his wife, there are ten thousand riders following and fifty thousand on foot, and two hundred elephants, all in golden armor; before them are one hundred trumpeters and one hundred dancers.

In his description of children captured by Hindustanis, Nikitin states that "they taught them to entertain," that is, to play and dance. As for the protection of a military leader, Meliktuchar, Nikitin comments that "every night his palace is guarded by one hundred men in armor, twenty trumpeters, ten drummers [*10 nagar*], and ten large *bubny,* each of which is played by two people."[303]

The luxury and the numbers of people Afanasii Nikitin describes as being involved in processions and in guarding these Eastern rulers might also have influenced the establishment of court ceremonies by the Muscovite grand princes. As we know, there was a continually increasing number of trumpeters, *nagar* (or *litavr*) players, and *nabatniki* playing huge drums ("bubny velikie") at the princely court. The increasing opulence of the Muscovite court found another outlet in the establishment of a special court cappella, whose members were known as *gosudarevy pevchie d'iaki* [the sovereign's singers or, literally, the sovereign singing clerics].

The date of the choir's establishment has not been fixed precisely. D. V. Razumovskii, who has studied this subject, is vague about its earliest period, saying that it began as a small ensemble of some thirty-five men and was gradually augmented until, by the end of the seventeenth century, it had seventy singers. The chronicles record that during Vasilii III's reign (r. 1505–33), the princely cappella was divided into ranks or stations [*stanitsy*], as it was in later times. The ensemble of thirty to thirty-five members (perhaps small from the viewpoint of a listener in the nineteenth and twentieth centuries but certainly not for the period in question!) was probably established during Ivan III's time (r. 1462–1505). Ivan was the great-grandson of Dmitrii Donskoi, and was nicknamed "the Great" by some historians, for he certainly placed early Muscovite court and social life on a new path. The idea of a rebirth of Byzantium and its courtly splendor must have been attractive. After Ivan married the Constantinopolitan princess Sofia, the famous architect Fioravanti was invited to Moscow, where in the fifteenth century he played a role analogous to that of Rastrelli in Peter's new capital in the eighteenth century.[303A] Fioravanti's newly constructed, grandiose Cathedral of the Dormition was consecrated on 12 August 1479 in the Kremlin, its main cupola rising more than 128 feet. "This church," states the chronicler, "was unusually beautiful in its majesty, its height, its brightness, and its size, and there was never such a church in Russia, except that in Vladimir."[304] Could Ivan have remained satisfied with a small choir for this grandiose new monument to church architecture? Might this not have led him to think of creating a new court ensemble suitable for this place?

In the old documents, thus far we have found the name of only one of the singers, Ivashka Kostitsa, who was sent as a commissioner to the Medinskii district to investigate a murder in the winter of 1538–39.[305] This is the earliest reference to a court singer, from the period of Ivan IV's regency. The reference indicates that Ivashka Kostitsa was a senior, respected singer and, as such, was apparently given the rank of commissioner in the early 1530s. If so, he must have begun his career as a singer in the time of Ivan III, who died in 1505. The reference also indicates that it had become customary to bestow commissionerships on court singers who had rendered special services or had reached the age of retirement. In 1551 the young Ivan IV conferred commissionerships on the singers Gavrilka Afonas'ev [or Afanas'ev], Matiushka Adamov, and Mitka Tsaryov, and after Tsaryov's death, on Tret'iak Zverintsev. It may be, however, that this custom was established only gradually, and Kostitsa's commissionership in the 1530s may support our assumption, not yet confirmed by documents, that the court choir was founded during the last quarter of the fifteenth century during the rule of Ivan III.

The singers had to take part in services at court churches and accompanied the ruler on his travels. It is known, for example, that Ivan the Terrible's singers went with him to Novgorod and to Kazan, and, as we have seen, they were constantly with him in the Aleksandrovskaia sloboda [outside Moscow] as well. They must have accompanied Ivan's grandfather, Ivan III, first at the time of his visit and later at his defeat of Novgorod.[306]

The singers were divided into groups or stations [*stanitsy*], generally with five singers in each. The stations represented a series of grades in the official hierarchy of singers, the first two being considered as senior. During church services at court, the first station was positioned to the right of the *kliros* and the second *stanitsa* was on the left.[306A] The ensemble had at its head a choir master called the *ustavshchik,* and each of the two sides [right and left] had its own leader, called a *golovshchik.* The lower [junior] stations were made up of young, inexperienced singers who were undergoing practical training. With the exception of the five singers mentioned above who were granted commissionerships and whose names thus happened to survive, we do not know the names of any of the earliest singers. Only after the Time of Troubles in the seventeenth century it is possible to establish more accurate data on the members of the tsar's choir.

Vasilii III succeeded his father, Ivan III, and carried on his rule. His reign did not leave traces in our area of interest, except that he maintained and strengthened relations with the West, especially with Poland. In this connection we should mention that the Muscovite envoy to Italy, Dmitrii Gerasimov, accompanied by the returning merchant Paul of Veng, visited Rome in September 1525. He was delighted with the Italian music he heard there, and certainly spoke of it on his return to Russia.[307] At that time in Rome the most famous composer was none other than Palestrina![307A] We soon shall see that, twenty-five years later, the polyphonic singing that had delighted Western European and Polish audiences spurred Ivan the Terrible's singers to attempt to create their own two-part singing in Moscow.

The reign of Ivan III's grandson, Ivan IV (r. 1533–84), on the other hand, left notable traces in the history of Russian music. Ivan the Terrible, the first Muscovite tsar of "all the Russias," was fond of folk songs, *skomorokh* buffoonery, and church music in almost equal measures. After having devastated Novgorod with bloody purges and abolished its franchise, he had both its experts in church music as well as its *skomorokhi* with their dancing bears sent to Moscow. From the history of the *skomorokhi,* we know that in 1571 the "merry folk" were deported from Novgorodian lands and sent to Moscow, which became the new center of their activities.[308] Prince Kurbskii had solid grounds for reproaching Ivan with collecting "*skomorokhi* who play the *dudka* and sang ungodly songs."[308A] Another contemporary eyewitness, a foreigner named Kelch, testifies that in Novgorod at the wedding of Ivan's niece, Princess Maria Vladimirovna Staritskaia, to the Danish Prince Magnus (1570), the tsar personally entertained the foreigners with bawdy songs and dances, both solo and choral, conducting them with a cane, which he used to beat the singers when they got out of rhythm.[308B]

The *skomorokhi* played an important role at Tsar Ivan's court and undoubtedly took part in his amusements and affairs. History has preserved a series of curious facts revealing the psyche of this insane and often evil despot. After the cruel reckoning with Novgorod (1570), the local archbishop Pimen, whom Ivan regarded as his personal foe, was seized and brought to Moscow. Contemporary foreign accounts speak of his being shamefully insulted by Ivan, who would have him seated on a white mare and surrounded by an escort of *skomorokhi* playing their instruments, at which time Ivan would pronounce: "Better for you to train dancing bears than to be a bishop!"[308C] At banquets in the Aleksandrovskaia sloboda, immediately after confession and prayer, Ivan often not only sang indecent songs with his private bodyguards [*oprichniki*] but sometimes even put on a buffoon's mask himself. And these wild orgies, which often ended either in fresh executions or in a new repentance, were ordinary occurrences in Moscow.

In his sober and penitent moments, Ivan probably found his clowning repugnant and devoted himself more enthusiastically to his other passion, church music, of which he was a connoisseur. He had undoubtedly studied church singing from childhood; the study of church singing was part of the education of the royal children and continued to be so even to the time of Peter the Great, which also explains the devotion to church singing of Peter's father, Tsar Aleksei. The composition of two *stikhiry* apparently may be ascribed to Ivan's better periods. One was written for the death of Metropolitan Pyotr, "Kymi pokhvalenymi venetsy ouviazemo" [To whom do we braid wreaths], and another was for the Virgin, "O velikoe miloserdie" [O, Most merciful]. They are preserved in one of the neumed manuscripts in the library of the Trinity–St. Sergius Lavra ([RGB, f. 304] no. 428), with the inscriptions "Tvorenie tsaria Ioanna despota rossiiskago" [The creation of Tsar Ivan, the Russian despot] and "Tvorenie tsarevo" [The creation of the tsar]. Both *stikhiry,* or at least the first one, may have been composed in 1547. This was a memorable year both in Ivan's life and for the city of Moscow. In that year a church council created a feast in commemoration of the memory of Pyotr, the metropolitan of Moscow and of all Russia. In the same year Ivan, at a very young age (he was born in 1530), married Anastasia Romanova, and soon thereafter a fire destroyed nearly half the city.[308D] This national disaster may have led to the composition of hymns appealing for the intercession of the canonized Muscovite saint and also of the Virgin, since the second *stikhira* was composed for the Feast of the Icon of the Vladimir Virgin (23 June). It is difficult to decide whether Ivan wrote only the texts of these *stikhiry* or whether he also composed the music (the melodies may have been notated later by one of his senior musicians, the priest Fyodor Kristianin or Ivan Nos, whom he brought in from Novgorod). Similar inscriptions in musical manuscripts, for example "Tvorenie Lva despota" [the creation of Leo the despot] and others, usually refer to the author of the literary text. But Tsar Ivan was certainly a learned and musically trained connoisseur of church singing. In any case, the two *stikhiry* published by Archimandrite Leonid reveal the author's exceptional talent.[309] Their origin cannot be doubted; they were preserved in a manuscript titled *Kniga glagolemaia Stikhirar' mesiachnyi, izhe est' Oko d'iachee* [Book called the monthly Stikhirar, which is the eye of the clerics] that belonged to Longin, a cleric at the Chudov Monastery at the beginning of the seventeenth century, that is, a close contemporary of Ivan IV. The chants are written in *kriukovaia* notation without *pomety* and the text is *razdel'norechnyi* [in which mute letters are substituted by vowels, as in the following words], with spellings like *venetsy, ouviazemo,* and *zastupenika.* Figure 91 shows a facsimile of the original notation, and musical example 8.1 is a transcription into modern notation.

Another document testifies to Tsar Ivan's knowledge of church chant. The Cathedral of St. Nicholas in the city of Pereiaslavl (in Vladimir province) was dedicated in 1564 in the presence of the tsar's family and his council. On the south wall of the vestibule [*papert*] is a large tablet of white stone with an inscription which, among other things, states that the tsar "was present at the All-Night Vigil, that he read the First Stasis [of the Prooemiac Psalm] and attended the Divine Liturgy and that, with beautiful song, together with his station [of singers] he sang at Matins and at Divine Liturgy."[310] It thus appears that there was a special station of the sovereign singers with which he sang both in his palace and in churches.

The well-known *Domostroi* (1547–50) by the Novgorodian Archpriest Sil'vestr (a contemporary of Tsar Ivan and his confessor in his youthful years) has preserved interesting evidence indicating that church singing was included in general education at that time. [The *Domostroi* was a guide to proper behavior and household management.] Sil'vestr had a school of his own, first in Novgorod and later in Moscow, in which pupils were taught church singing. In 1550 he wrote to his son: "You have seen, my child, many poor orphans and slaves and wretched people, both male and female and in Novgorod and here in Moscow, whom I fed and raised to maturity, and taught those who were worthy to read and write and to sing."[310A] Sil'vestr Medvedev's [later] school could hardly have been unique in Moscow in view of the considerable development of church singing and the art of *raspev* [chanting] which flourished there, especially in the last quarter of the sixteenth century.

Ivan summoned the Novgorodian singing masters to Moscow, where they lived in the Aleksandrovskaia sloboda. They so excelled in their art that their names are preserved in contemporary writings and by subsequent generations. From the passage already cited on the origin of the "octoechal chant in our Russian land," which is preserved in many seventeenth-century copies, we know many of the masters of Ivan's time and later, and we even know some of their works [see chapter 4, above]. Two of the singers summoned from Novgorod, Ivan Nos and the priest Fyodor Kristianin, lived in Ivan's "favorite village," the Aleksandrovskaia sloboda. There Ivan Nos composed the chants of the Triodion, the *stavrotheotokia,* and the *theotokia* of the Mineia.[310B] In Novgorod at the time lived the equally famous singer Markel, "reputed to be beardless," who, in 1555, was abbot of the Khutyn Monastery. He arranged the tunes for the Psalter and shortly thereafter,

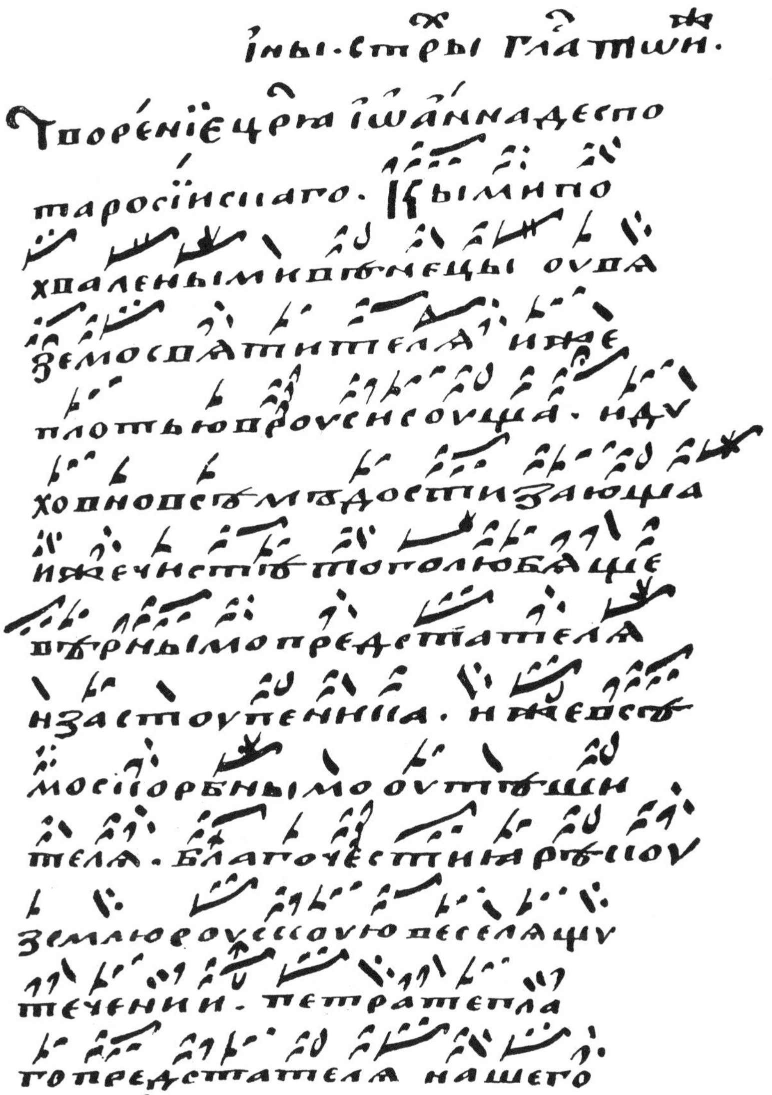

FIG. 91. The beginning of Ivan the Terrible's *stikhira* for the feast for Pyotr,
Metropolitan of Moscow, using *kriuki* (late sixteenth century; RGB, f. 304, no. 428).

in 1557, while living in a cell in the Antoniev Monastery, composed the *kanon* to Nikita,
Archbishop of Novgorod. Their teachers were the well-known Karelian singers Savva and
Vasilii Rogov, who were somewhat older. Savva taught Ivan Nos and Fyodor Kristianin,
and Vasilii, who took the monastic name Varlaam and died in 1603 as the metropolitan
of Rostov, "was a pious and wise man and was artful in *znamennyi* singing and composed
troestrochnye and *demestvennye* hymns as well."[311] Savva Rogov's third pupil was Stefan

Example 8.1. A composition by Ivan IV, "Kymi pokhvalenymi venetsy ouviazemo" [To whom do we braid wreaths]

Kymi pokhvalenymi venetsy ouviazemo sviatitelia izhe plot'iu v Rusi sushcha i dukhovno vsem
dostizaiushcha izhe chiste togo liubiashche vernyma predstatelia i zastupenika. Izhe vsemo
skorbnymo outeshitelia. Blagochesti reku zemliu Ruskuiu veseliashchu techenii, Petra teplago
predstatelia nashego i khranitelia.

To whom do we braid wreaths to honor the saint who bodily lived in Russia and with his spirit
reaching all, loved the faithful as their leader and representative. We praise the one who consoles
with virtue the whole of the Russian land, Peter, our representative and protector.

Golysh, also a well-known master who "composed many *znamennye* hymns" and who went
to various cities teaching the art of singing in the area around Usol'e and to the Stroganov
family, who at the time had settled around Perm. It is likely that he established a chapel
choir with the Stroganovs in Usol'e, where, in the second half of the seventeenth century,
[the composer and theorist] Nikolai Diletskii had contacts with the family.

The name Radilov should be added to these. He was a singer [*raspevshchik*] at the end
of the sixteenth century, also apparently a native of Novgorod, whose alleluia was performed
at the services on the Sunday of the Forefathers [before Christmas]. In the Chinovnik of
the Cathedral of St. Sophia in Novgorod, under 17 December, after the completion of the
Play of the Furnace, it was indicated that "the singers [*podiaki*] at the ambo sing . . . various
hymns to the Virgin and Radilov's alleluia."[312]

The second half of the sixteenth century thus marked a considerable advance in the
development of *znamennoe* singing. It was undoubtedly in that period that two- and three-
part singing was created, and the written documents name Vasilii Rogov, the future metropolitan Varlaam of Rostov, as one of its architects. And if, as we have seen, the sovereign
singers were rewarded with the rank of commissioner in large and wealthy monasteries—we learned of four such cases under Ivan IV—we have to realize that Vasilii Rogov's
outstanding services were so highly esteemed that he could attain the highest ranks in the
church hierarchy. Thus when, in 1589, Fyodor Ivanovich established the patriarchate, Vasilii
Rogov was elevated to the rank of metropolitan. And if it was not Vasilii Rogov himself,
then it must have been the pupils of his brother, Savva, who are listed above and who lived
with Tsar Ivan in the Aleksandrovskaia sloboda, who invented the so-called Kazan notation or signs and two-part church singing.[313] This invention was created in honor of Ivan's
conquest of the Kazan khanate (1552) and was dedicated to him in memory of that event. To
the earlier, well-established monophonic chant, the singing masters and composers added
a second, accompanying, voice and thus also created a new notation for two-part, and later
three-part, chanting. A new work was created in order to elucidate this new music, titled
Kniga glagolemaia Kokizy, sirech' kliuch k Kazanskomu znameni [Book called *Kokiza*, which
is to say the key to the Kazan notation; *kokizy* are melodic formulas collected together in
a book called a *Kokiznik*]. It contained a collection of 240 melodic patterns and 67 *fity*
[melismatic formulas]. Kazan notation consisted primarily of the *kriuki* (or *znamennyi*)
notational system, but in different combinations and with different meanings. The score
was written in two colors of ink: the lowest part in black ink; the middle part in red; and
the upper part also in black.

Figure 92 reproduces three pages from a *kokiznik* in the library of the Academy of
Sciences; two of the pages present a written introduction or explanation of the *Kliuch* [Key],
and the third page shows its notational signs.[314] The creators of Kazan notation utilized the

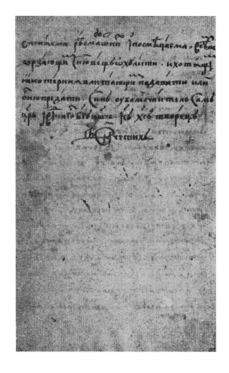

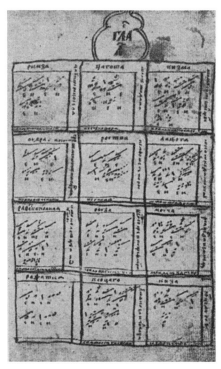

FIG. 92. Extracts from a seventeenth-century
kokiznik (BAN, 32.16.18, fols. 313–14).

basic types of signs, but whether they also preserved the meaning of those signs is uncertain, since the notation has not been studied. It did preserve the division into eight modes. The notation may have amounted mainly to combinations of various separate signs in order to denote different intervals and melodic sequences. For their two-part formulas, the inventors retained the designations used in previous singing practice; thus, for example, in Table 1 (Mode 1) for the *kokizy* in the reproduction we read [the following names of these melodic patterns]: *rymza, tsagosha, oudra . . . rafatka,* and so forth.

At about the same time as the conquest of Kazan, in 1551 the famous Stoglav Council [The Council of 100 Chapters] was assembled in Moscow "to set aright the good order of the church, the administration of the state, and the general organization of the land." The council touched on many questions concerning church music, folk song, and the *skomorokhi,* all of which demanded serious attention in Ivan the Terrible's time. Church music practice was at a high level of development and *znamennoe* singing was flourishing. We have already discussed the council's statutes dealing with folk customs and with the *skomorokhi* [in chapter 5]; they explain the views of the clergy and the higher administrative authorities concerning the creation of folk song. Russian society at that period required radical reforms, which, in turn, presented their own requirements. Instead, the Stoglav Council proved to be the starting point of our church schism by attempting to suppress the social unrest that had long foreshadowed the coming Time of Troubles.

The successors of Ivan the Terrible left no perceptible trace in the sphere of Russian art that is of interest to us. The brief reign of the so-called First False Dmitrii [r. 1605–1606], who inaugurated the Time of Troubles, was more striking in this regard. It should be mentioned, however, that under [Ivan's immediate successors], Fyodor Ivanovich and Boris Godunov, relations with the West were gradually strengthened (for example, the organ brought by the English envoy Jerome Horsey in 1586); court ceremonial, partly borrowed from Eastern potentates, was becoming more elaborate; and the *kriuki* notation had been perfected by the invention of the cinnabar signs by Novgorodian master Ivan Shaidur. There were undoubtedly contacts and influences from the West, if only from Poland, beginning in the period of the so-called First False Dmitrii.

The False Dmitrii was not, nor could he have been, the rough Cossack whom some recent historians have described. His contemporaries, even those who doubted his royal origins, knew him as a man who understood how to behave in the highest circles of Polish society, and his past revealed no traces of the "rough Cossack." His contemporary, Grevenbruch, the author of a pamphlet titled *Tragoedia Moscovitica* (Cologne, 1608), a detailed and interesting compilation of the rumors that circulated in Europe concerning Muscovite affairs, says that the murdered tsar "was a young man devoted to knowledge, particularly to the study of historical works, and that he also knew music and thereby was of service to the patriarch."[314A] This no doubt refers to church singing. The False Dmitrii's penchant for music, combined with his amazing carelessness and frivolity, were some of the causes of his downfall and could, at any rate, explain his savage reckoning and the brutal mockery of his corpse [at his death in May 1606].

All this became clear only after Dmitrii's brief reign. But during his rule a series of unprecedented and, from our point of view, very interesting events took place in Moscow. The tsarevich's entry [into the capital in 1605] was attended with typical Muscovite pomp and dramatic touches, and the people sobbed with emotion. The arrival of the tsar's bride, Marina Mniszech [the following year], however, was a different matter. At the gates of the palace a platform was erected, on which a band of trumpeters and buglers was stationed.

They had apparently arrived from Poland with Dmitrii and staged, in the words of contemporaries, "a magnificent concert."[314B] A reception such as this, so similar in spirit to festive occasions in the West, had never been seen in Moscow, of course. And the musical entertainments at the young tsar's court not only continued but increased, and the boyars grew ever more uneasy.

The tsar's wedding and Marina's coronation were accompanied by a series of balls and masquerades patterned on those at the Polish court. The palaces in the Kremlin resounded with music never before heard in Moscow. These banquets and festivities continued even on 9 May [1606], the feast of St. Nicholas the Miracle Worker, a saint the Muscovites held in special reverence. Finally, during Marina's stay at the Convent of the Ascension, the customary residence of the tsar's bride, Dmitrii entertained her with dances and *skomorokh* songs. All these events were set forth in the indictment advanced by the newly elected tsar, the two-faced Vasilii Shuiskii, after the ferocious reckoning with Dmitrii.[314C]

One more fact from Dmitrii's short reign requires clarification: some chronicles mention the "creation of hell in Moscow by Rastriga" [i.e., Dmitrii].[314D] P. O. Morozov relates this reference to a theatrical performance devised by Dmitrii, and assumes that the "hell" was part of the scenery for a morality play in a school drama, prepared by Jesuits who came with Dmitrii from Poland.[315] In actuality "hell" was a fort Dmitrii constructed for [military] maneuvers. It is described correctly and fully by a Dutch merchant, Isaac Massa, who lived in Moscow from 1601 to 1609 and whose writings were published by the Archaeographic Commission in 1874:

> He ordered a sort of engine or mobile fort on huge rollers, bearing several field pieces and completely filled with artifices. He intended it for use against the Tatars, desiring to sow fear among their horses. This device was truly ingenious. During the winter he set it up on the ice-bound [Moscow] river, and ordered a company of Polish cavalry to attack and bombard it. From the height of his palace he could observe the exercise in detail, and it seemed to him that it had succeeded according to his wishes. This machine was of very remarkable construction and entirely covered with paintings. The doors were in the shape of elephants, and the windows represented the mouths of furnaces spewing flames. Above these other apertures, serving as embrasures for small artillery pieces, were openings in the form of the heads of demons.[315A]

Massa adds that the Muscovites called it a "hellish monster" and accused Dmitrii of sorcery and of communicating with the devil, as evidenced by his ordering a representation of hell. After Dmitrii was murdered, they put a hideous mask over his face and a *dudka* either in his mouth or in his hand; they placed money by his side, with a placard reading: "Your wages as a *skomorokh*."[315B] But it did not stop with this. His mutilated body was burned along with the "hell" fort, and the ashes were shot out of a cannon, blown to the wind. Dmitrii's alleged sorcery long remained a subject of conversation. It was said that "pious people heard at midnight and even to the first cockcrow a screeching noise, *bubny* and *svireli* and other diabolical playing over his accursed corpse, Satan welcoming the arrival of his sycophant."[315C] On the other hand, the circumstances attending Dmitrii's murder perfectly paved the way for events to come. Skeptics had reason to argue that the corpse was masked for a definite purpose. They said it was not Tsar Dmitrii Ivanovich who had been killed but somebody else. The real tsar had saved himself once more and would come back.

In fact, the so-called False Dmitrii anticipated events in Moscow for the rest of the century. He had dreamed of conquering Azov and of founding a Russian empire; he wanted to establish an academy in Moscow; he planned to send young Muscovites to study abroad; he desired personally to teach them various skills, and staged maneuvers and exemplary military exercises; and he introduced masquerades and fashionable dances in the Kremlin. And for all this he was murdered and his corpse was brutalized in a beastly fashion. Each and every one of these points materialized in about one hundred years [under Peter the Great]; even the decorated Azov fortress was conquered in reality, and its conquest was celebrated in song. The ignorance of contemporary Muscovite society can be judged by the fact that even Peter, in his own lifetime, was proclaimed to be the Antichrist and a sycophant of Satan, because he, too, strove to make his capital a cultural center. Peter was successful in achieving a goal which, to Dmitrii, was but an unrealized dream.

9. Music in the Monastery. *Chashi* (Toasts). Bell Ringing. Sacred Performances (Sixteenth and Seventeenth Centuries)

The clergy's struggle against all manifestations of folk music, especially the remains of pagan rites and *skomorokh* instrumental performance, runs like a crimson thread throughout Russian society in the Middle Ages. Of course, the Church needed to find a substitute in order to satisfy to a certain extent its flock's demands for aesthetic distractions; these substitutions, however, had to be given a "soul-saving" or morally didactic character. At the same time, while preaching the Church's message of the salvation of the soul and the striving for an ascetic monastic life, it was important for the ecclesiastical hierarchy to make monastic life, and clerical life as a whole, more attractive, more colorful. And, in fact, the Church did color the rather gray and necessarily repetitive monastic ritual with more joyous and bright interludes. Some of them involved laymen, to whom the Church offered certain artistic diversions more or less closely connected with religious life.

Unfortunately it is not yet possible to paint a complete picture of the music of past monastic life. Many facts remain to be assembled and verified, even the content of the many notated books, which would shed some light on the music of old Russian church and monastic ritual. We must limit ourselves to the few facts that happen to be accessible, scattering a few crumbs to guide future researchers.

Old notated musical manuscripts and other literary documents (instructions for the ritual—Obikhodniki and Chinovniki—and various separate sources) contain many curious details of the events and customs established in monastic, religious, or public practice. Most of these sources have not yet been collected or interpreted, and only a few have so far attracted scholarly attention, such as some public events or the so-called *chashi gosudarevy* [literally, sovereign's cups, toasts honoring the ruler]. We are concerned here with the musical side of just such ordinary events, details which have since faded into the past; we are not concerned at this point with the music of the Russian Church, which has its own specialists and which continues to exist in musical and liturgical documents and in printed music books.

One of the forgotten pages of monastic life was the performance of a repentance verse known as the "Plach Adama" [Adam's lament]. Some versions of this verse, taken from manuscripts from the fifteenth through the eighteenth centuries, were published probably for the first time by P. Bezsonov in his book, *Wandering Pilgrims*. They include settings in *khomovoi* (*razdel'norechnyi*) text in musical manuscripts [texts in which mute letters are filled in by vowels]. Some of the texts are later and of a more literary character, from the Southwest, making their way into collections of *kanty* and psalms.[316] Bezsonov paid no attention to the tunes of the many Lament variants. The text was quite widespread, found in written documents and in oral transmission in various locations, as well as in books on liturgical practice and collections of religious verses for domestic use. These sources span a period of at least five hundred years, demonstrating the popularity of this particular verse in all strata of Russian society.[317]

One of the earliest copies is included in the well-known fifteenth-century collection of the St. Cyril–Belozersk Monastery, which contains many important literary documents.[318] It is inserted in the midst of *stikhiry* for the first week of Lent and has the curious title "An old poem [*starina*] for beer" [i.e., a poem to be performed at the time the beer (or mead) was passed around]. P. K. Simoni gives the text in an easy-to-read poetic form:

Plakasia Adam
pred raemo sedia:
"raiu moi, raiu,
prekrasnyi moi raiu,
mene bo radi
s"tvoren esi
i Evgy radi
zatvoreno byste.
Uzh' iaz ne vizhiu
raiskyia pishcha,
uzh iaz ne slyshiu
glasa arkhangil'skago.
Uvy mne greshnomu
i bezakonenomu!
Gospodi, gospodi ne otoverzi
mene pogiboshaago."

Adam lamented, sitting at the gate of Paradise:
"Ah Paradise, my beautiful Paradise,
Thou wert created for my sake,
And, because of Eve, thou art closed.
No longer do I behold the food of Paradise,
No longer do I hear the voice of the archangel.
Woe is me, sinner and transgressor!
Do not reject me, oh Lord, a man come to naught."

The *polnorechnyi* text of the poem may be regarded as the oldest, if not the original, form, which was later extended and varied. [A *polnorechnyi* or *pravorechnyi* text was written as it was spoken; cf *razdel'norechnyi* above.] We find a musical setting (with *kriuki* notation) in a notated manuscript collection of hymns from the first half of the sixteenth century, presently located in Moscow's Historical Museum ([GIM], Uvar. 694, fols. 285–285v) [fig. 93; musical example 9.1]).

A manuscript Obikhodnik from the time of Fyodor Ivanovich [d. 1598] shows the Lament's connection to everyday life. The Obikhodnik, which represents a collected summary of rules for the practice of the Trinity–St. Sergius and St. Cyril–Belozersk Monasteries, describes in detail the ritual of the dismissal of the monks after Vespers during *syropustnaia nedelia* (usually on Thursday of *Maslenitsa* [*syropust* is the last day of *Maslenitsa*, the Sunday before Lent, and *syropustnaia nedelia* refers to this week]).

Upon completion of Vespers, the singers on the right side begin to sing "Come to the Triune Divinity," and on the left side they sing "Let us be sent." At that time they set out the icon of the Most Pure Mother of God with the Christ Child that they have put up for the feast, the archimandrite with the clergy kiss the icon and that of the Miracle-worker, and the icon, which is on the lectern. Then [the archimandrite] bows to the singers. Then the clergy approach the icon in pairs. The brethren also [approach] in pairs. The clergy and the brethren then go to the archimandrite, bow, and the archimandrite blesses them with his hand, and [turning] from the archimandrite, they ask the singers for forgiveness, they then

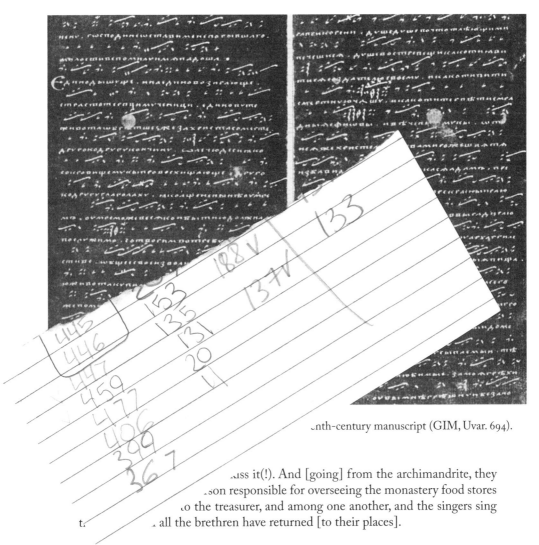

...nth-century manuscript (GIM, Uvar. 694).

...iss it(!). And [going] from the archimandrite, they ...son responsible for overseeing the monastery food stores ...o the treasurer, and among one another, and the singers sing t... ...all the brethren have returned [to their places].

After this, as all the monastic brethren quietly file in for the evening meal in pairs to the singing of the verses, the archimandrite distributes mead (in some places beer) to all the brethren, the singers, and to those who have served:

> While the mead is distributed to the brethren, the archimandrite rises and the greater deacon with the large candle, the singers stand at their places at the table, and the brethren sit. The archimandrite goes around to the clergy, then [also] to the singers, and gives a ladle of mead to each pair [of brethren]. Then to all the brethren. Standing, the singers chant the verses, and when he [the archimandrite] has gone round to all the brethren, he sits across from Varsanof'ev's place and sets a cover on a bench and distributes ladles of mead to the acolytes, and to all those who served.[319]

This repentance verse thus formed a part of the Lenten Triodion and appeared in various musical manuscripts for Lenten services. The designation of Adam's Lament in the

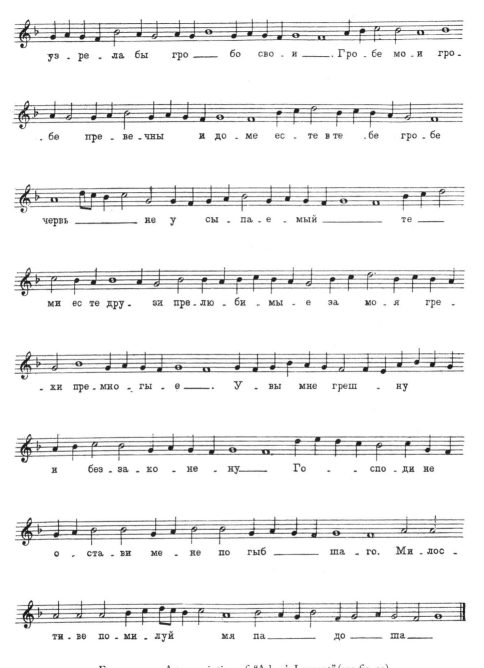

EXAMPLE 9.1. A transcription of "Adam's Lament" (see fig. 93)

St. Cyril–Belozersk manuscript as a poem "for beer" thus becomes understandable. The singers performed this Mode 6 chant in monasteries long ago during the distribution of beer or mead (the latter in Novgorod, whence this custom came to the Trinity–St. Sergius Lavra, near Moscow). Later the monastic practice of chanting this repentance poem became widespread as a domestic custom in the homes of both the clergy and the laity. The Lament can be found, as we have seen, in many collections of spiritual verses throughout the nineteenth century, and it may even be sung today in remote places. From old liturgical books we also see that the theme of Adam's Lament was the basis for the elaboration of several hymns not confined to Lent. In an eighteenth-century manuscript in my own collection, a Triodion that once belonged to the Savvin-Storozhevskii Monastery, there is on folio 9v a *stikhira* for the Sunday of Shrovetide, with the text: "Plachiu i rydaiu egda v chiuvstvo priimu" [I cry and weep as I face the eternal flame].[319A] The content is similar to Adam's Lament, and a whole series of *stikhiry* for Shrovetide (on fols. 14v–19v) has the overall heading "Izgnanie adamovo" [The expulsion of Adam]; one of them ("Sede Adam priamo raia" [Adam sat facing Paradise]), with a page heavily covered by wax, was undoubtedly performed frequently in the monastery. Musical example 9.2 is a transcription of that *stikhira*, with the note values of the original halved.

Singing appropriate *stikhiry* or *troparia* during the meal and dispensing and drinking mead or beer was a regular occurrence in monastic life. There, from the earliest times, it was customary to accompany the "Toast [literally, cup] to the Virgin" and the "Toast to the Ruler" with the chanting of *troparia*. This custom led to the musical accompaniment of other "cups," especially on ceremonial occasions. Around 1068 the Blessed Feodosii Pecherskii issued instructions concerning the blessing of meals and the drinking of toasts accompanied by *troparia*, that is, toasts in honor of the Virgin and the Grand Prince

EXAMPLE 9.2. "Adam's Lament" (a *stikhira* from an eighteenth-century Triodion)

Sede Adam priamo raia i svoiu nagotu rydaia plakashe[:] Uvy mne prelestiiu lukavoiu uveshchannu byvshu i okradenu[.] Mne prostotoiu nagu nyne zhe nedoumennu no ot raiu k tomu tvoeia sladosti ne naslazhdusia k tomu ne uzriu Gospoda i Boga moego i sozdatelia[;] v zemliu bo poidu ot neia zhe i vziat bykh[.] Milostive shchedryi vopiiuti po milui mia padshago.

Adam sat facing Paradise and, weeping because of his nakedness, lamented: Alas, though admonished, I am robbed by sly charms. My naked simplicity, now, bewildered, and I shall not rejoice in the sweetness of Paradise, and I shall not see the Lord and my God and Creator. I shall go into the dust as I was taken out of it. Gracious and Generous One, I cry unto Thee, have mercy on me, sinful as I am.

during which appropriate *troparia* or chants were sung.[320] Another of Feodosii's instructions confirms these toasts to the Virgin and to the ruler in early times. The fifteenth-century *Matitsa Zlata* [Golden queen bee] states that "no more than three toasts are to be offered at the meal with the chanting of the *troparia:* those in honor of Christ our Lord at the beginning of the meal, for the Virgin Mary at the end of the meal, and one for the ruler" (that is, *troparia* or singing accompany the three toasts).[321] Thus, already in the eleventh century, the final toast at the end of the meal was prescribed for the sovereign.

The subject of monastic toasts accompanied by singing is more interesting from a historical point of view than it might appear at first glance. Their establishment in the monasteries was most likely preceded by a similar custom in the pagan past, when a toast was offered to a pagan god, an honor subsequently transferred to the Virgin. We know that such transfers were practiced in early times to extirpate pagan rituals. In the well-known twelfth-century *Inquiry* of Kirik, addressed to Bishop Nifont of Novgorod, we read the warning "woe to those who drink to Rozhenitsa."[322] In this we see a reference to hymns to the Slavic pagan deities Rod and Rozhanitsa, which still existed at that time and perhaps even later as well. These hymns were sung at feasts and the Church had already replaced them with toasts in honor of the Virgin and Christ (Feodosii specifies the text "Slavitsia Khristos bog nash" [We glorify Christ our Lord]). This matter, of course, requires further study and corroboration. The "Cup of Christ" is not found in literary or musical documents from the sixteenth century or later, and we do not know when it was abolished.

The widespread dissemination, over time, of this custom of toasts accompanied by *troparia* and selected verses is evident from the fact that in January 1589, at the installation of Patriarch Job, "the tsar himself," after the meal, "toasted the Virgin, then [there were toasts to] Peter the Miracle Worker, to the tsar and the grand prince Fyodor Ivanovich, the tsaritsa and the grand princess Irina Fyodorovna, and then a toast honoring the newly installed Job, the patriarch of Moscow and all the Russias."[323] This happened at court, of course, not in a monastery, but in monasteries there were obligatory toasts honoring the Virgin, the patriarch, the metropolitan, the ruler, and possibly also the local father superior or authority. During such toasts, various *troparia* were sung according to the established "rite of pourings" ("chin za prilivok"): to the Virgin ("Vladychitse, priimi" [Heavenly Mother, accept or take us]), as well as the *mnogoletie* [Many years] to the religious hierarch and the ruler.

In this early period the toast honoring the ruler consisted of drinking to the health of the tsar at the end of the meal, when a special "sovereign's toast" was sung; the rite itself was both secular and religious. Originally, in addition to the toast to the tsar's health, they sang a *troparion* in Mode 1 ("Spasi, Gospodi, liudi tvoia" [Save, O Lord, thy people]), concluding with a *mnogoletie.* One of the earliest edicts "Concerning the Toast to the Tsar's Health" comes to us from the time of Ivan the Terrible. It is in a manuscript in the Tolstoi collection in the Russian Public Library [RNB], written in miniscule handwriting with the concluding *mnogoletie* notated with *kriuki.*[324] The vocal accompaniment of this rite was apparently altered and even extended at various times.[325] Thus, in a seventeenth-century Irmologii and Octoechos from the Titov collection ([RNB] no. 353), after the *troparion* to the Cross ("Spasi gospodi" [Save, O Lord]) the following were sung: a *kontakion* "Voznesyisia na krest voleiu" (You have been raised onto the cross), a *bogorodichen* [a theotokion or hymn to the Virgin] "Predstatel'nitsa strashnaia i nepostydnaia" [The appearance terrifying and unashamed], and the *mnogoletie* to Tsar Mikhail Fyodorovich. In the rite of the toast in a seventeenth-century *kriukovaia* manuscript from the collection of Prince Viazemskii, there is an indication that the *mnogoletie* to Tsar Aleksei Mikhailovich is sung by the *demestvo* [*demestvennoe penie* is a special type of chant and the *demestvennik,* a special singer; the manuscript in question is O.LXXX in the library of the Society of Friends of Old Literature, now in RNB, f. 536].[326] In another, slightly later *kriukovaia* manuscript from the seventeenth century belonging to the Novgorod Monastery of St. Anthony of Rome, an inscription reads: "when the toast to health is taking place we sing the *troparion* to the cross, "Spasi Gospodi," then "Slava" [Glory], then "Spasi blagovernago tsaria nashego Feodora" [Save our Orthodox Tsar Feodor], and after that the singers sing "Izhe neizre- chennago mudrostiiu sostavivshii" [In the unspoken wisdom having created] in Mode 8" (fol. 64).[327]

Finally, the most original and, from a musical point of view, the most extensive rite on such occasions was practiced in the time of Peter the Great. Peter was fond of all kinds of ceremonies and he probably permitted and possibly ordered the extended version of this rite. It consisted of the same Mode 1 *troparion* ("Spasi Gospodi"), the Mode 4 *kontakion* ("Voznesyisia na krest"), and the *theotokion* ("Predstatelstvo strashnoe i nepostydnoe"); the choir then sang the *mnogoletie* to the tsar in a new and curious version, apparently per- formed by two choirs alternately, as can be seen from the inscribed words "in put'" [another path] on the second variant of the *mnogoletie* at the words "neizrechennoiu mudrostiiu." The choir concluded with a resounding performance of the *stikhira* of praise in Mode 8, the sonorous Petrine *kant* "Dnes' vozgreme truba dobroglasna" [Today the sonorous trumpet thunders].[328] This rite is characteristic of Peter's time and was most likely instituted in con- nection with the founding of St. Petersburg.

Of all the events in monastic life, the arrival of the tsar on a pilgrimage was just about the busiest. Only a few monasteries were honored with visits of such highly placed digni- taries, of course, but other monasteries also had their aristocratic patrons, especially in the period of the independent principalities. In Moscow, however, where life pulsed so intensely, the visits of foreign hierarchs from the East added enormous variety, even from the musical point of view. Information on such ceremonies from earlier periods has not survived; what has survived are data from the sixteenth and seventeenth centuries, when the Muscovite state was established, and we know of customs that were introduced and reached the peak of their development at that time. This took place during the reign of the "most serene" tsar, Aleksei Mikhailovich, a great and solicitous admirer and connoisseur of magnificent church ceremonies. The traditions prevailing at that time, of course, were reflections of old monastic, ecclesiastical, and social customs. The solemn and festive processions accompa- nying the royal and patriarchal excursions were described and even illustrated by visiting foreigners, and many details have been preserved in contemporary documents published in the series *Historical Acts* and their supplements.

The preparation and organization of these receptions may be seen from Patriarch Nikon's document of 1657 addressed to the Iverskii Monastery, announcing the visit of Tsar Aleksei Mikhailovich as well as Nikon's own visit as patriarch. It contains orders to the authorities concerning all aspects of the festivities, including those portions to be sung. Announcing that the distinguished guests were due to arrive after Christmas, Nikon ordered that "the icons and all other items should be properly cleaned and by the right *klyros*, by the column, make a special wooden throne for the tsar, have it carved and gilded so that it looks especially glorious and well-made." The Muscovite court and Nikon himself admired the new Kievan polyphonic, *partesnoe* singing [from the Latin *partes,* indicat- ing part-singing or polyphony], and Nikon instructed the local prelate "to select from the brethren part-singers who are good, with beautiful voices, so that each of the parts can be filled appropriately" (that is, fully ["nabrat' khotia i slishkom"]). Furthermore, he ordered that a new tent-belfry should be built quickly so that all the bells would be installed by the time the guests arrived—bell ringing played an extremely important role in such circumstances. Nikon also ordered guards to be placed through the town near the monastic towers, saying that "the musketeers and gunners should be well selected and placed, and that the gunners should be able to shoot." He also took care to list the kinds of food and drinks that were to be prepared: "raspberry and two kinds of cherry *kvas* [a fermented drink] and apples in syrup, and other supplies and regular necessities in abundance."

The patriarch also added special character to the ceremonies with some welcoming verses, which were popular at the time. This was a novelty that carried into Petrine times and to the last quarter of the eighteenth century. Here we encounter its beginnings, as Nikon wrote:

> You should select some twelve brothers from the Iverskii Monastery who will deliver an oration [*oratsiia*] in front of the tsar and me, it should be short, religious, and laudatory; also select twelve youngsters or more, as many as you can find, and teach them an oration for the arrival of the tsar and myself, short, religious, and laudatory; also prepare an oration to be delivered at the time of the tsar's and my departure from the Iverskii Monastery; and select these youngsters carefully; just as the bishop's retinue in the service is distinguished by people carrying candles, so [those giving the orations] should be distinguished by gilded robes so that everything looks glorious; and you should also have candles which should number more than a hundred, so as to make it full of light as you welcome the Great Tsar and me.[329]

From these instructions, one can imagine the solemn ceremony surrounding the tsar's visits to monasteries and how these visits enlivened monastic life. The oratorical verses, probably sung or intoned, were the forerunners of the triumphal *kanty* of Peter the Great's time and the later welcoming *kanty* from the period of Anna Ioannovna, Elizabeth Petrovna, and Catherine II. The setting was of unusual splendor, lighted by many candles and with the sounds of polyphonic singing, and stirred by the mellow chime of the monastic bells. Bell ringing was strictly regulated, with special rules determining when and how to sound the bells. The local authorities and monastic representatives awaited the arrival of the tsar or spiritual leader at specific points, and special scouts were posted to announce the location of the guests and to signal the accompanying *perezvon* [an especially festive and elaborate sounding]. The ceremonial entrance progressed in *crescendo,* and the elaborate external splendor was accompanied by the superb singing of the brethren against the background of an exultant *perezvon* of the monastic bells. Then followed the ritual of divine services in the church, which was illuminated by hundreds of candles, and copious repasts with toasts, and so on.

The visits of the Eastern patriarchs to Moscow were also attended with magnificent and picturesque ceremonies.[329A] In the records of patriarchal excursions one finds a detailed and, regarding the musical aspects, rather curious description of the reception in Moscow in 1666 for Patriarch Paisius of Alexandria and Patriarch Macarius of Antioch. The tsar had invited them to help settle the dispute with his former favorite, Nikon, as well as to participate in a grand council. Of the numerous and verbose (but very interesting) details, here I cite a few concerning the role of the sovereign and patriarchal singers and the music they performed in the ceremonies. The first reception was marked by this imposing and elaborate setting:

"*Blagovest* (a call to service) sounded in the cathedral (obviously one of the main cathedrals in the Kremlin). Crosses were carried to the meeting; by the Earthen Fort stood Pavel, Metropolitan of the Sarsk and Podol regions, with [local] authorities and priests. The patriarchs arrived with amphora [*amfory*], with special vestments and crowns and with pastoral staffs in their arms. Metropolitan Pavel made a speech which was translated, sentence by sentence, by Archimandrite Dionysius . . . After that, both patriarchs took the life-giving cross, each had one, and blessed the people on all four sides; they then kissed the icons with which they were met. Metropolitan Pavel and all the authorities conveyed their blessing and they entered the city. The archimandrites led Paisii by the hand (also Macarius) . . . [On the next day] the patriarchs called on the tsar with gifts and dined at the Faceted Palace [in the Kremlin]; they went from the lodgings together, in sleds, preceded by their monks, and the sovereign singers sang ahead of them. Their gifts were carried by about two hundred men. And when they left . . . they were preceded by the surpliced singers of the Metropolitan of Novgorod . . . Then Divine Liturgy was conducted by archimandrites and abbots . . . The Novgorod singers were on the right side and the Krutitsa singers on the left." After the liturgy they dined again in the Faceted Palace and "after the meal there were toasts honoring the Virgin and the tsar; the tsar was toasted by both patriarchs and he raised his cup to each of the patriarchs; and at the table toasts were sung by the patriarchal singers."

Later in the patriarchs' Russian visit, during Lent of the following year, the patriarchal records note that "at Matins on Holy Saturday, the tsar attended the service with all the patriarchs (by that time a new Russian patriarch had been elected to replace the deposed Nikon); when the 'tomb of the Lord' was placed in the center of the church and singers from both choirs [*liki*] stood in the middle of the church, on the right side the Greek monks Meletii and Archimandrite Dionysii sang with others, while on the left the (Moscow) patriarchal singers sang." In July, while visiting the tsar in the village of Preobrazhenskoe, "the patriarchal singers sang the liturgy, and on the other side of the *krylos* they sang in Greek." On 1 September, at the consecration of a new icon of the Most Gracious Savior in Moscow, "the patriarchal singers sang the *troparion* "Prechistomu tvoemu obrazu poklon- iaemsia blagii" [We bow before your most immaculate image] and they sang briskly [*bodro*], and afterward they sang a *mnogoletie* to the tsar." A month earlier, the foreign patriarchs and the tsar had made a religious procession to the [representation of the River] Jordan. "At the Cathedral at the beginning [of the service] the [Russian] patriarchal singers sang the *troparia* for the consecration of the water, "Raduisia iazhe ot angela radost' priemshaia" [Rejoice as thou received joy from the angel]; along the road to the Jordan they sang these *troparia*. The last [stanzas of the] *troparia* at the Jordan were sung by the priests and the Gospel text was read by both patriarchs; both patriarchs also dipped their crosses [into the water], and sang in Greek "Spasi gospodi liudi tvoia" [Save, O Lord, thy people] twice, and on the third time it was sung in Russian. Returning from the Jordan the singers sang polyphonically ["peli . . . soglasie"] "Iako shchedr gospod'" [How generous is the Lord]. The patriarchs, while walking, kept blessing the people with holy water."[330]

The musical portion of these ceremonies was thus staged with great variety and splendor. The sovereign singers, the patriarchal singers, the singers of visiting provincial prelates (from Novgorod, Krutitsa, and possibly others), and even monastic singers (called elders) of the foreign dignitaries headed by the Greeks Meletii and Dionysii—all participated in various ways.

Generally the singers' part in all ritual services and church practices was strictly regulated by the church authorities. Special instruction books, called Chinovniki, contained full and detailed listings of church ceremonies for the whole year, with instructions for the music to be performed on every occasion. The Chinovnik of Novgorod's Cathedral of St. Sophia, published by A. Golubtsov, is an example of this kind of literary document.[331] Similar documents have been preserved from the Cathedral of the Dormition in Rostov, from the archiepiscopal house in Riazan, and one from Moscow belonging to the Moscow Synodal Library. They are all from the seventeenth century, a flourishing period for the Church in the Muscovite state.

The Chinovniki reveal the detailed religious ritual of churches and, to a certain extent, monasteries, including the role of singers and singing as well as a variety of bell-ringing practices. Everything was strictly regulated, day by day, and anyone interested in researching the musical past of Russia's monastic and public life will find rich material here, revealing the meaning of the ordering of melodies in old books with *kriuki* notation.

The fundamental tunes ([*napevy*] or *raspevy*) of the Russian Church in the sixteenth and seventeenth centuries were Muscovite and Novgorodian. Books provide a few surviving references to Bulgarian *raspev*, which was probably transferred into other chants and forgotten. There were, of course, local chant dialects (from Rostov, Iaroslav, and elsewhere) which have yet to be studied. When the Eastern patriarchs arrived in Moscow, they transmitted some melodies of the Greek (*gretskie, malogretskie*), Jerusalem, and Antioch chants. In Moscow at that time one might also encounter Kievan chant brought by the Ukrainian singers [*spevaki*] who settled in the city, which was sometimes called *soglasie* (that is, harmonic, polyphonic singing). It can hardly be doubted that the tunes, chants, and even the manner of performance which became fashionable in Moscow were also adopted in the provincial religious centers, especially in those monasteries visited by the tsar, as well as the patriarch and important secular and religious authorities from Moscow.

The Chinovniki, as noted, prescribed the music to be used in church services. The following are some of the regulations concerning the various tunes in Novgorod's Cathedral of St. Sophia in the sixteenth and seventeenth centuries:

> 7 September ([Eve of the] Birth of the Virgin). "At the Divine Liturgy, the choir on the right sings *demestvennyi* chant; the choir on the left the Novgorod polyphonic chant ["strochnaia novgorodtskaia"], and the singers [*pod"iaki*] at the ambo sing everything *demestvennyi.*"
>
> 14 September (Elevation of the Cross). "At the Divine Liturgy, the choir on the right sings *demestvennyi* chant; and on the left, Novgorod polyphonic chant ["strochnaia novgorodtskaia"]."
>
> The same for 15 September for the presentation of the Vladimir icon [of the Mother of God; see n. 149A].
>
> 25 September. "At the *deistvo* [action or procession], the singers sing the *stikhi* of the saint, and at the Divine Liturgy both choirs sing Muscovite polyphonic chant ["strochnaia moskovskaia"].
>
> 1 October (The Shroud of the Virgin). "At the Liturgy the singers sing the Obikhod to the Novgorod tune [*rospev*]."
>
> 4 October. "On this day [the Feast of] the Holy Father John, miracle worker, Archbishop of Novgorod . . . and by the orders of St. John to keep memorial services each year honoring the gracious tsars and tsaritsas . . . in all of Russia and in Great Novgorod and in all neighboring localities . . . at the Liturgy the singers on both sides sing the Moscow polyphonic chant, and those at the ambo do not sing anything. . . . At the vestment . . . and at the Liturgy they sing the Novgorod polyphonic chant."[332]

It appears, then, that at feasts of local saints, they performed the chants and order of service singing local tunes, whereas for feasts of a general, national significance they used the Muscovite tunes. Whether the two were completely independent in their music, and what their music was like, can hardly be determined at this time. The St. Sophia Chinovnik does not mention the melodies but rather their arrangements, and not the monophonic but the so-called *strochnye* arrangements. The term *strochnaia* is used because these tunes were arranged for two-, three-, and even four-part ensembles, each individual part written out in a separate line of neumes—*stroka*—above the text. This was one of the earliest and, from a theoretical point of view, poorly founded aspects of *partesnoe* singing, which originated in the sixteenth century in Southwestern churches and was soon transferred to Novgorod and Moscow. The lowest line of these arrangements, called the *demestvennik*, was copied in black ink; the next line, called the *niz* [bottom], was written in red ink; the third line, in black ink, was the *put'* [path, way]; and the fourth line, in red ink, was the *verkh* [top]. Figure 40 [in chapter 4] is a three-part *strochnaia* score written using neumes and serves as an example of this kind of attempt to harmonize the old melodies of the Russian Church.

The singers took an active role in many aspects of monastic and church life, and it is important to add that they also had a voice in monastic affairs. Thus the *ustavshchik* [leader] Gurii and the singers [*kryloshane*] of the St. Cyril–Belozersk Monastery, together with the abbot and other monastic representatives, signed a petition to Ivan the Terrible in 1583 concerning the willfulness of the elder Aleksandr.[333] The history of the Russian Church includes the unsavory role played by *golovshchik* Login from the Trinity–St. Sergius Lavra and his fight with his superior. Prominent singers could count on joining the patriarchal or sovereign singers eventually, and, in any case, many singers were quite well known in Moscow. Thus their support and influence in the capital were guaranteed to a certain extent. Moreover, the sovereign singers who, of course, had links with their provincial brethren, were often appointed as commissioners at monasteries. We have documentary evidence of this practice from the period of Ivan the Terrible (1551) to the time of Fyodor Alekseevich (1680).[334]

In addition to references to the melodies, the Novgorod Chinovnik also contains interesting regulations concerning bell ringing. We have already discussed the well-deserved reputation of Novgorod's bells and bell ringing, and here we present some of the regulations from the Novgorod Chinovnik [see also above, chapter 4]:

> 1 September. Beginning of the New Year:[334A]
>> For Prime, *blagovest* is struck on the large bell after the fourth hour of the day. Following Matins at the beginning of the first hour of the day, they strike *blagovest* at the cathedral on the large bell and alternately on the [or on a] middle-sized and small bell, as customary for the call to worship on Sunday. And at that time the bell ringers create a place for the prelate opposite the Church of Praises for the Mother of God, and the *kliuchari* above the ringers carefully watch him [the prelate].
>
> 13 September. Renovation of the Church of the Resurrection. "*Trezvon* with all [the bells] except the large one."
>
> 15 September. The day of the miracle-working icon from Vladimir. "*Trezvon* with all the bells . . . At the beginning of the first hour, *blagovest* sounds at the cathedral with the big, medium, and small bells; at the beginning of the third hour, *zvon* with all bells and gather the hierarchs with the celebrant in the sacred cell ["v krestovuiu kel'iu"]."

2 January. Forefeast of Theophany [Epiphany]. "*Zvon* of four bells and to the Royal Hours lasting all day."

5 January. "*Blagovest* at the time of the Royal Hours at the beginning of the second hour; *zvon* with five bells."

On Saturday before the beginning of Lent ["v subbotu miasopustnuiu"]: "At Vespers *blagovest* [sounds] at all times and *trezvon* with five bells."

"On Thursday evening and at Friday Matins Prime (during *syrnaia nedelia*, or *Maslenitsa*) at hours, *blagovest* with the Makar'evskii bell, and at hours, *blagovest* at the beginning of the fourth hour of the day, and at Vespers with five bells."

On Friday of the sixth week of Lent, "at hours *blagovest* [sounds] with the Makar'evskii bell; *trezvon* at Vespers with all except the large bells . . . at Compline, *blagovest* [sounds] with the Makar'evskii bell; a single *zvon* with two bells."

"On Holy Saturday, *blagovest* sounds at the end of Compline at the beginning of the fourteenth hour of the day, or as the day concludes with the Makar'evskii bell, and another *zvon* with two bells together."

On the same day, "*blagovest* sounds at Matins at four hours in the large *kamban* [see below]."

At Easter Matins: At the end of the liturgy,

> the protodeacon reads the gospel facing east and stresses those verses that the prelate exclaims. And by each exclamation of the protodea-con's gospel text, in the *kuteinik* they strike the *kandeia* [see below] individually, and in the small signal bell, and in the belfry from the smallest bell to the largest, they strike each one separately . . ." When the protodeacon "reaches the end of the gospel reading and after the exclamation, the singers sing "Slava tebe gospodi" [Glory to you, oh Lord] and the *kandeia* is struck three times, three times in the small signal bell and one clear strike in all bells.[335]

Thus each service and each holiday had its specified *zvon*, with a particular set of bells prescribed for use.

From the Novgorod Chinovnik and similar documents from other cities, we learn that in church practice until the seventeenth century, the bell was known also by the ancient designation *kamban*, a term usually designating the hand-held *bilo* (the large one, called the great [*bol'shoi*], and the small one). The *kandeia* (*kandiia*) refers to a small metal bowl with feet, which stood on the table and was struck with a hammer.

The Chinovnik also describes the duties of the bell ringers. The instructions for 1 September show that they were supervised by the sextons [*kliuchari*] and that one of the duties for the day was to erect a platform for the prelate for the "ushering in" of the new year (more about that later). Another of the bell ringers' duties was to prepare the so-called [River] Jordan for Epiphany (6 January): "The [River] Jordan is made by bell ring-ers who bring in the supplies, logs and planks, on horses belonging to the Cathedral, and the logs and planks are the Great Lord's" (Chinovnik, 82). We read further that the bell ringers "strongly" guarded the prelate's place "until his arrival, watching with the great-est apprehension" (150). The bell ringers were also closely involved in other church and monastic festivities and performances, for example, Palm Sunday and other holidays. The Chinovnik uses the term *zvontsy* not for the main bell ringers (*zvonary*) but for their assistants and pupils.

All these details reveal, if only partially, some aspects of daily life in monasteries and churches in the past. Further research may provide a more complete picture of the musical side of this life; for this, one must examine the numerous literary documents and musical manuscripts which have by no means been investigated sufficiently, even in some of our main libraries.

Now let us examine what the church offered the pious layman in exchange for the worldly, secular music it rejected, even cursed.

One encounters a variety of poetic types in old musical manuscripts: spiritual verses, penitential verses, and more tender, emotional verses [*stikhi umilyonnye*], written in Old Church Slavonic prose and in monophonic *znamennye* settings. These verses constituted the repertory of the domestic—*demestvennoe*—singing, and they were considered paraliturgical.[335A] In the seventeenth century they gradually gave way to the *kanty* and psalm-settings which came to Moscow from the South, in southern Russian [Ukrainian] and Polish versions. The earlier *stikhi* became the property of the Old Believers and, like the *skomorokhi* and secular song, retreated into the depths of the remote provinces.

A novelty in its own time, *demestvennoe* singing has its own curious document in the form of a Bogoglasnik, and in the *kanty* and psalms that grew out of it. The Bogoglasnik was a collection of spiritual and moral chants, regulated and approved by the Church. It first appeared in Cracow in 1631, and later, from the end of the eighteenth century, various versions were produced in the Pochaevskaia Lavra by the Basilians, monks of the order of St. Basil the Great.[336] These *kanty*, which gradually made their way to Moscow, were adopted by the southern Russian religious fraternities [*bratstva*], which developed them into three-part harmonized chants of a spiritual and moral character, although their texts were sometimes simple verses of congratulation or thanksgiving. The first examples of these types spurred a voluminous literature of *kanty* and psalm settings of local, Muscovite provenance. Hieromonk Simeon Polotskii (1629–1680) first introduced *kanty* and psalms into general practice. Polotskii was a well-known writer who taught Tsar Aleksei Mikhailovich's children and was a preacher in the Zaikonospasskii Monastery; he was educated at the Kiev Academy. In his *Stikhotvornaia psaltir'* [Versified Psalter] (1680) he stated that the Muscovites, "having become fond of the sweet and harmonious singing of the Polish Psalter, set poetically, became accustomed to sing those psalms knowing but few words, or none at all, obtaining only sweet spiritual entertainment."

The widespread dissemination of *kanty* as a sort of domestic "spiritual entertainment" led to abundant musical settings. One of the most talented composers of these pieces, as we shall see below, was the singer Vasilii Titov. Many *kanty* and psalm settings from the end of the seventeenth to the beginning of the eighteenth century have been preserved. Later they were supplemented by musical settings of versified psalms by [the poets] Lomonosov, Sumarokov, and Kheraskov. But by this time the *kant* as a musical genre had become old-fashioned. Our ancestors, following Western fashions, accepted the more easily accessible romances and instrumental pieces as their domestic music, genres that flourished thanks to the new foreign influences. Instead of the old spiritual *kanty*, new songs appeared, whose purpose was solely devotional.

Finding it difficult to supervise and control the laity's domestic artistic diversions, the Church undertook the creation of a series of dramatic actions or acts [*deistva*] of a moral and spiritual nature, supplementary to the divine worship and representing a kind of "spiritually supervised spectacle." Thus in church practice there appeared the Procession on the Ass as a ritual action on Palm Sunday, and the actions of the Last Judgment and the Fiery Furnace.

The Procession on the Ass was not strictly a theatrical action, although it was a festive scenic event supported by music. It was, in fact, an old Russian ceremony performed at the time of the installation of a prelate, known as *nastolovanie* [enthronement]. The ceremony was mentioned as early as the eleventh century by Metropolitan Illarion, and it took place inside a church. According to a 1652 description, at the end of the service at which the new bishop was to be installed, the patriarch and all the authorities present took off their sacred vestments, but the new bishop retained his. The *kliuchari* had prepared a carpeted seat by the choir on the left. The archpriest and protodeacon led the new bishop to the seat and had him sit; they then raised him by the arms and seated him again. This was done three times, and three times the exclamation "Ispolla eti despota" [For many years; from the Greek "Eís pollá étē, déspota"] was repeated. After this, the singers sang a *mnogoletie* for the newly installed prelate. The completion of the ceremony took place outside the church, where the new bishop blessed the assembled people. This was followed by his procession on an ass (or a horse) through the city, the blessing of the city, and the reading of prayers at the town gates. The installation of the prelate and the festal procession around the city were integral to the ceremony.[337]

A similar procession in a more imposing setting took place at the installation of a metropolitan. At Metropolitan Ioasaf's procession in 1539, he rode on an ass led by the equerry of the grand prince and his boyar. He was preceded by four *ognenniki* (men of rank who attended the enthronement of prelates and wore red costumes) with palm branches in their hands. After them came the singers of the grand prince and the metropolitan, singing *stikhi*. The metropolitan, in the midst of the people, made his way to the grand prince and returned in the same order to his own residence. Special solemnity attended the procession of Patriarch Ioasaf II (1667), as on that occasion the foreign hierarchs visiting Moscow at the time, the patriarchs of Alexandria and of Antioch and the metropolitans of Gaza and of Georgia, participated in the ceremony.

The Palm Sunday Procession was a repetition of the Procession on the Ass and was performed at a specific time in the church year. If the procession accompanying the celebration of the installation of a new prelate had a spiritual and administrative significance, then the Palm Sunday action had a certain moral and aesthetic influence on the populace, namely, to implant a sense of the chief prelate's loftiness and importance. It was thus a more elaborate ceremony. The action took place on Palm Sunday, representing a recollection and reenactment of Christ's entry into Jerusalem riding on a donkey. We find the first documented reference to the procession in 1548, in the expense books of the archiepiscopal house at the Cathedral of St. Sophia in Novgorod. By this time, undoubtedly, it was already an established custom in the Muscovite state. Its popularity may be gauged from Martin Beer's remarks in his *Moscow Chronicle;* Beer was a Lutheran pastor who visited Russia between 1600 and 1612 [the work is actually by Conrad Bussow; see the introductory notes to this chapter].[338] In 1611 military authorities prohibited the Palm Sunday procession as a consequence of the Time of Troubles. [Bussow writes:] "But since the prohibition of this festival the people had become even more incensed and were given the excuse to say that it would be better for them all to die than leave this festival uncelebrated, they were permitted to observe it, only instead of the tsar one of the Russian lords, Andrei Gundorov, was to hold the bridle of the donkey on which the patriarch was seated as far as the Jerusalem church."[338A] This ceremony was performed not only in Moscow but in other ecclesiastical-administrative centers as well. There is information indicating that it took place at different times in Novgorod, Riazan, Rostov, Astrakhan, Tobolsk, and other cities.

The Novgorod Chinovnik from the Cathedral of St. Sophia describes the performance of this procession in some detail, depicting what must have been an imposing and moving scene:

> The singers of the choir on the right, preceding the prelate, sing the verse "Imeiai prestol nebo" [With heaven as the throne]; the prelate, sitting on the ass, blesses the people on either side with the cross; . . . then follow priests and then the pussy willow (decorated and carried atop a carriage and surrounded by singers); by the willow the *podiiaki* sing "Dnes' blagodat'" [Today the grace] and "Imeiai prestol nebo." The willow is also followed by the singers and behind them come the acolytes with candles; then come deacons with censers censing the cross and the gospels and the prelate himself, going around the ass, and the authorities following after the ass, as is customary.[339]

[Conrad Bussow] was not the only one to have left a record of the Palm Sunday procession. Other foreigners visited Moscow during the seventeenth century, for example, Prince Johann of Denmark (1603), Jacques Margeret, who served under Tsar Boris and the False Dmitrii (1606), Samuel Maskiewicz (1611), Petrus Petrejus (1613), Adam Olearius (1636), and Baron Meyerberg (1661). The last two wrote accounts of their travels and appended illustrations representing the Procession on the Ass and vividly depicting the magnificent ceremony. The illustration from Meyerberg's 1662 volume is reproduced in figure 94.

According to Olearius's drawing, the procession also took place inside the Kremlin. It set out from the Spasskii Gate (later from the Place of Execution) to the pealing of all the bells. Ahead of the procession was a cart with a beautiful tree, whose branches and boughs were adorned with apples, figs, or dates. Beneath the tree stood six choirboys in white vestments with their heads uncovered; they sang "Osanna v vyshnikh" [Hosanna in the highest]. The people spread a cloth in front of the cart, which was followed by throngs of secular clergy and monks carrying willow branches and palm leaves, banners, icons, and the cross. This was followed by the patriarch riding on a caparisoned ass led by the tsar. The tsar was richly attired and, in turn, was supported and led by two of his most distinguished boyars. Children of the nobility, dressed in red, ran before the tsar and the patriarch, having strewn a path for them. In the cathedral the patriarch blessed the people, then appropriate excerpts from the gospels were read in the form of a dialogue, and the procession returned. In later versions of the procession some dramatic details were added, such as the special ceremony in which the prelate dispatched two people who conversed with the group by the tethered ass. The Palm Sunday procession was no longer held in the last years of the patriarchate (1697–1700), and when Peter I abolished the office, he also suppressed the rite, which he regarded as demeaning the tsar's dignity before the Church.

The old act of the Ushering In of the New Year [*letoprovodstvo*], which took place on 1 September, New Year's Day according to the Church calendar, was also part of the cycle of ecclesiastical and public festivities. It was staged on a public square, except if it rained on that day, and consisted of singing *stikhiry* and antiphons. A space covered with Persian carpets and with raised seats for the tsar and the patriarch was prepared at the Cathedrals of the Archangel and the Annunciation in Moscow. In the 1670s that place was even surrounded with spiked latticework painted in various colors, and the tsar's throne took the form of a cathedral with five cupolas glittering with mica and gilded eagles. We have documentation concerning this rite from the end of the fourteenth century. Like other actions in which the patriarch participated, it was discontinued in the last decade of the seventeenth century.

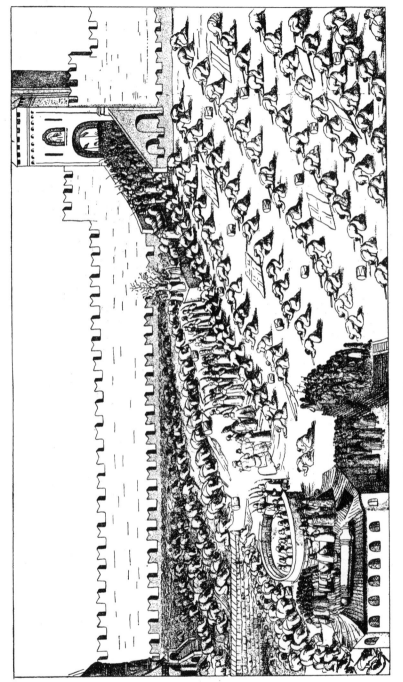

FIG. 94. The Palm Sunday Procession in Moscow, 1662 (after Meyerberg).

The Action of the Last Judgment took place on Sunday of *miasopustnaia nedelia* (before *Maslenitsa* [see above]) and served as a reminder of a future Judgment Day. This was also usually presented outside a church (in Moscow, behind the altar of the Cathedral of the Dormition). Places covered with velvet and carpets and surrounded by latticework were prepared for the tsar and the patriarch. There was a lectern in the center, on which an icon depicting the Last Judgment was placed, with a candlestick beside it. The ceremony consisted mainly of the patriarch and the protodeacon reading chapters of the Last Judgment from the gospels and the singing of *stikhiry*.

The performance of the Peshchnoe deistvo [Play of the Furnace] was incomparably more dramatic and theatrical, conveying a moral and instructive lesson. It took place on Sunday of the Holy Fathers on the Sunday before Christmas [which could fall as early as 17 December or as late as 23 December], and was supposed to remind the faithful in a dramatic way of the salvation of the three Old Testament children, Ananias, Azaria, and Misail, who were thrown into the fiery furnace for refusing to worship the Babylonian idol. In Novgorod preparations were made already on the preceding Wednesday, and the performance took place on Saturday and during the liturgy on Sunday. In Moscow's Cathedral of the Dormition it was performed at a more rapid tempo. Inside the cathedral, an enormous furnace was placed on the ambo; a specimen is preserved in the Russian Museum (figs. 95–96).[340]

FIG. 95. The furnace used in the Play of the Furnace (seventeenth century), now in the Russian Museum.

FIG. 96. The same furnace shown in figure 95, showing its entrance.

The acting roles were as follows: the three children, wearing surplices and little wreaths and with candles in their hands were accompanied by their preceptor, who also acted as stage manager; the acolytes [*pod'iaki*] with oil lamps and candles were followed by the Chaldeans, suitably attired, carrying iron tubes filled with stag-moss (Licopodium). The furnace was lighted by 150 candles. About 54 pounds of candles were needed for the performance, along with some 36 pounds of stag-moss, which was used to produce the effect of huge flames.[341]

The participants assembled in the Krestovaia Palace together with the clergy and the prelate. The prelate exclaimed, "Budi imia Gospodne blagoslovenno otnyne i do veka" [Let the name of the Lord be blessed from now and for ever and ever], the signal to proceed into the Cathedral of the Dormition accompanied by the children singing "Blagosloven esi, gospodi" [Blessed art thou, o Lord]. The same procession was repeated before Matins, when the actual performance took place. After singing the *irmos* of the sixth ode [of the Kanon], the priests intoned the seventh ode with the *stolpovyi* tune shown in musical example 9.3.[341A]

EXAMPLE 9.3."Na pole molebne" [The tyrant would place a furnace on the place of prayer]

Na pole molebne inogda muchitel' peshch' postavi na muchenie bogomudrykh.

The tyrant would place a furnace on the place of prayer to torture the god-fearing.

During that time the preceptor tied the children with a silk towel-like cloth. The Chaldeans held the ends of this cloth as they escorted the children from the altar and had them stand in front of the furnace. The following dialogue then took place:

1st Chaldean:	Are these the tsar's children?
2nd Chaldean:	Yes, the tsar's.
1st Chaldean: (to the children)	Do you see this furnace with burning flames and scorching hot?
2nd Chaldean:	This furnace is prepared to torture you.
Ananias:	We do see this furnace, but we do not fear it, as our God is in the heavens, and we worship Him, and He is powerful enough to lead us out of this furnace.
Azaria:	And He shall deliver us from your hands.
Misail:	And this furnace will not torture us, but reveal your shame.

The children were then escorted to the prelate's seat, they bowed to him and sang the verse shown in musical example 9.4.

EXAMPLE 9.4. "I potshchisia na pomoshch'" [And harken to help us]

I potshchisia na pomoshch' na nashu, iakozhe mozheshi khotiai.

And harken to help us as you can and wish.

The protodeacon then lit the children's three candles at the altar. Each child approached the prelate for his blessing, received the candle, and stood in his proper place. There followed another dialogue:

1st Chaldean:	Friend!
2nd Chaldean:	What is it?
1st Chaldean:	Are those the tsar's children?
2nd Chaldean:	Yes.
1st Chaldean:	They are not obeying our ruler's commands?
2nd Chaldean:	No.
1st Chaldean:	And they are not worshiping the golden calf?
2nd Chaldean:	No.
1st Chaldean:	Then we will cast them into the furnace.
2nd Chaldean:	And begin to burn them.

The preceptor then handed the youths, one by one, to the Chaldeans, who led them to the furnace "honorably and gently." Then the protodeacon's exclamations, "Blagosloven esi," alternated with the singing of the children in the furnace and the singers at the *klirosy*. The Chaldeans produced flames from the furnace with the stag-moss. At the exclamation "Angel gospoden' snide kupno s sushchimi" [The angel of the Lord descends with others], the sextons lowered the angel from above into the furnace. Giles Fletcher, who visited Moscow in 1588–89, tells of the extraordinary effect produced when the angel flew from the roof of the church to the children in the blazing flames. Apparently it is this episode of the angel's appearance to the three youths in the ambo that formed the subject for one of the miniature paintings in the Godunov Psalter of 1594 (fol. 568, "The prayer of the three children"). There followed another dialogue among the Chaldeans:

1st Chaldean:	Friend!
2nd Chaldean:	What is it?
1st Chaldean:	Do you see that?
2nd Chaldean:	I do.
1st Chaldean:	There were three but now there are four and the fourth is stern and very fearful, like the son of God.
2nd Chaldean:	He surely flew down and conquered us.

The chanting of hymns continued and the Chaldeans released the youths, one by one, to the following dialogue:

1st Chaldean:	Ananias! Come out of the furnace!
2nd Chaldean:	What happened? Nothing changed! They show no signs of fire or pitch or brimstone!
1st Chaldean:	We were going to burn you, but we were burned ourselves!

The three youths emerged and sang "Ispolla eti despota." The act was performed at Matins; an early meal was provided for the preceptor, the youths, the Chaldeans, and the singers, and the furnace was removed in time for the liturgy.[342]

The Play of the Furnace as described in detail here may serve as an example of a dramatized didactic religious action. We do not know when the play first appeared in Russia, but it was discontinued in the second half of the seventeenth century. Olearius, in his *Travels*, maintains that some of the actors' roles did not end with the staging of the show. In their buffoon-like Chaldean costumes, and with the permission of the clergy, the actors were set loose on the city of Moscow during the Christmas season. They were regarded as heathens, however, and, together with the mummers, had to undergo purification at Epiphany, on 6 January.

Like the Palm Sunday procession, the Play of the Furnace was one of the most popular entertainments of the Muscovite period. Its dramatic form (with sung and spoken dialogue) and its theatrical staging and effects (the burning furnace, the descent of the angel) were so remarkable that even Tsar Aleksei Mikhailovich and his wife attended it annually. Undoubtedly its theatricality aroused great interest in court circles and paved the way for the secular theater, whose early repertory, as we shall see, in its primitive literary form was not far removed from the dialogues of the Play of the Furnace.

The various actions described above, with their readings, dialogues, and musical numbers (ordinary church chant, and recitative-like passages and inserted ensembles in the Play of the Furnace), represented the showy extra-liturgical side of church practice. They came to an end while still in the preliminary stages of their dramatic evolution. The gradual extinction of these very beautiful and original manifestations of the church's musical life was, to some extent, a result of changes in Muscovite society. These changes occurred during the Time of Troubles under pressure from Polish and Western influences and the ever-increasing relations with various foreign elements. The struggle between secular powers and the church hierarchy also played a part in this process.

In church chant, too, there were also fashionable trends, which were reflected in other facets of society. The seventeenth century was the turning point in this respect. Although it is incomprehensible in our time, for centuries there had been the custom of embellishing a tune with vocal adornments of all kinds, involving the extension and curtailment of liturgical texts with all sorts of the *fafaki* and *ananeiki* with *khabuvy* that were used in the *putevoi* notation, apparently without much selectivity [see below for a description of these melodic ornaments and practices]. These practices suddenly began to be discarded. As we shall see, it was both the singers and the theorists who rebelled against them. And instead of the old chanting, the new polyphonic singing, *partesnoe penie*, was increasingly fashionable. This style, with all its excesses, was also popular, until it in turn gave way as serious church music was replaced by the frivolous, almost theatrical tunes introduced by the foreign *maestri* attached to the Russian court [in the eighteenth century].

The seventeenth century, which began by banishing secular, popular music to the remote corners of the Muscovite state, proved to be equally severe with other kinds of music, marking a turning point in the history of the ancient *kriukovoe* singing. The defects of this singing led to an arbitrary and often unnecessarily hasty correction of the liturgical texts, and included *ananeiki*, a kind of prefix often encountered in the midst of added syllables and words and sung in *razdel'norechie* texts.[343] The other defect was *khomoniia*, in which mute letters received vocal values (again, in *razdel'norechie* texts), for example, when the ending *-khom* was sung *-khomo* (e.g., instead of *sogreshikhom*, the word was sung *sogreshikhomo*, or *ne opravdakhom* sung as *ne opravdakhomo*). This also involved filling in the [partially] voiced letters ъ, ь, and ŭ with semi-vowels, which disrupted the melody; for example, the word *s"pas"* [съпасъ] was sung *sopas"* [сопасъ], the word *pozh"ru* [пожъру] was sung *pozheru* [пожеру], or *v"mene* [въ мѣнѣ] as *vo mone* [во монѣ], and so forth. Finally, the influence of Western and Polish "musical art" laid bare the necessity of a reexamination of musical manuscripts and led to the introduction of choral singing, which better reflected the new tastes of contemporary Russian society.

The prominent church singers (the sovereign and patriarchal singers) were also the composers and teachers of the new style. They received comprehensive training in schools, and their education was then completed by their practical singing experience. This explains why the first attempts at two-part singing were carried out by the singers themselves in the mid-sixteenth century. The second vocal line provided an accompaniment, a counterpoint of sorts to the fundamental, monophonic melody. An example of this is the sixteenth-century two-part setting of the chant "Na reke vavilonstei" [By the waters of Babylon] published by Smolenskii, in which the lower, bass voice sings the prescribed melody (called the *put'* or cantus firmus), while the *verkh* [top voice] sings a counterpoint to it.[344]

From a number of surviving theoretical treatises on church chant, we learn that the precentors and senior members of the profession received thorough training. One of the copies of Nikolai Diletskii's *Musikiiskaia grammatika* [Musical grammar] contains an illustration of a seventeenth-century singing school (fig. 97), showing a class of senior students (seated at the table) and boys with their teacher, who may be the renowned deacon I. Korenev, one of the authors of the treatise.[345]

FIG. 97. A Russian singing school in the seventeenth century [from Nikolai Diletskii's *Grammar* in RGB, f. 205, no. 146, published by Smolenskii].

In addition to Nikolai Diletskii, the seventeenth century boasted a whole series of music theorists, some better known than others. Even a century earlier, according to the *Stoglav,* some priests and deacons in Moscow had opened schools in which reading, writing, church singing, and "singing the Psalter and reading at the lectern" were taught. Every prominent church or monastic choir was also a school of church singing, especially for junior singers. The names of many famous masters and teachers of chanting are known, including Stefan Golysh, the brothers Savva and Vasilii Rogov, Ivan Lukoshkov [or Lukoshko], Ivan Nos, and others.

It is quite curious in this respect that during Tsar Aleksei Mikhailovich's reign (1645–76), several distinguished music theorists lived and worked almost simultaneously: the choirmaster [*regent*] Nikolai Pavlovich Diletskii and *d'iak* Ioann [or Ioannikii] Trofimovich Korenev, as well as the elder [*starets*] Aleksandr Mezenets and the monk Tikhon Makar'evskii. To these names may be added the earlier Novgorodian theorist Ivan Akimovich Shaidur. They were all active at almost the same time but, in spite of their common subject matter, church chant, each worked in his own sphere and their results were often contradictory.

In 1655 a committee of fourteen experts was appointed and summoned to Moscow with the task of reforming church chant, making it conform to the standards of *istinnorechie,* as well as making it uniform and beautiful. War and an epidemic of plague in Moscow prevented that commission from completing its work, and any results it may have achieved remain unknown. In 1668 a second commission of six members was assembled from those who were "well versed in *znamennoe* singing." Among the six was Aleksandr Mezenets, an elder from the Zvenigorod Monastery of St. Savva.[346] [See the prefatory notes to this chapter for significant revisions to Findeizen's presentation.] The commission's task was to correct the texts in musical manuscripts *na rech'* [that is, to eliminate the inserted vowels that distorted words and made them incomprehensible], and to standardize the chant melodies. The written document from the commission is a theoretical textbook called *Izveshchenie o soglasneishikh pometakh* [Report about the most harmonious notational signs], commonly known as *Azbuka znamennago peniia* [Alphabet of *znamennoe* singing] by Mezenets. The text, together with explanations and extremely valuable comparative tables of neumatic notations from the eleventh to the seventeenth century, was published by S. V. Smolenskii. Despite its brevity, Mezenets's *Alphabet* has not lost its significance to this day and can be viewed as perhaps the best guide to learning the *znamennaia* (*kriukovaia*) notation. Mezenets was later appointed corrector [*spravshchik*] at the Moscow Printing Office. The edition of music books envisaged by the commission never materialized.

The results of the second commission's activities were limited to the correction of Irmologii texts and the preparation of the *Report,* which was completed on 11 June 1668 and which was the collective work of the commission headed by Mezenets. This is supported by the acrostic of the final segment of the text ("Konets i bogu slavu" [The end, praise the Lord]) which reads: "Aleksander Mezenets and others worked on this." Undoubtedly Mezenets was the chief editor of the *Report.*

Biographical data on Mezenets are available in manuscripts in the library of the former Synodal School, currently located at the Historical Museum in Moscow. Thus in a chant anthology dated 1666 ([GIM, Sin. pev. sobr.] 728), on folio IV, one finds the signature "monach Alexander Stremmouchow" [in Latin letters] beneath the introductory verses:

> V znameni edinom tochiiu, i v pometakh:
> > svershen ouchitel'skikh soglasnykh primetakh.
> Aleksandera monakha rodom inozemtsa:

klirosskim prozvaniem vlastnago mezentsa.
Starozhitelstvom, ottsa imushcha belorostsa:
severskiia strany byvshago novgorodtsa.

Only in the neumes and in the *pomety* is the pedagogical
purpose completed by Monk Aleksander, a foreigner by
birth, in clerical name the masterful Mezenets; in terms
of his ancestry, his father was a White Russian, of the
Seversk area, former Novgorodian.

In another manuscript in the same library which includes a similar conclusion in verse,
Mezenets's father is called Ioann Malorosets [from Little Russia, Ukraine]; see manuscript
no. 98, a general Mineia dated 1677, fol. 1.[346A] One may reasonably presume, in any case,
that Aleksandr Ioannovich (his secular name is unknown and his secular family name is
Stremoukhov) was called Mezenets from the site of the monastery in which he took his
monastic vows, and that he was by birth either a White Russian or a Little Russian from
Novgorod-Severskii.

The activities of an earlier theorist, Ivan Akimovich Shaidur, were in agreement with
Mezenets's ideas. Shaidur, too, aimed at improving the old *znamennoe* singing. Shaidur, a native
of Novgorod and a master of church chant, was the author of the *Skazanie o pometkakh ezhe
pishutsia v penii pod znamenem* [A treatise on additional signs as these are written in chant
underneath the neumes], which appeared in the last quarter of the sixteenth century. According
to the evidence in Mezenets's *Alphabet,* Shaidur provided a grammar of *znamennoe* singing and
explained the use of the cinnabar signs (*pomety*), which he invented and became accepted in
general practice. To date, we do not know if Shaidur left any written explanation of his theoretical invention or improvements, or whether his ideas were disseminated through the various,
mostly later, singing treatises, such as the *Alphabet* by Mezenets and his collaborators. So far
nothing in Shaidur's own hand has come to light in neumed musical manuscripts.

The monk and patriarchal treasurer Tikhon Makar'evskii was a contemporary of
both these theorists.[347] He was the author of a manual for *partesnoe* singing titled *Kliuch
ili pravila musikiiskago peniia, soglasno i chinno sochinennago* [The key, or rules of musical
singing, harmoniously and decorously composed]. The significance and authenticity of
Tikhon's treatises have not yet been established. Archpriest V. M. Metallov, an authority on
church chant, considers that the *Pervoe uchenie musikiiskikh soglasii* [First lesson in musical concordances] which, according to Razumovskii, formed the second part of the *Key,*
was written by N. P. Diletskii (the work was published in 1877 by the Society of Lovers of
Old Literature). Metallov bases his opinion on the fact that a paragraph on tones [*ton*] in
Diletskii's *Musikiia* says: "as I said in Tikhon's music."[347A] Tikhon Makar'evskii's authorship
is proved by an acrostic, a device often used at the time, which adorns the first page of the
Skazanie [the title on one of the copies of Tikhon's treatise].[348] This acrostic is quoted in
V. Undol'skii's *Observations on the History of Church Singing in Russia,* and reveals that "the
monk Tikhon Makarievskii worked on this."[349] Tikhon's *Key,* which seems to have appeared
at the same time as Mezenets's *Alphabet,* indicates that the author was acquainted with
Diletskii's *Grammar.* In his exposition Tikhon used an early version of Diletskii's work,
which might have given Diletskii grounds for quoting "Tikhon's music" in his own treatise.

The most authoritative and most popular theorist of the second half of the seventeenth
century was Nikolai Diletskii. One of the versions of his theoretical treatise, *Musikiia*
[Music], was published in 1910 in an edition by S. V. Smolenskii. Diletskii's work appeared

at a time when the struggle between the advocates of the new polyphony and the adherents of the old *znamennoe* singing was at its height. One of the most interesting examples of this polemical literature was included in the latest version of Diletskii's treatise, namely, in deacon Ioann Korenev's *Musikiia* [Music].[349A]

Long before *partesnoe* singing appeared in Moscow, where it was brought by Kievan singers and supported by Tsar Aleksei Mikhailovich and Patriarch Nikon, the singing world had been in turmoil; this was because of the awareness of imperfections in the old *znamennoe* singing which prevailed in the ruling church. In this context, there is a very informative letter ["Poslanie"] by an unknown author, addressed to Patriarch Germogen and dating from the Time of Troubles, when one would hardly think anyone had the time to ponder questions of improvements in church singing. This is one of the first polemical writings about singing practices, although it is couched in the form of a request to "the most honorable majesty and most distinguished holiness" to clarify certain issues. The letter probably dates from about 1608 and describes some of the defects in chant as follows:[350]

> There is, Lord, in *stolpovoe* and *troestrochnoe* singing used by singers and *raspevshchiki* old and new in many places and in Stikhirari, something called *khabuva*, and also pronounced sometimes "ine ine khebuve" and these words, "ine ine khebuve" throughout the book for the Canonarch [the leader of the chant] are used in Stikhirari in *stroki* [lines] and they put a [notational] sign over them; and "khabuva" indicates a *fita,* and when they sing it, they say "khabuva." But there is a kind of singing in which it is placed in a few places in *stroki* and a sign is placed on it and these words, Lord, do not mean the same things: one says that you say "khebuve" which indicates "Khriste bozhe," but "khabuva" means "Khrista boga" and "khabuvu" means "Khristu bogu."[351] Others say that praise of God is pronounced, and others think that it is done for the sake of beauty, and still others think that it doesn't mean anything, and they just sing the *fity.* We, the poor [meek], think this: It seems, Lord, that we are lost in the fog and do not know the truth and it remains unknown, from where this is taken and in what language is said.

The author of the letter also inquired among the Greeks residing in Moscow:

> And they, Lord, said that we did not hear about and do not know that you say "khabuva" or "ine khabuve" and we in our Greek language do not have that in any books, nor in the Canonarch, nor for singers, nor in any other language we know; we have not heard this word in singing or in *fity.*

We do not know how the patriarch answered this inquiry. This, at any rate, was certainly not the only time at which the imperfections in contemporary musical practice were acknowledged. The next episode, from that same stormy period, around 1610, involves the well-known *golovshchik* Loggin (whom contemporaries nicknamed Korova [cow]) at the Trinity–St. Sergius Lavra. After a perhaps excessively free performance of the chant "Velichit dusha moia, gospoda" [My soul doth magnify the Lord], Archimandrite Dionisii scolded the singer: "On the word 'seed' [in the Magnificat] there is a *stat'ia* [a neume indicating a long note] and what do you yell?" The archimandrite was upset that Loggin sang an elaborate ornamentation instead of a long, drawn-out note.[351A] The ranks of those opposed to earlier singing practices grew as the defects of *razdel'norechnoe* singing were fully revealed; there were distortions of the liturgical texts, in addition to the nonsensical additions like *khabuva, ananeiki,* and so forth, and the discord in church services was further increased by the simultaneous performance of various portions in order to save time. Two opponents, the monk Evfrosin and the deacon Ioann Korenev, both contemporaries of Diletskii, became quite prominent. Evfrosin was the author of a polemical treatise, *Skazanie o razlichnykh eresekh i khuleniiakh na gospoda boga i prechistuiu bogoroditsu, soderzhimykh ot nevedeniia v znamennykh knigakh* [An account of various heresies and blasphemies against the Lord God and the Blessed Virgin, retained through ignorance in the notated musical books], preserved in several manuscript copies.[352]

From the author's preface we learn that the treatise was written in 1651, that is, it preceded the first commission of teachers convened in 1655. The author was an educated man for his time and had a good knowledge of church singing, with which he became acquainted during a pilgrimage to Jerusalem. In his treatise he notes what he heard in Kiev and among the Greeks: "I, sinner that I am, heard with my own ears: the Greeks under the Jerusalem Patriarch and in the holy churches in Kiev sing those psalms ('Gospodi vozzvakh tebe' [I cried unto the Lord; Revised Standard Version Psalm 142]) without refrains [*bez pripel*] all the way to the *stikhira*." He adds: "In our chanting we do not embellish the mode and we preserve the notational neumes [in manuscripts] while the sacred words and elevated and awe-filled terms are distorted against the printed and written books, both old and new." In addressing the origins of these bad habits, Evfrosin enumerates the defects of the liturgical singing of his time and attributes them "to the work of the devil, who brought discord instead of concord into singing." In answering the question of the origins of this "evil thorn," Evfrosin lists the shortcomings of the liturgical singing of his time and points to the guilty party, "the devil, that false teacher and enemy." It was the devil who has "secretly sown the seeds of discontent [literally, sown weeds in the wheat] among those we consider blessed his soul-destroying abuse against God, and has created discord in beautifully voiced singing and dissent regarding the holy writings and has corrupted the holy doctrine." In supporting his charges, Evfrosin details the "lawless" manner of performing some music, and a substantial part of his work is filled with sharp attacks on adherents of *znamennoe* singing. "Even among themselves," he writes, "these singers, with their ornamented singing, scold one another; each raises himself above the others and boasts, saying 'I am a student of Shaidur' and another praises himself as a student of Lukoshko." Loggin's pupils, according to him, "no matter where they are, must defend themselves." He even puts the singing leaders to shame: "But about this *znamennyi* singing of ours and about its distortion and its origins no one can find out anything anywhere by any means, because many of these glorious teachers in our days, lying around the taverns, died a shameful death and the memory of them died with [their] noise."[352A]

Another no less fervent opponent of the old church chanting was Ioann Trofimov Korenev, mentioned above, deacon of the Moscow Cathedral of the Presentation "na seniakh" at court.[352B] His *Music* was included in Diletskii's textbook, suggesting that the two authors may have collaborated. Thus Korenev, as a member of the court clergy which supported the new manner of church chant presented "through composition," might have been an authoritative conduit for Diletskii's theoretical innovations, which departed completely from the immovable foundations of *znamennoe* singing. It seems, however, that Korenev died before the last Russian version of Diletskii's treatise appeared (in 1681), since his work is mentioned there in the past tense. Korenev was probably responsible not only for the introductory part of the book based on the writings of early authors but also for the general revision of the Russian text of Diletskii's treatise.

Korenev's basic tone, as we have seen, was polemical. "It is to the devil," he says, that one must attribute the "envy, slander, and other such feelings" on the part of those who supported the old manner of singing. He also stated that instead of ridicule, the adherents of the old should weep and stop calling part singing the devil's deed and an act of heresy, as they did, just because it uses various clefs.[352C] Korenev presents his material in the form of a catechism, a series of questions and answers based on extensive quotations from the writings of church fathers and church history; in memorizing this material, students at singing schools were thus convinced that the new musical art was proper. Korenev's tone was polemical. Smolenskii and other scholars even claim that this book was one of the indirect causes of the decline of the ancient *kriukovoe* singing, although the introduction of part singing demonstrated the need for accurate and clearly presented notation. Nevertheless, Korenev's *Music* must be recognized as probably the earliest Russian work, and, moreover, one written by an ecclesiastic, to admit the wider significance of music, that is, beyond the framework of religious services.

It should also be noted that Korenev's treatise was titled *Music;* Diletskii's theoretical portion was didactic, a grammar, or *An Idea of a Musical Grammar,* as it was called in the 1679 version. Korenev defined the word "music" as "a harmonious art and an elegant distribution of voices . . . Music is the second philosophy and grammar." Finally, Korenev asks: "What is music?" He says that it is "twofold: one part is vocal and the other, instrumental," thus acknowledging both types of music. For the seventeenth century, which rejected "honking instruments" of every kind and banned both the *skomorokhi* and folk songs, the recognition of music alongside philosophy and grammar was a great step forward. Korenev's view, characterized by impatience and harshness toward his opponents,[353] may have been taken from Diletskii, whose artistic viewpoint he shared. Korenev undoubtedly believed deeply in Diletskii and greatly admired him, but it was nevertheless Korenev himself who expressed these views, and the credit for this important service belongs to him. In any event, he prepared the way for the dissemination of Diletskii's *Grammar,* whose outstanding and influential contribution to the theory of Russian church music is acknowledged by all students of the subject.

Korenev's *Music* appeared as an introductory polemical and didactic explanation of the second, and most important, part of the volume, Diletskii's *Grammar.* This work played an important role in the history of religious music of the seventeenth and eighteenth centuries, educating several generations of composers. The *Alphabet* by Mezenets and his co-workers, on the one hand, represented the crowning jewel in the tradition of *znamennoe* singing, explaining, a posteriori, its artistic value and the practical meaning of the neumatic notation which, over time, had played its historical role and was now doomed to extinction in the religious practices of the ruling church. Diletskii's *Musical Grammar,* on the other hand, became an indispensable manual for learning the technical skills necessary for freely composed sacred music.

Nikolai Pavlovich Diletskii, a native of Kiev, spent only the last part of his career in Moscow, where he found a wealthy patron in the eminent person of Grigorii Dmitrievich Stroganov (d. 1715). We have only approximate data for his life. Fétis, citing Belikov, the former inspector of the Court Chapel, says that Diletskii was born in 1630 and died in the last decade of the seventeenth century (ca. 1690). The last version of his *Grammar* is dated 1681, and there is no reason to think that he would not have reissued it from time to time, as he had in the past. In addition to the first (Wilno) edition of his *Musical Grammar* in Polish, which has not survived, there are dated manuscripts of his treatise from Smolensk in 1677, and from Moscow in 1679 and 1681.[353A] Diletskii was educated in Poland, probably in Wilno and in Warsaw, because in his manual he quotes as examples of the new concerted style excerpts from works by "the best Polish artists": Ivan Ziusk; precentor Stanisław [Jacek] Różycki (from the beginning of the seventeenth century); Nikolai Zamarevich; and Marcin Mielczewski. Perhaps only the last two were Diletskii's teachers, since he calls Ziusk an "old artist." Mielczewski, whom Diletskii cites most frequently, served in the court chapel in Warsaw around the year 1643.[354] His extant works are dated between 1651 and 1659, the period when Diletskii was his pupil. As a precentor and teacher of church singing, Diletskii lived in Wilno, then in Smolensk around 1677, and finally in Moscow, where he found a rich patron, Stroganov, whose Usol'e cappella was famous in its time. Ivan Lukoshkov, the famous arranger [*raspevshchik*] of neumatic chant and a pupil of Stefan Golysh, came from this establishment. Diletskii undoubtedly conducted Stroganov's choir since he dedicated the Moscow edition of his *Musical Grammar* to the "most noble among the noble, the most distinguished among the distinguished, to my lord Grigorii Dmitrievich Stroganov."[355]

Diletskii is less well known as a composer. His setting of the Cherubic Hymn is in a manuscript of church music written in staff notation from ca. 1690–96, belonging to the museum in Tver.[356] It is also known that he wrote music for the so-called Josephian texts (texts revised at the time of Patriarch Joseph, who died in 1652). Smolenskii views Diletskii as the founder of a new, Westernized school of singing in Russia. As a theorist and teacher, he created a whole school from which a series of Russian composers emerged at the end of the seventeenth and the beginning of the eighteenth centuries, most prominently the gifted *d'iak* Vasilii Titov. Diletskii was renowned in Poland as a theorist; in Wilno, in 1675, his book was published under the title *Toga złota w nowej świata metamorphosi, szlachetnemu magistratowi Wileńskiemu, na nowy rok przez Mikołaia Dileckiego, akademika Wileńskiego [ogłoszona] w Wilnie. Typis Franciscanis anno 1675* [The golden toga in the new metamorphosis of the world, dedicated to the noble Wilno magistrate on the new year, written by Mikolai Dilecki, a Wilno academic, printed in Wilno. The Franciscan Press, 1675]. It seems that, later on, this volume was revised and translated into various Russian versions [see n. 353A above].[357]

The earlier so-called explanations of neumes contained lists of neumes and *fity* [melodic formulas] listed according to the [eight] modes; they were comprehensible only with oral explanations and with repeated exercise and practice, and they contained no theoretical rules. In contrast, Diletskii's *Musical Grammar*, for its time and for Muscovite Russia, must be recognized as a complete theoretical treatise which explained in detail the grammatical and technical essentials of staff notation, part-singing, and *partesnoe* composition.

Diletskii's manual is based on the old system of hexachords, which was waning in the West but was a novelty in Russia. He introduced musical terminology that sounds harsh to the modern ear but that expressed specific meanings: *bemoliarnaia* [from *b moll*, or flat], *diezisovaia* [from *diezis*, or sharp], and *dural'naia* [from *dur*, indicating natural] music; *chvartki* (quarter note); *chetveroguboviaznye* (sixty-fourth note); and *kliavishi* (clefs, divided into three types: C, F, and G).[357A] Although the Venetian theorist Giuseppe Zarlino (1517–1590) had established an accurate understanding of major and minor triads, Diletskii had no knowledge of these concepts and speaks of harmony as producing cheerful singing (major) and mournful singing (minor). His teaching on fugue, in a chapter on contrary motion or counterpoint ("O protivotochii"), is reduced to a simple imitation of parts. His main purpose was to produce a guide to composition in the *kontsert* style so widely used in church music. As a representative of technical methods developed in Western singing practice, Diletskii views our eightfold modal tunes only as raw material suitable for development in a symmetrical and regulated tempo. "The Irmologii," he wrote, "and its notes and melodies do not have regular bars, but one can place [its music] into regular bars." He also treats chant texts in an interesting fashion. In the chapter "On Disposition" he states that, "if you want to set any *stikh*, you must decide and lay out where the *kontsert*, that is the struggle between the voice and the words, will be and where all will be together" (that is, *tutti*).[358] In a chapter on "ateksalis" (singing without words), he advises one first to compose the music and only then to add appropriate text. From the fragments of Diletskii's *Grammar* cited above, it is apparent that the treatise was not originally written in Russian but in all likelihood was translated from Polish, probably by a clergyman (Korenev). The heavy-handed terminology introduced in this treatise was long preserved in the vocabulary of our singers and composers.

In addition to these treatises, we have a series of manuscripts preserving music-theoretical works by unknown authors. For example, the *Kniga, glagolemaia Musikiia, izdannaia prezhde v Moskve o penii bozhestvennom radi blagochiniia tserkovnago ot liubomudrykh khudozhnikov* [A book called music, issued earlier in Moscow on sacred singing for the sake of a churchly good deed by wisdom-loving artists] of 1671, preserved in [RNB] Q.XII.1.[358A] Another work is titled *Nauka vseia musikii, ashche khoshcheshi razumeti Kievskoe znamia i penie, soglasno i chinno sochinennoe* [The complete science of music, if you wish to understand Kievan notation and singing, harmoniously and decorously prepared] in manuscript no. 267 in the Gorskii library collection of the Moscow Divinity School.[358B] These treatises have not generally been examined, and they do not seem to have had great significance compared to those that were copied and spread, like Mezenets's manual (for adherents of the old chant) and Diletskii's (for followers of the *kontsert* style).

The great practical value of Diletskii's *Musical Grammar* was in the fruitful activities of many Muscovite singers and choir leaders in the second half of the seventeenth century. The large number of surviving *kontserty* show that part singing and the *kontsert* style established deep roots in the Moscow singing community. In addition to Diletskii himself, the list of composers includes Nikolai Bavykin, Fyodor Redrikov, Vasilii Titov, Mikhail Sifov, and other Muscovite composers. Because of the large number of anonymous manuscripts, the list is far from complete.

Of all the old Russian masters, the talented *d'iak* Vasilii Polikarpovich Titov deserves special mention. Titov, a member of the sovereign singers, worked in the last quarter of the seventeenth and the first decade of the eighteenth centuries and must be ranked as one of the most gifted and fruitful Russian composers of his time.[359] Of all his works, his well-known *Mnogoletie* is quite national in character, and, in the people's memory, it represents the essence of his more developed *Great Mnogoletie*, which was at one time part of the liturgy. Succeeding generations have removed many of its interesting details, retaining only the triple repetition of the main subject. This work, which has survived more than 225 years, has become part of the national consciousness.[360] Titov knew how to vary a basic phrase in different voices quite ingeniously. His repeated use of the seventh formed by a passing tone in the bass is particularly characteristic; Glinka later introduced this into our secular music as an indication of folk-like harmonization. The clever combinations and easy flow of the voices must be recognized as original and masterly for their time, and the national character is fully preserved. Titov's historical importance does not depend solely on this popular melody, for he must be acknowledged as one of the greatest and most versatile composers of his era. The simplicity of the *Mnogoletie's* vocal style and the agility with which he handled the polyphonic chorus testify to his amazingly free mastery. Titov is credited with as many as thirty *kontserty* and settings of the liturgy for twelve voices, and he also wrote a number of works for eight, sixteen, and twenty-four voices.

Although he may have been a direct pupil of Diletskii, which is highly likely, or have been brought up on his *Musical Grammar,* Titov did not break with the past; he wrote an eight-part setting of the liturgy using traditional *znamennyi raspev,* and this is probably not the only example. His position as a church singer and his training specifically in choral practice influenced his work, but he always endeavored to go beyond the confines of composing only religious music. This can be seen in his works in a different genre. Titov can be viewed as the creator of a musical form new to Moscow, the *kanty* and psalm settings [*psal'my*] mentioned earlier, which were intended to serve as domestic chamber music. They were, in general, secular works, although their texts were of a religious and edifying nature—the Church did not permit any other kind of secular music. In the archives of the former Synod there is a manuscript copy, submitted by Titov to Tsar Fyodor Alekseevich in 1680, of his musical setting of Simeon Polotskii's *Versified Psalter.*[361] Another manuscript copy, presented to Tsarevna Sofia Alekseevna in 1687, is in the library of the Academy of Sciences [see figs. 98 and 99].[362]

FIG. 98. The title page of Vasilii Titov's *Versified Psalter,* 1687 [dedicated to Tsarevna Sofia; BAN, 16.15.11].

Titov's vast output includes 165 musical numbers for Polotskii's psalms. This collection marks the beginning of the genre's importance as domestic music, and Titov's settings were highly original and varied in their melodies and rhythms. Whereas in his *Great Mnogoletie* Titov used the future "Russian seventh," in his psalm settings he often inserted rhythmic

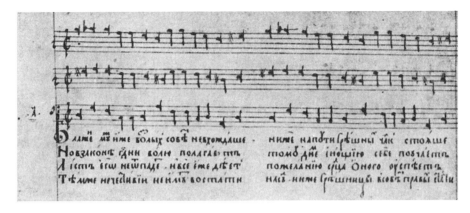

FIG. 99. The first psalm setting in Titov's *Versified Psalter*.

and harmonic (more rarely, melodic) turns characteristic of folk song. In Psalm 45, "Bog nam sila pribezhishche" [God is our strength and refuge; musical example 9.5], he uses a turn from original folk rhythms, accenting the penultimate quarter note in the bar, a procedure analogous to Tchaikovskii's chorus "Uzh kak po mostu, mostochku" [Along the bridge, the little bridge] in the opera *Eugene Onegin*.[363]

In the music for Psalm 51, "Silne v zlobe chto blazhishi" [Powerful in evil], completely modernized by S. V. Smolenskii, the similar descending passages at the end of the phrases are rhythmically identical, indicating, as Smolenskii justly remarks, that Titov had guessed the secret of our folk rhythm; see musical example 9.6.

EXAMPLE 9.5. "Bog nam sila pribezhishche" [God is our strength and refuge]

Bog nam sila pribezhishche,
Ot voln skorbei pristanishche;
Ashche zemlia vsia smutitsia
Nashe serdtse ne boitsia.

God is our strength and refuge,
A harbor from waves of grief;
Even if the whole earth were to be disturbed
Our heart is not afraid [cf. Revised Standard Version Psalm 46].

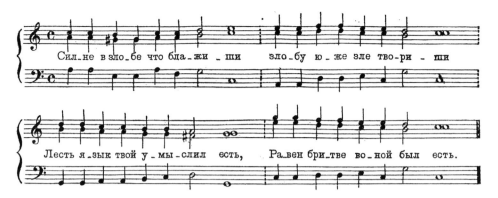

EXAMPLE 9.6. "Silne v zlobe chto blazhishi" [Powerful in evil why do you stray]

Silne v zlobe chto blazhishi
Zlobu iuzhe zle tvorishi;
Lest' iazyk tvoi umyslil est',
Raven britve vonoi byl est'.

Powerful in evil why do you stray
And from malice more evil make;
Your tongue, like a sharp razor
Plots flattery [cf. Revised Standard Version Psalm 52].

The folk spirit is maintained in Psalm 29, "Voznesu tia syi v nebesi" [I shall praise Thee to the skies], joyous, exultant, and requiring an animated performance (musical example 9.7).

EXAMPLE 9.7. "Voznesu tia syi v nebesi" [I shall praise Thee to the skies]

Voznesu tia syi v nebesi
Iako ty mia podnial esi,
Ne dav mene vo utekhu
Vragom moim na utekhu.

I shall praise Thee to the skies
As you have raised me,
Not giving me to my enemies as prize
[see Revised Standard Version Psalm 30].

The beautiful Psalm 9, "Gospodi, tebe sia az vsem serdtsem" [O Lord, I shall praise Thee with all my heart] sounds quite different, sterner and more severe in its coloring, as in musical example 9.8.

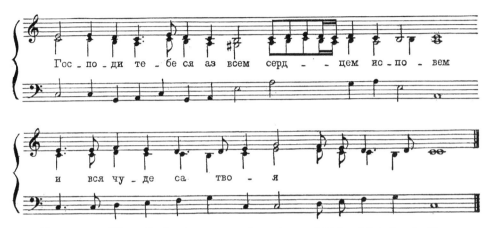

EXAMPLE 9.8. "Gospodi tebe sia az vsem serdtsem ispovem" [O Lord, I shall praise Thee with all my heart]

Gospodi tebe sia az vsem serdtsem ispovem
i vsia chudesa tvoia.

O Lord, I shall praise Thee with all my heart
and all your miraculous deeds.

The final Psalm 150, "Khvalite boga v sviatykh rabekh ego" [Praise God in the sanctuary of His servants; musical example 9.9] contains some interesting imitation.

EXAMPLE 9.9. "Khvalite boga v sviatykh rabekh ego" [Praise God in the sanctuary of His servants]

Khvalite boga v sviatykh rabekh ego (repeated)
I tverdi nebes sozdannei ot nego.

Praise God in the sanctuary of His servants
And the heavens created by Him.

Titov's psalm settings show great variety in their formal structure. The *kanty* and psalms were usually written in the form of a simple statement consisting of two periods (A + B). Titov alters this formula considerably. He often uses A + A + B (that is, a repeated A plus a new period, as in Psalms 29 and 45), or his period is composed of three, four, or five statements. The formula of the ninth ode appended to the Psalter, "Velichit dusha moia gospoda vsekh boga" [My soul doth magnify the Lord], is very interesting. It breaks down into two independent statements, which in turn are divided into the following periods:

I.   "Velichit . . ."   Phrase A repeated twice
      "Dukhu moemu . . ."   Phrase B once
II.   "Refrain"   (so designated by the composer;
                                          consists of the following):

      "Chestneishuiu . . ."   Phrase C once
      "i slavneishuiu . . ."   Phrase D twice
      "Bogoroditsu velichaem"   Phrase E once

From this we get the complete formula: A + A | B | + C | D + D | E.

Thus, within a single composition in the *Versified Psalter,* Titov shows his mastery of technique and rhythmic variety, and at the same time preserves to a degree the folk-like character of the music, even though it is set to [a series of] identical verse types. In Psalm 45 the contemporary ear is offended by the discord between the rhythmic stress [in the musical setting] and the stress of the syllabic verse [see musical example 9.5 above]:

Bog nam sila pribezhíshche,
Ot voln skorbei pristaníshche.

But this was a common phenomenon in contemporary vocal practice, not only in Russia but throughout Europe. Our singers may often have encountered such curious stresses as *póklon ot angél, Iordaná* (instead of *Iordána*), *pribezhíshche, slavíashchikhsia,* and so forth [all these examples illustrate misplaced stress in these words]. Even the western Meistersinger songs (fully analogous to our *kanty* and psalms) are filled with similar unnatural rhythmic accents in the musical settings of their versified texts. Nevertheless, it should be explained in Titov's defense that in his music for Psalm 45 he fully appreciated the basic rhythm of Polotskii's verses, but Polotskii's lack of poetic talent prevented him from maintaining that rhythm, especially in the first two lines [in which the stress is incorrect]:

Bog nam sila pribezhíshche
Ot voln skorbei pristaníshche;
Ashche zemlia vsia smutítsia
Nashe serdtse ne boítsia.
Ashche gory prelozhátsia

> V serdtse morsko obratïatsia,
> Dusha nasha ne smutítsia,
> V boze sil'nom utverdítsia.

This text should convince us that the composer interpreted the original rhythm of this psalm versification correctly, and that the irregular stresses must be attributed to Polotskii's deficient sense of rhythm; these niceties, however, attracted no attention in the seventeenth century. Equally unnatural stresses in the musical treatment of verses and literary texts in general can be found in Russian romances of a far later date, even at the beginning of the nineteenth century.

Another of Titov's large-scale works is his *Pesn' sviatym* [Hymn to the saints], a versified setting of the church calendar for the entire year. Polotskii wrote this text also, as a substitute for an older version of the *Pesn' sviatym* for which the music had been assembled from various popular *kanty*. Titov composed new music for the calendar, and, judging from the examples known to us, the musical setting is inferior to that for the *Versified Psalter*. Indeed, the text of the calendar is trivial and monotonous, resulting in verses such as the following for the month of May:

> Pafnutiia Borovska dnes' zhe ublazhaem,
> Da molit boga o nas, mol'by vozsylaem.

> Paphnutius of Borovsk we extol today
> We beseech him to God for us to pray.[364]

There was nothing in this to inspire the composer; he had to write music to the monotonous rhythms of the tedious verses (for example, [the rhymes] proslavliaem/ublazhaem, vossylaem/sovershaem), and his music followed suit.[365] It is possible that Polotskii requested or commissioned Titov to write the musical settings.

Of Titov's many other compositions, only the *Great Mnogoletie* remained in church practice to our day. Another interesting example of his sacred music is the six-part setting of "Blagoslovi dushe moia gospodi" [Praise the Lord, O my soul], which is as characteristically Russian in its liveliness and energy as is his *Mnogoletie*.[366]

Titov's contemporaries, who were trained in Diletskii's school or brought up on his *Musical Grammar*, also left a considerable number of vocal compositions quite similar in style to this master's works. These works include the twelve-part *kontsert* "Nebesa ubo dostoino da veselitsia" [Let heavens rejoice] by Nikolai Bavykin, who also wrote a twelve-part Liturgy of the Presanctified Gifts (manuscript formerly in the library of the Synodal School, presently in the Historical Museum in Moscow [GIM]), both of which testify to that composer's considerable technical mastery; Vasilii Vinogradov, author of a twelve-part *kontsert*, "Glasom moim k gospodu vozzvakh" [I cried unto the Lord with my voice], and a twelve-part setting of the Divine Liturgy; the sovereign singer D'iakovskii is mentioned in various sources without listing his works; Nikolai Kalachnikov [or Kalashnikov], author of twenty-three *kontserty* for twelve parts, four Cherubic Hymns, and a setting of the Divine Liturgy for twenty-four voices; Kolpenskii, who wrote four *kontserty*, two liturgies for twelve parts, and *zadostoiniki* [the *zadostoinik* is a hymn sung to the Virgin at the Divine Liturgy; see the glossary]; Ivan Leont'ev (mentioned by Smolenskii); Pyotr Naritsyn, author of a set of four-part *zadostoiniki* on Greek tunes and a setting of the Beatitudes; sovereign singer and choir leader Ivan Mikhailovich Protopopov, one of the creators of the *partesnoe* style (his polyphonic settings are preserved in the former archive of the Ministry of Court [RGIA]); the Muscovite choir leader Fyodor Redrikov, author of two *kontserty* and eight settings of the Divine Liturgy for twelve parts; sovereign singer Mikhail Sifov, one of the creators of the *partesnoe* style (D. V. Razumovskii does not list his works); deacon Simeon Iakovlev, author of a twelve-part *kontsert*—for the time being, this serves as a catalog of the first Russian composers of *partesnoe penie*. Undoubtedly, in time, a whole new series of works and composers from the end of the seventeenth and the beginning of the eighteenth century will come to light. According to Smolenskii, who assembled an invaluable collection of manuscripts of church music at the Moscow Synodal School, there are many sacred works from that particular period, composed for three, four, five, six, eight, twelve, sixteen, twenty-four, and even forty-eight voices; there are as many as five hundred *kontserty* for twelve voices (for triple choir) in that library.[367]

These works were widely performed by contemporary singers, as demonstrated by the tattered state of many of the manuscript books. They remained in use until the arrival of the new Italianate style, introduced by Italian masters who were invited to serve at the Imperial Court in Russia from the mid-eighteenth century on.

The new choral music, which eliminated the old monophonic chant from official church practice, thus accepted the forms and technical aspects developed by Western masters and transmitted them in a ready-made form to the Russian musical world. In that extensive vocal literature, there appeared for the first time polyphonic *kanty* in public life [outside the church], psalm settings intended for domestic use, and the more complex *kontserty* for church practice. Essentially they were all based on the Western motet in its simplest form, which was quickly assimilated and developed by Russian vocal composers. The varied makeup and sonorities of the choirs, the beauty of the vocal ensemble, which had not yet lost its links with folk music and retained some of its rhythms and melodies, and the new and ingenious vocal effects developed with experience—all this undoubtedly led to the rapid dissemination of *partesnoe* singing and the banishment of the old monophonic *znamennyi* singing to the depths of the provinces. Internal political circumstances were, of course, a contributing cause, especially the persecution of the Old Believers. A variety of interesting compositional methods appeared, their titles providing a guide to their character: "Umilitel'naia s vykhodkami" [An emotional song with elaborate ornamentation]; "Kheruvimskaia veselogo raspeva s vykhodkami" [Cherubic hymn with a merry tune and elaborate ornamentation]; variously named alleluia melodies ("bird," "leap," "trumpet," "from the garret," "named bagpipe," and so forth).

The enthusiasm in court circles for Western-style instrumental music, evidenced by the invitations to horn players and trumpeters to enter the tsar's service, now spread to vocal music, where it found an echo in various "horn openings" [or fanfares], for example, in the eighteenth-century *kant* "Vospoem pesn' novu" [Let us sing a new song], shown in musical example 9.10, in which the opening melodic turns truly imitate a horn.[368] An interesting example of a vocal composition entirely instrumental in character is the *kant* "Vozdvigni nas lezhashchikh i spiashchikh ot odra bolezni" [Raise us lying and sleeping from the sickbed], shown in musical example 9.11. This *kant* may serve as an example of the development of vocal composition in the *kontsert* style, illustrating what Diletskii called the "struggle of voices" (that is, concerto-type singing, solo) followed by the *tutti*, that is, the full choir. In examples like these, ingenuity and inventiveness were undoubtedly refined at the expense of folk characteristics. We must also mention another popular Western vocal technique, called *ekstsellentovanie* (from *excellente canere*), which remained in use almost to our own day. It consisted of embellishing the bass part with *roulades*. As an example I quote the following *kant* from a collection of the seventeenth–eighteenth century (Public Library [RNB], Q.XIV.25), in which the *roulades* in the bass part are clear enough; see musical example 9.12.

EXAMPLE 9.10. "Vospoem pesn' novu gospodevi bogu" [Let us sing a new song to the Lord God]

> Vospoem pesn' novu gospodevi bogu
> Iako sotvoril nam nyne milost' mnogu.
> Ne da de nam vrago mo pozherati,
> Izhe nas khoteshi vsekh predati smerti.

> Let us sing a new song to the Lord God
> For He created for us many favors.
> He did not let our enemies win,
> Our enemies, who wanted us all destroyed.

EXAMPLE 9.11. "Vozdvigni nas lezhashchikh i spiashchikh ot odra bolezni" [Raise us lying and sleeping from the sickbed]

> Vozdvigni nas lezhashchikh i spiashchikh ot odra bolezni

> Raise us lying and sleeping from the sickbed

This, then, is the state of vocal music at the beginning of the eighteenth century. This new style increasingly acquired the character of harmonized singing, moving away from the recent attempts, in the late sixteenth century, at creating a Russian counterpoint with freely moving voices. In their general movement, the voices in the new *partesnoe* singing were connected vertically, that is, chordally; the vocal counterpoint did not go beyond the use of

EXAMPLE 9.12. "Vsederzhiteliu Khriste bozhii syne" [Almighty Christ, Son of God]

Vsederzhiteliu Khriste bozhii syne
Slovo otchee veliko vsesilne
Prosveti dushu moiu pomrachennu
V bezdne grekhovnei v strastekh pogruzhennu.

Almighty Christ, Son of God,
Word paternal, great and all mighty,
Illumine my clouded soul
Plunged in old age in the sinful abyss.

imitation. Vocal practice, of course, might easily have developed in that direction, and its Lutheran foundation made it responsive to the Western influence which continued to permeate Muscovy's court and social life. The singers merely yielded to the spirit of the times and, to the best of their abilities, strove to preserve the links to the melodies and rhythms inherited from folk songs. The best of these musicians, such as the highly gifted V. P. Titov, mastered the problem, but the weaker vessels could only drift on the surface of the stream.

10. Music in Court Life in the Seventeenth Century

The sovereign singers. Foreigners in Russian service. The first theatrical performances in Russia

Life in the royal household dictated the tastes and fashions of Moscow's social elite. That courtly life, rooted in ancient tradition and isolated from everything external, particularly anything foreign, gradually began to be permeated by new influences. These changes were undoubtedly strongly condemned by the vast majority, who clung to the superstitions of the dark and distant past. A Pskov chronicler declared the English doctor Elisei Bomelius, who came to Moscow in 1570 and was appointed the tsar's physician, to be a "cruel sorcerer" who led Tsar Ivan the Terrible away from his faith.[368A] Even much later, when relations with foreigners began to improve, our ancestors could not rid themselves of their superstitious views of non-Russians. Thus, in 1638, Fyodor Zaval'skii [Zawalski], organ master for Tsar Mikhail Fyodorovich, had to swear that "he would serve with the sovereign's organists and would not engage in any sly tricks [*khitrosti*]." Shortly before this, an incident in Moscow illustrated the people's superstitious and prejudiced attitude toward foreigners. In about 1630 a Dutch doctor named Quirinus Bremburgh, an amateur lute player, lived in the city.[369] One day when he was playing by the open window of his room, a strong wind stirred the bones of a skeleton hanging on the wall. Some passing soldiers noticed this and spread the report that the doctor was forcing the dead to dance to the lute! Quirinus was accused of sorcery and, without the intercession of Prince I. B. Cherkasskii, would have been burned at the stake. Only the skeleton suffered this punishment; the doctor was deported from Muscovy.

Of course, as foreigners appeared more frequently, people were able to observe them and grow accustomed to them. And so, just outside the city in Kokue, a separate quarter was set aside in 1649, the Foreign Quarter (now Lefortovo). [The Foreign Quarter was called the Nemetskaia sloboda, literally, the German Suburb.] There the foreign residents lived their own lives, but Muscovite society gradually began to feel their influence.

It appears that music played a role in court life, insofar as we can judge artistic developments from surviving documents and sources. The sovereign singers, as well as *skomorokhi* and various instrumentalists, were in the tsar's service, and the instrumentalists were gradually joined by real musicians from abroad.

The sovereign singers were the tsar's household choir and sang at religious services; the patriarchal singers played the same role for the patriarch. (When the patriarchate was abolished and the Synod established, the patriarchal singers became the Synodal choir, and the sovereign singers came to be known as the court chapel or cappella.) As we know, the ensemble was not large at first, with only about thirty-five singers, although it gradually increased in size; by the end of the seventeenth century there were about seventy singers. This growth was a function of the increasing number of churches attached to the court and to the development of part singing, which required a full-sounding choir. The choir was divided into several stations [*stanitsy*] of varying rank, usually five singers in each. The first two stations were highest in rank and at court services, the first station stood to the right and the second station to the left [looking from the church toward the altar area]. The head

of the choir was the *ustavshchik,* and we know some of the leaders of the sovereign singers in the last quarter of the seventeenth century: Pavel Mikhailov, Pyotr Pokrovets, and
Fedot Ukhtomskii. The leader of the choir of Peter the Great was his favorite singer, Stepan
Beliaev. The lower-ranking stations were made up of young and inexperienced singers who
were being trained in their art. We have already discussed the prominent role this ensemble
played in the development of choral literature, especially in the seventeenth century.[370] The
singers were also leaders as performing, practical musicians.

After learning how successful part singing had been in Kievan church choirs, Tsar
Aleksei Mikhailovich ordered a transfer of teachers and singers from Kiev to the capital.[371]
The sovereign singers mastered the new art quickly, thus contributing to the dissemination
of the new style. They were also renowned for their skillful music copying, both neumatic
notation and staff notation for part singing. It is known, for example, that around 1640 the
singer Ivan Koniukhovskii copied a complete neumed two-part Obikhod on six hundred
folios with extraordinary clarity, despite the minute handwriting, and another singer, Potap
Maksimov (d. 1632), was renowned for his copying music *na rech'.*[371A] Court documents
preserve the names of others who copied *narechnoe penie;* before 1682 they include Semyon
Denisov, Bogdan Zlatoustovskii, Fyodor Konstantinov, Ivan Nikiforov (a *stol'nik* of Prince
M. N. Odoevskii), Mikhail Osipov, and Grigorii Kherugovskii.[371B] The latter two were
among the clergy of the metropolitan of Krutitsa, yet the music manuscripts they copied
were in the tsar's collection in Moscow. There is little doubt that many of the best surviving
manuscripts of both neumatic and staff notation were copied by the sovereign singers. As
experienced copyists, they probably often fulfilled private commissions as well. Finally, the
high opinion in which some of them were held is shown by singer Nikifor Kondratovich
Viazemskii's appointment as Tsarevich Aleksei Petrovich's chant teacher.[372] Following the
model set by the tsar and the patriarch, there were singers in Moscow attached not only to
the churches but probably also to the homes of wealthy boyars and aristocrats, for example,
the Stroganov choir, led by Diletskii.

The duties of the court instrumentalists were more restricted and less important. Among
the musicians at Tsar Mikhail Fyodorovich's court were the *tsymbal'niki* [keyboardists]
Andrei Andreev (in 1613), Tomilo Mikhailov Besov (in 1613–14), and Melentii Stepanov (in
1626–32). They were assigned to the Poteshnaia palata [Hall of Entertainment], about which
we have little information. Nevertheless, from the expense accounts of the Tsar's Treasury
from 1616 into the 1620s, we learn that the Hall of Entertainment in that period had seven
windows and four doors; in 1613 the *tsynbal'nik* Tomilo Mikhailov (Besov) received nearly
four yards of purple material, and in 1614 nearly seven yards of cloth were issued for hang-
ings for the doors and windows.[373] This gives some idea of the fairly large dimensions of this
hall, where the "tsar's entertainments" took place, including even foreign musicians. Later
on, the court organists were attached to the Poteshnaia palata as well.

Among the few extant documents on instrumental music, there is information about
Tsar Mikhail Fyodorovich's wedding festivities, which took place at the beginning of
February 1626. The second day of the festivities started with music. When the tsar left the
bedroom [*sennik,* literally a hay mattress] and entered the bathing room, they began to "play
the *surny* and trumpets and to beat the *nakry.*" At the meal in the Faceted Palace in the
Kremlin, they played *tsimbaly* and *nakry* "to the tsar's delight." Olearius further states that
he saw a girl in the tsar's apartments dancing to the harp and the fiddle. They probably also
had music with other impromptu diversions.[374]

During Mikhail Fyodorovich's reign (1613–45), however, the folk-like domestic musical
entertainments began to be blended with music introduced by visiting foreigners. Foreign

musicians, as we know, had appeared in old Russia long before the Time of Troubles. Tsar Mikhail established closer relations with foreigners during his reign, especially after the end of the war with Poland in 1635, and non-Russians were now invited and engaged for all sorts of useful undertakings, revitalizing the Poteshnaia palata.

The Dutch organ builders (and brothers) Johann and Melhart Luhn, along with their assistants Adamsen and Burmann, were engaged in 1630. They brought with them an organ ["strement na organnoe delo"] which they finished with carvings and with gold and painted decorations. At its top they placed images of a nightingale and a cuckoo so that "when the organ was played, the birds sang by themselves, without human hands." For this clever work the builders received 2,676 rubles from the tsar. The Luhn brothers lived in Moscow for eight years and taught their craft to several Russian apprentices. An organ built in Moscow by Russian masters was [later] presented, along with an organist, as a gift from the Russian tsar to the Persian shah. Around 1638 the Luhn brothers were succeeded in the "organ entertainment" ["organnaia potekha"] by another foreigner, a Pole named Fyodor Zaval'skii [Zawalski], who was assisted by another Pole named Iurii Proskurovskii [Proskurowski]. Zaval'skii has been mentioned previously, and Iushka Proskurov had been in service earlier, as he was in charge of the organ at the time of Tsar Mikhail Fyodorovich's second wedding, in 1626.[374A]

Organs were no doubt installed by some of the boyars, but demand increased with the growing number of foreigners in Moscow. Adam Olearius, who arrived there with the Holstein embassy in 1634, tells us that many foreigners lived in Moscow at that time, including about one thousand Protestant families. At first they were allowed to live anywhere in the city, and they built chapels in their own courtyards; these chapels were demolished when most of the foreigners were settled in the Foreign Quarter, where there were also several churches. These churches required organs, of course, and wealthy people had them in their own homes. In the early 1670s various singers and organists served in churches in the Foreign Quarter. Justus Mertz from Mühlhausen (1648–1702), who lived in Moscow between 1668 and 1671, was the cantor of the Saxon church, with an annual salary of one hundred thalers and all expenses. He was followed by Simon Gutovskii, who also took part in the first theatrical performances in Moscow.[374B] Both were contemporaries of the Polish organist Kazimir Vasilevskii (Kazimerko Leont'ev Vasilevskii [Waszilewski]), a native of Smolensk, who belonged to the Polish nobility and was attached to the Poteshnaia palata ["v gosudarevoi potekhe"] in the 1670s.[375] In the eighteenth century activities associated with the organ were established on a sound footing in Moscow. Builders extended their operations to include harpsichords and clavichords, and they sold their instruments in the new capital and in the provinces.[375A]

Aleksei Mikhailovich's reign (1645–76) was one of the most interesting and eventful in the history of Russia's artistic culture. During his rule the ceremonies staged by the church (including the "actions" discussed above) attained their final, most elaborate flowering. The appointment of two commissions, in 1655 and 1668, to correct musical manuscripts; the rapid development of part singing; the growth of the sovereign singers and the appearance among them, or in connection with the tsar's church reforms, of a series of composers of vocal music, theorists, and writers on music; the closer links with the West and the reinforcement of the foreign craftsmen and musicians in Moscow; and, finally, the staging of the first theatrical performances and the founding of a theatrical school in Moscow—all these events were closely connected with the personality and tastes of the tsar himself. Foreigners visiting Moscow had reason to be amazed at the majesty and splendor of the court. According to the Earl of Carlisle, who was Charles II's ambassador and a frequent visitor in Moscow during Aleksei's reign: "The court of the Moscow emperor is so beautiful and is maintained in such an orderly manner that among all the monarchs, one could hardly find one which could surpass it."[375B]

In November 1655 the tsar returned from a campaign against Sweden and his triumphal entrance into the city was staged in an especially festive and solemn manner. Patriarch Nikon, accompanied by the visiting patriarchs of Alexandria and Antioch, and with an assemblage of clergy carrying a multitude of icons, welcomed the tsar, who went on foot through the city, bare-headed and wearing a sable cloak, accompanied by the Siberian prince and a high-ranking boyar. He was preceded by a mass of young men singing from music they held in their hands. To the pealing of bells and salvos from captured enemy guns, he arrived at the Place of Execution and ordered an inquiry into the health of the populace. In response, according to Kostomarov, the dense crowd shouted "Long life to his Majesty" and prostrated themselves.[375C]

This picture gives us a glimpse of the elaborate ceremony surrounding Tsar Aleksei Mikhailovich. Actually, during his reign, Muscovite court life experienced two distinctly different periods. The first, which might be called the Nikonian period, dates from the tsar's accession to the throne and his close relationship with Patriarch Nikon; this period was marked by excessive piety. The second period, after the tsar's break with the omnipotent patriarch (1660), witnessed a change in his artistic tastes. The contrast is quite noticeable in the public ceremonies surrounding the celebration of the tsar's two weddings. When the tsar's marriage to his first wife, Maria Il'inichna Miloslavskaia, was celebrated in January 1648, the sovereign singers sang *stikhiry* from the Prazdniki and the Triodion during the wedding banquet, while the trumpets, organs, and *nakry* used at previous royal weddings were silenced. But at his second marriage, to Natalia Alekseevna Naryshkina in 1671, things were quite different. Court records inform us that "after the banquet, the Tsar ordered entertainments, and the Great Lord was entertained by organs, and a foreigner [*nemchin*] played the organ,[376] and they played on *surny* and blew on the trumpets, and played *surenki* [small *surny*], and they beat on the *nakry* and *litavry* throughout." Four years later, in September 1674, when the tsar celebrated the proclamation of his son, Fyodor Alekseevich, as heir to the throne, he staged a banquet at which there was music and which went on until 6 AM.[376A] These events show the differences in Aleksei Mikhailovich's tastes and entertainments at the beginning and at the end of his reign. If, in the early part of his reign, ecclesiastical authorities rigorously and resolutely persecuted the *skomorokhi* and waged war against any manifestation of popular and secular art, during his last years the tsar permitted even the organization of theatrical performances at court. To the end, however, he was a faithful supporter of church services and liturgical singing, and was anxious that they should be on a splendid scale. This is completely understandable, because Aleksei Mikhailovich was not only an admirer but a true connoisseur of church singing, which, as we know, was taught as part of the royal children's education. The tsar himself was a diligent student of the subject. In the music library of his son, Fyodor Alekseevich, there are several neumed manuscripts which Aleksei copied, probably in his youth.[377] In 1668, at a time when passions were running high between the advocates of the new choral style, on the one hand, and the defenders of the old neumatic notation and the pre-Nikonian texts, on the other, the Eastern patriarchs bestowed their blessing on the use of *partesnoe penie* in the churches, undoubtedly reflecting the tsar's wishes. The patriarchs were received in Moscow with fitting respect and cordiality.

During Tsar Aleksei Mikhailovich's reign, relations with the West acquired a more progressive character, and his ambassadors to other countries did not restrict themselves to observations on etiquette and public formalities, points that were stressed in most of the diplomatic reports [*stateinye spiski*] from ambassadors to foreign courts. Vasilii Likhachyov, in the report of his embassy to Florence in 1659, indicates that they drank a toast to the tsar's health during which "they played music on *kimvaly* and organs and there were two trumpeters and eight *gudok* players" (probably lutenists).[377A] He also describes a brilliant ball attended by "members of the Grand Council and their wives, about 400 people, and they danced all night—the prince himself (Ferdinand de' Medici, Duke of Tuscany), his son, brothers, and the Princess." But Likhachyov's account of the "comedies," undoubtedly staged in honor of the Muscovite ambassadorial party, is the most important element of his report:[377B]

> The Prince ordered the entertainment to start and chambers appeared and [first] there was one chamber, which then sank out of sight, and in this manner there were six changes [of scenery]; and in those chambers the ocean appeared, disturbed by waves, and there were fish in the sea and people rode on the fish, and at the top of the room was the sky and people sat on the clouds. And the clouds with the people on them sank down, and they grabbed a man on the earth under his arms, and they went back up again. And the people sitting on the fish also rose up to the sky after them. And then a man sitting in a carriage was lowered from the sky, and across from him in another carriage there was a beautiful maiden, and the valuable horses [*argamachki,* an Asiatic horse] beneath the carriages moved their legs as if they were alive. And the Prince said that one represented the sun, and the other the moon.
>
> And in a different scene, in the chamber there appeared a field full of human bones, and blackbirds flew in and started pecking at the bones. And then the sea appeared in the chamber and on the sea were small ships and people inside were sailing [them].
>
> And in a different scene, there appeared 50 men in armor; they started fighting with sabers and swords and they fired from pistols [harquebuses] and it was as if three men were shot. And young men and girls came out from behind the golden curtain and danced and did many marvelous things, and a boy came out and asked to eat and they kept on giving him many loaves of unleavened bread and they couldn't fill him up.
>
> And that entertainment [*igra*] was put together eight weeks before the ambassadors got there, and it cost 800 *efimki* [Joachimsthalers, silver thalers]. The same kind of comedy [*komediia*] was given as a present to the Spanish king, who had just had a son. And there were three different comedies staged for us in Florence.[378]

It is difficult at present to ascertain what plays the Muscovite emissaries saw in Florence in the months of January and February 1660. As far as I was able to determine the repertory of Italian theaters for the seventeenth and eighteenth centuries, it appears that one of the three operas staged in Florence in 1660 was Melani's *Il ritorno d'Ulisse.* Its subject matter resembles Likhachyov's description.[379] It is also certain that the boy who appeared during one of the changes of scenery performed one of the typical Italian *intermedi* which were later introduced on the Russian stage.

A few years later another Muscovite ambassador, *stol'nik* Pyotr Potyomkin, was sent to Spain and France.[379A] In September 1668 he and his entourage attended several court theatrical performances in Paris. On 16 September the Théâtre du Marais staged *Les Coups d'amour et de fortune* with changes of scenery and a ballet, which seems to have pleased them greatly; on the next day Molière's troupe staged *Amphitryon*. And yet the report by Potyomkin's embassy does not mention these plays (see *DRV* 4), and the only record we have of them is in the notes of the master of ceremonies, Sainctot.[380]

It is scarcely possible that, back in Moscow, Potyomkin did not discuss the theatrical marvels he had witnessed at Saint Germain, where he had seen the sparkling ballet and heard harmonious orchestral music ("pas de ballet et symphonie, sans aucune cacophonie" to quote the last lines of the *Gazette rimée,* a rhymed review).[380A] At any rate, Muscovite ambassadorial reports must have interested the inquisitive tsar and he must have taken them under consideration. Aleksei Mikhailovich also heard of the amateur theatricals produced in the Foreign Quarter. The Earl of Carlisle says that, in 1664, a comedy was staged in the embassy's quarters which "afforded the spectators some pleasant hours."[380B] Theatrical performances in the Foreign Quarter were apparently not exceptional events.

Shortly afterward the tsar himself wished to have the pleasure of witnessing theatrical spectacles at court. Circumstances were favorable. The deaths of his first wife, Tsaritsa Maria Il'inichna, and of a newborn daughter and, a few months later, of Princes Simeon and Aleksei, led the tsar to seek solace in the friendship of boyar Artemon Sergeevich Matveev. Matveev was one of the most progressive and enlightened Russian residents of Moscow. He had served in foreign regiments and was a cavalry colonel, familiar with foreign customs. His wife was a Scottish lady, Miss Hamilton, from the Foreign Quarter; on joining the Orthodox Church she assumed the name Avdot'ia Grigor'evna. Matveev's home was built in European fashion and contained a private theater in which plays were performed by Germans and by his domestic servants.[381] The tsar's second wife, Natalia Naryshkina (whom he married in 1671), was brought up in Matveev's home. The tsar involuntarily yielded to the influence of his young bride and Matveev, and when Tsarevich Peter was born on 30 May 1672, the tsaritsa's influence over her husband became even greater. The joyful events in the tsar's household—the birth of Peter and the proclamation shortly thereafter of Tsarevich Fyodor as heir to the throne—stimulated a desire to celebrate them in Western fashion, and Tsar Aleksei was fully prepared to do so.

About two weeks before Peter's birth, the tsar ordered Colonel Nicolay von Staden to "travel to Prince Jacobus of Courland [Latvia] and while in Courland to recruit for the service of the Great Lord mining experts who understood ores of all kinds and knew how to smelt them; also [two] skilled trumpeters and [two] knowledgeable people who could produce comedies."[381A] Staden's mission was not at all successful. At first he did manage to engage for the "entertainments of his royal majesty" a famous actor named Felten, and among other members of the troupe the no less famous Copenhagen singer, Anna Paulsen. But in the end things went badly. Both the miners and the actors refused to travel to distant Moscow, partly because of the lengthy journey and partly out of fear, for they heard absurd rumors to the effect that, once in Muscovy, foreigners were not allowed to leave the country and were threatened with beatings and exile to Siberia.[382] In December 1672 Staden returned to Moscow with only one trumpeter and four musicians. According to a document from the Foreign Office, published by S. K. Bogoiavlenskii:

In this year [1672], on the third day of December, Colonel Nicolay von Staden returned to the Tsar (complete list of his titles follows) from Sweden and appeared at the Foreign Office. According to the order of the Tsar, while in Stockholm and in Courland province, he contracted and brought back with him to the Tsar's service in Moscow a trumpeter from Imperial lands, Iohann Waldonn, and four musicians: from Prussia, Friederich Platenschleger; from Courland, Iacob Philips; from Gdansk, Gottfried Berge; from Saxony, Christophor Achermann, and with them seven various musical instruments. With the trumpeter he also brought his brother, Lieutenant Meller, because the trumpeter could not travel without him. And regarding the salaries in the Imperial service, they have agreed that Nicolay will provide monthly food from September of the present year; the trumpeter shall receive 8 rubles per month and the musicians 6 rubles each per month, and for the year the total will be 384 rubles; and the lieutenant will serve with the foreigners without any fixed salary.[383]

Staden's musicians stayed until about the middle of 1674, when some of them were dismissed from Moscow and others simply ran away. They were replaced by another group of foreign musicians: Ianus [Janus] Branten, Maximilian Markus, Frantsishek Annibal, Iagan [Johann] Teringeren, Ianus Kral'tson, and Maximilian Kreikenau. The first two "stayed in Moscow after [having arrived there with] an Imperial embassy," and the others were probably residents in the Foreign Quarter. In any case, both groups of musicians participated in the "tsar's comedy plays,"[384] although the first party, Waldon and his associates, arrived too late for the first performances.

While Staden was still absent from Moscow, the comedy [*komidiinoe deistvo*] had already been staged in Moscow. Three days after the birth of Tsarevich Peter, his young wife's first child, Aleksei Mikhailovich ordered the pastor of the Saxon church in the Foreign Quarter, Magister Johann Gottfried Gregory, to "prepare a comedy from the biblical Book of Esther, and for this purpose to have a new hall built" in Preobrazhenskoe village. There is little doubt that Matveev suggested Gregory to the tsar. But before ordering that a place be built for such hitherto unheard-of theatrical amusements, Tsar Aleksei consulted his confessor, Archpriest Andrei Savinov, who cited the precedent set by other Christian rulers, particularly the emperors of Orthodox Byzantium, who organized productions in their theaters. Four and a half months later the tsar's wish was fulfilled: on 17 October 1672, *Artakserksovo deistvo* [The Play of Artaxerxes] was staged.[385]

We are chiefly interested in the musical side of these earliest theatrical productions in Moscow. These first plays staged at Aleksei Mikhailovich's court included musical numbers, songs that were sometimes accompanied by instruments. So far only two short fragments have been discovered, and yet the complete repertory of dramatic productions, collected and assembled by N. S. Tikhonravov, clearly indicates that musical numbers were not neglected, although they appeared in the plays only incidentally.[385A]

During the first period of Moscow's court theater (1672–76), the following plays were produced:[386]

1672	17 October, *Artakserksovo deistvo* [The play of Artaxerxes] by Gregory
1673	around 2 February, Gregory's *Iudif'* [Judith];
	around 9 February, the ballet *Orfei i Evridika* [Orpheus and Euridice] with music by Schütz;[386A]
	in October, Simeon Polotskii's *Aleksei, bozhii chelovek* [Aleksei, man of God];[387]
	2 November, Gregory's *Tovii mladshii* [Tobit the younger];

1674–75[388]   *O Navukhodonosore tsare, o tele zlate i triekh otrotsekh, v peshchi ne sozhzhennykh* [King Nebuchadnezzar, the golden calf, and the three youths not burned in the furnace];

Komediia pritchi o bludnom syne [The comedy of the parable of the Prodigal Son] by Simeon Polotskii;

Zhalostnaia komediia ob Adame i Eve [The woeful comedy of Adam and Eve];

Malaia prokhladnaia komediia ob Iosife [The little pleasing comedy of Joseph];

Malaia komediia Baiazet i Tamerlan [The little comedy of Bajazet and Tamerlane] by Gregory.

Gregory's first plays were certainly presented in German, as they were performed exclusively by residents of the Foreign Quarter; with the immense cast of sixty-four actors, it would have been impossible to rehearse the "comedies" with native Muscovites in so short a time. Translations of *The Play of Artaxerxes* and other plays by Gregory were made for the tsar, and these must have helped to clarify these works, as did the printed translations of foreign opera libretti later on.

It is curious that the deepest impressions on the audiences were created by the following episodes in the first two plays by Gregory: "How Artaxerxes ordered Haman's execution in response to the petition by Esther and Mordecai's instruction," and "The Beheading of Holofernes by Judith." These scenes provided the titles to both plays in contemporary documents. Both plays were revived more than once and consequently enjoyed some popularity, as did *The Comedy of the Parable of the Prodigal Son*, of which several editions were published, containing illustrations by Picart.[388A]

These first Russian comedies were either borrowed (by Gregory) or simply translated (by Simeon Polotskii) from Western models, and they were varied by inserting crude comic episodes and vocal numbers.[389] Thus a musical *intermedium* (*mezhdusenie* [literally, a between-scenes]) was interpolated between the third and fourth acts of *Judith*, in which the kings captured by Holofernes bewailed their bitter fate; at the close, each of them sang a solo verse "very sorrowfully." Amarfal's music for the fourth verse survived; it was doubtless similar to those sung by the other three characters (Salmanasar, Ader, and Agag) and was published by I. A. Shliapkin.[390] Music played other roles, of course, in the early repertory of the Russian theater. There were other separate musical numbers, for example, Esther's song in *Artaxerxes* and the song of the four kings in *Judith*, noted above. Three soldiers sang a drinking song, "Vospoite bogu v timpanekh" [Praise the Lord with drums], in *Judith*, and there was also a concluding chorus of Jews taken from a biblical canticle. In *Bajazet and Tamerlane* the character Kalist sings a comic song, and in the *Woeful Comedy of Adam and Eve*, three angels sing a hymn of praise to God at the end of act 1. At the end of the second act there is another song (presumably with a chorus):[390A]

> Chrez adamovo padenie
> Vsi rody pogubleny.
>
> Through Adam's fall
> All mankind is lost.

At the conclusion of each act of the *Prodigal Son*, there was singing "followed by an *intermedium*"; the last word in the citation was written by the author himself, Simeon

Polotskii, [in Latin letters], thus establishing the use of this foreign term in our early theater.

In the play *King Nebuchadnezzar,* an elaboration of the popular Play of the Furnace, the youths, after the angel descends into the furnace, sing the same hymn of praise that was used in the liturgical drama:

> Blagosloven esi gospodi bozhe otets nashikh,
> i khvalen, i prevoznosim vo veki.

> Blessed art Thou, o Lord, God of our fathers
> Praised and glorified forever.

Similar indications may be encountered in annotations and remarks in the plays Tikhonravov published, for example, the note "Here trumpets sound out," and, in *Judith,* Nebuchadnezzar follows this with: "The trumpets are calling us to the table; rise councilors and follow me." After Judith beheads Holofernes, the text states: "Here to the blast of trumpets and drums the head is hung on the wall and Vanaia sings a song." In the *Prodigal Son,* in addition to the *intermedia* and singing mentioned above, there was a drinking song at the feast of the Prodigal Son and "talented musicians" [*sladkoigrateli*] appear, playing and singing to console the impoverished son. At the conclusion of the play a note indicates that "all make their bows, and the music starts up and the guests depart." Finally, in *Nebuchadnezzar* the king announces to the boyars (!) at the beginning of the play:

> Vy dnes' pechali nam ne pominaite,
> O musikii sladtsei pomyshliaite.

> Today do not remind us of sorrows,
> But think of the delights of music.

whereupon the musicians [*musikii*] enter.

Very little of the music for these early Russian theatrical works has survived. So far we know only the two songs from *Artaxerxes* and *Judith* published by Shliapkin. From *Artaxerxes* the song of Esther (as it is called in Shliapkin's edition) is preserved in a late-eighteenth-century manuscript copy. It is presented here as musical example 10.1 for two voices, moving almost entirely in parallel thirds.[391]

Esther was performed in Moscow in the first quarter of the eighteenth century, and "Esther's lament" may have been popular enough to have been included and maintained in the repertory of simple *kanty,* as the two styles of music were similar.[392] It appears here in a setting for two voices, and in the play itself it may have been performed in the same way at the ending of any of the acts.

Amarfal's song in *Judith* is even more interesting. Shliapkin published it in a transcription prepared by Professor L. A. Sakketti. Here I omit only the time signature and the sharp in the key signature which, apparently, were inserted accidentally in one of the printed versions of this song; I follow the original, however, in leaving out the bar lines in musical example 10.2.

This motif undoubtedly has much in common with Russian psalm settings from the end of the seventeenth century. It is remarkable that the opening melodic phrase (marked *a* in musical example 10.2) is identical to the well-known motif characterizing Ivan the Terrible

EXAMPLE 10.1. "Kako vosplachiu, kako vozrydaiu" [How I weep, how I lament]

Kako vosplachiu; kako vozrydaiu
S rodom Evreiskim, bedne pogibaiu.
Kto mia uteshit, ot placha tolika,
Zhalost' velika.

How I weep, how I lament
I shall perish in misery with the Jewish people.
Who shall console me from such weeping,
Such great sorrow.

in Rimskii-Korsakov's opera *Pskovitianka* [The maid of Pskov]; this fortuitous coincidence only demonstrates how purely Russian both motifs are. The vocal numbers in *Nebuchadnezzar*, specifically for the three children, were directly borrowed from the Play of the Furnace.

Other questions are equally important in examining the role of music in our first theatrical performances, for example, who performed the music in these shows and, especially, who composed the inserted musical numbers? We know that, in the first performances, the organist Simon Gutovskii and a musician [*igrets*], Timofei Gasenkrukh ([Hasenkruch], probably a violinist or lutenist), participated, and Laurentius Rinhuber and the previously mentioned organist Kazimir Vasilevskii may also have taken part. In addition to these musicians, the instrumental ensemble consisted of musicians in Matveev's service and then, beginning with *Judith,* the musicians Staden brought in 1672 were added. Later on, Pastor Gregory's church school and theatrical school may have formed the necessary group of musicians. The musicians played the "organs, viols (*ryle*), and *stramenty.*"[393]

We can answer only hypothetically the question of the composers for these dramatic plays. Judging from the two fragments in Shliapkin's edition, these works were not borrowed from the West, as the compiler of the collection apparently suggests. The melodies of the two songs resemble the Russian *kanty* of the period, which may suggest that the first Russian theatrical music was composed (perhaps on Matveev's orders) by members of the sovereign singers. Music like this would have been comprehensible to the tsar and his court. It seems quite likely, in any case, that Simeon Polotskii collaborated with V. P. Titov on his theatrical work. Titov had already set to music Polotskii's *Versified Psalter* and the collection of hymns to the saints. This would have been true, of course, only for the vocal numbers, and when contemporary *kanty* and psalm settings are published, we may find that some of them

EXAMPLE 10.2. "O prognevannyi bozhe" [Oh, furious God]

O prognevannyi bozhe,
Estli Befulii koe eshche spasenie
To Gospodi nash pomozi
Ashche li ny to na(s) vozmi ot seia zhizni.

Oh, furious God,
If there is still salvation for Bethulia
Then, oh Lord, help!
If not, then take us from this life.

were also used for the theater.[393A] The instrumental music was apparently played by experts from the Foreign Quarter following foreign models; the music was quite simple, consisting mainly of trumpet fanfares.

Yet in this first period in the history of the Russian theater at Aleksei Mikhailovich's court, a complete work by a foreign master was performed, namely, the ballet *Orpheus and Euridice,* staged in Moscow at the end of Carnival week in 1673 (presumably on 9 February). Jacob Reutenfels, from Courland, gives the following account in his *De Rebus Moschoviticis* (Padua, 1680):

> The fact is that hearing from many ambassadors that theatrical presentations were often given for European monarchs, with choruses and other amusements, in order to pass the time and disperse boredom, he [Tsar Aleksei], somewhat unexpectedly, ordered the presentation of a similar small production for himself, in the form of some sort of French dance. For that reason, in view of the shortage of time, in one week, with all possible haste, everything necessary for the chorus was prepared. In any other place but Moscow the performance would not have been able to be seen without anticipated apologies, but to the Russians it appeared so unusual and artistic that everything—the new costumes, never seen before, the unfamiliar sight of the stage, even, finally, the word "foreign" and the graceful strains of the music—easily created a sense of wonder. At first, it is true, the Tsar did not want to allow music as being new and in some ways pagan, but when they pleaded with him that without music it was impossible to put together a chorus, just as it is impossible for dancers to dance without legs, then he, a little unwillingly, left everything to the discretion of the actors themselves.[394]

The *Orpheus* presented in Moscow could not have been the Italian opera based on Rinuccini's libretto (first staged in Florence in 1600), as some scholars have assumed. It was rather, apparently, the ballet by the German composer Heinrich Schütz on the text by Professor August Buchner of Wittenberg. This ballet was first produced in 1638 in Dresden, where it was quite successful. Evidently the Moscow production was hastily copied from this Dresden performance, as Pastor Gregory and the inhabitants of the Foreign Quarter had close relations with the Saxon capital at that time. Just as Orpheus's singing caused the woods and rocks to move in the ancient Greek myth, so in the Moscow ballet pyramids danced to his music. The performance started with Orpheus greeting the tsar, praising his wisdom and the fine qualities of his soul. On either side of the ancient Greek god pyramids stood, adorned with transparencies and illuminated. At the end of his song, Orpheus turned to the pyramids and invited them to dance; after this, the ballet began.[395]

Two drawings from a contemporary publication give us some idea of the first Moscow stage productions in Aleksei Mikhailovich's time. The work is Polotskii's *Comedy of the Parable of the Prodigal Son* (Moscow, 1685), illustrated with engravings by the Dutchman Picart, who later worked at the Moscow Armory (fig. 100).[396] The staging of Gregory's and

FIG. 100. Two scenes from Simeon Polotskii's *The Comedy of the Prodigal Son* [probably from the early eighteenth century].

Polotskii's plays was undoubtedly copied from foreign productions, so these engravings can give us information about the stage, the footlights, and even the costumes and gestures of the Muscovite actors.

The presentation of comedies at court came to an end with Tsar Aleksei Mikhailovich's death on 29 January 1676 and the succession of his son, Fyodor Alekseevich (r. 1676–82). The theater's initiator and patron, A. S. Matveev, fell into disgrace and shortly thereafter was banished to Pustozersk. The new group of boyars surrounding the young tsar was opposed to Matveev's foreign amusements. The rooms used for the comedies were cleaned out, and the theatrical properties were taken to a residence that had belonged to Nikita Ivanovich Romanov. At the same time the theatrical school was closed and foreign musical entertainments were halted. No information concerning them has been preserved. The school at the Zaikonospasskii Monastery in Moscow may have continued with performances of Polotskii's plays but on a much more restricted scale than at court.

During Fyodor Alekseevich's reign, the creative activities of the sovereign singers continued, arousing the well-known controversy between the defenders of the old *znamennoe* singing and the creators of the new *partesnoe* and concerted style (Korenev's treatise is dated 1681).[397] The sacred performances discussed earlier, like the last of the Moscow patriarchs, had come to the end of their days. Regardless of the wishes of the young tsar, who reigned only briefly, much of the past was lost, and closer relations with the West necessarily revealed new perspectives to Moscow.

When Fyodor was succeeded by his younger brother, Peter I, the Muscovite state was steered on an entirely new course: theatrical performances were revived; the compositional activities of the sovereign singers blossomed; and the influence of foreign music became very powerful, swiftly and for many years overwhelming the fundamental national element of Russian music. In his *On Russia during the Reign of Aleksei Mikhailovich,* Grigorii Kotoshikhin rightly stressed the idea that ancient Russia's ignorance was the result of alienation from "other kingdoms." Tsar Peter Alekseevich seems to have imbibed this conviction with his mother's milk, and he broke decisively with all the past traditions of the state he inherited.

11. A Brief Survey of Singers, Composers, and Music Theorists of the Sixteenth and Seventeenth Centuries[398]

Adamov, Matiusha, sovereign singer, in 1551 appointed as a commissioner for the Trinity–St. Sergius Monastery by Ivan the Terrible [see chapter 8 on these appointments].

Afanas'ev, Gavrilka, sovereign singer, in 1551 appointed as a commissioner for the Trinity–St. Sergius Monastery by Ivan the Terrible.

Afanas'ev, Maksim, sovereign singer from Siberia, where he belonged to the choir of the Archbishop of Siberia. In 1691 he presented a petition to the tsar.

Anan'in, Ivan, singer and apparently choirmaster [*ustavshchik*] in the choir of Simon, Archbishop of Vologda and Belozersk (1666); his "Pokazaniia" [Testimonies] on the training of church singers were published by the Moscow Archaeological Society.[398A]

Andreev, Grigorii, patriarchal singer (1613–14); rehearsed the Play of the Furnace with singers in Moscow. Documents on this singer are in A. Viktorov, *Description of Expense Books*.

Babin, Semyon Fyodorov, one of the Bishop of Novgorod's singers; celebrated for the art of his *raspevy* at the end of the seventeenth century.

Baryshevskii, Andrei, sovereign singer (1683).

Baskakov, Petrushka, a singer of the Archbishop of Riazan and Murom (1596–98). He may be the author of the so-called Baskakov version ([*baskakov perevod*]; *raspev* or arrangement), well known in the history of chant.

Bavykin, Nikolai, Moscow conductor [*regent*] and composer. The library of the former Synodal School of Church Singing in Moscow [in GIM] contains his twelve-part setting of the Presanctified Liturgy.

Beliaev, Stefan Ivanovich, sovereign singer in Moscow, a pupil of South Russian singers; one of the creators of *partesnoe* singing in the second half of the seventeenth century and from 1699 leader of the tsar's choir. Some of his works are in the library of the former Synodal School in Moscow [GIM]: an Octoechos, four-part hymns for feasts, and so on. He was one of Peter the Great's favorites.[398B]

Beliai, Ivan Terent'ev, sovereign singer (1699–1701 and later).

Berezhanskii, Pyotr Ivanov, "a recently arrived foreigner from Kiev" and later a sovereign singer. In 1652 he joined with his "brethren" in petitioning the tsar for an increase in pay (see under Bykovskii).

Bezborodyi, Markell, well-known singer and Novgorodian monk; in 1555 abbot of the Khutyn Monastery in Novgorod. He arranged chants in his "Psalter and a whole cycle of chants honoring men and women venerated in Russia as new miracle workers, the cycle consisting of hymns and processionals and *stikhiry* covering the church year from September to the end of August" (at that time, the church calendar year started on 1 September). From 1557 he lived as a retired monk in the Antoniev Monastery, where he composed a *kanon* for Nikita, Archbishop of Novgorod.

Bogdanov, Efim, tsar's singer and clerk of the cross [*krestovyi d'iak*, an ecclesiastical rank]. Died in Moscow in 1678.

Borzakovskii, Andrei Fyodorovich, and Iakov Fyodorovich, sovereign singers in Moscow (1682–89).

Burmistrov, Larion (Lavrentii), sovereign singer (1679–83).

Bykovskii, Mikhail Osipov, "a recently arrived foreigner from Kiev" and later a sovereign singer. In May 1652 he applied for an increase in his daily pay. The tsar granted him a salary of eight *dengi* per day.

Denisov, Semyon, sovereign scribe-copyist of reformed chant [*narechnoe penie*] in the second half of the seventeenth century.

D'iakovskii, a Pole by birth; sovereign singer in Moscow, pupil of South Russian singers, and one of the creators of *partesnoe* singing at the end of the seventeenth and the beginning of the eighteenth centuries.

Diletskii, Nikolai Pavlovich, well-known theorist of the second half of the seventeenth century (ca. 1630–ca. 1690). A native of Kiev, he studied with the Polish theorists Mielczewski, Zamarevich, and Ziusk. Diletskii lived in Kiev, Wilno, Smolensk, and Moscow, where he was the conductor of G. D. Stroganov's choir. His famous *Musical Grammar* was published, that is, transmitted in several manuscript versions, first in Polish in Wilno and then in a Russian translation in Smolensk (as the *Grammatika peniia musikiiskago ili izvestnyia pravila v soiuze [sloze] musikiiskom, v nikh obretaiutsia 6 chastei. Izdadesia [v] Smolensku Nikolaem Diletskim v leto ot Rozhdestva Khristova 1677* [A grammar of musical singing, or known rules of singing in musical word[s], in which there are six parts; issued in Smolensk by Nikolai Diletskii in the year 1677 from the birth of Christ]. A copy of this version is in the Archive of the Ministry of Foreign Affairs in Moscow; another Russian translation was made in Moscow in 1679, and there are four copies: (1) Manuscript 994 in the Rumiantsev Museum [RGB]; (2) Undol'skii's copy, Manuscript 177 in the library of the Moscow Society for Russian History and Antiquities [RGB]; (3) Manuscript 532 in the Moscow Archive of the Ministry of Foreign Affairs [RGADA]; and (4) in the Library of the Synodal School of Church Chant [GIM].[398C]

Dmitrii, a monk, one of the singers associated with the Greek patriarch; in Moscow in 1589.

Evfrosin, a monk who wrote a polemical treatise in 1651 titled *Skazanie o razlichnykh eresekh i khuleniiakh na gospoda boga i prechistuiu bogoroditsu, soderzhimykh ot nevedeniia v znamennykh knigakh* [An account of various heresies and blasphemies against the Lord God and the Blessed Virgin, retained through ignorance in the notated musical books]. The three existing copies of this treatise are in the Public Library [RNB], Pogod. 1559; the Khludov Library [GIM], 91; and the former Synodal School in Moscow [GIM], 74 [see above, chapter 9].

Falaleev, Dimitrii, patriarchal singer of the first *stanitsa* at the time of Patriarch Filaret (1619–33).

Golutvin, Vladimir Sergeevich, sovereign singer, 1669–81, at the Cathedral of the Resurrection and at the Church of the Precursor in Moscow; in 1683 at the Verkho-Spasskii Cathedral. He accompanied Peter I to Voronezh in 1701.

Golysh, Stefan, singer, teacher of church chant and arranger [*raspevshchik*] in the sixteenth and seventeenth centuries. Golysh visited many towns and taught in the area of Usol'e and for the Stroganovs; he arranged many books of *znamennyi* chant. Among his pupils, Ivan Lukoshkov (as a monk, known as Archimandrite Isaiah) was very well known.

Grabovskii, Il'ia, sovereign singer, ca. 1682.

Iakovlev, Simeon, deacon and composer of sacred music at the end of the seventeenth century. Wrote a *kontsert* for twelve voices.

Iaroslavets, Vasilii, a supernumerary [*neokladnyi*] of the sovereign singers; in 1668 submitted a petition to the tsar.

Ilarionov, Kondratii, a deacon from Iaroslav, member of the second commission (1668) for the revision of notated liturgical books in Moscow.

Il'in, Iakushko (Iakov), a "newly arrived singer [*spevak*] from Kiev" who came to Moscow in April 1652 "to live forever" there; he joined the sovereign singers. In the same year he petitioned for a daily allowance of food.

Iosifov, Tit, patriarchal singer of the second *stanitsa* under Patriarch Filaret (1619–33).

Ivanov, Bogdan, patriarchal singer of the first *stanitsa* under Patriarch Filaret (1619–51); in 1651 he became a member of the sovereign singers.

Ivanov, Daniil, patriarchal singer of the second *stanitsa* under Patriarch Filaret (1619–51).

Ivanov, Grigorii, a Kievan singer who came to Moscow in April 1652 "to live forever" there; still serving as a sovereign singer in 1677.

Ivanov, Pyotr, a Kievan singer who came to Moscow in April 1652 "to live forever" there.

Kalachnikov, Nikolai, a prolific composer of sacred music at the end of the seventeenth and the beginning of the eighteenth centuries. The library of the former Synodal School of Church Singing [GIM] has manuscript scores of his compositions: (1) Divine Liturgy, for twenty-four voices; (2) a *kontsert*, "Izhe zapovedi" [As commandments], also for twenty-four voices; (3) Divine Liturgy for twelve voices; (4) All Night Vigil for twelve voices; (5) twenty-three *kontserty* for twelve voices.

Karsakov, Ignatii, a hieromonk of the Solovki Monastery (ca. 1678). On Archimandrite Makarii's orders, he copied "from approved arrangements of the imperial city of Moscow" a notated Irmologii, an Obikhod, the Twelve Great Feasts of the Lord, and others.

Kherugovskii, Grigorii, sovereign copyist of *narechnoe penie* in the second half of the seventeenth century.

Khrisanf, a Greek monk, *raspevshchik* in Moscow at the end of the seventeenth century. Manuscript no. 3983 of the Synodal Archive [GIM] contains the "*znamennye* Dostoino settings in all eight modes . . . by Khrisanf" and four Greek *raspevy* and *demestvennye* settings (see Viktorov, *Description of Expense Books* 2, pt. 2: 812).

Khristianin [Kristianin], Fyodor, a Moscow priest, *raspevshchik* of *znamennye* chants. Pupil of Savva Rogov and, in turn, educator of many singers himself. In Ivan the Terrible's time he lived in the Aleksandrovskaia sloboda. His arrangement ["perevod Khristianinov"] of *znamennyi raspev* is well known. According to contemporaries, Khristianin was "famous and knew *znamennyi* chant well, and many have learned from him."

Kolenda, Ioann (Ian), a singer of Polish origin, from Kiev, later a conductor [*regent*] in the tsar's cappella (1666) and a composer. His works are cited in Diletskii's *Musical Grammar*. He composed a number of *kontserty* for twelve, twenty-four, and thirty-two voices.

Kolpenskii, a composer of church music from the end of the seventeenth century in Moscow. The library of the former Synodal School contains his settings of all the *zadostoiniki* [hymns sung instead of the usual hymn to the Virgin beginning with the words "Dostoino est'" (It is meet)]; also two settings of the Divine Liturgy for twelve voices and four *kontserty*.

Koniukhovskii, Ivan, sovereign singer; in 1640 wrote a set of all the chants for the Obikhod, for two voices, on six hundred folios. Kostomarov (fasc. 4) states that in 1650 a certain Koniukhovskii ran away from Moscow to Lithuania, then to Constantinople and Stockholm, together with a self-styled clerk [*d'iak*], Timoshka Ankudinov. It is possible that this Koniukhovskii was the former sovereign singer. [See n. 398D, below, on Kostomarov.]

Konovskii, Klim, sovereign singer in Moscow; in 1655 he was sent to Kiev with Aleksandr Leshkovskii to bring the elder Iosif Zagvoiskii to Moscow to teach part singing. The report of their failure and their stopover in Putivl, on their return trip in February 1656, were published by Undol'skii [see n. 398, above].

Konstantinov, Fyodor, patriarchal singer; served as early as the 1640s. In 1652 he entered the sovereign singers but shortly thereafter returned to the patriarch's service. He went on a pilgrimage with the patriarch in 1667 and kept records of the patriarch's whereabouts. In 1668 he was a member of the second commission for the correction of musical liturgical books in Moscow. He was also a skillful copyist of *narechnoe* singing.

Korenev, Ioann Trofimov, deacon of the court Cathedral of the Visitation in Moscow; author of the polemical treatise *Musikiia* [Music] in defense of part singing, appended to the last (1681) Moscow version of Diletskii's *Musical Grammar.*

Korsakov, Grigorii Leont'ev, sovereign singer; in 1691 sent to the Siberian Office.

Kostitsa, Ivashka, sovereign singer under Vasilii III. In 1538–39 granted a commissionership.

Kriuk, Iurii, sovereign copyist of reformed [*narechnoe*] chant in the second half of the seventeenth century.

Kuz'min, Andrei, patriarchal singer of the first *stanitsa* under Patriarch Filaret (1619–33).

Leont'ev, Ivan, composer of church music in Moscow at the end of the seventeenth century.

Leshkovskii, Aleksandr, sovereign singer in Moscow; in 1655 sent with Klim Konovskii to Kiev to bring the elder Iosif Zagvoiskii to Moscow (see Konovskii).

Litvinov, Paisii, leader [*golovshchik*] of the right *kliros* at the Trinity–St. Sergius Lavra (1609).

Loggin [Login], leader and *raspevshchik* at the Trinity–St. Sergius Lavra (d. 1635). He composed to one and the same text five, six, ten, and even seventeen arrangements of *znamennyi* chant. Archimandrite Dionisii of the Trinity–St. Sergius Lavra told the choir leader Filaret: "You keep reasoning, and yet in Loggin's chant he puts signs wherever he wants them." For biographical data and accounts of Loggin's quarrels with Archimandrite Dionisii, see N. Kostomarov and P. Znamenskii.[398D]

Lukoshkov, Ivan, well-known *raspevshchik* of *znamennyi* chant from Usol'e, where he was probably either a singer or a conductor for the Stroganovs. There he studied with Stefan Golysh. His arrangements of *znamennyi* chant called "Lukoshkov" and "bol'shoi [great] Lukoshkov" are well known. In manuscript no. 32.16.18 of the library of the Academy of Sciences ([BAN] a notated Stikhirar from the beginning of the seventeenth century), on folio 205 there is a *stikhira* for the Feast of the Descent of the Holy Spirit, with the inscription: "Lukoshkov's *rospev.*"

Makar'evskii, Tikhon, monk and treasurer of the patriarchal court in Moscow during Fyodor Alekseevich's reign (1676–82). He wrote the *Kliuch ili pravila musikiiskago peniia, soglasno i chinno sochinennago* [The key, or rules of musical singing, harmoniously and decorously composed].[398E]

Maksimov, Potap, sovereign singer, copyist of reformed [*narechnoe*] chant, died in 1682 in Moscow.

Martem'ian, Shestak (i.e., Martem'ian's sixth son), *spravshchik* [corrector, redactor] at the Moscow Printing Office; in 1652 wrote the "Slovo o edinoglasii" [A commentary on monophonic chant], which was published in abridged form by A. V. Preobrazhenskii.[398F] Martem'ian died in 1653. Among the singers of the lower *stanitsa* in 1652–53 there was a Kir'iak Martem'ian, who was probably a younger brother.

Matveev, Ivan, patriarchal singer of the first *stanitsa* in Moscow, 1649–50.

Meletii, a deacon, a Greek singer, invited by Tsar Aleksei Mikhailovich to teach Greek singing to his singers. He also taught the patriarchal singers in the years 1656–59. He was an expert copyist of reformed [*narechnoe*] chant.

Mezenets, Aleksandr, an elder monk of the Zvenigorod Monastery of St. Savva, later corrector of the Moscow Printing Office. He was appointed to the second commission for the correction of musical liturgical books in Moscow in 1668, and he edited the *Izveshchenie o soglasneishikh pometakh* [Report about the most harmonious notational signs], which was published by S. V. Smolenskii in 1888. Manuscript copies of this treatise are in the Public Library [RNB] in the anthology Q.XII.1, and in the Rumiantsev Museum [RGB] Undol'skii Collection, nos. 176 and 1218. Mezenets also planned the printing of notated liturgical books. In Bezsonov's collection, there was a manuscript of verses provided with late *kriuki* notation with additional signs [*pomety*] by A. Mezenets. The library of the former Synodal School in Moscow has a book notated with *kriuki* ([GIM, Sin. pev.] 98) presented as a gift by Mezenets to a clerk of the Iamskii Prikaz, Pavel Chernitsyn, and containing an autobiographical poem from which it is evident that Mezenets was a native of the city of Cherkas in Little Russia; his father was called Ioann (Stremoukhov?). He lived for a time in Novgorod. See S. V. Smolenskii, who also quotes another poem by Mezenets signed "Monach Alexander Stremmouchow" [in Latin letters] but doubts whether it is in Mezenets's own handwriting. [See chapter 9, above, for updated information on Mezenets.][398G]

Mikhailov, Andrei, sovereign singer, copyist of reformed [*narechnoe*] chant (1678–82).

Mikhailov, Leontii, patriarchal singer of the second *stanitsa* under Patriarch Filaret (1619–33).

Mikhailov, Pavel, *ustavshchik* of the sovereign singers; accompanied the tsar on a pilgrimage in 1680.

Mikhailov, Savin, patriarchal singer of the second *stanitsa* under Patriarch Filaret (1619–33).

Mikhailov, Semyon, patriarchal singer of the first *stanitsa* in Moscow (1649–50).

Naritsyn, Pyotr, composer of sacred music at the end of the seventeenth century. In the library of the former Synodal School of Church Singing are his Beatitudes for four voices and *zadostoiniki* for four voices "from old Greek [models]." An eighteenth-century staff-notated manuscript, no. 3933, in the Synodal Archive, contains Naritsyn's *zadostoiniki* with the annotation "*dostoiny* in *znamennaia* notation in eight modes [*glasy*], notation by Naritsyn" and also "Greek by Naritsyn."[398H]

Nektar'ev, Ivan, Kievan singer who arrived in Moscow in April 1652 "to live forever" there and joined the sovereign singers.

Nikiforov, Ivan, sovereign singer; in 1659 he presented the tsar with an icon of the Holy Martyrs Sofia, Vera, Nadezhda, and Liubov' [Wisdom, Faith, Hope, and Love]. Nikiforov was also an expert copyist of reformed [*narechnoe*] chant.

Nikitin, Faddei, *d'iachok* from Usol'e, member of the second commission (1668) for the reform of the notated liturgical books in Moscow.

Nikitin, Ivan, patriarchal singer of the first *stanitsa* (1619–50).

Nikitin, Prokofii, sovereign singer of the third *stanitsa*, where he was a *putnik,* that is, he performed the middle line in the choir (1671).

Nizhegorodets, Andrei Vasil'ev, a native of Nizhnii Novgorod and sovereign singer in the time of Peter I. In the library of the Academy of Sciences [BAN] there is a notated Psalter containing compositions by Vasilii Titov (no. 16.15.9), with an inscription in Nizhegorodets's handwriting: "This book belongs to the singer Andrei Nizhegorodets, who is in service to the Great Lord Tsar and Great Prince Peter Alekseevich, autocrat of Great, Little, and White Russias."

Nos, Grigorii, *d'iachok,* member of the second commission (1668) for the reform of the notated liturgical books in Moscow.

Nos, Ivan, sovereign singer of the sixteenth and the seventeenth centuries, pupil of Savva Rogov. He lived in the Aleksandrovskaia sloboda in the days of Ivan the Terrible and arranged the "Triod for Lent and the Pentecostal Period, *stikhiry*-hymns of praise, *theotokia,* and *stavrotheotokia* of the Mineia for many saints."[398I]

Opekalov, a *raspevshchik* of the seventeenth century, either from Moscow or from Novgorod. In a notated manuscript of the Octoechos from 1672, in my possession, there is a setting of the chant "Sviatyi Bozhe, sviatyi krepkii" [the Trisagion], with the annotation "by Opekalov" (fol. 100). [See the prefatory comments to this chapter.]

Osipov, Mikhailo, a Kievan singer who came to Moscow in April 1652 "to live forever" there; he was also a sovereign copyist of reformed [*narechnoe*] chant.

Panfilov, Grigorii, sovereign copyist of reformed [*narechnoe*] chant in the second half of the seventeenth century.

Pavlov, Roman, a Kievan singer who came to Moscow in April 1652 "to live forever" there and joined the sovereign singers.

Pecherskii, Aleksandr, an elder of the Chudov Monastery, member of the second commission (1668) for the correction of notated liturgical books in Moscow.

Pikulinskii, Vasilii, singer and conductor for Metropolitan Sil'vestr Kossov of Kiev (1656), who knew *nachal'stvo* (conducting) and *partesnoe penie.* In answer to an invitation to Moscow to join the tsar's singers, the metropolitan stated: "We cannot do without Vas'ka the singer in the monastery and I cannot let him go."

Pokrovets, Pyotr Vasil'ev, sovereign singer ca. 1671, later an *ustavshchik.* In 1671 he lived on Tverskaia Street. By order of Peter I, dated 21 November 1682, after the death of Tsar Fyodor Alekseevich he was given four cases and seven baskets of books of *narechnoe penie,* "*znamennye* [books], three-part settings, and a variety of arrangements [*perevody*] of sacred music."[398J]

Polianinov, Matvei, horse-stable groom, promoted to sovereign singer in 1679.

Popovskii, Ivan, sovereign singer, choral conductor of Catherine I's cappella. In 1725 he copied a notated Irmologii, presently in the manuscript division of the Public Library in St. Petersburg ([RNB] F.I.863), with the following inscription: "This book, an Irmologii, was written with God's help in the imperial city of St. Petersburg by the singer Ivan Popovskii, choral conductor [*regent*] of the all-eminent Ruler and Empress Catherine Alekseevna, in the year 1725, on 16 January."

Protopopov, Ivan Mikhailov, sovereign singer, later *ustavshchik;* a pupil of the South Russian singers. One of the creators of *partesnoe penie* in the seventeenth century. His harmonizations are in the archive of the former Ministry of the Imperial Court [RGIA] (fascicles nos. 37, 53, 56).

Radilov, conductor and composer, apparently from Novgorod, at the end of the sixteenth and the beginning of the seventeenth century. The "Alelluia by Radilov" ("Alliluiia Radilova") can be found in staffless musical manuscripts from the time of Tsar Mikhail Fyodorovich and Patriarch Joseph. Contemporary records state that on the Sunday of the Forefathers at the liturgy, the Novgorodian singers always sang the alleluia by Radilov (*DRV* 4:387).

Redrikov, Fyodor, conductor and composer from Moscow. He composed eight settings of the Divine Liturgy, two *kontserty* (in the library of the former Synodal School of

Church Chant in Moscow [GIM]). In 1795 Gene's music store in Moscow advertised the sale of his *stikhiri* for the Twelve Great Feasts, for two choirs (eight voices); see the newspaper *Mosk. vedomosti* 1795, no. 98. Apparently his father or a relative by the name of Bogolep Redrikov, an elder of a cathedral (d. 1636), was buried in the Trinity–St. Sergius Lavra.[398K]

Rezvitskii, Iakov, a Little Russian; in Kholmogory, in June 1723, he set a Divine Liturgy for eight voices and made a setting of *zadostoiniki* for the Twelve Great Feasts (the Perm collection).

Rogov, Savva, brother of Vasilii; a resident of Novgorod and Karelian by birth. He was a famous singer and teacher of chant at the end of the sixteenth and beginning of the seventeenth centuries. Among his pupils were Stefan Golysh, Ivan Nos, and Fyodor Khristianin.

Rogov, Vasilii (monastic name Varlaam), a Karelian by birth; one of the creators of three-part chanting (sixteenth–seventeenth century). In 1587 he was installed as Archbishop of Rostov, and, in 1589, he was promoted to the rank of Metropolitan of Rostov. According to the author of a preface to an old notated Stikhirar, Varlaam was a "revered and wise man who was also a good singer. He was one of the creators and singers of traditional *znamennye* chants, three-part settings, and *demestvennyi* chant."

Sedoi, Osip, sovereign singer; in 1686 he accompanied the tsar on a pilgrimage.

Seliverstov, Ivan, a Kievan singer who arrived in Moscow in April 1652 "to live forever" there. He joined the ranks of the sovereign singers.

Shaidurov [Shaidur], Ivan Akimovich, a native of Novgorod, a master of church chant in Moscow in the first half of the seventeenth century. He is credited with the invention of the cinnabar additions to the neumes, which were universally accepted, and was the author of a grammar of *znamennyi* singing, the *Skazanie o pometakh, ezhe pishutsia v penii pod znamenem* [A treatise on additional signs as these are written in chants underneath the neumes]. "This Ioann diligently and with great care invented beautiful *znamennoe* singing; God revealed to him the model for *pomety*" (Razumovskii, *Church Singing in Russia,* fasc. 2:159).

Shestak, Martem'ian, see Martem'ian, Shestak.

Shila, Nikita, singer for the archbishop of Tver, died in the last quarter of the sixteenth century; according to land registers of the sixteenth century, he owned the village of Migunov.

Shishkov, Gurii, leader of the left *kliros* of the Trinity–St. Sergius Lavra in 1609.

Sifov, Mikhail, sovereign singer, pupil of South Russian singers, one of the creators of *partesnoe penie* at the end of the seventeenth century.

Simonov, Nikifor, sovereign singer in 1678.

Simonovskii, Timofei, patriarchal singer in 1677.

Sofia Alekseevna, tsarevna [daughter of Tsar Aleksei Mikhailovich] (1657–1704), as a nun named Susanna, she copied a notated Octoechos in semi-uncial script, with gold and colored ink, now preserved in the church of the village of Novospasskoe in the Moscow district.[398L]

Ternopol'skii, Fyodor, an important singer from Kiev who arrived in Moscow in February 1652 together with other singers and entered the sovereign singers. Ternopol'skii is one of the creators of *strochnoe penie.*

Timofeev, Stepan, a Kievan singer who arrived in Moscow in April 1652 "to live forever" there and became a sovereign singer.

Titov, Vasilii Polikarpovich, sovereign singer and highly talented composer in Moscow. He was active from 1680 to 1710. He set to music Simeon Polotskii's *Versified Psalter* (1680) and Polotskii's *Hymn to the Saints*, a calendar in verse for the entire year. The most popular of his works is his *Great Mnogoletie*; among other works are his settings of the Divine Liturgy for eight, sixteen, and twenty-four voices (one of the eight-part settings uses *znamennyi raspev*); a *theotokia* for six and eight voices; a liturgy for twelve voices; twenty-eight *kontserty* for twelve voices; *dogmatiki* for eight voices; and *kontserty* for the Twelve Great Feasts (1709). Many of his works are in the library of the former Synodal School of Church Chant in Moscow [GIM]. Two manuscript copies of his notated Psalter containing the 150 psalms and a musical *mesiatseslov* (Hymns to the Saints) as well as other compositions can be found in the manuscript division of the library of the Academy of Sciences ([BAN] nos. 16.15.11 and 16.15.9); in the Synodal Archive there is a manuscript copy of Polotskii's *Versified Psalter* "set to music in staff notation by the singer Vasilii Titov," which was presented to Tsar Fyodor Alekseevich.[398M]

Trofimov, Ivan, patriarchal singer of the first *stanitsa* in Moscow (1649–50).

Tsaryov, Mit'ka, sovereign singer, in 1551 appointed as a commissioner for the Trinity–St. Sergius Monastery by Ivan IV.

Ukhtomskii, Fedot, *ustavshchik* of the sovereign singers (1697).

Vasil'ev, Aleksandr, "a foreigner," a Kievan singer who came to Moscow in 1651. In June 1652 he petitioned the tsar for release with other singers to return to Kiev. It is unknown whether his appeal was successful.

Vasil'ev, Mikhaila, sovereign singer; in 1614 he was a *putnik* [sang the cantus firmus part] of the senior choral station (*bol'shaia stanitsa*).

Viazemskii, Nikifor Kondratovich, sovereign singer; he was Tsarevich Aleksei Petrovich's chant teacher and close friend, and was involved in the affair of the Tsarevich [Aleksei] who "perished" in 1718.[398N] He set to music the processional verse "Vrag kresta Khristova" [The enemy of the cross of Christ]. For further data on him see, among others, the study by S. F. Platonov, cited above under Beliaev.

Vinogradov, Vasilii, a Moscow choral conductor and composer of the late seventeenth century. His compositions are in the library of the Synodal School [GIM]: a setting of the Divine Liturgy for twelve voices and a *kontsert* for twelve voices, "Glasom moim ko Gospodu vozzvakh" [I cried unto the Lord with my voice].

Zagvoiskii, Iosif, an elder of the Bratskii Monastery in Kiev who taught part singing. Despite an urgent summons to the tsar's chapel in Moscow, he went to the monastery in Vygovsk, in Chigirin.[398O] Undol'skii published the decree of his release from Kiev and the report of the Kievan governor F. F. Volkonskii on the unsuccessful search for him.

Zlatoustovskii, Bogdan, sovereign copyist of *narechnoe penie* in the second half of the seventeenth century.

Zverintsev, Tret'iak, sovereign singer; around 1560 Ivan the Terrible awarded him a commissionership.

12. Music and Theater in the Age of Peter the Great

Russian travelers abroad at the end of the seventeenth and the beginning of the eighteenth century. Theatrical performances in the time of Peter I. Musicians from abroad. Music at court and in public life. Peter the Great's successors.

The Moscow period of Peter I's reign coincides with the end of the seventeenth century and rounds out the Muscovite epoch in the development of Russian music. With the beginning of the new century, music culture was transferred from the old capital [in Moscow] to the new one [in St. Petersburg], where it developed along entirely different lines.

Unlike his father [Aleksei Mikhailovich], Tsar Peter Alekseevich had no artistic inclinations. He was not attracted to music, and although a harpsichord was included in his entertainments as a child, it is not known who played it.[398P] When in 1697 he traveled abroad for the first time, the princesses of Hanover and Brandenburg proposed to entertain him with Italian singers, but Peter admitted frankly that he did not care for music: "I would prefer to go sailing and let off fireworks," he said. During his visit to Paris in 1717, he was invited to the opera by the regent, the Duke of Orleans, but he could not sit through to the end of the performance. Both these instances, especially Peter's reply to the German princesses, reveal a fundamental trait in his character. He attached only a utilitarian significance to music and theater. He preferred the art of pyrotechnics to the art of music, and our country's passion for fireworks and ingenious illuminations, in which music played a largely functional role, dates from this time. Peter was a remarkably expert performer on the drums, but, apart from that, his only interest in music was in church singing, an interest he inherited, no doubt, from his father.

Foreigners describe him in the same way. Bergholz, for example, says that Peter had little liking for music but was fond of drinking and compelled others to join him. He was in very high spirits at the celebration marking the conclusion of the Treaty of Nystadt [1721], drinking heavily and even dancing on tables. But during banquets he frequently silenced the music because it interfered with conversation. His attitude toward church singing was quite different; he often sang in the *kliros* reading from the choir books, preferring the *ekstsellentuiushchii* bass part [an ornamented bass line]. Preserved in the Moscow Armory are the vocal scores from which he sang, cleanly copied, bound in parchment, and inscribed "the Great Lord Peter Alekseevich was pleased to sing from this music."

Peter visited the Solovki Monastery with his singers on the eve of the Feast of the Assumption in 1701 and the chronicler there noted: "His Majesty the Emperor stood with the singers in the *kliros* on the right and was pleased to sing the All Night Vigil himself. The next day, on 15 August, he again stood and sang in the *kliros*." There is also a manuscript with the *irmosy* of Greek tunes [*grecheskii raspev*], formerly housed in the Kozel Hermitage of the Presentation to the Temple and presently in the Historical Museum in Moscow (in the collection of the Synodal School Library [GIM]) with the following inscription: "His Majesty the Emperor Peter the Great sang these *irmosy* on his name day at the All Night Vigil with the singers in the *kliros,* as His Majesty was fond of the Greek tunes [*grecheskii napev*], and he took the tenor part."

Peter often took the court singers with him on trips. One of his favorite servants was a singer named Vasilii, and another favorite was Stepan Beliaev, a pupil of South Russian singers who, in 1713, became a choir leader (he composed a four-part setting of hymns for the feasts of saints, now in the library of the former Synodal School [GIM]).[398Q] In 1712 Beliaev was granted "in perpetuity" a plot in Frolovskoe, in the Kolomenskoe district; it can hardly be doubted that he was one of Peter's drinking companions and an active participant in the tsar's assembly of jokesters [*vseshuteishii sobor*].[399] Peter also liked to have choral singing at his victory celebrations, and this undoubtedly stimulated a new type of *kant* of a solemnly festive, secular, and triumphal character. As we shall see, this new kind of *kant* produced a vast literature of a novel and well-defined nature.

Much closer relations with the West began from the first years of Peter's reign. Foreigners were now commonly invited to work in Russia, and Russian embassies and missions abroad became more frequent and assumed an entirely new character, as we see from official diplomatic reports and other contemporary writings. We have already looked at the diplomatic accounts from Aleksei Mikhailovich's reign; the notes of Russian travelers in Peter's time are much more interesting. In the past, Muscovites had marveled at cunning Western ingenuity, yet they held themselves aloof from foreigners, fearing infection by some sort of heresy. By the eighteenth century, however, that very same West had become an object of admiration and imitation. As A. N. Pypin perceptively observed, Russian travelers in Peter's time were thus standing at a kind of crossroad between these two contrasting outlooks, and their reactions are extremely interesting. On the one hand, the old view was more or less firmly fixed in their minds, but on the other hand, their imagination was involuntarily seized by the rich and astonishing impressions of the new.[400]

In this fresh outlook, due attention was paid to the arts, including music. Muscovites now conceived a genuine admiration for the superb masterpieces of sculpture and painting. In Naples, *stol'nik* Peter Andreevich Tolstoi visited a temple built in the time of the "accursed tyrant Nero," where he saw "many pagan gods," noting: "I cannot describe the marvelous and splendid craftsmanship or the lifelike depiction of these pagan gods."[400A] In previous times Muscovites would have been afraid even to look at such heathen deities.

The diplomatic reports of ambassadors B. P. Sheremetev (1697) and P. A. Tolstoi (1697–99), as well as Prince B. I. Kurakin's notes, provide a fascinating glimpse of Muscovite musical impressions from abroad. Sheremetev heard a good deal of music of various kinds: a Roman nobleman "entertained him with much music," and at Malta a trumpeter was assigned to him by the Master of the Order and played constantly during the ambassador's meals. Sheremetev's mission was brief, but even his fragmentary reports contain the formula for the musical entertainments and mealtime trumpet fanfares that were soon introduced in Moscow.[400B]

P. A. Tolstoi, who lived in Italy for sixteen months and visited many Italian cities, provides more details concerning music in his reports. Tolstoi returned to Russia in January 1699 completely enchanted by the Italian way of life. On his way to Italy he passed through Vienna and here are his impressions. At first, the instrumental music he heard in St. Stephen's Cathedral seemed to him to be simply extraordinary noise, for Muscovites were used to soft church chanting without instrumental accompaniment. Shortly afterward, having heard the organ in a church in Padua, Tolstoi began to revise his ideas on the subject.[401] No less interesting are his descriptions of Italian theaters he visited in Venice as well as other social amusements he experienced. He says that Venice had five opera houses at that time: "nowhere in the world are there such marvelous operas and comedies," he exclaims.[402] He also describes the exterior of the "teatrum" and is amazed to learn that "in one opera there are 100 to 150 or more men and women in costume." He gives an account of the Venetian Carnival, during which many people wear masks, amusing themselves "shamelessly," and so forth. In Naples he admired the duke's small children, who entertained the ambassador with singing "from notes" and with dances "in the French manner," and in private homes he saw *tsimbaly* (obviously clavichords) and other musical instruments for entertainment. His reports also contain information about music in other cities.

Prince B. I. Kurakin visited Holland early in the eighteenth century and reported on his trips abroad. After seeing the statue of Erasmus in a Rotterdam square, he describes it as follows: "There stands a fellow, cast in bronze, with a book as a sign that this was a very learned man who often taught others and thus they made the statue." He enumerates the amusements of fashionable society in The Hague, including assemblies of various kinds, and notes that "there was music in churches [*kerkhi*] and in Roman [Catholic] churches." In Amsterdam, "local inhabitants have collegia or gatherings of their companies which, as they assemble, play on various instruments and sing in the evenings; but foreigners are not admitted unless invited by someone from the company. And in both these cities (The Hague and Amsterdam) the public entertainment is comedy and opera." Prince Kurakin attended concerts given by the Amsterdam musical societies, and he also describes public concerts in Rome: "serenades, that is, music with singers similar to the opera, except that it is not in a theater but in chambers." He also heard oratorio performances by the congregation of San Filippo Neri and others.[403] The historical value of these notes by our forefathers is beyond question. They show how the Russian people's interest in the arts of the West gradually developed at the end of the seventeenth century, and how, remembering their impressions, they transmitted models to the next generation. Everything mentioned in these reports by the Muscovite noblemen was gradually transplanted to Russian soil.[404] Assemblies were begun during Peter's reign and fanfares at meals became customary in the homes of the wealthy; in the second half of the eighteenth century the capitals had public theaters and concerts, and even oratorios were performed.

On the other hand, foreign visitors to Moscow, especially foreign ambassadors, brought musicians and musical instruments with them. The Russian nobles were surprised at first but then began to copy them. Some of the foreigners kept records of these musical festivities and of their impressions of Muscovite public life. The diaries of Johann Korb and Kammerjunker F. W. von Bergholz are the most detailed in this respect, and we shall soon acquaint ourselves more closely with the latter. Johann Georg Korb, secretary to the Imperial ambassador Guarient, has interesting things to say in his *Diarium itineris in Moscoviam* [Diary of a trip to Muscovy (1698–99)].[405] There were two trumpeters in the ambassador's retinue, Johann Zimmer and Constantin Hoelleman, and some of the servants apparently also played kettledrums and perhaps trumpets and flutes, since Korb mentions various occasions on which the ambassador's "orchestra" participated in services at the Catholic Church in the Foreign Quarter, at dinners (to the sound of "trumpets and timpani"), at dances, and at Easter. Once, while walking in Izmailovo, Guarient even arranged a complete serenade for the tsar's family who heard, perhaps for the first time, "the most delightful sounds of a symphony."[406]

These kinds of musical performances no longer troubled Muscovites. According to Korb, musicians were employed not only by high-ranking foreigners but also by Russian high society. Korb tells us that when Peter's favorite, General Lefort, was on his deathbed, "on the doctors' orders, musicians were summoned and they lulled the patient to sleep with sweet-sounding symphonies"; on the day of his death, "General Lefort's mind wandered; at times he called for musicians, at other times for wine."[406A] In another passage from his diary

(26 July 1698), Korb records that Prince Boris Alekseevich Golitsyn, receiving Ambassador Guarient "with amazing kindness, ordered his Polish musicians to play various pieces for the company's amusement."[407] Thus, in addition to foreign musical ensembles, Moscow undoubtedly had bands of its own, made up of trumpeters, flautists, oboists (employed more for military requirements), and kettledrummers.

Even very early in the eighteenth century, not only were foreigners of all kinds freely admitted to the Muscovite state, but also (to quote Kurakin's autobiographical notes again) Russians "began to be sent to European countries for the purpose of study and learning." Tsar Peter Alekseevich himself traveled abroad more than once and observed the society of other countries, although he did not enjoy their music. Nevertheless, soon after returning from his first trip abroad (1697–98), from which his reforms arose, he introduced music and theater into Moscow's public life. Orders were issued to organize assemblies with music and dances, new musicians and actors were recruited from abroad, and a public theater was established in Moscow.

The management of the public theater was entrusted to foreign "principals" imported to Moscow for this purpose, and theatrical performances were also staged at the Moscow Slavo–Greco–Latin Academy and later at the Surgical School under the direction of Doctor Bidloo.[407A] Plays were produced for the court in the village of Preobrazhenskoe, where the theater was renovated by Tsarevna Natalia Alekseevna [Peter's sister]; later, plays were produced at Tsaritsa Praskov'ia Fyodorovna's residence in the village of Izmailovo. Copies of plays performed at the Kiev Academy, in the Metropolitan of Rostov's Krestovaia Palace, and even in Novgorod have been preserved. The repertory of all these theatrical enterprises can be divided into three basic categories: mystery plays and school plays of a similar character; regular theatrical plays (comedies and *intermedi*); and theatrical plays with political subtexts.

Mystery and school plays were performed at the Kiev Academy, and from there they passed to Moscow and Rostov. It is known that at the founding of the Kiev Academy, Metropolitan Pyotr Mogila [Mohyla] required the poetry teachers to prepare a play for the annual summer festivities. The subject matter was taken from the Bible, but over time, as Russian actors were brought in, topics from Russian history were selected (the tragicomedy *Vladimir* was staged in 1706). These theatrical productions were slavish imitations of Western models, although the same might be said of the Russian theatrical repertory of this period as a whole. The extent of this borrowing may be seen in the text of Dimitrii Rostovskii's *Deistvie na strasti Khristovy* [Passion play], a mystery play in which one of the two musical numbers was sung in Polish. St. Dimitrii Rostovskii ([St. Dimitrii of Rostov] 1651–1709) was one of the most popular authors of mystery plays performed in schools; during his residence in Rostov, the plays were staged in the Metropolitan's Krestovaia Palace.

The public theater in Moscow was managed by Johann Kunst and later by Otto (Artemii) Fürst. Its repertory, comprising some thirty plays, was nearly identical to that of contemporary French and German theaters. Most of the plays, with the exception of a few original Russian *intermedi* of a local character, were translated in the Moscow Foreign Office. These plays were also presented in both court theaters. Among the works included in the repertory of these theaters are the following:

> Before 1700, at the Kiev Academy: Dimitrii Rostovskii, *Rozhdestvenskaia drama* [Christmas drama] and his *Deistvie, na strasti Khristovy spisannoe* [A drama written on the Passion of Christ];
>
> November 1701 at the Moscow Slavo-Latin Academy: the comedy *Uzhasnaia izmena slastoliubivago zhitiia s priskorbnym i nishchetnym* [The terrifying change of voluptuary life into dire and indigent];[407B]

2 February 1702 at the Moscow Slavo-Latin Academy: *Strashnoe izobrazhenie vtorogo prishestviia gospodnia na zemliu* [The fearful representation of the second coming of the Lord on earth][407C] and *Tsarstvo mira, idolosluzheniem prezhde razorennoe i propovediiu sviatogo verkhovnago apostola Petra paki vozstanovlennoe* [The kingdom of the world destroyed by idolatry and reestablished by sermons of the holy and revered Apostle Peter];[407D]

1703 in Novgorod: *Dragyia smeianyia* (French comedy by Molière [*Les précieuses ridicules*]);[408]

1704 in Rostov: Dimitrii Rostovskii, *Venets slavno pobedonosnyi Dobropodvizhniku khrabrenniku Khristovu sv. velikomuchenniku Dimitriiu, v den' preslavnago prazdnika ego torzhestvenna* [A victorious crown for the greatly suffering St. Dimitrii, courageous disciple of Christ, on his feast day];[408A]

25 May 1708 at the Kiev Academy: *Iosif, patriarkha, svoim predaniem, uzami, temnitseiu i pochteniem tsarskago prestola Khrista syna bozhiia, predannago, strazhduiushchago i voznesshagosia so slavoiu preobrazuiushchii* [Patriarch Joseph, through his devotion, chains, the dungeon, and his reverence for the royal throne of Christ the Son of God, who suffered and ascended [to Heaven], transfigured with glory.]

February 1710 at the Moscow Slavo-Latin Academy: *Bozhie unichizhitelei gordykh, v gordom Izrailia unichizhiteliu chrez smirenna Davida unichizhennom Goliafe unichizhenie* [God's castigation of proud castigators in proud Israel by means of the castigation of the castigator Goliath through the meek David.][408B]

The dates of Kunst's and Fürst's productions have not yet been established. Between 1702 and 1707 (when the theatrical quarters were abandoned), their repertory included *Stsipio Afrikan, vozhd' rimskii, i pogublenie Sofonizby, korolevy numidiiskoi* [Scipio Africanus, the Roman general, and the destruction of Sophonisba, the Numidian queen] and *Chestnyi izmennik, ili Frideriko fon Poplei i Aloiziia, supruga ego. Komediia* [The honest traitor, or Friderico von Poplei and his wife Aloiziia, a comedy]. To the latter may be added one of the *intermedi* published by N. Tikhonravov (in *Russian Dramatic Works*, 2:489), in which a Polish nobleman sings a song. Another play published by Tikhonravov, *Dafnis, goneniem liubovnago Apollona v drevo liavrovoe prevrashchennaia* [Daphne, pursued by amorous Apollo, transformed into a laurel tree], may have been performed in St. Petersburg in about 1714, although there is no documentary evidence.

The plays listed above represent only a small portion of the contemporary Russian theatrical repertory; I have mentioned only those that appeared in print and contained musical numbers, and thus had some significance in the history of music in Russia. With regard to music, we can be certain only that there were vocal and instrumental numbers in these plays, adding variety to the dramatic action, but the music itself has not yet been found. In the religious mystery plays there were occasional choruses on religious subjects. The music of these choruses, as well as the music in the plays by Pastor Gregory and Simeon Polotskii [in the seventeenth century], was undoubtedly similar to that of the *kanty,* since the *kanty* themselves grew out of the musical numbers of the mystery plays staged at the Kiev and Moscow Academies. In one of these plays, *Bozhie unichizhitelei gordykh . . . unichizhenie* [God's castigation of proud castigators], we even find a "Dance of [Army] Officers."

The music in the secular theaters must have been of a totally different character, especially in Kunst's and Fürst's repertory. Here one encounters solo arias and songs with music, probably imported or written by the German organizers. Thus, in the comedy with songs *Stsipio Afrikan,* there are three arias for the character Masiniza, as well as arias for the character Eolus, for Ersil "with the monkey," and for the priest Bogudes; in the comedy *Chestnyi izmennik* there are songs for the Ghost Marquis and two for the jolly musician Leptulo; and in the comedy *Dragyia smeianyia* there is a chorus and a song for Maskarilo. The music for the Kievan tragicomedy *Vladimir* may have been similar in style. It included the singing of the priest Kuroiad, a dance with the singing of idols and priests, and a chorus of the Charms (of seduction). The play *Dafnis* could not have been an opera in the contemporary meaning of the term, contrary to some scholars' opinions. It contained only three separate vocal numbers, including the hymn and song of Cupid; the remainder of the text could hardly have been presented musically as there are no other discrete musical numbers in the work. Moreover, there were no available opera performers in our country at that time, either vocalists or instrumentalists.

Public performances in Moscow were given by Johann Kunst's company. Kunst was brought to Moscow in 1702 through the mediation of a certain Ian Splavskii and a subclerk, Sergei Liapunov. Splavskii, a Hungarian by birth and an adventurer by profession, entered Russian service in 1698, calling himself a captain. In June 1701 he was sent abroad to bring a troupe of actors to Moscow, but he was unsuccessful. Six months later he was sent off again with the same assignment, but this time *pod'iachii* Sergei Liapunov went with him, and in Danzig he signed a contract with the head of a traveling German troupe, Johann Christian Kunst; the troupe arrived in Moscow in June 1702. Kunst had assumed that he was to stage operas that were becoming fashionable in Europe, but this did not work out and he had to limit himself to dramatic spectacles.[409]

At that time the Moscow theater was under the jurisdiction of Fyodor Alekseevich Golovin, head of the Foreign Office in Moscow. At first the palaces of the False Dmitrii, the Rasstriginy Palaty near the Church of the Presentation, were assigned to the theater, but the site did not work well and Golovin ordered a hall to be built on Moscow's Red Square. After all kinds of delays and much correspondence with the clerks of the Foreign Office, the theater was opened, probably only for the 1702–03 Christmas season. To prevent Kunst's troupe from standing idle, the huge stone Italian-style mansion in the Foreign Quarter which had belonged to the late General Franz Iakovlevich Lefort was assigned for preliminary performances. At first the plays were given in German, but later also in Russian.[410] Kunst was also entrusted with the training of some ten Russian youngsters for the comedies. Their numbers subsequently increased and they formed the first group of professional Russian actors. In 1703 Kunst's directorship came to an end: he fled abroad to escape his debts. In the following year, the goldsmith Otto (Artemii) Fürst was appointed as the new head of the troupe and of the theater. Fürst was probably personally known either to the tsar or to Golovin, as it is otherwise difficult to account for his appointment. Kunst's, and later, Fürst's, troupe was made up of nine foreign actors, supplemented by the Russian trainees. Female roles were for some time performed by a girl named Johanna von Willich [Vilikh] and the wife of a doctor, Hermina Poggenkampf (in Russian as Pogankov), who probably sang the arias set for women's voices mentioned above.[411]

Fürst's theatrical productions ended shortly after the whole court moved to the new capital city of St. Petersburg. In 1707 the comedy hall was dismantled and the properties were transported to Preobrazhenskoe village for theatrical performances at Tsarevna Natalia Alekseevna's court. But in Moscow there were theatrical shows staged by the pupils of Dr. Bidloo's Surgical School, in the great hospital building on the Iauza River, and this continued until the 1740s.

Immediately following the actors, musicians from abroad were also recruited for service in Moscow. On 5 August 1702 a small wind ensemble was engaged through the agency of the Poppe brothers in Hamburg. There were seven musicians in the band, including the leader, probably the oboist Heinrich Sienknecht who, together with the trumpeter Gottfried Mollinius, received an annual salary of 140 rubles; the other musicians were paid 114 rubles each. At the same time the ambassador to Berlin, Izmailov, was allotted the sum of 1264 gold coins [zolotye] "for the purchase of small children with oboes and siposhi (an old flute) such as he purchased previously in Krolevets." In the following year, Prince Grigorii Oginskii [Oginski] sent for four more musicians from Poland, each of whom received an annual salary of 146 rubles. Sienknecht, the head of the Hamburg orchestra, was entrusted with teaching the oboe to twelve young singers (russkie spevaki; eleven of their names are cited by E. Barsov). The names of another twelve musicians who were in Peter's service at various times are also known.[412] Thus in Moscow and later in St. Petersburg, there was a sufficient number of musicians in service to the tsar who taught regimental oboists, trumpeters, and drummers and who were members of the court orchestra.[413]

The court orchestra was apparently formed after the court moved to the new capital where, generally speaking, orchestras and individual musicians in service became commonplace among the most thoroughly Europeanized nobles. It would be premature to speak of the existence of a special theater orchestra, in the accepted meaning of the term, although some historians of the Russian theater assert that Sienknecht's Hamburg orchestra was engaged in 1702 for that purpose. Stringed instruments had predominated in Italian theatrical orchestras ever since the beginning of the seventeenth century, as may be observed in the scores of works by Monteverdi and A. Gabrieli.[413A] In addition to strings, orchestras of that period included flutes and harps, instruments which were probably unknown in Moscow in Peter's time, except for piccolos in military bands. Nearly all of the musicians mentioned above played wind instruments. Until the beginning of the second quarter of the eighteenth century, one encounters reports either about individual musicians or complete bands made up of oboists, horn players, and trumpeters. Violinists are rarely mentioned and then singly and in connection with dance music. No operas were staged in the theaters of Peter's period, choral numbers did not need accompaniment, and soloists could, as before, be accompanied on a clavichord (cembalo) and small organs (regals, with reed ranks). In individual instances, of course, some stringed instruments could be added when the wind players were able to play them. A case in point was Johann Hübner who, although later a violinist and concertmaster, was originally a horn player.

In Moscow at the beginning of the eighteenth century, many external aspects of court and public life changed considerably. The terem [literally, tower chambers], in which the tsar's wife and daughters had been secluded from public view and in which Russian women in general had been sequestered, was opened up. Peter's favorite sister, Tsarevna Natalia Alekseevna, would accompany her brother to the Foreign Quarter. In July 1698 the Austrian ambassador Guarient arranged an impromptu serenade in the village of Izmailovo, to which the tsarevich and his sisters listened as they strolled through the woods. Guarient's wind band often played in the Foreign Quarter's Lutheran church and on holidays in the Mar'ina Grove. Johann Korb, the secretary of the Imperial embassy, even recorded in his diary a nocturnal serenade arranged for Guarient's name day which kept all of the embassy's neighbors awake.

In 1699, for the first time in Moscow, there was a funeral with music, for the tsar's favorite, General Lefort (who, it should be stated, had his own band of musicians). On that occasion the tsar himself put together the burial ceremony, for which he ordered three regiments of the Guard with nine flute players at the head of each regiment; these players "filled the air with the gentle sounds of mournful tunes," according to Korb.

In addition to instrumental music, vocal music also began to play a more prominent role in Moscow's public life. The triumphal celebrations of fresh victories and conquests were attended with the kind of ceremony Peter loved so dearly, and they gradually became more complicated and longer, with the addition of gun salvos and special *kanty,* theatrical performances, illuminations, fireworks, and even masquerades. Upon Kunst's arrival in Moscow, the Foreign Office demanded that he "prepare as soon as possible a new comedy about the victory and surrender to the Great Lord of the fortress Oreshka [Oreshek, Nöteborg]." A sizable collection of manuscript *kanty* has survived, created after Peter's various victories. These *kanty* accompanied the public ceremonies. The first of these ceremonies apparently took place in 1696 after the conquest of Azov when, following Western models, triumphal arches were erected, underneath which the victors entered to the accompaniment of music and the singing of *kanty.* The arches were decorated with various symbolic images and inscriptions. The first victory over the Swedes (1703, the conquest of Schlotburg, Iamburg, and Kopor'e) was celebrated with greater ceremony. Three triumphal arches were erected and, to greet the victors, special festive *kanty* were composed to be sung by the pupils of the Moscow Slavo-Latin Academy.[414] After the fall of Narva and Dorpat in December 1704, the celebrations were even more elaborate. Seven triumphal arches were erected, through which Peter rode followed by captured Swedish officers, standards, and guns. The victory at Poltava, according to the *Pokhodnyi iurnal* [Campaign journal] of 1709, was accompanied by a "great triumph" which lasted several days. The *kanty* performed at Peter's triumphal entry after his victory at Poltava are preserved in a later copy (1775), which contains marginal commentary about the performance of "Stikhi" [Verses] in 1709.[415] There is also a score of a thirteen-voice *kontsert,* "Na primirenie Poltavskoi batalii" [On the peace at the Battle of Poltava], preserved in the archive of the former Moscow Armory.[416] This *kontsert* was, of course, performed at the time of the festive church service.

Most brilliant of all were the celebrations at the signing of the Peace of Nystadt, which brought an end to the long Northern War. According to the published "Relation about the festive entry of His Imperial Majesty of all the Russias into Moscow on the 18th day of December 1721," Peter was greeted by Archbishop Feodosii of Novgorod with a speech, "at which meeting," says the "Relation," "Peter showed his imperial, gracious benevolence and rejoiced in hearing trumpets and musical voices from the arches for many hours. From the students, there echoed songs in many languages." Thus, at such festive receptions there must have been trumpet fanfares and perhaps some marches and choruses, probably performed at the triumphal arches not only by the sovereign singers but also by pupils of the Slavo–Greco–Latin Academy, who were able to sing "songs in many languages."

The Peace of Nystadt gave rise to a considerable number of *kanty.* One of these was apparently performed when Peter visited Prince Menshikov or some other participant in the conquest of the "Swedish Lion," King Charles (the *kant* is in manuscript Q.XIV.141, fols. 178v–80 in the Public Library [RNB]). The score of this piece, "Raduisia Rosko zemle" [Rejoice Russian land], is No. 1 in the music appendix in this volume. This interpretation is supported by repeated exclamations of *vivat* to the "Extraordinary Guest" [Peter], and the concluding verses of the *kant* refer to the year 1721, that is, the year of the Peace Treaty:

V Sione voskliknem
I vechnyi mir kliknem
Orlu dvoeglavnu
Petru khrabru slavnu
Orlu usmirennu
So lvom pomirennu.

In Zion we shall rejoice
And hail the eternal peace
For the two-headed eagle
For Peter, courageous and famous,
The eagle pacified
With the [Swedish] lion reconciled.

The festive songs of Peter's era resound with *vivaty,* borrowed from Polish court customs and even forming entire, separate *kanty.* Apparently these exclamations opened and concluded each triumphal procession under the arches erected along the parade routes. It thus appears that this long series of *kanty,* filled with hosannas, *mnogoletiia* [Many years], and *vivaty,* and with their characteristic texts ("With glory and honor," "And you conquered," "Rejoice, sing praises, Bellona glorious," and so forth), constitutes a single, complete, multi-sectional parade composition performed during the celebrations of the conclusion of the Peace Treaty of Nystadt. It is preserved in its entirety in the historically precious manuscript anthology in the Buslaev collection in the Public Library (see No. 2 in the music appendix in this volume, *kanty* from the time of Peter the Great).[417] Some long pauses in the *kanty* at rest stops of the triumphal procession were undoubtedly filled with gun salvos and bell ringing, which accompanied or concluded the *vivaty* or *mnogoletiia* described above. In this instance, the Petrine *kanty,* apparently composed by the sovereign singers, were thus predecessors of the festive cantatas of Catherine the Great's time composed by Sarti and his contemporaries, who added special horn music, even fireworks, to the fusillade and bell ringing.

In the same Buslaev manuscript we find two more *kanty* from 1721. The following work appears on folios 174v–75:[417A]

Raduisia Rossie radosti skazuiu
Orla so lvom shvetskim mirnym pokazuiu.

Rejoice as I tell of Russia's joy
And show the eagle with the pacific Swedish lion.

And on folios 184v–85 there is a *kant* with these primitive verses:

Tsariu Rossiiskii voine preslavnyi
V Evrope pervyi monarkho preslavnyi.

Russian Emperor, in war all-glorious
In Europe the first monarch all-glorious.

Both *kanty* were performed, in considerably altered versions, at the celebration of the two hundredth anniversary of the founding of St. Petersburg [in 1903]. One might find a whole series of similar compositions in the Buslaev manuscript, in addition to those mentioned above, written for the festivities surrounding the celebration of the Peace of Nystadt.

One of the last Petrine *kanty* was the "Pesn'" [Song] honoring the victorious return from the conquest of Derbent and other cities, and sung by students of the Moscow Academy as they welcomed Peter on 18 December 1722. Its text was printed for the occasion, and the music is also preserved in the Buslaev manuscript (fols. 218–19).[418] There is an interesting detail in the music, which is flowing and truly triumphant. For the verses that follow, the composer of the *kant,* which was created at the Academy and performed by its students, illustrated the word *vostochnyia* [eastern] with a melisma, thereby attempting to give it an eastern character:[419]

> Torzhestvennaia paki vam otrada
> Speshno prikhodiat Rossiiskaia chada
> Ot vostochnyia voennyia brani
> Marsovoi dani.
>
> For you a festive delight
> The children of Russia are returning
> From eastern battlefields
> A tribute to Mars.

The repertory of old Petrine *kanty* was thus enriched with a multitude of festive songs for triumphal entrances, banquet music, *vivaty,* and other vocal pieces. The public musical and theatrical performances described above were repeated even more often in Moscow during the second half of Peter's rule, when the center of the state and administrative authority had been moved to St. Petersburg, and when the old "imperial and ruling city" was preferred primarily for the celebration of large-scale festivities, from coronations to victory celebrations.

The beginning of the eighteenth century was marked by changes in the public life of the Muscovite state that were so violent and decisive as to destroy any hope for a return to the old, traditional ways. In December 1699 an edict was issued altering the reckoning of the calendar; henceforth the calendar would calculate years from the birth of Christ and no longer from the creation of the world. Following the European custom, New Year's Day was to be 1 January instead of 1 September, and celebrations were to be continued for a week with gun salvos, the firing of rockets, the lighting of tar barrels, and the decorating of houses. This was followed by a series of edicts which caused considerable agitation among the people: on shaving beards; wearing German-style clothing; establishing assemblies, and so forth. Adrian, the last of the Moscow patriarchs, died in October 1700, and the patriarchate was abolished in Russia. The city of St. Petersburg was founded in 1703 on the shores of the Neva River on the conquered Swedish territory of Ingermanland [Ingria]. It soon became Peter's favorite residence and the laying out of the new capital was one of his chief preoccupations. All these external facts, combined with the taxation imposed to meet the cost of the war and Peter's other undertakings, compulsory recruitment, and so forth, profoundly affected the internal life of the state. In public life, too, there were major changes.

With the new capital, the history of Russian music entered a new era: the St. Petersburg period. It began with an intense admiration for, and imitation of, Western Europe. The assemblies instituted by Peter's edict accomplished far more than we might imagine now, so long after the fact. Everything that had been dear to ancient Moscow, everything reminiscent of that city's former isolated existence, was now outmoded. Dress, manners, amusements, even one's appearance—all had to bear a different stamp and comply unfailingly with the Western manner, which, following the tsar's example, became the indisputable model. Peter's orders were always quite strict: the disobedient were fined, flogged, and even imprisoned.

In this new society music was to have a much wider role. Military music, which already existed, was supplemented by the introduction of other types of instrumental music. Truth to tell, with the exception of the vocal *kanty* (which were probably a privilege of the sovereign singers), our native musical creativity had hitherto remained silent, particularly in the realm of instrumental music. The instrumental music performed at assemblies, masquerades, serenades, and all kinds of *Tafelmusik* and fanfares was undoubtedly of foreign origin, as the primary conductors were foreigners.

It was not just the conductors; most of the musicians themselves were also foreigners, if only in the European-style orchestras. An interesting picture of this kind of ensemble, playing viols, appears in a large engraving titled "A Picture of the Great Tsar's Wedding" by A. Zubov (1712), a well-known engraver of the Petrine era. A copy of the complete engraving, reduced in size, appears in the third volume of D. A. Rovinskii's *A Detailed Dictionary of Russian Engraved Portraits.*[419A] Under the lower left corner of the engraving, by the number 8 [in the engraving], is a depiction of "Music etc." In a considerably enlarged image of that instrumental ensemble (fig. 101), one can see musicians standing around a table on which there are pitchers, goblets, and notated music (the "etc." of the title), playing on large and small bowed viols.

Orchestral music began to play a considerable role in everyday life. Thus, according to "A description of St. Petersburg and Kronshlot," published in 1710–11 (p. 36), "a band of twelve trained German trumpeters and kettledrummers played from time to time,

FIG. 101. Musicians playing viols, from the engraving "A Picture of the Great Tsar's Wedding" by A. Zubov (1712).

at noon, following the custom of German cities," in the upper gallery of the newly erected Post House (located at the site of the present Marble Palace).[419B] It should be noted that in those days, before there were any hotels in St. Petersburg, the Post House functioned as a sort of inn.

Contemporary memoirs include significant information on music in Peter's time. In this respect the diary of Kammerjunker F. W. von Bergholz, spanning the years 1721 to 1725, is of considerable interest. Bergholz was a member of the suite of Karl Friedrich, Duke of Holstein, the future husband of Tsarevna Anna Petrovna (1725).[420] Bergholz came to know St. Petersburg in the second decade of its existence, and by then Russian society was more or less accustomed to Peter's innovations. Bergholz's diary is valuable as a documentary record and a reflection of contemporaries' views of Russia in general, despite the superficiality of many of his conclusions, his misunderstanding of the Russian people, and occasionally the triviality and fragmentary state of the facts he noted. The Holsteiners, of course, like the other foreigners, considered themselves a superior race and in their hearts regarded everything Russian with contempt or patronizing condescension. This did not prevent them, however, from currying favor with the Russian nobles and matching them in their drunkenness and debauchery, or from taking part in the tsar's generous fund of crude and vulgar practical jokes of which the tsar was unsparing.

It is curious that Bergholz's diary is silent on Russian artistic creativity. Apart from church singing, the repertory of *kanty* was substantial, and among these works one could find some that were just as interesting as the *Tafelmusik* or serenades that so delighted him; no doubt Bergholz often heard *kanty*. As he became acquainted with performances on folk instruments, especially the *bandura* players, he viewed them merely as ethnographic relics.[421] Yet his diary contains fragmentary but reliable information concerning orchestras, serenades, shows, dances, masquerades, and other contemporary court and social amusements.

The assemblies Peter introduced were an important factor in training the population to observe the rules of etiquette. The special rules drawn up for these assemblies give us some idea of the character of public life in Peter's time.[422] Music played no small part at assemblies, as dancing was a feature of public and family gatherings. At that time the fashionable dances at court and in private homes were a German dance (probably the *Grossvater*, in which the tsar took part and which generally opened a ball), the minuet, and Polish and English dances. A special ceremonial dance was performed at weddings. According to Bergholz, this dance began with a kind of funeral march (that is, a piece in slow tempo, in 4/4 time, and in a minor key), during which the leading couple, as well as those following them, bowed or curtsied; after this came the Polish dance. The musicians often had a difficult time. Bergholz reports, for example, that at an evening party given by one of his superiors, the dancing went on from 5:00 PM until 5:30 AM—more than twelve hours without pause—even though the same musicians had probably also played *Tafelmusik* during the meal. In an interval of only a quarter of an hour the band members had their supper! At another assembly, at the home of Count Gavriil Ivanovich Golovkin, two Polish and two English dances were performed in succession, followed by a new endless dance lasting more than half an hour. In this dance, ten or twelve couples tied themselves together with their handkerchiefs, and each couple in turn, stepping forward, had to invent a new dance step. It was very hard luck on the musician, probably the band leader, who had to skip ahead at each of these changes, "with the result that he was utterly exhausted" (1:81). And that was not all! The dancers made for the garden or went into various rooms and even into the attic.[422A]

That music had become quite an ordinary part of life in the new capital is evident from the fact that Bergholz encountered musicians even at a baker's wedding. He tells us not only that Tsaritsa Catherine Alekseevna had a full orchestra, but that bands were maintained by many Russian noblemen and distinguished foreigners, including Admiral Fyodor Matveevich Apraksin (d. 1728); Prince Aleksandr Danilovich Menshikov (exiled in 1727), who had trumpeters and kettledrummers; Grigorii Andreevich Stroganov, whose orchestra consisted of eight musicians; General-procuror Pavel Ivanovich Iaguzhinskii (d. 1736), a great music lover and performer on the clavichord, who had his own horn players and who in 1722 sold his music library to the Duke of Holstein; Princess Maria Iur'evna Cherkasskaia (d. 1747), daughter of Iurii Iur'evich Trubetskoi, who had her own *bandura* player and an excellent orchestra of ten good musicians, German and Swiss performers among them. Bergholz praised this orchestra repeatedly.[423]

Among the foreigners, the Duke of Holstein and the Imperial ambassador Count Kinsky both had bands. Kinsky arrived in St. Petersburg in September 1721. The leader of his select ensemble was Johann Hübner, who later became a famous violinist and, after Kinsky's departure from Moscow in July 1722, worked for the Duke of Holstein. Kinsky's musicians participated, among other events, at an Easter service in Moscow, where the court had arrived to celebrate the Peace of Nystadt. The ensemble, which was undoubtedly well organized by Hübner, who was making a name for himself at the time, also played in private homes. Probably other notables also had private bands which Bergholz did not mention, and those who did not have their own bands hired them; the tsaritsa's orchestra often played for people closely associated with the court.

The household band, in its simplest form, was made up of trumpets and kettledrums (for example, Prince Menshikov's band and the *Tafelmusik* at Admiral Apraksin's), or of several horns (the Duke of Holstein's was the first to do this), or of a combination of these instruments. This structure was unchanged until the end of Peter's reign and was conditioned by the repertory, which was borrowed from the West. Musicians participated at receptions, banquets, dances, and serenades, and also attended their masters at social festivities and masquerades.[424] This instrumental repertory has not come down to us, but we are probably safe in assuming that it was similar to the fanfares used in the army and for the hunt. Models for such pieces were quite popular in the West and, of course, were well known to the musicians, so that only in extremely rare instances was it necessary to compose new *Tafelmusik* which, because of the simplicity of its form and the homogeneity of the wind band, could easily be written by any capable and experienced horn player and leader such as Hübner. Examples of such fanfares may be found in a rare old book, *Les dons des enfans de Latone: La musique et la chasse du cerf, Poëmes dédiés au Roy* (Paris, 1734), which includes in its final section trumpet calls and fanfares for one and two trumpets. The book presents a whole collection of short fanfares (8–16 bars), with various names and subjects, mostly in the 6/8 time so characteristic of solo horn music. Later on, undoubtedly, this rhythmic pattern was transferred to the French *quadrille*. The collection ends with a more complex concert fanfare for two horns composed by B. Morin, a chamber musician to the Duke of Orleans.[425] Much later, in 1786, a similar publication, *Truby na dni narochitye* [Trumpets (fanfares) for special days] was on sale for 15 rubles in Glazunov's bookshop, according to the *Spb. vedomosti* (1786, no. 72).

The Duke of Holstein's band and its public appearances may serve as an example of the activities of orchestral musicians during Peter's reign. It is therefore of interest to try to follow its birth and development as recorded in Bergholz's diary. In 1721 the duke brought two horn players from Vienna, Johann Leutenberger [Leitenberg] and Rummel, who initially made up the duke's band. Leutenberger, who had previously been in the service of the Holstein minister Bassewitz, was a virtuoso performer: "all who heard him admitted that they had never before listened to such delicate and superb horn playing. He accompanied all the instruments and could sustain as many as eighty-five bars without a pause, which made a great impression on his audiences" (Bergholz 1:16). Both musicians received an annual salary of one hundred ducats [*chervontsy*] from the duke, not counting some income on the side. Their duties included playing during the duke's dinners as well as on more ceremonial occasions. Thus, on 23 July 1721, both horn players performed several pieces at Ekaterinhof for the tsaritsa, and "the tsaritsa and the princesses listened very attentively and with great delight" (1:76); for this the musicians received twelve ducats. On that occasion a flotilla of more than fifty boats and wherries conveyed the party on the Neva to Ekaterinhof, and most of the noblemen had their own bands with them. The tsaritsa's horn players took turns with those of the duke (1:75). In the evening the duke ordered his rowers to stop in front of Ekaterinhof Palace while the musicians played "a beautiful nocturne" (1:76).[425A]

Bergholz's diary has a detailed description of a serenade the duke arranged in honor of the empress on 24 November [1721]. There was an orchestra of seventeen to eighteen musicians, including five who belonged to the duke's suite and ten from Count Kinsky's band. The Kapellmeister was the great music lover Assessor Surland, a member of the duke's suite.[425B] Two rehearsals were held the previous day, and guests were invited. The serenade took place early in the morning in the courtyard of what was then the Winter Palace, which was located on Millionaia Street by the Winter Canal (on the site of the Preobrazhenskii Regiment's former barracks), and provides an interesting picture of court life in old St. Petersburg. The band was ready at 6:00 AM on the appointed day, as the duke wanted the serenade to start before dawn in torchlight. The participants in the serenade, according to Bergholz, were in the following order: the procession was headed by the quartermaster, followed by twelve soldiers who carried tables, chairs, and candlesticks for the musicians; then came Bergholz, "to see that no time was lost in posting the torchbearers about the courtyard," and twenty men with torches, in double file; between them were the duke and his suite, and "behind them, after everyone else, the musicians." On entering the courtyard the quartermaster hastily set up the music stands opposite the empress's windows, and Bergholz posted the torchbearers, fifteen of whom, wearing the duke's full-dress livery and holding big wax torches, were lined up in front of the musicians and facing the Imperial apartments. The others, not in livery, stood behind the musicians. The instruments were tuned outside the gates, the music was distributed, the bandsmen took up their positions, and the performance began. "It lasted for nearly an hour and was the more enjoyable because the weather was calm and clear. Both princesses in morning dress stood at the windows and listened most attentively. The older princess clearly showed on this occasion that she was very fond of music, as she was constantly beating time with her hand and head. His Highness (the duke) often gazed in her direction and probably sighed in secret. We could not look around," writes Bergholz, "as the emperor came out of the house. He came up to His Highness and embraced him firmly and then approached the band, turning one ear toward the [musicians'] tables, but after listening for a little while he walked rapidly away." Shortly thereafter General Iaguzhinskii came out and thanked the duke on behalf of the empress. When the music was finished, the duke and his retinue departed, followed by Bergholz with the musicians and the torchbearers. "Vodka to the value of 80 or 90 rubles" was distributed to the musicians who participated in this serenade (1:169–70).

This serenade was certainly performed by a band of wind instruments. For special occasions, therefore, the two horn players were supplemented by amateurs belonging to the [duke's] suite and by hiring foreign musicians; the Kapellmeister was an official of the duke's court. The band gradually increased in size. In [late January] 1722, during a grand masquerade which took place in the streets of Moscow and lasted several days, the duke's two horn players were joined by four performers of "peasant music": a bagpipe, two fiddles, and an oboe.[426] The person responsible for this arrangement may have been the leader of Count Kinsky's band, Johann Hübner, who shortly afterward entered the duke's service. Hübner played the horn and the violin, and later distinguished himself as a Kapellmeister at court. It is certain that under his leadership the Holstein band was improved and enlarged by the addition of stringed instruments. Duke Karl Friedrich was soon to become betrothed to Tsarevna Anna Petrovna, and this involved an augmentation of his household.

In Moscow, and then in St. Petersburg, not only rehearsals of *Tafelmusik* and serenades but even regular concerts began to be organized. In the fall of 1722 the Duke of Holstein acquired a quantity of music from the departing Kinsky, as well as from some Russian noblemen, so that his band, which Bergholz now calls an orchestra, possessed scores of "many beautiful pieces" (2:19). This circumstance in turn facilitated the staging of concerts, which were usually given on Wednesdays after dinner and attracted many listeners from embassy circles and from the Foreign Quarter. At the time of Catherine's coronation in Moscow, on 7 May 1724, a large orchestra consisting of more than forty musicians conducted by Hübner played in the Kremlin palaces. These musicians were assembled from various bands: from the court, from the duke, and from those in service to various noblemen.[426A]

All these external forms embodying Peter's musical innovations affected only certain parts of Russian society. They did not touch the masses of the people, who remained faithful to and fought for their ancient customs. Even in high society, some connections to the past were maintained. We know from Bergholz that *bandura* players were still to be found at court, in the empress's household as well as in the service of the Duchess of Mecklenburg, Catherine Ivanovna (a niece of the emperor), and Princess Cherkasskaia.[427] It was here that the Holsteiners heard them and learned a few folk songs from them.

In addition to the *bandura* players retained in court service, other representatives of folk music were undoubtedly in the service of some noblemen. But this involuntary tribute to the native heritage was completely overwhelmed by the din and pomp of the new sounds and ceremonies that marked the Europeanization of the Russian state. Nevertheless, one finds similar survivals of folk music in subsequent reigns, sometimes expressed in the buffoon's cap (under Anna Ioannovna), sometimes in the caftan of the nobleman (under Elizabeth)—evidence of a lingering attachment to the legacies of the past. But these were the last, belated blossoms, crushed by French *galanteries* and the splendor of the court, which made folk song seem like a wild, uncultivated flower. Foreigners who heard this music without comprehending its pristine beauty or originality tried to dress it up in a more cultured form, but succeeded merely in bequeathing to posterity a caricature. The work of several generations was needed in order to cleanse folk song of its alien garb and restore its original simplicity and profound artistic significance.

It is particularly interesting to consider to what extent Peter's reign was reflected in folk art as a whole. This can be answered only after a comprehensive examination of the varied artistic phenomena which the events and reforms of Peter's reign evoked in the popular imagination. It is beyond the scope of a history of Russian music to discuss such subjects as folk woodcuts, manuscript illustrations, the considerable manuscript literature, and texts of folk songs that have reached us only in their latest variants. For our purposes here, the primary musical material is contained in the manuscript collections of vocal music from Peter's time and that of his immediate successors. It is still useful, nevertheless, to present a general overview of folk art as a context for the development of various musical forms.

On the one hand, there is an expression in this [folk] artistic consciousness of a spirit of protest against Peter's innovations and harsh measures. In the people's imagination, the great tsar was even identified as the Antichrist. Rumors of the end of the world were spurred by the novelties and restrictive edicts affecting the old way of life: the abolition of the patriarchate, the cruel persecutions of schismatics, decrees about the shaving of beards and the wearing of Western-style clothes, and so forth. Many schismatics fled to the outlying regions of the empire. "The religious fanaticism that was aroused found increasingly rich nourishment, and the imagination was stimulated by contemporary stories of the Second Coming," states A. Pypin, "and it reached the utmost extremes." In contemporary schismatic manuscripts, one finds many drawings of the Antichrist with his retinue in which there are clear hints of Peter and the events caused by his edicts. Even the tsar's favorite instrument, the drum, is not forgotten. These drawings, which indicate the agitation of the folk masses against Peter's reforms, also testify to the complete rupture between the people and the upper classes of society.[428] The ancient neumed chant retreated, along with the Old Believers, to the most distant regions and to the Kerzhensk forests. Even the death of the great reformer evoked a peculiar funeral monument created by Peter's enemies among the folk: the well-known woodcut "The Mice Bury the Cat." According to D. A. Rovinskii and other scholars, this woodcut expresses in a sharply satirical form passionate hatred of Peter, the destroyer of the old traditions [see n. 228E above].

On the other hand, Peter's reign also left traces in folk songs extolling many of the events of his era. The texts of these songs were collected by P. Bezsonov in the eighth fascicle of *The Songs of P. V. Kireevskii*. At present, however, these songs have only a literary and historical significance, since their tunes (except for those in the collection of Kirsha Danilov) have not come down to us. Bezsonov, who has studied them, asserts that the older forms of folk creativity had gradually but inevitably died out. Already in these old forms, we see the beginnings and development of an individual [as opposed to a collective] art. This process, whereby folk art changed into a fundamentally individualized and constructed art form, is seen especially in the new song forms, that is, the *kanty* and psalms that came into being in the eighteenth century with the increasing enthusiasm for syllabic versification. Some elements of the latter, however, can be traced long before Peter's era. These were the first glimmerings of the creation of secular music, which, as we shall see, very quickly yielded to new trends, combining in its primitive forms the demands of the Europeanized court circles and, at the same time, the more intimate artistic needs of the folk masses. This compositional activity remained almost entirely uniform, since the Russian musicians' new creative roots were still feeble and impermanent, and the music lovers' tastes in that period were not very demanding.

Peter's immediate successors, Catherine I (r. 1725–27) and Peter II (r. 1727–30), ruled only briefly, so there was no opportunity for the appearance of any kind of new musical elements in Russia. This occurred only during Anna Ioannovna's reign, when the first signs of a more serious musical culture appeared with the arrival of Italian opera to the capital. Until her reign, music (apart from the activities of the sovereign singers) had been employed only at festivals, balls, and illuminations. No. 3 in the music appendix in this volume is a *kant* on the death of Peter and Catherine's accession to the throne, from an eighteenth-century collection of three-part *kant* settings now in my possession.[429] The *kant* singer gives a rather touching picture of sadness and sorrow:

> V slezakh Rossiia vsia pogruzhalas'
> Po Petre v sirotstve kak ostalas'.

> Drowned in tears, Russia wept
> Orphaned by Peter.

The composer was also successful in imparting the sorrowful minor mode. Some musical details of the *kant* have an appealing spiritual quality, a mood alien to Peter's earlier, and merely superficially effective, ceremonial *kanty*. The second stanza hails Catherine's accession to the throne in the following verses:[429A]

> Paki v male po tme svet uzrela
> Kak Ekaterinu vozimela
> Na prestole vsia po vole
> Petrovoi stoiashchu na dolze
> Monarkhinia, geroinia,
> O! liute ne zhive ko tvoei polze.

> Through the murk then came the brightness,
> As we see enthroned our Catherine:
> She commands by Peter's will
> By the trust our hearts instill:
> O! Our Queen, Our Sovereign's bride.
> Damned are those not on your side.

The author of these verses could only have been Feofan Prokopovich, who frequently bestowed such bombastic and nonsensical epithets on Catherine, for example, in his "Speech on the Coronation Day of Her Majesty Catherine Alekseevna," delivered on 7 May 1724 at the Cathedral of the Dormition in Moscow (where he called her "velikaia geroinia monarkhinia!" [great heroine and monarch]), or in his "Speech at the Funeral of Emperor Peter" on 1 March 1725 in St. Petersburg.[430]

We might mention again that during Catherine I's reign, the Kapellmeister of the Holstein orchestra, Johann Hübner, became a prominent musician. As for other musicians from the period of her reign, there is little reliable information. It is certain only that at the end of the year-long mourning for Peter, performances were revived at the Winter Palace. They were described as "fabulous comedies with German, French, English, and Polish dances," and a play was staged as a comedy-fable entitled *Iasnoe sokolinnoe peryshko* [The bright falcon's feather]. During Catherine I's reign, two Parisian dancers, Ernest and Juliette, appeared in St. Petersburg, where they introduced new dances, the *musette* and the *rigaudon,* and had great success.[431]

Far more interesting in this respect was the three-year reign of the young Peter II. There were performances in the court's presence with the assistance of the two French dancers; thus on 1 January 1730, at the theater by the Green Bridge (formerly the Police Bridge), there was a performance of *Orfei v Adu* [Orpheus in Hades]. This was a "musical comedy with a dance of the spirits, composed by Franz Fürst" (according to V. Svetlov [see n. 431, above]). Also at that time, a company of French players appeared for the first time in St. Petersburg and apparently staged vaudevilles with singing, at least if we are to judge from the only information we have of that company's performance. In the *Spb. vedomosti*

(16 September 1729, no. 74) we find the following announcement: "Herewith it is made known that the local French players [*komedianty*] will tomorrow, that is on Wednesday the 17th, give a free show on the occasion of the happy birth of the French prince, and all enthusiasts are invited. The comedy to be shown is *Le pédant scrupuleux* or *Sovetnyi shkolnyi master* [The counseling schoolmaster] and after the comedy, *Obmanutyi okhotnik* [*Le chasseur trompé;* The deluded hunter] will be presented."[432] The latter piece could have been either a vaudeville with songs or a little ballet, which is less likely.

Contemporary issues of the *Spb. vedomosti* also provide unimportant but interesting notes concerning musical doings of the time. There are reports about the tsar's triumphal entry into Moscow to the sound of trumpets and kettledrums (1728) and a brief report of a banquet with illuminations and two bands of musicians who played "extraordinary concertos" [*kontserty;* the term is applied here to instrumental, not vocal, music] at the festival organized by Professor Delisle on 29 October 1729 in St. Petersburg, in honor of the birth of the French dauphin. Another more interesting announcement is that of the Danzig organist Feofil [Theophile] Volkmar about the sale of organs and harpsichords.[433] This announcement indicates the source of the first keyboard instruments in Russia.[433A] Finally, in a 1729 issue of the *Spb. vedomosti,* we find a report from Rome about a performance of a new opera there in December 1728 in Cardinal Ottoboni's palace. This item was accompanied by an editorial note stating: "Opera is a musical action akin to comedy, in which verses are sung and at the same time various dances and extraordinary machines can be presented" (*Spb. vedomosti* 1729, no. 1).

In the Buslaev manuscript collection we mentioned earlier ([RNB] Q.XIV.141, fols. 169v–70) there is a *kant* from 1727–28 hailing Peter II's accession to the throne in terms similar to those applied to Peter I:

> Veselisia Rossiia so otrokom preslavnym,
> Veselisia i so vnukom orlom dvoeglavnym [*sic;* in original]
> Ego zhe v Rossii byvaet detishche preslavno
> Ego zhe rozhdenie ot orla dvoeglavna.

> Rejoice, Russia, with the all-glorious child
> Rejoice with the grandson of the two-headed eagle
> The most celebrated child in Russia is he,
> Born of the two-headed eagle.

Such is the scanty information concerning music during the reign of Peter II. Some supplemental material can, to a limited extent, be found in contemporary foreign accounts; the most detailed of these is the Duke de Liria's "Letters about Russia to Spain." These letters, in a sense, continue the diary of Bergholz and others from Holstein. But the Spanish ambassador was much more interested in court intrigues than in local customs and manners, and his accounts of certain festivals and ceremonies refer only to court functions.[434]

Summarizing these new data about the musical life in St. Petersburg and Moscow at the end of the 1720s, we find that attempts were made to perform French plays and that the orchestral ensemble was considerably enlarged and perfected (for Catherine I's coronation in 1724, Hübner conducted an ensemble of forty musicians, and there were two groups of musicians for Prof. Delisle's *Tafelmusik*). Finally, we have a reliable report about one of the first merchants supplying imported harpsichords and clavichords, which were more or less necessities in homes of the wealthy; at the time, among the Russian nobility, harpsichord players included Princess Cherkasskaia (mentioned above), Count Iaguzhinskii, and also Prince Kantemir and the Countesses Golovina, who were educated in Sweden.[434A] It is also of interest that at the same time the Academic Bookstore in St. Petersburg issued an announcement to "lovers of excellent books," saying that it would accept orders for delivery "via ships from Germany, Holland, and other places" of various printed editions (*Spb. vedomosti* 1729, no. 18). In that way, even ordering music from abroad was facilitated for Russian music lovers.

Music Appendix for Volume 1

Kanty from the time of Peter the Great

No. 1 The *kant* written in celebration of the Peace of Nystadt, "Raduisia Rosko zemle" [Rejoice Russian land; from RNB, Q.XIV.141]

No. 2 Petrine festive *kanty* [from RNB, Q.XIV.141]

2.1 "Vivat"
2.2 "Mnogaia leta" [Many years]
2.3 "Sotvorizh emu, gospodi" [Let us create for him, O Lord]
2.4 "Kirie eleison"
2.5 "Sotvorizh emu" [Let us create for him, O Lord]
2.6 "Vivat"
2.7a "Slavoiu i chestiiu" [With glory and honor]
2.7b "Vivat"
2.8 "Osanna"
2.8a "I pokorim" [And we shall vanquish]
2.9 "Torzhestvui, likovstvui Bellona preslavna" [Rejoice, sing praises, Bellona glorious]
2.10 "Poem, gospodevi" [We sing, Lord]
2.10a "Poem vsi gospodevi" [We all sing, Lord]
2.11 "Desnitsa tvoia gospodi" [Thy right hand, Lord]
2.12 "Pobeditel na tebe vospevaem" [We sing to you, the victor]
2.12a "Vivat"
2.13 "Napadet na nia strakh" [Fear descends]
2.13a "Dondezhe proidut liudie tvoi" [Until your people pass]
2.14 "Mnogaia leta" [Many years]
2.15 "Dondezhe proidut liudie tvoi" [Until your people pass]
2.16 "Vivat"
2.16a "Vivat"

No. 3 A *kant* on the death of Peter and the elevation of Catherine I to the throne, "V slezakh Rossiia vsia pogruzhalas'" [Drowned in tears, Russia wept; from a source in Findeizen's collection]

I. Кант на заключение Ништадского мира.

(по ркп. Публ. Библ. Q. XIV № 141)

II. Петровские торжественные канты.

(по ркп. Публ. Библ. Q XIV № 141).

(лл. 159—166 об.)

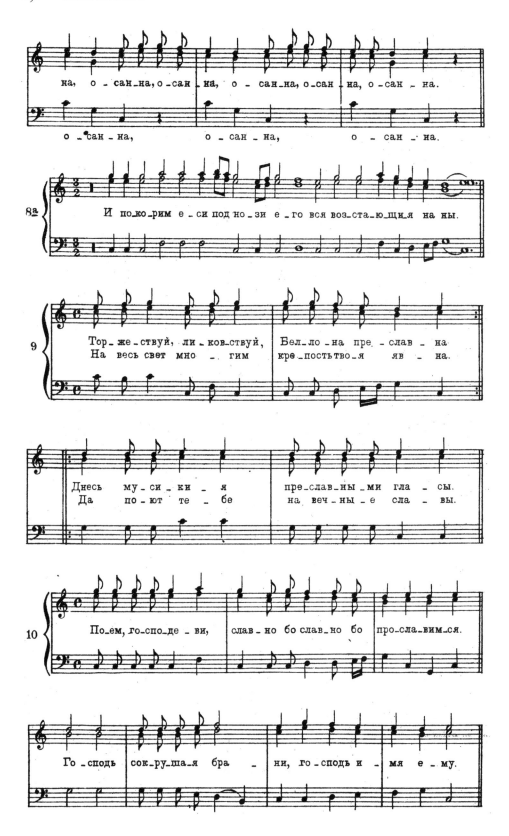

III. Кант на кончину Петра и восшествие на престол Екатерины I.

(Moderato)

1. В сле_зах Рос _ си _ я вся по _ гру _ жа _ лась   По Пе_тре

2. Па _ ки в ма _ ле по тьме свет уз _ ре _ ла   Как Е _ ка_

в си _ рот _ стве   как о _ ста _ лась.   Свет по _ мра _ чись

те _ ри _ ну воз _ и _ ме _ ла   На пре _ сто _ ле

столь со _ кру _ шись   Ве _ нец твой у _ вя _ де при гро_

вся по во _ ле   Пет _ ро _ вой сто _ я _ щу на дол_

бе.   Толь _ ко сте _ нать   Толь _ ко ры _ дать

зе.   Мо _ нар _ хи _ ня!   Ге _ ро _ и _ ня!

Толь _ ко дол_жно бы _ ло   у _ ныть у-тро _ бе.
                            бы _ ло

О!   лю _ те не жи _ ве   ко тво _ ей поль _ зе.

.

Notes

1. Introduction

[*Editors' note:* This chapter introduces and discusses the predecessors of the Slavs who lived in the territory that later became Russia and its neighbors. The references to Herodotus and other writers of ancient Greece, to the Scythians, and to the representations of musical instruments and dances depicted on artifacts unearthed during archaeological excavations provide ample materials for a musico-archaeological study, an approach seldom undertaken by present-day musicologists; some non-Russian comparative materials may be found, for example, in the volume on Greece edited by M. Wegner in the series *Musikgeschichte in Bildern* 2, no. 4 (Leipzig: Deutscher Verlag für Musik, 1963), and see also the many volumes that discuss ancient Greek musical instruments and references to music in writings from antiquity, as listed in *NG2*.

Most of the places Findeizen mentions in this chapter are on the northern coast of the Black Sea, although a few are in the vicinity of Kiev and other cities. Among the more important cities is Kerch, on the easternmost part of the Crimean Peninsula. The narrow pass connecting the Black Sea with the Sea of Azov has several names: Cimmerian Bosphorus, Kerch Straits, or Yeni-kale Straits (which refers to a tower or fortification on the tip of the peninsula on the western shore of the narrow pass). Ancient Greek Cherson appears to be the ancestor of present-day Kerch, although a later settlement named Kherson is located on the right bank of the Dnieper River a few dozen miles before it flows into the Black Sea. The city of Chernigov is located slightly to the northeast of Kiev; Ekaterinoslav was renamed Dnepropetrovsk in the 1920s and is the site of the well-known and much-touted Soviet hydroelectric power project, almost two-thirds of the way from Kiev down the Dnieper toward the Black Sea; and Aleksandropol and Nikopol are archaeological sites in the area.

It is interesting to note that the monumental multivolume history of Russian music, *Istoriia russkoi muzyki v desiati tomakh* [A history of Russian music in ten volumes] (Moscow: Muzyka, 1983–), does not include archaeological documentation predating the formation of the Russian state. Some earlier textbooks, including the first volume of Iu. V. Keldysh, *Istoriia russkoi muzyki* [History of Russian music] (Moscow: Muzgiz, 1948), had at least a brief mention of such monuments. The first volume of the new series begins *in media res*—with Russians already established in the lands which become their territories in the later Middle Ages.]

1. I. E. Zabelin, *Istoriia russkoi zhizni s drevneishikh vremen* [History of Russian life from the earliest times] (Moscow: Tip. Gracheva, 1876–79), 2:12; I. A. Khoinovskii, *Kratkie arkheologicheskie svedeniia o predkakh slavian i Rusi i opis' drevnostei* [Brief archaeological testimonies about the ancestors of the Slavs and of Rus' and a description of the artifacts] (Kiev: Tip. Imp. universiteta, 1896), 10. [Ivan Egorovich Zabelin (1820–1909) was a prolific writer on many aspects of life in ancient Russia; see the article in *GSE* 9:544. Findeizen also mentions the archaeologist August Schleicher (1821–1868; see the *Allgemeine Deutsche Biographie*, s.v. "Schleicher, August") and Vladimir Bonifat'evich Antonovich (Volodymyr Antonovych) (1834–1908), a Ukrainian historian and archaeologist (*GSE* 2:183; *EU* 1:85–86). Findeizen's uncritical acceptance of the hierarchical racial theories of writers such as Johann Friedrich Blumenbach (1752–1840), Joseph Arthur Gobineau (1816–1882), and others, is typical of his era.]

1A. [*Editors' note:* The names of the various tribes listed here and below in chapters 1 and 2 are taken, whenever possible, from the discussion in George Vernadsky, *Ancient Russia*, vol. 1 of George Vernadsky and Michael Karpovich, *A History of Russia* (New Haven: Yale University Press, 1943); we have also used this source as a guide in rendering the names of the early cities Findeizen discusses here.]

1B. [*Editors' note:* This is from Ode 62; there is an English-language translation by Thomas Moore, trans., *The Odes of Anacreon* (New York: Putnam's, 1903), 149.]

2. The *Thesmoforiazousai* were women who celebrated the *thesmoforia*, the feast honoring Demeter, goddess of agriculture and marriage. This feast was celebrated exclusively by women and included sacrificial offerings, libations, and dances. [Aristophanes' play, *Thesmoforiazousai,* is a satire dealing with the women participating in the ritual of *thesmoforiai* which Euripides is trying to attend. See Thomas Temple Wright, "The Presentation of Euripides in Old Comedy" (Ph.D. diss., University of Virginia, 1988).]

3. In the early 1900s, in one of the mounds at the village of Sakhnovka (Kiev province), a small gold plate was found; on it was depicted a group of ten persons led by an empress and, in front of her, a Scythian kneeling and playing on a lyre-like instrument. This plate was described in A. Miller and A. de Mortillet, "Sur un bandeau en or avec figures Scythes découvert dans un kourgan de la Russie Méridionale," *L'Homme préhistorique* 9 (1904), and was dated in the fifth century BC. Its authenticity is disputed by several Russian archaeologists (N. I. Veselovskii, M. M. Rostovtsev, and A. A. Spitsyn). The fragment of the plate reproduced here (fig. 1 in the text) with the figure of the player can scarcely admit any doubt about the existence among the Scythians of a "Greek" lyre with an excessively large body. [Findeizen refers to works by the Russian archaeologists Nikolai Ivanovich Veselovskii (1848–1918; *GSE* 4:624), Mikhail Ivanovich (not M. M.) Rostovtsev (1870–1952; *GSE* 22:292), and Aleksandr Andreevich Spitsyn (1858–1931; *GSE* 24:428).]

3A. [*Editors' note:* Throughout this section, Findeizen uses the term *svirel'* to describe the reed pipe instruments of ancient times. We have translated the term here simply as reed pipe, in order to distinguish this instrument from the folk instrument Findeizen discusses later in this chapter and at greater length in following chapters.]

4. Previous investigators have presumed that Anacharsis lived much later. See J.-J. Barthélemy, *Voyage du jeune Anacharsis en Grèce, vers le milieu du quatrième siècle avant l'ère vulgaire,* ed. Jean Denis Barbie du Bocage, 5th ed. (Paris: Garnery Libraire, 1817). [On Julius Pollux of Naucratia, see *Paulys Realencyclopädie der classischen Altertumswissenschaft,* s.v. "Iulius (Pollux)." The most recent edition of his *Onomasticon* is by Erich Bethe, ed., *Pollucis Onomasticon,* 3 vols. Lexicographi graeci 9 (Stuttgart: Teubner, 1967). The figure of Anacharsis is well known to Western scholars. The work by Abbe Jean-Jacques Barthélemy (1716–1795) was published both in French and in English in numerous editions, and a recent study is Jan Fredrik Kindstrand, *Anacharsis: The Legend and the Apophthegmata* (Uppsala: Distributed by Almqvist & Wiksell, 1981).]

5. Herodotus (d. 425 BC), who lived not long after Anacharsis, gives in his *History* (chaps. 76–80) interesting data about the unhappy end of this Scythian sage. "Like other barbarians, the Scythians avoid borrowing foreign customs," Herodotus writes,

> not only from other peoples but especially from the Greeks. This point was proven by Anacharsis and later by Skil [Scylas]. Anacharsis in particular, having visited many lands and acquiring much wisdom in his travels, on his return trip to his native Scythia passing the Hellespont arrived in Cyzicus (the old colony of Propontis near the present-day Sea of Marmara), where the inhabitants celebrated with great magnificence the feast honoring the mother of the gods. Anacharsis then made a vow to that goddess that if he reached home safe and sound, he would offer sacrifices to her in the same way as he had seen in Cyzicus and he would establish an all-night vigil for her. Upon returning to Scythia, he went to the so-called Woodland and celebrated fully the feast in honor of the goddess with *timpany* in his hands and hanging representations of the goddess. One of the Scythians, noticing this, informed the

> ruler, Saulius; the latter went personally, and seeing that Anacharsis celebrated this feast, killed Anacharsis with an arrow from his bow. And now, if one inquires about Anacharsis, the Scythians reply that they do not know about him because he traveled to Greece and accepted foreign customs.

Herodotus adds that Anacharsis was killed by his own brother. Concerning Anacharsis and citations from Aristophanes, Pollux, and other Greek authors, see V. V. Latyshev, *Izvestiia drevnikh pisatelei grecheskikh i latinskikh o skifakh i Kavkaze* [Reports of ancient Greek and Latin writers about the Scythians and the Caucasus] (St. Petersburg: Tip. Imp. Akademii nauk, 1893–1906 [published as an addendum to the *Zapiski Imperatorskogo russkogo arkheologicheskogo obshchestva* [Notes of the Imperial Russian Archaeological Society]), 1:32 [the quotation above], 322, 352, 495, and 590. [On Latyshev (1855–1921), see *GSE* 14:292.]

It may be noted here that some scholars view the Slavic folk festival *maevki* as derived from similar festivals honoring "the great mother of gods" Maja (Latin Majesta, the Greek Cybele), the goddess of fertility.

5A. [*Editors' note:* Thomas J. Mathiesen, *Apollo's Lyre* (Lincoln: University of Nebraska Press, 1999), 622 n. 47, reports that a modern scholar, Danuta R. Shanzer, believes that Martianus Capella's work was not written until the last quarter of the fifth century.]

6. Latyshev, *Izvestiia*, 2: fasc. 2:413; Martianus Capella, *De nuptiis Philologiae et Mercurii*, bk. 9.

7. Anton Ashik, *Kerchenskie drevnosti. O Pantikapeiskoi katakombe, ukrashennoi freskami* [Antiquities of Kerch. The Panticapaeum catacomb with frescoes] (Odessa: Tip. A. Brauna, 1845). The name of the author, Anton Ashik, appears in the dedication to Prince Vorontsov (fol. 2). Illustrations from this work were borrowed without acknowledgment of the source by the editors of the second fascicle of *Russkie drevnosti v pamiatnikakh iskusstva* [Russian antiquities in monuments of art], Count Tolstoi and N. P. Kondakov. [Anton Baltazarovich Ashik (1802–1854) was a Serbian, a native of Dubrovnik, who moved to Russia in the 1820s; see *ES-BE* 4:554.]

8. On the loss of this catacomb, which A. Ashik discovered and described, see V. V. Stasov, "Katakomba s freskami, naidennaia v 1872 g. bliz Kerchi" [Catacomb with frescoes, discovered in 1872 near Kerch] in *Sobranie sochinenii* [A collection of works] (St. Petersburg: Tip. M. M. Stasiulevicha, 1894), 1:214. [An additional volume was published with Stasov's *Sobranie sochinenii*, titled *Risunki k sochineniiam* [Illustrations to accompany the works] (St. Petersburg: Tip. A. Benke, 1894).]

9. Anton Ashik, *Vosporskoe tsarstvo s ego paleograficheskimi i nadgrobnymi pamiatnikami* [The Bosphorus Empire with its paleographic and funerary monuments] (Odessa: Neiman, 1848–49).

10. In antiquity the *timela* [thymele] represented the altar. [The term refers to round sanctuaries in Greek antiquity.]

11. *Otchet Imperatorskoi arkheologicheskoi komissii* [Report of the Imperial Archaeological Commission] for 1875.

12. *Imperatorskii Rossiiskii istoricheskii muzei. Ukazatel' pamiatnikov* [The Imperial Russian Historical Museum. A guide to the monuments], 2nd ed. (Moscow: Tip. A. I. Mamontova, 1893), 154, 200, 273ff.

13. The Simferopol horn is described in the *Otchet Imperatorskoi arkheologicheskoi komissii* for 1891, 76. Earlier issues of the *Otchety* and accompanying maps produced by the same commission contain many illustrations and valuable descriptions of numerous musical instruments depicted on artistic artifacts, discovered during excavations on the shores of the Black Sea. Thus two painted vases are described in the *Otchet* for 1861, one representing the education of the young Dionysus (an elaborate composition which includes, among other representations, an elderly man playing a double aulos), and the other showing Apollo and Dionysus at Delphi. Dionysus is depicted twice; in one image he is shown with a plectrum in his hand playing a six-string lyre, and in the other he plays a double aulos. The *Otchet* for 1868 has a reproduction and description of a vase at the Hermitage which was found in

1867 in one of the tombs of the Tauride peninsula and dates from the fourth century BC. The front part of the vase shows a joyous procession of five people, including a dancing youth and a maiden wearing a chiton and himation, the latter playing a double aulos, which seems to have been an attribute of joyful women. In the *Otchet* for 1869, among other things, we find the exterior of a *lekanos* with a painting representing the sacred dance of girls by an altar, accompanied by two women. One plays a ribbon-bedecked lyre using a plectrum, and the other, seated in the back, plays a double aulos. The same volume of the *Otchet* includes a reproduction and description of a vase in the Hermitage (fifth century BC) painted by Euphronius, found in Caere. It portrays *hetaera* at a feast; the third woman plays a double aulos, and behind her hangs the case for the instrument. The *Otchet* for 1870–71 contains a description of buccina-type trumpets which had been discovered. The *Otchet* for 1874 has a reproduction of a vase from the Hermitage with the representation of a satyr playing a double aulos, and so on.

14. For an illustrated description of the finds in the tumulus at Aleksandropol, see *Drevnosti Gerodotovoi Skifii. Sbornik* [The antiquities of the Scythia of Herodotus. A collection], 2 vols. (St. Petersburg: n.p., 1866).

15. Fig. 11 represents an ancient bas-relief from the Louvre, reproduced in Victor Duruy, *Histoire des Romains depuis les temps plus reculés jusqu'à l'invasion des barbares,* new and exp. ed. (Paris: Hachette, 1879), 1:90. It depicts an altar beside a sacred tree to which a boy leads an animal to be sacrificed. Behind him is a woman bringing fruits in a basket. In front of the tree (on which small bells are hanging) is a priestess, followed by an acolyte holding a double aulos who is also taking part in the ceremony. Similarly, in a Slavic document of a much later date, the well-known Khludov Psalter of the thirteenth century, we find a representation of the three Hebrew children (Anania, Azaria, and Misail) in Babylonian captivity (fol. 253). They are standing on the shore of the Babylon River (so labeled in the miniature) in front of a tree on which sacred bells hang (fig. N1.1).

[On Victor Duruy (1811–1894), see Sandra Horvath-Peterson, *Victor Duruy and French Education: Liberal Reform in the Second Empire* (Baton Rouge: Louisiana State University Press, 1984). The Khludov Psalter is a very well-known illuminated manuscript (presently in the State Historical Museum in Moscow, GIM, Khlud. 3); it is described in *SKSR* no. 384, where it is dated in the last quarter of the thirteenth century. There is a partial facsimile by M. V. Shchepkina, *Miniatiury Khludovskoi psaltyri* [Miniatures of the Khludov Psalter] (Moscow: Iskusstvo, 1977). In the same year N. N. Rozov published his study, "Muzykal'nye instrumenty i ansambli v miniatiurakh Khludovskoi (russkoi) psaltiri" [Musical instruments and ensembles in the miniatures of the Khludov (Russian) Psalter], in *Drevnerusskoe iskusstvo: Problemy i atributsii* [Old Russian art: Problems and attributions] (Moscow: Nauka, 1977), 91–105, which questioned some of Findeizen's identifications of musical instruments. A follow-up and fairly thorough examination of patterns of presentations of musical instruments in medieval Russian painting was published by V. I. Povetkin, "'Russkii' izobrazitel'nyi kanon na muzykal'nye instrumenty" [The "Russian" representational canon of musical instruments], *PKNO for 1989* (1990): 136–59. In Findeizen, *Ocherki* 1:18, n. 15 was appended to fig. 10; the location of this note has been repositioned for this edition.]

FIG. N1.1. A miniature from the Khludov Psalter.

16. Description and illustrations in *Drevnosti Gerodotovoi Skifii.* [We have reordered the numbering of figs. 8–13 to compensate for the lack of a fig. 13 in Findeizen's text.]

17. *Zapiski Imperatorskogo russkogo arkheologicheskogo obshchestva* 12, fasc. 1 and 2 (1901).

18. See D. A. Khvol'son, ed. and trans., *Izvestiia o Khozarakh, Burtasakh, Bolgarakh, Mad'iarakh, Slavianakh i Russakh Abu-Ali Akhmeda Ben Omar Ibn-Dasta* [Reports about the Khazars, Burtas, Bulgarians, Hungarians, Slavs, and Rus' by Abu-Ali Ahmad Ben Omar Ibn Dasta] (St. Petersburg: Tip. Imp. Akademii nauk, 1869); and A. Ia. Garkavi, *Skazaniia musul'manskikh pisatelei o slavianakh i russkikh s poloviny VII veka do kontsa X veka po R. Kh.* [The stories of Muslim writers about the Slavs and Russians from the second half of the 7th century to the end of the 10th century AD] (St. Petersburg: Tip. Imp. Akademii nauk, 1870). [On Daniil Abramovich Khvol'son (1819–1911), the well-known Semitic scholar, see *GSE* 28:622. The other author Findeizen mentions is Avraam Iakovlevich Garkavi (or Harkavi, Harkavy; 1835–1919), another Semitic scholar and Arabist; see *GSE* 6:97. He is also listed in *Encyclopedia Judaica,* 1971 ed., s.v. "Albert (Abraham Elijah) Harkavy." Ibn Fadlan was an Arab traveler and author from the first half of the tenth century who visited the Volga Bulgars in the early 920s. See Marius Canard, *La relation du voyage d'Ibn Fadlân chez les bulgares de la Volga,* Annales de l'institut d'études orientales 16 (Algiers: n.p., 1958); and A. P. Kovalevskii, *Kniga Akhmeda Ibn-Fadlana o ego puteshestvii na Volgu v 921–22 gg. Stat'i, perevody i kommentarii.* [Ahmad Ibn-Fadlan's book about his trip on the Volga in 921–22. Articles, translations, and commentary] (Kharkov: Izd-vo Khar'kovskogo universiteta, 1956). See also the *Encyclopedia of Islam,* 1968 ed., s.v. "Ibn Fadlan." Findeizen's account of the funeral customs Ibn Fadlan observed, probably of a chieftain of Rus', is apparently from Garkavi, *Skazaniia musul'manskikh pisatelei* (1870; reprint, Slavistic Printings and Reprintings, no. 96, The Hague: Mouton, 1969), 97–100. Some passages from Ibn Fadlan's account (based on Garkavi) are translated into English in Basil Dmytryshyn, ed., *Medieval Russia: A Sourcebook, 900–1700,* 2nd ed. (Hinsdale, Ill.: Dryden, 1973), 11–16. Ibn Dasta was an Arab writer from the tenth century, apparently traveling between AD 903 and 913. It is unknown whether he preceded Ibn Fadlan or drew on Ibn Fadlan's reports for his own writing; see *ES-BE* 24:741; and the *Encyclopedia of Islam,* where he is listed as Ibn Rusta. The only preserved volume of his *Book of Precious Treasures* is volume 7; it is located in the British Museum and contains descriptions of various cities and countries, including Constantinople. One of the most recent discussions of this writer appears in A. Miquel, *La géographie humaine du monde musulman jusqu'au milieu du XI siècle* (Paris: Mouton, 1980). On Al-Masudi, see Tarif Khalidi, *Islamic Historiography: The Histories of Masudi* (Albany: State University of New York Press, 1975); and A. Shboul, *Al-Masudi and his World: A Muslim Humanist and His Interest in Non-Muslims* (London: Ithaca, 1979).]

18A. [*Editors' note:* Findeizen refers to Aleksandr Aleksandrovich Kotliarevskii (1837–1881), *O pogrebal'nykh obychaiakh iazycheskikh slavian* [On the funeral customs of the pagan Slavs] (Moscow: [Sinodal'naia tip.], 1868); on this historian, see *ES-BE* 31:441.]

18B. [*Editors' note:* See Garkavi, *Skazaniia musul'manskikh pisatelei,* 263.]

19. In S. G. Rybakov, "Muzyka i pesni ural'skikh musul'man s ocherkom ikh byta" [Music and songs of the Muslims from the Urals, with an essay concerning their daily life], *Zapiski Imperatorskoi Akademii nauk* series 8 [Notes of the Imperial Academy of Sciences] 2, no. 2 (1897), one can find several folk songs that might have been sung at the kind of ceremonies Ibn Fadlan described, in which young girls took part. Here is a translation of one of them (Rybakov, *Muzyka i pesni,* 156):

> Vstavshi rano, ia smotriu:
> Sinitsy poiut pesni;
> I khotela by ia takzhe pet',
> No odinochestvo gnetet moiu sheiu
> V shirokoi stepi pered dver'iu
> Net sledov ot belogo zaitsa.

So mnoi igrali i smeialis' moi druz'ia,
A teper'—ni odnogo net.

Having risen early, I look about me
The titmice are singing their songs.
I, too, would join in the singing,
But loneliness hangs heavy on me.
In the wide plain, before the door
There is no trace of the white hare;
My friends played and laughed with me
But now they are all gone.

The remains of the ancient rituals in Russian and other songs, regrettably, has not yet been investigat-ed. [Sergei Gavrilovich Rybakov (1867–1921) was a student of Rimskii-Korsakov and an ethnographer as well as a composer; see *ME* 4:801.]

    20. Garkavi, *Skazaniia musul'manskikh pisatelei*, 125.

    20A. [*Editors' note:* From this point on, we are using Findeizen's term *svireli* to indicate the reed pipes of the Slavs; see n. 3A above. The passage from Ibn Dasta is from Garkavi, *Skazaniia musul'manskikh pisatelei*, 265.]

    21. During Igor Riurikovich's reign, Christianity was widespread even among the Kievan prince's military leaders. There is a curious record in the chronicles stating that in AD 945, to ratify a treaty with the Greeks, Igor and the pagan members of his troops swore in Perun's temple (in Kiev) on their weap-ons and gold, placing their shields, rings, and unsheathed swords at the feet of the idol. His Christian warriors swore on the cross in the Church of St. Elijah in the Podol district, probably the oldest church in Kiev (N. Zakrevs'kii, *Letopis' i opisanie goroda Kieva* [Annals and description of Kiev] [Moscow: Universitetskaia tip., 1858], 7). [Mykola (Nikolai) Zakrevs'kii (1805–1871) was a historian and ethnog-rapher who wrote extensively on the history of the city of Kiev; he also collected folklore, including songs. See *EU* 4:803. The translation of Ibn Dasta is from Garkavi, *Skazaniia musul'manskikh pisatelei*, 265. An English translation of the passage from the chronicles on the swearing of the oath is in Samuel Cross and Olgerd Sherbowitz-Wetzor, ed. and trans., *The Russian Primary Chronicle: Laurentian Text* (Cambridge, Mass.: Mediaeval Academy of America, 1973), 77. In Findeizen, *Ocherki* 1:24, n. 21 was attached to fig. 11; the location of this note has been repositioned for this edition.]

    22. The drawing in fig. 11 is taken from *Relation d'un voyage du Levant par Pitton de Tournefort*, vol. 1, as reproduced in an article by P. S. Kazanskii, "O prizyve k bogosluzheniiu v vostochnoi tserkvi" [The summons to the divine service in the Eastern Church], *Trudy I-go arkheologicheskogo s'ezda v Moskve, 1869 g.* [Report of the First Archaeological Congress in Moscow, 1869] (1871), 1:305. This may be the oldest way of suspending the *bilo* (or *klepalo*), which was probably already in use in pagan Rus'. [This refers to the use of wooden boards and planks beaten by a wooden hammer instead of—or before—the use of bells. The drawing is taken from the work of a French botanist, Joseph Pitton de Tournefort (1656–1708), which is available in many editions; the earliest are *Relation d'un voyage du Levant fait par ordre du roy enrichie de descriptions et de figures d'un grand nombre de plantes rares, de divers animaux, et de plusieurs observations touchant l'histoire naturelle . . .* (Paris: Imprimerie Royale, 1717); and *Relation d'un voyage du Levant: fait par ordre du Roy: Contenant l'histoire ancienne et moderne de plusieurs isles de l'Archipel, de Constantinople, des côtes de la Mer Noire, de l'Armenie, de la Georgie, des frontières de Perse et de l'Asie Mineure . . .* (Lyon: Anisson et Poseul, 1717). On the author, see *GSE* 26:265, which cites G. Becker and R. Heim, *Tournefort* (Paris: Muséum national d'histoire naturelle, 1957). The other author cited is Petr Simonovich Kazanskii (d. 1878; *ES-BE* 26:902). The best and most comprehensive study of Russian bells is Edward V. Williams, *The Bells of Russia: History and Technol-ogy* (Princeton, N.J.: Princeton University Press, 1985).]

22A. [*Editors' note:* Theophylact (or Theophylactus) Simocatta was a seventh-century Byzantine historian who wrote about the Slavs in his *Historiae,* which describes a series of wars between Byzantium and various surrounding states ca. 600.]

2. Pagan Rus'

[*Editors' note:* This chapter contains frequent references to various deities in Slavic mythology. On this subject, see, for example, Linda J. Ivanits, *Russian Folk Belief* (Armonk, N.Y.: M. E. Sharpe, 1992); Myroslava T. Znayenko, *The Gods of the Ancient Slavs: Tatishchev and the Beginnings of Slavic Mythology* (Columbus, Ohio: Slavica, 1980); and Mark Kulikowski, *A Bibliography of Slavic Mythology* (Columbus, Ohio: Slavica, 1989). References to Greek writers are easy to trace in any history of Byzantium. Findeizen also includes occasional references to some of the many Russian chronicles. There are entries on some of these sources in *GSE* (for example, for the Gustinskaia Chronicle mentioned in this chapter) and *MERSH,* and see the extensive references in R. P. Dmitrieva, comp., *Bibliografiia russkogo letopisaniia* [A bibliography of Russian chronicle writing] (Moscow: Akademiia nauk SSSR, 1962). Findeizen cites folk songs from various collections and collectors, which are identified below, and see also the discussion of Ivan Prach and other collectors in volume 2 of Findeizen's text. The first volume of *IRM* (1983), like earlier textbooks published roughly between 1940 and 1980, begins with a discussion of folk songs. The stress is on songs for seasonal work (such as spring seeding or summer harvest), presumably following the viewpoint that folk music precedes "art music." Compared to some fairly elaborate statements made in the past, the most recent publication is much more concise and modest in its coverage of this topic.]

23. For a drawing and description, see D. Ia. Samokvasov, "Drevnie zemlianye nasypi i ikh znachenie dlia nauki" [Ancient earthen mounds and their scholarly significance], *Drevniaia i novaia Rossiia* [Ancient and new Russia] 1, no. 3 (1876): 275ff. A folk tradition holds that Prince Chernyi, the founder of the town of Chernigov, was buried in the Black Mound or Grave [*chernaia mogila*]. [On the archaeologist Dmitrii Iakovlevich Samokvasov (1843–1911), see *ES-BE* 56:218 and *BSovE* 50:189.]

24. See the *Chernigovskie gubernskie vedomosti* [Gazette of Chernigov province] 44 (1852; this is the non-official part of the journal); and also Samokvasov, "Drevnie zemlianye nasypi," 278.

25. *Drevnosti Rossiiskogo gosudarstva* [Antiquities of the Russian state], drawings by academician F. Solntsev (Moscow: Tip. A. Semena, 1849–53; reprint, A. N. Chirva, comp., and E. P. Chernukha, ed. [Moscow: AO Kapital i Kul'tura, 1994], in a Russian-English parallel text). [The term *truba* is generally translated here as trumpet; it commonly signifies a straight cylindrical instrument, often made of metal. The term *rog* (or *rozhok*), usually translated as horn, refers to a curved, conical instrument often made of animal horn, wood, or leather. The instrument in fig. 7, to which Findeizen refers here, is a *rog,* although he uses the term *truba* immediately following to describe the large, loud instruments used for hunting and on the march; in this particular case, we have translated *truba* as horn. Many thanks to Robert Karpiak, at the University of Waterloo in Ontario, for his patient and careful discussions of terminology relating to musical instruments. Throughout his work, Findeizen refers to the Music History Museum, which has had a complex evolution from his time to our own, as recorded in Patricia Kennedy Grimsted, ed., *Archives of Russia: A Directory and Bibliographic Guide to Holdings in Moscow and St. Petersburg* 2 vols. (Armonk, N.Y.: M. E. Sharpe, 2000), 1:586–91. The "Muzykal'no-istoricheskii muzei" to which he refers was, in the 1920s, under the administration of the Leningrad Philharmonic, and at that time it had an extensive collection of manuscripts and other written sources, as well as a large collection of musical instruments. The instruments were eventually organized into what was called the Exhibit of Musical Instruments [Muzykal'nykh instrumentov vystavka], associated with the State Scientific Research Institute of Theater and Music; it is currently a branch of the St. Petersburg State Museum of Theater and Musical Arts. The manuscript collection

is now part of the Sector of Source Study (Sektor istochnikovedeniia) of the Russian Institute of the History of Arts in St. Petersburg [Rossiiskii institut istorii iskusstv, or RIII).]

25A. [*Editors' note:* Zabelin, *Istoriia russkoi zhizni,* 2:18.]

25B. [*Editors' note:* See N. M. Karamzin, *Istoriia gosudarstva rossiiskogo,* 5 vols. [History of the Russian state] (Moscow: Nauka, 1989–98), 1:44; Karamzin says that the musicians are playing "kitharas or *gusli.*" On the famous historian Nikolai Mikhailovich Karamzin (1766–1826), see *GSE* 11:43.]

25C. [*Editors' note:* S. A. Gedeonov, *Variagi i Rus'* [The Varangians and Rus'] (St. Petersburg: Tip. Imp. Akademii nauk, 1876). Stepan Aleksandrovich Gedeonov (1815–1878) was a historian and, from the 1860s, director of the Hermitage and the Imperial theaters; see *GSE* 6:153.]

26. Fuller details in I. I. Sreznevskii, *Sviatilishcha i obriady iazycheskogo bogosluzehniia drevnikh slavian, po svidetel'stvam sovremennym i predaniiam* [Sanctuaries and rituals of the pagan religious services of the ancient Slavs, according to contemporary testimonies and traditions] (Kharkov: Universitetskaia tip., 1846; reprint, Madison: University of Wisconsin Library, 1980). [Arkona was a temple site on the island of Ruegen in the Baltic Sea (linked to Germany from the city of Stralsund). The large temple of the Slavs there was described by Saxo Grammaticus (1140–1208) in his *Gesta Danorum.* The Danish king Waldemar I razed the city and the temple in 1169 and took all the treasures to Denmark; see *GSE* 2:312, which also adds that, in 1920, archaeological excavations confirmed Saxo's descriptions. See also the monograph by K. Schuchardt, *Arkona, Rethra, Vineta. Ortsuntersuchungen und Ausgrabungen* (Berlin: H. Schoetz, 1926).]

26A. [*Editors' note:* Translation from Jack Haney and Eric Dahl, trans., *The Discourse on Igor's Campaign: A Translation of the "Slovo o polku Igoreve"* ([Seattle]: n.p., 1989), 28.]

26B. [*Editors' note:* The description of the Arkona temple is in Saxo Grammaticus, *Danorum Regum Heroumque Historia,* trans. and ed. Eric Christiansen, BAR International Series 118(i) (Oxford: BAR, 1981), 2:494.]

26C. [*Editors' note:* This passage is in Saxo Grammaticus, *Danorum Regnum Heroumque Historia,* 2:505: "A demon was seen to leave the inner shrine in the form of a dark animal and suddenly vanish from the sight of the bystanders." For a description of the destruction of the temple, see 498–506. Findeizen's source for the tale of the idol in Novgorod is not clear; the passage is close to the version in the Tsarskii copy of the Sofia I Chronicle in *PSRL* 39 (1994), 35–36, according to Daniel Waugh.]

27. *Drevnosti. Trudy moskovskogo arkheologicheskogo obshchestva* [Antiquities. Works of the Moscow Archaeological Society] 1 (1865): 47.

27A. [*Editors' note:* Translation from Haney and Dahl, *The Discourse on Igor's Campaign,* 30.]

28. Sreznevskii, *Sviatilishcha i obriady,* 21.

29. The last two deities are, apparently, not yet clarified. The deity Moksha (in Sanskrit the term *moksha* means death) was still recalled in popular memory even in the sixteenth century; among the questions in the village nomocanons (ecclesiastical regulations) one asked: "Did she (the parishioner) still go to Mokosh?" (see E. V. Barsov, *Slovo o polku Igoreve* [The lay of the host of Igor] (Moscow, 1887–89; reprint, Slavistic Printings and Reprintings 95, nos. 1–3 [The Hague: Mouton, 1969], 1:360). [Elpidifor Vasil'evich Barsov (1836–1917) was a well-known historian and folklorist who collected manuscripts for Moscow libraries; see *GSE* 3:35. Translations of the passage on Vladimir and the following passage on Dobrynia are from Cross and Sherbowitz-Wetzor, *The Russian Primary Chronicle,* 93–94; transliteration slightly modified to conform to the practices of the present volume.]

29A. [*Editors' note:* Findeizen's source here is I. I. Sreznevskii, *Materialy dlia slovaria drevnerusskogo iazyka* [Materials for a dictionary of the old Russian language] (St. Petersburg: Tip. Imp. Akademii nauk, 1893–1903; reprint, Moscow: Gos. izdatel'stvo inostrannykh i natsional'nykh slovarei, 1958), 3:144 (all subsequent references are to this reprint edition).]

30. N. I. Kostomarov, *Ocherk domashnei zhizni i nravov velikorusskogo naroda v XVI i XVII stoletiiakh* [An essay on home life and customs of the Great Russian people in the 16th and 17th

centuries], 3rd ed. (St. Petersburg: Tip. M. M. Stasiulevicha, 1887), 263–64. [Nikolai Ivanovich Kosto-marov (1817–1885) was a well-known ethnographer and historian; see *GSE* 13:439. On the traditions of Rod and the Rozhanitsy, see Ivanits, *Russian Folk Belief,* 14ff.]

31. Manuscript no. 181 in the Rumiantsev Museum [RGB]. [Findeizen's source here may be Sreznevskii, *Materialy,* 2:164.]

32. *RIB* 6:31. The questions of Kirik, Savva, and Elijah, with answers by the Novgorod bishop Nifont and other hierarchs from the years 1130–56, from a parchment manuscript of the thirteenth century, the *Kormchaia.* [The *Kormchaia* is a compendium of various secular and ecclesiastical codes. On Kirik, see *MERSH* 17:26 and *SKK* 1:215–17; the source is GIM, Sin. 132, described in *SKSR* no. 183, primarily from ca. 1280.]

33. F. Buslaev, *Istoricheskaia khristomatiia [khrestomatiia] tserkovno-slavianskogo i drevne-russkogo iazykov* [Historical reader of the Church-Slavonic and Old Russian languages] (Moscow: Univer-sitetskaia tip., 1861), 403.

34. N. Petrov, "Podlinnost' pouchenii Feodosiia Pecherskogo o pitii i chashakh troparnykh i o kazniakh bozhiikh" [The authenticity of the instructions of Feodosii Pecherskii [of the Kiev Monastery of the Caves] about drinking and chanted toasts and about God's punishments], *Izvestiia Otdeleniia russkogo iazyka i slovesnosti Imp. Akademii nauk* [Proceedings of the Department of Russian Language and Literature of the Imperial Academy of Sciences] 2, bk. 3 (1897): 783. [These toasts (literally, cups) to the Virgin are discussed in greater detail in chapter 9.]

35. The phrase "fruzhskiia slon'nitsa," which undoubtedly designated a musical instrument, re-mained without explanation by our scholars: A. Kh. Vostokov, *Slovar' tserkovno-slavianskogo iazyka* [Dictionary of Church Slavonic], 2 vols. (St. Petersburg: Izd. II-go otdeleniia Akademii nauk, 1858–61), and Sreznevskii, *Materialy* [although Sreznevskii cites this passage under "slon'nitsa" in 3:423, defining it as a wind instrument or possibly a curved horn]. Is not the term *fruzhskiia slon'nitsa* a translation of the French oliphant, a horn made of elephant ivory, well known in the Middle Ages in the West and which later appeared at the Moscow court? [On the *Slovo,* see *SKK* 1:437–38, where the Paisii collection is identified as RNB, Kir.-Bel. 4/1081.]

36. For notes concerning that document, see Buslaev, *Istoricheskaia khristomatiia,* 540. [Many thanks to Gregory Myers, who translated this difficult passage from the *Slovo.*]

37. Karamzin, *Istoriia gosudarstva rossiiskogo,* 4 n. 387. [The phrase "bel-goriuch' kamen'" is found frequently in songs (see chapter 4) and implies magical properties; see V. I. Dal', *Tolkovyi slovar' zhivogo velikorusskogo iazyka,* 4 vols. [A defining dictionary of the living Great Russian language] (St. Petersburg: M. O. Vol'f, 1880–82) (all references in this translation are to the reprint of this second, expanded edition, 1880–82, reprinted in Moscow: Russkii iazyk, 1981), 1:153. The phrase "kamy go-riushch'" (kamen' goriuch') describes biblical brimstone; see Sreznevskii, *Materialy,* 1:1188.]

37A. [*Editors' note:* Krasivyi Mech (or Krasivaia Mech') is a tributary of the Don River, also known as Krasnyi Mech for its beauty; *ES-BE* 32:512 (and thanks to Daniel Waugh for this refer-ence).]

38. Sreznevskii, *Sviatilishcha i obriady,* 25.

39. "Opyt russkogo prostonarodnogo slovotolkovatelia" [An essay in compiling a glossary of the Russian language of the simple folk], *ChOIDR* 9 (1847), section 4:5.

40. A curious report from Count Cherkasskii to Tsar Fedor Alekseevich is preserved in a register from 1678–79 in Moscow (*RIB* 11:508): "and according to reliable accounts, it is said that the vizier [*vezir'*] or many pashas with large numbers of troops went to the Zaporozh'e and they won't stay be-low Kiev, and they won't leave any undesirables along the way to Kiev, and on this side of the Dnieper, or the Bog [River], there aren't any . . ."

40A. [*Editors' note:* Garkavi, *Skazaniia musul'manskikh pisatelei,* 139.]

41. Sreznevskii, *Sviatilishcha i obriady,* 73.

42. One of these was, for example, a *zhrets-zvatel'* [a priest-summoner]; according to Sreznevskii, *Materialy*, 1:962, this is a musician or one who "summons people with horns [*truby*] to the place of [pagan] worship." He cites a thirteenth-century text, the *Skazanie Afroditiana* [The tale of Afroditian].

43. I. M. Snegirev, *Russkie prostonarodnye prazdniki i suevernye obriady* [Russian folk festivals and superstitious rituals] (Moscow: Universitetskaia tip., 1837), 2:69. [*Koliada* is the Yuletide season, during which *koliady*, or special songs or carols, were sung. See also *Russian Folk Lyrics*, trans. and ed. Roberta Reeder, introductory essay by V. Ja. Propp (Bloomington: Indiana University Press, 1993), 3, 57 n. 2. Ivan Mikhailovich Snegirev (1793–1868) was a professor at Moscow University who published widely on Russian antiquities and folklore; see *ES-BE* 60:616–17.]

43A. [*Editors' note:* Iosif Sreznevskii's publication was in the *Ukrainskii vestnik* [Ukrainian herald] in 1817, and was published later by I. P. Sakharov, *Pesni russkogo naroda* [Songs of the Russian people] (St. Petersburg, 1838), pt. 1.]

44. V. Borisov, *Opisanie goroda Shui i ego okrestnostei* [A description of the town of Shuia and its environs] (Moscow: V Tip. Ved. mosk. gorod. politsii, 1851), 154.

45. A. Titov, *Rostovskii uezd* [Rostov district]. [This is probably Titov's book, *Rostovskii uezd iaroslavskoi gubernii* [Rostov district of Iaroslav province] (Moscow: Sinodal'naia tip., 1885).]

46. *Russkie narodnye pesni, sobrannye N. A. L'vovym. Napevy zapisal i garmonizoval Ivan Prach* [Russian folk songs, collected by N. A. L'vov, tunes written down and harmonized by Ivan Prach], ed. A. S. Suvorin (St. Petersburg: A. S. Suvorin, 1896), 8. [This is the fourth edition; see the publication history as outlined in LPC, xi; LPC is a facsimile edition of the second edition of the collection. Findeizen discusses these eighteenth-century anthologies at length in volume 2, chapter 18.]

46A. [*Editors' note:* These Petrine-era prohibitions are listed in Alexander V. Muller, trans. and ed., *The Spiritual Regulation of Peter the Great* (Seattle: University of Washington Press, 1972), 14–15.]

47. *Krest'ianskie pesni, zapisannye v sele Nikolaevke Menzelinskogo uezda Ufimskoi gubernii N. E. Pal'chikovym* [Peasant songs collected by N. E. Pal'chikov in the village of Nikolaevka in the Menzelin district of Ufa province], ed. A. E. Pal'chikov (St. Petersburg: A. E. Pal'chikov, 1888). The value of this outstanding collection is enhanced by the fact that the folk songs are notated with their *podgoloski* [supporting voice or second part in folk polyphony] in choral performance; these parts are absent in the majority of other collectors' works. [Nikolai Evgrafovich Pal'chikov (1838–1888) worked extensively as a collector of folk songs; see *ME* 4:169.]

47A. [*Editors' note:* N. M. Lopatin and V. P. Prokunin, comps., *Sbornik russkikh narodnykh liricheskikh pesen* [A collection of Russian lyric folk songs] (Moscow: Tip. A. I. Mamontova, 1889), pt. 1, 63. Nikolai Mikhailovich Lopatin (1854–1897) published a collection of Russian folk texts (without music) in 1885. In the 1880s he collaborated with Vasilii Pavlovich Prokunin (1848–1910), another folklorist and collector; see *ME* 4:464f.]

47B. [*Editors' note:* Mikhail Dmitrievich Chulkov (1743–1793) published four volumes of texts of Russian folk songs in the 1770s. See LPC, 14ff. There is also a monograph on Chulkov in English by John G. Garrard, *Mixail Culkov. An Introduction to his Prose and Verse* (The Hague: Mouton, 1970); see also chapter 18 for further discussion of these eighteenth-century collections.]

48. Lopatin and Prokunin, *Sbornik russkikh narodnykh liricheskikh pesen*, pt. 1, 63.

49. Ibid., pt. 1, 65.

50. One of the best variants is in Rimskii-Korsakov's *Sbornik* [A collection], op. 100, no. 45.

51. *Russkie pesni, neposredstvenno s golosov naroda zapisannye i s ob"iasneniiami izdannye Iu. N. Mel'gunovym* [Russian songs, written down directly from the voices of the people and published with commentaries by Iu. N. Mel'gunov], fasc. 1 (Moscow: E. Lissner i Iu. Roman, 1879), 13; and *40 narodnykh pesen, sobrannykh T. I. Filippovym i garmonizovannykh N. A. Rimskim-Korsakovym* [40 folk songs, collected by T. I. Filippov and harmonized by N. A. Rimskii-Korsakov] (Moscow: P. Iurgenson,

1882), 30. [Iulii Nikolaevich Mel'gunov (1846–1893) was a folklorist; see *ME* 3:533. Tertii [Terentii] Ivanovich Filippov (1825–1899) was an amateur singer and art lover who gave Rimskii-Korsakov some forty songs which the composer arranged and published in 1882; see *ME* 5:811ff.]

51A. [*Editors' note:* Nikolai Semenovich Klenovskii (1853–1915) was a conductor, a composer, and a musical ethnographer who arranged concerts of music by various nationalities; see *ME* 2:833–34.]

52. It is quite curious to note that the terms *pop* and *popeitsa* [priest and priest's wife] existed even in pre-Christian Russia in the sense of male singer and female singer.

3. Kievan Rus'

[*Editors' note:* This chapter deals with the early Russian state, or Kievan Rus', in the period from about the tenth through the thirteenth centuries, when the Tatars conquered most of the land and imposed a rule which was to last until the end of the fourteenth century. The chapter is divided into three segments: (1) Kiev and information about Russia's conversion to Christianity; (2) references to old Russian musical instruments; and (3) old Russian church music.

In the first section, on Kiev and the conversion, Findeizen discusses *byliny,* epic narrative poems comparable to the Western European epics of the Middle Ages. There are many studies of these poems, easily located in any history of Russian literature. English-language studies include Alex E. Alexander, *Bylina and Fairy Tale, the Origins of Russian Heroic Poetry* (The Hague: Mouton, 1973); Russell Zguta, "*Byliny:* A Study of Their Value as Historical Sources" (Ph.D. diss., Penn State University, 1967); and Patricia M. Arant, *Compositional Techniques of the Russian Oral Epic, the* Bylina (New York: Garland, 1990). See also James Bailey and Tatyana Ivanova, trans., *An Anthology of Russian Folk Epics* (Armonk, N.Y.: M. E. Sharpe, 1998).

Probably the most famous of all Russian epics is the *Slovo o polku Igoreve,* often translated as the *Lay of the Host of Igor;* a lay [*lai*] is a long narrative poem meant to be sung. We have retained this common translation, in part because it is familiar, and in part because of its resonance, to musicians, with later medieval French poetry and music. However, for our translations from the work, we are relying on the lovely and evocative rendition in Haney and Dahl, *The Discourse on Igor's Campaign.* In this translation, Jack Haney discusses the term *slovo,* which is a common title in early Russian literary works, describing his choice of the word *discourse* for the title. As Haney says, the word *song* as a translation for *slovo* "implies fixed melos and more than the metrical accompaniment which the poem was likely to have had; a 'lay' suggests not only a song but also much more of a narrative structure than the *Slovo* seems to be. The 'tale' would suggest more fiction than is the case, while 'poem' overemphasizes the formal aspects of the work, which is nonetheless a poem" (53–54).

There are many studies of this work, which was preserved in a single manuscript copy that was destroyed in the great Moscow fire of 1812. Most scholars believe it to be a work roughly contemporaneous to the events it describes (either ca. 1187, immediately after Igor's return from captivity, or from a decade or so later); some believe it to date from the fifteenth century (from the time of the *Zadonshchina,* discussed below). A few scholars believe the work to be an eighteenth-century creation; see the views expressed, most recently, in Edward L. Keenan, *Josef Dobrovský and the Origins of the Igor Tale* (Cambridge, Mass.: Harvard University Press, 2004). One scholar, Lev Vladimirovich Kulakovskii, not only believes that the tale was sung but has attempted to reconstruct the ancient melos; see his *Pesn' o polku Igoreve* [The song of the host of Igor] (Moscow: Sovetskii kompozitor, 1977). The Igor tale has been published in several versions in recent anthologies; see *PLDR XII vek,* 373–87, 679–88; and *BLDR* 4:254–67, 628–34, and the series of three poetic translations into modern Russian on 530–82. Findeizen also discusses two interrelated poems, the *Skazanie o Mamaevom poboishche* [The tale of Mamai's bloody battle] and the *Zadonshchina* (the land beyond the Don River where the battle took place); see the extensive bibliography on both in *SKK* 2: pt. 1, 345–53; 2: pt. 2, 371–84.

References to Byzantium and to the organs used in ceremonies at the Imperial court are frequently cited in Western literature. In addition to the concise statements in *NG2*, see Jean Perrot, *L'orgue de ses origines hellénistiques à la fin du XIIIe siècle* (Paris: A. et J. Picard, 1965); the English translation, slightly abridged, appeared under the title *The Organ from Its Invention to the End of the Thirteenth Century*, trans. Norma Deane (New York: Oxford University Press, 1971). The most recent study of this subject dealing specifically with the organ in Byzantium in the ninth and tenth centuries is Nikos Maliaras, *Die Orgel im byzantinischen Hofzeremoniell des 9. und 10. Jahrhunderts*, Miscellanea Byzantina Monacensia 33 (Munich: Institut für Byzantinistik und Neugriechische Philologie der Universität, 1991). These volumes also contain full bibliographical references to the frequently quoted writings by Liutprand and information about the "wonders" and "automata" he witnessed in Constantinople. On organs in Russia, see L. I. Roizman, *Organ v istorii russkoi muzykal'noi kul'tury* [The organ in the history of Russian musical culture] (Moscow: Muzyka, 1979).

The one reference requiring special attention, and not well known in Western musicology, concerns the fresco depicting musicians and musical instruments in the Cathedral of St. Sophia in Kiev, dating from the mid-eleventh century. This fresco, located in the southwest stairway leading up to the gallery, shows a group of entertainers such as one might have encountered at public festivities in Byzantium. Recent reconstruction after the 1964 cleaning of the fresco and a new interpretation of a damaged segment reveal that it contains a fine representation of a pneumatic organ with bellows. There are some color facsimiles of the fresco; see, for example, S. A. Vysotskii, *Svetskie freski Sofiiskogo sobora v Kieve* [Secular frescoes in the Cathedral of St. Sophia in Kiev] (Kiev: AN Ukrainskoi SSR, 1989), at the beginning of chapter 4, and *Gosudarstvennyi arkhitekturno-istoricheskii zapovednik* [State architectural-historical monument] (Kiev: Mistetstvo, 1984), 132–33. There is a color facsimile (pl. 269) of one of the musicians in H. N. Lohvyn, *Kiev's Hagia Sophia: State Architectural-Historical Monument* (Kiev: Mistetstvo, 1971), and excellent black-and-white reproductions of the organ and the musicians are shown in plates 255–56.

The reinterpretation of this fresco concerns the image that Findeizen, quoting N. P. Kondakov, interpreted as follows: "[an actor] raises a curtain covering the entryway to admit the next act, a clown and harlequin" (*Ocherki* 1:56). The two persons presumably about to enter are, in fact, two men pumping the bellows of the organ, and the "actor" who supposedly "raises a curtain" is actually an organist playing the instrument; the lower part of the organ is damaged in the fresco, and hence the earlier interpretations and speculations. The revised view of the fresco was offered by S. A. Vysotskii and I. F. Totskaia, "Novoe o freske 'Skomorokhi' v Sofii Kievskoi" [New information about the fresco "Skomorokhi" at St. Sophia in Kiev]), in *Kul'tura i iskusstvo drevnei Rusi* [Culture and art in early Rus'] (Leningrad: Izdatel'stvo Leningradskogo universiteta, 1967), 50–57 (a volume honoring the Soviet art historian M. K. Karger); see also André Grabar, "Les Fresques des escaliers à Sainte-Sophie de Kiev et l'iconographie impériale Byzantine," *Seminarium Kondakovianum: Recueil d'études* 7 (1935): 103–17, which sets out a context for the frescoes in Byzantine practices. Totskaia and A. M. Zaiaruznyi later published an additional article on the topic, "Muzykanty na freske 'Skomorokhi' v Sofii Kievskoi" [Musicians in the fresco "Skomorokhi" at St. Sophia in Kiev], in *Drevnerusskoe iskusstvo. Khudozhestvennaia kul'tura X–pervoi poloviny XIII v.* [Old Russian art. Artistic culture from the tenth to the first half of the thirteenth century] (Moscow: Nauka, 1988), 143–55. In her report on this fresco presented at the Eighteenth International Congress of Byzantine Studies in Moscow, 1991, Totskaia seems to have accepted Vysotskii's suggestion that the whole repertory of frescoes, including that of the musicians, represents illustrations of the reception Princess Olga received in Constantinople while visiting the Byzantine emperor Constantine VII Porphyrogenitus; see the photocopied "Summaries of Communications" in volume 2 (Moscow, 1991), 1162–63. Findeizen idealizes his interpretation of the musicians, seeing in the fresco a representation of a Russian *khorovod* (round dance), which modern scholarship no longer accepts. Furthermore, Findeizen uses the term *skomorokhi* for these entertainers, equating them with Russian buffoons or itinerant entertainers (see chapter 5 below). His interpretations of musical instruments in this fresco also require some reinterpretation in light of recent research on musical instruments. See the editorial comments prefacing chapter 1 on the Khludov Psalter.

References to various Russian chronicles, including more than forty volumes in the series *Polnoe sobranie russkikh letopisei* [A complete collection of Russian chronicles]), are of great interest. Several of the chronicles have been translated into English: Cross and Sherbowitz-Wetzor, *The Russian Primary Chronicle;* George A. Perfecky, trans. and ed., *The Hypatian Codex Part Two: The Galician-Volynian Chronicle,* Harvard Series in Ukrainian Studies 16, no. 2 (Munich: Wilhelm Fink Verlag, 1973); and Serge A. Zenkovsky and Betty Jean Zenkovsky, trans., *The Nikonian Chronicle,* 5 vols. (Princeton, N.J.: Kingston, 1984–89). In the notes, all references to published chronicles have been expanded to include the volume number and date in the *PSRL* series; many of the volumes exist in multiple editions, and not all of these include the same texts. References to names of churches and monasteries in this chapter and throughout the text are based, whenever possible, on William Craft Brumfield, *A History of Russian Architecture* (Cambridge: Cambridge University Press, 1993; first paperback edition, Cambridge: Cambridge University Press, 1997).]

53. I. Shtritter [Johann Gotthelf von Stritter], *Izvestiia vizantiiskikh istorikov* [Reports of Byzantine historians] (St. Petersburg: Tip. Imp. Akademii nauk, 1770), 1:120. [This is a translation by Vasilii Svetov of Stritter's *Byzantinae historiae scriptores* (Paris: Ex. Typ. Regia, 1648–1702); Findeizen gives the date of publication as 1771. Roizman, in his *Organ,* 12–13, discusses this passage, noting that the Greek original (τα οργανα) might mean either an organist or an instrumentalist in general. Roizman also emphasizes that the word may refer to any number of Slavic peoples, not necessarily Russians specifically.]

53A. [*Editors' note:* See, for example, *PVL,* 38 (translation into modern Russian on 175); English translation in Cross and Sherbowitz-Wetzor, *The Russian Primary Chronicle,* 95.]

54. *Patriarshaia, ili Nikonovskaia, letopis'* [The Patriarchal or Nikonian chronicle] (St. Petersburg: Arkheograficheskaia komissiia, 1862), 10 (also *PSRL* 22 [pt. 2, 1914], 151). [See also *PSRL* 9 (1965), 10. The translation above is from Zenkovsky and Zenkovsky, *The Nikonian Chronicle,* 1:19, under the year 876.]

55. An incomprehensible word apparently designating some kind of artistic treasures at the Constantinopolitan palace. [The term *gripsos,* in *PSRL* 9 (1965), 10 n. 4, means *griffin* and is rendered as such in the Zenkovsky translation.]

55A. [*Editors' note:* Roizman, in *Organ,* 18, discusses Findeizen's use of the phrase "percussion organs" (*udarnye organy*), noting that it is an error Findeizen repeats from his source, Ainalov (see n. 57 below). The confusion results from the dual meaning of the Greek term for organ, which can mean either an organ specifically or simply instruments in general; see, for example, S. K. Shambinago, ed., *Skazanie o Mamaevom poboishche* [The tale of Mamai's bloody battle], Izdaniia OLDP, no. 125 ([St. Petersburg]: Tip. M. A. Aleksandrova, 1907), 28 for the latter usage. On the use of organs and other instruments at the Byzantine court around the time of Olga's visit, see Roizman, *Organ,* 14–19. The passage from Liutprand is translated from Findeizen's Russian sources; cf. the English translation in F. A. Wright, trans., *The Works of Liudprand of Cremona* (New York: Dutton, 1930), esp. 207–12. Findeizen calls Liutprand's work the *Istoriia* (History).]

56. Theophilos died in 842. Already in the first centuries of the Christian era, the art of organ building had passed from Rome to Byzantium. A pneumatic organ—and such were undoubtedly the organs at the Constantinopolitan palace—may be seen on the well-known relief from the fourth century [on the base of the obelisk] of Theodosius the Great (for a picture, see François-Joseph Fétis, *Histoire générale de la musique depuis les temps les plus anciens jusqu'à nos jours* (Paris: Firmin Didot frères, fils et cie., 1874), 4:499) [see also Roizman, *Organ,* foll. 48]. Later, in the middle of the eighth

century, a similar organ, but more richly ornamented and more complex, was given as a gift by the Byzantine emperor Constantine Kopronymos to the king of the Franks, Pepin the Short.

56A. [*Editors' note:* Findeizen's description of Olga's reception at the Byzantine court is apparently taken from secondary sources, such as Zabelin, *Istoriia russkoi zhizni,* 2:180ff., which suggest the kind of reception Olga might have had in Constantinople but which are not based on primary accounts of her trip. These descriptions of Byzantine court ceremony ultimately derive from Constantine VII Porphyrogenitus, *De ceremoniis;* in the edition by Albert Vogt, trans. and ed., *Constantin VII Porphyrogénète: Le Livre des cérémonies,* vol. 2 (Paris: Société d'édition "Les Belles Lettres," 1939), these general prescriptions for the reception of an ambassador come primarily from chapters 73 (64) and 74 (65), on pp. 94–104.]

56B. The word *kamelavki* [καμηλαύκι(ν) or καμελαύκι(ν), το] indicates a hat or a cap, or the cap of Orthodox priests or monks; the reference in the passage Findeizen cites thus indicates priests. See Ἐμμανουὴλ Κριαρᾶς, Λεξικὸ τῆς Μεσαιωνικῆς Ἑλληνικῆς Δημώδους Γραμματείας, *1100–1669,* τόμος ε' (Θεσσαλονίκη, 1977); *Lexiko tes mesaionikes Hellenikes demodous grammateias, 1100–1669* [Emmanouel Kriaras, *Lexicon of Medieval Hellenic Folk Literature, 1100–1669*], vol. 5 (Thessaloniki, 1977).

57. D. V. Ainalov, *Istoriia drevnerusskogo iskusstva* [History of old Russian art] (Petrograd: Tipo-Litografiia I. Iudelevicha, 1915), 1:117ff.

57A. [*Editors' note:* The term *polychronion* (in Russian *mnogoletie,* acclamation) is well known to students of Byzantine chant; see the examples in Egon Wellesz, *A History of Byzantine Music and Hymnography,* 2nd ed. rev. and enl. (Oxford: Clarendon, 1961), 98–122, and musical examples on 114ff. See also entries for both these terms in *NG2.*]

58. Zabelin, *Istoriia russkoi zhizni,* 2:197–98.

59. Ainalov, *Istoriia drevnerusskogo iskusstva,* 145–46, 162 [Findeizen's quotation, inexact in places, is at 145–46].

59A. [*Editors' note:* Ainalov, *Istoriia drevnerusskogo iskusstva,* 146.]

59B. [*Editors' note:* Ainalov, *Istoriia drevnerusskogo iskusstva,* 162–63.]

59C. [*Editors' note:* Findeizen does not give his source for this tale. For a translation of a *bylina* about Diuk Stepanovich, see N. Kershaw Chadwick, *Russian Heroic Poetry* (New York: Russell & Russell, 1964), 101–15; see, esp., 110–11 for an incident involving molded buttons that is reminiscent of the passage above. See also Bailey and Ivanova, *An Anthology of Russian Folk Epics,* 253–63, on the figure of Diuk Stepanovich, esp., 263 on the roaring, hissing buttons. Many thanks to Jack Haney for his help in translating this and other *bylina* texts.]

59D. [*Editors' note:* The German bishop Thietmar of Merseburg lived ca. 976–1018. His *Chronicon* covers the period between 908 and 1018. There is a recent annotated Russian edition by A. V. Nazarenko, ed., *Nemetskie latinoiazychnye istochniki IX–XI vekov. Teksty, perevod, kommentarii* [German sources in Latin from the 9th–11th centuries. Texts, translation, commentary], in *Drevneishie istochniki po istorii Vostochnoi Evropy* [The earliest sources for the history of Eastern Europe] (Moscow: Nauka, 1993), 131ff.]

60. *Historia Ecclesiastica,* lib. 2, cap. 13. [This work by Adam of Bremen (d. ca. 1076) is also known as *Gesta Hammaburgensis Ecclesiae Pontificum;* see the English translation by Francis J. Tschan, *History of the Archbishops of Hamburg-Bremen* (New York: Columbia University Press, 1959), where Kiev is mentioned on p. 67. It is not clear to which edition or translation Findeizen refers.]

61. [Thietmar of Merseburg], *Dithmarus restitutus Chronicon* (Hanovere, 1707), 1:426; Karamzin, *Istoriia,* 1 n. 522.

62. The excavations of the Church of the Tithe, carried out in Kiev by A. S. Annenkov (from 1828 on), led to the discovery, among many other objects, of two bells made of Corinthian copper, evidently brought by Vladimir from Greece (*Istoricheskii vestnik* [Historical herald], September 1910, 983). This

establishes, then, that cast bells first appeared in Russia already in the period of the conversion. [Findeizen's reference is to P. I. Korenevskii, "Arkheologicheskie raskopki v Kieve" [Archaeological excavations in Kiev], *Istoricheskii vestnik* 121 (1910): 980–84; see the discussion in Williams, *The Bells of Russia,* 33ff., esp. fig. 27, which reproduces bells discovered during the excavations of the church. Findeizen uses the term "choir" (*khor*) in this passage; Vladimir Morosan, *Choral Performance in Pre-Revolutionary Russia,* Russian Music Studies 17 (Ann Arbor: UMI Research Press, 1986), chap. 1, esp. 9–10, discusses the ways in which this term is used, and misused, in writings on Russian music.]

62A. [*Editors' note:* The passage from the Gustinskaia Chronicle is in *PSRL* 2 (1843), 256, under the year 988. The description of Anna's household is in *PVL,* 50, and the reference to the summoning of the three Greek singers by Iaroslav the Wise is from the *Stepennaia kniga* [The book of degrees], *PSRL* 21 (1908), 171, as is the reference to the Slavs learning *demestvennoe penie.* See *PSRL* 1 (1926), col. 55 (Cross and Sherbowitz-Wetzor, *The Russian Primary Chronicle,* 78) for the reference to the *domestiki* near the Church of the Tithe. On the term *domestiki,* see n. 86F below, and also see the editorial comments prefacing the notes to chapter 4.]

62B. [*Editors' note:* Findeizen refers here to V. A. Prokhorov, *Khristianskie i russkie drevnosti* [Christian and Russian antiquities] (St. Petersburg, 1871).]

62C. [*Editors' note:* Findeizen's references here (*Ocherki* 1:56) are difficult to unravel; see also nn. 63 and 73B below. The first reference of the two reads as follows: "ovy gusel'nyia glasy ispushchaiushche, druzii zhe organnyia glasy poiushche, a tem zamar'naia pisky glasiashche." It does not appear in Nifont but in the *Life* of St. Feodosii (compare the passage referring to musical instruments in Nifont, published by S. I. Kotkov, ed., *Vygoleksinskii sbornik* [The Vygoleksinskii collection] (Moscow: Nauka, 1977), 115, to the *Life* of St. Feodosii, in "Zhitie prepodobnogo ottsa nashego Fedosiia, igoumena Pecher'skogo" [The life of St. Fedosii, Father Superior of the Caves Monastery], *ChOIDR* 1 (1879): 34v). Findeizen's quotation is not exact; his source for this material is Ainalov, *Istoriia drevnerusskogo iskusstva,* 235–36, 237–38; see also Sreznevskii, *Materialy,* 1:610, 1021. The source for Findeizen's second reference has not been identified; the second passage, in full, reads: "ovy biiakhu v bubny, drugie v kozitsy i v sopeli sopiakhu, inii zhe vozlozhisha na ia skuraty, deekhu na glumlenie chelovekom i narekosha igry te rusaliia."]

63. Ainalov, *Istoriia drevnerusskogo iskusstva,* 235ff. [The passage from the *Life* of St. Feodosii is from Ainalov, *Istoriia drevnerusskogo iskusstva,* 242; Ainalov gives no source. The descriptions of hunting are in Vladimir Monomakh's "Instructions to his Children"; see the translation in Serge A. Zenkovsky, ed. and trans., *Medieval Russia's Epics, Chronicles, and Tales,* rev. ed. (New York: Dutton, 1974), 99–100, which is based on *PSRL* 1 (1926). Findeizen again uses the passage describing musical instruments played in the presence of the prince (*Ocherki* 1:56); the variant does not match those described in nn. 62C or 73B; the passage reads: "mnogie igraiushche pred kniazem, drugie zhe organnye glasy poiushche . . . i tako vsem igraiushchim i veseliashchimsia iako zhe obychai est' pred kniazem."]

64. I. Tolstoi and N. Kondakov, *Russkie drevnosti v pamiatnikakh iskusstva* [Russian antiquities in monuments of art], vol. 4, *Khristianskie drevnosti Kryma, Kavkaza i Kieva* [Christian antiquities of the Crimea, the Caucasus, and Kiev] (St. Petersburg: Tip. Ministerstva putei soobshcheniia, 1891), 151–52.

64A. [*Editors' note:* The Greek aulos is related to the oboe rather than to the flute. The question mark here is Findeizen's, for he does not agree with Kondakov's reference to *sopeli.*]

64B. [*Editors' note:* Findeizen, *Ocherki* 1:57 refers here to Al-Farabi, who is not mentioned in his previous chapters. Although Al-Farabi (d. 950) was an important philosopher and did write a treatise on music, he did not write the kind of travel accounts Findeizen describes here, and the reference is probably a typographical error.]

65. Guillaume André Villoteau, "Description historique, technique et littéraire des instruments de musique des Orientaux," in *Description de l'Egypte,* vol. 13 (Paris: Impr. Impériale, 1823). [There

are several editions of this work and it is not clear to which edition Findeizen refers. He specifies an octavo format of the work as volume 14 of the series; the listing above, as volume 13 in an octavo format, is the closest match.]

66. Fétis, *Histoire générale de la musique*, 2:122.

67. A. S. Famintsyn, *Domra i srodnye ei muzykal'nye instrumenty russkogo naroda* [The *domra* and related musical instruments of the Russian people] (St. Petersburg: Tip. E. Arngol'da, 1891). [We have retained Findeizen's spelling; in chapter 3 he refers to the *dombra,* and in later chapters to the *domra.* On these terms, see G. V. Keldysh, main ed., *Muzykal'nyi entsiklopedicheskii slovar'* [Musical encyclopedic dictionary] (Moscow: Sovetskaia entsiklopediia, 1990), 179–80.]

68. Fétis, *Histoire générale de la musique*, 4:347. Pictures of other miniature paintings of the ninth and tenth centuries with the representations of similar four-cornered harps are reproduced in A. S. Famintsyn, *Gusli—russkii narodnyi muzykal'nyi instrument* [The *gusli,* a Russian folk musical instrument] (St. Petersburg: OLDP, 1890), 78–79. For the shapes of harps in ancient Egypt, see Fétis, *Histoire générale de la musique*, 1:197, 199, 212, 255–56, 258–60, and 266–69ff.

69. Even our folk designations of priests as *pop* might have Old Slavonic roots where, as we know, the term *pop* and the female form *popeika* signified a male and a female singer [see n. 52 above, where Findeizen uses the term *popeitsa*]. According to G. Voltiggi's dictionary, this meaning was preserved even in the nineteenth century in Illyria. "This common noun can be found in Poland proper, as a designation for thirty-six populated settlements, as well as designating uninhabited places, and not including the areas of Silesia, Bohemia, and Moravia, where, although there is no memory of this (i.e., although there are now no traces), a *pop* was at one time involved in ceremonial rites" ([Khodakovskii], "Istoricheskaia sistema" [Historical system], in *Russkii istoricheskii sbornik* [Russian historical collection], ed. M. Pogodin (Moscow: Universitetskaia tip., 1838), 1: bk. 3: 64). The author of the article thus presumes that the term *pop,* meaning a singing priest, existed among the Western Slavs even before the acceptance of Christianity. [Giuseppe Voltiggi (1750–1825) published a dictionary of the "Illyrian" language (i.e., of the Balkan Slavs) with translations of words into Italian and German; see his *Ricsoslovnik (vocabolario-Woerterbuch) illiricskoga, italianskoga i nimacskoga* [A dictionary of Illyrian, Italian, and German] (Vienna: U Pritesctenici Kurtzbecka, 1802). Khodakovskii was correspondent of the *Russkii istoricheskii sbornik* and had been involved in some of the early excavations of ancient archaeological sites in Russia; see *GSE* 2:247.]

69A. [*Editors' note:* Findeizen's source here is apparently V. P. Avenarius, *Kniga bylin* [A book of *byliny*], 3rd ed. (St. Petersburg: Tip. S. Dobrodeeva, 1885), as it is for the same passage in n. 75 below. For a translation of a related version of the tale, see Bailey and Ivanova, *An Anthology of Russian Folk Epics*, 204–13, esp. 212; and Chadwick, *Russian Heroic Poetry*, 116–22, esp. 121.]

69B. [*Editors' note:* In this section, names and identifications of Arab and Western scholars already well known are taken for granted without further elaboration; see references in chapters 1 and 2. Some of the names of the various musical instruments appear in *NG2,* and there is a useful reference tool by Manfred Aumayr, *Historische Untersuchungen an Bezeichnungen von Musikinstrumenten in der russischen Sprache,* Dissertationen der Universität Wien 169 (Wien: VWGÖ, 1985); see also the discussions of instruments in Roizman, *Organ; IRM* 1; *ME;* and Sreznevskii, *Materialy.* Among the various *byliny* heroes Findeizen mentions, Boian is of interest as he may be viewed as a sort of counterpart to Orpheus.]

69C. [*Editors' note: IRM* 1:73 identifies Findeizen's source as the Voskresenskaia Chronicle; see *PSRL* 7 (1856), 127, under the year 1220. The passage reads, in full: "povele voem obolochites'... poide polk po poltse b'iushche v bubny i v truby" (*Ocherki* 1:61).]

69D. [*Editors' note:* The passage from the Hypatian Chronicle of 1151 is in *PSRL* 2 (1962), col. 436; the passage from the Suzdal Chronicle of 1216 is in *PSRL* 1 (1926), 499; it reads, in full: "molviakhut bo i pro Iaroslava: stiagov u nego 17, a trub i bubnov 40" (*Ocherki* 1:61).]

69E. [*Editors' note:* This passage from the Nikonian Chronicle from 1219 is in *PSRL* 10 (1965), 84; it reads, in full: "Kniaz' zhe Sviatoslav Vsevolodovich' povele svoim vooruzhatisia i stiagi navolochiti i izriadi polki v nasadekh i udarisha v bubny i v truby i v surny" (*Ocherki* 1:61–62).]

69F. [*Editors' note:* Findeizen gives no source; there are slight variants in T. Dianova et al., ed. and trans., *Skazanie o Mamaevom poboishche* [The tale of Mamai's bloody battle] (Moscow: Kniga, 1980), 1:85 (transcription), and 125 (translation into modern Russian, on which the present translation is based.]

69G. [*Editors' note:* Translation of the two following passages are from Haney and Dahl, *The Discourse on Igor's Campaign,* 28.]

70. The text of the Manasses Chronicle was published by A. Chertkov, *Opisanie voiny velikogo kniazia Sviatoslava Igorevicha protiv bolgar i grekov v 967–97 godakh* [A description of the war between the Great Prince Sviatoslav Igorevich and the Bulgars and Greeks in 967–97], in *Russkii istoricheskii sbornik,* vol. 6, bk. 3–4; the miniature painting described here is in the appendix, and it was reprinted by Pogodin in the third volume of *Drevniaia russkaia istoriia do mongol'skogo iga* [History of early Russia to the Mongol yoke] (Moscow: Sinodal'naia tip., 1871) [reprint, Slavistic Printings and Reprintings 256, no. 3 (The Hague: Mouton, 1971)]. The best reproduction of the miniature (and in color) is in the OLDP edition by V. V. Stasov, ed., *Miniatiury nekotorykh rukopisei vizantiiskikh, bolgarskikh, russkikh, dzhagataiskikh i persidskikh* [Miniatures in some Byzantine, Bulgarian, Russian, Chagatai, and Persian manuscripts] ([St. Petersburg]: Tip. I. N. Skorokhodova, 1902), plate 3. [The Manasses Chronicle is Cod. Vatic. Slav. II; a facsimile is available in Ivan Duichev, ed., *Letopistsa na Konstantin Manasi. Fototipno izdanie na Vatikanskiia prepis na srednebʺlgarskiia prevod* [The Chronicle of Konstantin Manasses. A photo-facsimile edition of the Vatican manuscript in old Bulgarian] (Sofia: Izd-va na Bʺlgarskata Akademiia na naukite, 1963.]

70A. [*Editors' note:* Findeizen, *Ocherki* 1:62 adds *bubny* (tambourine) in parenthesis after the term *kimvaly* (cymbals).]

71. [Fig. 18 is from] a miniature in a twelfth-century manuscript in the Strasbourg University library, *Hortus deliciarum,* reproduced in Edward Buhle, *Die Blasininstrumente,* vol. 1 of *Die musikalischen Instrumente in den Miniaturen des frühen Mittelalters: Ein Beitrag zur Geschichte der Musikinstrumente* (Leipzig: Breitkopf & Härtel, 1903), plate 2.

72. Archimandrite Amfilokhii, "O Slavianskoi Psaltiri XIII–XIV veka biblioteki A. I. Khludova" [On the Slavic psalter of the thirteenth-fourteenth centuries in A. I. Khludov's library], *Drevnosti. Trudy moskovskogo arkheologicheskogo obshchestva* 3 (1873): pt. 1: 1–28.

73. In his description of the miniatures (numbering eighty-four in the manuscripts), S. Shambinago states that all copies of this document (listed above) "are derived from a single artistic original, much older than the existing translations." The appearance of the document itself can be dated in the fifteenth century. [Sergei Konstantinovich Shambinago (1872–1948) was a well-known historian of literature; see Shambinago, *Skazanie o Mamaevom poboishche,* 63. There is a listing of manuscripts transmitting the Mamai texts in Roman Jakobson and Dean S. Worth, ed. and trans., *Sofonija's Tale of the Russian-Tatar Battle on the Kulikovo Field,* Slavistic Printings and Reprintings 51 (The Hague: Mouton, 1963), 8–10; on p. 10, the authors identify Uvarov 492 as GIM 1831. For an illustration of the fresco in the Cathedral of St. Dmitrii, which Findeizen mentions below, see V. N. Lazarev, *Drevnerusskie mozaiki i freski XI–XV vv.* [Old Russian mosaics and frescoes, 11th–15th centuries] (Moscow: Iskusstvo, 1973), illustration no. 166.]

73A. [*Editors' note:* Translation of this phrase based on Roizman, *Organ,* 10 n. Findeizen's source is probably Sreznevskii, *Materialy,* 1:610, which reads "stroim" rather than "stroil." The Putiatina Mineia is in RNB, Sof. 202 (*SKSR* no. 21); see the detailed study, with a facsimile of the service for 4 May, by L. I. Shchegoleva, *Putiatina mineia (XI vek): 1–10 maia* [The Putiatina Mineia (11th century): 1–10 May] (Moscow: Territoriia, 2001).]

73B. [*Editors' note:* The passage reads in full as follows, in *Ocherki* 1:68: "ovy gousl'nyia glasy ispoushchaiushche, drougyia zhe or"gan'nyia glasy poiushche, i inem zamar'nyia pisky glasiashchem, i tako v'sem igraiushchem i veseliashchem"sia, iakozhe obychai est' pr'd kniaz'm'." The Poteshnaia palata, or Hall of Entertainment, is where the tsar's private entertainments were held in the seventeenth century. The reference to wine drinking is in *PVL*, 62; and see Cross and Sherbowitz-Wetzor, *The Russian Primary Chronicle*, 130. This is the fourth time Findeizen refers to the passage on instrumental music at the court of Sviatoslav Iaroslavich; see nn. 62C and 63 above. Roizman makes several corrections to this appearance of the passage in Findeizen's text (*Organ*, 20). The reference in this paragraph is not from the Russian Primary Chronicle but from the *Life* of St. Feodosii ("Zhitie prepodobnogo ottsa nashego Fedosiia," 34v). The passage also appears, in similar form, in the *Paterik Kievskogo Pecherskogo monastyria* [Paterik (a manuscript collection describing the lives of saints and monastic life) from the Kievan Caves Monastery] (St. Petersburg: [Izd. Imperatorskoi arkheograficheskoi komissii], 1911), 50; in fact, both references in this paragraph—to Sviatopolk drinking wine and to the musical performances—appear in slightly varied form in both sources. (An English translation of the *Paterik* is in Muriel Heppell, trans., *The* Paterik *of the Kievan Caves Monastery,* Harvard Library of Early Ukrainian Literature, English Translations 1 [Cambridge, Mass.: Harvard University Press, 1989], 77, although the instruments are not clearly identified in this translation.) Roizman also notes that the phrase "zamar'nyia pisky" may refer to an instrument (from the Arabic *zamir,* an aulos-like instrument) rather than to foreign (*zamorskii*) practice; Roizman cites A. N. Veselovskii, "Razyskaniia v oblasti russkogo dukhovnogo stikha" [Investigations in the realm of the Russian spiritual verse], *Zapiski Imperatorskoi Akademii nauk* 45 (1883), prilozhenie 1:147–48. Roizman discusses Sviatoslav Iaroslavich on pp. 20–21, placing the instruments in the context of Byzantine court practice.]

73C. [*Editors' note: PVL,* 74; cf. the translation in Cross and Sherbowitz-Wetzor, *The Russian Primary Chronicle,* 147.]

73D. [*Editors' note: PVL,* 83 (modern Russian translation on p. 220); Cross and Sherbowitz-Wetzor, *The Russian Primary Chronicle,* 161, on which the present translation is based. The reference to the eldest of the demons appears several lines after the listing of instruments. The passage is also quoted in Sreznevskii, *Materialy,* 1:610.]

73E. [*Editors' note:* On the phrase "v gusli gudut'" in Kirill of Turov, see the reference in A. S. Famintsyn, *Skomorokhi na Rusi* [The *skomorokhi* in Rus'] (St. Petersburg: Tip. E. Arngol'da, 1889), 41 and n. 2; and in Sreznevskii, *Materialy,* 1:610; in both sources, the quotation is listed as taken from Kirill Turovskii 95. The phrase does not appear in the English-language translation of Kirill's writings in Simon Franklin, *Sermons and Rhetoric of Kievan Rus',* Harvard Library of Early Ukrainian Literature, English Translations 5 ([Cambridge, Mass.]: Harvard University Press, 1991). These authors may have been referring to one of the many texts which, until recent times, had been attributed to Kirill in various nineteenth-century editions. See the brief survey in *PLDR XII vek,* 660–63, with reference to the major study on Kirill, by I. P. Eremin, "Literaturnoe nasledie Kirilla Turovskogo" [The literary legacy of Kirill of Turov], *TODRL* 11 (1955): 342–67; 12 (1956): 340–61; and 13 (1957): 409–26. Findeizen's reference to Andrei Iur'evich's *Life* is apparently from Sreznevskii, *Materialy,* 1:610.]

73F. [*Editors' note:* Cosmas of Alexandria was a sixth-century traveler and monk. His *Topographia Christiana,* written in the mid-sixth century, was known in a Russian translation from the sixteenth century, *Kniga naritsaema Koz'ma Indikoplov;* see the most recent edition by V. S. Golyshenko and V. F. Dubrovina (Moscow: Indrik, 1997) for an extensive bibliography. This is an edition of GIM, Uvar. 566, which does not include the phrase "guslenoe khudozhestvo," although it does mention the *gusli* and includes a constellation of musical instruments in the illustration of King David composing the Psalter (illustration 24, and see the text on fol. 62); the phrase does appear in Sreznevskii, *Materialy,* 1:610. Illustrations depicting the same scene from two other variants of Cosmas's treatise are in Roizman, *Organ,* foll. 48, and in the edition of the work in OLDP 86; the instruments in these scenes include *gusli,* organs, a wide variety of horns, and percussion instruments. Findeizen discusses Cosmas further in chapter 4.]

73G. [*Editors' note:* Findeizen's source here is apparently Sreznevskii, *Materialy,* 1:610.]

74. Avenarius, *Kniga bylin,* 4–5. [For a translation of a Dobrynia tale, see Chadwick, *Russian Heroic Poetry,* 80–90.]

75. Avenarius, *Kniga bylin,* 62.

75A. [*Editors' note:* On the Great Eagle, a bowl of wine or brandy at Petrine-era assemblies, see Robert Massie, *Peter the Great: His Life and World* (New York: Ballantine, 1980), 809.]

76. P. A. Bezsonov, ed., *Pesni, sobrannye P. V. Kireevskim* [Songs collected by P. V. Kireevskii] (Moscow: Obshchestvo liubitelei rossiiskoi slovesnosti, 1861), fasc. 2:35, written down in Olonetsk province. [A second, expanded edition of the work was published in 1868–79.]

76A. [*Editors' note:* Translation from Haney and Dahl, *The Discourse on Igor's Campaign,* 27.]

76B. [*Editors' note:* Findeizen refers here to the *Trudy I-go arkheologicheskogo s'ezda v Moskve, 1869 g.* (1871), XCVII. The church in question is the twelfth-century Church of the Intercession of the Virgin on the Nerl River, near Vladimir; extensive photos are in G. K. Vagner, *Skul'ptura drevnei Rusi. XII vek. Vladimir. Bogoliubovo.* [The sculpture of ancient Rus'. Twelfth century. Vladimir and Bogoliubovo] (Moscow: Iskusstvo, 1969), where the figure of King David is discussed at 130–31, with photos at 137, 161, and 163; see also the discussion in Brumfield, *A History of Russian Architecture,* 47–51.]

76C. [Editors' note: See the color reproduction of this image in O. Popova, *Les miniatures russes du XIe au XVe siècle* (Leningrad: Aurora, 1975), 55.]

77. Fétis, *Histoire générale de la musique,* 4:505. The representation of David with the *crwth* is in ibid., 4:345. [The *organistrum* players at the abbey church of St. Georges at Saint Martin-de-Boscherville are identified in *NG2.*]

77A. [*Editors' note:* F. E. Korsh, ed., *Slovo o polku Igoreve* [The lay of the host of Igor] (St. Petersburg: Akademiia nauk, 1909). Feodor Evgenievich Korsh (1843–1915) was a distinguished investigator of *byliny* who, from 1904, together with E. Lineva, published transcriptions of Russian folk songs as recorded by Lineva. Evgeniia Lineva was an extremely significant scholar in this area; see the article in *NG2* by Barbara Krader (s.v. "Linyova") and Alfred Swan, *Russian Music and Its Sources in Chant and Folk Song* (London: J. Baker, 1973). The editorial notes to chapter 3 above discuss the meanings of the term *slovo.*]

78. *Vestnik Evropy* [European herald], October (1878): 786, 796. The singer Or is mentioned in the Hypatian Chronicle in the year 1201; see below.

79. N. Bitsyn, "Slovo o polku Igoreve" [The lay of the host of Igor], *Russkii vestnik* [Russian herald] 109 (February 1874): 764.

80. *Zadonshchina velikogo kniazia gospodina Dmitriia Ivanovicha i brata ego Volodimira Andreevicha* [*Zadonshchina* of the Great Prince Lord Dmitrii Ivanovich and his brother, Vladimir Andreevich] (St. Petersburg, 1858). [The word *zadonshchina* carries the meaning of "the epic events beyond the River Don."] In his discussion, Sreznevskii states (p. 4) that the *Zadonshchina* "is not a historical story or a legend, but a poem, similar to the Great Russian *bylina* or a Little Russian *duma,* such as may sometimes be heard in the wailing of blind beggars." [Findeizen's reference to Sreznevskii is apparently to a separate offprint of the article, appearing in the *Izvestiia Imperatorskoi Akademii nauk* [Proceedings of the Imperial Academy of Sciences] 6 (1858): cols. 337–62; 7 (1858): cols. 96–100; the quotation above is in 6: col. 338.]

80A. [*Editors' note:* This and the following passages are quoted from Haney and Dahl, *The Discourse on Igor's Campaign,* 28, 44; Findeizen quotes these passages from Sreznevskii (see n. 81 below).]

81. Sreznevskii, *Zadonshchina,* 12–13.

81A. [*Editors' note:* The description of Roman Galitskii is in *PSRL* 2 (1962), col. 716; and *PLDR XIII vek,* 236–37. Findeizen refers to Buslaev, *Istoricheskaia khristomatiia,* col. 578.]

81B. [*Editors' note:* Translation from Haney and Dahl, *The Discourse on Igor's Campaign,* 26.]

82. Sreznevskii, *Zadonshchina,* 9 n., cites a number of poetic fragments from our chronicles, unquestionably influenced by popular poems of the time, especially the *Lay of the Host of Igor.* [In the article cited in n. 80 above, the reference is to 6: col. 342 n., and the three references Findeizen gives here also appear in Sreznevskii, *Materialy,* 1:850–51 from the Laurentian Chronicle; 3:390 from the Hypatian Chronicle; and 2:19 again from the Hypatian Chronicle, in a slightly expanded translation in Perfecky, *The Galician-Volynian Chronicle,* 45. The passage reads as follows (square brackets are Perfecky's): "However, when they saw that they could not restrain the [whole] city, they came out like cowards who feared [the consequences] of the city's surrender, with tears in their eyes and downcast faces, and licking their dry lips, since they no longer had the power to rule."]

82A. [*Editors' note:* The translation of the first passage is based partially on Jakobson and Worth, *Sofonija's Tale,* l. 29, which is close to, but not identical with, Findeizen's source. All subsequent references to Jakobson and Worth are to line number, which points the reader to the corresponding line in the original text, the critical notes, and the translation. We have modified the layout in Jakobson and Worth, however, which is a prose translation, to conform to the poetic style cited here in Findeizen. Findeizen does not give a source for the second passage, which is apparently from a tale of Dobrynia Nikitich.]

82B. [*Editors' note:* Translation based partially on Jakobson and Worth, *Sofonija's Tale,* l. 17, which is close to, but not identical with, Findeizen's source.]

82C. [*Editors' note:* The translation is from Haney and Dahl, *The Discourse on Igor's Campaign,* 27–28; for a discussion of the Troian Trail, see 63. Findeizen, *Ocherki* 1:78, indicates the opening phrase "O Boian," the concluding phrase "grandson of Igor," and the phrase roughly corresponding to "weaving glories together" as the "superfluous poetic feet."]

83. Korsh, *Slovo o polku Igoreve.* [See n. 82C above, on the italicized words.]

83A. [*Editors' note:* Kirsha Danilov was an early collector of Russian folk songs. Although his identity is in doubt, a collection attributed to him circulated in manuscript in the eighteenth century and was first published early in the nineteenth century; see *IRM* 2:252–55. Findeizen discusses Kirsha Danilov further in chapter 4, where additional bibliographical sources are listed.]

83B. [*Editors' note:* See the similar passage in Jakobson and Worth, *Sofonija's Tale,* ll. 13–14.]

84. Sreznevskii, *Zadonshchina,* 18 [in the article in n. 80 above, the reference is to 6: col. 345]. The oldest, although incomplete, copy of that work (from the 1470s) is in a fifteenth-century manuscript in the collection from the St. Cyril-Belozersk Monastery, RNB, Kir. 9/1086, fols. 122–29; its text was published by P. K. Simoni [1859–1939] in the third fascicle of his valuable *Pamiatniki starinnogo russkogo iazyka i slovesnosti, XV–XVIII st.* [Sources of old Russian language and literature, 15th–18th centuries] (St. Petersburg: Akademiia nauk, 1922). [On the passage from the *Zadonshchina,* cf. Jakobson and Worth, *Sofonija's Tale,* l. 15.]

84A. [*Editors' note:* See Haney and Dahl, *The Discourse on Igor's Campaign,* 28.]

85. *PSRL* 2 [1962], col. 716. [See also *PLDR XIII vek,* 236–37; and Perfecky, *The Galician-Volynian Chronicle,* 17.]

86. *PSRL* 2 [1962], col. 794. [See this passage also in *PLDR XIII vek,* 302–303; and Perfecky, *The Galician-Volynian Chronicle,* 52. Findeizen's clarifications—omitted in this translation—are somewhat confusing because he leaves out several lines of text. Russell Zguta, *Russian Minstrels: A History of the Skomorokhi* ([Philadelphia]: University of Pennsylvania Press, 1978), 83–84, cites other references to musicians in the Hypatian Chronicle.]

86A. [*Editors' note:* Jakobson and Worth, *Sofonija's Tale,* l. 14.]

86B. [*Editors' note:* Findeizen cites the description of Roman above; see n. 81A.]

86C. [*Editors' note:* The Daniil reference is in *PSRL* 2 (1843), 186–87; on the song in praise of Aleksandr Nevskii, see *PSRL* 7 (1856), 151, as Findeizen notes in the Russian text.]

86D. [*Editors' note:* This source is now in RGB, Vol. 519; see the description in Iosif, *Opis' rukopisei perenesennykh iz biblioteki Iosifova Monastyria v biblioteku Moskovskoi dukhovnoi akademii* [A listing of manuscripts transferred from the library of the Joseph [of Volokolamsk] Monastery to the library of the Moscow Divinity School] (Moscow: Universitetskaia tip., 1882), 166–69; and in Pavel Stroev, *Opisanie rukopisei monastyrei Volokolamskogo, Novyi-Ierusalim . . .* [A description of manuscripts of the Volokolamsk [and] New Jerusalem . . . monasteries] (St. Petersburg: Tip. Stasiulevicha, [1891]), 132–33; on the current numbering, see A. A. Zimin, "Iz istorii sobraniia rukopisnykh knig Iosifo-Volokolamskogo monastyria" [From the history of the collection of manuscript books of the Joseph of Volokolamsk Monastery], *Zapiski otdela rukopisei* [Notes of the Manuscript Division] 38 (1977): 15–29.]

86E. [*Editors' note:* While for all the preceding segments of Findeizen's text the attainments of Western scholarship on Russian music are woefully inadequate, this particular topic—the early stages of Russian church music—represents one area in which there has been a fair amount of progress in the West, especially in the last several decades. At the time Findeizen was writing on neumatic notation, he was unaware of the progress in the study of Byzantine chant made by Western scholars, particularly H. J. W. Tillyard and Egon Wellesz, which changed the discipline considerably and superseded all earlier thinking on the subject. Only after Findeizen's death did some Russian scholars become aware of these studies, but by that time research dealing with church music inside the Soviet Union was discouraged.

Findeizen gave a thorough description of the ekphonetic notation as he understood it. His presentation may be compared to the article in *NG2*. Among his references, Findeizen cites the well-known Abbé J. B. Thibaut and also K. I. Papadopulo-Keramevs [Papadopoulos-Kerameus] (1856–1912), whose work deserves attention and even reexamination, since he may have been the first to carry out a comparative study of the earliest Byzantine and Slavic musical manuscripts. Findeizen's overview of the historical developments of Russian chant is based on studies by Russian pioneers in this area: Dmitrii Vasil'evich Razumovskii, Stepan Vasil'evich Smolenskii, Vasilii Mikhailovich Metallov, and Antonin Viktorovich Preobrazhenskii (see biographies for some of these figures in *NG2*). For a modern evaluation of their contributions to scholarship, see Miloš Velimirović, *Byzantine Elements in Early Slavic Chant*, Monumenta Musicae Byzantinae, series Subsidia, vol. 4 (Copenhagen: Munksgaard, 1960), esp. chap. 2; and his "Der Stand der Forschung über kirchenslavische Musik," *Zeitschrift für slavische Philologie* 31 (1963): 145ff.; "The Present Status of Research in Slavic Chant," *Acta Musicologica* 44 (1972): 235–65; and the entry "Russian and Slavonic Church Music" in *NG2*, with an extensive bibliography. Another comprehensive bibliographic resource is V. V. Protopopov, *Russkoe tserkovnoe penie: Opyt bibliograficheskogo ukazatelia ot serediny XVI veka po 1917 god* [Russian church singing: An essay in creating a bibliographic index from the mid-16th century to 1917] (Moscow: Muzyka, 2000). There is a two-volume report of papers produced for a conference dedicated to Razumovskii in M. Lozovaia, main ed., *Gimnologiia: Materialy Mezhdunarodnoi nauchnoi konferentsii "Pamiati protoiereia Dimitriia Razumovskogo" (k 130-letiiu Moskovskoi konservatorii) 3–8 sentiabria 1996 / Hymnology: Papers of [the] Musicological Congress "Rev. Dimitry Razumovsky's ad memoriam" (on the occasion of the 130th Anniversary of the Moscow Conservatory) September 3–8, 1996* (Moscow: Kompozitor, 2000), which includes several articles on early chant scholars.

In recent years there have been additional studies on this subject, although a fully satisfactory and systematic history of Russian church music from the acceptance of Christianity through the subsequent centuries has not yet been written; most of the work done so far consists of paleographical studies and investigations of the relationship between the Byzantine neumatic notation and the notation transmitted in Russian medieval manuscripts. The English translation of Johann von Gardner's magisterial study of Russian chant, by Vladimir Morosan (as *Russian Church Singing*, vol. 1, *Orthodox Worship and Hymnography*, and vol. 2, *History from the Origins to the Mid-Seventeenth Century* [Crestwood, N.Y.: St. Vladimir's Seminary Press, 1980 and 2000] with additional volumes forthcoming) will probably also be the first musicological discussion in English of the subject of *istinnorechie* and *razdel'norechie* and the concept of *khomoniia* (linguistic topics not dealt with sufficiently in existing English-language studies—for example, by Alfred Swan). Findeizen discusses these issues as well; the terms *istinnorechie* and *razdel'norechie* refer to the linguistic practice of substituting fully voiced vowels in place of semi-vowels, which did have length and which were always notated in older manuscripts. Over time, especially in the sixteenth century, these semi-vowels changed into the fully voiced vowels *o* and *e*. Because of the repeated appearance of the ending *-khomo* in these texts, the term *khomoniia* was also used to describe this linguistic shift.

Findeizen's list of preserved musical manuscripts from the early centuries of Christianity in Russia in n. 109 (and n. 152 in chapter 4) is amazingly complete for its time, based, as it is, primarily on Metallov's studies, which listed only twenty-five manuscripts. In 1972 Velimirović expanded this list from thirty-one to around fifty musical manuscripts (see his "Present Status of Research"), and at present (2004) it would seem that the list can be further expanded to include about eighty musical manuscripts written before AD 1500.

Findeizen's discussion of *kondakarian* notation as well as that of *znamennaia* notation (both mentioned in the article "Neumatic notations" in *NG2*, which uses a slightly different transcription system than that used in the present volume) is a valuable historical document, yet it essentially demonstrates the author's bafflement about their possible meaning and the likelihood of their transcription, which he wisely did not tackle. Some of the problems posed by the Russian documents have become critical components of the study of Byzantine neumatic notation and, as such, may be found in recent studies by O. Strunk, K. Levy, C. Floros, and some younger scholars (see bibliography in *NG2*). Findeizen's reference to the two "alphabets" of neumatic notation known at that time is of great interest, and he lists the fifty-one neumes he found in one of these documents, from the fifteenth century. Since then, the late Maksim Viktorovich Brazhnikov (1906–1973) was able to uncover and examine some forty specimens of these lists in manuscripts of the fifteenth and sixteenth centuries, and his successors in Russia have increased even further the number of rediscovered sources. These alphabets (or simply "lists of neumes," some of which offer attempts at interpreting how to sing them) are the focus of several recent studies, all currently in progress, so that new results may soon be forthcoming in rapid succession.

We should mention that, in addition to a few Western scholars (Nicolas Schidlovsky, Nina Konstantinova Ulff-Moeller, and Gregory Myers, the latter devoting himself to a large-scale examination of *kondakarian* notation in a monograph, *The Hierarchical Chant Tradition of Kievan Rus': A Historical, Liturgical, and Musical Exegesis of Kondakarnoie Pienie*) who are investigating the Byzantine-Russian relationship of the early centuries, several younger Russian scholars are also currently contributing to this research, particularly Irina Lozovaia and Irina Shkol'nik in Moscow and Zivar Guseinova and S. V. Frolov in St. Petersburg. One of Frolov's articles deserves particular attention: "K probleme zvukovysotnosti bespometnoi znamennoi notatsii" [On the problem of pitch in "un-reformed" neumatic notation], in *Problemy istorii i teorii drevnerusskoi muzyki* [Problems in the history and theory of early Russian music], ed. A. S. Belonenko and M. V. Brazhnikov (Leningrad: Muzyka, 1979): 124–47. Evgenii Vladimirovich Gertsman in St. Petersburg has devoted himself to the study of ancient Greek and Byzantine music theory, and his book *Vizantiiskoe muzykoznanie* [Byzantine musicology] (Leningrad: Muzyka, 1988) was the first on this subject to be published in the former Soviet Union.

Finally, modern research since Findeizen's days has made a few serious attempts at least at a partial transcription of some medieval Russian chant melodies. This was done by comparing the notation of the Russian melodies to those in the Byzantine tradition and finding a few points of contact, facilitating an insight into a few melodic segments of the earliest stages of Russian liturgical singing. Iurii Keldysh, who was the dean of Russian scholars and the author of the first volume of the *IRM* series, presented in 1983 a fair overview of research into the origins of Russian chant and its links with Byzantine tradition (*IRM* 1:79–118). This may have been the first presentation in Russian of a well-informed statement about Western scholars' attainments in this field, using their own examples to show their methodology and results.]

86F. [*Editors' note:* Findeizen refers here to the *Stepennaia kniga,* published in *PSRL* 21 (1908), 171, discussed at greater length below. The passage on Metropolitan Mikhail is in *PSRL* 9 (1965), 64; a translation of this passage can also be found in Zenkovsky and Zenkovsky, *The Nikonian Chronicle,* 1:110–11 (for the year 991). Morosan, *Choral Performance,* 10, discusses the term *domestik* and the possible duties of these singers in medieval Russian church practice. The *kliros* (or *krylos;* cleros) is "the place set apart at each side [of the altar] for the readers and singers" (D. P. Sokolov, *A Manual of the Orthodox Church's Divine Services,* trans. from Russian [1899; reprint, Jordanville, N.Y.: Holy Trinity Russian Orthodox Monastery, 1968], 18), and it can also refer to the singing ensembles themselves; see also Morosan, *Choral Performance,* 9–10.]

86G. [*Editors' note:* On the singer Stefan, see the *Paterik Kievskogo Pecherskogo monastyria,* 9ff.; and the translation in Heppell, *The Paterik of the Kievan Caves Monastery,* 13, where other chronicle references are listed in n. 41; on Kirik, see I. A. Gardner, *Bogosluzhebnoe penie russkoi pravoslavnoi tserkvi* [Liturgical singing of the Russian Orthodox Church] (Jordanville, N.Y.: Holy Trinity Russian Orthodox Monastery, 1978), 1:272, where he refers to the commentary section of V. P. Adrianova-Peretts, ed., *Povest' vremennykh let* [The tale of bygone years] (Moscow: Akademiia nauk SSSR, 1950), 2:162; and on Luke, see the reference in *PSRL* 1 (1926), col. 370, from the year 1175.]

86H. [*Editors' note:* The term *aprakos* gospel refers to the way in which the texts are arranged; it contains excerpts of gospel texts ordered for Sunday readings. Another ordering, as an *Evangelie tetr (tetroevangelium),* is laid out according to the order of the Evangelists in the Bible rather than the order of readings as they are used in the liturgical year. See Gardner, *Orthodox Worship and Hymnography,* 128 n. 59.]

87. The Ostromir Gospel is in RNB, F.п.I.5 [see *SKSR* no. 3, where it is dated 1056–57]; the Kupriianov leaflets are in RNB, F.п.I.58 [see *SKSR* no. 12].

88. The notation of the cantillation of the gospel readings was so designated by the Greek scholar I. D. Tzetzis in his Η Επινόησις της Παρασημαντικής των κατά τον Μεσαίωνα Λειτουργικών και Υμνολογικών Χειρογράφων των Ανατολικών Εκκλησιών [The invention of Byzantine musical notation in the medieval liturgical and hymnological manuscripts of the Eastern churches] (Athens: n.p., 1886), and his term [ekphonetic notation] was accepted by the learned Abbé J. B. Thibaut in his two works, *Monuments de la notation ekphonétique et neumatique de l'église Latine* (St. Petersburg: Impr. Kügelgen, Glitsch & Cie, 1912 [reprint, Hildesheim: Georg Olms, 1984]) and *Monuments de la notation ekphonétique et hagiopolite de l'église Grecque* (St. Petersburg: Impr. Kügelgen, Glitsch & Cie, 1913 [reprint, Hildesheim: Georg Olms, 1976]). Tzetzes, in writing about various aspects of chanting, mentions the existence of a special way of "reading aloud the books of the Old and New Testament, used by priests and deacons" that he called ekphonetic (*veleglasnyi*). He adds that this practice was "also used for reciting psalms and prayers in some monasteries even to this day." (This reference is from K. I. Papadopulo-Keramevs, "Proiskhozhdenie notnogo muzykal'nogo pis'ma u severnykh i iuzhnykh slavian po pamiatnikam drevnosti, preimushchestvenno vizantiiskim" [The origin of musical notation among the northern and southern Slavs according to documents from antiquity, primarily Byzantine], *Vestnik arkheologii i istorii* [Archaeological and historical journal] 17 [1906], otdel 1:134).

89. Bychkov's work appears in *Izvestiia arkheologicheskogo obshchestva* [Proceedings of the Archaeological Society] 5 (1865), fasc. 1. Nevertheless, the late S. V. Smolenskii, in his review of V. M. Metallov, *Bogosluzhebnoe penie russkoi tserkvi* [Liturgical singing in the Russian Church], *Otchet Akademii nauk* [Report of the Academy of Sciences] (1909), stated, among other points: "recently, thanks to information obtained from academician A. I. Sobolevskii, I discovered ekphonetic signs on pages of the Ostromir Gospel (for example, fol. 211v)." As we can see, there was no need to discover the

signs, for they were already known by the scholars I mentioned, and yet they long remained uninvestigated.

89A. [*Editors' note:* N. M. Karinskii, *Khrestomatiia po drevne-tserkovno-slavianskomu i russkomu iazykam* [A reader in the Old Church Slavonic and Russian languages] (n.p.: Savinov, 1883 and 1889). Available catalogs list only a later edition, from 1904, published by Akademiia nauk, and a second edition issued in St. Petersburg by Ia. Bashmakov in 1911.]

90. [*Editors' note:* Findeizen refers in the text to I. I. Sreznevskii, *Drevnie slavianskie pamiatniki iusovogo pis'ma* [Old Slavic monuments of uncial writing] (St. Petersburg: Akademiia nauk, 1868; reprint, Nendeln, Liechtenstein: Kraus Reprint, 1966).] A most interesting study was published by Papadopulo-Keramevs, "Proiskhozhdenie notnogo muzykal'nogo pis'ma," 134–71, correctly comparing them to the ekphonetic signs in Greek gospel manuscripts in the St. Petersburg Divinity School dated 985 and 1033. It is truly remarkable that the ekphonetic signs in the Ostromir Gospel were completely ignored by several serious scholars who studied that document, including A. Kh. Vostokov (*Filologicheskie nabliudeniia* [Philological observations] (St. Petersburg: Tip. Imp. Akademii nauk, 1865); M. M. Kozlovskii in his study of the language in the Ostromir Gospel, *Issledovaniia po russkomu iazyku* [Findeizen apparently refers here to Kozlovskii's *Issledovanie o iazyke Ostromirova evangeliia* (A study of the language of the Ostromir Gospel)] (St. Petersburg: Akademiia nauk, 1885), vol. 1; N. M. Karinskii, "Ostromirovo evangelie kak pamiatnik drevnerusskogo iazyka" [The Ostromir Gospel as a document of the Old Russian language], *Zhurnal Ministerstva narodnogo prosveshcheniia* [Journal of the Ministry of Public Enlightenment] 5 (1903): 94–110; and even Sreznevskii, *Drevnie slavianskie pamiatniki iusovogo pis'ma*.

91. "Otryvki evangel'skikh chtenii XI v., imenuemye Kupriianovskimi (Novgorodskimi)" [Fragments of the gospel readings from the 11th century, called Kupriianov (Novgorodian)], *Izvestiia II-go otd. Russk. Akademii nauk* [Proceedings of the second section of the Russian Academy of Sciences] 28 (1923): 273–320. This study is especially valuable for us as it contains reproductions of all four pages of the Kupriianov leaflets in their actual size.

92. See the reproduction appended to volume 1 of A. Nikol'skii, *Opisanie rukopisei khraniashchikhsia v arkhive Sviateishego pravitel'stvuiushchego sinoda* [Description of manuscripts in the archive of the Holy Ruling Synod] (St. Petersburg: Sinodal'naia tip., 1904). In addition to that particular manuscript (no. 24), Smolenskii, in his review of Metallov's work, mentioned that gospel manuscripts nos. 9 and 55 in the same collection [now in GIM] also contain ekphonetic signs not mentioned in Nikol'skii, *Opisanie rukopisei*.

93. Names of signs in the sixteenth-century Slavonic gospel [middle column of Table 3.1] are only those of signs represented on folio 35. Their total number is undoubtedly much larger.

93A. [*Editors' note:* This manuscript is apparently GIM, Usp. 1163. Many thanks to Sysse Engberg and Nicolas Schidlovsky for their help in identifying this source, which dates from the eleventh century, with a later section dating from the fourteenth century.]

94. Seventeenth-century theorist Aleksandr Mezenets calls the *paraklit* the first sign: "The first sign—*paraklit*—in all eight modes at the beginning of whatever verse . . . is invariably sung on a single step." The name *paraklit* is from the notated *kanons* [a poetic form] of the daily service of the *oktoechos*, written in a separate book called the Paraklitike. A notated parchment Paraklitike of the twelfth century is found in the library of the former Moscow Synodal Typography no. 1204/69. [This is RGADA, f. 381, no. 80; see *SKSR* no. 160, which dates it sometime between the end of the eleventh and the beginning of the twelfth centuries.] (See D. V. Razumovskii, "O notnykh bezlineinykh rukopisiakh" [On notated staffless manuscripts], in *Chteniia v Moskovskom Obshchestve liubitelei dukhovnogo prosveshcheniia* [Readings of the Moscow Society of Friends of Religious Education] (1863), 58 n. [The Mezenets reference is from S. V. Smolenskii, ed., *Azbuka znamennogo peniia ("Izveshchenie o soglasneishikh pometakh") startsa Aleksandra Mezentsa 1668* [Alphabet of *znamennoe* singing ("Report

about the most harmonious notation signs") by the monk Aleksandr Mezenets, 1668] (Kazan: Tip. Imp. universiteta i Tipo-litografiia N. Danilova, 1888), 10; on Mezenets, see the editorial notes to chapter 9 for updated information.]

94A. [*Editors' note:* The chapter references here, to John and Luke, may be to a series of readings rather than to numbered chapters; thus the reference to chapter 186 of John may indicate the 186th reading from John.]

94B. [*Editors' note:* The Byzantine calendar reckoned time from the creation of the world, with the New Year beginning on September 1; with the acceptance of Christianity, the Russians also adopted this system, which was in use until the time of Peter the Great. A convenient reference point for most Westerners is the year AD 1492, which corresponds to the year 7000 from the creation of the world in the Byzantine/Russian system. The reference to Manuel is in *PSRL* 2 (1962), col. 300; the reference to Princess Anna is in *PVL,* 50; this is a reference to ecclesiastical figures in general, not specifically to singers.]

95. *Kniga Stepennaia tsarskago rodosloviia, soderzhashchaia istoriiu Rossiiskuiu s nachala onyia do vremen gosudaria tsaria i vel. kniazia Ioanna Vasil'evicha, sochinennaia trudami preosv. mitropolitov Kipriiana i Makariia, a napechatannaia pod smotreniem Kol. Sov. i Ak. Nauk Chlena Gerarda Friderika Millera* [The Book of Degrees of the Imperial genealogy, containing the history of Russia from its beginnings to the times of the Sovereign Tsar and Great Prince Ivan Vasil'evich, compiled by the labors of the Most Reverend Metropolitans Kipriian and Makarii and printed under the supervision of the Collegial Councilor and Member of the Academy of Sciences, Gerard Frederick Miller] (Moscow: Universitetskaia tip., 1755), pt. 1: 224. [English translation taken, in part, from Morosan, *Choral Performance,* 4 (and see his discussion of this passage; note that the transliteration is slightly altered to conform to the editorial practices of the present volume); see *PSRL* 21 (1908), 171, where the passage appears at the end of chapter 5 and continues into chapter 6.]

96. S. V. Smolenskii, "O drevnerusskikh pevcheskikh notatsiiakh" [On old Russian chant notations], in *Pamiatniki drevnei pis'mennosti i iskusstva* [Documents of early literature and art] 145 (1901), 23. Smolenskii also says, and justly so: "We love to refer to the well-known and, as it were, straightforward testimony of the *Stepennaia kniga.*" At the conclusion of his evaluation of the *Stepennaia kniga,* Smolenskii states: "The incompleteness of its evidence, recorded three hundred years after the events, is therefore obvious." Unfortunately, as we shall see, Smolenskii's erroneous point of departure was to try to prove Russian invention of the notational signs and even the melodies in our earliest musical documents.

97. *Martirii* were special signs corresponding to the present-day clefs and indicating a change of mode or tonality. Similar Greek signs are seldom found in known sources. The meaning of this term in singing practice was investigated by J. B. Thibaut, "Etiud o vizantiiskoi muzyke" [Study of Byzantine music], *Vizantiiskii vremennik* [Byzantine annals] 6 (1899): pt. 1, 1–12.

97A. [*Editors' note:* For definitions and descriptions of Russian liturgical terms and sources, see Vladimir Morosan, ed., *Tysiacha let russkoi tserkovnoi muzyki / One Thousand Years of Russian Church Music,* vol. 1 of Monuments of Russian Sacred Music series 1 (Washington D.C.: Musica Russica, 1991); Gardner, *Orthodox Worship and Hymnography;* and articles in *NG2.*]

98. The *Stepennaia kniga* was compiled at the initiative of Metropolitan Makarii (d. 1564) in 1563 by his collaborator and successor, Afanasii. See the study by P. G. Vasenko, *"Kniga Stepennaia tsarskogo rodosloviia" i ee znachenie v drevnerusskoi istoricheskoi pis'mennosti* [The *Book of Degrees* and its significance in old Russian historical writing] (St. Petersburg: Tip. I. N. Skorokhodova, 1904); see also N. S. Derzhavin, *Stepennaia kniga kak literaturnyi pamiatnik* [The *Book of Degrees* as a literary document] (St. Petersburg, 1903). [There is an earlier edition of Derzhavin's work from Batum: Tip. Kiladze, 1902. For updated information and bibliography on the *Stepennaia kniga,* see *SKK* 2: pt. 1: 73–79 (s.v. "Afanasii").]

99. M. M. Shcherbatov, in his *Istoriia Rossiiskaia* [Russian history] (1771; [reprint, ed. I. P. Khrushchev and A. G. Voronov, St. Petersburg: Izdanie kniazia B. S. Shcherbatova, 1901–3]), citing excerpts from the still unpublished *Stepennaia kniga,* spoke of "mythical traditions" on which it is based. The well-known historian A. A. Shletser [August Ludwig von Schlözer] declares in his *Nestor* (in the translation by D. Iazykov, vol. 1) that, in the *Stepennaia kniga,* "where ancient times are discussed they are full of intolerable fables"; that "the *Stepennaia kniga* . . . has created a great deal of suffering for Russian history" since, because of its official character, it has been accorded great importance and its "fables" were copied anew from ancient times. [Findeizen refers here to Avgust Ludovik Shletser, *Nestor. Ruskiia Letopisi na drevle-slavenskom iazyke* [Nestor. Russian sources in old Slavonic], trans. Dmitrii Iazykov (St. Petersburg: V Imperatorskoi tip., 1809), 1:91–92; on the historian Schlözer, see *MERSH* 33:145–54.] An even sharper reaction to this document is to be found in an article by "K" in *Korifei* (St. Petersburg, 1802), pt. 1, which accuses the authors of that book of the following: "They departed from the meaning of the old chroniclers, substituting for it false and ridiculous legends . . . There is nothing more tedious than their florid and bombastic style." [Findeizen's reference here is probably to the eleven-volume serial *Korifei, ili kliuch literatury* [Korifei, or the key to literature] (St. Petersburg: V Tip. Shnora, 1802–7).] M. Kachenovskii, "Ob istochnikakh dlia russkoi istorii" [On sources for Russian history], *Vestnik Evropy* (1809), states that the authors of the *Stepennaia kniga* accepted and introduced into the book "many made-up stories of foreign historians." K. F. Kalaidovich, a contemporary of the latter writer and a serious researcher, also points out that "the main shortcoming of the *Stepennaia kniga* is the multitude of fictions" ("Ob uchenykh trudakh mitr. Kipriiana" [On the scholarly works of Metropolitan Kipriian], *Vestnik Evropy* [1813]), Not only early Russian scholars but later researchers agree on the fictitious and florid content of the *Stepennaia kniga* concerning events of the earliest period of Russian history. Thus A. N. Pypin, *Istoriia russkoi literatury* [History of Russian literature] (St. Petersburg: M. M. Stasiulevich, 1898), 2:467, comments that the "narrative (of the *Stepennaia kniga*) proceeds in a pompous style which the rhetoric of the period (of compilation) had accepted as the official style," whereby even the historical introduction of the *Stepennaia kniga* speaks in the language "of lives of saints or *kanons* decorated with a web of words." P. G. Vasenko, who studied this document in great detail, testifies to its "rhetorical style and prolix language" (*"Kniga Stepennaia tsarskogo rodosloviia" i ee znachenie,* 21). [The second, expanded edition of Pypin's work, issued in St. Petersburg by M. M. Stasiulevich in 1902–1903, is reprinted in Slavistic Printings and Reprintings 92, nos. 1–4 (The Hague: Mouton, 1968). The word *kanon* here can refer either to the poetic form or perhaps also to the customary, and elaborate, vocabulary used to describes the lives and works of the saints.]

100. V. V. Stasov, "Zametka o demestvennom i troestrochnom penii" [A note on the *demestvennoe* and tri-partite chant], *Sobranie sochinenii,* 3:107. [The article is reprinted in V. V. Stasov, *Izbrannye sochineniia* [Selected works], ed. P. T. Shchipunov (Moscow: Iskusstvo, 1952), 1:123–40.]

101. The Roman philosopher Boethius (ca. 475–526) wrote his famous *De Musica* in five books in which he laid out the essence of the Greek musical system, which by then had been lost. His work was published three times toward the end of the fifteenth century and again in 1570; it enjoyed great authority in the West. [Findeizen (and his source, Stasov's "Zametka o demestvennom i troestrochnom penii" noted above) quotes from the theoretical work by Sebastian of Felstin (or Sebastian Felsztyna, *Opusculum musices noviter congestum* (Kraków: Hieronim Vietor, 1534), A2, available in a facsimile edition in *Monumenta musicae in Polonia,* seria D: Bibliotheca antiqua 4 (Kraków: Polskie wydawnictwo muzyczne, 1976). There was an earlier edition of the treatise, from 1524–25 (and a still earlier, and significantly different, edition from 1517); the 1534 edition was reprinted in 1539. See *NG2* s.v. "Sebastian z Felsztyna." The Boethius text is readily available in translation in any number of sources, for example, Oliver Strunk, ed., *Source Readings in Music History: From Classical Antiquity through the Romantic Era* (New York: Norton, 1950): 79–86. Many thanks to Thomas Mathiesen for information on the text and the translation from Latin.]

102. Stasov, "Zametka o demestvennom i troestrochnom penii," 126.

102A. [*Editors' note:* Findeizen, *Ocherki* 1:90 identifies this as manuscript no. 148, fol. 165; the current location is RGADA, f. 381, no. 148, as described in *SKSR* no. 169, which assigns a date of the twelfth to the thirteenth century.]

103. A. Potebnia, *K istorii zvukov russkogo iazyka* [On the history of the sounds of the Russian language] (Voronezh: V Tip. V. I. Isaeva, 1876), 36.

104. A. Vostokov, *Opisanie russkikh i slovenskikh rukopisei Rumiantsovskogo muzeuma* [Description of Russian and Slavonic manuscripts in the Rumiantsev Museum] (St. Petersburg: Tip. Imp. Akademii nauk, 1842), 650.

105. Potebnia, *K istorii zvukov,* 36.

105A. [*Editors' note:* This example comes from D. V. Razumovskii, *Tserkovnoe penie v Rossii* [Church singing in Russia] (Moscow: Tip. T. Ris, 1867), 64.]

106. In his *Istoriia russkoi tserkvi* [History of the Russian Church] (St. Petersburg: Tip. R. Golike, 1883), 12:113, Metropolitan Makarii states:

> During the period in which *khomovoe* chant was prevalent, words were stretched out to nonsense, with the changing position of stresses, changing the semi-vowels into full vowels, and the addition of new vowel-like sounds. Even the Stoglavyi Sobor [The Council of 100 Chapters] and Patriarch Germogen protested against such transgressions. During the time of Patriarch Joseph even some of the lay congregation protested, along with two of the most authoritative Moscow archpriests, Neronov of the Kazan Church and the tsar's confessor, Vonifat'ev of the Cathedral of the Annunciation. They were joined by the metropolitan of Novgorod, Nikon, as well as by the tsar himself. Patriarch Joseph was hesitant at first but then requested that Parthenius, Patriarch of Constantinople, decide, along with the other Greek hierarchs, "whether to preserve monophonic chanting during services in churches as well as in the monasteries?" The answer from Constantinople stated that the readings [lessons] in churches ought to be performed by a single voice and that singers ought to sing harmoniously and not in an unseemly bellowing.

[A brief discussion, in English, of this issue and of the practice of *mnogoglasie,* or simultaneous performance of musical portions of the liturgy, is in Vladimir Morosan, "*Penie* and *Musikiia:* Aesthetic Changes in Russian Liturgical Singing during the Seventeenth Century," *St. Vladimir's Theological Quarterly* 23, nos. 3–4 (1979): esp. 162–63; see also A. V. Preobrazhenskii, *Vopros o edinoglasnom penii v russkoi tserkvi XVII-go veka* [The question of monophonic singing in the Russian Church in the seventeenth century], Pamiatniki drevnei pis'mennosti i iskusstva 155 ([St. Petersburg]: OLDP, 1904). The Stoglav (from *sto glav* = one hundred heads [i.e., chapters]) was the chief legal code for the clergy, put together at a council in the year 1551; see *SKK* 2, pt. 1: 423–27, for current bibliography. There is a recent edition by E. B. Emchenko, *Stoglav: Issledovanie i tekst* [Stoglav: Analysis and text] (Moscow: Indrik, 2000).]

107. Concerning the *khomovoe* chanting, one should mention the article by Gavriil Artamonov (a Moscow merchant and member of the priestless sect [*bespopovtsy*] who died in 1756) published in *Trudy Kievskoi dukhovnoi akademii* [Proceedings of the Kiev Divinity School] January 1876. [Findeizen refers here to the article "O russkom bezlineinom i v chastnosti khomovom penii" (On Russian staffless and partially *khomovoe* singing) on pp. 163–99 of that volume.] He writes in opposition to the shortcomings of *khomovoe* chanting and certainly does not support it, as some scholars have surmised.

108. For the neumatic notation of text I, as found in manuscript GIM, Sin. 589, fol. 18, see the reproduction in the first volume of D. V. Razumovskii, I. A. Fortunov, and G. Karpov, *Krug tserkovnogo drevnego znamennogo peniia* [The cycle of old *znamennoe* church singing] (St. Petersburg: Tip. V. S.

326 NOTES TO PAGE 68

Balasheva, 1884), xxv. [*Editors' note:* R. Palikarova Verdeil, *La musique byzantine chez les Bulgares et les Russes (du IXe au XIVe siècle)* (Copenhagen: Munksgaard, 1953), 74, presents portions of all three of the texts used here in fig. 27d, usefully laid out so that the different syllable counts are visible.]

109. The following is a more detailed listing of these sources [and see also sources listed in n. 152 below]:

KONDAKARI

1. Rule [*Ustav*] with the Kondakar of the former library of the Moscow Synodal Typography of the eleventh century [Moscow, Tret'iakov Gallery, Manuscript Division K-5349; the same date is given in Gregory Myers, comp., *The Lavrsky Troitsky Kondakar,* Monumenta Slavico-Byzantina et Mediaevalia Europensia 4 (Sofia: Heron, 1994), 5; and see *SKSR* no. 50, which dates it from the late eleventh to the early twelfth century];

2. The Nizhnii Novgorod or the so-called Blagoveshchenskii Kondakar (RNB, Q.п.I.32). [This manuscript is published in facsimile in vol. 2 of Antonín Dostál and Hans Rothe, eds., *Der altrussische Kondakar': Auf der Grundlage des Blagověščenskij Nižegorodskij kondakar',* Bausteine zur Geschichte der Literatur bei den Slawen 8 (Giessen: Wilhelm Schmitz, 1976); in *SKSR* no. 153, the manuscript is dated from the late twelfth to the early thirteenth century];

3. Manuscript 23 in the Trinity-St. Sergius Lavra [RGB, Tr. 23; published in Myers, *The Lavrsky Troitsky Kondakar;* the manuscript is currently dated from the end of the twelfth century];

4–5. Two Kondakari from the twelfth century in the Moscow Synodal Library. [These are GIM, Sin. 777, dated from the mid-thirteenth century in Myers, *The Lavrsky Troitsky Kondakar,* 5; in *SKSR* no. 205 from the first half of the thirteenth century; and in GIM, Usp. 9, dated 1207. The Uspenskii Kondakar is published in Arne Bugge, ed., *Contacarium Palaeoslavicum Mosquense,* Monumenta Musicae Byzantinae, main series, vol. 6 (Copenhagen: Munksgaard, 1960). Myers, *The Lavrsky Troitsky Kondakar,* 5, citing Velimirović, "The Present Status of Research," 264, notes that there is a sixth Kondakar, RGB, f. 205, no. 107 (described in *SKSR* no. 124, from the end of the twelfth century; a fragment of this manuscript is in RNB, Pogod. 43 and is listed as *SKSR* no. 125), with a published facsimile of one folio in N. B. Tikhomirov, "Katalog russkikh i slavianskikh pergamennykh rukopisei XI–XII vekov, khraniashchikhsia v otdele rukopisei Gosudarstvennoi Biblioteki SSSR im. V. I. Lenina. Chast' II (XII vek)" [Catalog of Russian and Slavonic parchment manuscripts from the 11th–12th century in the Manuscript Division of the USSR State Lenin Library. Part II (12th century)], *Zapiski otdela rukopisei* [Notes of the Manuscript Division] 27 (1965): 102.]

STIKHIRARI: Twelfth Century

1. Fragment in RNB, Q.п.I.39;

2. Manuscript RNB, Q.п.I.15;

3–4. Two manuscripts in the Moscow Synodal Typography Library [these are probably RGADA, f. 381, nos. 145 and 152, which are two parts of a single source; see *SKSR* nos. 103–104. *SKSR* nos. 168–69 lists two additional Stikhirari from the late twelfth to the early thirteenth century in this collection: RGADA, f. 381, nos. 147 and 148. Findeizen, here and in the text below, refers to manuscript no. 151 in the Synodal Typography Library; this is probably a typographical error and has been changed throughout to no. 152];

5–7. Three manuscripts in the Moscow Synodal Library, one of which is dated 1157 [the source dated 1157 is GIM, Sin. 589; the other two sources are probably GIM, Sin. 572 and 279, both from the twelfth century; *SKSR* no. 135 also lists GIM, Sin. 278, a Stikhirar from the second half of the twelfth century];

8. Manuscript in the St. Petersburg Divinity School library dated 1163 [RNB, Sof. 384; see *SKSR* no. 54].

Stikhirari: Thirteenth Century

9. Manuscript in the Russian Academy of Sciences [BAN, 34.7.6, from the twelfth century; facsimile published in Nicolas Schidlovsky, ed., *Sticherarium paleoslavicum Petropolitanum: Codex Palaeoslavicus no. 34.7.6, Bibliothecae Academiae Scientiarum Rossicae*, Monumenta Musicae Byzantinae 12 (Hauniae: C. A. Reitzel, 2000)];

10. Manuscript in the Moscow Divinity School (from the Joseph Monastery) [RGB, Iosif-Vol. 3, from the fourteenth century];

11. Manuscript in the Rumiantsev Museum in Moscow, no. 420 [RGB, Rum. 420, from the fourteenth to the fifteenth century].

Stikhirari: Fourteenth Century

12–13. Two manuscripts in the library of the Trinity-St. Sergius Lavra [RGB, Tr. 439, from the fourteenth to the fifteenth century, and RGB, Tr. 22, dated 1303].

Irmologii

1–2. Two twelfth-century manuscripts in the library of the Moscow Synodal Typography [RGADA, f. 381, no. 149 (twelfth century) and no. 150 (fourteenth century); published in E. Koschmieder, ed., *Die ältesten Novgoroder Hirmologien-Fragmente,* 3 vols. (Munich: Verlag der Bayerischen Akademie der Wissenschaften, 1952–58). These are two parts of a single manuscript; see *SKSR* nos. 121–22, which dates them from the late twelfth or the early thirteenth century];

3. The merchant Samsonov's manuscript, dated 1249, mentioned by Sreznevskii, *Drevnie pamiatniki* [according to V. M. Metallov, *Russkaia simiografiia* [Russian sign notation] (Moscow: Izd. Mosk. arkheologicheskogo instituta, 1912), 12, the manuscript is lost; a translation of Metallov's work, as *Russische Semeiographie,* is available as volume 7 of Sagners slavistische Sammlung (Munich: O. Sagner, 1984).]

4–5. Two manuscripts in the Moscow Synodal Library, one from the Resurrection [New Jerusalem] Monastery dating from the thirteenth century and the other from the fourteenth century [GIM, Voskr. 28 (twelfth century; *SKSR* no. 120 specifies the end of the twelfth century); and GIM, Sin. 748].

Triodi: Twelfth Century

1–2. Two manuscripts in the Moscow Synodal Library [GIM, Sin. 278 and 319; *SKSR* no. 135 describes GIM, Sin. 278 as a Stikhirar];

3. One in the St. Petersburg Divinity School Library [this may duplicate no. 5 below];

4. One in the library of the Moscow Synodal Typography [this may be GIM, Voskr. 27 or RGADA, f. 381, no. 148; *SKSR* no. 49 also lists RGADA, f. 381, no. 138, a Triod from the eleventh to the twelfth century and the thirteenth century; *SKSR* no. 64 describes RGADA, f. 381, no. 139, which includes some twelfth-century notation.]

Triodi: Thirteenth Century

5. St. Petersburg Divinity School (Sofiiskoe sobranie) [RNB, Sof. 96; Velimirović, "The Present Status of Research," 263, lists this as a twelfth-century source; and *SKSR* no. 220 dates it from the first half of the thirteenth century];

6. Moscow Synodal Library (formerly the Uspenskii Cathedral [the Cathedral of the Dormition]) [GIM, Usp. 8].

Minei

1. Early thirteenth century in RNB, Q.п.I.12 [*SKSR* no. 126 dates this source from the second half of the twelfth century; see also n. 118 below];

2. End of the thirteenth century in [GIM] Sin. 168 [and see n. 118A below, where Findeizen dates this source to the twelfth century, which is the date assigned in *SKSR* no. 94].

Bibliography for these sources include N. V. Volkov, *Statisticheskie svedeniia o sokhranivshikhsia drevnerusskikh knigakh XI–XIV vv. i ikh ukazatel'* [Statistical data about old Russian books preserved from the 11th–14th centuries and an index], Pamiatniki drevnei pis'mennosti 123 (St. Petersburg: Tip. I. N. Skorokhodova, 1897); Vostokov, *Opisanie russkikh i slavianskikh rukopisei*; N. K. Nikol'skii, Kh. M. Loparev, V. I. Sreznevskii, A. A. Titov, et al., *Opisanie rukopisei Kirillo-Belozerskogo monastyria, sostavlennoe v kontse XV veka* [Description of manuscripts of the St. Cyril–Belozersk Monastery, compiled at the end of the fifteenth century], Pamiatniki drevnei pis'mennosti 113 (St. Petersburg: Sinodal'naia tip., 1897). [See also the detailed listing in Velimirović, "The Present Status of Research," 261–64; and in *SKSR,* passim. Many thanks to Daniel Waugh for important help in compiling this updated listing.]

110. The first such chants were probably the *stikhiry* honoring Princes Boris and Gleb (in 1072); in memory of the transport of the relics of St. Nicholas the Miracle-worker to Bari (in 1087); and honoring the Blessed St. Feodosii of the Monastery of the Caves [in Kiev] (in 1095).

110A. [*Editors' note:* Razumovskii, *Tserkovnoe penie v Rossii,* 62.]

111. *Ananeiki* are found in the oldest musical manuscripts and in music books of the seventeenth century. In the large collections of rules [*Ustavy*] of the seventeenth century (Moscow 1610 and 1641), during the All-Night Vigil, at the prooemiac psalm after the words "fullfillment of all blessings," it was prescribed that singers should sing: "Slava ti Gospodi, anenenenaani stvorivshemu vsia . . ." [Glory to you, O Lord, anenenenaani, who created all . . .]. In that same century there even appeared *ananeiki* for two voices that were to be added to the singing in Greek of the *Eís pollá étē, déspota* [acclamation wishing many years to the bishop or any high hierarch celebrant; see n. 57A above] at the altar, during the procession of the hierarch after the Little Entrance. Smolenskii, "O drevnerusskikh pevcheskikh notatsiiakh," 97, gives a modern transcription of an elaborate *ananeika* which has been preserved to recent times among the Old Believers.

112. This manner is practiced, for example, among contemporary Christians in Asia Minor, especially in Syria and Palestine, where the choir on the left side sings in Greek and the one on the right sings in Arabic, but the tunes are the same. [Findeizen does not give a source for the bilingual singing in thirteenth-century Rostov, but similar references are in E. Golubinskii, *Istoriia russkoi tserkvi* [History of the Russian Church] (Moscow: Universitetskaia tip., 1901), 1: pt. 1: 359, and n. 2; many thanks to Gregory Myers for information on this passage.]

113. See the list of manuscripts above [n. 109; this is Moscow, Tret'iakov Gallery, Manuscript Division K-5349]. A reproduction of folio 102v of that manuscript appears in Metallov, *Russkaia simiografiia,* pl. IV.

114. Formerly this manuscript belonged to the Monastery of the Annunciation [Blagoveshche-nie] in Nizhnii Novgorod, from which it received its designation. A photo-reproduction of the manu-script appears in the first edition of N. Karinskii, *Khrestomatiia po drevne-tserkovno-slavianskomu i russkomu iazykam*, pt. 1. [See n. 89A above; Findeizen apparently refers to the 1883 edition.] In Metallov, *Russkaia simiografiia*, Plates XVIII–XXII reproduce pages from this manuscript; the call number of the manuscript is RNB, Q.II.I.32 [see n. 109 above].

115. A *kondak* is a short song celebrating a feast or a saint. Thus a collection of *kondaki* is a *Kondakar*. The Hypatian Chronicle, under the year 1111, records that "Vladimir ordered his priests, in procession, ahead of the populace, to sing the *troparia* and *kondaki* of the Holy Cross"; in the twelfth-century travelogue of abbot Daniel [to the Holy Land]: "We approached the Lord's Tomb singing the *kondak* "Ashche i v grobe snide besmert'ne" [And He descended into the tomb immortal]." [The reference from the Hypatian Chronicle is in *PSRL* 2 (1843), 2; the reference to Daniel is in *PLDR XII vek*, 112–13.]

116. Papadopulo-Keramevs, "Proiskhozhdenie notnogo muzykal'nogo pis'ma," in a special table juxtaposes some fourteen signs (apparently only from the upper layer) from Slavic *kondakaria* with the signs from the Greek *papadikai* (Greek ecclesiastical chant, performed by the leaders or *protop-salts*). [Findeizen's reference here is to the *papadikē* (plural, *papadikai*), the introductory segment of a musical manuscript, containing a basic introduction to notation; see *NG2*.] But comparing Keramevs's table with the few samples of *kondakarnaia* notation published so far, among them the five pages of the Blagoveshchenskii manuscript (folio 103 in Karinskii, *Khrestomatiia po drevne-tserkovno-slavian-skomu i russkomu iazykam*; folios 20, 52v, and 85 in Metallov, *Russkaia simiografiia*; and our reproduc-tion of folio 113v), one realizes that in these five pages only, the upper line contains no fewer than sixty-three different signs, some of which reappear more than once in the same plates, while a number of signs may be found without changes in the Kondakari of the Trinity–St. Sergius Lavra, the Mos-cow Synodal Typography, and the Stikhirar from the year 1303. Thus Keramevs has by no means given a complete list of all the signs of the upper layer of *kondakarnaia* notation; the shape of some of the signs may even now be assembled, to a certain degree, into some systematic order, as some signs are put together (fig. N3.1), similar to the later *kriuki*. There are also variants of the same sign, which were not a result of the copyist's hand or of defects in copying but may have designated various manners of performance or variants in the melodic outline (fig. N3.2).

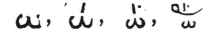

Fig. N3.1. Ordering of *kondakarnaia* notation.

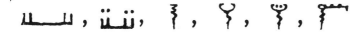

Fig. N3.2. Variants in *kondakarnaia* notation.

117. S. V. Smolenskii, "Neskol'ko novykh dannykh o tak naz. kondakarnom znameni" [Some new data about the so-called *kondakarnaia* notation], *RMG* 1913, nos. 44–47, 49, discusses mostly the literary side of *kondakarnaia* singing. Smolenskii's basic idea, that the "*kondakarnaia* notation was a Russian invention" and that the "*kondakarnaia* melodies, the *kondakarnaia* notation, could not have been particularly complicated or difficult" since such notation was followed by "simple laymen or sex-tons" is refuted not only by the Greek features of the signs in the upper notational layer but also by the

great variety, in number and complexity, of these signs. The "simple laymen" or "simple sextons" could hardly sing these settings, which appear to be for two or even three voices, the meaning of which has remained inaccessible to later learned investigators.

118. The manuscript was described by Vostokov, *Filologicheskie nabliudeniia,* 202. Vostokov has also noted (p. 204) that, in addition to the *stikhira* mentioned above, on three different places (fols. 102 and 134 of the new numbering) above the text, one encounters the Greek letter *theta* as a musical sign. At the present time the text and notation of the *stikhiry* for the Feast of the Dormition, which, incidentally, were written by a different scribe, have almost totally faded and can be read with great difficulty, except for a few "bright" spots. [This is RNB, Q.п.I.12 which, in n. 109 above, Findeizen ascribes to the thirteenth century; *SKSR* no. 126 dates this source from the second half of the twelfth century.]

118A. [*Editors' note:* In n. 109 above, Findeizen dates this manuscript from the late thirteenth century; according to *SKSR* no. 94, the source dates from the twelfth century.]

119. S. V. Smolenskii, *Kratkoe opisanie drevnego (XII–XIII veka) znamennogo Irmologa, prinadle-zhashchego Voskresenskomu, "Novyi Ierusalim" imenuemomu, monastyriu* [A brief description of the old notated Irmologii (12th–13th century) belonging to the Resurrection Monastery, called New Jerusa-lem] (Kazan: Tip. Imp. universiteta, 1887). On pp. 15–16, Smolenskii lists all the notational signs in this document, which was later transferred to the Moscow Synodal Library. Some of these are reproduced in table 3.2.

120. A reproduction was published in Hugo Riemann, *Muzykal'nyi slovar'* [Music dictionary] (Moscow: P. Iurgenson, 1901–4), 702.

120A. [*Editors' note:* Findeizen refers here to the theorist Henricus Glareanus; see his *Dodecachordon,* trans., transcribed, and commentary by Clement A. Miller (n.p.: American Institute of Musicology, 1965). See also *NG2* on Glareanus and the Octoechos, as well as for important bibli-ography on the relationships between Eastern and Western chant systems.]

121. Razumovskii, *Krug tserkovnogo drevnego znamennogo peniia,* 1:iii. In addition to Razumovskii, who gave the simplest and most understandable explanation of the structure of our modal system, other writings about the Octoechos include I. I. Voznesenskii, *O tserkovnom penii pravoslavnoi greko-rossiiskoi tserkvi: Bol'shoi i malyi znamennyi rospev* [On the church singing of the Greek–Russian Orthodox Church: The great and lesser *znamennyi* chant] (Riga: Tip. G. T. Korchak-Novitskogo, 1889), and the same author's *Osmoglasnye rospevy trekh poslednikh vekov pravoslavnoi russkoi tserkvi* [The octoechal melodies of the three last centuries of the Russian Orthodox Church] (Kiev: Tip. S. V. Kul'zhenko, 1888) [and the accompanying volume, *Obraztsy osmoglasiia rospevov kievskogo, bol-garskogo i grecheskogo s ob"iasneniem ikh tekhnicheskogo ustroistva, prilozheniia k sochineniiu "Osmoglasnye rospevy trekh poslednikh vekov pravoslavnoi russkoi tserkvi"* [Examples of octoechal Kievan, Bulgarian, and Greek melodies, with an explanation of their technical construction, appended to the work "The octoechal melodies of the three last centuries of the Russian Orthodox Church"] (Riga: Tip. Ernesta Platesa, 1893).] See also the work by V. M. Metallov, *Osmoglasie znamennogo rospeva* [The Octoechos of the *znamennyi* chant] (Moscow: Sinodal'naia tip., 1899). [Findeizen gives the publication date of Metallov's work as 1900. In this chart, the final of glas 4 should probably read sol; however, many scholars have expressed reservations about applying such rigid theoretical constructs to the Russian tradition, and it is not at all clear how well this system might reflect medieval practice and conceptions in Russian chant. Many thanks to Nicolas Schidlovsky for sharing his thoughts on this question.]

122. A. Preobrazhenskii, "O skhodstve russkogo muzykal'nogo pis'ma s grecheskim v pevcheskikh rukopisiakh XI–XII vv." [On the resemblance of the Russian notation to the Greek in musical manu-scripts of the 11th–12th centuries], *RMG* 16 (1909), nos. 8, 9, 10.

4. Novgorod the Great

[*Editors' note:* This chapter deals with the history and cultural significance of Novgorod, a city with distinct social, political, and cultural traditions that was annexed into the Muscovite state by Ivan III in 1478, as part of the long process of the consolidation of the Muscovite princes' power; as Findeizen discusses, this effort lasted for a century, during which Novgorodian cultural traditions were gradually eroded. The end of this process, at least externally, was marked by Ivan IV's destruction of the city in 1570. Novgorod was an important commercial city with connections to Western Europe, and the Hanseatic League had offices there (although it was not, as Findeizen states, actually a full-fledged member). Findeizen discusses the city's political and social structure as it might relate to its musical culture, for, unlike Moscow, Novgorod had elements of a republican form of government, in which, although the real political power was oligarchical, there was an elected mayor (or *posadnik*), as well as a popular assembly (*veche*). A basic source on the Novgorodian populace and social structure is V. L. Ianin, *Novgorodskie posadniki* [The Novgorodian *posadniki*], 2nd ed., rev. and exp. (Moscow: Iazyki slavianskoi kul'tury, 2003).

Important excavations have taken place in Novgorod beginning in the 1920s, and a great deal of the medieval city's infrastructure of roads and outlines of its buildings have been preserved, as well as written documents on birchbark and wooden implements of various sorts. An overall description of the rich process of excavation is summarized in M. W. Thompson, *Novgorod the Great: Excavations at the Medieval City Directed by A. V. Artsikhovsky and B. A. Kolchin* (New York: Praeger, 1967). Musical instruments are among the surviving wooden objects of Novgorod, and, although Findeizen discusses musical instruments at length in chapters 6 and 7, it is useful here to cite several recent studies dealing with the instruments discovered there; Findeizen, given his interest in archaeology, would surely have appreciated their significance. These studies include B. A. Kolchin, "Kollektsiia muzykal'nykh instrumentov drevnego Novgoroda" [A collection of musical instruments of old Novgorod], *PKNO for 1978* (1979): 174–87; idem, "Gusli drevnego Novgoroda" [*Gusli* of old Novgorod], in *Drevniaia Rus' i Slaviane* [Ancient Rus' and the Slavs] (Moscow: Nauka, 1978): 358–66; V. I. Povetkin, "Gudebnye sosudy drevnego Novgoroda" [Musical vessels of old Novgorod], *PKNO for 1984* (1986): 155–67; and idem, "Drevnii novgorodskii odnostrunnyi muzykal'nyi instrument (K voprosu o drevnerusskom smyke)" [An old Novgorodian single-stringed musical instrument (On the question of the old Russian *smyk*)], *PKNO for 1998* (1999): 180–86. The most recent reports from the continuing work in the city appear in the series *Novgorod i novgorodskaia zemlia: Istoriia i arkheologiia / Novgorod and [the] Novgorod Region: History and Archaeology,* where V. I. Povetkin has issued a series of annual reports documenting each season's excavation. See also Povetkin's "V mire muzyke drevnego Novgoroda i Rusy. Arkheologicheskie otkrytiia 2000 g." [In the musical world of ancient Novgorod and Rusa: Archaeological discoveries in 2000], *Novgorod i novgorodskaia zemlia: Istoriia i arkheologiia / Novgorod and [the] Novgorod Region: History and Archaeology* 15 (2001): 59–66; and idem, "Mir muzyki drevnikh novgorodtsev. Arkheologicheskie otkrytiia 2000 goda" [The musical world of the ancient Novgorodians. Archaeological discoveries in 2000], *Proshloe Novgoroda i novgorodskoi zemli: Materialy nauchnoi konferentsii 2001–2002 gg.* [The past in Novgorod and the Novgorodian lands: Materials from a scientific conference, 2001–2002] (Novgorod: Novgorodskii gos. universitet imeni Iaroslava Mudrogo, 2002), pt. 1: 23–34.

In this chapter Findeizen discusses at length the long narrative poems called *byliny*. Many of these texts refer to legendary heroes associated with the city, including figures such as Vasilii Buslaev and Sadko. Although their names appear in the later Novgorodian chronicles, they do not appear in the early texts and should not be regarded as actual historical figures, as Findeizen presents them. One might note, in general, that Findeizen takes the chronicle accounts quite literally, although there has been considerable scholarly debate about the content of many of the accounts, for example, the story of the "calling of the Varangians" from the North to provide order and stability among the Slavs.

A. Stender-Petersen looks at the story of the calling of the outsider to provide order in a broader European context (*Die Varägersage als Quelle der Altrussischen Chronik* [Aarhus: Universitetsforlaget, 1934]).

Kirsha Danilov was one of the first to compile these *byliny*, apparently in the mid-eighteenth century (after 1742). The first edition of the Danilov collection appeared in 1804, and, in 1818, an edition with music appeared under the editorship of K. F. Kalaidovich. The latest edition is by A. P. Evgen'eva and B. N. Putilov, *Drevnie rossiiskie stikhotvoreniia, sobrannye Kirsheiu Danilovym* [Old Russian poems, collected by Kirsha Danilov], 2nd enl. ed. (Moscow: Nauka, 1977). The Soviet musicologist Viktor Mikhailovich Beliaev (1888–1968) prepared a reconstruction of the melodies, published posthumously as *Sbornik Kirshi Danilova: Opyt restavratsii pesen* [The collection of Kirsha Danilov: An attempt at reconstructing the songs] (Moscow: Sovetskii kompozitor, 1969). Zguta, *Russian Minstrels*, also discusses the *byliny* and the Novgorodian *skomorokhi* in chapters 2 and 4 of his work.

In this chapter Findeizen also discusses the famous Novgorodian bells and bell-ringing traditions, a topic covered by Edward V. Williams in his important and substantial study, *The Bells of Russia*, where there are ample references to Novgorod. Williams has generously shared with us his unmatched understanding of the complexities of Russian bells and bell ringing, for which the editors of this volume are most grateful. See also the recent work by I. A. Shalina, "Pskovskie zvonnitsy i kolokol'ni XVI v." [Belfries and bell towers in Pskov in the 16th century], *PKNO for 1997* (1998): 473–84; and T. B. Shashkina, "Kolokola domongol'skoi Rusi po dannym arkheologii" [Bells in pre-Mongol Rus' according to archaeological data], *PKNO for 1995* (1996): 477–83.

The period of the sixteenth century is unquestionably a pivotal point in the history of Russian church music. There are hundreds of musical sources from this period, a wealth of primary source material that contrasts dramatically with the period before 1500, for which there are approximately fifty (or perhaps as many as eighty) musical manuscripts preserved. Findeizen's summary of this century may still serve as a good starting point, which should be supplemented by the extremely important studies by Maksim Viktorovich Brazhnikov, especially his *Drevnerusskaia teoriia muzyki* [Old Russian music theory] (Leningrad: Muzyka, 1972). The data on the sixteenth-century singers in Novgorod and their move to Moscow, as well as the filiation of teachers and their pupils, represents one of Findeizen's significant contributions, and it has been restated by Western scholars, for example, by Alfred Swan in his series of three articles titled "The Znamenny Chant of the Russian Church," *Musical Quarterly* 26, no. 2 (1940): 232–42; no. 3 (1940): 365–80; and no. 4 (1940): 529–45. An excellent and accessible survey of this material appears in Vladimir Morosan, *Choral Performance in Pre-Revolutionary Russia*, which, although focused on nineteenth- and twentieth-century singing practice, presents an overview of early monophony and polyphony in Russian practice.

The Novgorodian singers Findeizen discusses in this chapter are the first documented, named creators of Russian liturgical music (although the concept of creativity in Eastern Orthodox liturgical music admitted to reworking and elaborately recomposing preexisting models). Findeizen gives more information about these Novgorodian singers than had appeared in any earlier Russian scholarly work, and he resumes this discussion about individual singers and the organized singing ensembles (the sovereign and patriarchal choirs) in chapter 8, on Moscow in the fifteenth and sixteenth centuries, as the Novgorodian singers had all been ordered to Moscow by Tsar Ivan IV in the last decades of the sixteenth century. His presentation has been supplemented in recent works, particularly by the scholar N. P. Parfent'ev, whose *Drevnerusskoe pevcheskoe iskusstvo v dukhovnoi kul'ture rossiiskogo gosudarstva XVI–XVII vv.* [The old Russian art of chanting in the religious culture of the Russian state in the 16th–17th centuries] (Sverdlovsk: Izd. Ural'skogo universiteta, 1991), adds many new names of singers and singing teachers. The opening chapter of Parfent'ev's book is devoted to Novgorod's chant tradition and its singers, and later chapters move to Moscow and the singers who were established there, as well as the singing tradition associated with the Stroganov family in Sol'vychegodsk. See also N.

Parfent'ev and N. Parfent'eva, *Usol'skaia (Stroganovskaia) shkola v russkoi muzyke XVI–XVII vekov* [The Usol'e (Stroganov) school in Russian music in the 16th–17th centuries] (Cheliabinsk: Kniga, 1993). Parfent'ev's *Professional'nye muzykanty rossiiskogo gosudarstva, XVI–XVII vekov. Gosudarevy pevchie d'iaki i patriarshie pevchie d'iaki i pod'iaki* [Professional musicians of the Russian state, 16th–17th century. The sovereign singers and the patriarchal singers] (Cheliabinsk: Kniga, 1991) is an impressive and comprehensive evaluation and listing of known singers in the organized ensembles in the sixteenth and seventeenth centuries, relying on extensive archival work; see also Natal'ia Parfent'eva, *Tvorchestvo masterov drevnerusskogo pevcheskogo iskusstva XVI–XVII v.* [Works of masters of old Russian singing, 16th–17th century] (Cheliabinsk, 1997).

Findeizen links to Novgorod the name of Ivan Shaidur, who is credited with the first "reform" of the Russian neumatic notation, which is presumed to have taken place around 1600. The number of documents preserving Shaidur's innovations appears to be extremely small, however, which raises significant questions about the effectiveness of this reform, which Findeizen discusses fairly well in his text. He also presents a summary of the theoretical framework and notational signs associated with the designation of pitches in the "modernized" tonal range used for chants by the end of the sixteenth century. Excerpts from Shaidur's treatise are in A. I. Rogov, *Muzykal'naia estetika Rossii XI–XVIII vekov* [Musical aesthetics in Russia in the 11th–18th centuries] (Moscow: Muzyka, 1973), 95–96, and additional bibliography appears in chapter 9, where Findeizen resumes his discussion of chant theory.

Recent studies have tackled the issue of the complex terminology and attributions of several other types of chants and neumatic notations (such as Kazan signs and *putevoi rospev* and its notation) that were current in the sixteenth century. Although many younger Russian scholars are focusing on this period, at present there is no final unanimity in the interpretation of the great wealth of data from the sixteenth century. One of the important chant types Findeizen considers in this chapter is *demestvennyi* chant, a topic for which there is considerable literature, including the extensive treatment in Johann von Gardner, *Das Problem des altrussischen demestischen Kirchengesanges und seiner linienlosen Notation*, Slavistische Beiträge 25 (Munich: Sagner, 1967). The interpretation of the term *demestvo* and a singer of this music as a *demestvennik* has undergone various transformations. The most frequently accepted theory is that the term was derived from the Greek *domestikos* [δομέστιχος, or δομέστιχος], meaning the leader of a church choir. (See Κριαρᾶς [Kriaras], Λεξικὸ τῆς Μεσαιωνικῆς Ἑλληνικῆς *Δημώδους Γραμματείας* [Lexicon of medieval Hellenic folk literature], vol. 5, where the term is defined as indicating an ecclesiastical rank given to singers or to other low-ranking hierarchs.) One intriguing set of references, however, points out that *demestvo* was also a technical term for a single part in a polyphonic context. This suggests that with the appearance of terms like *verkh* and *niz* (designating high and low) as well as *put'* (literally, road or path, but in function apparently akin to the term *tenor* in the sense of "one who holds the tune" or "is on the right track"), the ingredients of a polyphonic score are on hand as early as the mid-sixteenth century. See Galina A. Pozhidaeva, "Formy izlozheniia demestvennogo mnogogolosiia" [The presentation of *demestvennyi* polyphony] in *AE* 1981 (1982): 123–33; and also her "Vidy demestvennogo mnogogolosiia" [Aspects of *demestvennyi* polyphony], in *Russkaia khorovaia muzyka XVI–XVIII vekov* [Russian choral music of the 16th–18th centuries] (Moscow: Gos. muzykal'no-pedagogicheskii institut im. Gnesinykh, 1986): 58–81 (this is volume 83 in the series of occasional publications put out by the Institute). Pozhidaeva is a very prolific writer, yet not all of her publications should be accepted at face value. Her most recent work, "Prostrannye raspevi drevnei Rusi XI–XVII vekov" [The long (or drawn-out) chants of early Russia of the 11th–17th centuries] (Moscow, 1999), leaves some doubts about her understanding of the earliest medieval layers (her basic point is that, in her terminology, the terms *demestvennyi*, melismatic, and *prostrannyi* are synonyms used interchangeably!). But her collection of transcriptions of what she calls *demestvennyi raspev* is worth studying for the wealth of melodies she offers. See also her *Traditsii russkogo tserkovnogo penii, Vypusk I, Demestvennyi raspev XVI–XVIII vv.* [Traditions of Russian church singing, pt. 1, *Demestvennyi* singing, 16th–18th centuries] (Moscow: Kompozitor, 1999). B. A. Shindin has also worked on *demestvennyi* chant; see his study, written with I. V. Efimova, *Demestvennyi rospev. Monodiia i mnogogolosie* [*Demestvennyi* singing. Monody and polyphony] (Novosibirsk: Novosibirskaia gos. Konservatoriia im. M. I. Glinki, 1991). Keldysh (*IRM* 1:147–51) also cites another work by Shindin which suggests that this type of chant has links with folk music; see his "Problema proiskhozhdeniia demestvennogo rospeva v otechestvennom muzykoznanii" [The problem of the origin of *demestvennyi* chant in our country's musicology], in *Problemy istorii i teorii drevnerusskoi muzyki* [Problems in the history and theory of old Russian music] (Leningrad: Muzyka, 1979), 109–23. In her *Drevnerusskoe pevcheskoe iskusstvo* [The old Russian art of chanting] (Vladivostok: Izd-vo Dal'nevostochnogo universiteta, 1983), Galina Vasil'evna Alekseeva carries out an interesting structural analysis of the melodic patterns in Russian chant as documented in sixteenth- and seventeenth-century manuscripts.

The problem of the alphabets [*azbuki*] of neumes is being studied by Guseinova and by Dmitrii Semenovich Shabalin of Kemerovo University (east of Novosibirsk, in Siberia). The so-called *putevoi rospev* has been studied by M. V. Bogomolova (of Dushanbe); see her "Putevoi raspev i ego mesto v drevnerusskom pevcheskom iskusstve" [*Putevoi raspev* and its place in the art of early Russian singing], *Muzykal'naia kul'tura srednevekov'ia* [Musical culture of the Middle Ages] 2 (1992): 122–24; and her "Modelirovanie drevnerusskikh pesnopenii putevogo rospeva po printsipu podobiia (na primere stikhir rukopisi inoka Khristofora 1602 goda" [The structuring of early Russian *putevoi raspev* on the principles of *podoben* (on the example of the *stikhiri* in the 1602 manuscript of monk Khristofor], *Problemy muzykoznaniia* [Problems in musicology] 4 (1990): 47–61. Some of these sources have been explored in detail by the Bulgarian scholar Bozhidar Karastojanov who, after having lived for some twenty years in Moscow, has returned to Sofia, where he is publishing the results of his studies. Finally, Findeizen mentions the work of the chant theorist Aleksandr Mezenets briefly in this chapter; see chapter 9 for more information, including a crucial rethinking of the chronology of Mezenets's work.]

122A. [*Editors' note:* Findeizen's source is *PSRL* 1 (reprint, 1962), col. 422.]

122B. [*Editors' note:* This series of quotations from the Buslai *bylina* is from Avenarius, *Kniga bylin;* in the eighth edition (Moscow: Izdanie A. A. Stupina, 1913) the passages appear on pp. 293–94 and 308.]

122C. [*Editors' note:* These passages are in Avenarius, *Kniga bylin,* 8th ed., 306–307.]

122D. [*Editors' note:* *PSRL* 9 (1965), 247; and see the editorial comments above on the reference to these figures only in the later Novgorodian chronicles, which are probably drawing from the *bylina* tradition. Many thanks to Daniel Waugh for clarifying this point.]

123. Bezsonov, *Pesni, sobrannye P. V. Kireevskim,* fasc. 5:LXV.

124. Avenarius, *Kniga bylin,* xxiii [endnotes].

125. Ibid., 243ff.

125A. [*Editors' note:* The quotation is from the Novgorod III Chronicle, *PSRL* 3 (1841), 215; see the Pskov I Chronicle, *PSRL* 4 (1848), 177; and the edition by A. N. Nasonov, *Pskovskie letopisi* [Pskov chronicles] 1 (Moscow: Izd. AN SSSR, 1941), which was reprinted as *PSRL* 5, vyp. 1 (2003), 10. See also the Novgorod I Chronicle, *PSRL* 3 (1841), 14; and the more recent edition by A. N. Nasonov, ed., *Novgorodskaia pervaia letopis' starshego i mladshego izvodov* [The Novgorod I Chronicle in the earlier and later recensions] (Moscow: Izd-vo AN SSSR, 1950), 32.]

125B. [*Editors' note:* A variant of this passage appears in Avenarius, *Kniga bylin,* 8th ed., 323.]

125C. [*Editors' note:* Sadko's patronymic, Sotnich', as recorded in the Novgorod II Chronicle, is similar to the term *sotnik;* see *PSRL* 30 (1965), 203. The term *sotnik* also had an administrative meaning in Muscovy; see Sergei G. Pushkarev, *Dictionary of Russian Historical Terms from the 11th century to 1917* (New Haven: Yale University Press, 1970), 139.]

125D. [*Editors' note: PVL*, 37; this translation is from Cross and Sherbowitz-Wetzor, *The Russian Primary Chronicle*, 94 (transliteration slightly modified to conform to the editorial practices of this volume). It is the sentence immediately preceding this passage to which Findeizen refers when calling Dobrynia a *posadnik*, which was an elected official in Novgorod. In *PVL*, 37, the passage reads: "Volodimer zhe posadi Dobrynu, uia svoego, v Novegorode," which suggests that Vladimir installed or appointed Dobrynia, his uncle, in Novgorod, not that Dobrynia was elected to the position of *posadnik* by the populace. Thanks to Daniel Waugh for this clarification.]

125E. [*Editors' note: PSRL* 21, pt. 1 (1908), 139.]

126. Bezsonov, *Pesni, sobrannye P. V. Kireevskim*, fasc. 2:35.

127. P. N. Rybnikov, ed., *Pesni, sobrannye P. N. Rybnikovym* (Moscow: A. Semen, 1861), pt. 1: 369. [There is a modern edition of the work by B. N. Putilov, ed., *Pesni, sobrannye P. N. Rybnikovym* [Songs collected by P. N. Rybnikov] (Petrozavodsk: Kareliia, 1989–91).]

128. Rybnikov, *Pesni*, 319.

129. A. F. Gil'ferding, "Onezhskie byliny" [*Byliny* from Onega], *Sbornik Otd. Rus. iazyka i slov. Ak. nauk* [Papers of the Section for Russian Language and Literature of the Academy of Sciences] 59–61 (1894): 954.

130. Bezsonov, *Pesni, sobrannye P. V. Kireevskim*, fasc. 5:54.

131. Ibid., fasc. 5:58–59.

132. *Drevniia Rossiiskiia Stikhotvoreniia, sobrannyia Kirsheiu Danilovym i vtorichno izdannyia, s pribavleniem 35 pesen i skazok, dosele neizvestnykh, i not dlia napeva* [Old Russian poems, collected by Kirsha Danilov and published for the second time with an addition of 35 songs and tales hitherto unknown and with music for singing] (Moscow, 1818). For this, as well as for the first edition, from 1804, the music was "corrected" by Shprevich, a former music teacher at the University's Boarding School for the Nobility in Moscow [Universitetskii blagorodnyi pansion]. These "corrections" to some extent mutilated the original version of the music, which was restored in a more complete and more scholarly edition of this collection by P. N. Sheffer, ed., *Sbornik Kirshi Danilova* (St. Petersburg: Tip. Imp. Akademii nauk, 1901), in which the musical lines are printed with photographic accuracy.

133. A. V. Markov, "Materialy i issledovaniia po izucheniiu narodnoi pesni i muzyki" [Materials and investigations on the study of folk songs and music], *Trudy muzyk. etnogr. komissii* [Reports of the musical ethnographic commission] 1 (1906): 156 (materials collected in Arkhangel'sk province in the summer of 1901). [Grigor'ev's book is *Arkhangel'skie byliny i istoricheskie pesni* [The Arkhangel'sk *byliny* and historical songs] (Moscow: Imp. Akademii nauk, 1904.]

134. *Velikorusskie pesni v narodnoi garmonizatsii: Pesni novgorodskie* [Songs from Great Russia in folk harmonization: Songs from Novgorod] (St. Petersburg: Imp. Akademii nauk, 1909), fasc. 2. [On the distinguished musical ethnographer Evgeniia Lineva (d. 1919), see the editorial notes prefacing chapter 3 above.]

135. The music is cited from the published manuscript from the Public Library [RNB], edited by P. N. Sheffer [see n. 132 above], 31; subsequent examples are from this edition. The notated music was undoubtedly written down by a fiddler or from a performance on a violin. The attempt to fit the text with Kirsha Danilov's music, perhaps not so successful, was mine [i.e., Findeizen's].

136. See n. 133 above. [Findeizen's reference to Markov's *Belomorskie byliny* is unclear here, but he may be referring to A. V. Markov, A. L. Maslov, and B. A. Bogoslovskii, *Materialy sobrannye v Arkhangel'skoi gubernii letom 1901 goda* [Materials collected in Arkhangel'sk province in the summer of 1901] (Moscow: Tip. K. L. Men'shova, 1905), of which the first volume is about the White Sea.]

137. Grigor'ev, *Arkhangel'skie byliny*, 1:163.

137A. [*Editors' note:* Findeizen refers in his text to V. V. Stasov, *Slavianskii i vostochnyi ornament* [Slavic and Oriental ornament] (St. Petersburg: Kartograficheskoe zavedenie A. A. Il'ina, 1887). A selection of images from Stasov's book is reproduced in Zguta, *Russian Minstrels*, 71–75.]

137B. [*Editors' note:* fig. 31a is from RNB, F.п.I.1 (*SKSR* no. 300, a thirteenth-century psalter); fig. 31b is from RNB, Frolov. 3; and fig. 31c is from RNB, O[Q?].п.I.7. The initial is also reproduced in Povetkin, "'Russkii' izobrazitel'nyi kanon," 148 (the source is identified on p. 149). Fig. 32 is from GIM, Sin. 69; the image is reproduced in G. I. Vzdornov, *Iskusstvo knigi v drevnei Rusi: Rukopisnaia kniga severo-vostochnoi Rusi XII–nachala XV vekov* [The art of the book in ancient Rus': The manuscript book in north-east Rus' in the 12th–beginning of the 15th centuries] (Moscow: Iskusstvo, 1980), plate 31, and see pp. 76–77, where he notes that the manuscript is from Moscow, not from Novgorod.]

138. Cosmas Indicopleustes [in Russian, Koz'ma Indikoplov] was a merchant from Alexandria in the first half of the sixth century who later became a monk; he traveled to India (hence his name, Indikoplov or Indoplavatel' [one who sailed to India]). His work, which contained valuable information about geography, cosmography, and the history of the East, was exceptionally popular in medieval Europe and in Russia, where it has been preserved in several translations and manuscripts. One such text appears in a manuscript of the Makar'evskaia chet'ia Mineia (a Novgorod copy of the sixteenth century) and was published by the OLDP (St. Petersburg, 1886), as vol. 86 in the *Pamiatniki* series. [See n. 73F above. A chet'ia Mineia is a large collection of readings organized for each month. There is a recent edition of the Koz'ma Indikoplov treatise by Golyshenko and Dubrovina, *Kniga naritsaema Koz'ma Indikoplov,* mentioned above in chapter 3.]

138A. [*Editors' note:* F. I. Buslaev, *Istoricheskie ocherki russkoi narodnoi slovesnosti i iskusstva* [Historical studies of Russian folk literature and art], 2 vols. (St. Petersburg: V Tip. tovarshchestva "Obshchestvennaia pol'za," 1861). The complete title of the miniature is: "Postem David pobedi diavola, i tsarstvo obrete imy v zderzhaniem pobedi venchaetsia, tsar' David biiashe medvedia" (*Ocherki* 1:123).]

139. This complex miniature depicting various musical instruments is fully reproduced below in figs. 45 and 46 [in chapter 6].

140. The Icon of the Miraculous Intervention is fully described, with a reproduction of a fragment depicting the view of Novgorod, in *Izvestiia Imp. arkheol. obshch.* [Reports of the Imperial Archaeological Society] 5 (1864), fasc. 3. [There is a color reproduction of another version of this icon, from ca. 1460–70, in V. N. Lazarev, *Novgorodskaia ikonopis' / Novgorodian Icon-Painting* (Moscow: Iskusstvo, 1969), plate 5, which shows only two trumpets.]

141. See the article by P. L. Gusev (with reproductions of various parts of the icon) in "Novgorod XVI veka po izobrazheniiu na khutynskoi ikone: 'videnie ponomaria tarasiia'" [Novgorod in the sixteenth century according to the depiction in the Khutyn icon, The Vision of the Sexton Tarasii], *Vestnik arkheologii i istorii* [The archaeological and historical herald] 13 (1900): 7–66. [A color reproduction of this icon appears in D. Likhachov [Likhachev], V. Laurina, and V. Pushkariov [Pushkarev], *Novgorod Icons 12th–17th Century* (Leningrad: Aurora, 1980), plate 239; see also the brief description on 334; the icon is in the Novgorod Museum, no. 7632.]

142. Stasov, *Slavianskii i vostochnyi ornament,* Tablitsa, fol. lxix, no. 8. [This image is reproduced in Povetkin, "'Russkii' izobrazitel'nyi kanon," 149, where it is identified as BAN 34.5.20, fol. 113v (in the *tetr,* not the *aprakos* format, as Findeizen says; on these terms, see n. 86H above). According to Vzdorov, *Iskusstvo knigi,* 77 n. 2, the source (the Mikulino Evangelie) is from Moscow, not Novgorod.]

142A. [*Editors' note:* PSRL 4 (1848), 24.]

142B. [*Editors' note:* Findeizen gives no source for this passage, although it is close to Sreznevskii, *Materialy* 3:464, under the word *sopel'k''* from a thirteenth-century life of St. Nifont. On the "twitterings" from overseas, see n. 73B above.]

142C. [*Editors' note:* Many thanks to Edward Williams and Malcolm Brown, who explain the terminology relating to bells as follows: The largest bell in the tower was called the *blagovestnik* or *prazdnichnyi blagovestnik* bell (the festal herald bell), which was used on major feasts and on which *blagovest* (ringing a single bell to announce services) was sounded. Next in size was the *voskresnyi krestovyi* bell, that is, the Sunday (*voskresen'e*) or, literally, the "Resurrection" bell, referring, of course, to

Easter but, by extension, also to the weekly celebration of the Resurrection every Sunday, when the liturgy commemorates the Paschal Sacrifice and the Resurrection. The word *krestovyi* refers to the cross, signifying this large bell to be the *blagovestnik* not only for Sundays but also for Feasts of the Cross. The third largest in size is the *polieleinyi* bell; the name is from the Greek *polyeleos* ("many mercies") and refers to the Polyelaion Psalms (esp. Psalms 134 and 135) sung during Matins. These Psalms include numerous repetitions of the line "His mercy endureth forever," hence the name "many mercies." The *povsednevnyi*, or everyday, bell is the ferial (weekday) *blagovestnik*. On ordinary (non-festal) weekdays, there is no *Polyelion* at Matins, and this would be the largest bell appointed for use.]

143. Aleksandr Golubtsov, "Chinovnik Novgorodskogo Sofiiskogo sobora" [Book of Rites of the Novgorod Cathedral of St. Sophia], *ChOIDR* 2 (1899), pt. 1: i–xx, 1–272.

143A. [*Editors' note:* The term *trezvon* indicates a collective and especially festive and complex ringing of all the bells; it is quite lengthy and is rendered in three sections or movements. A *zvon* is a simpler sounding of some of the bells in the tower, and the term can also mean a set of bells or the sound produced when bells are rung. For more on bell terminology, see Williams, *The Bells of Russia*, 243–46. Many thanks to Edward Williams, who generously shared his thoughts on this section of Findeizen's work and on this particular passage; the translation here is his.]

143B. [*Editors' note:* The passage reads in full as follows (Findeizen, *Ocherki* 1:131): "blagovest ko vsenoshchnomu za 5 chasov dni, a zvoniat na Sofeiskoi kolokolni vo vsia po sobornomu peniiu, a u praznika po praznichnomu peniiu zvon byvaet a blagovestiat i zvoniat v sennie kolokola." The term *sennye* here (which means literally hall or vestibule) is unclear in the context of St. Sophia's bells. Edward Williams makes the tentative suggestion that here it refers to bells which later are called *zazvonnye* bells, that is, the smallest and highest-pitched bells in a *zvon*. Thus the five arches in the St. Sophia bell tower, which Findeizen describes below, might have included the four largest bells (*prazdnichnyi, voskresnyi, polieleinyi,* and *vsednevnyi*), with the fifth arch containing several small *zazvonnye/sennye* bells.]

144. Golubtsov, "Chinovnik," 1, 27, 33–34, 73, 93, and 106. [Thus, apparently on this particular day, the Makar'evskii bell had a dual function: it was used to sound *blagovest* and also served as the bell on which the hours were struck.]

145. A similar specimen existed (until 1925) in the museum of the former Archaeological Institute in Leningrad. It came from Novgorod and can be dated not later than the fifteenth century. The Novgorod Museum has two such old *bila;* one is a curved strip of forged iron about eighteen feet, eight inches, long, approximately four inches wide, and less than half an inch thick. It was suspended by an iron chain passed through two holes in the middle, and it dates from the sixteenth century. The other is a rectangle of cast iron and has an intriguing shape and history of its own. It was presented by Peter I as a gift to a Novgorod monastery at the beginning of the eighteenth century in exchange for old guns that had been confiscated. On the upper side is a figure of an eagle's head, while the remains of another are broken off. Between them is a semi-circle pierced with holes for the iron chain. Thus, in some churches in Novgorod, *bila* were used along with bells even in the eighteenth century.

145A. [*Editors' note:* See Williams, *The Bells of Russia*, Appendixes A and B.]

146. Cf. Archimandrite Makarii, *Arkheologicheskoe opisanie tserkovnykh drevnostei v Novgorode i ego okrestnostiakh* [Archaeological description of ecclesiastical antiquities in Novgorod and its environs], Part 2 (Moscow: V Tip. V. Got'e, 1860); and *Sbornik Imperatorskogo Russkogo istoricheskogo obshchestva* [Anthology of the Imperial Russian Historical Society], vols. 60, 62 (1887, 1888) [in which the entire contents of these volumes is] an alphabetical index of names of Russian masters.

147. "Materialy dlia arkheologicheskogo slovaria" [Materials for an archaeological dictionary], *Drevnosti. Trudy moskovskogo arkheologicheskogo obshchestva* 2 (1870), section 11:5. [Williams, *The Bells of Russia*, 17–19, has a brief discussion of *bila* in Russia, including their use in Novgorod. In Findeizen's fig. 38, there seems to be only one figure striking a *bilo;* the image is reproduced in Williams's *Bells of*

Russia, 1, 118, where it is identified more specifically as appearing under the term *bilo* in "Materialy dlia arkheologicheskogo slovaria," listed above.]

148. The full text of the *Tsarstvennaia kniga* without the illustrations is published in *PSRL* 13, pt. 2 (1906); the reference to bells is on 453–54. [This edition of the *Tsarstvennaia kniga* is from the manuscript Findeizen cites in the text. There is a typographical error in Findeizen's text (*Ocherki* 1:133); the passage should read "i pade z drevianye kolokolnitsy" instead of "i pade 3 drevianye kolokolnitsy," as in Findeizen. On the Tsar's Book, part of a large illuminated codex, see O. I. Podobedova, *Miniatiury russkikh istoricheskikh rukopisei. K istorii russkogo litsevogo letopisaniia* [Miniatures in Russian historical manuscripts: Toward a history of Russian illuminated manuscript writing] (Moscow: Nauka, 1965).]

148A. [*Editors' note:* On Anthony, see Williams, *The Bells of Russia*, 34, and n. 15.]

148B. [*Editors' note:* Williams, *The Bells of Russia*, 40, 203 n. 66, identifies this reference as coming from the Novgorod I Chronicle; see Nasonov, *Novgorodskaia pervaia letopis'*, 354.]

148C. [*Editors' note:* Translation from Williams, *The Bells of Russia*, xv, from *PSRL* 3 (1841), 148 (the Novgorod II Chronicle; Williams discusses the passage further on p. 44.]

149. Data about the ancient bells of Novgorod may be found in the work by Makarii, "Arkheologicheskoe opisanie"; see also S. G. Rybakov, *Tserkovnyi zvon v Rossii* [Church bell ringing in Russia] (St. Petersburg: Tip. E. Evdokimova, 1896); N. F. Okulich-Kazarin, *Sputnik po drevnemu Pskovu* [Guide to old Pskov] (Pskov: Izd. Pskovskogo arkheologicheskogo obshchestva, 1911); and V. P. Laskovskii, *Putevoditel' po drevnemu Novgorodu* [Guide to old Novgorod]; and other works. [Findeizen gives no date for the Laskovskii book; there is a first edition from 1910, published in Novgorod by Gubernskaia tipografiia and a second, corrected edition from the same press issued in 1913. On the Novgorod assembly bell, see Williams, *The Bells of Russia*, 41 and n. 79, and the illustrations in Podobedova, *Miniatiury russkikh istoricheskikh rukopisei*, figs. 122–24. A. N. Chudinova, *Penie, zvony, ritual: Topografiia tserkovno-muzykal'noi kul'tury Peterburga* [Singing, bell ringing, and ritual: The landscape of the church-musical culture of Petersburg] (St. Petersburg: Ut, 1994), carries the topic into the eighteenth century.]

149A. [*Editors' note:* According to E. A. Gordienko, *Novgorod v XVI veke i ego dukhovnaia zhizn'* [Novgorod in the 16th century and its spiritual life] (St. Petersburg: Bulanin, 2001), 332 and plate LI, there was a church dedicated to the *Sreteniia* [presentation] of the Icon of the Vladimir Virgin in Novgorod, built in 1548–54, so it is possible that the 15 September date in the St. Sophia Chinovnik is related to this. Two other events are also associated with a procession or presentation of this icon, both in Moscow and neither on 15 September. The icon was brought from Vladimir to the Cathedral of the Dormition in Moscow in connection with the invasion of Tamerlane in August 1395, and it was again brought to Moscow in June 1480 (see *Gosudarstvennaia Tret'iakovskaia Galereia. Katalog sobraniia*, vol. 1, *Drevnerusskoe iskusstvo X–nachala XV veka* [State Tret'iakov Gallery. A catalog of the collection, Vol. 1, *Early Russian art from the 10th–beginning of the 15th century*] (Moscow: Krasnaia ploshchad', 1995), 38. Thanks to Daniel Waugh for pointing out these references.)]

150. Golubtsov, "Chinovnik," 21, 31–32, 36, 42, 48, 53, 55–56, 110, 131.

151. Metropolitan Evgenii, "Svedenie o Kirike, predlagavshem voprosy Nifontu Novgorodskomu" [Information about Kirik, who posed questions to Nifont of Novgorod], *Trudy i letopisi Obshchestva istorii i drevnostei rossiiskikh* [Works and Annals of the Society of Russian History and Antiquities] 4 (1828): 129. [There is a recent study of Kirik by R. A. Simonov, *Kirik Novgorodets—uchenyi XII veka* [Kirik the Novgorodian, a twelfth-century scholar] (Moscow: Nauka, 1980).]

152. The most remarkable of these manuscripts are (a) in the library of the Moscow Synodal Typography [RGADA] and all dating from the twelfth century, that is, from the earliest period of our literacy:

> 1. Manuscript no. 285, Ustav [rule] with notated Kondakar [now in Moscow, Tret'iakov Gallery, Manuscript Division K-5349; see *SKSR* no. 50];

2–3. Two festal Stikhirari: manuscript no. 303 [*SKSR* no. 103, describing RGADA, f. 381, no. 145] and no. 330 [probably *SKSR* no. 104, in RGADA, f. 381, no. 152, although *SKSR* lists its former shelf number as 331, not 330];

4–5. Manuscript nos. 307, 308, two notated Irmologii [*SKSR* nos. 121–22, two parts of a single manuscript, in RGADA, f. 381, nos. 149, 150];

6. Manuscript no. 306, Triod postnaia [Lenten Triodion, containing hymns and prayers for Lent and Passion Week] and Triod tsvetnaia [Festal Triodion, with hymns and prayers from Easter through the first Sunday after Pentecost; RGADA, f. 381, no. 148, described in *SKSR* no. 169 as dating from the twelfth to the thirteenth century];

and (b) in the Moscow Synodal Library [GIM]:

7–8. Two notated Stikhirari from the twelfth century, manuscript no. 589 (dated 1157) and no. 572 [GIM, Sin. 589, 572, the latter listed as 571 in Findeizen; *SKSR* nos. 100, 99];

9–10. Manuscript nos. 278, 319, two notated Triodi from the twelfth century [GIM, Sin. 278, listed in *SKSR* no. 135; and GIM, Sin. 319, listed in *SKSR* no. 106];

11. Manuscript no. 777, notated Kondakar from the thirteenth century [GIM, Sin. 777, listed in *SKSR* no. 205].

For a listing of *znamennye* and *kondakarnye* manuscripts from Novgorod, see Volkov, *Statisticheskie svedeniia*; and A. A. Pokrovskii, *Drevnee pskovo-novgorodskoe pis'mennoe nasledie* [The written heritage of old Pskov and Novgorod] (Moscow: Sinodal'naia tip., 1916). For a more detailed description of some fragments and for reproductions from manuscripts, see Metallov, *Russkaia simiografiia*. [See also n. 109 above for a more complete listing of sources.]

153. The Novgorod monk Vasilii Rogov served twice as abbot of the St. Cyril-Belozersk Monastery and for some time in the Monastery of the Nativity of the Virgin in Vladimir. The Rostov chronicler mentions his place of origin as the village Ivanovy Gory in Bezhetsk county. He died on 23 August 1602 and was buried in the Rostov Cathedral (A. A. Titov, commentary, *Letopis' o rostovskikh arkhiereiakh* [The Chronicle of Rostov church hierarchs], OLDP Izdaniia 94 (St. Petersburg: Tip. S. Dobrodeeva, 1890), primechaniia, 20.

154. The full text of the preface was published by V. Undol'skii in the appendixes to his "Zamechaniia o tserkovnom penii v Rossii" [Notes on church singing in Russia], *ChOIDR* 3 (October 1846), pt. 1: 19–23. [This translation, beginning with the phrase "with our own ears," is taken from Morosan, *Choral Performance*, 17–18; editorial annotations in square brackets are Morosan's. The passage is also published in Rogov, *Muzykal'naia estetika*, 42–44. An important publication of Kristianin's music is M. V. Brazhnikov, ed., *Fedor Krest'ianin: Stikhiry / Fyodor Krestyanin: Canticles*, PRMI 3 (Moscow: Muzyka, 1974), which includes a full color facsimile, transcription, and extensive commentary. Here and throughout this volume, Findeizen speaks of Usol'e, in the Urals, and the Stroganov family's holdings there and in that area in general. As N. P. Parfent'ev points out, this description has been used fairly loosely; see chapter 3 of his *Drevnerusskoe pevcheskoe iskusstvo*, where he unravels the specific geographical locations in the many references relating to singing masters and chant types in the period under consideration.]

155. *Drevniaia rossiiskaia vivliofika* [Ancient Russian library], 2nd ed. (Moscow: V Tip. Kompanii Tipograficheskoi, 1788): 6:387. The Chinovnik (published by Golubtsov) also directed that after performing the Play of the Furnace, on 17 December, "the singers [*podiaki*] at the ambo sing . . . Radilov's alleluia [*alliluiia Radilovu*]" (70).

155A. [*Editors' note:* The term Findeizen uses here is *pevchii d'iak,* literally a singing deacon or clerk; singers were associated with various state and ecclesiastical figures. On this term, see the discussion in chapters 8–11 of this volume.]

155B. [*Editors' note:* See the introductory editorial remarks to chapter 11 for updated thinking on "opekalovskii raspev," which refers to a monastery, not to a singer or a composer.]

155C. [*Editors' note:* This system is discussed in *NG2* (s.v. "Notation"), where it is compared to the Byzantine system, which also indicates specific intervals between pitches. In his reference to Hermannus Contractus, Findeizen calls him a "vergenskii monakh," which may be a typographical error for *vengerskii,* Hungarian; on the theorist's origins, see the biographical article in *NG2*. In his discussion of this system of notation, Gustave Reese, *Music in the Middle Ages* (New York: Norton, 1940), 137, gives the following terminology: *equisonus; semitonium;* and *tonus cum semitonio.*]

156. Apparently the text of Shaidur's *Skazanie* was dispersed among the many theoretical textbooks of *kriukovaia* notation in the seventeenth and eighteenth centuries; at any rate, its original version remained unknown to Razumovskii, Smolenskii, and other researchers.

156A. *PSRL* 6 (1853), 16–17. [This is Findeizen's note 156a, in *Ocherki* 1:143.]

157. *PSRL* 3 (1841), 167. [*PSRL* 30 (1965), 189, under the date 1572.]

158. V. V. Maikov, *Kniga pistsovaia po Novgorodu Velikomu kontsa XVI v.* [The Cadastres of Great Novgorod from the end of the sixteenth century] (St. Petersburg: Tip. M. A. Aleksandrova, 1911). The registers of the 1580s have preserved the following names of the Novgorodian singers [*pevchie d'iaki*]: the Cathedral of St. Sophia, Sergei (94), "the prelate's singers" [*vladychnye*]: Kirill, Iakov Andreev, Fedor Stepanov, and Ivan Selivanov (96–97), and probably also the prelate's singers: David Nikiforov, Vasilii Vorob'ev, Iakusha (97–98), and Stepan Lukin (102). The untaxed dwellings of all these singers are listed as deserted. The Novgorodian bell ringers who are listed in these books include Denis Iakovlev in the Church of Egor the Sufferer (7); Onkudin at the Church of St. Nicholas (12); Proshka (full name Prokopii), died at age seventy-nine in 1662 (18); and Okul Terent'ev at the Church of St. Dimitrii (24). Bell ringers at the Cathedral of St. Sophia included Dmitrii Petrov (95), Mosorga Leont'ev (102), and Trofim (103); Mikhail Ivanov at the Church of St. Konstantin (127); Isak at the Church of St. John the Baptist and Ivan Timofeev at the Church of the Archangel (237); Onton and Grishka at the Church of St. John the Baptist (238, 244); Vaska Abramov the ringer on Fridays [*piatnitskii zvonets*] (239); two "Filippovskie" ringers, Stepan (d. 1671) and his probable successor, Grisha Sidorov. Their names may be useful for a history of bell ringing in Russia. [These bell ringers may have been associated with the Church of the Apostle Philipp in Novgorod, which was built in 1528–29 (on its history, see Gordienko, *Novgorod v XVI veke,* 147–51). Also, the "Filippovskii post" was the forty days leading up to Christmas, so these bell ringers may have had some special traditions for this period.]

5. The Activities of the *Skomorokhi* in Russia

[*Editors' note:* Findeizen's discussion of the *skomorokhi*—the jesters, buffoons, or *jongleurs* of Russia—is truly a masterpiece of research involving a great wealth of archival data. It also qualifies as a sociological and ethnographic study of the subject, for Findeizen reasoned that the generic term *skomorokh* (and related vocabulary), when used as a geographical name, might indicate the presence of actual *skomorokhi* in the area; he thus collected the names of a series of villages, settlements, plots of land, and so forth, all bearing witness to the activities of these entertainers.

In this chapter Findeizen refers to the well-known writer and traveler Adam Olearius (1603–1671), whose work has also been used in a number of Western writings. An English translation of his travels appeared as early as 1669, and the most recent English edition, which we have relied on for this study, was translated and edited by Samuel Haskell Baron, *The Travels of Olearius in Seventeenth-century Russia* (Stanford: Stanford University Press, 1967), based on the second German edition of 1656. Olearius's book is an important source not only for its woodcuts depicting the *skomorokhi* and the puppet theater but for many other descriptions of Russian life in a variety of settlements in the first half of the seventeenth century.

The only full-length study in English on the subject of the *skomorokhi* is by Russell Zguta, *Russian Minstrels: A History of the Skomorokhi* ([Philadelphia]: University of Pennsylvania Press, 1978).

Russian scholarship on the subject is naturally considerably larger, although not generally relating to music. One work in particular traces Findeizen's evolving treatment of the subject: N. V. Ramazanova, "'Skomorosh'e delo' v ocherkakh N. F. Findeizena po istorii muzyki v Rossii" ["*Skomorokh* activities" in N. F. Findeizen's works on the history of music in Russia], which appears in the important collection *Skomorokhi: Problemy i perspektivy izucheniia* [*Skomorokhi:* Scholarly problems and perspectives], ed. V. V. Koshelev (St. Petersburg: Rossiiskii institut istorii iskusstv, 1994), 41–50; this volume contains a series of articles from a symposium on the topic held in St. Petersburg in November 1994. Additional references appear in the following notes.]

159. On the origin of the word *skomorokh* (or *skomrakh* and the adjective *skomrash'skyi* or *skomoroshii*) and also about the dances and other features of the daily life of that profession, see the following works: I. D. Beliaev, "O skomorokhakh" [About the *skomorokhi*], *Vremennik Imp. Obshchestva istorii i drevnostei Rossiiskikh* [Annals of the Imperial Society for Russian History and Antiquities] 20 (1854): 69–92; A. S. Famintsyn, *Skomorokhi na Rusi* [The *skomorokhi* in Rus'] (St. Petersburg: Tip. E. Arngol'da, 1889 [reprint, St. Petersburg: Aleteiia, 1995]; A. Kirpichnikov, "K voprosu o drevnerusskikh skomorokhakh" [On the question of the old Russian *skomorokhi*], *Sbornik II-go otd. Imp. Akademii nauk* [Collection of the Second Section of the Imperial Academy of Sciences] 52, no. 5 (1891): 1–22. [See also the bibliography cited in Zguta, *Russian Minstrels*; and V. V. Koshelev, *Skomorokhi: Annotirovannyi bibliograficheskii ukazatel' 1790–1994 gg.* [*Skomorokhi*: An annotated bibliographic guide, 1790–1994] (St. Petersburg: Liki Rossii, 1994). Two fairly recent Russian monographs on the subject are Z. I. Vlasova, *Skomorokhi i fol'klor* [The *skomorokhi* and folklore] (St. Petersburg: Aleteiia, 2001); and A. A. Belkin, *Russkie skomorokhi* [Russian *skomorokhi*] (Moscow: Nauka, 1975).]

160. *Povest' vremennykh let* [The Russian Primary Chronicle], from the year 6576 (*PSRL* 1:73 [see *PSRL* 1 [1926], col. 170]; cf. the Nikon Chronicle, 1:157 [see *PSRL* 10 [1862], 95]). [See also *PVL*, 75; and Cross and Sherbowitz-Wetzor, *The Russian Primary Chronicle*, 147. Zguta discusses this passage in *Russian Minstrels*, 3–6, where he also discusses the rites associated with the festival of *rusaliia*, a pre-Christian tradition later identified with the week before Trinity Sunday.]

161. *Russkie dostoprimechatel'nosti* [Russian sights], pt. 1: 9. [Findeizen's reference here is, in fact, to *Russkie dostopamiatnosti* [Russian monuments], issued in three parts by the Obshchestvo istorii i drevnostei Rossiiskikh between 1815 and 1844; part 1 (1815) includes a study by R. Timkovski, "Poucheniia arkhiepiskopa Luki k bratii" [The sermons of Archbishop Luke to the brethren], 3–16. This sermon is reprinted in T. V. Chertoritskaia, comp. and ed., *Krasnorechie drevnei Rusi (XI–XVII vv.)* [The oratory of ancient Rus' (11th–17th centuries)] (Moscow: Sovetskaia Rossiia, 1987); quoted passage appears on p. 40. On Archbishop Luke, see *SKK* 1:251–53.]

162. "Letopisets' Pereiaslavlia Suzdal'skogo s predisloviem i opisaniem rukopisei: Letopisets' ruskikh tsarei" [The Pereiaslavl-Suzdal short chronicle, with a preface and a description of the manuscripts: The short chronicle of the Russian tsars], *Vremennik Imp. Obshchestva istorii i drevnostei Rossiiskikh* 9 (1851), pt. 2: 3. [This passage (which is quoted in full in Findeizen, *Ocherki* 1:145) appears in *PSRL* 41 (1995), 6, and reads, in part: "I nachashia pristroati sobe koshiuli, a ne srachitsy, i mezhinozhie pokazyvati, i krotopolie nositi ... aki skomrasi." See also Zguta, *Russian Minstrels*, 18, for a brief reference to this passage, including a definition of the *krotopolie* as a jacket or tunic.]

163. *Russkiia dostopamiatnosti*, 114. [See n. 161 above; the article to which Findeizen refers is "Pravilo Kiurilla mitropolita rus'skago" [The rule of Kirill, Russian metropolitan], which appears in part 1 (1815): 104–18. On Kirill, see *SKK* 1:225–27.]

164. Manuscript in the Public Library [RNB], chap. 51, 191. [See *SKSR* no. 186, where the source is identified as RNB, F.II.II.1.]

165. Sreznevskii, *Materialy*, 3:379.

166. Buslaev, *Istoricheskaia khristomatiia*, 504. [The translation here is based on Rogov, *Muzykal'naia estetika*, 50.]

167. Sreznevskii, *Materialy,* 3:380. [The cleric John Malalas was a sixth-century Byzantine chronographer; Sreznevskii cites a passage from his *Chronicle* and its translation from a fourteenth-century Russian source. Malalas mentions the role of music (or, more generally, all kinds of sound), popular theatrics and the stage, performers, and equestrians, as does the Russian translation. Many thanks to George-Julius Papadopoulos for his help with this passage. On Malalas, see *SKK* 1:471–74.]

168. A detailed study of the puppet theater is V. N. Peretts, "Kukol'nyi teatr na Rusi" [Puppet theater in Rus'], *Ezhegodnik Imp. teatrov* [Annual of the Imperial theaters], for the 1894–95 season, appendix to vol. 1. We shall not concern ourselves with the origin and development of the puppet theater in Russia and the traits it shares with Western performances by *jongleurs* or in puppet shows. Peretts correctly refers to D. A. Rovinskii's conjecture about the puppet theater described by the seventeenth-century traveler Olearius, which was "the well-known *petrushka* [Punch and Judy show] which survived to this day, more than two centuries, almost without change; it assumed the traits of the Russian *skomorokh* and, as such, spread throughout Russia." The author makes another valuable statement when he notes that the "*petrushka* was formed by melding elements of Russian buffoonery with the traits of the German Hanswurst-Pickleherring character. Its prototype was the *polichinelle,* the Italian Pulcinella," which should be recognized as the ancestor of all European jesters and *skomorokhi.* [A brief overview of the subject of the *skomorokhi* and puppet theater is in Zguta, *Russian Minstrels,* 112–14.]

169. This custom has been preserved by the people to the most recent times. In Orel province and in the district of Samara, as well as in many other places, evidence attests to the required participation of *skomorokhi* in wedding rites (see V. Varentsov, *Sbornik pesen Samarskogo kraia* [Collection of songs from the Samara district] (St. Petersburg: Izd. N. A. Serno-Solov'evicha v. tip. O. I. Baksta, 1862), 169 [reprint, Samara: Obl. tsentral'nogo narodnogo tvorchestva, 1994]). The lyrics of one song from Orel province, cited in Beliaev, "O skomorokakh," 76, are the following:

> A kak by kto zhe skomoroshechka da podvez?
> Igrai, igrai, skomoroshichek, v selo do sela,
> Uzh chtob byla Natal'iushka vesela.

> Who would want to give the *skomorokh* a lift?
> Play, oh play, *skomorokh,* from village to village
> To make little Natal'iushka merry.

Varentsov's collection (listed above) includes a similar wedding song:

> Zaprech' zhe by vorona konia,
>   Chtoby vez,
> Posadit'-to by skomoroshnichka,
>   Chtob igral:
> Igrai, poigrai, skomoroshnichek,
>   S sela do sela,
> Chtoby nasha Praskov'iushka
>   Byla vesela.

> Get a black horse
>   to pull [the cart]
> Put the *skomorokh* in
>   so he will play.
> Play, oh play, *skomorokh*
>   from village to village
> To make our dear Praskov'ia merry.

169A. [*Editors' note:* See Emchenko, *Stoglav,* 313.]

170. *Akty istoricheskie* [Historical acts] 4:124–26. The document excerpted here is by a Tobol'sk governor dated 7158 [1649], and it is similar to orders for the collection and destruction of the "honking instruments" ["gudebnye sosudi"] of the *skomorokhi* in Moscow itself, which is described by Olearius. One might conclude, therefore, that this was a state-ordered measure aimed at the eradication of the *skomorokhi* and of folk instruments. [Findeizen refers here to the destruction of musical instruments described in Adam Olearius, *Vermehrte Newe Beschreibung Der Muscowitischen vnd Persischen Reyse,* ed. D. Lohmeier (Tübingen: Max Niemeyer Verlag, 1971), 302, and in Baron, *The Travels of Olearius,* 262–63, although "honking instruments" are not mentioned in these passages.]

171. Beliaev, "O skomorokakh," 70. [There is an edition of Cosma of Prague in G. E. Sanchuk, ed., *Koz'ma Prazhskii, cheshskaia khronika* [Cosma of Prague, Czech chronicle] (Moscow: Izd-vo AN SSSR, 1962), where this passage appears on 169.]

172. Ibid., 92.

173. Cf. N. D. Chechulin, *Goroda Moskovskogo gosudarstva v XVI v.* [Towns of the Muscovite state in the sixteenth century] (St. Petersburg: Tip. I. N. Shorokhodova, 1889) [reprint, Slavistic Printings and Reprintings 198 (The Hague: Mouton, 1969)], which contains brief but interesting statistical data about the activities of the *skomorokhi* in many Muscovite towns of that period. P. Simson, *Istoriia Serpukhova* [History of Serpukhov] (Moscow: T. Ris, 1880) [reprint, Moscow: Arkheograficheskii tsentr, 1992] records names of local *skomorokhi* in the mid-sixteenth century. [Nikolai Dmitrievich Chechulin (1863–1927) was a historian and librarian who wrote extensively on sixteenth- and eighteenth-century Russia (see *GSE* 29:86). Pavel Fedorovich Simson's comprehensive manuscript collection is described in *Opisanie rukopisei, prinadlezhashchikh P. F. Simsonu* [A description of manuscripts belonging to P. F. Simson] (Tver: Izd. Tverskoi uchenoi arkhivnoi komissii, 1902).]

174. The data for this study were compiled from the following sources (in addition to the works by Chechulin and Simson, mentioned in n. 173 above):

1. "Perepisnaia okladnaia kniga po Novugorodu Vot'skoi piatiny" [Census and tax register of Novgorod's Vot'ska county], *Vremennik Imp. Obshchestva istorii i drevnostei Rossiiskikh* 11 (1851): materialy, 1–464, for the years 7003 and 7008 [1495 and 1500].

2. *Novgorodskie pistsovye knigi izdannye Arkheograficheskoi komissiei* [Novgorod cadastres published by the Archaeographic Commission] (St. Petersburg: Tip. Bezobrazova, 1859–1910), 6 vols. and index [reprint, Slavistic Printings and Reprintings 212, vols. 1–3 (The Hague: Mouton, 1969)].

3. A. M. Andriiashev, "Materialy po istoricheskoi geografii Novgorodskoi zemli: Shelonskaia piatina po pistsovym knigam 1496–1576 gg." [Documents on the historical geography of Novgorodian lands: The Shelon county cadastres for 1496–1576], *ChOIDR* 3 (1914) [entire volume].

4. N. V. Kalachev, ed., *Pistsovye knigi Moskovskogo gosudarstva,* pt. 1, *Pistsovye knigi XVI veka* [Cadastres of the Muscovite state, part 1, Cadastres of the sixteenth century] (St. Petersburg: Izd. Imp. Russkogo geograficheskogo obshchestva, 1872 [2nd ed., St. Petersburg: Tip. II-go otd. Sobstvennoi E. I. V. Kantseliarii, 1877].

5. *Pistsovaia i perepisnaia knigi XVII veka po Nizhnemu Novgorodu* [A cadastre and census record from the 17th century for the city of Nizhnii Novgorod], *RIB* 17 (St. Petersburg: Sinodal'naia tip., 1896).

6. Archimandrite Leonid, ed., *Akty Iverskogo sviatoozerskogo monastyria (1582–1706)* [Acts of the Iverskii Sviatoozerskii Monastery, 1582–1706], *RIB* 5 (St. Petersburg: V Tip. A. Transhelia, 1878); and *Akty kholmogorskoi i ustiuzhskoi eparkhii* [Acts of the Kholmogorsk and Ustiug bishoprics], *RIB* 14 (St. Petersburg: Tip. A. Katanskogo, 1894).

7. *PSRL.*

8. V. Borisov, *Opisanie goroda Shui.*

9. *Perepisnaia kniga goroda Moskvy 1638 goda* [The Moscow census book of 1638] (Moscow: Tip. M. P. Shchepkina, 1881).

10. *Pistsovye knigi Riazanskogo kraia* [Cadastres of the Riazan district] (Riazan: Tip. M. S. Orlova, 1898–1904).

11. V. V. Maikov, *Kniga pistsovaia po Novgorodu Velikomu kontsa XVI v.* [Cadastre for Great Novgorod from the end of the sixteenth century] (St. Petersburg: Tip. M. A. Aleksandrova, 1911).

12. "Pskov i ego prigorody: Pistsovaia kniga po Pskovu i ego prigorodam XVI v." [Pskov and its suburbs: A cadastre from Pskov and its suburbs from the sixteenth century], *Sbornik Moskovskogo Arkhiva Ministerstva iustitsii* [Collection of the Moscow Archive of the Ministry of Justice] 5 (1913), entire volume, and 6 (1914).

13. Mikulin Chronicle: (a) *Mikulinskaia letopis', sostavlennaia po drevnim aktam, ot 1354 do 1678 goda* [The Mikulin Chronicle, compiled according to ancient acts, 1354–1678] (Moscow: V Tip. V. Got'e, 1854); and (b) A. Vershinskii, ed., "Mikulinskaia letopis'" [The Mikulin Chronicle], *Tverskaia starina* [Antiquities of Tver] February (1911): 46–53; March (1911): 38–46; April (1911): 35–45; May (1911): 41–44; June (1911): 41–48; July (1911): 34–41; August (1911): 48–52; September (1911): 25–29; October–November (1911): 27–34; December (1911): 23–30; January–February (1912): 63–67.

14. A. A. Titov, ed., *Dozornye i perepisnye knigi drevnego goroda Rostova* [Overseers' records and census books of the old town of Rostov] (Moscow: M. N. Lavrov, 1880).

15. A. A. Titov, *Iaroslavskii uezd* [The Iaroslav district] (Moscow: I. A. Vakhrameev, 1884).

16. *Akty istoricheskie* [Historical acts], collected and published by the Archaeographic Commission (5 vols.) and the Supplements (12 vols.), St. Petersburg, 1841–72. [Vols. 1–3, St. Petersburg: V Tip. E. Pratsa, 1841; vols. 4–5, St. Petersburg: V Tip. II-go Otdeleniia Sobstvennoi E. I. V. Kantseliarii, 1842; supplements, St. Petersburg: V Tip. II-go Otdeleniia Sobstvennoi E. I. V. Kantseliarii, 1846–72.]

[*Editors' note:* For explanations and definitions of the technical administrative terminology appearing throughout this section, see Pushkarev, *Dictionary of Russian Historical Terms;* Dal', *Tolkovyi slovar';* Sreznevskii, *Materialy;* and S. G. Barkhudarov, main ed., *Slovar' russkogo iazyka XI–XVII vv.* [A dictionary of the Russian language, 11th–17th centuries], vols. 1– (Moscow: Nauka, 1975–). In Findeizen's original text, there is a map showing the geographical distribution of the *skomorokhi;* this map is not included in this translation.]

175. Maikov, *Kniga pistsovaia po Novgorodu Velikomu,* 69, 118, 159, 263–64. [There were five such "ends" or neighborhoods, each under an "end assembly" (*veche*), according to Thompson, *Novgorod the Great,* 2.]

176. Settlements [*pogosty*] of Derevskaia *piatina,* where there were villages named Skomorokhovo or where individual members of this profession lived, include Posonskii (the new clearing [*pochinok*] and hamlet of Skomorokhovo); Kolomenskii; Mlevskii (in the hamlet of Gryzhino, Ivashka Skomorokh's house); Mikhailovskii (in the hamlet of Trubakha, Mikitka Skomorokh's house, and a Skomorokhovo hamlet); Vel'evskii (in the hamlet Fishkovo, the house of Senka Skomorokh; in the hamlet Pestovitsy, the house of Senka Skomorokh); Molviatitskii (Sysoiko Skomorokh's house in the hamlet of Sviattsovo; Mikhal. Skomorokh's house in the hamlet of Bykovo); Bukhovskii (Isachko Skomorokh's house in the hamlet of Zakhozhai; in the hamlet of Mikhalevo, Mikulka Skomorokh's house; in the hamlet of Ilomlia, Stepanko Skomorokh's house; Semenovskii (Vasko Skomorokh's house in the hamlet of Stavtsovo); Iazholobitskii (Eremka Skomorokh's house in the hamlet of Ontsiforovo); Lokotskoi (in the hamlet of Paltsovo, Gridka Skomorokh's house); Belgskii (the hamlet of Iashkovo, Iakimko

Skomorokh's house); Bronnitsskoi and Sytinskii (two hamlets named Skomorokhovo). All cited in *Novgorodskie pistsovye knigi*, 1:50, 65, 73, 152, 156, 208, 219, 238, 653, 658, 756, 758, 760, 788, 817; 2:43, 416, 446, 474, and 477).

177. In the town of Demon [the same meaning in English] (the hamlet of Skomorokhovo and in the hamlet of Domashevo, Gridka Skomorokh's house; Iakush Skomorokh's house in the recent clearing [*pochinok*] of Kozlovo); the *pogosty* of Polonovskoi (the hamlet Skomorokhovo) and Borkovskii (in the hamlet of Drest'ianka, Borisko Skomorokh's house); listed in *Novgorodskie pistsovye knigi*, 2:499, 508, 548, 581, 591.

178. Mikheiko Skomorokh of the Kursk district; see *Novgorodskie pistsovye knigi*, 2:624, 631.

179. In the *pogost* of the Zhabenskaia *desiatina* [2.7 acres], the homes of Luk'ianka Skomorokh, Minka and Sofronka Skomorokh (*Novgorodskie pistsovye knigi*, 2:704).

180. Ibid., 2:821.

181. Ibid., 2:827. [Findeizen's references in nn. 181–84 are to "Nov. per. knigi"; the references are from *Novgorodskie pistsovye knigi*.]

182. Ibid., 3:236.

183. Ibid., 3:494, 518, 528.

183A. "Perepisnaia okladnaia kniga po Novugorodu Vot'skoi piatiny," 112. [This is Findeizen's note, labeled in his text as 183a.]

184. *Novgorodskie pistsovye knigi*, 3:556.

185. "Perepisnaia okladnaia kniga po Novugorodu Vot'skoi piatiny," 177.

186. *Novgorodskie pistsovye knigi*, 4:117, 211, 379, 401, 403, 466, 480; 5:694. In the hamlet of Zakhol'e in the Kotor settlement, Ontonka Skomorokh's house; in the settlement of Pazherevitskii in the hamlet Lamovo, the house of the landless peasant Ivanka Skomorokh; in the hamlet of Ostrov Gorodenka, the houses of Stepanka and Mishuka Skomorokh; and in the hamlet of Baikovo, the house of the landless peasant Kuzemka Marka Skomorokh.

187. Ibid., 6:219, 403.

188. Chechulin, *Goroda Moskovskogo gosudarstva*, 51; "Perepisnaia okladnaia kniga po Novugorodu Vot'skoi piatiny," 12 (1852): 3. In the town of Iama there were houses belonging to the following *skomorokhi*: Ignat, Kuzemka Olukhnov, Ofonoska and Radivonko, Zelenka and Olekseika. In the town of Korela, listed as "young men without trade settled in the area by the Fedorovka River," are the houses of the *skomorokhi* Belavo, Vasko Pribytok, Suverets Maloi, Ivashko Rysko, Vorobei, and Polezhai. From this list it is clear that the *skomorokhi*, when listed in the census books, are sometimes listed not by their first names (always in the diminutive form) but by their nicknames.

189. The data concerning the towns of Toropets, Ustiuzhna, Kolomna, Mozhaisk, Tula, Kazan, and Sviiazhsk are taken from Chechulin, *Goroda Moskovskogo gosudarstva;* the author did not cite more detailed data from manuscript sources.

190. Karamzin, *Istoriia gosudarstva rossiiskogo* 6: n. 629.

190A. [*Editors' note:* A *dudka* is a kind of flute or recorder-like pipe. Aumayr, *Historische Untersuchungen an Bezeichnungen von Musikinstrumenten*, 29–32, notes that the term can also refer to bagpipes.]

190B. [*Editors' note:* Thanks to Daniel C. Waugh and Henry Cooper for interpreting this term.]

191. *Pistsovye knigi Moskovskogo gosudarstva*, pt. 2: 76, 113, 126, 136, 197, 277, 281, 289, 297, 310, 342, 350, 462, 512, 717, 739.

192. Ibid., 1082, 1090, 1203.

193. *Pistsovaia i perepisnaia kniga XVII veka po Nizhnemu Novgorodu*, 130, 140, 143, 163, 279.

194. *RIB* 14:244.

195. Leonid, *Akty Iverskogo sviatoozerskogo monastyria (1582–1706)*, 333, 1018, 1063.

196. Titov, "Iaroslavskii uezd," 75.

196A. [*Editors' note:* Dal', *Tolkovyi slovar'*, 4:203: "*skomorokh* s Presni naigryval pesni."]

197. Adam Olearii, *Opisanie puteshestviia v Moskoviiu i cherez Moskoviiu v Persiiu i obratno* [Description of travels to Muscovy and through Muscovy to Persia and back], introduction, translation, notes, and index by A. M. Loviagin, with nineteen drawings on separate sheets and sixty-six drawings in the text (St. Petersburg: A. S. Suvorin, 1906).

198. Olearii, *Opisanie puteshestviia v Moskoviiu*, 18. [Translation from Baron, *The Travels of Olearius*, 48–49. See also Adam Olearius, *Vermehrte Newe Beschreibung*, 19 ("mit einer Lauten und Geigen").]

198A. [*Editors' note:* Olearius mentions lutes [*Laute*] again; in Gruzino "the *streltsi* [musketeers], having drunk several cups of vodka, helped entertain us with two lutes and games with the bear" (Baron, *The Travels of Olearius*, 51); see also Olearius, *Vermehrte Newe Beschreibung*, 23; on p. 213 there is apparently another depiction of dancing, in which several people have joined hands and formed a circle.]

199. D. A. Rovinskii, *Russkie narodnye kartinki* [Russian folk drawings] (St. Petersburg: Tip. Imp. Akademii nauk, 1881–93), 5:225. [Also reproduced in Baron, *The Travels of Olearius*, foll. 150; and in Olearius, *Vermehrte Newe Beschreibung*, 193.]

200. Olearii, *Opisanie puteshestviia v Moskoviiu*, 190. [Translation from Baron, *The Travels of Olearius*, 142; see also Olearius, *Vermehrte Newe Beschreibung*, 193–94.]

201. Ibid., 189. [See Olearius, *Vermehrte Newe Beschreibung*, 193; and Baron, *The Travels of Olearius*, 142, where the ambassador is identified as Jakob Ulfeldt.]

202. *Akty, sobrannye v bibliotekakh i arkhivakh Rossiiskoi Imper. Arkheograficheskoi ekspeditsiei Imp. Akad. nauk* [Documents collected in libraries and archives by the Russian Imperial Archaeographic Expedition of the Imperial Academy of Sciences] (St. Petersburg: V Tip. II-go otdeleniia Sobstvennoi E. I. V. Kantseliarii, 1836), 1:62, no. 86.

203. Ibid., 117, no. 145.

204. Ibid., 122, no. 151. ["A skomorokhom u nikh lovchei i ego tiun po derevniam silno (i.e. nasil'no—N.F.) igrati ne osvobozhaet: kto ikh pustit na dvor dobrovol'no, i oni tut igraiut; a uchnut u nikh skomorokhi po derevniam igrati silno, i oni ikh iz volosti vyshliut von bezpenno" (Findeizen, *Ocherki* 1:156).]

205. Ibid., 140, no. 171.

206. Ibid., 153, no. 181.

207. Ibid., 180, no. 201.

208. Ibid., 207, no. 217.

209. Ibid., 257, no. 241.

209A. Ibid. 267, no. 244. [This is Findeizen's note, labeled n. 209a in the text.]

210. Borisov, *Opisanie goroda Shui*, 451–52.

210A. [*Editors' note:* Prince Andrei Kurbskii was one of Tsar Ivan's friends and advisers; he broke with the ruler over his harsh treatment of the aristocracy, instigated as an attempt to consolidate the power of the throne over the quasi-independent principalities. Kurbskii sent a series of highly critical letters to Ivan from his self-exile in Lithuania. See J. L. I. Fennell, *The Correspondence between Prince A. M. Kurbsky and Tsar Ivan IV of Russia, 1564–1579* (Cambridge: Cambridge University Press, 1955), 242–43. Edward L. Keenan, however, in his *Kurbskii-Groznyi Apocrypha: The Seventeenth-century Genesis of the "Correspondence" Attributed to Prince A. M. Kurbskii and Tsar Ivan IV* (Cambridge, Mass.: Harvard University Press, 1971), considers this correspondence to be a later forgery.]

211. Bands of *skomorokhi* existed long before the onset of the Time of Troubles. Thus chapter 41, question 19, of the Stoglav established their presence: "in remote parts *skomorokhi* move, assembled in bands of 60, 70, and up to 100 persons, and they go around to villages and peasants' houses and eat and drink to excess; they steal cattle from pens and beat people up on the roads" [Emchenko, *Stoglav*, 311].

One therefore understands why the administrative order banning *skomorokhi* from performing in villages without invitation was issued; documents relating to that ban were cited above. By covering up their activities with singing and dancing, the *skomorokhi* did commit robbery, giving their deeds a humorous character. Sakharov, *Pesni russkogo naroda,* 4:103, cites one such act of thievery by *skomorokhi,* recollected in folk memory as follows:

> Akh, Suzdal'tsy, Volodimertsy,
> Ni skakat', ni pliasat' s kolokol'chikami,
> S kolokol'chikami, bolobol'chikami!
> Akh, stanesh' govorit'-vygovarivati,
> Cherno na belo vyvorachivati!

> Ah, you folks from Suzdal' and from Vladimir,
> Don't jump or dance with jingle-bells,
> With jingle-bells, bingle-jells,
> Ah, you start talking and arguing,
> And things turn inside out [black turns into white].

Beliaev pointed out the *skomorokh* character of this song in his interesting study of the *skomorokhi* ["O skomorokhakh"]. "To this day," he tells us (that is, in the 1850s), "you can hear from many old-timers stories of how *skomorokhi* would split into two groups, one of which would be in the village to steal things, while the other would entertain the inhabitants with singing and fortune telling, often telling them the very thing that was happening at the time in their own homes" (83). (That is exactly what our first operatic *skomorokh,* Toropka-Golovan, does in Verstovskii's opera, *Askol'dova mogila* [Askold's tomb], in the scene in which Nadezhda is kidnapped while the ballad "Blizko goroda Slavianska" [Near the city of Slaviansk] is sung, and the same scene occurs in the source for this opera, the novel by Zagoskin.) According to Beliaev, in the village of Likova in Moscow province, near Mozhaisk Road, there is a story about a band of wandering *skomorokhi* who take up position near the village and entertain the inhabitants with this song:

> Ai, matushka Likova,
> Prishei k shube rukava!

> Ai, mother Likova,
> Sew the sleeve on the fur coat!

"When they returned home from that performance," says Beliaev, "they found most of their sheep missing" (Beliaev, "O skomorokhakh," 83 n.). Later singers [*volochebniki*] recalled the earlier *skomorokhi,* as in this song from Belorussia (published in P. V. Shein, *Belorusskie narodnye pesni* [Belorussian folk songs] (St. Petersburg: Tip. Maikova, 1874), 82 [reprint, *Belaruskiia narodnyia pesni* (Minsk: Dziarzh. vyd-va BSSR, 1962)]:

> Ishli-briali volochebniki,
> Vo tsiamnoi nochi, da po griaznoi griazi,
> Volochilisia, da i obmochilisia,
> Shatalisia i boutalisia,
> K bogatomu domu pytalisia.

> The dragging singers went with a bang and a clatter
> Through a dark night on a muddy dirt road;
> They dragged themselves and got soaking wet,
> They roamed around noisily,
> And tried for a wealthy house.

Even the music of their songs is similar to the songs of the *skomorokhi*. Rimskii-Korsakov, in his collection *Russkie narodnye pesni* [Russian folk songs] (1870), no. 47, includes a song of the *volocheb-niki* from Smolensk province in which singers extend Easter greetings. The tune is fast, joyful, and *skomorokh*-like; the text, except for the refrain "Khristos voskres" [Christ is risen], also reminds one of the bygone adventures of the *skomorokhi:*

> Dala lyn', dala lyn'! Po iaichen'ku!
> Ty doma ne doma khoziainushko?
> On ne kazhetsia—velichaetsia.
> On sidit za stolom podpershis' kostylem;
> Kto ne dast kontsa piroga—my korovu za roga;
> Kto ne dast paru iaits—my progonim vsekh ovets;
> Kto ne dast soloniny kusok—my svin'iu zavalim.

> Dala-lyn, dala-lyn, an egg for each!
> Are you home, at home, dear host?
> He pretends he's not, he's too good for us.
> He sits by the table, leaning on a crutch;
> Whoever doesn't give us the end-piece of a pie—we'll take his cow by the horns;
> Whoever doesn't give us a couple of eggs—we'll chase away all his sheep;
> Whoever doesn't give us a piece of salted meat—we'll grab his pig.

212. *Akty, sobrannye v bibliotekakh i arkhivakh Rossiiskoi Imp. Arkheograficheskoi ekspeditsiei*, 3:264.

213. Ibid., 4:138.

214. Along with these repressive measures, in the same period one encounters even in literary documents statements directed against *skomoroshestvo*. Thus, for example, in a seventeenth-century manuscript in the collection of Count Viazemskii (manuscript in the Society for Old Literature [RNB], no. 79, fol. 128v) there is a chapter on *skomorokhi:* "When a musician [*gudets*] or *skomrakh* [*skomorokh*] or anyone of this sort invites you, you eagerly accept and spend most of the day only in such doings. [Yet when] God and His prophets and apostles summon us, we yawn in church and scratch ourselves and think of other things. When there are *skomrasy* or [at the time of the] *rusaliia*, you don't mind the rain, and the wind and water beating you in the face, and stand there enduring the cold and wet and the distant travel you had to make and nothing restrains you from going. But if it is to come to church, rain is quite an obstacle. And if one were to ask you who Amos or A[v]diia are, or about the number of prophets or apostles, you can't even open your mouth, but if it is about horses or *skomrasy* or about horror stories, well, then you can talk."

215. In a foreword to his collection of Arkhangel'sk *byliny*, A. D. Grigor'ev [in *Arkhangel'skie by-liny*] refers to the preservation in that part of the country of a whole repertory of *skomorokh* relics, thus confirming the influence of the *skomorokhi* along the river Pinega. "Most of the *skomorokh stariny*," he writes, "are characterized not only by their joking content, but by the setting and cheerfully fast tune . . . [1:xx] If the repertory of the bygone *skomorokhi* allows us only to presume the existence of *skomorokhi* in this area, that in the village of Shotogorka in the Pinega district there are several peas-ant families with the name Skomorokhov [. . .] definitely indicates that the *skomorokhi* did at one time live along the river Pinega, at least in Shotogorka" [1:xxiii]. Grigor'ev thus presumes with good reason that having been persecuted in the central districts, the *skomorokhi* hid in remote and faraway areas of the Muscovite state. [Our thanks to Jack Haney for his advice and expertise in translating this series of texts.]

216. The subject matter of this old tale, so characteristic of the *skomorokh* creations, relates to the second marriage of Ivan the Terrible to Princess Maria Temriukovna Cherkasskaia. Although such a subject would seem to prevent it from becoming part of the *skomorokh* repertory, the light character of

the tune and the joking details in the text permit us to make that assumption; apparently this a very old *skomorokh* creation:

> A Kostriuk poskakivaet,
> A Kostriuk popliasyvaet;
> A Kostriuk tseres stol skotsil,
> A Kostriuk pit'ia spleskal.

> And Kostriuk keeps on hopping,
> And Kostriuk keeps on dancing,
> And Kostriuk jumped over the table,
> And Kostriuk splashed the drinks.
> (Grigor'ev, *Arkhangel'skie byliny,* 1:363)

216A. [*Editors' note:* Zguta, *Russian Minstrels,* 49–50, discusses these "Usy" or "Usishcha" songs as a confluence of *skomorokh* traditions and brigand or outlaw songs; see also Propp, *Russian Folk Lyrics,* 29–30. Variants of this type appear in the eighteenth-century collection by Kirsha Danilov, discussed above in chapter 4 and in volume 2 of Findeizen's work. Many thanks to Dan Newton for his help in deciphering this text.]

216B. [*Editors' note:* N. Abramychev, *Sbornik russkikh narodnykh pesen* [Collection of Russian folk songs] (St. Petersburg: M. Vasil'ev, 1879).]

216C. [*Editors' note:* There are variants of Foma and Erema woodcuts in A. Sytova, *The Lubok: Russian Folk Pictures, 17th–19th century* (Leningrad: Aurora, 1984), nos. 34 and 64.]

217. T. Filippov and N. Rimskii-Korsakov, *40 narodnykh pesen* [40 folk songs] (Moscow: P. Iurgenson, 1882).

218. The refrain [bars 5-8] is repeated after every verse and is omitted here.

219. Pal'chikov, *Krest'ianskie pesni, zapisannye v sele Nikolaeve Ufimskoi gubernii.*

6. Music and Musical Instruments in Russian Miniatures, Woodcuts, and Glossaries

[*Editors' note:* Chapters 6 and 7 survey the musical instruments of Russia. Chapter 6 discusses pictorial documentation in miniatures in manuscripts and early broadsides, as well as references in interpretive dictionaries and glossaries which date from the sixteenth and seventeenth centuries and introduce new musical terminology to their Russian audience. Chapter 7 is devoted to folk instruments. On the subject of musical instruments in general, Manfred Aumayr's *Historische Untersuchungen an Bezeichnungen von Musikinstrumenten in der russischen Sprache* provides solid information, which may be supplemented with articles in *ME,* the *Muzykal'nyi entsiklopedicheskii slovar', IRM* 1, and Roizman, *Organ.* Among the many Russian-language studies of folk instruments, the one best known is Konstantin Aleksandrovich Vertkov, ed., *Atlas muzykal'nykh instrumentov narodov SSSR* [An atlas of musical instruments of the peoples of the USSR] (Moscow: Gos. muzykal'noe izdatel'stvo, 1963); there is an English translation by Natasha Bushnell Yampolsky (originally a B.A. thesis, University of Washington, 1972, with a second, revised edition from 1980). See also Vertkov's *Russkie narodnye muzykal'nye instrumenty* [Russian folk musical instruments] (Leningrad: Muzyka, 1975).

In these chapters Findeizen refers to Karion Istomin (1640s–1717), who worked in the Printing Office, finally rising to become its head in 1698–1701. Istomin wrote or compiled a variety of sources, in particular an illustrated primer, published in Moscow in 1694, which is a valuable source containing many images of musical instruments. A complete facsimile edition of this primer, based on a copy in RNB, has been issued as Karion Istomin, *Bukvar'* [Primer], commentary by V. I. Lukianenko and M. A. Alekseevna (Leningrad: Avrora, 1981); see also the article in *MERSH* 15:16 and the survey in Max J. Okenfuss, *The Discovery of Childhood in Russia: The Evidence of the Slavic Primer* (Newtonville, Mass.: Oriental Research Partners, 1980).

Findeizen also uses information from Grigorii Karpovich Kotoshikhin (ca. 1630–1667), *O Rossii v tsarstvovanie Alekseia Mikhailovicha* [On Russia during the reign of Aleksei Mikhailovich], which was re-edited, with commentary, by Anne E. Pennington (Oxford: Clarendon; New York: Oxford University Press, 1980) and which is also available in a reprint of the 4th edition, from St. Petersburg, 1906, reprinted in Grigorii Karpovich Kotoshikhin, *O Rossii v tsarstvovanie Alekseia Mikhailovicha* [On Russia during the reign of Aleksei Mikhailovich], *Moskoviia i Evropa* [Muscovy and Europe], ed. A. Liberman and S. Shokarev, in the series Istoriia Rossii i doma Romanovykh v memuarakh sovremennikov XVII–XX vv. [A history of Russia and the house of the Romanovs in memoirs by contemporaries, 17th–20th centuries] (Moscow: Fond Sergeia Dubova, 2000), 11–146. Kotoshikhin's career is summed up briskly by Pennington in her article in *MERSH* 17:236–39, as follows: "Civil servant. Traitor. Emigrant. Writer. Murderer." He worked in the Foreign Office, passed information to the Swedish government, and finally fled Muscovy; his treatise was written in Sweden.

Findeizen's position as a musical ethnographer must have impressed upon him the necessity of discussing repeatedly the role and evolution of musical instruments and their use in folk practice. Yet in spite of its similarity to the preceding chapter, Findeizen's discussion of folk instruments in chapter 7 brings out new material. Although some of the instruments he refers to in this chapter have been mentioned earlier, Findeizen manages to offer elaborate presentations of the musical instruments in the folklore of Russia and Ukraine (in those days called "Little Russia" and thus a part of "all the Russias"—we have retained Findeizen's terminology in this translation).]

219A. [*Editors' note:* The names of the musicians are listed as in Findeizen, transliterated from the Cyrillic text of the illustration. See 1 and 2 Chronicles.]

220. Buhle, *Die musikalischen Instrumente in den Miniaturen des frühen Mittelalters,* Plate 13.

221. Ibid., Plate 14.

222. The *azbukovniki* were also known under other names. A. Karpov, who published a study of the *azbukovniki* of the Solovetskii [monastic] library, lists four remarkable dictionaries of ancient writing, in both full and abridged versions, which were widely used in Russia:

> 1. *Slovesa ot grecheskago iazyka i ot sirskago, i ot evreiskago, i ot latyn'skago, i ot sloven'skago* [Words from the Greek language, and from Syrian, from Hebrew, from Latin, and from Slavonic];

> 2. *Tolkovanie o nerazumnykh slovesekh pervoe nachnetsia psaltyr' krasen s gusl'my* [Interpretation of incomprehensible words starting first with the Psalter, [made] beautiful with the *gusli*];

> 3. *Se zhe pritochne rechesia* [How to say it correctly];

> 4. *Tolkovanie neudob' poznavaemym v pisanii rechem, ponezhe polozheniia sut' rechi v knigakh ot nachalnykh prevodnik, ova sloven'ski, i na ser'bski, i drugaia bolgar'ski, i na grecheski, i po prochikh iazyk, ikhzhe neudovolishasia prelozhiti na russkii* [Interpretation of difficult words found in writings, as the words have appeared in books from the original translators, in Slavonic, Serbian, Bulgarian, Greek, and other languages, which are unsatisfactorily translated into Russian].

Our ancestors liked the *azbukovniki* for they provided readings in all branches of learning; a single book contained a great deal of interesting material culled from a variety of works that came to Russia from the East and the West. But, as Karpov justly remarks, the *azbukovniki* and similar books also spread quite a few strange errors, superstitious tales, and absurd falsehoods. In the absence of any kind of scholarly education, everything was received and accepted indiscriminately with full faith. See A. Karpov, *Azbukovniki, ili alfavity inostrannykh rechei, po spiskam Solovetskoi biblioteki* [*Azbukovniki* or alphabets of foreign words, based on manuscripts in the Solovetskii Library] (Kazan: Tip. Imp. universiteta, 1878 (in 1877 published as an appendix to the periodical *Pravoslavnyi sobesednik*

[The Orthodox interlocutor]); A. V. Prussak, *Opisanie azbukovnikov, khraniashchikhsia v rukopis-nom otdelenii Imperatorskoi publichnoi biblioteki* [Description of the *azbukovniki* in the Manuscript Division of the Imperial Public Library], in *Pamiatniki drevnei pis'mennosti* [Monuments of early writing] 186 (St. Petersburg: M. A. Aleksandrov, 1915); Shirskii, "Ocherki drevnikh slaviano-russkikh slovarei" [Essays on old Slavonic-Russian dictionaries], *Filologicheskie zapiski* [Philological notes] 1869, fasc. I and II; Batalin, "Drevne-russkie azbukovniki" [Old Russian *azbukovniki*], *Filologicheskie zapiski* (1873); Buslaev, "Dopolneniia i pribavleniia k 2-mu tomu 'Skazanii Sakharova'" [Addenda to the second volume of "Sakharov's Tales"]; and the first volume of N. Kalachev, *Arkhiv istoriko-iuridicheskikh svedenii, otnosiashchikhsia do Rossii* [Archive of historical-legal information relating to Russia], 3 vols. (Moscow: Tip. A. Semena, 1850). [There is a second edition from St. Petersburg: Tip. i lit. A. E. Landau, 1876; it is not clear to which edition Findeizen refers. See the discussion and textual analysis of many of these sources in L. S. Kovtun, *Azbukovniki XVI–XVII vv.* [Alphabets of the 16th–17th centuries] (Leningrad: Nauka, 1989); and in V. V. Protopopov, *Russkaia mysl' o muzyke v XVII veke* [Russian thought about music in the 17th century] (Moscow: Muzyka, 1989), 8–15; see also Morosan, "*Penie* and *Musikiia*," esp. 152f. Sakharov's *Skazaniia russkogo naroda* [Tales of the Russian people] was recently reissued in Tula: Priokskoe knizhnoe izdatel'stvo, 2000.]

222A. [*Editors' note:* Although this text contains an internal date of 1596, the manuscript itself is of a later date, with watermarks pointing to as late as the 1630s; see Kovtun, *Azbukovniki*, 16 n. 20.]

222B. [*Editors' note:* On Sakharov's work, see n. 222 above. Kovtun, *Azbukovniki*, 19–20, notes that Sakharov combined text from two different manuscripts (GIM, Uvar. 310 (2088) and 311 (2094).]

222C. [*Editors' note:* An edition of Berynda's work is available as V. V. Nimchuk, ed., *Leksykon slovenoros'kyi Pamvy Beryndy* [Pamva Berynda's Slavonic-Russian lexicon] (Kiev: AN URSR, 1961).]

222D. [*Editors' note:* There is a typographical error in Findeizen, *Ocherki* 1:179ff, where the manuscript is placed in the Solov'ev collection instead of the Solovetskii; see Kovtun, *Azbukovniki*, 9–10 (an extensive classified listing of sources). References have been corrected throughout.]

222E. Dal', *Tolkovyi slovar'*, 1:236, clarifies: "band of *volochebniki* [wandering or, literally, dragging singers] go with a *gudok* and a bagpipe [*volynka*]." [See n. 211 above. Note 222E is Findeizen's, listed in his work as n. 222a.]

223. The Chudov manuscript is similar to manuscript no. 376 in the Rumiantsev Museum [RGB, Rum. 376; see below on the identification of this source], which dates from the end of the seventeenth century, 7 *svobodnykh mudrostei* [Seven liberal arts; the word *mudrosti* means, literally, wisdoms]: (1) Grammar, (2) Dialectics, (3) Rhetoric, (4) Music, (5) Arithmetic, (6) Geometry (actually, Geography), and (7) Astronomy. The Society of Friends of Old Literature published the *Pervoe uchenie musikiiskikh soglasii* [First lesson in musical concordances] in 1877 from a manuscript in the library of Count P. P. Viazemskii. In the manuscript that lesson is headed "Moudrost' chetvertaia Musika" [The fourth art—music]. [For a brief summary, in English, of the seven liberal arts in Muscovy, see Claudia Jensen, "Nikolai Diletskii's 'Grammatika' (Grammar) and the Musical Culture of Seventeenth-century Muscovy" (Ph.D. diss., Princeton University, 1987), 254–60, and the bibliography cited therein; see also the discussion of these sources in Protopopov, *Russkaia mysl' o muzyke*, 16–21, with a listing of sources on p. 18. Spafarii's text is published in Nikolai Spafarii, *Esteticheskie traktaty* [Treatises on aesthetics], ed. O. A. Belobrova (Leningrad: Nauka, 1978), where, on p. 153, the author describes the source from the Rumiantsev collection in RGB as no. 375 rather than no. 376, as in Findeizen. *Pervoe uchenie* was published in OLDP Izdaniia 6 (St. Petersburg: Lit. A. Beggrova, 1877); Protopopov, *Russkaia mysl' o muzyke*, 18 n., identifies this source as RNB, OLDP, 129.]

224. Buslaev, *Istoricheskaia khristomatiia*, 1114.

224A. [*Editors' note:* In his description of the first Russian music his party encountered, in Ladoga, Olearius labels the instrument he heard as a violin ("mit einer Lauten und Geigen . . ."). See Olearius, *Vermehrte Newe Beschreibung*, 19.]

224B. [*Editors' note:* This is probably an old number for this source; Kovtun, *Azbukovniki,* 9–10, lists several sources from the Solovetskii collection, all with different numbers. Findeizen mentions this source in n. 222 above.]

225. *Katalog tserkovnykh i dr. predmetov drevnostei, nakhodiashchikhsia v drevlekhranilishche Kostromskogo tserk.-ist. obshch. v pokoiakh Mikhaila Fedorovicha Romanova, chto v Ipat'evskom mona-styre* [Catalog of ecclesiastical and other ancient objects presently in the repository of the Kostroma Society for Church History in the chambers of [Tsar] Mikhail Fedorovich Romanov, in the Ipat'ev Monastery] (Kostroma, 1914), 72.

226. The work is described by Rovinskii in *Russkie narodnye kartini,* 2: no. 696; the primer is reproduced in the fourth volume [containing illustrations]. Before the revolution, the original was in the home of the Romanov boyars in Moscow. In Count Viazemskii's manuscript collection [now in RGB], there is an eighteenth-century manuscript (F.CXXIX) titled *Azbuka Kariona Istomina s aglitskim perevodom* [Karion Istomin's Primer with an English translation]; see *Opisanie rukopisei kn. P. P. Viazemskogo* [A description of the manuscripts of Prince P. P. Viazemskii], Pamiatniki drevnei pis'mennosti i iskusstva [Monuments of early writing and art] 119 (St. Petersburg: Tip. glavnogo upr. delov, 1902), 132. [As noted above, a facsimile edition of Karion's alphabet is available in an edition by V. I. Lukianenko and M. A. Alekseevna.]

227. Karion (Istomin), a *ieromonakh* [monk with the rank of a priest] of the Chudov Monastery, died in September 1717. He was a member of Patriarch Ioakim's retinue and was a humane pedagogue and prolific writer, translator, and poet attached to the court. On Karion, see *RBS* 8:525.

228. Some of them were reproduced in the less expensive second edition: *Russkie narodnye kartinki, sobral i opisal D. Rovinskii* [Russian folk drawings, collected and described by D. Rovinskii], posthumous publication printed under the supervision of N. Sobko, 2 vols. (St. Petersburg: Izd. P. Golike, 1900). [A brief discussion, in English, of the *lubki* is in Alison Hilton, *Russian Folk Art* (Bloomington: Indiana University Press, 1995), 107–13.]

228A. [*Editors' note:* This image appears in Dianne E. Farrell, "Medieval Popular Humor in Russian Eighteenth-century *lubki,*" *Slavic Review* 50, no. 3 (1991): 551–65. Farrell discusses most of the figures appearing in the woodcuts Findeizen presents here.]

228B. [*Editors' note:* There are variants of Foma and Erema and Savos'ka and Paramoshka woodcuts in Sytova, *The Lubok: Russian Folk Pictures,* nos. 33, 34, 64.]

228C. [*Editors' note:* There is a color reproduction of "The Parable of the Wealthy and Wretched Lazarus" in Sytova, *The Lubok: Russian Folk Pictures,* no. 13; no. 14 in that volume is a color reproduction of Findeizen's fig. 57, "The Banquet of the Pious and the Profane," which also includes a bagpipe.]

228D. [*Editors' note: Maslenitsa,* or Butter Week, corresponds to Shrovetide; on its rituals and traditions, see D. S. Likhachev, A. M. Panchenko, and N. V. Ponyrko, *Smekh v drevnei Rusi* [Laughter in early Rus'] (Leningrad: Nauka, 1984), esp. 175–202. *Semik* was a spring fertility holiday occurring on the seventh Thursday after Easter; a brief discussion of its rituals (and those of *Maslenitsa*), in English, is in Hilton, *Russian Folk Art,* 110, 149–51, and see also Farrell, "Medieval Popular Humor." There is a color engraving from the nineteenth century illustrating the *semik* festival in Moscow in Sytova, *The Lubok: Russian Folk Pictures,* no. 131; other musical instruments appear in color reproductions in this volume in nos. 20, 38, 119, 126, 148–49, 157, 164, 166, and elsewhere. A color reproduction of Findeizen's fig. 60 can be found in Iu. Ovsiannikov, *Lubok. Russkie narodnye kartinki XVII–XVIII vv. / The Lubok. Russian Broadsides of the 17th–18th Centuries* (Moscow: Sovetskii khudozhnik, 1968), no. 42; see also the instruments depicted in nos. 36 and 37.]

228E. [*Editors' note:* There are several versions of "The Mice Bury the Cat" in Sytova, *The Lubok: Russian Folk Pictures,* nos. 17, 92, 144, from the eighteenth and nineteenth centuries; a somewhat sim-plified variant of Findeizen's version is in Ovsiannikov, *Lubok,* no. 31. For a reinterpretation of the sub-ject matter of this series of images, see M. A. Alekseeva, "Graviura na dereve 'Myshi kota na pogost volokut'—pamiatnik russkogo narodnogo tvorchestva kontsa XVII–nachala XVIII v." [The woodcut "The Mice Bury the Cat": A monument of Russian folk creativity of the end of the 17th–beginning of the 18th century], *XVIII vek* [18th century] 14 (1983): 45–79; Farrell, "Medieval Popular Humor," summarizes this view, which sees the topic in the context of late seventeenth-century popular culture predating Peter's death, and not as a work by the Old Believers.]

7. A Survey of Old Russian Folk Instruments

228F. [*Editors' note:* The full text of the eleventh-century psalter reference reads: "Tserkvi glagolet' devy iako i iuny soushcha, voroia toum pal'nitsa zhe iako v tekh briazdaiushcham gouslem dukhov'nem" (*Ocherki* 1:201). The source transmitting Ephrem the Syrian is apparently BAN 4.9.38 from the thirteenth century, Parenesis Efrema Sirina, as described in *SKSR* no. 289. The reference from the Primary Chronicle is in *PVL*, 220; the translation is based on Cross and Sherbowitz-Wetzor, *The Russian Primary Chronicle*, 161. The Mineia from 1096 is quoted from Sreznevskii, *Materialy*, 3:1147; cf. the term *briatsalo* in the alphabets in chapter 6 above. *SKSR* nos. 7–8 lists RGADA, f. 381, no. 84, for September 1095–96; and RGADA, f. 381, no. 89, for October 1096.]

228G. [*Editors' note:* The passage from the Efrem nomocanon, which Findeizen dates in the eleventh century [GIM, Sin. 227, dated in *SKSR* no. 75 as twelfth and thirteenth centuries] is "Igr'nitsi eretitsi zhe ili Elini," and the passage from the Novgorod nomocanon, from 1280 [GIM, Sin. 132, in *SKSR* no. 183], is "Oblich'ia igr'ts' i lik''stvenik." Findeizen, *Ocherki* 1:202, also cites GIM, Sin. 1043 [*SKSR* no. 4], from 1073, also illustrating the word *igrets:* "I postavliu iunoshu kniazia ikh, i igr'tsi gospod'stvouiut' im glagolet Gospod'."]

229. All the quotations from ancient documents cited here are taken from Sreznevskii, *Materialy*. [Findeizen, *Ocherki* 1:202, gives another series of examples to illustrate the term *gudenie* and its variants: from the sixteenth-century *Slovo* [Discourse] ("Ne podobaet khristianom igr besovskykh igrati, izhe est' pliasanie, gudba, pesni mirskyia") and from the *Zadonshchina* ("Voskhvalim veshchago Boiana v gorode Kieve, gorazda gudtsa," for which the translation is taken from Jakobson and Worth, *Sofonija's Tale*, l. 13, but with the phrase "gorazda gudtsa" translated here as "skilled player" rather than "skilled singer" and the transliteration modified). Findeizen's other examples are similar: "Gudenie ikh slysha" (in the *Thirteen Orations* of Gregory of Nazianzus, eleventh-century manuscript source, probably RNB, Q.II.I.16, listed in *SKSR* no. 33); "Otritsaiusia . . . semekha, guzhen'ia, svirelii" (from the teachings of Ephrem the Syrian, in a manuscript from 1288; there is no such dated source in *SKSR* but see n. 228F above); "Pishchemoe ili gudimoe" (from a fourteenth-century source); "Ne poveleno est' khrist'ianom gusti i pleskati" (Paisii collection, fifteenth century, which, according to *SKK* 1:437–38, is RNB, Kir.-Bel. 4/1081); and, from the same source, "No ashche pliastsi ili gudtsi, ili in kto igrets' pozovet' na igrishche idol'skaia to vsi tamo tekut raduiasia."]

229A. [*Editors' note:* The passage from Gregory of Nazianzus reads: "Rtsy mi, o chiudes'ny, dobro li est' pliasati ili pipolovati?" in Findeizen, *Ocherki* 1:202, where there is another series of examples illustrating terms associated with wind instruments, again taken from Sreznevskii: "Ouslyshite glas truby, sirinin zhe i gusl'n [giasl'n], pipely i pesn'nitsa. S pipolami, gusl'mi" (*Materialy*, 2:932 and elsewhere, citing Daniel 3:5 ("at what time ye hear the sound of the cornet, flute, harp, sackbut") from the Upyr' Likhii manuscript of 1047, in the Moscow Synodal Library and the library of the Academy of Sciences; the identity of this source is unclear); "Glas trouby, pishchalii zhe i guslii, tsevnitsia zhe i pregudnitsia i pisk" (*Materialy*, 2:938, from the same source, from Daniel 3:10); "Ashche episkop . . . obriashchetsia na bratse, a v nem zhe boudut piskove, a sego ne lshiitsia, da izvr"zhetsia sana" (*Materialy*, 2:938, from the Dubenskii collection of laws and sermons, sixteenth century, from the St. Petersburg Divinity School, no. 129).]

229B. [*Editors' note:* The passage from the Novgorod IV Chronicle is in *PSRL* 4, pt. 4 (1848), 59. The passage from the Nikonian Chronicle is from 1348; see *PSRL* 10 (1965), 220; and the translation in Zenkovsky and Zenkovsky, *The Nikonian Chronicle*, 163.]

229C. [*Editors' note:* N. I. Privalov, *Muzykal'nye dukhovye instrumenty russkogo naroda* [The musical wind instruments of the Russian people] (St. Petersburg: Tip. I. N. Skorokholova, 1907), 58. Available catalogs list the publication as comprised of two volumes, from 1906 to 1908; it is not clear to which volume Findeizen refers.]

230. Guthrie, *Dissertations sur les antiquités de Russie* [(St. Petersburg: Impr. du Corps Impérial des cadets nobles, 1795)], is the first investigation of Russian folk songs and musical instruments. Although it is now obsolete, it is of interest to us as it contains illustrations and brief descriptions of musical instruments as they were then used in folk life. [This work by Matthew Guthrie (d. 1807) is a French translation of the first part of his English-language work, *Noctes Rossicae, or Russian Evening Recreations.* See A. G. Cross, "Early British Acquaintance with Russian Popular Song and Music (The Letters and Journals of the Wilmot Sisters)," *Slavonic and East European Review* 66 (1988): 24–25, where further bibliography on Guthrie is cited on 24 n. 13.]

231. Similar wooden horns [*rozhki*], subsequently giving rise to metallic ones and making up horn ensembles in Tver and Vladimir provinces, are described in detail by Privalov, *Muzykal'nye dukhovye instrumenty.*

232. It is difficult to say whether horns made of ivory (so-called oliphants), similar to Petrine-era horns, were used in early times in princely homes. The Paisii collection (fourteenth to the fifteenth century [dated fifteenth century in n. 229]) apparently alludes to this kind of instrument: "to be rejected . . . satanic dances, Frankish oliphant [*fruzhskiia slon'nitsa;* in another manuscript, *slom'nitsa*], and musical *gusli.*" In this case, the term *slonnitsa* may designate the curved horn made of ivory (the oliphant). [See chap. 2 n. 35 above.]

233. For detailed descriptions and illustrations of these instruments, see Privalov, *Muzykal'nye dukhovye instrumenty,* 110–26, 134–43.

233A. [*Editors' note:* Findeizen's quotations also include the following, from John Malalas (see n. 167), in a fifteenth-century source: "Svirtsa poem, v dom vedet po vecher, da sviriuiut ou nego" (*Ocherki* 1:206); his source is Sreznevskii, *Materialy,* 3:273.]

233B. [*Editors' note:* The Riazan nomocanon is cited in Sreznevskii, *Materialy,* 3:273; see also *SKSR* no. 186, describing RNB, F.II.II.1; the passage from Grigorii is from Sreznevskii, *Materialy,* 1:608; and both Malalas and the *Zlatoustroi* are from 3:273. Findeizen quotes the passage on the use of the reed as follows: "T"n"koiu tr"st'tseiu svirim." Although this passage does not appear in V. N. Malinin, *Desiat' slov Zlatostruia XII veka* [Ten sermons of the *Zlatostrui* of the 12th century] (St. Petersburg: Imp. Akademii nauk, 1910), a series of instruments are mentioned on pp. 49 and 71 of that volume. The *Zlatostrui* manuscript is RNB, F.II.I.46, described in *SKSR* no. 74.]

234. "Hear the voice of the *truby, pishchali,* and the *gusli, tsevnitsy,* and *pregudnitsy*" in the Upyr' Likhii manuscript of 1047, in the library of the Academy of Sciences [see n. 229A above]; and in the Nikonian Chronicle under 1204: "Ashche by zlyi sluga, davaiai dukh napevaniem tsevnitsa i bretsaniem guslei Davydovykh, Saula otbegashe, kolmi pache strashnyia truby, izhe Troitsu sviatuiu vo edinom bozhestve ispovedaiushche, ustrashites'i bezhati ishchut'."

235. For an illustration and description of the *kuvichka,* see A. Mordvinov, "Vesna v Kurskoi gubernii" [Spring in Kursk province], *Vsemirnaia illiustratsiia* [Illustrated world] 120 (1871).

235A. [*Editors' note:* Color reproductions of both these images are in E. A. Mishina, *Russkaia graviura na dereve XVII–XVIII vv. / Russian Woodcuts of the 17th–18th Centuries* (St. Petersburg: ARS and Dmitrii Bulanin, 1998), nos. 96, 106.]

235B. [*Editors' note:* Findeizen, *Ocherki* 1:208, supplies a series of proverbs and sayings about the *volynka,* all taken from Dal', *Tolkovyi slovar',* 1:238.]

236. *Slovar' russkogo iazyka, sostavlennyi vtorym otdeleniem Imperatorskoi Akademii nauk* [A dictionary of the Russian language, compiled by the Second Section of the Imperial Academy of Sciences] (St. Petersburg: Tip. Imp. Akademii nauk, 1895) 1: col. 501. Perepelitsyn's statement in his

Istoriia muzyki v Rossii [History of music in Russia] (St. Petersburg: M. O. Vol'f, 1888), 6, that at archaeological excavations of old Slavic tombs, a representation in metal of a Slavic soldier playing a bagpipe was found in one of the burial mounds, is not supported by reference to any source; the statement remains on the author's conscience, as he embellished quite freely in his *Istoriia*. The picture of the bagpipe he reproduced is taken from Guthrie's book, as is our fig. 70. [Findeizen gives Belorussian sayings in this passage in *Ocherki* 1:208, also taken from Dal', *Tolkovyi slovar'*, 1:238.]

237. Kargarateli, *Kratkii ocherk gruzinskoi muzyki* [A short study of Georgian music] (Tiflis, 1901). [G. B. Bernandt and I. M. Iampol'skii, *Kto pisal o muzyke. Bio-bibliograficheskii slovar' muzykal'nykh kritikov i lits, pisavshikh o muzyke v dorevoliutsionnoi Rossii i SSSR* [Who wrote about music. A bio-bibliographical dictionary of music critics and figures who wrote about music in prerevolutionary Russia and in the USSR] (Moscow: Sovetskii kompozitor, 1971), 2:24, identifies this scholar as I. G. Kargareteli (1867–1939), who published his *Ocherk gruzinskoi narodnoi muzyki* (A study of Georgian folk music) in 1901.]

238. Buhle, *Die musikalischen Instrumente,* plate 13, reproduces thirteenth-century miniatures from sources in the Stiftsbibliothek in St. Blasius and in the city library in Leipzig, in which the bagpipes are depicted as having been made of the entire animal skin, including the head.

239. H. Mendel, *Musikalisches Conversations-Lexikon* (Berlin: Robert Oppenheim, 1878), 9:12. The article "Sackpfeife" contains interesting and detailed information on the spread of bagpipes in Europe. This article was also used by Buhle, *Die musikalischen Instrumente.*

240. Dal', *Tolkovyi slovar'*, 1:238.

241. Mendel, *Musikalisches Conversations-Lexikon,* 9:11.

241A. [*Editors' note:* The passage from the Nikonian Chronicle from 1219, cited above in chapter 3, is in *PSRL* 10 (1965), 84. The passage from the St. Sofia Annals [Sofiiskii Vremennik] is from *PSRL* 6 (1853), 313, under the year 1552. The source is treated as an appendix to the Sof. II Chronicle in *PSRL,* vol. 6.]

242. Preserved in a Moscow register from 1664–65, among other things, is the name of a *surna* player in the tsar's service, Andrei Klimashevskii, who left Poland in June 1665 to enter the tsar's service "in eternal servitude" (*RIB* 11:267, 285). [Findeizen joins two widely separated passages from Kotoshikhin, *O Rossii v tsarstvovanie Alekseia Mikhailovicha,* ed. Liberman and Shokarev, *Moskva i Evropa,* 21, 81.]

243. Sreznevskii, *Materialy,* 1:424 (Antioch Pandect, eleventh century) [which reads: "Ashche oubo vidit' strazh' oriazh'e griadoushche i v"stroubit'" (If the watchman sees someone coming [. . .] and sounds the trumpet); see *SKSR* no. 24, which describes GIM, Voskr. 30].

243A. [*Editors' note: PSRL* 1 (1926), 499; see chapter 3 and n. 69D above.]

244. According to the Moscow census book of 1669, in Belgorod on the ecclesiastical lands of the Zachateiskii Monastery there was a "house of the trumpeter [*trubachei*] Andrei Lebedev" (*Perepisnye knigi goroda Moskvy* [Census records of the city of Moscow] (Moscow: Gorodskaia tip., 1886), 90.

245. Dal', *Tolkovyi slovar'*, 4:436, defines the word *trubnik* as "someone who works with the fire pipes [or tubes]; on fire brigades there are *trubniki* and sub-*trubniki.*" He does not refer to a *trubnik* as a trumpeter. In seventeenth-century records, however, the term *trubnik* in the sense of trumpeter appears frequently. In addition to Kotoshikhin (cited above) for example, the expense book for 1613–14 reads: "By the sovereign's decree a *funt* [pound] of *ladan* [a fragrant resin] was provided for the icon of the Sign of the Pure Mother of God, which is being sent to the regiments at Belyi . . . the *trubnik* Saltan Ofremov Fomin took it" (*RIB* 9:163).

246. Savvaitov, *Opisanie starinnykh russkikh utvarei* [Description of old Russian utensils] (St. Petersburg: Akademiia nauk, 1865), 38. [See also Sreznevskii, *Materialy,* 3:1005.]

246A. [*Editors' note:* The passage from the Igor tale is from Haney and Dahl, *The Discourse on Igor's Campaign,* 27; and the passage from the *Zlatostrui* is from Sreznevskii, *Materialy,* 3:559.]

246B. [*Editors' note:* Findeizen refers in the text to the *Akty istoricheskie. Dopolneniia,* 1: no. 22.]

247. The Riazan nomocanon of 1284, manuscript in the Public Library [RNB, F.п.II.1], fol. 51, includes the *svirets'*, the *goudets'*, the *smychek* [referring to someone who plays a bowed instrument], and the dancer, among others, in a list of people to be banished [quoted fully in Findeizen's n. 247]. The Russian Primary Chronicle, in the year 6976 (1468), states: "The devil alienates us from God by all manner of craft, through trumpets and *skomorokhi*, bowed instruments, *gusli* and pagan festivals [*rusal'i*]." [The quotation from the Primary Chronicle is from the year 6576 (1068); see *PVL*, 74 (where the phrase "i smykami" [bowed instruments] does not appear) and 211; the English translation is based on Cross and Sherbowitz-Wetzor, *The Russian Primary Chronicle*, 147. This passage is cited above in chapter 3.]

248. N. Privalov, *Gudok, drevne-russkii muzykal'nyi instrument* [The *gudok*, an old Russian musical instrument] (St. Petersburg, 1904), 21.

249. Ibid., 18. [In the caption for fig. 73 in *Ocherki* 1:212, Findeizen attributes the drawing to Fétis; in the text, he notes that it is a late eighteenth-century illustration from Guthrie. According to *Muzykal'nyi entsiklopedicheskii slovar'*, 507, *smyk* could mean either a bow or a *gudok*-type stringed instrument.]

249A. [*Editors' note:* The Stoglav reference is in Emchenko, *Stoglav*, 313.]

250. Sreznevskii, *Materialy*, 2:1627, citations from fourteenth- and fifteenth-century Bibles. [In his text (*Ocherki* 1:213), Findeizen includes two additional citations: "Se be skazaia gusli i pregud'nitsa pesni" (These are what are called songs of the *gusli* and *pregudnitsa*) and "Ouslyshit' glas truby, pishchali zhe i guslin, tsevnitsia zhe i pregudnitsa," from Daniel 3:10 (Thou, O king, hast made a decree, that every man that shall hear the sound of the cornet, flute, harp, sackbut, psaltery, and dulcimer, and all kinds of musick, shall fall down and worship the golden image; see also n. 229A above).]

251. See campaign diaries from 1724 and 1725: "On 22 August 1724, His Imperial Majesty was pleased to baptize the infant of the *gudok* player [*gudoshnik*] Iakov Konev"; on 9 January 1725, "there took place the wedding of Mishka, the servant of His Majesty's orderly [*den'shchik*] Vasilii Pospelov, to the *gudok* player Nastas'ia, attended by His Imperial Majesty, Her Imperial Majesty the Empress, and many other persons; for this wedding all the *gudok* players were assembled." [On the term *den'shchik*, see n. 398Q below.]

252. *Trudy I-go arkheologicheskogo s"ezda v Moskve, 1869 g.*, 471. The *gudok* is mentioned in folk songs from Chernigov province collected by P. N. Rybnikov, *Pesni, sobrannye P. N. Rybnikovym*, 3:453, who points out that it was made of birch or mountain ash.

252A. [*Editors' note:* This passage, with minor differences, is cited above in chapter 6; the manuscript source is GIM, Sin. 353.]

253. Famintsyn, *Domra i srodnye ei muzykal'nye instrumenty*, 43.

253A. [*Editors' note:* On Guagnini, see the article in *MERSH* 13:173–76.]

253B. [*Editors' note:* Findeizen refers here to the definition in the seventeenth-century alphabet discussed above in chapter 6; a typographical error in *Ocherki* 1:215 results in a reference to an eighteenth-century alphabet.]

254. Famintsyn, *Domra i srodnye ei muzykal'nye instrumenty*, 12.

255. Ibid., 10–11.

256. *Izvestiia Imp. arkheol. komissii* [Reports of the Imperial Archaeological Commission] 32 (1909): 14. The church was built ca. 1750. When an iconostasis was erected in the refectory in 1885, the icon was repainted along with some other old icons, according to the author of the note in the *Izvestiia*, although he called it a "remarkable" icon.

257. Rovinskii, *Russkie narodnye kartinki*, 1: figs. 166, 170, 98.

258. I. I. Golikov, *Dopolnenie* [Addenda] to *Deianiia Petra Velikogo* [Acts of Peter the Great] (Moscow: Universitetskaia tip., 1790–97), 10:23. [This elaborate mock ceremony, so typical of Peter's entertainments, involved the wedding of the eighty-four-year-old Nikita Zotov (who was Peter's

tutor and later served as mock-pope at his court) to a young woman. It is described in Massie, *Peter the Great*, 618–19, which quotes from the account of Friedrich Christian Weber, the ambassador from Hanover, who witnessed the spectacle. No balalaika is mentioned in this passage, but Weber does refer to a mock-tsar who was dressed to represent King David, carrying a lyre covered with a bearskin.]

258A. [*Editors' note:* The proverb reads: "Na slovakh—chto na gusliakh, a na dele—chto na balalaike." Many thanks to Dan Newton for insights into this saying.]

259. B. Babkin, "Balalaika. Ocherki po istorii ee razvitiia i usovershenstvovaniia" [The balalaika: Studies of its development and improvement], *Russkaia beseda* [Russian conversation] (March 1896).

259A. [*Editors' note:* The term *razlad* here refers to a special type of balalaika tuning in which all three strings are tuned to different pitches; many thanks to Elena Dubinets for clarifying this point.]

259B. [*Editors' note:* The Dashkov and Rumiantsev ethnographic collections form part of the Rossiiskii etnograficheskii muzei [Russian Ethnographic Museum] in St. Petersburg; see Grimsted, *Archives of Russia*, 2:1004.]

260. "As he approached the porch, [Chichikov] noticed . . . a man's face, as wide as the Moldavian pumpkins called *gorlianki*, from which balalaikas are made in Russia, two-stringed ones, light balalaikas" (*Polnoe sobranie sochineniia Gogolia* [Complete collected works of Gogol], 5th ed. [Moscow, 1884] 3:951).

261. A detailed study of the balalaika and its origins is in Famintsyn, *Domra i srodnye ei muzykal'nye instrumenty.* On the modernized balalaika, see V. K., *V. V. Andreev i ego velikorusskii orkestr* [V. V. Andreev and his Great Russian orchestra] (St. Petersburg: Tip. A. S. Suvorova, 1909). There were many balalaika virtuosos in the eighteenth and nineteenth centuries. In addition to those mentioned in the sources already cited, we should note the well-known performer, singer, and dancer Khrunov, renowned in St. Petersburg in the early 1800s. He was a noncommissioned officer of the Izmailov Regiment, and S. P. Zhikharev wrote about him in his memoirs in his description of the promenade on 1 May 1807 at Ekaterinhof (*Zapiski Stepana Petrovicha Zhikhareva* [Memoirs of Stepan Petrovich Zhikarev] (Moscow: Izd. Russkogo arkhiva, 1890), 403). At the end of the nineteenth and the beginning of the twentieth century, the outstanding virtuoso B. S. Troianovskii appeared in Andreev's orchestra. The following variation of the folk song "Svetit mesiats" [The moon shines], as he performed it in a very fast tempo, demonstrates the level of virtuosity that may be achieved on a balalaika (example provided by N. I. Privalov; see musical example N7.1). [The initials "V.K." above stand for Viktor Pavlovich Kolomiitsov (1868–1936), so identified in *Kto pisal o muzyke*, 2:58.]

261A. [*Editors' note:* Findeizen's source is Sreznevskii, *Materialy* 1:610 (and see also 2:1620), and he gives another passage, also from 1:610, from the Paisii collection: "Rekut nerazumnii: kuiu pakost' gusli tvoriat'" (Stupid people say that *gusli* are responsible for any kind of foulness).]

262. For the text of the story and an analysis, see M. Speranskii, "Devgenievo deianie. K istorii ego teksta v starinnoi russkoi pis'mennosti. Issledovanie i teksty" [The deeds of Devgenii. On the history of its text in old Russian writing. Investigation and texts], *Sbornik Otd. russkogo iazyka i slovesnosti Ross. Akademii nauk* 99, no. 7 (1922). [See the text and translation in *PLDR XIII vek*, 28–65; the passages Findeizen notes are on 46–49. There is also an edition by V. D. Kuz'mina, *Devgenievo deianie. (Deianie prezhnikh vremen khrabrykh chelovek)* [The deeds of Devgenie (The deeds of brave men of former times)] (Moscow: Izd-vo AN SSSR, 1962).]

263. F. J. Fétis, "Résumé philosophique de l'histoire de la musique," in the first edition of his *Biographie universelle* (Paris: H. Fournier, 1835), cites the following tune of the Little Russian song "Akh pod vyshnei" [Ah, under the cherry tree] as written down in St. Petersburg in the early 1800s by A. Boieldieu, with the accompaniment of a five-string *gusli* (see musical example N7.2). [Adrien Boieldieu (1775–1834) was a leading French opera composer who spent the first decade of

EXAMPLE N7.1. "Svetit mesiats" [The moon shines]

the nineteenth century in Russia; see *NG2*. On the song "Akh pod vyshnei," see volume 2, chapter 18, of the present work; this song was published in the late eighteenth century in a Russian music journal.]

264. The two following tunes from the *Kalevala,* written down by Elias Lenrot, *Kalevala, finskii narodnyi epos* [*Kalevala,* the Finnish folk epic], trans. L. Bel'skii, 2nd ed. (Moscow: Izd. M. i S. Sabashnikovykh, 1915 [3rd ed., 1933]), 420, may serve as examples (see musical examples N7.3 and N7.4).

265. The following song from Saratov province ("Zelena grusha v sadu shataetsia" [In the garden the green pear tree sways]) is an example of a Great Russian tune in 5/4 and using a pentatonic scale (see musical example N7.5). It was published in Rimskii-Korsakov's *Russkie narodnye pesni* [Russian folk songs], op. 24, no. 75. The last two bars may have altered the 5/4 meter through the process of transmission or in the notation of the tune.

265A. [*Editors' note:* Findeizen probably refers here to the music theorist Grigorii Alekseevich Marenich, 1833–1918; see *Kto pisal o muzyke,* 2:184–85.]

266. Jakob von Stählin, "Nachrichten von der Musik in Russland," in *M. Johann Joseph Haigolds Beylagen zum neuveränderten Russland* (Riga: J. F. Hartknoch, 1769–70), 2:19 [and see below, and volume 2, for a more detailed discussion of Stählin's work]. The popularity of the tabletop *gusli,* not only in the capital cities but also in the provinces, is amply demonstrated in the many contemporary memoirs from the late eighteenth and first half of the nineteenth century. In his "Zapiski irkutskogo zhitelia" [Notes

EXAMPLE N7.2. "Akh pod vyshnei" [Ah, under the cherry tree]

EXAMPLE N7.3. A song from the *Kalevala*

EXAMPLE N7.4. A song from the *Kalevala*

of a resident of Irkutsk], *Russkaia starina* [Russian antiquity] (July 1905), 215, I. T. Kalashnikov states that, at the beginning of the nineteenth century, piano playing in Irkutsk was "barely known . . . Instead, *gusli* were used a great deal and two of the exiles [to Siberia] were excellent performers." Count S. D. Sheremetev, in his memoirs, *Staraia Vozdvizhenka* [Old Vozdvizhenka Street] (St. Petersburg: Tip. M. M. Stasiulevicha, 1892), 24, tells of the "old, gray-haired *gusli* player with an unusual nose" who, in the 1850s, lived in the Moscow home of the Count's grandmother and "delighted my grandmother and all of us with his beautiful playing." In the *Vospominaniia* [Reminiscences] of A. V. Shchepkina (Sergiev Posad: Tip. I. I. Ivanova, 1915), 213, we read: "Although M. S. Shchepkin himself (a celebrated

EXAMPLE N7.5. "Zelena grusha v sadu shataetsia" [In the garden the green pear tree sways]

Akh! Zelena grusha v sadu shataetsia,
svet i Mamen'ka dusha rasplakalas'.

Ah, the green pear tree sways in the garden,
and mother dear burst into tears.

artist) had studied music only a little, as a child he had been taught to play the *gusli;* that instrument was often found at that time and it took the place of the small fortepiano, which appeared later in provincial domestic life."

267. A. M. Vodovozov's *popovskie gusli* is presently in the Music History Museum (Inventory no. 1324). The range of the instrument is from C two octaves below middle C to f four and one-half octaves above middle C. In the same museum are portraits of the *gusli* players Vodovozov and Artamonov.

267A. [*Editors' note:* See n. 228F above on this source.]

268. *Trudy I-go arkheologicheskogo s"ezda v Moskve, 1869 g.,* 473.

269. "Oruzhie tsaria Borisa Godunova" [Armaments of Tsar Boris Godunov], Manuscript no. 665, dated 1589. [Findeizen's source is Sreznevskii, *Materialy,* 2:265. His reference to Viskovatyi is unclear; Ivan Mikhailovich Viskovatyi (d. 1570) worked in the government of Ivan IV in the 1550s to the 1560s, particularly in the Foreign Office. He was suspected of being involved in a boyar plot against the tsar and was executed.]

270. Ibid.

270A. [*Editors' note:* See n. 243A above.]

270B. [*Editors' note:* The passage suggests some kind of elaborate engraving: "travy rezany na proem" (*Ocherki* 1:223). In the passage from the *Zadonshchina,* Jakobson and Worth, *Sofonija's Tale,* l. 19, reads "bubni b'iut' v Serpukhove" (they are beating the *bubny* in Serpukhov); Findeizen's source is Sreznevskii, *Materialy,* 1:188.]

270C. [*Editors' note:* Findeizen, *Ocherki* 1:224, offers a series of examples of the association with *skomorokhi,* all taken from Sreznevskii: "Gore . . . chaiushche vecheri s gusl'mi i sopel'mi i bubny i pliasan'em" (Woe [to him who] anticipates evenings with *gusli* and *sopeli* and *bubny* and dancing; Paisii collection, fourteenth century [dated fifteenth century in n. 229]); "v selekh vozbesiatsia v bubny i v sopeli" (in villages they raise Cain [stir up the devil] with *bubny* and *sopeli;* Pskov I Chronicle, under the year 1505); and with women: "varisha kniazi zapiat' poiashtiikh posrede devits' bub"nits'" (Chudov Psalter, eleventh century) and "Posrede molodits' bubennits" (the Psalter of Maksim Grek, sixteenth century, both from Sreznevskii, *Materialy,* 1:188). These are from Psalm 68 in the Revised Standard Version: "the singers in front, the minstrels last, between them maidens playing timbrels"). We thank Daniel Waugh for his help in identifying and translating passages throughout this chapter. The numbering of the Psalms differs slightly in the Hebrew and the Greek systems. The Russian Orthodox

Church numbering, which Findeizen uses throughout, follows the Greek system. Concordance tables are readily available; generally, in the Greek ordering, the Psalms are assigned a lower number than in the Hebrew system (followed also by Protestant churches). Thus, for example, Psalms 11–113 in the Hebrew numbering correspond to Psalms 10–112 in the Greek and Russian Orthodox system.]

270D. [*Editors' note:* As Daniel Waugh notes, this reference to the *nakry* is from the *Tale of the Capture of Constantinople,* which is attributed to Nestor Iskander; see the text in *PLDR vtoraia polovina XV veka* [second half of the 15th century], 224, which is based on the earliest surviving manuscript source, from the early sixteenth century (RGB, Tr. 773). This seems to be the basis for the entry in the Nikonian Chronicle (*PSRL* 12 [1965], 84), which Findeizen cites here.]

271. *PSRL* 6 [1853]. [Text and translations from Afanasii Nikitin are taken from *PLDR vtoraia polovina XV veka,* 466–67, 470–71; Findeizen has joined two widely separated passages in his citation. A partial English translation of Nikitin's journey is in Zenkovsky, *Medieval Russia's Epics, Chronicles, and Tales,* 333–53; see also the interpretation of Nikitin's experiences in Gail Lenhoff, "Beyond Three Seas: Afanasij Nikitin's Journey from Orthodoxy to Apostasy," *East European Quarterly* 13, no. 4 (1979): 431–47. On the term *nagarniki* (and variants), see chapter 8 n. 303 below.]

272. The *bubny velikie* undoubtedly refer to *nabaty.*

273. Manuscript no. 482 in the Rumiantsev Museum [RGB]. [Findeizen's source for the citations from the St. Sofia Annals and the inventory of Boris Godunov's armory is Sreznevskii, *Materialy,* 2:293–94.]

274. The small copper drum [*litavra*] (Inventory no. 7) is stamped with a scene of Peter receiving a deputation from the Senate, with the inscription: "P. I p. t. i. v.," that is, "Petr I prinimaet titul imperatora vserossiiskogo" [Peter I accepts the title of Emperor of All the Russias].

275. *Doklady i prigovory, sostoiavshiesia v Pravitel'stvuiushchem Senate v tsarstvovanie Petra Velikogo* [Reports and comments made in the ruling Senate during the reign of Peter the Great] (St. Petersburg: Tip. Imp. Akademii nauk, 1887), vol. 3, bk.1, 445.

276. *RIB* 5:406–409.

277. A picture of these Kokshaisk musicians appears in the journal *Zhivopisnaia Rossiia* [Picturesque Russia] 56 (1902); and in *RMG* 7 (1902): 206.

278. Dal', *Tolkovyi slovar',* 1:165, states that "the *vargan* is a musical instrument of the simple folk; a *zubanka,* a small piece of iron in the shape of a lyre with a metal tongue lengthwise in the center." Dal' derives its name from the Karelian *varga* (*varega*), meaning mouth or jaws. [Dal' also cites a folk saying relating to the instrument, reproduced in Findeizen's note 278. On the use of the term *vargan* in medieval chronicles, see Roizman, *Organ,* 39–43.]

278A. [*Editors' note:* The sistrum was associated with the worship of Isis. It had a U-shaped frame with crossbars, which rattled when shaken, and sometimes metal discs and jingles were added to intensify the effect. See *NG2.* V. I. Povetkin discusses wooden noisemakers discovered during the course of excavations in Novgorod in his "Otkrytie treshchotok novgorodskikh" [The discovery of Novgorodian rattles], *PKNO for* 2000 (2001): 160–66 .]

279. *Russkii istoricheskii sbornik* 3:26.

279A. [*Editors' note:* Findeizen's reference to the Nikonian Chronicle here is apparently taken from Sreznevskii, *Materialy,* 1:227. Earlier Findeizen had cited a slightly different version of this passage, in which *vargany* were not mentioned; see above, n. 270D. Surviving *vargany* from the thirteenth to the fifteenth centuries are discussed in Kolchin, "Kollektsiia muzykal'nykh instrumentov," 187.]

280. N. I. Privalov, in his article on *lozhki* (*RMG* [1908], nos. 28–36), quotes an interesting statement from the memoirs of General-Major Tuchkov from the late eighteenth to the early nineteenth century, and he also clarifies the role of *lozhki* in the later Great Russian orchestra. [Findeizen refers here to Pavel Alekseevich Tuchkov (1775–1858), who took part in the wars with Sweden and with France in the early nineteenth century; see *GSE* 26:408.]

281. D. I. Evarnitskii, *Istoriia zaporozhskogo kazachestva* [History of the Zaporozhian Cossacks] (St. Petersburg, 1892), 1:282. [Findeizen's information on Cossacks comes from Dmitrii Ivanovich Evarnitskii (Dmitro Ivanovych Iavornytskyi, 1855–1940), whose history of the Zaporozhian Cossacks was reprinted in Kiev as late as 1990; see his *Istoriia zaporoz'kykh kozakiv* [A history of the Zaporozhian Cossacks] (Kiev: Nauk. dumka, 1990–91). Natalie O. Kononenko also discusses Ukrainian folk practice in her *Ukrainian Minstrels: And the Blind Shall Sing* (Armonk, N.Y.: M. E. Sharpe, 1998).]

282. Such are all specimens of the Kirghiz *kobyz* in the Museum of Anthropology and Ethnography of the Academy of Sciences in St. Petersburg and in the Dashkov Museum in Moscow [see n. 259B above], used in Siberia, Orenburg, and Turkestan, and also by the Karachaev highlanders of Kuban province [fig. N7.1]. It is inconceivable that in the remote past among these people there existed more developed types of the *kobyz* that delighted the Zaporozhian Cossacks, as it is difficult to accept the notion that any folk instrument could undergo a change for the worse. Another instance of the similarity in the names of instruments is the case of two Slavic instruments that have nothing in common: the Serbian bowed *gusle* with either one or two strings [illustrated in the *Muzykal'nyi entsiklopedicheskii slovar'*, 157] and the multi-stringed, plucked *gusli* of the northern Slavs.

283. D. I. Evarnitskii, *Istoriia zaporozhskogo kazachestva* [History of the Zaporozhian Cossacks], 2nd ed. (Moscow, 1900), 300. This archaeologist made the curious statement that of the twelve ravines crisscrossing the landscape of Khortitsa (where remnants of the Zaporozhian Sich [see below] are preserved), one, in early times, was called *muzychika* (143).

Fig. N7.1. A Kirghiz *kobyz* (from Findeizen's collection).

284. [Ostap Veresai], *Kobzar' Ostap Veresai, ego muzyka i ispolniaemye im narodnye pesni* [*Kobza* player Ostap Veresai, his music, and the folk songs he performed] (Kiev, 1874), 38. The tuning varied by geographical location and by player; see A. K. Bich'-Lubenskii, "Banduristy i lirniki na khar'kovskom XII arkheolog. s"ezde" [*Bandura* and *lira* players at the 12th Archaeological Congress in Kharkov], *RMG* 38 (1902). [The entry in *Kto pisal o muzyke*, 1:98, lists this author as Konstantin Mikhailovich Bich-Lubenskii, an ethnographer active around 1900.]

285. M. Petukhov, "Ivan Aleksandrov, odin iz poslednikh predstavitelei igry na torbane" [Ivan Aleksandrov, one of the last representatives of *torban* playing], *Vsemirnaia illiustratsiia* 12 (1891). [This article by the music historian and ethnographer Mikhail Onisiforovich Petukhov (1843–1895) is not included in *Kto pisal o muzyke*, 2:281, although the author wrote widely about many folk instruments.]

286. *Letopisnoe povestvovanie o Maloi Rossii i eia narode i kazakakh voobshche . . . Sobrano i sostavleno chrez trudy inzhen.-gen.-maiora i kavalera Aleksandra Rigel'mana, 1785–86* [Annals-Chronicle about Little Russia and its people and about Cossacks in general . . . collected and compiled by the labors of engineer, general-major, and cavalier Aleksandr Rigel'man, 1785–86] (Moscow: Universitetskaia tip., 1847), pt. 4, bk. 6, p. 87. [Aleksandr Ivanovich Rigel'man (1720–1789) was a military engineer who worked in Ukraine and served in the Russo-Turkish wars from 1735 to 1739 and from 1768 to 1771; his rank of general-major was fourth in the Table of Ranks (see Pushkarev, *Dictionary of Russian Historical Terms*, 19). He later devoted his attention to the study of the Don Cossacks, and although his book was written in the 1780s, it was published only in the 1840s, in *ChOIDR* 5 (1846); 6–9 (1847); and 6 (1848). A recent Ukrainian edition of his work has been issued

under the title *Litopysna opovid' pro Malu Rosiiu* (Kiev: Lybid, 1994). See the biographical information in *GSE* 22:186.]

287. Ibid., 81. Interesting pictures of Cossacks are appended to this work, one playing the *bandura* and the other dancing, as well as eighteenth-century Ukrainian landowners dancing. The first of these is reproduced in Evarnitskii, *Istoriia zaporozhskogo kazachestva.* [The territory of the Zaporozhian Cossacks (the term means, literally, "beyond the rapids," referring to the Dnieper River) covered the southern part of Ukraine in the mid-sixteenth through the late eighteenth centuries. Their culture was centered around the Sich, a fortress or keep; there were several such fortresses, with large garrisons attached, in this period. See the articles by B. Krupnytsky and A. Zhukovsky, "Zaporizhia"; and by A. Zhukovsky, "Zaporozhian Sich" in *EU* 5:812–14, and 818–20, respectively, and the survey in Philip Longworth, *The Cossacks* (New York: Holt, Rinehart and Winston, 1970), esp. chap. 1.]

288. *Iuzhnaia Rus'* [Southern Rus'] 41 (22 April 1912). [Many thanks to Geoffrey Schwartz, of the University of Washington, for his translations of the Ukrainian texts throughout this chapter. On the Mamai paintings, see M. Hnatiukivsky, "Kozak-Mamai," in *EU* 2:650–51.]

289. *Dnevnik kamer-iunkera F. V. Berkhgol'tsa* [Diary of Kammerjunker F. W. Bergholz], trans. I. F. Ammon, novoe izd. s dopolnitel'nymi primechaniiami (Moscow: Universitetskaia tip., 1902), pt. 1, 70. [Friedrich Wilhelm von Bergholz (1699–1765) was in Russia in the 1720s as part of the diplomatic mission headed by Karl Friedrich, Duke of Holstein-Gottorp. The diary he wrote during that period is examined in more detail in chapter 12; the first part of Ammon's translation has been reprinted in *Dnevnik kamer-iunkera Fridrikha-Vil'gel'ma Berkhgol'tsa* [The diary of Kammerjunker F. W. von Bergholz], *Neistovyi reformator* [The frenzied reformer], ed. A. Liberman and V. Naumov, in the series Istoriia Rossii i doma Romanovykh v memuarakh sovremennikov XVII–XX vv. [A history of Russia and the house of the Romanovs in memoirs by contemporaries, 17th–20th centuries] (Moscow: Fond Sergeia Dubova, 2000), 109–502, referred to hereafter as Bergholz, *Dnevnik* (2000), where the passage on Prince Kantemir's *bandura* player appears on p. 168. Dmitrii Konstantinovich Kantemir (1673–1723) was *hospodar* of Moravia who strongly supported the ambitions of Peter the Great against the Ottoman Turks and who became a significant figure in Peter's government; his son, Antiokh Dmitrievich, was an important literary figure and is discussed below in Findeizen's account. There is a brief biographical sketch of Kantemir *père* in William Edward Brown, *A History of 18th-century Russian Literature* (Ann Arbor: Ardis, 1980), 31–32.]

290. For data on the *bandura* and Ukrainian performers, see Famintsyn, *Domra i srodnye ei muzykal'nye instrumenty,* 119–70.

290A. [*Editors' note:* P. O. Kulish, *Zapiski o iuzhnoi Rusi* [Notes on southern Rus'] (St. Petersburg: A. Iakobson, 1856; reprint, Kiev: Izd-vo khudozhestvennoi literatury "DNIPRO," 1994).]

290B. [*Editors' note:* Samuel Maskiewicz's diary is published in Samuel and Bogusław Maskiewicz, *Pamiętniki Samuela i Bogusława Kazimierza Maskiewiczów* [The diaries of Samuel and Bogusław Kazimierz Maskiewicz], ed. A. Sajkowski (Wrocław: Zakład narodowy im. Ossolińskich, 1961), where the passage on the *lira* is on p. 141.]

291. On the *lira,* see M. Petukhov, *Narodnye muzykal'nye instrumenty Muzeia S.-Peterburgskoi konservatorii* [Folk musical instruments in the Museum of the St. Petersburg Conservatory] (St. Petersburg: Tip. Imp. Akademii nauk, 1884); A. Maslov, "Lira," *RMG* (1902): 353; K. Bich-Lubenskii, "Malo-rossiiskaia lira i 'rylia'" [The Little Russian *lira* and "*rylia*"], *RMG* (1900): 960; and N. I. Privalov, *Lira, russkii narodnyi muzykal'nyi instrument* [The *Lira,* a Russian folk musical instrument] (St. Petersburg, 1905). An interesting description of the tuning and dimensions of the large Don *lira,* which resembles the Ukrainian instrument but differs in size and in some details of construction, is given in A. M. Listopadov's report about the song-collecting expedition in 1902–1903, "Narodnaia kazach'ia pesnia na Donu" [Cossack folk song in the Don area], in *Trudy muzykal'no-etnograficheskoi komissii* [Reports of the Musical-Ethnographic Commission], 1:161.

291A. [*Editors' note:* The term *tsymbaly* has a variety of meanings. Dal', in *Tolkovyi slovar'*, 4:575, defines the term as a kind of zither or *gusli;* see also Aumayr, *Historische Untersuchungen*, 91, 130–33. Roizman, in *Organ*, 54–57, discusses the term in its seventeenth-century context as a keyboard instrument. See also chapter 6 above.]

292. On the *tsimbaly*, see Famintsyn, *Gusli*, 121–32; see also N. Findeizen, "Evreiskie tsimbaly i tsimbalisty Lepianskie" [Hebrew *tsimbaly* and the *tsimbaly* players of Lepiansk], *Muzykal'naia etnografiia* [Musical ethnography] (1926): 37–42.

293. Published in the journal *Sever* [The North] (1897): 2514. [Vasilii Vasil'evich Mate (1856–1917) was a Russian engraver who studied in St. Petersburg and then in Western Europe; he returned to St. Petersburg in the 1880s, where he taught at various institutions until his death; see *GSE* 15:552.]

294. *Materialy dlia izucheniia byta i iazyka russkogo naseleniia Severo-Zapadnogo kraia* [Materials for the study of the daily life and language of the Russian population of the north-western territory], collected and arranged by P. V. Shein (St. Petersburg: Tip. Imp. Akademii nauk, 1887) vol. 1, pt. 1, 530. [Shein (1826–1900) collected Russian and Belorussian folk materials beginning in the 1850s and produced many volumes of songs, texts, and studies of folk life; see *GSE* 29:571.]

294A. [*Editors' note:* Thanks again to Geoffrey Schwartz of the University of Washington for his advice on this text.]

295. *Materialy dlia izucheniia byta i iazyka russkogo naseleniia severo-zapadnogo kraia*, musical supplement, p. 4, song no. 648.

296. Ibid., 539ff.

296A. [*Editors' note:* Olearius, *The Travels of Olearius*, 262–63.]

296B. [*Editors' note:* See chapter 5 n. 170 above.]

8. Music in Ancient Moscow (Fifteenth and Sixteenth Centuries)

[*Editors' note:* Findeizen's study in this chapter of Moscow's musical life in the fifteenth and sixteenth centuries was the most thorough to have appeared in print. Ivan III's marriage in 1472 to the last Byzantine princess, Zoe-Sofia of the house of the Paleologues, legitimized the presumptive transfer of Constantinople's power and significance to Moscow and, although contacts with the West were already in evidence, Sofia's arrival in Russia from Italy contributed to the direct penetration of Italian and, more generally, Western influences on many aspects of Russian culture. One example is the Bolognese architect Aristotle Fioravanti (d. 1486?), who built the Cathedral of the Dormition of the Virgin in the Moscow Kremlin and who was able to use his skills in metal casting to construct guns for Ivan III's army. He was brought to Moscow by Semen Ivanovich Tolbuzin, Russia's first emissary to Italy, who was in Venice in 1474–75 (see *ES-BE* 65:420; and on Fioravanti, see *MERSH* 11:173–74).

Findeizen also discusses the arrival in Moscow of the Augustinian monk and organist known as Ivan Spasitel' (presumably Giovanni Salvatore in Italian). That he was referred to as an organist has raised questions about the presence of organs in Russia in that period, and some have speculated that there may have been a Roman Catholic church in Moscow. Although there was no such church in Moscow at that time, later writers have suggested that there may have been an organ in the royal household, a point which remains unconfirmed. Findeizen suggests, in n. 300 below, that a craftsman called Ivan Friazin (i.e., Frank, or a general term for a foreigner) in the Russian sources was also called Ivan Spasitel', although it is unclear from Findeizen's text whether he believes the two Ivans were, in fact, the same person, the organist. Later scholars have made two different suggestions. The Swiss-Russian musicologist Robert-Aloys Mooser believes that Ivan Friazin refers to a different person, one Gian-Battista della Volpe, who was in Moscow in 1469 and was involved in preparations for Ivan's wedding (*MA* 1:17 n. 2). Iurii Keldysh, on the other hand, in *IRM* 1:128, writes that the names Ivan Friazin and Ivan Spasitel' referred to the same person. In this Keldysh follows Leonid Isaakovich Roizman (1916–1989), the foremost authority on the history of organs in Russia, who makes the same connection between the two figures in his book, *Organ v istorii russkoi muzykal'noi kul'tury,* 28–30. Roizman goes further by stating that, since there are no documents indicating that Salvatore brought an organ with him in 1490, it must be presumed that the Russians already had such an instrument; their emissaries in Italy and elsewhere half a century earlier at the Council of Florence had presumably encountered organs on their trip. (For a bibliography on the Russian representatives at the Council of Florence in 1438–39, see Miloš Velimirović, "Liturgical Drama in Byzantium and Russia," *Dumbarton Oaks Papers* 16 (1962): 374 n. 66; and see the additional account published in *BLDR* 6: 464–87.)

That Western European musical instruments did present a novelty in sixteenth-century Russia was recorded by the British emissary Jerome Horsey (d. 1626), who reported the Russians' interest in the musical instruments he had brought with him in 1586. Horsey's comments have been cited frequently in the musicological literature; see the editions of his work in *Russia at the close of the sixteenth century. Comprising the treatise "Of the Russe common wealth," by Dr. Giles Fletcher; and the travels of Sir Jerome Horsey, knt., now for the first time printed entire from his own manuscript,* ed. Edward A. Bond (London: Printed for the Hakluyt Society, 1856); and in Lloyd E. Berry and Robert O. Crummey, eds., *Rude and Barbarous Kingdom: Russia in the Accounts of Sixteenth-Century English Voyagers* (Madison: University of Wisconsin Press, 1968).

In describing the increasingly elaborate ceremony at the Russian court, Findeizen suggests that the special choir, the *gosudarevy pevchie d'iaki,* was established already in the first half of the sixteenth century, during the reign of Vasilii III (r. 1505–1533). Keldysh notes that Findeizen assumed only tentatively that the formation of the choir went hand in hand with the building of the Cathedral of the Dormition in the Kremlin, from 1479 (see *IRM* 1:132 n.1). The earliest documented presence of singers in the ruler's retinue in Moscow dates, in fact, only from 1526, as established by Svetlana G. Zvereva in her excellent article, "O khore gosudarevykh pevchikh d'iakov v XVI v." [On the choir of the sovereign singers in the 16th century], *PKNO for 1987* (1988): 125–30. See also N. P. Parfent'ev, *Professional'nye muzykanty rossiiskogo gosudarstva XVI–XVII vekov* [Professional musicians of the Russian state in the 16th–17th centuries] (Cheliabinsk: Kniga, 1991), another extremely valuable study of this ensemble, with extensive archival documentation of individual singers. Parfent'ev gives another thorough summary in *Drevnerusskoe pevcheskoe iskusstvo.*

In this chapter (and throughout volume 1) Findeizen refers to a German, or Foreign, Quarter and to the Aleksandrovskaia Quarter or settlement. The Russian term used for both is *sloboda,* a large village, often inhabited by free, non-serf peasants; the term came to designate a tax-free zone and therefore a district of a city established for foreign merchants and settlers who came to live and trade there. There is a useful English summary in Samuel H. Baron, "The Origins of Seventeenth Century Moscow's Nemeckaja Sloboda," *California Slavic Studies* 5 (1970): 1–17, and reprinted in his *Muscovite Russia: Collected Essays* (London: Variorum Reprints, 1980). See also Martha Luby Lahana, "Novaia Nemetskaia Sloboda: Seventeenth-Century Moscow's Foreign Suburb" (Ph.D. diss., University of North Carolina at Chapel Hill, 1983).

Findeizen dutifully records the oft-repeated statement that Ivan IV was a composer of church hymns, an issue which has engendered considerable literature. Keldysh summarizes the basic information in *IRM* 1:132–33, noting that Dmitrii Likhachev has identified a *kanon* as Ivan's, although the work is preserved under a different name. Note 309 below includes additional information on transcriptions of hymns attributed to or associated with Ivan IV. Keldysh rightly refutes Findeizen's assumption that Ivan IV had someone else write down the notation for his musical works, as both of the hymns are *podobny,* that is, the pattern of verse and melody is based on a preexisting model. Experienced singers thus undoubtedly already knew the melodies and fitted the new text into the traditional melodies as indicated. If the tsar had learned to sing from the notation existing at that time, he might have been able to record his compositions as well. The question of Ivan the Terrible as hymnographer and composer has been discussed recently, with convincing examination of sources and attribution of works, by Natal'ia Semenovna Seregina, "Otrazhenie istoricheskikh sobytii v stikhire o Temir-Aksake i v drugikh pesnopeniiakh vladimirskoi ikone i problema avtorstva Ivana Groznogo" [The reflection of historical events in the *stikhira* about Tamerlane and in other chants to the Vladimir icon and the problem of Ivan the Terrible's authorship], *PKNO for 1985* (1987): 148–64, with references to previous literature; see also the discussion in Parfent'ev, *Drevnerusskoe pevcheskoe iskusstvo*, 99–102. The entire eleventh volume of *BLDR* is devoted to Ivan's works, including his hymns, and see also *SKK* 2, pt. 1: 371–84 for extensive bibliography. There has been a great deal of scholarly debate about the authenticity of Ivan's literary works; see Keenan, *The Kurbskii-Groznyi Apocrypha.*

In this chapter Findeizen also mentions the *Domostroi,* which was a basic code for Orthodox family life and household management from the sixteenth century. Sil'vestr (d. before 1577) may have compiled or written parts of the work; see *SKK* 2, pt. 2: 323–33, for a survey of his life and relevant bibliography. A recent edition is V. V. Kolesov and V. V. Rozhdestvenskaia, eds., *Domostroi* (St. Petersburg: Nauka, 2000); and there is also an English translation by Carolyn Johnston Pouncy, *The Domostroi: Rules for Russian Households in the Time of Ivan the Terrible* (Ithaca: Cornell University Press, 1994).

Finally, Findeizen cites a "key" to the Kazan notation, titled *Kniga, glagolemaia Kokizy, sirech' kliuch k Kazanskomu znameni* [Book called *Kokiza,* which is to say the key to the Kazan notation]. Although the term *kokiza* does designate a collection of melodic formulas (and several additional names are used to describe such formulas, for example, *litso* and *fita*), at the time of this writing no definitive key to understanding Kazan notation is known. Brazhnikov's pupils, N. S. Seregina and A. N. Kriukov, edited one of Brazhnikov's larger works, the *Litsa i fity znamennogo raspeva* [The *litsa* and *fity* of znamennyi singing] (Leningrad: Muzyka, 1984), which discusses some of these problems. See also Rogov, *Muzykal'naia estetika,* 155–59.]

296C. [*Editors' note:* Findeizen's "[o] veshchannom boiarine" (the eloquent boyar; *Ocherki* 1:237) should probably be "boiane," that is, referring to the figure of Boian. The term *gudets* in this passage is probably best translated as singer or player; see Dal', *Tolkovyi slovar',* 1:405–406; and Jakobson and Worth, *Sofonija's Tale,* l. 13. There is an enormous literature on the various versions of the *Zadonshchina* and the ways in which it might relate to the Igor tale; see, for example, J. L. I. Fennell, "The *Slovo o polku Igoreve:* The Textological Triangle," *Oxford Slavonic Papers,* n.s. 1 (1968): 126–37, which provides a summary of the different views and a history of the scholarly exchanges.]

296D. [*Editors' note:* Findeizen's first text is very close to that in Jakobson and Worth, *Sofonija's Tale,* l. 17; the translation is taken from this source, with some modifications in transliteration to conform to the editorial practices of this volume. Findeizen's second passage is close, but not identical, to line 30 in the same source; the translation of the first two lines here is taken from Jakobson and Worth.]

296E. [*Editors' note:* This passage corresponds to Jakobson and Worth, *Sofonija's Tale,* ll. 55–56, from which this translation is taken.]

297. A later version of the *Zadonshchina,* from a seventeenth-century copy, was published by V. Undol'skii in the *Vremennik Mosk. obshch. istorii i drevnostei rossiiskikh* 14 (1852). Buslaev referred to this copy, as cited above [in chapter 3], stating that it is distinguished by its "folk-poetic quality" (see his *Istoricheskaia khristomatiia,* 1323). An even older copy, closer to the original text, is preserved in a manuscript from the St. Cyril–Belozersk Monastery from the fifteenth century (Public Library [RNB] Kir. 9/1086), published by P. K. Simoni, *Pamiatniki starinnogo russkogo iazyka i slovesnosti* [see n. 84 above].

297A. [*Editors' note:* Ivan Nikitich Bersen' Beklemishev was tried, along with Maksim Grek, in 1525, as a result of his criticisms of Ivan's foreign policies; the testimony of the trial, from which Findeizen took his quotation, is in *Akty, sobrannye v bibliotekakh i arkhivakh Rossiiskoi imperii Arkheo-*

graficheskoi ekspeditsiei (St. Petersburg: V. Tip. II-go otdeleniia Sobstvennoi E. I. V. kantseliarii, 1836), vol. 1, document no. 172, 141–45; it is also cited in A. A. Zimin, *Rossiia na poroge novogo vremeni* [Russia on the threshold of the modern age] (Moscow: Mysl', 1972), 283. Thanks to Daniel Waugh for these references. Maksim (1470?–1556) was a Greek monk who had been close to Lorenzo de Medici's circle in Florence who came to Moscow as a translator in 1518. He eventually wrote many important works in Russian, but his views on ecclesiastical holdings led to a trial and to his eventual exile; he never returned to Greece. There is a brief summary of his life in *MERSH* 21:26–28. The Third Rome theory, also mentioned in Findeizen's text, said that Russia was the successor of Byzantium as the heir to Rome; *MERSH* 23:118–21 gives an account of the complex origins and evolution of this doctrine.]

298. *Drevnosti Rossiiskogo gosudarstva* [Antiquities of the Russian state], pt. 2, plate no. 85. [There is a photograph of the throne in *Gosudarstvennaia Oruzheinaia palata* [The State Armory] (Moscow: Sovetskii khudozhnik, 1988), 365; there is some debate as to its date and origin, but scholars generally suggest a Western origin in the sixteenth century.]

299. Ibid., plate no. 62.

300. In addition to other craftsmen, Ivan Friazin, a chaplain of the Augustinian order of white monks, was brought to Moscow; in some documents he is named Ivan Spasitel'. The "Jewish physician Mistro Leon from Venice" was brought to Moscow as well (see *Vremennik Mosk. obshch. istorii i drevn. Ross.*, 3 and 16:21, correction by K. M. Obolenskii). [See the introductory remarks, above, on the figure of Ivan Friazin.]

301. Irina, sister of Boris Godunov [and wife of Tsar Fedor].

302. *Zapiski o Moskovii XVI v. sera Dzheroma Gorseia* [Notes about Muscovy in the 16th century by Sir Jerome Horsey] (St. Petersburg: Suvorin, 1909), 74. [This passage is cited here from Horsey, *Russia at the close of the sixteenth century*, 222. On p. 217, Horsey notes that, while in London at the beginning of 1586, "in the interim . . . [I] had made my provicion of lyons, bulls, doggs, guilt halberds . . . organes, virgenalls, musicions . . . and other costly things of great value, according to my commissions." He returned to Moscow in April of that year.]

302A. [*Editors' note:* The Fitzwilliam Virginal Book is generally believed to have been copied about a decade earlier than Findeizen states; it is not known, from Horsey's description, what pieces may have been played on those "organes and virgenalls" at the Muscovite court.]

303. *PSRL* 6 (1853), 335. It is interesting to note that Afanasii Nikitin had learned many Persian and other foreign words and loved to show off in his *Travels*, even if he pronounced them incorrectly. This Russian imitative trait goes far back into the past. [These translations are based on the text and modern Russian translation in *PLDR vtoraia polovina XV veka*, 454–57 (the first two passages); and 470–71. See Lenhoff, "Beyond Three Seas," for a different interpretation of the significance of the many non-Russian passages in the text; on p. 438, she identifies "Meliktuchar" ("the prince of merchants") as Mahmud Gawan of Khorassan. The word *nagarniki* (and variants) in the modern Russian translation in *PLDR* is translated simply as *barabanshchiki* (percussionists, or variants), but see Roizman, *Organ*, 41 and note for a discussion of this term in the context of military instruments; in other sources transmitting Nikitin's account, the word appears as *varganniki*. Findeizen's reference to children taken prisoner by the Hindustanis is from a passage in Nikitin retelling a local legend about a monkey prince and his army. The offspring of this monkey kingdom are sometimes taken in by the local people and are taught various skills. See the partial English translation in Zenkovsky, *Medieval Russia's Epics, Chronicles, and Tales*, 333–53; the tale of the monkey army is on 342.]

303A. [*Editors' note:* Carlo Bartolomeo Rastrelli (1675–1744) was a sculptor and artist who worked in St. Petersburg; his son, Bartolomeo Francesco (1700–1771), was an important architect who worked on many of the buildings in the city in mid-century, during the reigns of Empresses Anna and Elizabeth. See *MERSH* 30:199–200.]

304. The Cathedral of St. Dmitrii in Vladimir was also built by foreign architects in the thirteenth century. It is interesting to note that Fioravanti went to Vladimir to examine this church and that he recognized it as a model for ecclesiastical architecture. [The chronicle reference is from *PSRL* 12 (1965), 192; the translation is from Zenkovsky and Zenkovsky, *The Nikonian Chronicle,* 5:209. On the cathedral, which dates from the twelfth century, see Brumfield, *A History of Russian Architecture,* 51–61.]

305. *RIB* 2:784–86. Ivashka Kostitsa is mentioned in the documents several times. [See also the brief entry in Parfent'ev, *Professional'nye muzykanty,* 254.]

306. The author of the St. Sofia Annals enumerates in detail all of Ivan III's banquets in Novgorod in the year 1476 (*PSRL* 6 [1853], 16) as well as all the rich gifts he received on such occasions [see chapter 4 above]. The famous Novgorod *skomorokhi* undoubtedly entertained the ruler at that time.

306A. [*Editors' note:* See n. 86F above, on the term *kliros.*]

307. P. Pierling, *L'Italie et la Russie au XVI siècle* (Paris: E. Leroux, 1892). [The figure Findeizen refers to as Paul of Veng is Paolo Chenturione [Centurione], a Genoese merchant who was in Muscovy as a representative of Leo X; see Zimin, *Rossiia na poroge novogo vremeni,* 205, 302; and the sources cited there. Our thanks to Daniel Waugh for this reference.]

307A. [*Editors' note:* It is, of course, hardly possible that Gerasimov heard music by Palestrina. As pointed out, for example, in MA 1:19 n. 1, the year 1525 is roughly the date of Palestrina's birth. On Gerasimov and his activities, see the concise summary in Robert M. Croskey, *Muscovite Diplomatic Practice in the Reign of Ivan III* (New York: Garland, 1987), 271.]

308. *PSRL* 3 (1841), 167 (Novgorod II Chronicle). [*PSRL* 30 (1965), 189, under the year 1572.]

308A. [*Editors' note:* On Prince Andrei Kurbskii, see n. 210A above.]

308B. [*Editors' note:* Christian Kelch (1657–1710) was a priest in Estonia and a historian of Livonia (Latvia). Findeizen uses his work, *Liefländische historia* (Reval, 1695), as a source for Ivan the Terrible's behavior at the wedding of his niece to the Danish prince Johan Magnus in Novgorod in 1570. This was the date of the betrothal; the actual date of that event was 12 April 1573, and Magnus occupied the throne of Livonia until his death in 1583.]

308C. [*Editors' note:* Olearius, *Travels,* 91–92, cited earlier.]

308D. [*Editors' note:* On Anastasia, see *MERSH* 31:148–50.]

309. See the article "Stikhiry, polozhennye na kriukovye noty. Tvorenie tsaria Ioanna despota Rossiiskogo" [*Stikhiry* set to *kriukovye* notation, composed by Tsar Ivan, autocrat of Russia] after manuscript 428 in the library of the Trinity–St. Sergius Lavra, communicated by Archimandrite Leonid, *Pamiatniki drevnei pis'mennosti* [Monuments of early writing] (St. Petersburg, 1886). [This source is currently located in RGB, f. 304, no. 428. Additional *stikhiry* from the cycle of works appearing under the attribution to Ivan IV are included in N. A. Uspenskii, *Obraztsy drevnerusskogo pevcheskogo iskusstva* [Examples of the old Russian art of chanting] (Leningrad: Muzyka, 1971), 130–33; and in his *Drevnerusskoe pevcheskoe iskusstvo* [Old Russian singing] (Moscow: Sovetskii kompozitor, 1971), 21 n. 2; as well as in Morosan, *One Thousand Years,* 16–19, 677–78. See also the transcription in Gardner, *Bogosluzhebnoe penie,* 1:460–63. Keldysh, *IRM* 1:132–33, lists a third text attributed to the ruler. Many thanks to Irina Lozovaia for information on and clarification of this group of pieces.]

310. Leonid, "Stikhiry," p. III.

310A. [*Editors' note:* See the passage and modern Russian translation in *PLDR seredina XVI veka* [mid-16th century], 166–67, on which the present translation is based.]

310B. [*Editors' note:* On this terminology, see chapter 4 above.]

311. Manuscript no. 1885, fol. 155, in the collection of Count Uvarov [in GIM]. See Archimandrite Leonid, *Sistematicheskoe opisanie slaviano-rossiiskikh rukopisei sobraniia grafa A. S. Uvarova* [Systematic description of the Slavonic-Russian manuscripts in the collection of Count A. S. Uvarov] (Moscow: Tip. A. I. Mamontova, 1893–94), pt. 4, 244. [The descriptions of Vasilii Rogov and, below, of Ivan Nos are cited in chapter 4; see also Protopopov, *Russkaia mysl' o muzyke,* 27.]

312. Golubtsov, "Chinovnik novgorodskogo Sofiiskogo sobora," 70. [The music historian Alfred Swan (1890–1970) in his own copy of Findeizen's *Ocherki*, now at the University of Virginia, corrected this reference to p. 130. See also chapter 4 and n. 155 above.]

313. It is entirely possible that the Moscow singers Gavril Afonas'ev, Matvei Adamov, Dmitrii Tsarev, and Tret'iak Zverintsev, all of whom Ivan promoted in the 1550s, may have participated in this work. [A typographical error in *Ocherki* 1:249 places the establishment of the patriarchate in 1689 rather than in 1589.]

314. After manuscript no. 32.16.18 in the library of the Academy of Sciences [BAN]. [This manuscript is described in F. V. Panchenko, comp., *Pevcheskie rukopisi v sobranii biblioteki Rossiiskoi Akademii nauk* [Notated musical manuscripts in the collection of the library of the Russian Academy of Sciences] (St. Petersburg: Biblioteka Rossiiskoi Akademii nauk, 1994), 16–17. Findeizen, in his caption to figure 92, assigns the manuscript a date in the eighteenth century, which is probably a typographical error.]

314A. [*Editors' note: Tragoedia Moscovitica: sive de vita et morte Demetrii* (Cologne: Gerard Greuenbruch, 1608); Findeizen's source is a Latin-Russian parallel translation by A. Braudo and I. Rostsius, eds., *Moskovskaia tragediia, ili rasskaz o zhizni i smerti Dimitriia* [A Moscow tragedy, or a narrative of the life and death of Dmitrii] (St. Petersburg: V. S. Balashev, 1901), 58. This work (published, not written, by Greuenbruch) is one of several closely related accounts of the events of Dmitrii's rule that came out in Western Europe between 1606 and 1607; see Isaac Massa, *A Short History of the Beginnings and Origins of These Present Wars in Moscow under the Reign of Various Sovereigns Down to the Year 1610,* trans. and ed. G. Edward Orchard (Toronto: University of Toronto Press, 1982), xxiii. On the False Dmitrii, see Philip L. Barbour, *Dimitry Called the Pretender, Tsar and Great Prince of All Russia, 1605–1606* (Boston: Houghton Mifflin; Cambridge, Mass.: Riverside, 1966); for general background, see Maureen Perrie, *Pretenders and Popular Monarchism in Early Modern Russia: The False Tsars of the Time of Troubles* (Cambridge: Cambridge University Press, 1995); and Chester S. L. Dunning, *Russia's First Civil War: The Time of Troubles and the Founding of the Romanov Dynasty* (University Park: Pennsylvania State University Press, 2001); as well as the extensive bibliographies cited in these works.]

314B. [*Editors' note:* Braudo and Rostsius, *Moskovskaia tragediia,* 46.]

314C. [*Editors' note:* Findeizen's source appears to be Braudo and Rostsius, *Moskovskaia tragediia,* 61, although the anonymous author does not mention *skomorokhi* specifically but describes dancing, secular music, and general festivities.]

314D. [*Editors' note:* Contemporaries referred to Dmitrii as *rastriga,* as Massa explains in his account, saying that the term "means 'the untonsured.'" . . . In the end, he was given several other such epithets . . . but they called him nothing but 'the Renegade Monk'" (Massa, *A Short History,* 74–75). His residence in Moscow, the Rasstriginy Palaty, was used in the early eighteenth century for a theater; see chapter 12 below.]

315. P. O. Morozov, *Istoriia russkogo teatra* [History of the Russian theater] (St. Petersburg: Tip. V. Demakova, 1889), 113. [Petr Osipovich Morozov (1854–1919) was a well-known historian of the theater; see *BSovE,* 40:821.]

315A. [*Editors' note:* Massa's work is cited here from Massa, *A Short History,* 117–18. Massa describes the celebration of Dmitrii's wedding, complete with music, on pp. 131–34. The musicians at Dmitrii's court were killed at the same time that he was; see p. 140 of Massa's account.]

315B. [*Editors' note:* The account of the mask and *dudka* appears in Braudo and Rostsius, *Moskovskaia tragediia,* 53–54. Massa, *A Short History,* 138, also mentions the presence of masks at the time of Dmitrii's death, as does Conrad Bussow in *The Disturbed State of the Russian Realm,* trans. and ed. G. Edward Orchard (Montreal: McGill-Queen's University Press, 1994), 77. Bussow was in Muscovy during the first decade of the seventeenth century. On the broader symbolic implications of this treatment of Dmitrii's corpse, see B. A. Uspenskij, "Tsar and Pretender: *Samozvančestvo* or Royal Imposture in Russia as a Cultural-Historical Phenomenon," in Ju. M. Lotman and B. A. Uspenskij, *The Semiotics of Russian Culture,* ed. Ann Shukman, *Michigan Slavic Contributions* 11 (1984): 259–92.]

315C. [*Editors' note: RIB* 13: col. 59 (and cf. col. 831). Similar stories are recounted in Bussow, *The Disturbed State of the Russian Realm,* 78.]

9. Music in the Monastery. *Chashi* (Toasts). Bell Ringing. Sacred Performances (Sixteenth and Seventeenth Centuries)

[*Editors' note:* The topics treated in this chapter are seldom found in books dealing with Russian music. Russian scholars have been studying the repentance verses since the nineteenth century, and scholars today are currently examining these texts and their surviving music, particularly Adam's Lament, which appears in variants both with and without music. One version of this text was discussed recently by N. S. Seregina, "Pokaiannyi stikh 'Plach Adama o Rae' rospeva Kirila Gomulina" [The repentance verse "Adam's Lament for Paradise" in the version by Kiril Gomulin], *PKNO for 1983* (1985): 258–62. A less frequently encountered example of the repentance verse was surveyed by S. V. Frolov, "Iz istorii drevnerusskoi muzyki (Rannii spisok stikhov pokaiannykh)" [From the history of old Russian music (an early copy of the repentance verses)], in *Kul'turnoe nasledie drevnei Rusi* [The cultural heritage of old Rus'] (Moscow: Nauka, 1976), 162–71, which includes a transcription of the music. See also the texts, translations into modern Russian, commentary, and bibliography in *PLDR vtoraia polovina XVI veka* [second half of the 16th century], 550–63, 635–40; *BLDR* 10:556–61; and the article "Stikhi pokaiannye" [Repentance verses] in *SKK* 2, pt. 2: 421–23.

The subject of "toasts to the ruler" (*chashi gosudarevy*) was studied primarily by prerevolutionary Russian scholars; their work is summarized in the article on the subject in *SKK* 2, pt. 2: 508–11; see also the article on Ivan Semenovich Kurakin by L. V. Sokolova and Ia. G. Solodkin in *SKK* 3, pt. 2: 206–12. (Kurakin [ca. 1575–1632] is listed as the author of a toast in honor of Tsar Mikhail Fedorovich, the first Romanov tsar, whose reign began in 1613.) A recent study of these toasts is by E. L. Burilina, "Chin 'za prilivok o zdravii gosudaria' (istoriia formirovaniia i osobennosti bytovaniia)" [The rite of the "pouring to the health of the tsar" (a history of its development and contextual details)], in D. S. Likhachev, ed., *Drevnerusskaia literatura: istochnikovedenie* [Old Russian literature: Source studies] (Leningrad, Nauka, 1984), 204–14, which includes an extensive listing of sources.

Findeizen frequently refers to Patriarch Nikon (lay name Nikita Minov, 1605–1681), who served as Patriarch of the Russian Church from 1652 to 1667. Nikon was a highly controversial figure, a supporter of some liturgical reforms which led to the great schism in the Russian Church (for a biographical survey, see *MERSH* 25:4–10; and *SKK* 3, pt. 2: 400–404, pt. 4: 757–61). Although Nikon was ultimately forced to resign and sent into exile, his reforms were upheld and his main opponents eventually withdrew from the official church. To this day they are known as Old Believers [*staroobriadtsy*]; the schism itself was known as the *raskol,* and the followers of the schism were termed *raskol'niki.*

It was during this period, in 1654, that the union of Ukraine and Russia took place, although this event was followed by more than a decade of war with both Poland and Sweden; at the 1667 "eternal peace" signed with Poland, Moscow gained claim to Kiev and territories east of the Dnieper River, as well as retaining the cities it had taken during the course of hostilities, particularly Smolensk. It is from the time of the 1654 union that Kievan singers began to be called to Moscow in significant numbers, and it is from this time that we can date the beginning of the strong Western influences in Muscovite music, particularly the widespread use of polyphony in religious services as well as in non-liturgical and secular music. (Findeizen also discusses this process in chapter 10.) In this context it is useful to note the rediscovery of a Kievan manuscript with staff notation dating from about the year 1600. It has been examined and described in several brief studies by Anatol V. Konotop, particularly in his "Drevneishii pamiatnik ukrainskogo notolineinogo pis'ma—Suprasl'skii irmologion

1598–1601 gg." [The oldest document of Ukrainian staff notation: The Irmologii from Suprasl' of ca. 1598–1601], *PKNO for 1974* (1975): 285–93.

It is entirely possible that some polyphonic practices may already have existed in the Russian tradition, and recently uncovered documentation suggests that certain aspects of *demestvennyi raspev* may have been polyphonic in the mid-sixteenth century. Yet through the influx of Kievan singers, who seem to have been exposed to contemporary Western trends then current in Poland, the beginning of the second half of the seventeenth century presents a definite reorientation in the singing practices of the official church, which not only condoned but even fostered these new settings. There are also references in this period to many different types of chants, although some of these may date from an earlier time. By mid-century one can no longer speak of a single, unified Russian chant; instead, there were many different types, including Kievan, *znamennyi, bol'shoi raspev* (large, great), and *malyi raspev* (little or short), as well as Bulgarian, Greek, and Serbian chant. This is in addition to the previously discussed *demestvennyi* and *putevoi* chant types. On the so-called Greek chant in the Russian tradition, see the discussion in L. A. Igoshev, "Proiskhozhdenie grecheskogo rospeva (opyt analiza)" [The origin of Greek chant (an essay in analysis)], *PKNO for 1992* (1993): 147–50; and see the general survey in Parfent'ev, *Drevnerusskoe pevcheskoe iskusstvo,* chaps. 1 and 2.

In addition to chants for the religious ritual, nonliturgical and secular music also began to appear in polyphonic settings in this period. The most prominent genre is the *kant* (pl. *kanty*), which takes its name from the Latin *cantus,* clearly showing the Western origins of both its name and its style. Furthermore, some of the first significant treatises on music made their appearance in Russia at this time and, with them, polyphonic compositions on a large scale. The term *partesnoe penie* in this period indicated singing according to the individual parts, from the Latin *partes;* there were more than five hundred so-called *partesnye kontserty,* polyphonic, polychoral, a cappella works for four, eight, twelve, sixteen, twenty, and even more parts. In this chapter we use the term *kontsert* as a way of distinguishing these works from eighteenth-century concerti; we also use the terms *partesnoe penie* and part singing interchangeably.

In this chapter Findeizen discusses the cleric Simeon Polotskii (1629–1680; secular name Samuil Petrovskii-Sitnianovich), a poet, teacher, and author of dramatic plays. Simeon arrived in Moscow in 1663 or 1664, and in 1667 was entrusted with the education of the tsar's children. There is an extensive survey, plus a very large bibliography, in *SKK* 3, pt. 3: 362–79, by A. M. Panchenko, D. M. Bulanin, and A. A. Romanova, with updated bibliography in *SKK* 3, pt. 4: 790–94, and a selection of his works is readily available in I. P. Eremin, ed., *Simeon Polotskii: Izbrannye sochineniia* [Simeon Polotskii: Collected works] (Moscow: Akademiia nauk, 1953; reprinted in St. Petersburg: Nauka, 2004). The best English-language study of Polotskii's works is by Anthony Hippisley, *The Poetic Style of Simeon Polotsky,* Birmingham Slavonic Monographs 16 (Birmingham: Department of Russian Language and Literature, University of Birmingham, 1985). Simon Karlinsky, in his fine book *Russian Drama from Its Beginnings to the Age of Pushkin* (Berkeley: University of California Press, 1985), discusses "Simeon of Polotsk" on pp. 111–14, and see the general survey of his life in *MERSH* 29:8–11. Findeizen discusses Simeon's plays in chapter 10.

Among Polotskii's works was a verse translation of the complete Psalter, a text which was set to music several years later by Vasilii Polikarpovich Titov (ca. 1650–1715), probably the most impressive and outstanding composer of choral music at the end of the seventeenth and the early years of the eighteenth centuries. There are brief entries on Titov in *MGG* 13: cols. 436–37; *NG2;* and *ME* 5: col. 533, and see also Keldysh's more detailed survey in *IRM* 1:243–49, 287–92 (including some brief musical examples). An excellent survey of Titov's works is in Olga Dolskaya-Ackerly, "Vasilii Titov and the 'Moscow' Baroque," *Journal of the Royal Musical Association* 118, no. 2 (1993): 203–22; and see also idem, "The Early Kant in Seventeenth-Century Russian Music" (Ph.D. diss., University of Kansas, 1983). Titov's settings of Polotskii's *Versified Psalter* are studied in a dissertation by N. A. Solov'ian,

"Pesennyi sbornik V. Titova na teksty S. Polotskogo—kak vydaiushchiisia pamiatnik russkoi kamer-noi vokal'noi muzyki vtoroi poloviny XVII veka" [V. Titov's song collection on texts by S. Polotskii as an outstanding monument of Russian chamber vocal music in the second half of the 17th century] (unpublished *diplomnaia rabota*, Moscow Conservatory, 1978), and there is also a discussion of the composer and his works in V. V. Protopopov's important work, *Muzyka na Poltavskuiu pobedu* [Music for the victory at Poltava], PRMI 2 (Moscow: Muzyka, 1973). Some of Titov's works are available in Olga Dolskaya, ed., *Vasilii Titov i russkoe barokko: Izbrannye khorovye proizvedeniia / Vasily Titov and the Russian Baroque: Selected Choral Works*, in Vladimir Morosan, ed., Pamiatniki russkoi dukhovnoi muzyki / Monuments of Russian Sacred Music, series 13, vol. 1 (Madison, Conn.: Musica Russica, 1995), and in Morosan, *One Thousand Years*.

A sizable part of this chapter deals with the discussion of what were called *deistva* (acts or actions), which we translate as "liturgical dramas" but which could also indicate some other kind of religious ceremonial action or procession. Although it is uncertain when these "actions" came into existence, it appears that their introduction into the ritual served a didactic function, illustrating in clear and approachable form the meaning and the moral of the liturgical message. They are well documented in the sixteenth and first half of the seventeenth century, after which time they seem to have fallen out of use. Findeizen mentions several of these actions, particularly the Palm Sunday procession, during which the patriarch was seated on a donkey and led by the tsar, impersonating Christ's entry into Jerusalem. Interpretation of the symbolism of this and other actions is presented by Michael S. Flier, "Breaking the Code: The Image of the Tsar in the Muscovite Palm Sunday Ritual," in Michael S. Flier and Daniel Rowland, eds., *Medieval Russian Culture*, vol. 2 (Berkeley: University of California Press, 1994), 213–42 (this is vol. 19 of *California Slavic Studies*); and Robert O. Crummey, "Court Spectacles in Seventeenth Century Russia: Illusion and Reality," in *Essays in Honor of A. A. Zimin*, ed. Daniel C. Waugh (Columbus, Ohio: Slavica, 1985), 130–58; see also Richard Wortman, *Scenarios of Power: Myth and Ceremony in Russian Monarchy*, vol. 1, *From Peter the Great to the Death of Nicholas I* (Princeton, N.J.: Princeton University Press, 1995); and Paul Bushkovitch, "The Epiphany Ceremony of the Russian Court in the Sixteenth and Seventeenth Centuries," *Russian Review* 49, no. 1 (1990): 1–17. A half-dozen other, less developed actions or plays are known to have existed, including one depicting the Last Judgment.

The most elaborate was the Play of the Furnace, which reenacted the story of the Three Children in the Fiery Furnace, performed on the Sunday of the Holy Fathers (the Sunday before Christmas, which could fall between 17 and 23 December). The documentation for this play is plentiful and most elaborate, as discussed in Velimirović, "Liturgical Drama in Byzantium and Russia," 351–85. Keldysh has also discussed this action several times, for example, in his "Renessansnye tendentsii v russkoi muzyke XVI veka" [Renaissance traits in Russian music of the 16th century], in *Teoreticheskie nabliudeniia nad istoriei muzyki* [Theoretical research in the history of music] (Moscow: Muzyka, 1978), 174–99, esp. 191–99 (this is a Festschrift for V. V. Protopopov); and in *IRM* 1:152–60. See also Karlinsky's *Russian Drama from Its Beginnings*, 1–6; and Likhachev, Panchenko, and Ponyrko, *Smekh v drevnei Rusi*, 156ff. It has been suggested that *skomorokhi* might have participated in the Play of the Furnace, based on foreign accounts of the wild behavior of the actors who played the Chaldean jailers in the play and who ran about the city after the performance throughout the Christmas season, until Epiphany, when they were supposed to cleanse themselves by jumping into the river (see Velimirović, "Liturgical Drama," 373). The English traveler Giles Fletcher, who was in Muscovy in 1588–89, said that the Chaldeans "run about the towne all the twelue dayes, disguised in their plaiers coats, and make much good sport for the honour of the Bishops pageant" (Lloyd E. Berry, ed., *The English Works of Giles Fletcher, the Elder* (Madison: University of Wisconsin Press, 1964), 293; and see later descriptions by Olearius (*The Travels of Olearius*, 241) and Guy Miege, *A Relation of Three Embassies from his Sacred Majestie Charles II to the Great Duke of Muscovie, the King of Sweden, and the King of Denmark* (London: Printed for

John Starkey, 1669), 104–105. Other evidence comes, indirectly, from payment records. Ivan Zabelin, *Materialy dlia istorii, arkheologii i statistiki goroda Moskvy* [Sources for the history, archaeology, and statistics of the city of Moscow] (Moscow: Moskovskaia gorodskaia tip., 1884), 1:55–58, lists the names of several people who played the roles of Chaldeans in the late 1620s and into the early 1630s; although they are not specifically called *skomorokhi*, they are also not labeled as *pod'iaki* or as members of the established singing ensembles, as were the other participants.

Findeizen's reference to a contemporary description of the Palm Sunday procession by Martin Beer (or Behr, the pastor of the Lutheran Church in Moscow) needs correction. According to *ES-BE* 9:69, the actual writer was Behr's son-in-law, Conrad Bussow (d. 1617); Findeizen relied on an early edition of the publication by Nikolai Gerasimovich Ustrialov (1805–1870), listed in n. 338 below, which was apparently corrected in later editions but which seems to have escaped Findeizen's attention. On Bussow, see *MERSH* 6:51–53; and the edition by I. I. Smirnov, *Moskovskaia khronika, 1584–1613* [Moscow chronicle, 1584–1613] (Moscow: AN SSSR, 1961). The English translation by G. Edward Orchard, *The Disturbed State of the Russian Realm* (Montreal: McGill-Queen's University Press, 1994), also addresses the issue of the authorship of the work.

Findeizen mentions several other foreigners who described the Palm Sunday procession: the Danish Prince Johann; Jacques Margeret; Samuel Maskiewicz; Petrus Petrejus; Olearius; and Baron Augustin von Meyerberg, whose account includes drawings showing a panoramic view of Red Square and the procession itself, as seen in Findeizen's fig. 94 [in this volume]). Some of these works are available in accessible editions. On Jacques Margeret (ca.1565–?), see *The Russian Empire and Grand Duchy of Muscovy: A 17th-Century French Account*, trans. Chester S. L. Dunning (Pittsburgh: University of Pittsburgh Press, 1983); and *Un mousquetaire à Moscou: Mémoires sur la première révolution russe, 1604–1614*, ed. Alexandre Bennigsen (Paris: La Découverte/Maspero, 1983). On Samuel Maskiewicz (ca. 1580–ca. 1640), see the *Wielka Encyklopedia Powszechna*, 7:9; see also the *Polski Słownik biograficzny*, 20:120–22). His son, Bogusław (1625–1683), was later a witness to events in Moscow in 1660. Their joint memoirs were edited by A. Sajkowski, *Pamiętniki Samuela i Bogusława Kazimierza Maskiewiczów.*

The accounts by Petrus Petrejus (or Petreius, 1570–1622) survive in several languages; see *MERSH* 28:18, and Marshall Poe, *Foreign Descriptions of Muscovy: An Analytic Bibliography of Primary and Secondary Sources* (Columbus, Ohio: Slavica, 1995), 152–53. The *Reliatsiia Petra Petreia o Rossii nachala XVII v.* [Petrus Petrejus's *Relatio* on Russia at the beginning of the 17th century] is available in an edition by Iu. A. Limonov and V. I. Buganov (Moscow: AN SSSR, 1976); his larger history (issued in Leipzig in German in 1620), which was based on his earlier *Relatio,* was translated by A. N. Shemiakin (1867) and has been reprinted in Petrus Petrejus [Petr Petrei], *Istoriia o velikom kniazhestve Moskovskom* [History of the great principality of Moscow], *O nachale voin i smut v Moskovii* [On the beginning of the wars and the Time of Troubles in Muscovy], ed. A. Liberman and S. Shokarev, in the series Istoriia Rossii i doma Romanovykh v memuarakh sovremennikov XVII–XX vv. [A history of Russia and the house of the Romanovs in memoirs by contemporaries, 17th–20th centuries] (Moscow: Fond Sergeia Dubova, 1997), 151–464. Baron Augustin Meyerberg (1622–1688) served Emperor Leopold I several times as ambassador and was sent to Moscow between 1661 and 1663. His report, *Iter in Moschoviam* (1661), was published in Burchard von Wichmann, *Sammlung bisher noch ungedruckter kleiner Schriften zur ältern Geschichte und Kenntniss des russischen Reichs* (Berlin: Bey Georg Reimer, 1820). A reprint of a translation by A. N. Shemiakin (1874) is in Augustin Meyerberg [Avgustin Meierberg], *Puteshestvie v Moskoviiu barona Avgustina Meierberga* [A journey through Muscovy by Baron Augustin Meyerberg], *Utverzhdenie dinastii* [The establishment of the dynasty], ed. A. Liberman and S. Shokarev, in the series Istoriia Rossii i doma Romanovykh v memuarakh sovremennikov XVII–XX vv. [A history of Russia and the house of the Romanovs in memoirs by contemporaries, 17th–20th centuries] (Moscow: Fond Sergeia Dubova, 1997), 43–184. Meyerberg's account includes a number of fascinating pictures documenting contemporary Russian scenes drawn by an artist in his retinue; see Friedrich Adelung, ed., *Al'bom Meierberga: Vidy i bytovye kartiny Rossii XVII veka* [Meyerberg's album: Views and scenes of daily life in Russia in the 17th century] (St. Petersburg: A. S. Suvorin, 1903). A brief entry on Meyerberg in English can be found in *GSE* 16:241, and a more detailed entry in *ES-BE* 36:946–47.

The remainder of this chapter discusses the appearance of theoretical treatises in Russia in the second half of the seventeenth century. Some of these works deal with the chant tradition and some introduce Western polyphonic idioms and concepts such as the hexachord. Findeizen was apparently unaware of an important treatise from 1604 by the monk Khristofor titled "Kliuch znamennoi" [A key to *znamennaia* notation]); the work is discussed in M. V. Brazhnikov and G. Nikishov, eds., *Kliuch znamennoi*, PRMI 9 (Moscow: Muzyka, 1983). This somewhat rambling treatise is quite important for understanding the *putevaia* notation and contains some early examples of the interpretation of these signs in another notational system. The treatise was published with an extensive commentary by Nikishov, who completed the work of his deceased teacher.

Probably the most frequently mentioned chant treatise is the work by Aleksandr Mezenets, who has been viewed as the second great reformer of chant notation after Shaidur. Mezenets was believed to have cleared up any remaining notational problems by adding clarifying signs to the neumes, creating a notation that was fully readable and easily transcribed into Western staff notation. By the end of the seventeenth century, staff notation was widely used in Russian practice (it was called Kievan notation, indicating its origins for Muscovy) and manuscripts called *dvoznamenniki* contained both neumatic and staff notation for the same melodies, a sort of Rosetta stone for establishing the meaning of neumes.

Mezenets's treatise was first published by Stepan Vasil'evich Smolenskii (1848–1909), under the title *Azbuka znamennogo peniia (Izveshchenie o soglasneishikh pometakh) startsa Aleksandra Mezentsa (1668-go goda)* [Alphabet of *znamennoe* singing (Report about the most harmonious notational signs) by the monk Aleksandr Mezenets, 1668] (Kazan: Tip. Imp. universiteta, 1888), which was Findeizen's source for his discussion. All of the older literature concerning the dates of the two commissions of which Mezenets was a member, and, of course, all of Findeizen's statements on this subject, require radical revision following the recent research by Nikolai Pavlovich Parfent'ev. The most concise statement on Mezenets by this scholar appears in *SKK* 3, pt. 1: 63–68; and see his expanded presentation, focusing on manuscript sources and handwriting, in "Aftografy vydaiushchegosia russkogo muzykal'nogo teoretika XVII v. Aleksandra Mezentsa (Stremoukhova)" [Autographs of the outstanding seventeenth-century Russian music theorist Aleksandr Mezenets (Stremoukhov)], *PKNO for 1990* (1992): 173–85. The first significant step in reevaluating the work was taken by Zivar M. Guseinova, professor at the St. Petersburg Conservatory, with her monograph *"Izveshchenie" Aleksandra Mezentsa i teoriia muzyki XVII veka* [The "Report" by Aleksandr Mezenets and music theory in the 17th century] (St. Petersburg: St. Petersburg Conservatory, 1995). Nikolai Parfent'ev, in his *Drevnerusskoe pevcheskoe iskusstvo*, after a thorough examination of contemporary documents, proved that the date of the treatise must be moved to 1670, as a result of misdated council meetings dealing with chant reform. Parfent'ev and Guseinova have published jointly a magnificent volume titled *Aleksandr Mezenets i prochie, Izveshchenie . . . zhelaiushchim uchitsia peniiu, 1670 g.* [Aleksandr Mezenets and others, the "Report . . . for those who wish to learn singing," 1670], introduction, [facsimile] publication, translation of the documents, and historical study by N. P. Parfent'ev, commentary and analysis of the documents and deciphering of the notation by Z. M. Guseinova (Cheliabinsk: Kniga, 1996). The volume contains both the long (88 pp.) and the short (31 pp.) version of the treatise in facsimile.

In his reevaluation of the treatise, Parfent'ev begins with the fact that Mezenets's family name was Stremoukhov and that his father's name was Ivan. Contrary to earlier belief, Mezenets was already a monk in the 1640s and was active as a copyist of musical manuscripts. It is no longer possible to support the traditional view that, in 1668, Mezenets introduced the so-called added signs in black ink to supplant the cinnabar signs which had presumably been invented and used earlier by Shaidur. On the basis of a thorough analysis of manuscripts from various scriptoria, Parfent'ev concludes that both types of signs (the red cinnabar signs and the black ink signs) appeared more or less simultaneously and coexisted before the mid-seventeenth century. Mezenets was not the only one to use them, moreover, for they can be found in other manuscripts. The assumption that Mezenets was a member of the first commission for the correction of manuscripts, in the session from 1652 to 1654, can no longer be assumed. Although he may indeed have participated in the work of that commission, there is no documentary proof that he did so. Furthermore, Uspenskii's statement that, from 1657 on, Mezenets was working at the Printing Office as a *spravshchik* (a censor or corrector) must be abandoned, since the handwriting of the "Monk Aleksandr" at that institution is, in fact, that of Aleksandr Shestakov and not of Aleksandr Mezenets, whose handwriting can be followed in a number of manuscripts.

In the preface to his treatise Mezenets also mentioned that the process of the correction of books by some less "learned" persons had created a situation in which it was impossible for two singers, let alone three or more, to sing in concord. This deficiency led to the second commission, which was in session from 8 February 1669 to 1 May 1670. Parfent'ev has written on this new dating of the commissions in his "O deiatel'nosti komissii po ispravleniiu drevnerusskikh pevcheskikh knig v XVII v." (On the work of the commission for the correction of old Russian singing books in the 17th century), *AE for 1984* (1986): 128–39. Based on this new chronology, he suggests that the date of the treatise should be revised from 1668 to the second half of 1670, after the end of the second commission's work (and, of course, Findeizen's date of 1655 for the first commission and 1666–67 for the second commission must also be revised). Although Mezenets was a member of the second commission, there is no proof that he was its chairman, as many scholars have presumed. Mezenets was probably born in the early years of the seventeenth century, and the last document suggesting that he was alive dates from 1677; there is no recorded date of death. Mezenets is not listed in any of the Western reference tools, although there is a brief article in *ME* 3: col. 493, by N. D. Uspenskii. It is an irony of history that Mezenets's work on clarifying and codifying the meaning of neumes, thus perpetuating their use for future years, was superseded by the rapid penetration of Western staff notation. The only group that consistently retained the use of neumatic manuscripts in Russia, and uses them to this day, is the Old Believers, who were opponents of all the reforms in the seventeenth century.

Several other theorists and composers were active in the seventeenth century in Russia: Nikolai Pavlovich Diletskii (d. after 1681); Ioannikii Trofimovich Korenev (d. ca. 1680–81); and Tikhon Makar'evskii (d. 1707); there are also some anonymous theoretical works from this period. Although all three of these theorists wrote treatises of varying length and significance, Diletskii is the only one known to have been a composer as well. An anonymous treatise (or rather a collection of melodic formulas as a guide to the "weaving of a composition") has been discussed by Alina N. Kruchinina and B. A. Shindin, "Pervoe russkoe posobie po muzykal'noi kompozitsii" [First Russian handbook on musical composition], *PKNO for 1978* (1979): 188–95.

Although Findeizen discusses Tikhon Makar'evskii first, he was chronologically the latest of the three theorists. He was the author of a treatise known as the *Kliuch* [Key] in which he presents comparative versions of neumatic and staff notation. He was thus a champion of the new and modern staff notation in the manuscripts containing both, namely, the *dvoznamenniki* or doubly notated sources that appeared around 1700. There is no mention of Tikhon in Western reference tools, but see *ME* 5:537–38; and Protopopov, *Russkaia mysl' o muzyke*, 65–69.

The most significant of these late-seventeenth-century theorists was Nikolai Pavlovich Diletskii (in Ukrainian, Mykola Pavlovych Dylets'kyi), who appears to have been a native of Kiev. Three complete versions of Diletskii's treatise are available: S. V. Smolenskii, ed., *Musikiiskaia grammatika Nikolaia*

Dilets'kogo [The musical grammar of Nikolai Diletskii], OLDP Izdaniia 128 ([St. Petersburg]: Tip. M. A. Aleksandrova, 1910), which is a version of the treatise from Moscow, 1681; V. V. Protopopov, *Idea grammatiki musikiiskoi* [An idea of a musical grammar], PRMI 7 (Moscow: Muzyka, 1979), which contains a full facsimile, transcription, translation into modern Russian, and extensive study of a source transmitting the Moscow 1679 version; and O. S. Tsalai-Iakymenko, *Hramatyka muzykal'na* [Musical grammar] (Kiev: Muzychna Ukraina, 1970), a full-color facsimile and transcription of a Ukrainian-language source from St. Petersburg, 1723, which transmits a variant of the Smolensk, 1677 version. A selection of Diletskii's compositions is available in N. O. Herasymova-Persyds'ka [N. A. Gerasimova-Persidskaia], ed., *Mykola Dylets'kyi: Khorovi tvory* [Nikolai Diletskii: Choral works] (Kiev: Muzychna Ukraina, 1981); and in Morosan, *One Thousand Years.* The most important work on Diletskii's treatise has been carried out by Vladimir Vasil'evich Protopopov, who has brought to light many new sources transmitting the work; see also the English-language studies by Claudia Jensen, "Nikolai Diletskii's 'Grammatika' (Grammar) and the Musical Culture of Seventeenth-century Muscovy" (Ph.D. diss., Princeton University, 1987); and her article, "A Theoretical Work of Late Seventeenth-century Muscovy: Nikolai Diletskii's *Grammatika* and the Earliest Circle of Fifths," *JAMS* 45 (1992): 305–31.

Korenev is discussed in Protopopov, *Idea grammatiki musikiiskoi,* and he includes a more extended discussion of the theorist in his *Russkaia mysl' o muzyke,* 44–58 (where the author disentangles the complex manuscript transmission, unclear in Findeizen); see also Jensen, "A Theoretical Work of Late Seventeenth-century Muscovy," 320–31; and, for additional context for Korenev's work, see Morosan, *"Penie* and *Musikiia,"* 149–79. There is a survey of his writings by A. M. Panchenko and M. A. Salmina in *SKK* 3, pt. 2: 181–82; pt. 4: 733, and see also Ellon DeGrief Carpenter, "The Theory of Music in Russia and the Soviet Union, ca. 1650–1950" (Ph.D. diss., University of Pennsylvania, 1988), although the author's focus was the period after 1800.]

316. P. Bezsonov, *Kaleki perekhozhie* [Wandering pilgrims] (Moscow: A. Semen, 1864), fasc. 6, "Two words" (from the publisher, xvi); "Adam's Lament," nos. 632–68, 236–314. [There is a reprint of vol. 1 of *Kaleki perekhozhie,* with a new introduction by Sergei Hackel, from Farnborough: Gregg International, 1970.]

317. One of the earliest copies is in a fifteenth-century manuscript from the St. Cyril–Belozersk Monastery [see n. 318 below], and one of the most recent is in a nineteenth-century manuscript, no. 4048 of the Society for Old Literature (collection of spiritual verses of the nineteenth century [the collection is now in RNB]); see Kh. M. Loparev, *Opisanie rukopisei Imperatorskogo Obshchestva liubitelei drevnei pis'mennosti* [Description of the manuscripts of the Imperial Society of Friends of Old Literature] (St. Petersburg: Tip. Imp. Akademii nauk, 1899), pt. 3: 76.

318. The manuscript, dated in the 1470s, is currently located in the State Public Library [RNB] (Kir. no. 9/1086). A description of the manuscript and some of its texts is in Simoni, *Pamiatniki starinnogo russkogo iazyka i slovesnosti.* I am sincerely grateful to P. K. Simoni for bringing to my attention some publications related to Adam's Lament and also for his assistance in obtaining photographs of the sixteenth-century copy of the Lament with musical notation, graciously supplied by the academician M. N. Speranskii. The transcription of the neumatic notation published here has been prepared, at my request, by the protodeacon of the church at the Gromovskii Cemetery of the Old Believers, Father Kh. I. Markov, an expert in singing according to neumatic notation.

319. Manuscript no. 400 of the Moscow Synodal Library [GIM], fols. 190v and 191v. Cf. A. V. Gorskii and K. I. Nevostruev, *Opisanie slavianskikh rukopisei Moskovskoi Sinodal'noi biblioteki* [Catalog of Slavic manuscripts in the Moscow Synodal Library] (Moscow: Sinodal'naia tip., 1869), pt. 3, sec. 1, 382 [a reprint edition is available from Wiesbaden: Otto Harrassowitz, 1964]. Varsanofii, who is mentioned in the manuscript, was a well-known monk of the Trinity Lavra during the reign of Tsar Fedor Ivanovich. [Many thanks to Gregory Myers, who translated this text for this edition.]

319A. [*Editors' note:* The title of this Triodion, given in Findeizen, *Ocherki* 1:261, is "Triodion si est' tripesnets, s bogom sviatym, obderzhai podobaiushchee emu posledovanie." The complete title of the piece reads: "Plachiu i rydaiu egda v chiuvstvo priimu, ogn' vechnyi, tmu kromeshnuiu i tartar liutyi cherv' skrezhe" (I cry and weep as I face the eternal flame, the darkness of hell and the ferocious Tatar gnashes the worm).]

320. The earliest texts of the *Pouchenie* [Instruction] were published by the Very Rev. Makarii Bulgakov in "Zhitie prepodobnogo ottsa nashego, igumena pecherskogo, Feodosiia" [Life of the Revered Father, the Father Superior of the Caves Monastery, Feodosii], *Uchenye zapiski II-go otdeleniia Imp. Akademii nauk* 2, fasc. 2 (1856): 197. The authenticity of the Blessed Feodosii's instruction is confirmed by Petrov, "Podlinnost' pouchenii prep. Feodosiia Pecherskogo," 783. [There are two articles on Feodosii in the *Uchenye zapiski* 2, fasc. 2 (1856): "Zhitie prepodobnogo Feodosiia Pecherskogo v perevode na sovremennyi russkii iazyk Preosv. Filareta, Episkopa Khar'kovskogo" [The life of the Reverend Feodosii Pecherskii, translated into modern Russian by the Rev. Filaret, Bishop of Kharkov], 129–192; and "Sochineniia prepodobnogo Feodosiia Pecherskogo" [The works of the Rev. Feodosii Pecherskii] prepared by Makarii], 193–224.]

321. Buslaev, *Istoricheskaia khristomatiia,* 692. [Many thanks to Henry Cooper, of Indiana University, for his explanation of the context of the word *matitsa* in the title of this document. The word has a dual meaning, indicating in many Slavic languages an organization dedicated to the promotion of national cultures; it also refers to a queen bee, probably from the Greek, and appears frequently as a title for works, as Cooper says, of "sweet usefulness."]

322. Ibid., 386.

323. *RIB* 2 (1875): 316.

324. Manuscript Q, no. 67, fol. 111. [This source is listed in K. Kalaidovich and P. Stroev, *Obstoiatel'noe opisanie slaviano-rossiiskikh rukopisei, khraniashchikhsia v Moskve v biblioteke . . . grafa Fedora Andreevicha Tolstogo* [Detailed catalog of Slavo-Russian manuscripts preserved in Moscow in the library . . . of Count Fedor Andreevich Tolstoi] (Moscow: V. Tip. Selivanovskogo, 1825), sec. 2, no. 195. The current number is RNB, Q.XVII.67; see the concordance tables in D. Uo [Waugh], *Slavianskie rukopisi sobraniia F. A. Tolstogo* [The Slavic manuscripts in the collection of F. A. Tolstoi] (Leningrad: BAN SSSR, 1980), 26.]

325. The "rite of the pouring" is described in detail by K. Nikol'skii, *O sluzhbakh russkoi tserkvi, byvshikh v prezhnikh pechatnykh bogosluzhebnykh knigakh* [About the services of the Russian Church in early printed liturgical books] (St. Petersburg: V Tip. Tovarshchestva "Obshchestvennaia pol'za," 1885), 237–56.

326. In another, earlier notated manuscript in the Viazemskii collection [RNB, f. 166] O.XX, there is a different rite for the toast to health (fol. 115).

327. Nikol'skii, *Opisanie rukopisei, khraniashchikhsia v Arkhive Sviateishego pravitel'stvuiushchego sinoda* 2, fasc. 2: 606.

328. See the study by A. Orlov, "Chashi gosudarevy" [Toasts to the tsar], *ChOIDR* 4 (1913), pt. 2: 53, where this ritual is described and presented in full with musical notation.

329. *Akty istoricheskie* 4, no. 110: 251.

329A. [*Editors' note:* On the visits of the Eastern Patriarchs to Russia, see the discussions in Borys Gudziak, *Crisis and Reform: The Kyivan Metropolitanate, the Patriarchate of Constantinople, and the Genesis of the Union of Brest* (Cambridge, Mass.: Distributed by Harvard University Press for the Ukrainian Research Institute, Harvard University, 1998); and George-Julius Papadopoulos and Claudia Jensen, "'A Confusion of Glory': Orthodox Visitors as Sources for Muscovite Musical Practice (late 16th–17th century)," *Intersections* 26, no. 1 (2005): 3–33. The account by Paul of Aleppo, who recorded his travels in Muscovy in the mid-1650s and in the 1660s, is an important source for musical practice; there is an English translation in Paul of Aleppo, *The Travels of Macarius, Patriarch of*

Antioch: Written by his attendant Archdeacon Paul of Aleppo, trans. and ed. F. C. Balfour, 2 vols. (London: Printed for the Oriental Translation Committee, 1829–36). Charles Halperin, "In the Eye of the Beholder: Two Views of Seventeenth-century Muscovy," *Russian History/Histoire Russe* 24, no. 4 (1997): 409–23, includes extensive bibliographical information on Paul's treatise.]

330. *Vykhody patriarshie* [Patriarchal excursions (processions)], in the Addenda to the *Akty istoricheskie* 5:98, 105, 112, 133.

331. Golubtsov, "Chinovnik Novgorodskogo Sofiiskogo sobora."

332. Ibid., 21, 31–32, 34–36, 42ff. See also Gorskii and Nevostruev, *Opisanie slavianskikh rukopisei Moskovskoi sinodal'noi biblioteki*, pt. 3, sec. 1.

333. *Akty istoricheskie*, 1:405.

334. *Drevnosti. Trudy Moskovskogo arkheologicheskogo obshchestva* 1 (1865): 24.

334A. [*Editors' note:* This passage is slightly abridged here; see the text in *Ocherki* 1:271. On the term *indikt*, see chapter 4 above.]

335. Golubtsov, "Chinovnik Novgorodskogo Sofiiskogo sobora," 1, 27, 32, 82, 83, 149, 156, 180, 208–209, 214.

335A. [*Editors' note:* Findeizen, and other early scholars, equated the terms *demestvennyi* and *domashnii* [domestic] because the words seemed to refer to the same practice. Contemporary scholars use the term *demestvennyi* to refer to a special type of ecclesiastical singing, but in this passage Findeizen apparently presumed that parts of domestic or household (i.e., *domashnii*) practice might be labeled *demestvennyi*. Although the *kanty* were intended for domestic use, they were not part of the *demestvennyi* repertory.]

336. Apparently the Pochaevskaia Lavra began printing a Bogoglasnik in 1790; in 1805 a somewhat abridged edition appeared (*Bogoglasnik. Soderzhashch pesni blagogoveinyia prazdnikom gospod'skim, bogorodichnym i narochitykh sviatykh chrez ves' god prikliuchaiushchymsia. Dlia Ounitskikh tserkvei* [Bogoglasnik, containing reverential songs for the feasts of the Lord, the Virgin, and special saints taking place throughout the year, for Uniate churches]); later editions appeared in 1825, 1850, and so on. See Ia. Golovatskii [Holovats'kyi], *Dopolnenie k ocherku slaviano-russkoi bibliografii V. M. Undol'skogo* [Addendum to the essay on Slavonic-Russian bibliography by V. M. Undol'skii] (St. Petersburg: Imp. Akademii nauk, 1874). The most recent edition of the Bogoglasnik, from 1903, was edited by the Pedagogical Council of the Synod especially for schools in the church parishes. The foundation of this edition is the old Basilian Bogoglasnik. The first part of the 1903 edition contains monophonic chants, and the second part has polyphonic *kanty* for three voices. A comparison of the 1903 version with the 1805 edition shows that many of the psalms have been taken note for note from the earlier edition, and that the only change is the introduction of bar lines for easier reading. V. N. Peretts, in the first volume of his *Istoriko-literaturnye issledovaniia i materialy* [Historical and literary studies and materials] (St. Petersburg: Tip. F. Vaisberga i P. Gershunina, 1900), has an interesting chapter on the history of the Bogoglasnik, with information on the origin and composition of this collection as well as notes on the authors of some of the psalms.

337. For details about this ritual and also about other, now forgotten "actions" practiced by the Orthodox Church, see Nikol'skii, *O sluzhbakh russkoi tserkvi*. Reports and data about the Play of the Furnace and others are in Nikolai Novikov, *Drevniaia rossiiskaia vivliofika 1773–75*, with a new edition in 5 volumes by the Myshkin district public library in Myshkin, 1894–97 [not listed in available catalogs]. The Play of the Furnace was restored recently by Nikol'skii and A. Kastal'skii, *Peshchnoe deistvo: Starinnyi tserkovnyi obriad* [The Play of the Furnace: An old church rite] (Moscow: P. Iurgenson, 1909). A description of the Chaldean furnace and historical data about the structure are in A. Spitsyn, "Peshchnoe deistvo i khaldeiskaia peshch'" [The Play of the Furnace and the Chaldean furnace], *Zapiski Russkogo arkheologicheskogo obshchestva* 12 (1901), fasc. 1 and 2 (and see the additional note by I. Shliapkin).

338. See N. G. Ustrialov, *Skazaniia sovremennikov o Dimitrie Samozvantse* [Contemporary reports about Dimitrii the Pretender] (St. Petersburg: Tip. Imp. rossiiskoi akademii, 1859), pt. 1.

338A. [*Editors' note:* This passage, slightly expanded, is from Orchard, ed. and trans., *The Disturbed State of the Russian Realm*, 160–61.]

339. Golubtsov, "Chinovnik Novgorodskogo Sofiiskogo sobora," 182–86.

340. The furnace in the Russian Museum, of Novgorodian origin, is viewed by some researchers not as a furnace, but as an ambo [or pulpit], yet its structure and dimensions confirm that it was used during the Play of the Furnace. It is built on two levels with a solid wooden floor on which (on the upper level) the children stood; there were stairs leading up to that level with a special opening visible in the illustration (see fig. 96). The lower level, decorated with carved reliefs of saints with openings on the sides, was where the safe fire was made. The Novgorod Chinovnik confirms the designation of just such a sizable "furnace-ambo" for the Play of the Furnace in which, in addition to the three children (joined by an angel descending from the cupola), there was also room for a lectern as well as for the protodeacon and the priest. The text in the description reads: "When singers begin the glorification, the children enter the furnace, first Anania and Azaria, then the protodeacon with the Gospel and then the priest, and they are followed into the furnace by Misail. The protodeacon places the Gospel on the lectern and steps out of the furnace. And the children stand in the furnace by the lectern, all together, facing the priest" (Golubtsov, "Chinovnik Novgorodskogo Sofiiskogo sobora," 67). If the furnace were only decorative, would they place a lectern inside it and have the priest read the Gospel? In old miniature paintings (as in the Godunov Psalter of 1594, cited earlier), one may find representations that clarify the staging of this ecclesiastical rite.

341. In the expense accounts for 1613, on the occasion of the staging of the Play of the Furnace on December 21, it was recorded: "On the ruler's direct order, each of the three children for the Play of the Furnace was given 3 *arshiny* [about 7 feet] of cloth [*nastrafilo*]; and the singer Grigorii Ondreev, for teaching, three and a half *arshiny* [just over 8 feet] of cloth; to the four singers for the Play of the Furnace 4 *portishche* [a special measure of cloth] of *nastrofilo;* of these one *portishche* of the English cherry-colored cloth costing 2 rubles and 6 altyn, four [measures of] light green *nastrafilo* at a cost of 2 rubles, and 2 *portishche* of light blue, also at a cost of 2 rubles each. And to the two Chaldeans, Stepan and Savva, a *portishche* of *nastrofilo* each, light blue, at a cost of 2 rubles, 4 altyn, and 2 den'gi." See A. Viktorov, *Opisanie zapisnykh knig i bumag starinnykh dvortsovykh prikazov, 1584–1725* [Description of expense books and papers of old court departments, 1584–1725] (Moscow: S. P. Arkhipov, 1877), fasc. 1:104, and Razumovskii, *Patriarshie pevchie diaki i poddiaki* [The patriarchal singers] ([St. Petersburg,] N. F. Findeizen, 1895), 25. [See also the similar descriptions in Velimirović, "Liturgical Drama in Byzantium and Russia," 383–85.]

341A. [*Editors' note:* Findeizen's source for the two- and three-part musical examples is Kastal'skii, *Peshchnoe deistvo;* see also Velimirović, "Liturgical Drama in Byzantium and Russia," 363 n. 36.]

342. "And for the teacher (for example, in Moscow in 1613, the sovereign singer Grigorii Andreev, mentioned in n. 341 [as Ondreev]) and the children and the singers of both choirs [*liki*], and for the *podiiaki* and the Chaldeans there will be an early meal and [then they] ascend to the vault ["byvaet rannei stol v kliuche i vskhod na pogreb"]. And after Matins the furnace is removed and on that spot place an ambo and the Lord's angel is taken down and stored at a prepared place" (Golubtsov, "Chinovnik Novgorodskogo Sofiiskogo sobora," 68). According to that document, the children and the Chaldeans participated in the following services, because in these there were references to the biblical event for which the children sang "Iazhe obrete o peshchi khaldeistei" [As we found ourselves in the Chaldean furnace] and later "on the order of the celebrant the children sang furnace *stikhi* and the *diaki* sang selected *stikhi* [from Daniel 3]." Then, after the meal, which was accompanied by a toast to the ruler, "the celebrant, nobleman, children, and Chaldeans depart from the refectory to the *krestovaia* cell, the children sing "I iako vo tmakh agnets tuchen" [the text refers to "the lamb

in darkness"]. And coming into the *krestovaia* cell, they sing to the Most Reverend and then the *mnogoletie,* and the singers bow to the celebrant and go to an outer chamber [or annex; "otkhodiat v vykhodnuiu polatu"] to change the costumes. On the same day the children, Chaldeans, and *podiiaki* escort the prelate to and from Vespers as is customary" (ibid., 71). This ritual activity is also described in a manuscript in the Uvarov collection (see *Drevnosti,* 9). In the article cited above, Spitsyn has assembled many interesting details concerning the staging of the Play of the Furnace in many towns. In P. I. Savvaitov, *Opisanie Vologodskogo kafedral'nogo sobora* [Description of the Cathedral Church in Vologda] (Moscow: Bakhmetev, 1863), 134–38, we find the following concerning the construction of that important accessory to the action, the angel that is to be lowered (8 December 1637): "purchased two dried skins . . . for 1 ruble, 6 altyn, and 4 den'gi; from these skins, a form for the archangel ["pod Arkhangelov obraz"] was cut out, sewn, and glued for the Play of the Furnace, and the painter who decorated it was paid 1 ruble, 6 altyn, and 4 den'gi."

343. S. Smolenskii, in his article "O drevnerusskikh pevcheskikh notatsiiakh," 96, cites a long *ananeika* from the Prooemiac Psalm in a seventeenth-century version: "Slava ti, gospodi, ai ne-ne-nenai, nenenenanili, nenanai-nai-nali, sotvorivshemu vsia."

344. S. Smolenskii, "Znachenie XVII v. i ego 'kantov' i 'psal'mov' v oblasti sovremennogo tserkovnogo peniia t. n. 'prostogo napeva'" [The significance of the seventeenth-century and its *kanty* and psalm settings in the realm of contemporary church singing of the so-called simple chant], *Muzykal'naia starina* [Musical antiquity] 5 (1911): 87.

345. On one of the engravings of a 1701 primer (which begins: "To the glory of the Father and Son and the Holy Spirit, by order of the Great Lord our Tsar and Great Prince Peter Alekseevich . . . this book, the primer, is published with Slavonic, Greek, and Roman letters for those who desire learning") there appears a representation of a Moscow school (not a singing school). In that picture the instructor beats a pupil with a birch rod; another pupil, on his knees, reads a book; still another four pupils are busy at a table. This engraving shows the pedagogical methods of the period and fully confirms the saying that the root of learning is bitter. [See the reproduction in Gregory L. Freeze, ed., *Russia: A History* (Oxford: Oxford University Press, 1997), 96.] The following testimony of church singers from 1666 is quite interesting; it was written by Ivan Anan'in, a singer associated with the Archbishop of Vologda, and describes what they have learned [in the following citation the individual capital letters *V, P,* and *N* stand for *verkh,* the upper voice; *put',* the middle; and *niz,* the lower voice or part]: "liturgy of [St. John] Chrysostom (V P N); Lenten [liturgy] (P N); *zadostoiniki* (P N); *obikhod stroshnoi* (P N) and *demestvennoi* (P N) and *okhtai* [Octoechos] (P N); and feasts of the Lord (P N); and *trezvony* for the entire year (P N); I sang a *demestvennyi niz* and *put'* for the Divine Liturgy (P N); and *stikhiry* for the saints with *svetil'ny* [a type of hymn] and for the Virgin [?] (P N); and *stikhi* for the tsar for which we have arrangements ["kotorye u nas v perevodakh est'"] (P N); and for all three Royal hours (P N); and the Greek *kanon* "Vodu proshed" [Having parted the waters] (P N); the Beatitudes in the eight modes (P N); the Lenten Triodion (N P) and the weekly verses copied by the *pod"iaki,* that they sing in a measured way, I sing all the *niz* and *put'* [lines]" (*Drevnosti. Trudy Moskovskogo arkheologicheskogo obshchestva* 1 (1865) 23). [On the *kanon,* a liturgical poem chanted at the morning service, see *NG2.*] From Anan'in's testimony, it is evident how difficult the practical school was for the singers of the time. [On this document, see A. S. Belonenko, "Pokazaniia arkhiereiskikh pevchikh XVII veka" [The testimonies of the bishop's singers in the seventeenth century], *TODRL* 36 (1981): 320–28.]

346. The Moscow Synodal Typography has preserved the receipts for salaries signed by the members of that second commission, from which we can see its full membership. The names are Aleksandr Pecherskii, an elder of the Chudov Monastery; Aleksandr Mezenets, an elder of the Zvenigorod Monastery of St. Savva; patriarchal singer Fedor Konstantinov; Kondratii Ilarionov, deacon from Iaroslav, church *d'iachok* Grigorii Nos; and church *d'iachok* Faddei Nikitin from Usol'e.

346A. [*Editors' note:* Parfent'ev cites this manuscript in *Aleksandr Mezenets i prochie, Izveshchenie . . . zhelaiushchim uchitsia peniiu, 1670 g.,* 42ff. and see the discussion in his article in *SKK* 3, pt. 1: 63–68; the source is GIM, Sin. pev. 98, where the introductory verses read: "Rodovoditel'stvom cherkasinozemets / Ottsa imushcha Ioanna malorostsa / Severskikh zhe stran prezhde byvsha novgorodtsa." Parfent'ev explains that the term *cherkas* at the time referred to a Cossack; *malorosets,* of course, meant Ukrainian, and in other manuscripts, Mezenets is listed as a Belorussian. In the seventeenth century residents of the Seversk border districts may have been called either Belorussians or Little Russians (Ukrainians); Mezenets thus came from a family that lived at one time in a Cossack settlement in Novgorod Severskii and the family name, Stremoukhov, has been documented there as well.]

347. Tikhon Makar'evskii was born in Makar'evsk, in Karelia, from which he received his name, as did some Western musicians (Guido of Arezzo, Palestrina, etc.) as well as some Russian musicians (Aleksandr Mezenets, Andrei Nizhegorodets, and others). [On the theorists mentioned in this section, see the prefatory notes to this chapter; updated manuscript references are in Protopopov, *Russkaia mysl' o muzyke;* and *SKK.* Additional detailed biographical information is in Findeizen's chapter 11.]

347A. [*Editors' note:* The term *ton* in Diletskii's work encompasses the basic distinction between what he calls happy and sad music; see Jensen, "Nikolai Diletskii's 'Grammatika,'" 293–95, 337.]

348. One of the copies of Tikhon Makar'evskii's *Kliuch,* in the State Public Library (Tolstoi collection [RNB] Q.XII.1), has the following heading: *Skazanie o notnom glasobezhanii i o liternykh znamennykh pometakh i o znameni notnom iazhe v sem kliuche razumeniia napisano po liniiam i po spatsiiam prostogo klavesa* [Information on notated vocal movement and on additional letter signs, and on the notated signs, as in this key to understanding all that is written on the lines and in the spaces of the *prostoi* clef (or key)].

349. Similar acrostics ornament the two other treatises by our early theorists: Mezenets's *Azbuka* and Korenev's *Musikiia.* [Findeizen refers to V. Undol'skii, *Zamechaniia dlia istorii tserkovnogo peniia v Rossii* [Observations on the history of church singing in Russia] (Moscow: Imperatorskoe obshchestvo istorii i drevnostei rossiiskikh, 1846), 15.]

349A. [*Editors' note:* There are three distinct versions of Diletskii's treatise: the earliest, from Smolensk in 1677, is titled *Grammatika musikiiskago peniia* [A grammar of musical singing]; the second version, from Moscow in 1679 and 1681, is titled *Grammatika peniia musikiiskago* [also translated as "A grammar of musical singing"]; the third version, from Moscow in 1679, is titled *Idea grammatiki musikiiskoi* [An idea of a musical grammar]. On these three versions, see the extensive discussions in Protopopov, *Idea grammatiki musikiiskoi;* and Jensen, "Nikolai Diletskii's 'Grammatika.'"]

350. This anonymous letter is in a manuscript collection in the Public Library ([RNB] Q.XVII.270, fols.1–15); it was published by V. V. Maikov in the volume dedicated to S. F. Platonov. [Findeizen refers here to V. V. Maikov, "Poslanie k patriarkhu Germogenu o zloupotreblenii v tserkovnom penii 'khabuva'" [A letter to Patriarch Germogen on the abuse of the *khabuva* in church singing], in *Sergeiu Fedorovichu Platonovu ucheniki, druz'ia i pochitateli* [To Sergei Fedorovich Platonov from students, friends, and admirers] (St. Petersburg, 1911; reprint, Düsseldorf: Brücken-Verlag and Vaduz, Liechtenstein: Europe-Printing, 1970), 415–31. The translation of this passage is based, in part, on the slightly different version in Morosan, "*Penie* and *Musikiia,*" 160.]

351. In the old *azbukovniki,* the word *khabuva* was interpreted as "Khrista bogom" [of Christ the Lord]. [This passage repeats the phrase "Christ the Lord" in different grammatical inflections, for example, "of Christ the Lord," "to Christ the Lord," etc.]

351A. [*Editors' note:* A slightly different version of this passage is translated in Morosan, *Choral Performance,* 19, where the passage is quoted more fully.]

352. There are four known copies: in the Public Library [RNB], Pogodin collection no. 1559; Synodal School in Moscow [GIM] no. 74; Khludov Library no. 91; and Uvarov collection no. 1885

[the latter two collections also in GIM]. The latter is in a seventeenth-century manuscript which also contains another *Skazanie o razlichnykh eresekh . . . soderzhimykh ot nevedeniia v znamennykh knigakh* [Statement about various heresies . . . retained through ignorance in notated musical books], showing that this topic was of great interest to Muscovite readers in the seventeenth century (see Archimandrite Leonid, *Sistematicheskoe opisanie*, vol. 4, sec. 17, 241–44). [See the discussion in Protopopov, *Russkaia mysl' o muzyke*, 42–44, 83–90 (a long quotation from the treatise and translation); and *SKK* 3, pt. 1: 297–98, pt. 4: 698, for updated references to sources; see also Rogov, *Muzykal'naia estetika*, 69–77, based on the Khludov source, now GIM, Khlud. 91.]

352A. [*Editors' note:* Translation of this final passage from Evfrosin taken from Morosan, "*Penie* and *Musikiia*," 167.]

352B. [*Editors' note:* According to Irina Lozovaia, the church with which Korenev was associated was torn down in the early nineteenth century. The phrase "na seniakh" or "sen'" refers to a canopy or porch, suggesting that the church was connected by an inner porch or covered passageway to another church or building. Many thanks to Irina Lozovaia for her detailed information on this term.]

352C. [*Editors' note:* This is Findeizen's summary (*Ocherki* 1:291), which follows Korenev's text very closely. Findeizen also cites Korenev, as follows: "O nerazumie, pache vsiakogo bezumiia sitsevykh glagol! Ne smekhu, no placha dostoina sut', ezhe delo sviatoe i pravednoe eretichestvom vmeniati i besovskimi kliuchami imenovati."]

353. In their polemical zeal, the adherents of the old ways did not shy away from sharp criticism. Thus, in 1665, archpriest Avvakum, a contemporary of Korenev, gave his petition against the Nikonian heresy to Tsar Aleksei Mikhailovich (ultimately, in 1681, Avvakum was to be burned at the stake). "In Moscow," he wrote, "in many of the Lord's churches they sing songs, not the divine chants, and [they do it] in the Latin manner, with Latin rules and regulations, they wave their arms, bow their heads, stomp their feet as is usually done among the Latins to the accompaniment of organs." These rivals, deacon Korenev and archpriest Avvakum, were only representatives of the parties striving to maintain decorum in the church and in the chanting, and they were sharply defined representatives of the opinions then prevalent in various layers of Moscow society. [Findeizen does not cite a source for this passage from Avvakum, but it is likely that he quotes from V. M. Metallov, *Ocherk istorii pravoslavnogo tserkovnogo penii v Rossii* [An essay on the history of Orthodox church singing in Russia] (Moscow: A. I. Snegireva 1915), 82, or from Metallov's source, Makarii, *Istoriia russkoi tserkvi*, 12:613.]

353A. [*Editors' note:* Diletskii's Polish-language treatise, *Toga złota*, is known only from its title page, given below in Findeizen's text. It was printed in 1675 at the Franciscan Press in Wilno and preserved through the citation in Karol Estreicher, *Bibliografia polska* (1870–1939; reprint, Warsaw: Wydawnictwa Artystyczne i Filmowe, 1977), 15:207. Because of its brevity (only seven leaves), it does not appear to be a full-blown Polish version of the *Grammatika* but may have been some sort of panegyric address. See Jensen, "Nikolai Diletskii's 'Grammatika,'" 26–33, and the bibliography cited therein.]

354. Eitner, *Quellen-Lexicon*, 6:471, lists the following works by Mielczewski: (1) *Deus in nomine* for bass accompanied by three instruments and organ (1659) printed in the volume of Joh. Havemann; and (2) Mass *O gloria domina*, for six voices, in manuscript score in the Joachimsthal city library. The following works are in the former Royal Library in Berlin: (3) concerted motet *Benedictio et claritas* for six voices, two violins, four trombones, and continuo; and (4) *Veni domine et volit andare* for three voices and continuo. Mielczewski was in the service of Wladyslaw IV; for more detailed information about his activities, see A. Poliński, *Dzieje muzyki polskiej w zarysie* [A history of Polish music in outline] (Lwów: H. Altenberg, 1907). Poliński also mentions S. Różycki. In *RIB* 5:481 there is an interesting reference to the fact that, in 1664, Patriarch Nikon requested to have sent to him "canticles for nine voices, and psalms for eight voices, and the mass by Milevski." This must certainly refer

to Mielczewski, but it is also of note that Nikon knew Polish composers. [See *IRM* 1:171 n. 7.] The history of the concerted vocal style in Poland remains little studied to date, except for the article by Dr. J. Zurcinski, "Die alte polnische Kirchen-componisten und deren Werke," *Kirchenmusikalisches Jahrbuch* (1900). Of all the Polish masters listed by Diletskii, Mielczewski is the only one mentioned in that article. Thus the question of the influence of Italian masters on Polish musicians, who exercised indirect influence on the growth of the concerted style of our seventeenth-century Muscovite *d'iaki*, remains to be clarified. It is certain, however, that Giovanni Francesco Anerio (1567–1620), for example, served ca. 1609 at the court of the Polish King, Sigismund III, and thus probably had direct contacts with the Polish theorists and composers of the early seventeenth century. [On Mielczewski, see *NG2* for an expanded works list, including the edition, still in progress. On Różycki, see *NG2* for a brief survey. The Polish–Ukrainian–Russian musical connections have been explored in some depth since Findeizen's time; in addition to standard histories of Russian music and studies of *kanty* and *kontserty*, especially by Herasymova-Persyd'ska and Pozdneev, see works by Igor' Belza, for example, his "Rosyjsko-polskie stosunki muzyczne XVII i XVIII wieku" [Russian-Polish musical relations in the 17th and 18th centuries], in Z. Lissa, ed., *The Book of the First International Musicological Congress Devoted to the Works of Frederick Chopin* (Warsaw: Polish Scientific Publishers, 1963): 507–509; and articles in another collection edited by Lissa, *Polsko-rosyjskie miscellanea muzyczne* [A Polish-Russian musical miscellany] ([Kraków]: Polskie wydawnictwo muzyczne, 1967).]

355. The fame of G. D. Stroganov's chapel can be judged from the fact that, in 1689, on the tsar's command, Stroganov sent to Moscow two bass singers and two altos [*al'tistye spevaki*], who were placed under the jurisdiction of the Novgorod office. For this he received a letters-patent [*zhalovannaia gramota*] from the tsar (P. Mel'nikov, "Dorozhnye zametki" [Observations from on the road], in *Polnoe sobranie sochinenii* [Complete collected works] (St. Petersburg, 1898), 12:340). [Grigorii Dmitrievich Stroganov (1656–1715) was responsible for consolidating and increasing his family's vast landholdings and for expanding their important salt manufacturing works; see *MERSH* 37:219. On the musical establishment of the Stroganov family at a slightly earlier period, see V. V. Protopopov, "Notnaia biblioteka Stroganovykh v Sol'vychegodske (1627 g.)" [The music library of the Stroganovs in Sol'vychegodsk (1627)], *PKNO for 1981* (1983): 182–86. See, too, Parfent'ev, *Drevnerusskoe pevcheskoe iskusstvo*; Parfent'ev and Parfent'eva, *Usol'skaia (Stroganovskaia) shkola v russkoi muzyke*; and the additional bibliography in both works.]

356. *Drevnosti. Trudy Moskovskogo arkheologicheskogo obshchestva* 10 (1885): 187.

357. The following may be a complete list of the copies of Diletskii's *Grammar* [sources and current locations, given below, are taken from the far more complete listing in Protopopov, *Idea grammatiki musikiiskoi*, 454–92]:

    1. One copy with the title: *Grammatika musikiiskago peniia ili izvestnaia pravila peniia v sloze musikiiskom, v nikh zhe obretaiutsia shest' chastei ili razdelenii* [A grammar of musical singing or known rules of singing in musical phrases [or in a musical manner], in which there are six parts or divisions], "issued in Smolensk by Nikolai Diletskii, in the year 1677 AD." This is an eighteenth-century copy in Moscow in the Archive of the Ministry of Foreign Affairs, no. 532-1024. In the preface the author states: "I wrote my grammar in a shorter form than the one I did earlier in Wilno; I set it out now in abridged form and divided into two parts." [There are four known sources of the Smolensk, 1677 version of Diletskii's work, plus two lost versions, one cited by I. P. Sakharov, "Issledovaniia o russkom tserkovnom pesnopenii" [Studies of Russian church singing], *Zhurnal Ministerstva narodnogo prosveshcheniia* 61 (1849): 179–85; and another from the library of the Cathedral of St. Sophia in Kiev, from the late eighteenth century); the extant copies are in RGADA, f. 181, no. 541 (early eighteenth century, which Findeizen cites above); L'viv, Muzei ukrains'koho mystetstva, ruk. fond no. 87/510804 (from

St. Petersburg, 1723; available in a full-color facsimile by Tsalai-Iakymenko, *Hramatyka muzykal'na*); Kalininskii oblastnoi gosudarstvennyi arkhiv, f. 103, no. 651a (early eighteenth century); and St. Petersburg, Institut istorii, Rossiiskaia Akademiia nauk, f. 238, op. 1, no. 256 (last quarter of the eighteenth century).]

2–4. Three copies with the title: *Idea grammatiki musikiiskoi* [An idea of a musical grammar], "compiled earlier by Nikolai Diletskii in Wilno, then translated by him into the Slavonic dialect in the Tsar's city of Moscow, from the creation of the world 7187 [1679]." Copies of this version are in the Moscow Divinity School, no. 107 (this copy formerly belonged to the Stroganovs); in the Moscow Synodal School (described by V. Metallov in *RMG* 12 [1897]), and in the Rumiantsev Museum in Moscow, no. 994. [There are nearly a dozen manuscripts transmitting the Moscow, 1679 version of Diletskii's treatise; the most important (and accessible) is the source formerly in the Moscow Divinity School, RGB, f. 173, no. 107, which is available in facsimile by Protopopov, *Idea grammatiki musikiiskoi* (with inserted material from RNB, Q.XII.4, from the late seventeenth–early eighteenth century); Protopopov believes it to be an autograph source. The source from the Moscow Synodal School, which Findeizen mentions above, is GIM, Sin. pev. 777, from the first decade of the eighteenth century.]

5–6. Two copies with the title: *Musikiia* [Music] "first written on the basis of ancient writers, and second, through the research of deacon Ioannikii Korenev, who served [at the Cathedral of the Presentation] "na seniakh" of our Great Tsar [see n. 352B above], finally finished by Nikolai Pavlovich Diletskii in the year 7189 (1681) on 30 May." These are in the library of the Moscow Society for Russian History and Antiquities (Undol'skii's copy of the seventeenth century, published by S. V. Smolenskii in 1910 in the Society of Friends of Old Literature series [RGB, f. 205, no. 146]) and in the State Public Library (F.XII.56); this is the latest copy. [There are several additional sources transmitting this version, listed in Protopopov, *Idea grammatiki musikiiskoi.*]

357A. [*Editors' note:* Some of the terminology Findeizen presents in this passage appears in Korenev's treatise; see Smolenskii, *Musikiiskaia Grammatika Nikolaia Diletskogo,* 56.]

358. Here is how Diletskii proposes a plan for a composition: "As an example of the text "Edinorodnyi Syne" [Only-begotten son], I divide it as follows: "Edinorodnyi Syne"—*kontsert;* "izvolivyi"—tutti; "voplotisia"—*kontsert;* "i prisnodevy Marii"—all together; "raspnyisia zhe"—*kontsert,* and so forth.

358A. [*Editors' note: O penii bozhestvennom* is Korenev's, and circulates in several sources, some together with Diletskii's treatise; see Protopopov, *Idea grammatiki musikiiskoi,* esp. 559 (and see 531 for his corrections to Findeizen's presentation); and his *Russkaia mysl' o muzyke,* 44–58, where he disentangles the conflicting attributions. There is a summary of the debate in Jensen, "Nikolai Diletskii's 'Grammatika,'" 323–26.]

358B. [*Editors' note:* Protopopov, *Russkaia mysl' o muzyke,* 71, lists two known sources for the *Nauka vsea musikii:* RGB, Muz. sobr., no. 3893, and RNB, Q.XII.1; see also the brief discussion in Jensen, "Nikolai Diletskii's 'Grammatika,'" 331–32.]

359. Manuscript copies of V. P. Titov's works have preserved some rather exact dates. His setting of Polotskii's *Versified Psalter* was presented to Tsar Fedor Alekseevich in 1680 [see n. 361], and the manuscript of his *kontserty* for the Twelve Great Feasts was dated 1709. Thus the creative years of this master were probably from 1675 to 1715, and he likely lived in the period from around 1650 to 1715.

360. The version for three voices was printed by Smolenskii, "Znachenie XVII veka i ego 'kantov' i 'psal'mov,'" 101; and the version of the *mnogoletie* for six voices, together with the six-voice setting of the Prooemiac Psalm ("Blagoslovi, dushe moia, gospodi" [Praise the Lord, O my soul]), was published in 1910 by the School for Ecclesiastical Choral Conductors. [A modern edition of Titov's *Grand Mnogoletie* is in Dolskaya, *Vasily Titov and the Russian Baroque,* 189–92.]

361. Manuscript no. 3973, *Psaltyr' rifmotvornaia* [Versified Psalter], 226 folios, in paper binding; a lengthy inscription appears on folio 1: "For the glory of the Lord God in the Holy Trinity the Psalter of King David is artistically set in poetic verses and, of course, appropriate to the various texts; at the command of the Great Lord our Tsar and Great Prince Fedor Alekseevich, ruler of Great and Little and White Russia; issued in the Tsar's great city of Moscow at the Verkhnaia Tipografiia in the year 7188 from the Creation of the World, or from the birth of Christ the year 1680, *indikt* 3, in the month of April. Ieromonakh Simeon Polotskii wrote these poems, and the musical setting of the poems were at the request of the Great Lords our Tsars and Great Princes Ioann Alekseevich and Petr Alekseevich . . . and [they were set] by means of the composition, that is, the creation by the Tsar's sovereign singer Vasilii Titov." The last four words appear to have been written in Titov's own handwriting. From the inscription on the second folio, we learn that this copy was presented (or the entire composition was dedicated?) to Tsar Fedor Alekseevich. In the same copy (on fols. 200v–201r) there is a poem titled "K gliadateliu" [To the viewer], set to music: "Khulnik stikhov omirikh nekto zoil biashe, pisaniem si slavu onago terzashe" [There was a certain Zoilos, a curser of Homeric verse, who with his writing shredded his fame; the phrase "nekto zoil" refers to the ancient critic Zoilos (ca. 400–320 BC), famous for his attacks on Homer's writings and who came to be synonymous with any kind of nasty criticism; see *ES-BE* 24:624–25; and Dal', *Tolkovyi slovar'*, 1:690]. See Nikol'skii, *Opisanie rukopisei, khraniashchikhsia v arkhive Sviateishego pravitel'stvuiushchego sinoda* 2, pt. 2: 794–96. This appears to be one of the first (if not *the* first) secular vocal piece by a known composer of the seventeenth century. On folios 202–26 of the same manuscript is a versified calendar with texts by Polotskii set to music by Titov. [See *IRM* 1:244 on the date of Titov's setting.]

362. *Psaltyr' notnaia* [Notated psalter; the word is also spelled *Psaltir'* in Findeizen's text] in the library of the Russian Academy of Sciences (no. 16.15.11 [in BAN; see *IRM* 1:244]) bound in green leather with gold lettering, dated 1686; it was presented to Tsarevna Sofia with a dedication in verses on folio 6. Titov's role as a composer is spelled out. [The poem is abbreviated here; cf. Findeizen, *Ocherki* 1:xxvi; and see Protopopov, *Muzyka na Poltavskuiu pobedu*, 230, noting that the phrase "newly beautified" below suggests an earlier version of the musical setting]:

> Notami novoulepotstvovasia,
> Ei zhe Premudroi Tsarevne podasia
> Ot Vasiliia diaka pevchego
> Titova, raba ikh vsesmirennago.

> With music newly beautified,
> Presented to the All-wise Tsarevna
> From the singing *d'iak* Vasilii
> Titov, the most humble servant.

Titov's great popularity is indicated by a manuscript in the Uvarov collection ([in GIM] Leonid, *Sistematicheskoe opisanie* 4, manuscript no. 2166) and by the printed copies of the *Versified Psalter* of 1680 with added handwritten musical notation (Kiev notation) in the Historical Museum in Moscow ([GIM] Khlud. 257 and Muz. sobr.); for these data I am indebted to the academician M. N. Speranskii, who kindly communicated them to me. Apparently there are also manuscript copies of Titov's *Notated Psalter* among the manuscripts of the library of the former Synodal School (presently also in the Historical Museum). Notably Titov's name does not appear in the official documents and lists of singers during Peter's reign (except for one set of *kontserty* dated 1709). It is possible that Peter could not forgive him for the dedication to the "all-wise" tsarevna whom Peter had confined to a convent. [See Solov'ian, "Pesennyi sbornik V. Titova na teksty S. Polotskogo," 49–51, for updated information on sources; see also the references in *IRM* 1, listed in n. 362 above. Protopopov, *Muzyka na Poltavskuiu pobedu*, 230–31, discusses Titov's later career, with reference to Findeizen's presentation.]

363. There is another version of the same psalm in the notated psalter belonging to the sovereign singer Andrei Nizhegorodets, also in the library of the Academy of Sciences (no. 16.15.9) [on this source, see Solov'ian, "Pesennyi sbornik V. Titova na teksty S. Polotskogo," 50; and *IRM* 1:249—both of which list as BAN, IB, no. 117. On this collection, see E. I. Bobrova, comp., *Biblioteka Petra I: Uka-zatel'-spravochnik* [The library of Peter I: A reference guide] (Leningrad: BAN SSSR, 1978), esp. 15, and see 40 on the manuscript source]. In that manuscript, which is another copy of Titov's *Versified Psalter* but with various additions, the psalm in question was transcribed as follows, with the first phrase (which [in musical example 9.5] is repeated twice) omitted and the bass part slightly altered, as in musical example N9.1. In Smolenskii, "Znachenie XVII veka i ego 'kantov' i 'psal'mov,'" this psalm is changed even more. Generally all the musical examples cited by Smolenskii in that article (and especially Titov's compositions) are changed considerably relative to the manuscript originals. They are arranged quite elegantly and sometimes furnished with modern harmonizations, thereby giving an erroneous impression of the composers' level of technical proficiency and musical taste.

364. Doggerels of this kind were ridiculed even by contemporaries; there was good reason, for example, that the sharp-witted Kantemir had quite uncomplimentary things to say about Ioann

EXAMPLE N9.1. "Bog nam sila pribezhishche" [God is our strength and refuge]

Maksimovich, author of the *Alfavit sobrannyi, rifmami slozhennyi* [The alphabet compiled and set to verse]: "By hard labor I shall create two verses even if they did not come off; stiff and boring to the ears, they are just like those in the whole alphabet that tells of the lives of saints." [The "sharp-witted" Kantemir is Antiokh Dmitrievich Kantemir (1708–1744), a writer, poet, and diplomat (he was ambassador to Great Britain and France); in his satirical writings and poems, some of the first to be written in a modern, secular style, he defended the reforms of Peter the Great. On this writer, see Brown, *A History of 18th-century Russian Literature,* chap. 3. The poem Findeizen cites is from his Fourth Satire (written ca. 1730 and not published during his lifetime); see Antiokh Kantemir, *Sobranie stikhotvorenii* [A collection of poetic works], introduction by F. I. Priima (Leningrad: Sovetskii pisatel', 1956), 112.]

365. A few numbers from the Hymn to the Saints are published in Smolenskii, "Znachenie XVII veka i ego 'kantov' i 'psal'mov.'" The work includes other examples of *kanty* and psalms, especially by Titov, and, regrettably, they are not always reproduced accurately.

366. After having been forgotten for almost two hundred years, this work was performed for the first time at the historical concerts of the Synodal School in Moscow in 1895 and was published as a supplement to A. Preobrazhenskii, *Ocherk istorii tserkovnogo peniia v Rossii* [Essay on the history of church chant in Russia], 2nd ed. (St. Petersburg: n.p., 1910). In the archive of the Holy Synod (manuscript no. 1200 [probably in GIM, Sin. pev.], a collection of chants in staff notation), there are three of Titov's compositions: "Edinorodnyi syne" [Only-begotten son], the Cherubic hymn, and the *zadostoinik.*

367. Stepan Smolenskii, "O sobranii russkikh drevne-pevcheskikh rukopisei v Moskovskom Sinodal'nom uchilishche tserkovnogo peniia" [On the collection of old Russian singing manuscripts at the Moscow Synodal School of Church Singing], *RMG* nos. 3–14 (1899) and a separate offprint. Unfortunately a full descriptive catalog of this valuable collection has not appeared in print. Smolenskii

and D. V. Allemanov did compile a short, incomplete catalog of the collection in manuscript (presently in the Historical Museum in Moscow [GIM]), which also remains unpublished. Musical compositions by old Russian masters from the end of the seventeenth and the beginning of the eighteenth century have also remained unpublished. [For a summary of published works from this period, see the prefatory comments to chapter 12 below.]

368. Public Library [RNB] Q.XIV.141, fols. 182v–183.

10. Music in Court Life in the Seventeenth Century

[*Editors' note:* One of the starting points in this chapter, which begins with an overview of court music in the seventeenth century, is a reference to organs and the arrival in Moscow in 1630 of two Dutch brothers, Johann and Melchior Luhn (in Russia their names were Iagan and Mel'khert Lunevi, and the Dutch spelling may be Loon). In his book on the history of the organ in Russia, Roizman cites documents suggesting that they brought an instrument with them, which was then gilded and colored in Moscow and even had two mechanical birds—a nightingale and a cuckoo which were activated by playing the organ as a kind of special effect (Roizman, *Organ*, 61–62). Roizman also corrects an error that has been repeated several times, namely, that the Luhns had "several" pupils; according to him there was only a single pupil, Timofeev (63). There were to be more organists as well as organ builders in subsequent decades in Moscow. For an English-language survey of organs and organ playing in early Russia, see Miloš Velimirović, "The First Organ Builder in Russia," in *Literary and Musical Notes: A Festschrift for Wm. A. Little* (Bern: Peter Lang, 1995), 219–28; for a general survey of this period (including material covered in Findeizen's chapter 12, on the Petrine era), see idem, "Warsaw, Moscow and St. Petersburg," in *The Late Baroque Era: From the 1680s to 1740*, ed. George J. Buelow (London: Macmillan, 1993). In his discussion of the plays at the Muscovite court, Findeizen mentions the organ builder and jack-of-all-trades Simon (or Simeon) Gutovskii (d. 1685), who seems to have been a versatile builder of decorated organs. On Gutovskii, see the important discussion by Roizman (*Organ*, 54–55, 69–79, 83–85ff), as well as *ME* 2: col. 120 and the two sources in English listed above.

Although Findeizen did mention the decrees against the *skomorokhi* and their dispersal after 1649 (see chapter 5), he omits any reference to these events at this point in his chronology. According to Olearius, Tsar Aleksei not only banned further "entertainments" but also ordered that musical instruments be collected in Moscow and burned on a pyre. It strikes us as not terribly efficient that in a city the size of Moscow only five cartloads of instruments were collected and destroyed. There were, of course, many other musical instruments in Moscow at that time, some associated with the court itself and some with private figures. No one, for example, dared touch the collection of instruments owned by Nikita Ivanovich Romanov, and after Nikita's death in 1657 Tsar Aleksei conveyed his instruments to another nobleman as a gift (Roizman, *Organ*, 66–67). Among the other important figures who may have had their own instrumental ensembles, Findeizen mentions I. D. Miloslavskii (Tsaritsa Maria's father) and the Golitsyn princes; for general background on the latter family, see Lindsey Hughes, *Russia and the West, the Life of a Seventeenth-century Westernizer, Prince Vasily Vasilevich Golitsyn (1643–1714)* (Newtonville, Mass.: Oriental Research Partners, 1984).

During the course of the 1650s and 1660s there were several Muscovite embassies sent to Western Europe: in 1656, Chemodanov to Venice; in 1659, Likhachev to Florence; in 1662, Zheliabuzhskii to Venice and England; in 1668, Potemkin to Spain and Paris. Upon their return, these ambassadors provided a great deal of information about the music and the musical performances they witnessed. On Likhachev's report, see the sources cited in nn. 377A and 377B below; a part of Likhachev's report is also available in a French translation in MA 1:21. *RBS* 10:485–91 has a fairly extensive discussion of his life and excerpts from his report about experiences in Florence, and there is a brief discussion of the Likhachev family in *MERSH* 20:40–41; Vasilii Likhachev died after 1668.

Findeizen's assumption that while in Florence Likhachev may have seen a work by Jacopo Melani (1623–1676) entitled *Il ritorno d'Ulisse* is unlikely to stand. *NG2* lists Melani's *Il ritorno d'Ulisse* as being performed in February 1669 in Pisa at the Palazzo dei Medici. The opera was performed in Florence but only in 1689; see *NG2*. The work does not appear in Robert Lamar Weaver and Norma Wright Weaver, *A Chronology of Music in the Florentine Theater, 1590–1750*, Detroit Studies in Music Bibliography, no. 38 (Detroit: Information Coordinators, 1978), 130, in their listing of performances in 1659–61. Indeed, the work Likhachev described was probably not an opera at all. He mentioned no music in connection with the performance, although he does enumerate other music he heard at court (see the further discussion of Likhachev's account in Findeizen's text below).

On Potemkin's description of his embassy to Spain and France, see Claudia Jensen and John Powell, "'A Mess of Russians left us but of late': Diplomatic Blunder, Literary Satire, and the Muscovite Ambassador's 1668 Visit to Paris Theaters," *Theatre Research International* 24 (1999): 131–44. Findeizen also mentions reports by the Earl of Carlisle on entertainment during the embassy to Moscow. Charles Howard, Earl of Carlisle (1628–1685), was an ambassador to Moscow in the second half of 1663 and 1664. The record of his stay in Moscow was issued in 1669 by Guy Miege (1644–1718?), *A Relation of three embassies from His Sacred Majestie Charles II, to the great Duke of Muscovie, the King of Sweden, and the King of Denmark.*

Tsar Aleksei Mikhailovich's second marriage, to Natal'ia Naryshkina in 1671 (after the death of his first wife, Maria, two years earlier), represents a turning point in official attitudes toward music; Natal'ia was raised in the home of Artemon Sergeevich Matveev, the head of Aleksei's Diplomatic Chancellery and a strong proponent of Western culture. On Matveev's role in musical developments in Muscovy, see the sources cited in Jensen and Powell, "'A Mess of Russians,'" n. 7. As Findeizen notes, many of the documents pertaining to the establishment of the theater in the early 1670s are published in S. K. Bogoiavlenskii, "Moskovskii teatr pri Tsariakh Aleksee i Petre" [The Moscow theater under tsars Aleksei and Peter], *ChOIDR* 2 (1914): iii–xxi, 1–76. A survey of these materials, in English, is in Claudia Jensen, "Music for the Tsar: A Preliminary Study of the Music of the Muscovite Court Theater," *Musical Quarterly* 79, no. 2 (1995): 368–401.

Findeizen's discussion of the establishment of the court theater and the first performance of the play now known in Russian as *Artakserksovo deistvo* [The play of Artaxerxes (the biblical Ahasuerus)] is as complete as was possible at the time. As Karlinsky notes in his *Russian Drama from Its Beginnings*, 37–45, this play is an original work by Johann Gottfried Gregory (d. 1675), a pastor in Moscow's Foreign Quarter. No copies of the work were known in Findeizen's time but, by a strange coincidence, two copies of the play came to light in 1954, one in Vologda and the other in Lyon. The latter was published by André Mazon and F. Cocron, *La comédie d'Artaxerxès (Artakserksovo deistvo) présentée en 1672 au Tsar Alexis par Gregorii le Pasteur* (Paris: Institut d'études Slaves de l'Université de Paris, 1954) with its texts, in both German and Russian, on facing pages. A critical edition of the Vologda copy was published by V. P. Adrianova-Peretts and I. M. Kudriavtsev, *Artakserksovo deistvo: Pervaia p'esa russkogo teatra XVII v.* [*The play of Artaxerxes:* The first play of the Russian theater in the 17th century] (Moscow: Akademiia nauk SSSR, 1957); additional fragments from the play (filling in act 2, lacking in the Lyon copy) were published in K. Günther, "Das Weimarer Bruchstück des ersten russischen Dramas 'Artaxerxovo dejstvo' (1672)," *Studien zur Geschichte der russischen Literatur des 18. Jahrhunderts* 3 (vol. 28 of Veröffentlichungen des Instituts für Slawistik): 120–78. There is an excellent study, with extensive bibliography, of the earliest plays in A. N. Robinson, ed., *Pervye p'esy russkogo teatra* [The first plays of the Russian theater], vol. 1 of A. N. Robinson et al., eds., *Ranniaia russkaia dramaturgiia (XVII–pervaia polovina XVIII v.)* [Early Russian dramaturgy, 17th–first half of the 18th century] (Moscow: Nauka, 1972); and E. G. Kholodov, "K istorii starinnogo russkogo teatra (neskol'ko utochnenii)" [Toward the history of the old Russian theater (some clarifications)], *PKNO for 1981* (1983): 149–70. (The first part of Kholodov's article deals with the staging of the Artaxerxes play, and the second half concerns theatrical productions in Moscow in 1702–1706, a topic discussed in chapter 12.) Other literature on the Muscovite court theater is reviewed in Jensen, "Music for the Tsar," and there is an English translation of the first Russian court play by Yvette Louria, "The Comedy of Artaxerxes (1672)," *Bulletin of the New York Public Library* 72, no. 3 (1968): 139–210. An article in the journal *Muzykal'naia akademiia* 2 (1992): 119–20, includes an interview with the director Irina Muratova, who revived *Artakserksovo deistvo* in the 1990s.

In 1898 Il'ia Alekseevich Shliapkin published some melodies that he believed had been used in the Artaxerxes play as well as in the theater's next play, a setting of the story of Judith. Keldysh does not consider these melodies reliable or authentic, however, but rather as dating from the eighteenth century (*IRM* 1:199; 2:56 n. 34), and, indeed, Shliapkin published them in connection with the early-eighteenth-century theater organized by Natal'ia, Peter the Great's sister (see n. 390 below). It is of no small interest to note that prior to Gregory's work very few theatrical pieces were based on the Esther theme. There was apparently only one opera, *Artaserse, l'ormondo constante,* produced earlier, in Venice in 1668. All other operas with that title (and apparently almost all using Metastasio's libretto) or titled *Esther* seem to postdate the Moscow performance of 1672. *Judith,* like *Artakserksovo deistvo,* was not an opera but rather a play with some musical interludes; the text is published in Robinson, *Pervye p'esy russkogo teatra,* 351–458. Thus it appears that this topic was not widely set in the years before the Moscow theater, but see n. 379 below for a discussion of a performance of the story in Poland in 1635, witnessed by visiting Muscovite envoys.

Orfeo, the ballet by Schütz, was written for the marriage of Prince Johann Georg of Saxony and Princess Magdalena Sybilla of Brandenburg, which took place in Dresden in November 1638. Although Schütz's music is lost, the text, by August Buchner, survives (see *NG2*). On the possible relationship between this work and the Moscow performance discussed in this chapter, see Claudia Jensen, "Orpheus in Muscovy: On the Early History of the Muscovite Court Theater," *Gimnologiia 4, Vizantiia i Vostochnaia Evropa: Liturgicheskie i muzykal'nye sviazi; k 80-letiiu doktora Milosha Velimirovicha / Hymnology 4, Byzantium and East Europe: Liturgical and Musical Links; in Honor of Miloš Velimirović* (2003): 281–300; see also n. 386A below.

Karlinsky, *Russian Drama from Its Beginnings,* 10, notes the existence of the first "non-Latin Kievan drama," the play titled *Aleksei chelovek bozhii* [Aleksei, man of God] and appears to conclude that the play is of Polish origin, written more in Polish than in Russian (and/or Ukrainian). A study by L. I. Sazonova, "Teatral'naia programma XVII v., 'Aleksei chelovek bozhii,'" [A theatrical playbill of the 17th century: *Aleksei, man of God*], *PKNO for 1978* (1979): 131–49, provides important context for the work, which was prepared for a planned visit to Kiev by Tsar Aleksei; the visit did not take place, but this printed playbill survives. Although this is an important point for historians of drama, of special interest to musicologists is the terminology that appears in two places in the text, where the word *intermedium* is clearly printed in Cyrillic letters (see facsimiles of fols. 4r and 5r on pp. 139 and 141 of Sazonova's article). The first time the word is used, it indicates the insertion of an *intermedium* between scenes 3 and 4. Each scene is qualified with the term *iskhozhdenie,* which suggests "proceeding" or "issuing from" and thus seems to explain the term *stsena* (scene) to unfamiliar readers, and the term *intermedium* is followed by the words "ili smiekh" (or laughter), which surely clarifies the role of the *intermedium* within the larger play. Additional information on theatrical terminology is in P. N. Berkov, "Iz istorii russkoi teatral'noi terminologii XVII–XVIII vekov" [From the history of Russian theatrical terminology in the 17–18th centuries], *TODRL* 11 (1955): 280–99.

Finally, Findeizen again discusses the sovereign and patriarchal singers in this chapter; almost all the singers he names are in the excellent study by Parfent'ev, *Professional'nye muzykanty rossiiskogo gosudarstva.* Because Parfent'ev's listing of singers is in an easily accessible alphabetical format, we do not include specific references to each singer here.]

368A. [*Editors' note:* Findeizen, *Ocherki* 1:307, calls Bomelius a German, but although he was born in Westphalia, his education and career were in England, and he went to Russia from England; see A. A. Zimin, *Oprichnina Ivana Groznogo* [The *Oprichnina* of Ivan the Terrible] (Moscow: Mysl', 1964), 286; and *MERSH* 5:102–103. The description of Bomelius as a sorcerer is in A. N. Nasonov, ed., *Pskovskie letopisi* [Pskov chronicles], vol. 2 (Moscow: Izd-vo AN SSSR, 1955), 262.]

369. The Dutch Dr. Quirinus Bremburgh from Almer submitted a request on 5 December 1628 to be accepted into the tsar's service by presenting a certificate of his qualifications dated 1622 (*RIB* 8:233, 250). [This story is from Olearius; see Baron, *The Travels of Olearius,* 132. On the organist Zawalski, see Roizman, *Organ,* 63–64.]

370. An analogous position in the ecclesiastical world was that of the patriarchal singers [*d'iaki* and *pod'iaki*], whose institution had the same administrative divisions as the sovereign singers; the latter, however, were viewed as being of a higher rank. On solemn ceremonial occasions, when both groups of singers participated, the sovereign singers occupied positions of greater honor and always appeared first. Furthermore, it seems that the tsar's service was more lucrative, and not infrequently patriarchal singers passed into the sovereign's service. For a detailed investigation of the singers, see D. V. Razumovskii, *Patriarshie pevchie diaki i poddiaki i gosudarevy pevchie diaki.* [The organization of the two singing ensembles is discussed at length in Parfent'ev, *Professional'nye muzykanty rossiiskogo gosudarstva;* and idem, *Drevnerusskoe pevcheskoe iskusstvo.*]

371. These were "the foreigners, Kievan singers" [*spevaki*]: Mikhail Osipovich Bykovskii, Aleksandr Vasil'ev, Grigorii and Petr Ivanov, Iakushko Il'in, Ivan Nektar'ev, Mikhail Osipov, Roman Pavlov, Ivan Seliverstov, Fedor Ternopol'skii, Stepan Timofeev, and others, who arrived in Moscow in 1652. Some of them soon returned to Kiev, and others entered into the tsar's service. The Greek singer deacon Meletii arrived in Moscow, where he taught the sovereign singers (1656–59) and he also became a distinguished copyist of *narechnoe* singing. Later on, in 1666, the well-known theorist and composer Ivan Kolenda, who was mentioned in Diletskii's treatise, came from Kiev to Moscow. [See the discussion of the arrival of the Kievan singers in K. V. Kharlampovich, *Malorossiiskoe vliianie na velikorusskuiu tserkovnuiu zhizn'* [Ukrainian influence on Great Russian church life] (Kazan, 1914; reprint, Slavistic Printings and Reprintings, no. 119, The Hague: Mouton, 1968), 72–74, 317–28.]

371A. [*Editors' note:* Findeizen's reference here is unclear; there was a Potap Maksimov who worked as a music scribe, but his well-documented career spans the 1660s to the 1680s. See the documents in *RIB* 23: kn. 3: cols. 365–66; and V. V. Protopopov, "Notnaia biblioteka tsaria Fedora Alekseevicha" [The music library of Tsar Fedor Alekseevich], *PKNO for 1976* (1977): 119–33.]

371B. [*Editors' note:* A *stol'nik* was a high-ranking service office. *Stol'niki* served the tsar and others at banquets and worked in a variety of civil, diplomatic, and military positions, ranking immediately below the members of the boyar duma, according to Pushkarev, *Dictionary of Russian Historical Terms,* 149. Findeizen's reference to the *stol'nik*-copyist Ivan Nikiforov is unclear. There was an Ivan Nikiforov in the *gosudarevy pevchie d'iaki* in 1659 and 1663, but he is not listed either as a *stol'nik* or as a copyist; see D. V. Razumovskii, "Gosudarevy pevchie d'iaki XVII veka" [The sovereign singers in the 17th century], *Obshchestvo drevne-russkogo iskusstva* [Society for early Russian art] (1873): 165; and S. P. Luppov, "Prodazha v Moskve uchebnykh psaltyrei" [The sale in Moscow of educational psalters], in S. P. Luppov and N. B. Paramonova, eds., *Knigotorgovoe i bibliotechnoe delo v Rossii v XVII–pervoi polovine XIX v.* [Bookselling and bibliographic affairs in Russia in the 17th to the first half of the 19th century] (Leningrad: Biblioteka AN SSSR, 1981), 18. Parfent'ev, *Professional'nye muzykanty,* 302–303, lists an Ivan Nikiforov, a member of the sovereign singers, who was a copyist.]

372. N. K. Viazemskii received a salary of 73 rubles; he accompanied [the tsarevich] Aleksei Petrovich in 1711 to Dresden and later to Torun; for the latter trip he received 200 gold coins (*Doklady i prigovory, sostoiavsheisia v Pravitel'stvuiushchem Senate,* 7, bk. 2: 88, 117; 7, bk. 4: 847).

373. Viktorov, *Opisanie zapisnykh knig i bumag,* fasc. 1:100. [On the *tsymbal'niki,* see Roizman, *Organ,* 53–54; although the term can mean a cimbalom or dulcimer, in this period it seemed to refer to a keyboard instrument.]

374. In 1629–38 the tsar had in his service a *metal'nik* (a tightrope walker), a German who converted and took the name Ivan Semenov Lodygin; he taught his art to Russian youths and also taught them how to play the drums. [On the word *metal'nik,* see Barkhudarov, *Slovar' russkogo iazyka XI–XVII vv.,* 9:123. The term indicates some kind of performer or entertainer.] Tightrope walkers were provided with a special costume: jacket and pants of red cloth and a crimson skull cap. There is no doubt that other members of the Poteshnaia palata were also given special costumes and among these, besides those already mentioned, were the storytellers Petrushka Taras'ev, son of Sapog, Klimka Onofreev Orefin, the fool Moisei, and others (Viktorov, *Opisanie zapisnykh knig i bumag,* 1:69). [The passage from Olearius that Findeizen mentions does not describe Mikhail's wedding but rather is his description of the first Russian music the foreign party heard, in Ladoga, on their journey to Moscow. Olearius says that they heard lute and fiddle music accompanying a song about Tsar Mikhail; there was also dancing by men and by women. See Baron, *The Travels of Olearius,* 48–49. The *surny,* trumpets, and percussion were part of the traditional instrumental fanfare performed after the consummation of a marriage.]

374A. [*Editors' note:* Johann Luhn died in Moscow in 1637, and his brother left the following year. For additional information (and some corrections) on these instrumentalists at court, see Roizman, *Organ,* esp. 58–69; see, too, his listing of names on 361–72. Spellings throughout this passage are taken from Roizman, *Organ;* here Findeizen refers to the Luhn brothers as Gans and Mel'khart and to the assistant ["podmaster'e organnogo dela"] Adamsen as Adamen. As noted above in the prefatory notes to this chapter, Roizman says that the birds on the Luhn brothers' organ probably sounded through special organ pipes; he also notes, on p. 73, that there is no evidence that an organ built by Russian masters was given to the shah. Findeizen probably refers to the later organ built by the Pole Simeon Gutovskii, from Smolensk, which was indeed sent as a gift to the shah.]

374B. [*Editors' note:* Roizman, *Organ,* 81, notes that Mertz worked as a teacher and cantor ("uchitel' i kantor") at the Saxon church, not as an organist; he also notes that Gutovskii did not live in the Foreign Quarter. Roizman (p. 79) addresses Findeizen's remarks on the presence of organs in the churches of the Foreign Quarter, stating that there is no evidence that such organs were present among the foreign population of Moscow; Russian keyboard practice throughout most of the seventeenth century was concentrated at court.]

375. M. P. Zablotskii, comp., "Opis' moskovskoi meshchanskoi slobody" [A register of the Moscow *meshchanskaia* quarter], *ChOIDR* 2 (1860): pt. 5: 15, no. 464.

375A. [*Editors' note:* On terminology used to describe various keyboard instruments, see the prefatory notes to chapter 12 below. See also volume 2 for a more detailed discussion of keyboard instruments in Russia in the eighteenth century.]

375B. [*Editors' note:* Findeizen's source here has not been identified, but it does not appear to be from Miege's published account of the Carlisle mission; the ambassador was in Russia on a single mission in 1663–64.]

375C. [*Editors' note:* Philip Longworth, *Alexis: Tsar of All the Russias* (New York: Franklin Watts, 1984), 95–96, describes the departure ceremony in April 1654 and, on 102–103, Aleksei's return in February 1657 (delayed by an outbreak of plague in Moscow). The military goal was to take Smolensk from Polish control and, at the same time, to guard against any possible intervention from the north by Sweden. The Muscovite armies were successful, and Aleksei entered Smolensk in September 1654.]

376. Apparently the organist Simon Gutovskii, cited above. [The term *nemchin* refers to a foreigner in general, not necessarily a German specifically. Findeizen's source for this passage is unclear; he refers only to the *Dvortsovye razriady,* but the passage does not appear in available published volumes.]

376A. [*Editors' note:* Longworth, *Alexis, Tsar of All the Russias,* describes this ceremony (mentioning only elaborate sacred ritual), on 214–16.]

377. Thus in the inventory of music books (1682) belonging to Tsar Fedor Alekseevich, kept in the Moscow Armory, there are six manuscript notebooks "in twenty-five columns copied by the hand of the Great Lord Tsar and Prince Aleksei Mikhailovich of blessed memory, autocrator of all the Great, Little, and White Russias" as well as some other fascicle folios [*tetrati v poldest'*] with "Two [hymns] for the Nativity of Christ, the first in three lines "na peregovorkakh [?]," and the second, the lowest [voice], copied by the hand of the Great Lord" (see A. Uspenskii, *Materialy dlia istorii tsarskoi biblioteki v Rossii v XVII i XVIII vv.* [Materials for the history of the tsar's library in Russia in the 17th and 18th centuries], 54, in galley-proof copy). [Much of this collection went to Aleksei's son and successor, Fedor Alekseevich; see Protopopov, "Notnaia biblioteka tsaria Fedora Alekseevicha," which surveys the inventory (RGADA, f. 396, op. 2, ed. 601) and discusses the collection in general. For a general survey of Fedor's cultural interests, see *SKK* 3, pt. 4: 82–91. There are two studies devoted to Tsar Aleksei's abilities as a composer; see V. K. Bylinin and A. L. Pososhchenko, "Tsar' Aleksei Mikhailovich kak master raspeva" [Tsar Aleksei Mikhailovich as a master of *raspev*], *PKNO for 1987* (1988): 131–37; and V. V. Protopopov, "Chetyrekhgolosnaia khorovaia kompozitsiia tsaria Alekseia Mikhailovicha" [A four-part choral composition by Tsar Aleksei Mikhailovich], *PKNO for 1991* (1997): 107–10. A survey of Tsar Aleksei's own collection of books (or of books associated with him) is in Daniel C. Waugh, "The Library of Aleksei Mikhailovich," *Forschungen zur osteuropäischen Geschichte* 38 (1986): 299–324.]

377A. [*Editors' note:* Likhachev's account is in *DRV* 4:339–59. The account begins with his orders to go to Europe, in June 1659. The embassy arrived in Livorno in January 1660 and reached Florence later that month. They left the city in February.]

377B. [*Editors' note: DRV* 4:350–51, following the entry of 20 January. Throughout this passage, Likhachev's report uses the word *palata,* which can mean not only a room or a palace but also a special place where events occur. We have translated this term as *chamber;* to Likhachev, the different sets may indeed have suggested a series of rooms or chambers. On the term *palata,* see the Academy of Sciences' dictionary, *Slovar' sovremennogo russkogo literaturnogo iazyka* [A dictionary of the modern Russian literary language] (Moscow: Akademiia nauk SSSR, 1959), 9:44. Further on in the report are references to changes [*peremeny*] of scenery or sets. Part of Likhachev's report is translated in Longworth, *Alexis, Tsar of All the Russias,* 210.]

378. *DRV* 4:350–51 [Findeizen cites the edition from 1894, 1:84, not listed in available catalogs.] This report was undoubtedly the text reprinted verbatim in Nosov's fantastic *Khronika russkogo teatra* [Chronicle of the Russian theater] (Moscow: n.p., 1863) where, under 6 January 1661, we read of the very same spectacle taking place in Moscow! The investigators of our theatrical past, while considering Nosov's *Chronicle* as absurd, still have not yet presented a critical evaluation of his statements. Yet a reexamination of trustworthy sources proves convincingly that most of Nosov's statements are false, not to mention that the well-established data for the theatrical history (from 1672 on) do not appear in Nosov's work, and even later information about the court theater is not reliable. I was able to establish the repertory of these theaters for most of the eighteenth century on the basis of newspapers from St. Petersburg and Moscow (*Sankt-Peterburgskie* and *Moskovskie vedomosti*), with omissions only for those years missing in the Public Library [RNB] collection, and my findings are in total disagreement with Nosov's. Thus the assumption that Nosov utilized the original playbills or repertories of the state theaters assembled by the well-known actor I. A. Dmitrevskii can also be dismissed; undoubtedly Dmitrevskii would have collected materials from theaters from his own time. [Ivan Afanas'evich Dmitrevskii (1734–1821) was a very famous actor and director who was involved in all aspects of Russian theater in the late eighteenth and early nineteenth centuries. See *GSE* 8:316, and Findeizen's discussion in volume 2, chapter 17.]

379. Before that, in 1635, during Mikhail Fedorovich's reign, the boyars Prostev and Leont'ev were sent to Poland to negotiate the marriage of the Polish crown prince to Princess Irina Mikhailovna; they were invited to the court theater in Warsaw, where a mystery play, *Judith and Holofernes,* was staged for them. The same topic was the subject of one of the first plays staged thirty-seven years later in Moscow during the reign of Aleksei Mikhailovich. [Findeizen refers here to the embassy headed by A. M. L'vov-Iaroslavskii; see S. M. Solov'ev, *Istoriia Rossii s drevneishikh vremen* [A history of Russia from the earliest times], vol. 5 of *Sochineniia* [Works] (Moscow: Mysl', 1990), bks. 9–10, 171–74; English translation in S. M. Soloviev, *The First Romanov: Tsar Michael, 1613–1634,* vol. 16 of *History of Russia,* ed., trans., and with an introduction by G. Edward Orchard (Gulf Breeze, Fla.: Academic International, 1991), 237ff. This mission is also mentioned in Robinson, *Pervye p'esy,* 47. On the Florentine operas, see the prefatory remarks to this chapter, above; *NG2* gives a performance date of February 1669 in Pisa for Melani's *Il ritorno d'Ulisse.*]

379A. [*Editors' note:* We have corrected the spelling and identification of some of the French-language sources here without editorial comment. Details of Potemkin's 1668 trip are in Jensen and Powell, "'A Mess of Russians'"; a modern edition of Potemkin's report of the French portion of his trip is in D. S. Likhachev, ed., *Puteshestviia russkikh poslov XVI–XVII vv: Stateinye spiski* [Voyages of Russian ambassadors of the 16th–17th centuries: Diplomatic reports] (Moscow: Izd. Akademii nauk SSSR, 1954), 227–315. French translations of some passages are in E. M. Galitzin, *La Russie du XVIIe siècle dans ses rapports avec l'Europe occidentale: Récit du voyage de Pierre Potemkin* (Paris: Gide et J. Baudry, 1855). The performances Potemkin saw were not at court; see below. On the theaters, see John Powell, *Music and Theatre in France, 1600–1680* (Oxford: Oxford University Press, 2000).]

380. P. Pekarskii, *Nauka i literatura pri Petre Velikom* [Science and literature during the reign of Peter the Great] (St. Petersburg: V Tip. tovarshchestva "Obshchestvennaia pol'za," 1862), 1:388, took this information from Galitzin, *La Russie en XVII siècle,* which quotes the poem in full from the contemporary *Gazette rimée* devoted to Potemkin's embassy and the performance he saw. It begins thus:

> Ces deux Ministres remarquables
> Par leur air, par leurs vestemens
> Et leurs bizarres ornemens,
> Qui n'ont nul rapport à nos Modes,
> Mais qui leur sont bien plus commodes,
> Ont été menez, pour certain,
> Dans le même ordre, à Saint-Germain,
> Et du Grand SIRE en l'audiance,
> Avec pompe et magnificence.

[This passage is in Galitzin, *La Russie du XVIIe siècle,* 434. As described in Jensen and Powell, "'A Mess of Russians,'" just after Potemkin and his suite departed, the actor Raymond Poisson threw together a one-act farce titled *Les Faux Moscovites,* which was performed in October 1668 and was based on French impressions of the exotic foreign visitors.]

380A. [*Editors' note:* See Jensen and Powell, "'A Mess of Russians,'" 134 and n. 20.]

380B. [*Editors' note:* Guy Miege, *A Relation of Three Embassies* chronicles the Carlisle mission. On p. 142 he notes: "Our Musique-master composed a handsome Comedie in Prose, which was acted in our House." This kind of entertainment was necessary as the party's movements and contacts while in Moscow were highly restricted. On the mission, see the sources cited in Jensen, "Music for the Tsar," n. 20.]

381. At that time there were apparently quite a few boyars in Moscow with a taste for foreign customs and who kept musicians in their service. One of them, for example, was the tsar's cousin, Nikita Ivanovich Romanov (d. 11 December 1656), who had his own musicians. He is mentioned in

the tsar's letter to *sto'lnik* A. I. Matiushkin dated 13 March 1655: "Bring along Kuska (Kuz'ka, Kuz'ma), Mikita Ivanovich Romanov's trumpeter . . . as well as old, new, and young singers" (*Sobranie pisem tsaria Alekseia Mikhailovicha* [A collection of letters of Tsar Aleksei Mikhailovich] (Moscow: Tip. V. Got'e, 1856), 45). [Olearius twice mentions Romanov's love of foreign music; see Baron, *The Travels of Olearius*, 130, 263.] A 1689–90 inventory of the Golitsyn princes' possessions, which were taken to the Armory, includes organs; an inventory of the possessions of boyar I. D. Miloslavskii, made after his death in 1668, lists "14 German trumpets" (Viktorov, *Opisanie zapisnykh knig i bumag*, 2:394, 1:207). Miloslavskii evidently had his own band of wind instruments. [See also the references in Jensen, "Music for the Tsar," 384. The private orchestra is mentioned in Martha Lahana's forthcoming monograph on Matveev, and see the documents published in L. M. Starikova, "K istorii domashnikh krepostnykh teatrov i orkestrov v Rossii kontsa XVII–XVIII vv." [Toward a history of domestic serf theaters and orchestras in Russia at the end of the 17th and in the 18th century], *PKNO for 1991* (1997): 56–60 (petitions by Vasilii Repskii). For important corrections to Matveev's biography, see Lahana's forthcoming monograph, and see also the discussions and bibliography in Longworth, *Alexis;* and *SKK* 3, pt. 2: 341–43, and pt. 4: 746.]

381A. [*Editors' note:* Findeizen's source is Bogoiavlenskii, "Moskovskii teatr," 1.]

382. Among the documents published by Bogoiavlenskii, "Moskovskii teatr," 20–22, is a letter from the well-known singer Anna Paulsen of 4 April 1673 addressed to Colonel von Staden, in which she informs the "most gracious patron" that she had been unable to come to Russia in the preceding year (apparently along with other actors) because the Danish king in Copenhagen would not release her. The death of the Danish royal prince had set her free, and she was awaiting Staden's final decision. From this letter it is evident that she, together with other actors, had played previously in Riga. She also wrote: "The colonel also told us to find a good male singer and lute player; we are trying to do so every day, but because of the long trip nobody is willing to join us." Apparently by 1673 it was possible to do without her, as there are no further documents relating to her in the archives.

383. Bogoiavlenskii, "Moskovskii teatr," 6. Musicians' salaries were not as insignificant as it may seem, for at that time the value of the silver ruble was twelve times that of the ruble at the beginning of the twentieth century. Later documents published by Bogoiavlenskii give the exact names and destinies of these first foreign musicians in Muscovite service. The original contract with Staden was signed by the following: Iohann Waldon, Felt Trompter, Friederich Platenschleger, Iacob Philips, Gottfried Berge, and Christophor Achermann [Findeizen suggests that the proper spelling is Ackermann]. Of these, Waldon (whose name is spelled in various ways) was engaged in Stockholm, and the others, "former court musicians of the Duke of Courland," were engaged in Moscow. [The contract was signed in Mitau on 25 August 1672.] According to the contract they were able to play on various instruments: "organs, trumpets, tromba marina, flutes, clarinets, trombones, violins, and viola da gamba, together with vocal performances (i.e., as accompanists—N.F.) and also on other instruments." [Findeizen cites the Russian translation in Bogoiavlenskii, "Moskovskii teatr," 19; the document reads: "Orgeln, Trompeten, Trompeten-Marinen, Cinchen, Dulcian und Posaunen, Violen und Viol de Gambe, auch die vocalische Music dabey, und noch andere Instrumente mehr verstehen."] Upon their arrival in Moscow in early 1673, the musicians presented the following petition to the tsar:

> To the Tsar (list of titles) petition by your servants, the newly arrived foreign trumpeters Ivashko Valdov full trumpeter ["polnoi trubach" (possibly "polevoi trubach," i.e., field trumpeter—N.F.)] and Fedka Platonshleger, musician, with their fellows. In the past year [1672], Lord, as Colonel Mikolai Fan Staden was overseas on your business and invited us, your servants, to serve you and promised us a monthly salary with food allowance starting with September 1 of this [new] year [7]181 [September 1672 to August 1673]. Thus we your servants, on the basis of the contract, arrived

and were given only allowance for December, and for September and October and November nothing was given. Gracious Tsar (titles), have mercy on us your servants, and order, Lord, that we be given that allowance for those three months according to the colonel's contract. Lord Tsar, please be merciful. (Bogoiavlenskii, "Moskovskii teatr," 17)

[Findeizen notes that the phrase "polnoi trubach" may be a misprint for "polevoi trubach" (field trumpeter). The phrase "polnoi trubach" may also have associations with musicians' guilds; see Jensen, "Music for the Tsar," 376 and n. 38; Staden uses the phrase "polnye trubachei" in an earlier dispatch, cited in Bogoiavlenskii, "Moskovskii teatr," 3.] The musicians' request was fulfilled. As for the musicians, the trumpeter Waldon was released two years later and he returned to Sweden; two others, Philips and Berge, ran away in 1675, as can be seen from the petition of Captain Johann Rubert:

To the Tsar (titles) petition from your servant of the soldier's status, foreign captain Iaganka [diminutive of the German name Johann] Rubert. In this year [7]184 on 19 September [1675] the foreign musicians Iakov with his friend Kotfrid [Gottfried] ran away from my home, where they lived as renters in my rental quarters, and where they went from my home I, your servant, do not know; and whatever belongings and instruments they had, they took everything. Gracious Lord (titles) have mercy on me, your servant and order to have a statement written so that I, your servant, and with a wife and children at that, would not perish. (Bogoiavlenskii, "Moskovskii teatr," 47)

In accordance with the petition, on 20 September orders for arrest were sent "to Novgorod and Pskov, and to the border at Smolensk, on the road to Kaluga and to Briansk to the border, and on the road to Vologda and Arkhangel'sk, that the runaway musicians be caught, put in chains, and returned to Moscow under guard, with great care, and to speed things up, give to the four *streltsy*, for food on the road, one *poltina* each to carry out the orders for these runaways" (ibid.). There are replies preserved from local officials from Pskov, Putivl', and Sevsk reporting that they have taken measures to catch the musicians. Their further fate, as well as that of two others (Friederich Platenshleger and Christophor Ackermann) remains unknown.

384. The names of the foreign musicians in the second group are cited in two decrees of 1675, published by Bogoiavlenskii, "Moskovskii teatr," 62–63:

1. The year [7]184 [1675] on 2 November the Tsar (titles) ordered the foreign musicians Ianus Branten and Maksimilian Markus, who remained in Moscow after the Imperial emissaries Francisco Annibale and Johann Karl Teringeren, to register at the Foreign Office and to issue to them salary in the office as follows: body of beef [no legs or head], two carcasses of sheep; half of an eighth of oatmeal; allot them food and drink from the first day of this year [7]184 [1 September] as long as they shall be in Moscow, bread of 2 *dengi*, 3 cups of wine, 4 *krushki* [a wooden dish for measuring] of honey and 4 *krushki* of beer per person daily. Drinks to be given in ready-made dishes ["v gotovykh sudekh"] from the New Pharmacy, and for meat, flour, and for purchases of bread, give money from the Pharmacy income in the Novgorod Office;

2. On 8 November, [7]184 [1675] the Tsar (titles) ordered to give to the foreign musicians Ianus Kraltson and Maksimiialin Kreiken as salary daily food allowance from 7 November as long as they shall be in Moscow, 5 *altyn* per day per person from the Novgorod Office, from the New Pharmacy's income. This edict of the tsar was ordered to be written by boyar Artemon Sergeevich Matveev. Clerk Vasilei Bobinin. (Ibid.)

385. The preparatory period of the early theater in Russia was presented above. In those developments, one of the main roles was played by Pastor Johann Gregory. P. O. Morozov, in his *Istoriia russkogo teatra*, gives a fairly full biography of Pastor Gregory. Only a few additional new facts need to be added from the work of Ernst Koch, "Die Sachsenkirche in Moskau," *Neues Archiv für Sächsische*

Geschichte und Altertumskunde 32 (1911): 270–316. Gregory, born 15 May 1631 in Merseburg, as a young man served as a soldier and cavalryman in Sweden and Poland. In 1658 he accepted a position as a teacher in the Foreign Quarter in Moscow, and after passing an examination in Dresden, he was appointed as pastor in the new Lutheran, the so-called Saxon, church in that same quarter. He traveled twice to Germany from Moscow; the second time, his official mission was to invite his stepfather, Dr. Blumentrost, to the position of court physician, and his unofficial mission was to make a collection for the church, which was under the protection of the Saxon king. Having visited many German towns, Gregory not only saw widespread theatrical performances but wrote a letter in verse to his friends in Stuttgart, where he had been warmly received and where, apparently, there were often talks about faraway, barbaric Muscovy. The opening lines read:

> Der tapfre Reusse wird ein Barbar zwar genennet,
> Und ist kein Barbar doch, wie dieses Buch bekennet . . .
> (Koch, "Die Sachsenkirche in Moskau," 284)

This demonstrates that Gregory was able to express himself in verse, and it also explains the puzzle facing some scholars who wondered how a Saxon pastor could undertake the writing of theatrical plays. Blumentrost, who departed for Moscow with one of his stepdaughters and two of his own, still minor children, also invited the medical student Laurentius Rinhuber, in the capacity of private teacher for his son and as physician's assistant. The latter, who in 1683 changed his family name to Reinufer, played an important role in the staging of the first play in Moscow. Gregory, however, invited from Stettin Justus Mertz, mentioned earlier, to the position of teacher and cantor in the Saxon church in Moscow. Gregory's success in Saxony aroused the jealousy of his rival in Moscow, pastor [Johann Dietrich] Vockerodt. The German Quarter in Moscow was a nest of intrigue. Gregory was denounced for alleged improper use of the tsar's name during a sermon and for unwarranted collection of offerings; he was deposed, and Vockerodt was appointed in his place. Rinhuber intimates that the recommendation to Matveev that Gregory would be able to stage a theatrical play was made with the aim of finally ruining the pastor, as his enemies hoped that he would fail in that endeavor. But, as is well known, Gregory emerged victorious. The tsar selected a popular subject, the story of Esther, a reminder of the fate of his second wife and her guardian, A. S. Matveev. Gregory's play, *Esfir' i Agasfer* [Esther and Ahasuerus] was translated into Russian as *Artakserksovo deistvo*, as the biblical king Ahasuerus was renamed Artaxerxes. The translation was prepared by a teacher, Iurii Mikhailov, and by the translator at the Foreign Office, Georgii Huebner [Giubner]. The roles were rehearsed by Rinhuber; the role of Esther was apparently performed by Dr. Blumentrost's older son. A copy of the text of the play, bound in gilt morocco, was presented to the tsar but unfortunately it has not survived [see the prefatory notes to this chapter]. On 21 January 1673 Pastor Gregory received a reward for his labors: forty sables worth 100 rubles and two worth 8 rubles. On 6 April of the same year, during Holy Week, "the pastor Iagan Gotfrid [Gregory] and the teacher Iurii Mikhailov and with them the actors [*komedianty*] in the play *Artakserksovo deistvo* were received [to kiss the tsar's] hand and see the Great Lord's bright eyes. Never before had the pastor or the foreign children of the Great Lord's Foreign Office kissed his hand." Thus Gregory was fully rehabilitated and rewarded. As for Rinhuber, he had already been appointed secretary of the embassy that was about to go to Dresden, Vienna, and Italy. In 1673 a theatrical school in Moscow was established with Gregory as its principal, and twenty-six children of local middle-class families [*meshchanskie deti*] were accepted as students. Pastor Gregory died on 18 June 1675, before the beginning of Fedor Alekseevich's reign, when the theater and the school were abolished. In the inventory of goods received and disbursed by the sub-clerk of the Foreign Office Boris Mikhailov in the year [7]184 [September 1675 through August 1676], among other items are listed forty sables worth 70 rubles, according to a note on the petition by Ivan Evstaf'ev, issued to the "foreigner Iagan Ganfrit for staging a comedy with decorations" (*Dopolneniia k Aktam istoricheskim,* 7:196). [Shortly after the performance, Laurentius Rinhuber traveled to the West and returned once more to Russia in 1684. See *RBS* 16:224–27; his treatise was published as *Relation du voyage en Russie fait en 1684* (Berlin: A. Cohn, 1883); and see the review by A. Brikner, "Lavrentii Ringuber," *Zhurnal Ministerstva narodnogo prosveshcheniia* (February 1884): 396–421. On the background of the Foreign Quarter, see Lahana, "Novaia Nemetskaia Sloboda."]

385A. [*Editors' note:* Findeizen cites Tikhonravov's *Russkie dramaticheskie proizvedeniia 1672–1725 godov* [Russian dramatic works, 1672–1725], 2 vols. (St. Petersburg, 1874).]

386. The "theatrical mansion" [*komidiinaia khoromina*] where plays were staged was originally built in the village of Preobrazhenskoe; its dimensions were approximately 10 square *sazheni* [about 490 square feet], with a width of 6 *arshiny* [14 feet]; the walls were covered with cloth and the floor was carpeted. The tsar's seat was in front, and behind him, in the manner of an amphitheater, were benches for other viewers; for the tsaritsa and the children there was a kind of latticed box. The stage was separated by railings and a curtain that parted to the sides and was called a *shpaler* (*Spalier*). For lighting, tallow candles in candlesticks were used. The musicians were probably placed to the side, on the stage. The scenery was called "frames of painting in perspective" ["ramy perspektivnogo pis'ma"]. According to Rinhuber, the performance of *Artakserksovo deistvo* with its entr'actes [or intervals] lasted ten hours! Such a length of time was not surprising owing to the novelty of the enterprise and the slow tempo of the stage action and dialogue, as well as the number of participants. A performance of a play also on the Esther story in the late sixteenth century by Jesuits in Munich lasted three days and required 150 performers. Occasionally the theater would temporarily move from Preobrazhenskoe to Moscow, and the performances would be staged in the Kremlin rooms above the Pharmacy. Regrettably there are no preserved representations depicting the Russian theater of that time. Some idea about the contemporary theatrical staging may be obtained from the popular prints of the *Play of the Parable of the Prodigal Son* (Moscow, 1685; reprinted by D. Rovinskii in his *Russkie narodnye kartinki* and also in the posthumous, more accessible edition of Rovinskii's work, edited by N. Sobko, 2:403–4; see also the article "Nachalo stsenichnykh predstavlenii v XVII v. v Moskve" [The beginning of stage presentations in Moscow in the 17th century], *Vsemirnaia illiustratsiia* 1871, nos. 110–11. The illustrations of Polotskii's play in that edition are engraved after the drawings of Dutchman Picart [see n. 388A below] and represent a German or Dutch stage and not the one in Moscow. It is true, however, that Pastor Gregory's theater in Moscow was modeled on foreign examples. [The texts of *Artakserksovo deistvo* and *Iudif'* are published in Robinson, *Pervye p'esy russkogo teatra*, with extensive commentary and introductory material; see also Kholodov, "K istorii starinnogo russkogo teatra"; and A. N. Robinson, *Bor'ba idei v russkoi literature XVII veka* [The conflict of ideas in Russian literature in the 17th century] (Moscow: Nauka, 1974).]

386A. [*Editors' note:* Jensen, "Music for the Tsar," 374–75, suggests a date of February 1672, during *Maslenitsa*, for *Orfeo*, making it a direct antecedent for the plays at court. It is highly unlikely that the Moscow production reproduced Schütz's earlier ballet, although Findeizen is correct in noting the ties between some of the Germans in Moscow and the Saxon court. See also idem, "Orpheus in Muscovy."]

387. According to Pekarskii, *Nauka i literatura pri Petre Velikom*, 1:394, this play was written in honor of the angel [the holy protector] of Aleksei Mikhailovich and was produced, judging from a hint at the end of the prologue, at the beginning of the war with the Turks, which started early in 1673. The tsar's name day was on 5 October and the first performance of *Aleksei* may thus be assumed to have taken place in early October 1673. [On the play *Aleksei, bozhii chelovek*, see the article by Sazonova, "Teatral'naia programma XVII v." listed in the editorial preface above. This play was not written by Simeon Polotskii.]

388. The exact dates of the staging of the other plays have not been established. Ivan Zabelin, *Istoriia goroda Moskvy* [History of the city of Moscow], 2nd ed. (Moscow: Kushnerev, 1905), 338,

mentions a play on 13 November 1674 but does not give its name. P. O. Morozov, *Istoriia russkogo teatra,* 1:149, states that on Thursday of *Maslenitsa,* on 11 February 1675, there was a play given in the Kremlin, but he does not say which one. Very interesting data about the staging of the first theatrical plays in Moscow may be found in the *Arkhiv istoriko-iuridicheskikh svedenii, otnosiashchikhsia do Rossii* [Archive of historical-legal information about Russia], published by N. Kalachev (Moscow: Tip. A. Semena, 1850), 6:16ff. and in the valuable materials published by Bogoiavlenskii, "Moskovskii teatr." [The text of the remaining plays are all published, with extensive commentary, in O. A. Derzhavina, ed., *Russkaia dramaturgiia poslednei chetverti XVII i nachala XVIII v.* [Russian drama in the last quarter of the 17th century and the beginning of the 18th century], vol. 2 of A. N. Robinson, ed., *Ranniaia russkaia dramaturgiia (XVII–pervaia polovina XVIII v.)* (Moscow: Nauka, 1972). See also articles on the individual plays in *SKK* 3. On the historian Nikolai Vasil'evich Kalachev (1819–1885), mentioned above, see *GSE* 11: 344.]

388A. [*Editors' note:* The history of the illustrations for Polotskii's *Prodigal Son,* which have been widely reproduced, is complex and, apparently, unresolved (see, for example, reproductions in Eremin, *Simeon Polotskii: Izbrannye sochineniia,* foll. 168 and 176). The attribution to "Pikar" apparently comes from Rovinskii, *Russkie narodnye kartinki,* 4:520–22 (where he says that they are engravings from Dutch originals) and volume 5, where he says that they are the work of the "elder Picart." Rovinskii (who published the entire set of illustrations) refers here to Pieter Picart (Pickaerdt, Picaert), who worked in Russia between 1702 and 1737. Picart was the stepson and former student of Adriaan Schoonebeck, an Amsterdam etcher and printer hired by Peter the Great after they met during the tsar's European tour in 1698; see James Cracraft, *The Petrine Revolution in Russian Imagery* (Chicago: University of Chicago Press, 1997), 170–77. Cracraft includes examples of Picart's Russian work; its quality suggests that the *Prodigal Son* engravings may be the work of Picart's students. The date of Picart's tenure in Russia supports the evidence of the paper types used in the *Prodigal Son,* indicating that the print is not from 1685, the date on the title page, but from a slightly later period. See the summaries in V. N. Vsevolodskii-Gerngross, *Istoriia russkogo dramaticheskogo teatra* [History of Russian dramatic theater], ed. E. G. Kholodov et al. (Moscow: Iskusstvo, 1977), 1:393 n. 61; and Derzhavina, *Russkaia dramaturgiia poslednei chetverti XVII i nachala XVIII v.,* 313–24, which outlines the disputes over the publication date of Polotskii's play.]

389. In such episodes we encounter the Hanswursts and other theatrical buffoons of the Western theaters but in Russian guise. In *Judith,* the character Susakim appears in this type of role, subjected to a mock execution by being beheaded with a fox's tail, after which he looks for his chopped-off head and asks the audience about it. The buffoonery of Susakim and similar characters is analogous to Pedrolino in Orazio Vecchi's *L'Amfiparnaso* (1597). The quasi-biblical Susakim, at the end of the second act, turns to his companions, exclaiming: "Come along, brothers, let us have some sausages!" In these early Russian plays, clowning was interwoven with dramatic elements. Beginning with the plays of Simeon Polotskii and in the later repertory of the eighteenth century, comic intermedia were inserted between acts mechanically as comic entr'actes. [On a similar character, Pickleherring, who also appears in early Russian plays, see Jensen, "Orpheus in Moscovy," 291, and n. 33. The character appears in the play on Tamerlane; see Derzhavina, *Russkaia dramaturgiia poslednei chetverti XVII i nachala XVIII v.,* 71.]

390. I. A. Shliapkin, *Tsarevna Natal'ia Alekseevna i teatr ee vremeni* [Tsarevna Natal'ia Alekseevna and the theater of her time], Pamiatniki drevnei pis'mennosti 128 (St. Petersburg: V. Balashev, 1898), v. [See the prefatory comments to this chapter on these melodies, which modern scholars believe to date from the eighteenth century. There is a survey of Natal'ia's theater in *SKK* 3, pt. 3: 278–89, pt. 4: 783.]

390A. [*Editors' note:* This is a Russian translation of the well-known Lutheran hymn, "Durch Adams Fall," a text (and, presumably, a tune) that would have been familiar to the German performers in the court theater. See K. Günther, "Neue deutsche Quellen zum ersten russischen Theater," *Zeitschrift für Slawistic* 8, no. 5 (1963), 671–72.]

391. Shliapkin, *Tsarevna Natal'ia Alekseevna i teatr ee vremeni*, 82–83. I have corrected the second voice, as in Shliapkin's edition or in the manuscript copy, the harmony with the first voice sounded harsh and unnatural, especially since, in Shliapkin's book, the musical example was "edited" by Sakketti. [Liverii Antonovich Sakketti (1852–1916; see *ME* 4: col. 818) was a descendant of Italian musicians who settled in Russia; he studied and later taught at the St. Petersburg Conservatory, where he was the first to teach a course on musical aesthetics in Russia. His books on the theory and history of music were used as textbooks for some time in Russia.]

392. Shliapkin's assumption (ibid., ix n.) that the book mentioned in the inventory of possessions belonging to Pitirim, Archbishop of Nizhegorod, titled "Kniga Artakserks, dramma na muzyke, deistvuemaia v Zimnem dome 1738 g. na latinskom i rossiiskom dialektakh" [The book of Ahasuerus, a drama in music performed at the Winter Palace in 1738 in Latin and Russian] is a copy of *Esfir'* or Gregory's *Artakserksovo deistvo* is erroneous, as that booklet is simply the libretto, in Italian and Russian, of Francesco Araja's opera *Artaserse*, which was staged in St. Petersburg in 1738.

393. Morozov, *Istoriia russkogo teatra*, 1:136. The violins (viols) were renamed *ryli* because of their shape; their body, although somewhat flatter, reminded people of the Little Russian folk instrument *lira*, also called *ryla*, with its three gut strings [see chapter 7]. As for the term *stramenty*, we must presume it referred to wind instruments. [Roizman, "Iz istorii organnoi kul'tury v Rossii (vtoraia polovina XVII veka)" [On the history of organ culture in Russia (second half of the 17th century)], *Voprosy muzykoznaniia* [Questions of musicology] 3 (1960): 596–97, suggests that the *stramenty* may have been some sort of mechanical or wind-up instrument with a turning handle, or an instrument that produced sound by plucking wires. Gutovskii sometimes repaired them with wire, as did a metal craftsman, and Peter the Great had some as toys when he was a child. On Hasenkruch, see Roizman, *Organ*, 89–90.]

393A. [*Editors' note:* There is no evidence to date that Titov or any of the sovereign or patriarchal singers participated in the court theater.]

394. Reutenfels's statement that only a week was allowed for the staging of the ballet corresponds to the data published by Morozov: if *Judith* were staged on 2 February 1673, then on the 9th the ballet was performed for which "four blue decorated [pyramids] for the ballet" ["vykrashennye golubtsom chetyre balety"], that is, movable pyramids, were required for the performance (see Morozov, *Istoriia russkogo teatra*, 1:147). [The passage appears in Reutenfels, *De rebus Moschoviticis* (Padua: Typis Petri Mariae Frambotti, 1680), 105. There is a Russian translation of Reutenfels's work by Aleksei Stankevich in *ChOIDR* 3 (1905) and 3 (1906); the passage on the theater is in 3 (1905), pt. 2: 88–89. This translation has been reissued as Iakov Reitenfel's, *Skazaniia svetleishemu gertsogu toskanskomu Koz'me Tret'emu o Moskovii* [Reports on Muscovy to the honorable Duke of Tuscany, Cosimo III], *Utverzhdenie dinastii* [The establishment of the dynasty], ed. A. Liberman and S. Shokarev, in the series Istoriia Rossii i doma Romanovykh v memuarakh sovremennikov XVII–XX vv. [A history of Russia and the house of the Romanovs in memoirs by contemporaries, 17th–20th centuries] (Moscow: Fond Sergeia Dubova, 1997), 231–406. Many thanks to Martha Lahana for providing the text of Reutenfels's treatise, and to Kent Webb for advice on the translation from Latin.]

395. Reutenfels quotes the German text of Orpheus's prologue; see E. Koch, "Die Sachsenkirche in Moskau," 366. [See also Reutenfels, *De rebus Moschoviticis*, 106–107.]

396. A complete copy of the 1685 edition with all the scenes of the "Komediia" is reproduced in Rovinskii, *Russkie narodnye kartinki*, 3:8–31 [description and texts; see also the accompanying *Atlas*, and see n. 388A above on the illustrations of this play].

397. As already stated, some curious documents are preserved concerning Tsar Fedor Alekseevich's music library: an inventory of music books, which, after the tsar's death, were turned over to his *ustavshchik* [choir leader] in 1682. An approximate tally from the list shows that the library

contained 138 music books (manuscripts), more than 913 music notebooks [*tetradi*], and about 1,707 sheets, columns, and so on. These holdings were stored in seven chests and four cases. According to a contemporary description, the cases in libraries were as follows: "a case with an internal lock, painted, on the upper cover corners are reinforced by cut cast iron, in the middle covered by a chiseled brass plate." The chests were white. According to a description prepared for publication by A. Uspenskii, *Materialy dlia istorii tsarskoi biblioteki v Rossii* (galley-proofs at the Academy of Sciences), in Fedor Alekseevich's library there were music manuscripts copied in the seventeenth century by Semen Denisov, Bogdan Zlatoustovskii, Fedor Konstantinov, Iurii Kriuk, Meletii the Greek, Ivan Nikiforov, Mikhail Osipov, Grigorii Panfilov, and Grigorii Kherugovskii. There were also music books either given as gifts or bequeathed to him, previously belonging to Nikita Gorchakov, Prince Mikhail Nikolaevich Odoevskii, Ivan Semenov, and boyars Vasilii Ivanovich and Semen Luk. Streshnev. All these individuals had previously owned these musical manuscripts and were obviously music lovers.

11. A Brief Survey of Singers, Composers, and Music Theorists of the Sixteenth and Seventeenth Centuries

[*Editors' note:* This chapter is a short catalog of singers, composers, and theorists in the sixteenth and seventeenth centuries. Many of the figures here have already been discussed; see the new information about Mezenets and the brief comments about Tikhon Makar'evskii in the introductory remarks to chapter 9 above, and see also the entries in Parfent'ev, *Professional'nye muzykanty;* and Chudinova, *Penie, zvony, ritual* (for eighteenth-century Petersburg), which expand tremendously on the list of names Findeizen knew. An additional name needs correction: there was no singer or composer by the name of Opekalov. Irina F. Bezuglova has demonstrated in several studies that the term "opekalovskii rospev" should actually be interpreted to refer to the monastery by that name. The monastery had apparently been abandoned by ca. 1600 and was renovated in the second half of the seventeenth century; all documentation about "opekalovskii rospev" dates, in fact, from this later period of renovation. See her article "Opekalovskii rospev" [Opekalovskii chant], *PKNO for 1978* (1979): 196–204. N. Kalachnikov was a composer of religious music, including polychoral works, one of which is published, in part, by Tamara Livanova, *Ocherki i materialy po istorii russkoi muzykal'noi kul'tury* [Studies and materials on the history of Russian musical culture] (Moscow: Iskusstvo, 1938), foll. 104.]

398. The materials for this listing are from the following sources: "Azbuchnyi ukazatel' imen russkikh deiatelei dlia russkogo biograficheskogo slovaria" [Alphabetic index of names of Russian public figures for a Russian biographical dictionary], *Sbornik Imp. Russkogo istoricheskogo obshchestva* 60, 62 (1887–88), pts. 1, 2 [reprint, Nendeln, Liechtenstein: Kraus Reprint, 1976]; Razumovskii, *Patriarshie pevchie diaki;* idem, *Tserkovnoe penie v Rossii;* S. V. Smolenskii, *Azbuka znamennogo peniia startsa Aleksandra Mezentsa;* idem, *Obzor istoricheskikh kontsertov Sinodal'nogo uchilishcha tserkovnogo peniia v 1895 g.* [A survey of historical concerts of church singing at the Synodal School in 1895] (Moscow: Sinodal'naia tip., 1895); idem, "O sobranii russkikh drevne-pevcheskikh rukopisei"; Undol'skii, *Zamechaniia dlia istorii tserkovnogo peniia v Rossii;* and from descriptive lists [*opisi*] and catalogs of manuscript collections in the Public Library, the Academy of Sciences, the Synodal Archive, and other libraries and private collections. Readers should keep in mind, when referring to the location of manuscripts, that the library of the Synodal School in Moscow is presently in the Historical Museum in Moscow [GIM].

398A. [*Editors' note:* The "Pokazaniia" was published in *Drevnosti. Trudy Moskovskogo Arkheologicheskogo obshchestva,* 1:23; see also Belonenko, "Pokazaniia," 320–28; and n. 345 above.]

398B. [*Editors' note:* Findeizen cites the study by the academician S. F. Platonov, "Iz bytovoi istorii petrovskoi epokhi" [From the history of social customs of the Petrine era], *Izvestiia Akademii nauk* (1926): 673ff. See also S. B. Butskaia, "Stefan Ivanovich Beliaev—gosudarev pevchii d'iak" [Stefan Ivanovich Beliaev, sovereign singer], *PKNO for 1992* (1993): 151–56.]

398C. [*Editors' note:* See chapter 9 above, where Diletskii's works are discussed in greater detail; there are slight discrepancies in Findeizen's various presentations of the titles of Diletskii's treatises. Updated references to manuscript sources are also given in chapter 9. Although Diletskii cites works by the Polish composer Mielczewski, there is no indication that he actually studied with him, as Findeizen states here.]

398D. [*Editors' note:* On the singer Loggin, Findeizen cites the pamphlet *O khomovom penii* [On *khomovoe* singing] (Pskov, 1879), 113. He also refers to N. Kostomarov, *Russkaia istoriia v zhizneopisaniiakh* [Russian history in biographies], 4th ed. (St. Petersburg: M. Stasiulevich, 1896), 1:701; and P. V. Znamenskii, *Rukovodstvo k russkoi tserkovnoi istorii* [Manual for Russian church history] (Kazan: Universitetskaia tip., 1870), 229. Kostomarov's work was reprinted in Moscow by Terra Publishers, 1997. It is not clear to which edition of Znamenskii's *Rukovodstvo k russkoi tserkovnoi istorii* Findeizen refers. The first edition is from Kazan: Universitetskaia tip., 1870, and there are at least five editions from the same publisher, to 1888.]

398E. Tikhon Makar'evskii came from a lay family and was born in Nizhnii Novgorod in the parish of the Church of the Ascension. A wooden cross in that church bears the inscription: "this stone church of the Miraculous Ascension was built through the devotion and at the expense of the monk Tikhon, formerly a layman in that parish, who then voluntarily left this world and received tonsure in Makarii's Zheltovodskii Monastery and by God's intentions was taken into the household of the Holy Patriarch Adrian, where he was treasurer, to sing ["byst' domu ego kaznachei pet' dovol'no"]." Tikhon came to be called "Makar'evskii" after the name of the monastery. Tikhon later joined the Savvin-Storozhevskii Monastery, where he held the position of cellarer. In 1691, at the order of Patriarch Adrian, Tikhon traveled to Moscow to the affiliated Monastery of the Resurrection (called "the High" ["Vysokii, inache Savvinskoe podvor'e"]) for the dedication of its stone Church of the Ascension. Patriarch Adrian made Tikhon treasurer of the patriarchal household, and he served in that capacity for ten years; the patriarch also named Tikhon executor of his last will and manager of his affairs at his death (1700). Tikhon was still alive in 1706, for in that year he signed a chronograph which has been preserved in the seminary in Nizhnii Novgorod (see the biographical materials assembled by Razumovskii in his "Tserkovnoe russkoe penie" [Russian church singing], *Trudy I-go arkheologicheskogo s"ezda v Moskve* [1871]: 455). A complete copy of Tikhon's *Kliuch* written on paper, 1676–80, is in the library of the Academy of Sciences (library of K. I. Nevostruev). Manuscript Q.XII.1 in the Public Library [RNB] contains the "Skazanie o notnom glasobezhanii" [Information on notated vocal movement], which ends with the acrostic published by Undol'skii; the second part of the *Kliuch* was published by the Friends of Old Literature under the title *Pervoe uchenie musikiiiskikh soglasii* [First lesson on musical concordances; the source, RGB, sobr. OLDP, 129, contains a variety of material, not all of it Tikhon's; see Protopopov, *Russkaia mysl' o muzyke*, 18; and Jensen, "Nikolai Diletskii's 'Grammatika,'" 334–37]. In the Tolstoi collection, there is a "Nakaz stroitel'nyi kaznacheiskii" [Treasurer's building order] of 1689 addressed to the Purdyshevskii Nativity Monastery, signed, among others, by the *kelar'* Tikhon Makar'evskii (see Kalaidovich and Stroev, *Obstoiatel'noe opisanie slaviano-rossiiskikh rukopisei*, otd. 2, no. 236 [the manuscript number is now RNB, Q.II.28]). [This is Findeizen's note 398a. See also chapter 9 above on Tikhon's treatise.]

398F. [*Editors' note:* In his text Findeizen refers here to A. V. Preobrazhenskii, *Vopros o edinoglasnom penii v russkoi tserkvi XVII v.* [The question of monophonic chant in the Russian church in the seventeenth century], Pamiatniki drevnei pis'mennosti i iskusstva 155 (St. Petersburg: OLDP, 1904).]

398G. [*Editors' note:* Findeizen cites several sources in this passage. On Mezenets's plans for printing liturgical books, see P. A. Bezsonov, "Sud'ba notnykh pevcheskikh knig" [The fate of notated song books], *Pravoslavnoe obozrenie* 14 (1864); and on the manuscript of verses with late *kriuki* notation and *pomety*, see I. Bezsonov, "K voprosu o sobiranii i izdanii pamiatnikov narodnogo pesnotvorchestva"

[On the question of the collecting and publishing of documents of folk singing], *Mosk. vedomosti* 1896, no. 302). On Mezenets's biography, Findeizen cites Smolenskii, *O drevnerusskikh pevcheskikh notatsiiakh*, 35–36; for Smolenskii's doubts about the handwriting, see 36–37. The Iamskii prikaz was the government department responsible for managing communications and transportation (Pushkarev, *Dictionary of Russian Historical Terms*, 104). The term *iam* referred to a post-horse station, and *iamshchiki* were post riders, a term appearing in the title of an eighteenth-century Russian opera Findeizen discusses in chapter 18, *Iamshchiki na podstave* [Postal coachmen at the relay station].]

398H. [*Editors' note:* On the Naritsyn manuscripts, Findeizen cites Nikol'skii, *Opisanie rukopisei, khraniashchikhsia v arkhive Sviateishego pravitel'stvuiushchego sinoda*, 2, pt. 2: 812, manuscript no. 3983.]

398I. [*Editors' note:* In Findeizen, *Ocherki* 1:332, the title reads: "Triod' postnaia i tsvetnaia, mnogim sviatym stikhiry slavniki, bogorodichny i krestobogorodichny lineinyia"; this is corrected in Alfred Swan's copy of Findeizen's text to "mineinyia."]

398J. [*Editors' note:* On Pokrovets's residence on Tverskaia Street, Findeizen cites *Perepisnye knigi Moskvy, 1665–76*, 163.]

398K. [*Editors' note:* Findeizen cites V. I. Saitov and B. L. Modzalevskii, comp., *Moskovskii nekropol'* [Moscow necropolis], 3 vols. (St. Petersburg: Velikii kniaz, 1907–1908), 1:117.]

398L. [*Editors' note:* On the manuscript Sofia copied, Findeizen cites P. Kazanskii, *Selo Novospasskoe, Dedenevo tozh i rodoslovnaia Golovinykh, vladel'tsev onogo* [The villages of Novospasskoe and Dedenevo and the genealogy of the Golovins who possess them] (Moscow: S. Selivanovskii, 1847), 57. The current location of this manuscript is uncertain, but it is not mentioned in *SKK* 3, pt. 3: 487–88. For a biographical survey, see Lindsey Hughes, *Sophia, Regent of Russia, 1657–1704* (New Haven: Yale University Press, 1990).]

398M. [*Editors' note:* On Titov's setting of Polotskii's *Versified Psalter*, Findeizen cites Nikol'skii, *Opisanie rukopisei, khraniashchikhsia v arkhive Sviateishego pravitel'stvuiushchego sinoda*, 2, pt. 2: 794–96, manuscript 3973; in vol. 1:609–12, manuscript 1200 includes other works by Titov: "The only-begotten Son," the Cherubic Hymn, and *zadostoiniki*.]

398N. [*Editors' note:* On the death of the tsarevich, following his flight from Russia, his return, his disinheritance, and finally his torture, see Massie, *Peter the Great*, chap. 54.]

398O. [*Editors' note:* The full quotation is in Findeizen, *Ocherki* 1:328: "stoial v monastyre ego stroen'ia na krylose."]

12. Music and Theater in the Age of Peter the Great

[*Editors' note:* This chapter examines the reign of Peter the Great and the music and theater in his lifetime, and analyzes some of the reports made by Russians who traveled abroad in that period. Lindsey Hughes, *Russia in the Age of Peter the Great* (New Haven: Yale University Press, 1998), provides an overview of the period, focusing on the degree to which Peter's rule constitutes a break with Muscovite traditions; she has also written a shorter biography, *Peter the Great: A Biography* (New Haven: Yale University Press, 2002). Massie, *Peter the Great*, is aimed at a more popular audience and focuses on foreign policy. There is a comprehensive survey of Petrine-era music by Iurii Keldysh in *IRM* 2:29–64, and see the valuable series of articles in *MP.*

The musical compositions for two and three voices known as *kanty* begin to dominate the repertory of performances in the late seventeenth and early eighteenth centuries; Findeizen discussed this repertory briefly in chapter 9, when he introduced Vasilii Titov's *kant*-style settings of Simeon Polotskii's *Versified Psalter*. The only monograph in English on these *kanty* is Dolskaya-Ackerly, "The Early Kant in Seventeenth-century Russian Music." The same author has recently published an entire *kant* manuscript; see Olga Dolskaya, ed., *Spiritual Songs in Seventeenth-century Russia*, Bausteine zur Slavischen Philologie und Kulturgeschichte Reihe B, Neue Folge B. 4 (Cologne: Böhlau, 1996), which includes a generous selection of facsimiles from the source (GIM, Muz. 1938); in her introduction, Dolskaya provides references to some of the many important articles written by A. V. Pozdneev, in which he explored the Polish–Ukrainian–Muscovite connections in this repertory. On Pozdneev and his enormous output, see Gerald Smith, "A. V. Pozdneev and the Russian 'Literary' Song," *Journal of European Studies* 5 (1975): 177–89; see also Dolskaya's "Manuscript Collections of Seventeenth-century Russian Songbooks," *Australian Slavonic and East European Studies* 5, no. 1 (1991): 1–14. Additional references are in the editorial notes prefacing chapter 9; see also the notes to chapter 13 in volume 2, where Findeizen again discusses the topic.

Findeizen does not elaborate on the existence of the *partesnye kontserty*, polychoral works that became extremely popular in the last third of the seventeenth and into the eighteenth century, for this area was little explored before the 1960s and 1970s. According to the Kievan scholar Nina Herasymova-Persyd'ska (in Russian, Gerasimova-Persidskaia), who was one of the first scholars to focus on this type of musical composition in Ukraine and Russia, approximately five hundred works are preserved in manuscript sources, only a handful of which have been studied. See her anthology, compiled by L. V. Ivchenko, *Ukrains'kyi kant XVII–XVIII stolit'* [Ukrainian *kant* in the 17th–18th centuries] (Kiev: Muzychna Ukraina, 1990), which includes a brief English-language summary of the volume and its many musical examples. Among Herasymova-Persyd'ska's earlier publications, an important anthology is *Materiali z istorii ukrains'koi muzyky: Partesnii kontsert* [Materials from the history of Ukrainian music: Polyphonic *kontsert*] (Kiev: Muzychna Ukraina, 1976). This volume includes the complete score for Diletskii's setting, for eight voices, of the Easter Kanon (and see chapter 9 above on Herasymova-Persyd'ska's publication of other *partesnoe* works by Diletskii). See, too, her stylistic analysis in *Khorovyi kontsert na Ukraini v XVII–XVIII st.* [The choral *kontsert* in Ukraine in the 17th–18th centuries] (Kiev: Muzychna Ukraina, 1978). One of her recent works is a publication of newly discovered scores of five- and six-part Ukrainian pieces dating from ca. 1700 from a manuscript found in Novi Sad in Serbia: *Ukrains'ki partesni motety pochatku XVIII stolittia z Iuhoslavs'kykh zibran'* [Ukrainian choral motets of the early 18th century from Yugoslav collections], in Ukrainian and Russian, with an English summary (Kiev: Muzychna Ukraina, 1991). See also the earlier study by Iu. V. Keldysh, *Russkaia muzyka XVIII veka* [Russian music in the 18th century] (Moscow: Nauka, 1965), esp. chap. 1, and the English-language survey by Olga Dolskaya, "Choral Music in the Petrine Era," in *Russia in the Reign of Peter the Great: Old and New Perspectives*, ed. Anthony Cross (Cambridge: Study Group on Eighteenth-Century Russia, 1998), pt. 2: 173–85. All these works, in addition to the survey in *IRM* 1, include substantial bibliographies of this important genre.

In this final chapter of volume 1, Findeizen also discusses the Russian travelers who wrote about their experiences in Western Europe (in addition to those who accompanied Peter on his two trips to the West); the most important is Petr Andreevich Tolstoi (1645–1729), who traveled to Italy in 1697–99. His diary has been translated by Max J. Okenfuss, *The Travel Diary of Peter Tolstoi, A Muscovite in Early Modern Europe* (De Kalb: Northern Illinois University Press, 1987), and there is a modern Russian edition by L. A. Ol'shevskaia and S. N. Travnikov, eds., *Puteshestvie stol'nika P. A. Tolstogo po Evrope 1697–1699* [The travels of *stol'nik* P. A. Tolstoi in Europe, 1697–1699] (Moscow: Nauka, 1992).

Johann Georg Korb (1672–1741) visited Moscow in 1698–99; his *Diarium itineris in Moscoviam* (1700) was published in Vienna in 1717 as *Tagebuch der Reise nach Russland*. The only English translation appeared in two volumes as *Diary of an Austrian Secretary of Legation at the Court of Czar Peter the Great* (London: Bradbury & Evans, 1863), and the work has been reprinted in the series *Russia through European Eyes* 8 (New York: Da Capo, 1968). A well-annotated edition in German appeared in the same year: Johann Korb, *Tagebuch der Reise nach Russland*, ed. Gerhard Korb, commentary by Edmund Leingärtner (Graz: Akademische Druck-u. Verlagsanstalt, 1968). Korb was a secretary to Ignatius Christophorus von Guarient, a special emissary of Leopold I. While in Moscow, they were received by Boris Alekseevich Golitsyn (1654–1714), one member of the triumvirate overseeing Russia during Peter's Great Embassy to Western Europe in 1697 and 1698. See also *MERSH* 17:174–75. Another member of Peter's inner circle, Petr Alekseevich Golitsyn (1660–1722) was responsible for bringing back to Russia a young castrato singer, Filippo Balatri, who eventually wrote of the several years he spent in St. Petersburg; see the fascinating articles by Daniel Schlafly, "Filippo Balatri in Peter the Great's Russia," *Jahrbücher für Geschichte Osteuropas* (spring 1997): 181–98; and "A Muscovite *Boiarynia* Faces Peter the Great's Reforms: Dar'ia Golitsyna between Two Worlds," *Canadian-American Slavic Studies* 31, no. 3 (1997): 249–68. See also I. F. Petrovskaia, *Istochnikovedenie istorii russkoi muzykal'noi kul'tury XVIII–nachala XX veka* [Source studies in the history of Russian musical culture, 18th–beginning of the 20th centuries], 2nd exp. ed. (Moscow: Muzyka, 1989), 91.

Findeizen refers in this chapter to the Slavo–Greco–Latin Academy, which was established in the 1680s and which brought the traditions of the classical Latin grammar school to Muscovy. An extensive survey of Russian education and schools in this period can be found in Max J. Okenfuss, "Education in Russia in the first half of the eighteenth century" (Ph.D. diss., Harvard University, 1970). One of two educators Findeizen mentions who fostered performance of school dramas is Petr Simeonovich Mogila (Mohyla; 1597–1647), a native of Moldavia who was educated in L'vov, took monastic vows in 1625, and, by 1627, was already a high ranking archimandrite of the Kiev Monastery of the Caves. From 1632 until his death he served as the metropolitan of Kiev, and in 1632 he helped to found a school named in his honor as the Mogila Academy in Kiev, where plays (including music) are known to have been staged; see Karlinsky, *Russian Drama from Its Beginnings*, 8; and Paulina Lewin, "The Staging of Plays at the Kiev Mohyla Academy in the Seventeenth and Eighteenth Centuries," *Harvard Ukrainian Studies* 5, no. 3 (1981): 320–34 (although it does not seem likely that the Moscow court theater of the 1670s borrowed equipment from Kiev, as she suggests). Findeizen also mentions Dimitrii Rostovskii (1651–1709), the archbishop of Rostov (his secular name before taking monastic vows in 1668 was Daniil Savvich Tuptalo). In 1702, the year he became the metropolitan of Rostov, he founded a school which, from the outset, had some one hundred students. These students participated in performances of plays, some of which Dimitrii himself wrote. A full score of his *Rozhdestvenskaia drama* [Christmas drama] was published in 1989, edited by Evgenii M. Levashev (Moscow: Sovetskii kompozitor, 1989). A convenient summary of his works in English is in Karlinsky, *Russian Drama from Its Beginnings*, 14–24; his *Komediia na uspenie bogoroditsy* [Play of the Dormition of the Virgin] and *Komediia na rozhdestvo Khristovo* [Play of the birth of Christ] were published in *Russkaia dramaturgiia poslednei chetverti XVII i nachala XVIII v.* There are two recent studies of Petrine-era theater by L. M. Starikova, who has carried out important archival research relating to eighteenth-century music and theater as a whole: "Russkii teatr petrovskogo vremeni, komedial'naia khramina i domashnie komedii tsarevny Natal'i Alekseevny" [Russian theater of the Petrine era, the theatrical quarters ("comedy mansion") and the domestic theater of Tsarevna Natal'ia Alekseevna], *PKNO for 1990* (1992): 137–56; and "Dokumental'nye utochneniia k istorii teatra v Rossii petrovskogo vremeni" [Some documentary clarification on the history of the theater in Russia in the Petrine era], *PKNO for 1997* (1998): 179–90.

It is difficult to identify the origin (and even the genre!) of some of the works presented by Johann Kunst and his successor, Otto Fürst, in Moscow between 1702 and 1707. There were several German-language settings of the *Scipio Africanus* story based on libretti by Nicolò Minato (ca. 1627–1698), who worked in Vienna and whose libretti were widely set by German composers (see listings in *NG2*). Franz Stieger, *Opernlexikon*, pt. 3, *Titelkatalog* (Tutzing: Schneider, 1975), 3:1106, also lists an anonymous *Singspiel* setting titled *Scipio* (Durlach, 1684). Kunst may have been familiar with this German tradition. There are also, of course, many Italian-language operatic settings of the Scipio theme from the second half of the seventeenth century. It is similarly difficult to determine any specific models for the possible 1714 production of *Dafnis*. There were several Italian operas on that subject from around 1700, as well as an anonymous German work staged in Leipzig in 1710. The Moscow theater in the early years of the century was under the jurisdiction of the Foreign Office, headed by Fedor Alekseevich Golovin (1650–1706), who had been a member of the Great Embassy of 1697 to Western Europe and who might thus have seen or heard about Western theatrical productions of various kinds. On Golovin, see *GSE* 7:257 and *MERSH* 13:21–22.

Findeizen's discussion of celebratory processions after military victories and the erection of triumphal arches is of considerable interest. There are general discussions of Peter's victory parades and processions in Cracraft, *The Petrine Revolution in Russian Imagery;* and Wortman, *Scenarios of Power,* vol. 1, chap. 2; see also V. P. Grebeniuk and O. A. Derzhavina, *Panegiricheskaia literatura petrovskogo vremeni* [Panegyrical literature of the Petrine era] (Moscow: Nauka, 1979); and V. N. Vasil'ev, *Starinnye feierverki v Rossii, XVII–pervaia chetvert' XVIII veka* [Early fireworks in Russia, 17th–first quarter of the 18th century] (Leningrad: Izd-vo gos. Ermitazha, 1960). Some of the *kanty* and pieces written for such occasions have been published, especially for the celebrations after Peter's great victory at Poltava, where he defeated the Swedish King Charles XII in 1709. The *kant* celebrating the Peace of Nystadt (shown in the music appendix to this volume) was also published in *IRMNO* 1:5. See, too, V. V. Protopopov's detailed study in *Muzyka na Poltavskuiu pobedu,* which also includes scores to a number of works. The same author produced a shorter version of this material in his "Muzyka petrovskogo vremeni o pobede pod Poltavoi" [Petrine-era music on the Poltava victory], *SM* 12 (1971): 97–105; see also the article "Kant" in *MP* 2:20–37.

In his discussion of the 1720s Findeizen makes several references to Friedrich Wilhelm von Bergholz (1699–1765). He was the son of a professional soldier who was in Russian service at the time of Bergholz's birth and who later moved back to Germany. Bergholz returned to Russia in 1721 for a stay of some six years (until 1727), in the service of Karl Friedrich, Duke of Holstein-Gottorp, who, in 1725, married a daughter of Peter the Great, Anna Petrovna (1708–1728), the older sister of the future empress Elizabeth. Anna's only child was Peter III (1728–1762), who in 1745 married a German princess, the future Catherine the Great (1729–1796). Bergholz's *Diary* is a rich mine of information about life in St. Petersburg from 1721 to 30 September 1725, when the diary stops. There is no English translation of Bergholz's writings, but there is a comprehensive doctoral dissertation by Elizabeth C. Sander, "Social Dancing in Russia at the End of the Petrine Era: Friedrich Wilhelm von Bergholz's *Tagebuch,* 1721–1725" (Ph.D. diss., University of Western Ontario, 2002), which focuses on dance at the Russian assemblies and wedding ceremonies. She includes an extensive biography in her chapter 2, and see also the biography in *RBS* 2:755–57; Sander also provides a useful summary listing Bergholz's references to music and dancing on pp. 213–15. Throughout her dissertation, Sander cites (and translates) Bergholz's original diary; in the present work we have translated from the Russian translation Findeizen uses, by I. F. Ammon (1902–1903), the first part of which has been reprinted in an edition by Liberman and Naumov in the series *Istoriia Rossii i doma Romanovykh v memuarakh sovremennikov XVII–XX vv.* and refer to it as Bergholz, *Dnevnik* (2000); see chap. 7 n. 289.

Bergholz mentions the private orchestras owned by a number of prominent figures such as General-Admiral Fedor Matveevich Apraksin (1671–1728), who studied shipbuilding together with Peter in Holland in 1697–98 (*SKK* 3, pt. 4: 321–24, attributes the anonymous travel diary, the *Zhurnal,* from 1697 to 1698 to Apraksin's brother, Andrei Matveevich [1663–1731]). Bergholz also mentions one of Peter's close friends, Aleksandr Danilovich Menshikov (1672?–1729), who was in charge of building much of the newly founded city of St. Petersburg. There is an important study of Menshikov's orchestra and his singers (he employed more than fifty musicians) by I. V. Saverkina and Iu. N. Semenov, "Orkestr i khor A. D. Menshikova" [A. D. Menshikov's orchestra and choir], *PKNO for 1989* (1990): 160–66; see also the article on Menshikov in *MP* 2:204–208 by the same authors. Findeizen also discusses Grigorii Dmitrievich (not Andreevich) Stroganov (1656–1715), already mentioned in chapter 9 above. In 1722 Peter elevated three of Grigorii's sons (Nikolai, Aleksandr, and Sergei) to the rank of baron, as a reward for the merits and services of the family (see *ES-BE* 62:803). Other important figures in this chapter include Pavel Ivanovich Iaguzhinskii (1683–1736), son of a Lithuanian teacher who became the organist for the Lutheran community in Moscow, where the young Pavel prospered, reaching the highest ranks in the society (see MA 1:40 n. 4; and Roizman, *Organ*, 102), and Countess Maria Cherkasskaia (1696–1747), a daughter of Iurii Iur'evich Trubetskoi (1668–1739); see, too, the article in *MP* 3:254–55. Findeizen also mentions the assembly that took place at the home of Gavriil Ivanovich Golovkin (1660–1734), a prominent figure in Peter's retinue. Several of these figures are mentioned briefly as performers in Robert Karpiak, "The Culture of the Keyboard in 18th-century Russia," *Continuo* (December 1998): 5–8. Findeizen also mentions the Austrian emissary in St. Petersburg, S. W. Kinsky, who left Russia in 1722; see MA 1:37–38 and the *Allgemeine Deutsche Biographie*, 15:775ff., where he is identified as one of the sons of Wenzel Norbert Octavian Kinsky (1642–1719). There is a genealogy of the Kinsky family by Josef Folkmann, *Die gefürstete Linie des uralten und edlen Geschlechtes Kinsky* (Prague: K. André, 1861).

Johann Hübner (1696–1759) was a Warsaw-born Prussian who studied violin in Vienna, where he was hired to accompany Kinsky to St. Petersburg in 1721. After Kinsky departed in the following year, Hübner stayed, first in the service of Prince Karl Friedrich and then, after Friedrich's departure, as a musician at the Russian court. Findeizen presumed that the last known date of Hübner's stay was ca. 1750, an assumption quoted in *ME* 2: col. 121; the substantial article in *MP* 3:231–34 ("Khiubner") provides additional information on his career in Russia. Robert-Aloys Mooser corrects Findeizen's statement (in *Ocherki* 2:17) that Hübner came to Russia with his violin teacher Rosetti, attributing the error to Findeizen's misreading of data in J. G. Walther's 1732 lexicon (MA 1:37 n. 2). See also the important study by A. L. Porfir'eva, "Legenda o kapelle gertsoga golshtinskogo i podlinnaia istoriia pridvornogo orkestra v 1702–1728 gg." [The legend of the Duke of Holstein's cappella and the true history of the court orchestra, 1702–1728], *PKNO for 1996* (1998): 168–85.

Finally, a note on some of the terms Findeizen uses in this chapter. The Russian phrase *zastol'naia muzyka*, literally "at-table music," is translated here by the more familiar German term *Tafelmusik*; many works of this type were composed throughout the early eighteenth century. An article on "Stolovaia (zastol'naia) muzyka" appears in *MP* 3:105–107. Findeizen frequently uses the term *valtorn*, a transliteration of the German *Waldhorn*; we have translated this simply as horn or horn player (*valtornist*). The terminology for keyboard instruments is complex in this period. Findeizen uses the terms *chembalo*, *klavesin*, and *klavikord* frequently, and he seems to use them as direct equivalents of their Western counterparts; these terms are simply translated with their cognates as cembalo, clavecin (or harpsichord), and clavichord. The term *tsinbaly*, which appears in some of the contemporary documents Findeizen quotes, is more difficult. Roizman, *Organ*, 53ff., says that *tsinbaly* (*klavitsimbaly*) were apparently related to the *klavesin*/clavecin rather than the *klavikord*/clavichord (he discusses specifics of the materials used to construct and repair the two types of instruments). We simply refer to *tsinbaly* without further translation, keeping in mind that the term refers to a keyboard instrument. (One might point out, however, that the word has caused confusion in other studies. Max Okenfuss's excellent translation of Petr Tolstoi's diary, cited above, translates *tsinbaly* as cymbals; Tolstoi thus reports on pervasive, and apparently entertaining, cymbal playing throughout Western Europe!)]

398P. [*Editors' note*: Although Findeizen, *Ocherki* 1:337, describes Peter's instrument as a *klavesin*, Roizman, in *Organ*, 54, cites two sources in which the instrument is called a *klavikord* (or *klevikort*).]

398Q. [*Editors' note*: Findeizen uses the term *den'shchik*, which can also have a military connotation, to describe the singer Vasilii; see Dal', *Tolkovyi slovar'*, 1:428; and Pushkarev, *Dictionary of Russian Historical Terms*, 11.]

399. On S. Beliaev, see Viktorov, *Opisanie zapisnykh knig i bumag*; *Doklady i prigovory, sostoiavsheisia v Pravitel'stvuiushchem Senate*, vols. 1–3; and the *Kamer-fur'erskii tseremonial'nyi zhurnal* [The Court Chamberlain Ceremonial Journal, a record of daily life of the Imperial family] of the Petrine period [St. Petersburg: Ministerstvo Imperatorskogo dvora, 1818]. Peter's relationship to Beliaev was

clarified by Academician S. F. Platonov in his study "Iz bytovoi istorii petrovskoi epokhi" [From the history of daily life in the Petrine era], *Izvestiia Akademii nauk* (1926): 673. [See also the recent study by Butskaia, "Stefan Ivanovich Beliaev—gosudarev pevchii d'iak." Platonov's *Moscow and the West,* trans. J. L. Wieczynski (Hattiesburg, Miss.: Academic International, 1972), is readily available to English-speaking readers. Massie, *Peter the Great,* translates the *vseshuteishii sobor* as the Jolly Company; see his discussion on 117ff.]

400. A. Pypin, "Puteshestviia za granitsu vremen Petra Velikogo" [Travels abroad in the time of Peter the Great], *Vestnik Evropy* 9 (1897): 244–87; 10 (1897): 692–741. [See also Okenfuss, *The Travel Diary of Peter Tolstoi,* xi–xxv on the enormous changes Tolstoi experienced on his journey.]

400A. [*Editors' note:* Tolstoi's account was published as "Puteshestvie stol'nika P. A. Tolstogo" [The journey of *stol'nik* P. A. Tolstoi], *Russkii arkhiv* (1888), no. 2: 161–204; no. 3: 321–68; no. 4: 505–52; no. 5: 5–62; no. 6: 113–56; no. 7: 225–64; and no. 8: 369–400. This passage is in no. 5 (1888): 32; see also Okenfuss, *The Travel Diary of Peter Tolstoi,* 193.]

400B. [*Editors' note:* Boris Petrovich Sheremetev (1652–1719) was an important military figure in the age of Peter the Great; see the monograph by A. I. Zaozerskii, *Fel'dmarshal B. P. Sheremetev* [Field Marshal B. P. Sheremetev] (Moscow: Nauka, 1989); and the surveys in *RBS* 23:107–36 and *MERSH* 53:23.]

401. "This organ is wondrous," wrote Tolstoi, "it is so immeasurably loud that it seems like the church is shaking from the sound of that organ. On this organ is a golden star that shines when the organ is played [as the light] passes along the pipes of the organ; and in the organ hovers the likeness of a bird—a canary or a nightingale. In this organ, when they play all the voices and pipes, not a single instrument remains in all of music that does not echo as if it were played on this organ; at first there are the organ, *tsymbal,* violins, basses, *shtort* (a *basson,* an old type of a large flute [N.F.]), harps, flutes, viole da gamba [*vol'nogamby*], zithers, trumpets, kettledrums, and all other musical instruments. When they push in some of the stops the organ echoes trumpets exactly as if two trumpeters are blowing their trumpets together, calling to one another, one from afar and the other from nearby; and this organ has many other parts, which I do not describe now because I lack the time." This passage from Tolstoi's embassy report was printed in "Puteshestvie stol'nika P. A. Tolstogo," *Russkii arkhiv* 3 (1888): 360. [Translation, with modifications in the names of instruments, from Okenfuss, *The Travel Diary of Peter Tolstoi,* 100; the passage on his experience at St. Stephen's in Vienna is on p. 64 of Okenfuss's translation, where he says "such was the noise [from the various musical instruments] that it was impossible to hear the human voice." The same passage, on his experiences at St. Stephen's in Vienna, is in "Puteshestvie stol'nika P. A. Tolstogo," *Russkii arkhiv* 2 (1888): 333. Findeizen's definition of *shtort* (*stort*) above is somewhat perplexing. According to *NG2,* in English usage at about this time the term might have referred either to a dulcian or a bassoon; the *basson d'amor* was a bass shawm-type instrument of a slightly later period.]

402. At that time, as is well known, Venetian opera was in full flower. In the period between 1637 and 1699, some eleven theaters opened in Venice, in which at the time of Tolstoi's embassy the operas by Legrenzi, Lotti, and Alessandro Scarlatti predominated. [The passages on Venetian theater are in "Puteshestvie stol'nika P. A. Tolstogo," *Russkii arkhiv* 4 (1888): 546–47, and those on the children in Naples, 5 (1888): 48; translation from Okenfuss, *The Travel Diary of Peter Tolstoi,* 153 (on Venetian theater), and see p. 207 on the impressive Neapolitan children. Some excerpts from Tolstoi's travels are cited in French in MA 1:26–28, where the author lists Albinoni, Bononcini, Pollarolo, Ruggieri, and Ziani as popular composers in Venice at the time of Tolstoi's journey, a list substantiated by the repertory appearing in Charles H. Parsons, comp., *Opera Composers and Their Works,* 4 vols., The Mellen Opera Reference Index (Lewiston, N.Y.: Edwin Mellen, 1986), and in Irene Alm, *Catalog of Venetian Librettos at the University of California, Los Angeles,* in University of California Publications: Catalogs and Bibliographies 9 (Berkeley: University of California Press, 1993).]

403. This is how Count Kurakin describes his impressions: "During Lent they do oratorios and there is nothing in the world like them. Oratorio is a composition with verses about the Passion of Christ, and they sing them with music as if it were an opera, except that it is spiritual and performed in a church. During our stay, there was one in the church of San Filippo Neri under the patronage of Cardinal Pamphili. Then Cardinal Ottoboni stages the largest and best known at great cost. Thus one may say that of such great music, of such compositions, and such instruments there can be no better in the world, and especially what wild passages beyond expectation there were on trumpets, that suddenly gave chills to men." [Findeizen, *Ocherki* 1:340, says, literally, that Kurakin attended "oratorical gatherings of the congregation of San Filippo Neri and others" ("on prisutstvoval na oratorial'nykh sobraniiakh kongregatsii Filippa Neri i drugikh"). Boris Ivanovich Kurakin (1676–1727) was sent to Italy in 1697 to study naval science; he later served as ambassador in Paris and in Holland (see *ES-BE* 33:61 and *IRM* 2:34).]

404. See *Zapiski russkikh puteshestvennikov za granitsei* [Notes of Russian travelers abroad] in the series *Kul'turnaia istoricheskaia biblioteka* [Cultural historical library] (St. Petersburg, 1914).

405. Johann Georg Korb, *Dnevnik puteshestviia v Moskoviiu (1698 i 1699 g.)* [Diary of a trip to Muscovy in 1698 and 1699], Russian translation and commentary by A. I. Malein (St. Petersburg: A. S. Suvorin, 1906). [See the prefatory notes to this chapter for more recent editions. Sander discusses Korb's diary in her "Social Dancing in Russia," 12–19.]

406. Entry of 9 July 1708: "The ambassador was pleased to visit the most beautiful surroundings and much-praised woods and thus to be able to contemplate this famous, delightful place (Izmailovo). He was accompanied by musicians, in order to join to the rustling of the wind, softly gliding through the tops of the trees, their even sweeter melodies. The empress, the crown prince, and the unmarried princesses lived there . . . they happened to be out for a walk and when the beautiful sounds of the symphony of trumpets and flutes reached their ears, they stopped for a short time to listen, although they were about to return home. The musicians' vanity swelled; seeing that they were being observed with approval, they started vying with one another, seeing who might create the best impression in their art. The listeners, who remained for a quarter of an hour, admired the art of all of them" (Korb, *Dnevnik*, 158). It is possible that for this serenade, certainly planned in advance, Guarient may have added the musicians (flautists) of other distinguished foreigners in Moscow who had their own bands. Korb also reports that the Brandenburg envoy Markward von Prinz brought along some seven oboe players, young boys, whom the tsar then purchased from their instructor for twelve hundred gold coins (Korb, *Dnevnik*, 116). Evidently these are the young players acquired by Lefort during his stay in Brandenburg, by agreement with Ivan Tromk from the "Elector's chamber music" ("Posol'stvo Tsaria i Velikogo Kniazia Petra Alekseevicha k rimskomu imperatoru Leopol'du v 1697–1698 godakh" [Tsar and Great Prince Peter Alekseevich's embassy to the Roman Emperor Leopold in 1697–98], *Pamiatniki diplomaticheskikh snoshenii* [Monuments of diplomatic relations] 8 (1867): col. 833).

406A. [*Editors' note:* François Lefort (in Russian, Franz Iakovlevich Lefort) was born in Geneva in 1653 and became a professional soldier; upon his arrival in Russia he became a close friend of Peter I, who promoted him to the rank of general and grand admiral. Lefort died in 1699 in Moscow; see *GSE* 14:343; and *MERSH* 19:120–22.]

407. Korb, *Dnevnik*, 70, 132–33.

407A. [*Editors' note:* Dr. Nicolas Bidloo was the son of a renowned Dutch physician, Robert Godfried Bidloo. Nicolas was presumably born in the 1670s, and by 1697 had became a physician himself after schooling in Leiden. His reputation led to Peter the Great's invitation (through A. A. Matveev) to come to Moscow for six years. Bidloo arrived in June 1703 and was immediately appointed personal physician to the emperor. By 1706 Bidloo had made a proposal for a medical school and hospital to be built in Moscow, and the building was completed in record time by November 1707, becoming the first Surgery School in Russia. In 1723, for Peter the Great's return from Persia, Dr. Bidloo staged a play by V. Shtein with students from the school; see *RBS* 3:34–35.]

407B. [*Editors' note:* Translation of title (somewhat abbreviated) taken from Karlinsky, *Russian Drama from Its Beginnings*, 30, where there is a brief discussion of some of the plays listed here. The text is published in A. S. Demin, main ed., *P'esy shkol'nykh teatrov Moskvy* [School dramas in Moscow], vol. 3 of *Ranniaia russkaia dramaturgiia* (Moscow: Nauka, 1974), 51–83.]

407C. [*Editors' note:* The text of this play is published in Demin, *P'esy shkol'nykh teatrov Moskvy*, 84–126.]

407D. [*Editors' note:* The text of the play is lost, but an eighteenth-century summary is published in Demin, *P'esy shkol'nykh teatrov Moskvy*, 193–99, and see the commentary on 491–93.]

408. In the existing copy of this play, the subtitle states that this comedy was "performed before the Samoyed King." At Peter's court there resided a Pole (d. 1714 in St. Petersburg) who carried this jesting title and who wrote the tsar various documents. These were found in the tsar's private papers and, according to P. Pekarskii, they were written in the same handwriting as was the fragment of the play *Dragyia smeianyia*, also found in Peter's papers. It is possible that the "Samoyed King" may have translated Molière's *Les précieuses ridicules*, giving it this ungrammatical Russian title. [Karlinsky, *Russian Drama from Its Beginnings*, 48, describes the Russian title as meaning "something like 'dear ones laughed at.'"]

408A. [*Editors' note:* Karlinsky, *Russian Drama from Its Beginnings*, 30, has a brief description of this play, which is about the martyrdom of St. Demetrius of Salonika.]

408B. [*Editors' note:* The text of the play is lost, but a summary published in Moscow in 1710 is in Demin, *P'esy shkol'nykh teatrov Moskvy*, 228–38, and see the commentary on 501–503, where the play is linked to the Russian victory over the Swedes at Poltava.]

409. Upon his arrival in Moscow, Kunst submitted a denunciation [*donositel'noe pis'mo*] to the Foreign Office on 10 July 1702, in which, among other things, he complained that Splavskii, "whom I had asked, along with Liapunov, to give me two weeks to find good actors but also such who are experienced in little operas, namely in plays with singing, for the same price, but I could not prevail on them. They promised me that both shall go to Torun, some twelve leagues from Gdansk, where three such actors, skilled in operas, who for thirteen years were trained in instrumental and vocal music, were expecting [them]. But they bypassed [them] by two miles [*mil, milia;* about 5 versts]." Kunst's complaint and the clauses of the contract were published by E. B. Barsov in the supplement to the *Khronika russkogo teatra Nosova* (Moscow: Izd. Imp. obshchestva istorii i drevnosti rossiiskikh, 1883). A description of the theater building, Golovin's correspondence with the clerks of the Foreign Office about the construction of the theater, details about the theatrical box office and entrance tickets [*iarlyki*], and the income from plays in Peter's time are also published there. [For background on the establishment of Kunst's theater, see Kholodov, "K istorii starinnogo russkogo teatra," esp. 162–69; and Starikova, "Russkii teatr petrovskogo vremeni."]

410. An impression of Muscovite society's attitude toward the theater may be obtained from an edict issued by Peter on 5 January 1705: "Comedies [plays] in Russian and in German to be presented with musicians to play on various instruments, on selected days of the week, on Mondays and Thursdays; and viewers of all ranks, Russians and foreigners, can go at will and freely without any misapprehensions, and on those days the city gates of the Kremlin, Kitaigorod, and Belgorod are not to be closed before the ninth hour at night, and for those passing through the gates, no toll fee is to be charged, so that those going to see the plays can go readily."

411. Apparently Poggenkampf was still alive during Elizabeth Petrovna's reign, receiving, in 1748, a salary (or pension payment) of 200 rubles annually and food at court (*Kamer-fur'erskii zhurnal* [1748]: 88, 122, 150).

412. In 1702, in addition to the two main musicians, several others were recruited in Hamburg. One of the two primary musicians, Gottfried Otto Mollinius, has already been mentioned. He was

still in Russian service in 1715; he was apparently the "trumpeter Gotfried" who was sent by General Field Marshal B. P. Sheremetev on 30 April 1703 to Nöteborg (St. Petersburg) with a "letter of exhortation to surrender" according to the *Iurnal* (1703): 16 [this is a reference apparently to *Pokhodnyi iurnal* cited below], after a manuscript in the former archive of the Moscow Ministry of Foreign Affairs [RGADA]. [The rank of *general-fel'dmarshal* is the highest army ranking.] Those recruited in Hamburg were Henrich Jeronim Lorenz, Peter Mollinius, Franz Ernst Rompf (or Rumps), Thomas Schell (or Schelli), and Gerhart Drost. The orchestra was hired for two years and consisted of oboists and trumpeters. In 1703 four of Oginskii's men entered service: Henrich Kazius, Michael Pitian, Christian Richter, and Jan Sternzer. Barsov reports the name of still another musician, oboist Fedor Gopt [Hopt?] who was in Moscow probably before the arrival of those from Hamburg. A few more names of musicians who served under Peter are preserved: court musicians Peter Berendt (1715); Friedrich Brandt (1715); Johann Friedrich Wolff (d. 24 January 1724 at age thirty-eight); Peter Düben (1715); renowned horn player M. Kelbel (Köhlbel), a Czech who started his service under Peter and then served under Catherine I and Peter II and was later readmitted into Russian service under Elizabeth; Julius Christian Kergar (1715); Johann Andrea Kliber (ca. 1720 and later); Daniel Lemm (1717); Erich Adam Müss (1717); Nikolai Norman; Ivan Pomorskii, the probable ancestor (in Russia) of several generations of musicians; and Johann Konrad Rose (b. 1695, d. 1782 in St. Petersburg). Some of these men were apparently Swedish prisoners of war who later entered Russian service. These musicians must have taught a considerable cadre of Russian military band musicians as well as young clerks, singers, and serfs who were sent to them. Much new and valuable data about theatrical history and music, such as lists of musicians and their salaries, are in Bogoiavlenskii, "Moskovskii teatr." [See Porfir'eva's excellent archival study, "Legenda o kapelle gertsoga golshtinskogo," for current thinking on the musicians and musical establishments of this period, and see the article "Pridvornyi orkestr" (court orchestra) in *MP* 2:413–56 for a listing of names (there is a separate article on Köhlbel in *MP* 2:52–55, with important archival information); see also *MA* and the further discussion in volume 2 of this study. The Polish nobleman Prince G. Ogiński (d. 1709) is mentioned in the biography of his father in *Polski słownik biograficzny* 23:603–607, as well as very briefly in *Wielka encyklopedia powszechna* 8:169.]

413. In his diary, Bergholz mentions large numbers of military musicians: oboists, trumpeters, horn players, kettledrum players, and drummers, most of them foreigners. He also cites a serenade staged by German oboists of the guard unit, although in both guard regiments there were also six detachments of Russian oboists, one for each battalion. At the Epiphany parade in 1722, the tsar was preceded by a platoon of oboists. [Findeizen cites the Ammon translation of *Dnevnik kamer-iunkera F. V. Berkhgol'tsa;* the reference to the six detachments of oboists appears in Bergholz, *Dnevnik* (2000): 278; and for the Epiphany parade, see 286. Sander, "Social Dancing in Russia," 38–43, gives a publication history of Bergholz's diary.]

413A. [*Editors' note:* Better examples might be Venetian opera orchestras from the last half of the seventeenth century.]

414. Their texts were published at the time (in 1703) as a separate pamphlet, "Torzhestvo mira preslavnago" [Celebration of the glorious peace]. They were reprinted by Pekarskii in his *Opisanie slaviano-russkikh knig i tipografii, 1698–1725* [Catalog of Slavonic-Russian books and presses, 1698–1725] (St. Petersburg: V Tip. tovarshchestva "Obshchestvennaia pol'za," 1862), nos. 64–65. Music for the *kanty* is preserved in a manuscript in the Public Library ([RNB] Buslaev collection, Q.XIV.141). On this manuscript and for a more detailed description of Peter's festive ceremonies, see my study "Petrovskie kanty" [Petrine *kanty*], *Izvestiia Akad. nauk SSSR* [Proceedings of the Academy of Sciences of the USSR], 6th series, 7–8 (1927): 667–90.

415. A transcription of these *kanty* was kindly presented to me by A. V. Preobrazhenskii, to whom I am grateful for this communication. The manuscript with these *kanty* is in the library of the former

Synodal School in Moscow (presently in the Historical Museum in Moscow [GIM]). A manuscript copy made in 1775 has the following heading: "Verses to the Glory and Honor of the Great Lord and Tsar and Great Prince Peter Alekseevich, autocrator of all the Russias, etc., etc., etc., victorious over Charles, King of Sweden and his army as happened at Poltava in the year of our Lord 1709." In the margins of the manuscript there is also the note "and they were sung on the tsar's arrival from Poltava to Moscow at the triumphal gates by the singers." In this manuscript, the *kanty* are copied out as monophonic, using the Kievan [staff] notation in the *tsefaut* clef and comprising a total of ten separate compositions. [On names of clefs in eighteenth-century practice, see Jensen, "Nikolai Diletskii's 'Grammatika,'" chap. 4; and on the Poltava celebrations, see Protopopov's extensive study, *Muzyka na Poltavskuiu pobedu.* Reproductions of the engravings depicting the triumphal arches and the processions are in N. V. Kaliazina and G. N. Komelova, *Russkoe iskusstvo Petrovskoi epokhi* [Russian art of the Petrine era] (Leningrad: "Khudozhnik RSFSR," 1990), plates 148, 162; see also reproductions (including scores for Poltava compositions) in *IRM* 2, foll. 64.]

416. V. M. Metallov, "Sinodal'nye byvshie patriarshie pevchie" [The Synodal, formerly patriarchal, singers], separate offprint from *RMG* 1898, 13. The concerto was written for one discant, two altos, eight tenors, and two basses.

417. [RNB] Q.XIV.141, fols. 154v–66. It is printed for the first time in the music appendix to this volume and was performed (almost in its entirety) twice by the choir of the State Academic Chorus in January 1924 as an example for my lecture for the Society of Friends of Old Literature and in the Archaeological Institute in Leningrad for a lecture on *kanty* of the Petrine period. The *kanty* are reproduced here as they appear in the original, preserving perhaps some technical mistakes.

417A. [*Editors' note:* Keldysh, in his survey of Petrine music, discusses this piece in *IRM* 2:40 n. 7.]

418. The text appears in Pekarskii, *Opisanie slaviano-russkikh knig i tipografii,* no. 528.

419. The music for the *kant* celebrating the conquest of Derbent is printed in my study, "Petrovskie kanty."

419A. [*Editors' note:* D. A. Rovinskii, *Podrobnyi slovar' russkikh gravirovannykh portretov* [A detailed dictionary of Russian engraved portraits] (St. Petersburg, 1888), 3:1687. There are several editions of the work; Findeizen apparently refers to the four-volume edition issued by the Academy of Sciences, 1886–89. The first edition was from 1872. Aleksei Fedorovich Zubov (b. 1682, d. after 1750) was a famous Russian engraver who worked in both Moscow and St. Petersburg. He specialized in architectural landscapes, and among his many works is a well-known panorama of St. Petersburg from ca. 1716, which documents the city in its early stages of development. See *GSE* 9:695; and Kaliazina and Komelova, *Russkoe iskusstvo Petrovskoi epokhy,* plates 163 (the wedding), 168 (the panorama).]

419B. [*Editors' note:* "Opisanie Sanktpeterburga i Kronshlota v 1710-m i 1711-m gg." [A description of St. Petersburg and Kronshlot in 1710 and 1711] is published in *Russkaia starina* (October 1882): 32–60; (November 1882): 293–320; it includes many references to music, particularly in association with Anna Ioannovna's betrothal and wedding.]

420. A Russian translation of this valuable historical material was made by I. F. Ammon, and in 1902 Bartenev published the third edition in four parts [*Dnevnik kamer-iunkera F. V. Berkhgol'tsa, 1721–1725;* see n. 413 above].

421. Soon after their arrival in Russia the Holsteiners heard the *bandura* players, and Bergholz remembered a few "jovial" folk songs, for example, "Stopochki po stoliku" [The shot glasses on the table] and "Po boru khodila" [As I was walking through the woods; or, As she was walking through the woods], and consequently he was viewed as a connoisseur of Russian folk songs. In his *Diary* he records that, on one occasion, the Holsteiners "after supper started singing joyfully both of our Russian songs 'Stopotski postolisku' and 'Pobora godilla' [titles written in Latin letters] as many pranced about, and, standing on the table, emptied more than one glass!" (1:179). [Many thanks

to Elizabeth Sander and Elena Dubinets for their advice on these titles. The passage appears in Bergholz, *Dnevnik* (2000), 267; see also a reference to peasant music (*krest'ianskaia muzyka*) on 446, from September 1722.]

422. According to Bergholz, the assemblies were held during the winter at various homes of the nobility; the emperor (if he was present) or the general police-master, and, in Moscow, the commander [General Pavel Iaguzhinskii] announced to the assembled guests where to come the next time. Admission to the assemblies was free for everyone. The host was not obliged to meet or escort the guests outside the room, even if the guest was the emperor himself. In the ballroom there was a table prepared with pipes, tobacco, and wooden sticks (for lighting the pipes), as well as tables for playing chess and checkers; card playing was not allowed. Dancing was started by the host, either a minuet, anglaise, or Polish dance, but a rule applied to the minuet that it could only be started by a gentleman and a lady who, having danced the minuet, were then free to choose anyone they wanted as a partner. Everyone was free to do whatever he or she wanted: dance, smoke, play games, converse, or look around at the others. The guests were also free to ask for wine, beer, vodka, tea, or coffee, and the host was not obliged to insist that guests eat or drink but merely had to state what refreshments were available. Assemblies began at about 5:00 PM and ended no later than 10:00 PM, when everyone returned to their homes. "What I dislike at these assemblies," Bergholz wrote, "is, first of all, that they smoke and play checkers in the ballroom where the ladies are and where they dance, which creates a stench and noise. And, second, that the ladies sit apart from the men, so that not only is conversation with them impossible, but one can hardly manage to speak to them; when they do not dance, they sit as if they were mute and simply stare at one another" (2:71 [Bergholz, *Dnevnik* (2000), 338–39]). [On the assemblies, see Sander, "Social Dancing in Russia," esp. chap. 3; for the text of the decree on assemblies, see 73 n. 3; and for the complete text of Bergholz's comments on the assemblies, see 84–85. Balatri's observations, quoted in Schlafly, "A Muscovite *Boiarynia* Faces Peter the Great's Reforms," 261, give a sense of the difficulties some of the more traditional women had in adjusting to these new social requirements.]

422A. [*Editors' note:* The wedding Bergholz describes here is from 1 November 1721 (Bergholz, *Dnevnik* (2000), 233–37), and the gathering at Golovkin's house is from 25 July 1721 (*Dnevnik* (2000), 176–78. In several passages Bergholz mentions dancing into the morning hours; on p. 450 he describes dancing until 5:00 AM, and see also pp. 465–66, where he mentions the difficulties for the musicians. Sander, "Social Dancing in Russia," devotes chapter 4 to wedding celebrations.]

423. Kazanskii, *Selo Novospasskoe*, states that during Peter's reign the Golovin family was distinguished by its musicality and European education. Sergei Vasil'evich (1698–1715), son of the *blizhnii stol'nik* [lower rank of nobleman] V. P. Golovin (d. 1733), received a splendid education in his parents' home, had a beautiful voice, and knew music well; Countesses Maria Ivanovna (who married Count V. A. Repnin), Maria Alekseevna (wife of Count Prozorovskii), and Natal'ia Nikolaevna (d. 1763) were only a few of many Russian ladies at Peter's court who were musicians and singers. They were educated in Sweden, sang excellently, and played the harp and the piano (137–38). [See Karpiak, "Culture of the Keyboard," 7–8, on the compositions of another aristocratic Russian woman of the period, Ekaterina Siniavina Vorontsova.]

424. Upon the Duke of Holstein's arrival in St. Petersburg, he was met by the "magical sounds of trumpets" at the entrance to the Summer Palace, which was the summer residence of the Imperial family (1:42 [Bergholz, *Dnevnik* (2000), 156, from July 1721]); he was also met by fanfares when he visited the various nobles. In the duke's own guard there were eight oboists and two horn players. The translators of Bergholz's text, and probably his own contemporaries, translated the German term *Tafelmusik* quite literally into Russian [as *stolovaia muzyka*]. Thereupon that term, *stolovaia* [*muzyka*], was preserved for a repertory of similar works all the way to the beginning of the nineteenth century.

425. Jean Baptiste Morin (1677–1745), "Ordinaire de la musique de S. A. R. Monseigneur le Duc d'Orleans," was also the author of divertimenti about the hunt and of *Tafelmusik*. It is quite possible that Peter became acquainted either with these works or with their author during his visit to Paris in 1717, where he was met by the regent, the Duke of Orleans, who was Morin's employer. Morin's fanfares might easily have reached St. Petersburg in other ways as well, since the French court dictated the fashions and tastes of the period. In any case, musical example N12.1 from the first part of a concert fanfare by Morin provides a notion of the *Tafelmusik* of the period in Moscow and St. Petersburg. [The date Findeizen gives for Morin's death is probably a misprint; *NG2* gives his year of death as 1754. *Les dons des enfans de Latone* is by J. S. de Rieux.]

425A. [*Editors' note:* Leutenberger is described in Bergholz, *Dnevnik* (2000), 120; for the horn players at Ekaterinhof, see 174, and for the flotilla on the Neva, see 173.]

425B. [*Editors' note:* The position of assessor was part of Peter's reorganization of the Russian governmental structure. He set up colleges, or collegiate boards, headed by a president and vice president; they also included councilors (*sovetchiki*) and assessors (*assessory*). See Hughes, *Russia in the Age of Peter the Great,* 107–108. On this serenade, see Sander, "Social Dancing in Russia," 61–63; and Bergholz, *Dnevnik* (2000), 258–59.]

426. Of these four musicians, three were footmen of the duke and the bagpipe player was a servant of Privy Councilor Gespen. This was fully in keeping with the spirit of the times, when no distinction was made between musicians and livery servants, and any among the latter who could

EXAMPLE N12.1. Morin, fanfare

play an instrument of any kind could obtain a more profitable position. Bergholz reported that at the puppet court [in the sense of mini-court] of the Duke of Holstein in St. Petersburg, "the supervision of the kitchen, the cellar, the musicians, and the livery servants in general was entrusted to Marshal von Platen" (4:6). For the duke's band and for musicians belonging to other nobles, there was a special livery of green costumes edged with silver. In the description of a 1722 masked ball in Moscow, which took place in honor of the conclusion of the Nystadt Peace Treaty, Bergholz notes that in one group of masked people, representing Estenwald villagers, there were four musicians, one of whom played on a wonderful Polish bagpipe which was made in the shape of a goat with big golden horns; the instrument made quite an impression on the simple folk (see the illustration of this type of Polish bagpipe in fig. 47 [and fig. 70] above). Two other musicians played violins, and still another played the oboe. Thus all four represented village musicians; the two horn players were dressed as hunters and played in alternation with the other musicians (2:44 [and Bergholz, *Dnevnik* (2000), 314]).

426A. [*Editors' note:* According to Sander, quoting Bergholz in "Social Dancing in Russia," 59 and n. 82, the actual number was even higher: sixty musicians. The reference to the Duke of Holstein's acquisition of new musical scores is in Bergholz, *Dnevnik* (2000), 453–54.]

427. An inventory of Prince V. V. Golitsyn's property confiscated in 1690 shows, among the objects in his household, a "large bass *domra* inside a wooden box, value one ruble" (I. E. Zabelin, *Domashnii byt russkikh tsarei XVI i XVII stoletiiakh* [Domestic lives of the Russian tsars, 16th and 17th centuries], vol. 1 of *Domashnii byt russkogo naroda v XVI i XVII st.* [Domestic lives of the Russian people in the 16th and 17th centuries] (Moscow: Tip. Gracheva, 1872), 186, appendix 99). Thus Golitsyn must have had his own *domra* players. [The most recent reprint of Zabelin's work is from Moscow: Iazyki russkoi kul'tury, 2000, from various editions.]

428. A. Pypin, "Petr Velikii v narodnom predanii" [Peter the Great in folk legends], *Vestnik Evropy* (August 1897): 640–90; V. N. Shchepkin, "Dva litsevykh sbornika Istoricheskogo muzeia" [Two illustrated manuscripts in the Historical Museum], *Arkheologicheskie izvestiia i zametki* [Archaeological reports and notes] (1897). Rovinskii's *Russkie narodnye kartinki* also contains interesting materials about this subject. [On the popular woodcut "The Mice Bury the Cat," see n. 228E above.]

429. This collection preserves only two individual parts, the discant and the bass. For the performance of this *kant* by the Academic Chapel Choir as a musical example for my lecture on Petrine *kanty,* it was necessary to reconstruct the lost middle voice. It is in this [reconstructed] version that the "Kant na konchinu Petra" [*Kant* on the death of Peter] is printed here in the music appendix to this volume. [The collection is identified in *Ocherki* 1:361 as a seventeenth-century collection, surely a misprint.]

429A. [*Editors' note:* Many thanks to Alexander Levitsky for this lively translation, and also to Elizabeth Sander for her advice on this passage.]

430. *Sochineniia F. Prokopovicha* [Works of Feofan Prokopovich] (St. Petersburg, 1761), pt. 2: 103–11. [On Prokopovich (1681–1733), see the surveys in Karlinsky, *Russian Drama from Its Beginnings,* 24–29; and James Cracraft in *The Eighteenth Century in Russia,* ed. John G. Garrard (Oxford: Clarendon, 1973): 75–105.]

431. V. Svetlov, "Pridvornyi balet v Rossii" [Court ballet in Russia], *Ezhegodnik Imp. teatrov* [Annual of the Imperial theaters] for the season 1901–1902, supplement, p. 10.

432. The reliability of the *Spb. vedomosti* is beyond any doubt. However, the presence of a French company in St. Petersburg during the reign of Peter II is not mentioned either by Stählin or by the most recent investigators of the Russian theater. [On the origins of these works, see *IRM* 2:133, citing Robert-Aloys Mooser, *L'opéra-comique français en Russie au XVIIIe siècle* (Geneva: R. Kister, 1954), 13–14. It is interesting to note that Findeizen mentions the production of *Orfei v Adu* at the same time as the appearance in Russia of the two French dancers; there are two contemporary French works on the subject of Orfeo: M. A. Charpentier's *La descente d'Orphée aux enfers,* and, in 1699, A. Campra's "Orfeo nell'inferni" (the third act of his *Le carnaval de Venise*); see *NG2,* and Stieger's *Opernlexikon.*]

433. Here is the text of this advertisement: "Interested lovers of choral and chamber music are hereby notified that the following items are offered for sale in Danzig: (1) small organs with choral and chamber voices [ranks of pipes] with seven playing ranks and a tremulant, for 200 rubles; (2) extraordinary clavecin from F/F♯ (two and a half octaves below middle C) to C (two octaves above

middle C) with four ranks, of which one is about four *tony* [tones; this may refer to the lengths of the courses or strings], two about eight, the fourth about sixteen tones, for 100 rubles; (3) extraordinary clavichord with three courses [of strings] of wonderful voice and extraordinary workmanship for 30 rubles—all three of such harmonious voice and clean workmanship that there can be no better quality. Those interested in these extraordinary instruments should respond in writing within six to eight weeks to their owner, Theophilus Andreas Volkmar, the organist of the main Church of St. Catherine in the old city in Danzig. The indicated price shall not be reduced and the instruments can only be acquired by payment in Danzig." The advertisement mentions the mechanical chamber organs which, among their registers, had a tremolo [tremulant stop]; it also mentions a clavecin with four registers and a small clavichord with three strings for each key; the latter type, preceding the fortepiano, was preserved and was in use in Russia until the end of the eighteenth century. [Thanks to Robert Karpiak and Elizabeth Sander for their advice on this passage.]

433A. [*Editors' note:* Elizabeth Sander notes that Bergholz's diary also contains references to organs and harpsichords.]

434. "Pis'ma o Rossii v Ispaniiu Duka de Liriia, byvshego pervym Ispanskim poslannikom v Rossii pri imperatore Petre II i v nachale tsarstvovaniia Anny Ioannovny" [Letters about Russia to Spain by Duke de Liria, the first Spanish emissary in Russia during the reign of Emperor Peter II and the beginning of the reign of Anna Ioannovna], *Osmnadtsatyi vek* [Eighteenth century] (Moscow: P. Bartenev, 1869), 2:5–198, 3:27–132. A curious detail recorded by Duke de Liria is the list of expenses incurred in connection with a festival he prepared for the Russian court on 27 June 1728, at which there was also music. Whereas the carpenters were paid 177 rubles, the cooks and footmen 223 rubles, and the person in charge of fireworks 200 rubles, the musicians, who had quite a lot of work to do on such an occasion, received a total of 100 rubles. [On this mission, see also L. F. Il'ichev and E. S. Sanchez, eds., *Rossiia i Ispaniia: Dokumenty i materialy, 1667–1917* [Russia and Spain: Documents and materials, 1667–1917], 2 vols. (Moscow: Mezhdunarodnye otnosheniia, 1991). Duke de Liria, according to a paper read in 1989 at a regional conference of Slavic studies in Charlottesville, Virginia, by James Gerard Hart, was the first son of James Fitzjames, First Duke of Berwick (1670–1734). His son, James Fitzjames Jr. (1696–1738), was also Duke of Berwick, but the title Duca de Liria was bestowed on the twelve-year-old boy in 1708, when the King of Spain arranged to wed the boy to Donna Catherina de Veraguas. There have been many descendants with that title, which belongs to a distinguished Spanish family. He was in Russia from 1727 to 1730.]

434A. [*Editors' note:* On early keyboard music in Russia, see also Robert Karpiak, "Culture of the Keyboard in 18th-century Russia," which includes references to available recordings; and idem, "Researching Early Keyboards in Russia," *Continuo* 2 (February 1996): 2–6. Many thanks to Robert Karpiak for his advice on this material.]

Volume 1 Bibliography

[*Editors' note:* Not included here are most general reference works or works that appear in the list of abbreviations. It was not possible to find complete page numbers for some articles, and not all the editions Findeizen consulted are listed in available catalogs and databases. In these cases we list the most complete information possible, realizing that other editions and sources may be lurking in libraries that are not cataloged in the available sources. A few other works were impossible to verify; these have been omitted from this bibliography but are included in Findeizen's notes.]

Abramychev, N. *Sbornik russkikh narodnykh pesen* [Collection of Russian folk songs]. St. Petersburg: M. Vasil'ev, 1879.

Adrianova-Peretts, V. P., et al., eds. *Povest' vremennykh let* [The tale of bygone years]. 2 vols. Moscow: Akademiia nauk SSSR, 1950.

Adrianova-Peretts, V. P., and I. M. Kudriavtsev, eds. *Artakserksovo deistvo: Pervaia p'esa russkogo teatra XVII v.* [*The Play of Artaxerxes:* The First play of the Russian theater in the 17th century]. Moscow: Akademiia nauk SSSR, 1957.

Ainalov, D. V. *Istoriia drevnerusskogo iskusstva* [History of old Russian art]. Petrograd: Tipo-Litografiia I. Iudelevicha, 1915.

Akademiia nauk SSSR. *Slovar' sovremennogo russkogo literaturnogo iazyka* [A dictionary of the modern Russian literary language]. 17 vols. Moscow: Akademiia nauk SSSR, 1950–65.

Akty istoricheskie. Dopolneniia [Historical acts. Addenda]. 5 vols. with an additional 12 vols. St. Petersburg: Arkheograficheskaia komissiia, 1841–72.

Akty kholmogorskoi i ustiuzhskoi eparkhii [Acts of the Kholmogorsk and Ustiug bishoprics]. *RIB* 14. St. Petersburg: Tip. A. Katanskogo, 1894.

Akty, sobrannye v bibliotekakh i arkhivakh Rossiiskoi Imperii Arkheograficheskoi ekspeditsiei Imp. Akad. nauk [Documents collected in libraries and archives by the Russian Imperial Archaeographic Expedition of the Imperial Academy of Sciences]. 4 vols. St. Petersburg: V Tip. II-go otdeleniia Sobstvennoi E. I. V. kantseliarii, 1836.

Alekseeva, G. V. *Drevnerusskoe pevcheskoe iskusstvo* [The old Russian art of chanting]. Vladivostok: Izd-vo Dal'nevostochnogo universiteta, 1983.

Alekseeva, M. A. "Graviura na dereve 'Myshi kota na pogost volokut'—pamiatnik russkogo narodnogo tvorchestva kontsa XVII–nachala XVIII v." [The woodcut "The Mice Bury the Cat": A Monument of Russian folk creativity of the end of the 17th–beginning of the 18th century]. *XVIII vek* [18th century] 14 (1983): 45–79.

Alexander, Alex E. *Bylina and Fairy Tale, the Origins of Russian Heroic Poetry.* The Hague: Mouton, 1973.

Alm, Irene. *Catalog of Venetian Librettos at the University of California, Los Angeles.* University of California Publications: Catalogs and Bibliographies 9. Berkeley: University of California Press, 1993.

Amfilokhii, Archimandrite. "O Slavianskoi Psaltiri XIII–XIV veka biblioteki A. I. Khludova" [On the Slavic psalter of the thirteenth–fourteenth centuries in A. I. Khludov's library]. *Drevnosti. Trudy Moskovskogo arkheologicheskogo obshchestva* [Antiquities. Works of the Moscow Archaeological Society] 3, (1873), pt. 1: 1–28.

Andriiashev, A. M. "Materialy po istoricheskoi geografii Novgorodskoi zemli: Shelonskaia piatina po pistsovym knigam 1496–1576 gg." [Documents on the historical geography of Novgorodian lands: The Shelon county cadastres for 1496–1576]. *ChOIDR* 3 (1914) [entire volume].

Arant, Patricia M. *Compositional Techniques of the Russian Oral Epic, the* Bylina. New York: Garland, 1990.

Artamonov, G. "O russkom bezlineinom i v chastnosti khomovom penii" [On Russian staffless and partially *khomovoe* singing]. *Trudy Kievskoi dukhovnoi akademii* [Proceedings of the Kiev Divinity School] (January 1876): 163–99.

Ashik, Anton. *Kerchenskie drevnosti. O Pantikapeiskoi katakombe, ukrashennoi freskami* [Antiquities of Kerch. The Panticapaeum catacomb with frescoes]. Odessa: Tip. A. Brauna, 1845.

———. *Vosporskoe tsarstvo s ego paleograficheskimi i nadgrobnymi pamiatnikami* [The Bosphorus Empire with its paleographic and funerary monuments]. Odessa: Neiman, 1848–49.

Aumayr, Manfred. *Historische Untersuchungen an Bezeichnungen von Musikinstrumenten in der russischen Sprache.* Dissertationen der Universität Wien 169. Wien: VWGÖ, 1985.

Avenarius, V. P. *Kniga bylin* [A book of *byliny*]. 3rd ed. St. Petersburg: Tip. S. Dobrodeeva, 1885.

"Azbuchnyi ukazatel' imen russkikh deiatelei dlia russkogo biograficheskogo slovaria" [Alphabetic index of names of Russian public figures for a Russian biographical dictionary]. *Sbornik Imperatorskogo Russkogo istoricheskogo obshchestva* [Anthology of the Imperial Russian Historical Society] 60, 62 (1887–88), pts. 1, 2. Reprint, Nendeln, Liechtenstein: Kraus Reprint, 1976.

Babkin, B. P. "Balalaika. Ocherki po istorii ee razvitiia i usovershenstvovaniia" [The balalaika: Studies of its development and improvement]. *Russkaia beseda* [Russian conversation] (March 1896). Reprint, *RMG* 1896, in abridged form.

Bailey, James, and Tatyana Ivanova, eds. *An Anthology of Russian Folk Epics.* Armonk, N.Y.: M. E. Sharpe, 1998.

Barbour, Philip L. *Dimitry Called the Pretender, Tsar and Great Prince of All Russia, 1605–1606.* Boston: Houghton Mifflin; Cambridge, Mass.: Riverside, 1966.

Barkhudarov, S. G., main ed. *Slovar' russkogo iazyka XI–XVII vv.* [A dictionary of the Russian language, 11th–17th centuries]. Vols. 1–. Moscow: Nauka, 1975–.

Baron, Samuel H. "The Origins of Seventeenth Century Moscow's Nemeckaja Sloboda." *California Slavic Studies* 5 (1970): 1–17. Reprint, Samuel H. Baron, *Muscovite Russia: Collected Essays.* London: Variorum Reprints, 1980.

———, ed. *The Travels of Olearius in Seventeenth-century Russia.* Stanford: Stanford University Press, 1967.

Barsov, E. V. *Slovo o polku Igoreve* [The lay of the Host of Igor]. Moscow, 1887–89. Reprint, Slavistic Printings and Reprintings 95, nos. 1–3. The Hague: Mouton, 1969.

Barthélemy, J.-J. *Voyage du jeune Anacharsis en Grèce, vers le milieu du quatrième siècle avant l'ère vulgaire.* Edited by Jean Denis Barbie du Bocage. 5th ed. Paris: Garnery Libraire, 1817.

Batalin, N. I. "Drevne-russkie azbukovniki" [Old Russian *azbukovniki*]. *Filologicheskie zapiski* [Philological notes] 3 (1873): 1–34; 4–5 (1873): 35–68.

Becker, G., and R. Heim. *Tournefort.* Paris: Muséum national d'histoire naturelle, 1957.

Beliaev, I. D. "O skomorokhakh" [About the *skomorokhi*]. *Vremennik Imp. Obshchestva istorii i drevnostei rossiiskikh* [Annals of the Imperial Society for Russian History and Antiquities] 20 (1854): 69–92.

Beliaev, V. M. *Sbornik Kirshi Danilova: Opyt restavratsii pesen* [The collection of Kirsha Danilov: An attempt at reconstructing the songs]. Moscow: Sovetskii kompozitor, 1969.

Belkin, A. A. *Russkie skomorokhi* [Russian *skomorokhi*]. Moscow: Nauka, 1975.

Belonenko, A. S. "Pokazaniia arkhiereiskikh pevchikh XVII veka" [The testimonies of the bishop's singers in the 17th century]. *TODRL* 36 (1981): 320–28. The document is also published in *Drevnosti. Trudy Moskovskogo arkheologicheskogo obshchestva* [Antiquities. Works of the Moscow Archaeological Society] 1 (1865).

Belza, Igor'. "Rosyjsko-polskie stosunki muzyczne XVII i XVIII wieku" [Russian-Polish musical relations in the 17th and 18th centuries]. In *The Book of the First International Musicological Congress Devoted to the Works of Frederick Chopin,* ed. Z. Lissa, 507–509. Warsaw: Polish Scientific Publishers, 1963.

Bergholz, F. W. von. *Dnevnik kamer-iunkera F. V. Berkhgol'tsa* [Diary of Kammerjunker F. W. von Bergholz]. Translated by I. F. Ammon. Moscow: Universitetskaia tip., 1902. The first part of Ammon's translation is reprinted in *Dnevnik kamer-iunkera Fridrikha-Vil'gel'ma Berkhgol'tsa* [The diary of Kammerjunker F. W. von Bergholz]. *Neistovyi reformator* [The frenzied reformer], ed. A. Liberman and V. Naumov, 109–502. In the series Istoriia Rossii i doma Romanovykh v memuarakh sovremennikov XVII–XX vv. [A history of Russia and the house of the Romanovs in memoirs by contemporaries, 17th–20th centuries]. Moscow: Fond Sergeia Dubova, 2000. The second part of Ammon's translation is reprinted in *Dnevnik kamer-iunkera F. V. Berkhgol'tsa* [Diary of Kammerjunker F. W. von Bergholz]. *Iunost' der-zhavy* [The youth of a power], ed. V. Naumov, 9–324. In the series Istorii Rossii i doma Romanovykh v memuarakh sovremennikov XVII–XX vv. [The History of Russia and the house of the Romanovs in memoirs by contemporaries, 17th–20th centuries]. Moscow: Fond Sergeia Dubova, 2000.

Berkov, P. N. "Iz istorii russkoi teatral'noi terminologii XVII–XVIII vekov" [From the history of Russian theatrical terminology in the 17–18th centuries], *TODRL* 11 (1955): 280–99.

Bernandt, G. B., and I. M. Iampol'skii. *Kto pisal o muzyke. Bio-bibliograficheskii slovar' muzykal'nykh kritikov i lits, pisavshikh o muzyke v dorevoliutsionnoi Rossii i SSSR* [Who wrote about music. A bio-bibliographical dictionary of music critics and figures who wrote about music in pre-revolutionary Russia and in the USSR]. 4 vols. Moscow: Sovetskii kompozitor, 1971–89.

Berry, Lloyd E. ed. *The English Works of Giles Fletcher, the Elder.* Madison: University of Wisconsin Press, 1964.

Berry, Lloyd E., and Robert O. Crummey, eds. *Rude and Barbarous Kingdom: Russia in the Accounts of Sixteenth-Century English Voyagers.* Madison: University of Wisconsin Press, 1968.

Berynda, Pamva. *Leksykon slovenoros'kyi Pamvy Beryndy* [Pamva Berynda's Slavonic-Russian lexicon]. Edited by V. V. Nimchuk. Kiev: AN URSR, 1961.

Bethe, Erich, ed. *Pollucis Onomasticon.* 3 vols. Lexicographi graeci 9. Stuttgart: Teubner, 1967.

Bezsonov, I. "K voprosu o sobiranii i izdanii pamiatnikov narodnogo pesnotvorchestva" [On the question of the collecting and publishing of documents of folk singing]. *Mosk. vedomosti* 302 (1896).

Bezsonov, P. A. *Kaleki perekhozhie* [Wandering pilgrims]. Moscow: A. Semen, 1861–64. Reprint of vol. 1, with a new introduction by Sergei Hackel, Farnborough: Gregg International, 1970.

———, ed. *Pesni, sobrannye P. V. Kireevskim* [Songs collected by P. V. Kireevskii]. Moscow: Obshchestvo liubitelei rossiiskoi slovesnosti, 1861.

———. "Sud'ba notnykh pevcheskikh knig" [The fate of notated song books]. *Pravoslavnoe obozrenie* [Orthodox review] 14 (1864).

Bezuglova, I. F. "Opekalovskii rospev" [Opekalovskii chant]. *PKNO for 1978* (1979): 196–204.

Bich-Lubenskii, K. M. "Banduristy i lirniki na Khar'kovskom XII arkheolog. s"ezde" [*Bandura* and *lira* players at the 12th Archaeological Congress in Kharkov]. *RMG* 38 (1902).

———. "Malo-rossiiskaia lira i 'rylia'" [The Little Russian *lira* and "*rylia*"]. *RMG* 41 (1900).

Bitsyn, N. "Slovo o polku Igoreve" [The lay of the Host of Igor]. *Russkii vestnik* [Russian herald] 109 (February 1874).

Bobrova, E. I., comp. *Biblioteka Petra I: Ukazatel'-spravochnik* [The library of Peter I: A reference guide]. Leningrad: BAN SSSR, 1978.

Bogoiavlenskii, S. K. "Moskovskii teatr pri Tsariakh Aleksee i Petre" [The Moscow theater under Tsars Aleksei and Peter]. *ChOIDR* 2 (1914): iii–xxi, 1–192.

Bogomolova, M. V. "Modelirovanie drevnerusskikh pesnopenii putevogo rospeva po printsipu podobiia (na primere stikhir rukopisi inoka Khristofora 1602 goda" [The structuring of early
Russian *putevoi raspev* on the principles of *podoben* (on the example of the *stikhiri* in the
1602 manuscript of monk Khristofor]. *Problemy muzykoznaniia* [Problems in musicology] 4
(1990): 47–61.

——. "Putevoi raspev i ego mesto v drevnerusskom pevcheskom iskusstve" [*Putevoi raspev* and
its place in the art of early Russian singing]. *Muzykal'naia kul'tura srednevekov'ia* [Musical
culture of the Middle Ages] 2 (1992): 122–24.

Borisov, V. A. *Opisanie goroda Shui i ego okrestnostei* [A description of the town of Shuia and its envi-
rons]. Moscow: V Tip. Ved. mosk. gorod. politsii, 1851.

Braudo, A., and I. Rostsius, eds. *Moskovskaia tragediia, ili rasskaz o zhizni i smerti Dimitriia* [A Moscow
tragedy, or a narrative of the life and death of Dmitrii]. St. Petersburg: V. S. Balashev, 1901.
Originally published as *Tragoedia Moscovitica: sive de vita et morte Demetrii*. Cologne: Gerard
Greuenbruch, 1608.

Brazhnikov, M. V. *Drevnerusskaia teoriia muzyki* [Old Russian music theory]. Leningrad: Muzyka,
1972.

——, ed. *Fedor Krest'ianin: Stikhiry / Fyodor Krestyanin: Canticles*. PRMI 3. Moscow: Muzyka,
1974.

——. *Litsa i fity znamennogo raspeva* [The *litsa* and *fity* of znamennyi singing]. Edited by N. S.
Seregina and A. N. Kriukov. Leningrad: Muzyka, 1984.

Brikner, A. "Lavrentii Ringuber." *Zhurnal Ministerstva narodnogo prosveshcheniia* [Journal of the
Ministry of Public Enlightenment] (February 1884): 396–421.

Brown, William Edward. *A History of 18th-century Russian Literature*. Ann Arbor: Ardis, 1980.

Brumfield, William Craft. *A History of Russian Architecture*. Cambridge: Cambridge University Press,
1993. First paperback edition, Cambridge: Cambridge University Press, 1997.

Bugge, Arne, ed. *Contacarium Palaeoslavicum Mosquense*. Monumenta Musicae Byzantinae. Main
series. Vol. 6. Copenhagen: Munksgaard, 1960.

Buhle, Edward. *Die Blasininstrumente*. Vol. 1 of *Die musikalischen Instrumente in den Miniaturen des
frühen Mittelalters: Ein Beitrag zur Geschichte der Musikinstrumente*. Leipzig: Breitkopf &
Härtel, 1903.

Bulgakov, Very Rev. Makarii. *Istoriia russkoi tserkvi* [History of the Russian Church]. 12 vols. St.
Petersburg: Tip. R. Golike, 1883–1903.

——. "Sochineniia prepodobnogo Feodosiia Pecherskogo" [The works of the Reverend Fedosi
Pecherskii]. *Uchenye zapiski II-go otdeleniia Imp. Akademii nauk* [Scholarly notes of the
Second Section of the Imperial Academy of Sciences] 2, fasc. 2 (1856): 193–224.

Burilina, E. L. "Chin 'za prilivok o zdravii gosudaria' (istoriia formirovaniia i osobennosti bytovaniia)"
[The rite of the "pouring to the health of the tsar" (a history of its development and contextual details)]. In *Drevnerusskaia literatura: istochnikovedenie* [Old Russian literature: Source
studies], ed. D. S. Likhachev, 204–14. Leningrad, Nauka, 1984.

Bushkovitch, Paul. "The Epiphany Ceremony of the Russian Court in the Sixteenth and Seventeenth
Centuries." *Russian Review* 49, no. 1 (1990): 1–17.

Buslaev, F. I. "Dopolneniia i pribavleniia k 2-mu tomu 'Skazanii Sakharova'" [Addenda to the 2nd
volume of "Sakharov's Tales"]. [There is a reprint ed. of *Skazaniia russkogo naroda*, Tula:
Priokskoe Knizhnoe izdatel'stvo, 2000].

——. *Istoricheskaia khristomatiia [khrestomatiia] tserkovno-slavianskogo i drevne-russkogo
iazykov* [Historical reader of the Church-Slavonic and Old Russian languages]. Moscow:
Universitetskaia tip., 1861.

——. *Istoricheskie ocherki russkoi narodnoi slovesnosti i iskusstva* [Historical studies of Russian folk literature and art]. 2 vols. St. Petersburg: V Tip. tovarshchestva "Obshchestvennaia pol'za," 1861.

Bussow, Conrad. *The Disturbed State of the Russian Realm.* Translated and edited by G. Edward Orchard. Montreal: McGill-Queen's University Press, 1994.

[————.] *Moskovskaia khronika, 1584–1613* [Moscow chronicle, 1584–1613]. Edited by I. I. Smirnov. Moscow: AN SSSR, 1961.

Butskaia, S. B. "Stefan Ivanovich Beliaev—gosudarev pevchii d'iak" [Stefan Ivanovich Beliaev, sovereign singer]. *PKNO for 1992* (1993): 151–56.

Bylinin, V. K., and A. L. Pososhchenko. "Tsar' Aleksei Mikhailovich kak master raspeva" [Tsar Aleksei Mikhailovich as a master of *raspev*]. *PKNO for 1987* (1988): 131–37.

Canard, Marius. *La relation du voyage d'Ibn Fadlân chez les bulgares de la Volga.* Annales de l'institut d'études orientales 16. Algiers: n.p., 1958.

Carpenter, Ellon DeGrief. "The Theory of Music in Russia and the Soviet Union, ca. 1650–1950." Ph.D. diss., University of Pennsylvania, 1988.

Chadwick, N. Kershaw. *Russian Heroic Poetry.* New York: Russell & Russell, 1964.

Chechulin, N. D. *Goroda Moskovskogo gosudarstva v XVI v.* [Towns of the Muscovite state in the 16th century]. St. Petersburg: Tip. I. N. Shorokhodova, 1889. Reprint, Slavistic Printings and Reprintings 198. The Hague: Mouton, 1969.

Chertkov, A. *Opisanie voiny velikogo kniazia Sviatoslava Igorevicha protiv bolgar i grekov v 967–97 godakh* [A description of the war between the Great Prince Sviatoslav Igorevich and the Bulgars and Greeks in 967–97]. *Russkii istoricheskii sbornik* 6, bks. 3–4 (1843).

Chertoritskaia, T. V., comp. and ed. *Krasnorechie drevnei Rusi (XI–XVII vv.)* [The oratory of ancient Rus' (11th–17th centuries)]. Moscow: Sovetskaia Rossiia, 1987.

Chudinova, A. N. *Penie, zvony, ritual: Topografiia tserkovno-muzykal'noi kul'tury Peterburga* [Singing, bell ringing, and ritual: The landscape of the church-musical culture of Petersburg]. St. Petersburg: Ut, 1994.

Cracraft, James. "Feofan Prokopovich." In *The Eighteenth Century in Russia.* Edited by John G. Garrard, 75–105. Oxford: Clarendon, 1973.

————. *The Petrine Revolution in Russian Imagery.* Chicago: University of Chicago Press, 1997.

Croskey, Robert M. *Muscovite Diplomatic Practice in the Reign of Ivan III.* New York: Garland, 1987.

Cross, A. G. "Early British Acquaintance with Russian Popular Song and Music (The Letters and Journals of the Wilmot Sisters)." *Slavonic and East European Review* 66 (1988): 21–34.

Cross, Samuel, and Olgerd Sherbowitz-Wetzor, eds. and trans. *The Russian Primary Chronicle: Laurentian Text.* Cambridge, Mass.: Mediaeval Academy of America, 1973.

Crummey, Robert O. "Court Spectacles in Seventeenth Century Russia: Illusion and Reality." In *Essays in Honor of A. A. Zimin*, ed. Daniel C. Waugh, 130–58. Columbus, Ohio: Slavica, 1985.

Dal', V. I. *Tolkovyi slovar' zhivogo velikorusskogo iazyka* [A defining dictionary of the living Great Russian language]. 2nd exp. ed. 4 vols. St. Petersburg: M. O. Vol'f, 1880–82. Reprint, Moscow: Russkii iazyk, 1981.

Demin, A. S., main ed. *P'esy shkol'nykh teatrov Moskvy* [School dramas in Moscow]. Vol. 3 of the series Ranniaia russkaia dramaturgiia (XVII–pervaia polovina XVIII v.) [Early Russian dramaturgy (17th–first half of the 18th century)], ed. A. N. Robinson et al. Moscow: Nauka, 1974.

Derzhavin, N. S. *Stepennaia kniga kak literaturnyi pamiatnik* [The *Book of Degrees* as a literary document]. St. Petersburg, 1903. [Western catalogs list an edition of Derzhavin's work from Batum: Tip. Kiladze, 1902.]

Derzhavina, O. A., ed. *Russkaia dramaturgiia poslednei chetverti XVII i nachala XVIII v.* [Russian dramaturgy in the last quarter of the 17th century and the beginning of the 18th century]. Vol. 2 of the series Ranniaia russkaia dramaturgiia (XVII–pervaia polovina XVIII v.) [Early

Russian dramaturgy (17th–first half of the 18th century)], ed. A. N. Robinson. Moscow: Nauka, 1972.

Dianova, T. V., et al., eds. and trans. *Skazanie o Mamaevom poboishche* [The tale of Mamai's bloody battle]. 2 vols. Moscow: Kniga, 1980.

Diletskii, Nikolai [Dylets'kyi, Mykola]. *Hramatyka muzykal'na* [Musical grammar]. Edited by O. S. Tsalai-Iakymenko. Kiev: Muzychna Ukraina, 1970.

———. *Idea grammatiki musikiiskoi* [An idea of a musical grammar]. Edited and translated by V. V. Protopopov. PRMI 7. Moscow: Muzyka, 1979.

———. *Khorovi tvory* [Choral works]. Edited by N. O. Herasymova-Persyds'ka. Kiev: Muzychna Ukraina, 1981.

———. *Musikiiskaia Grammatika Nikolaia Diletskogo* [The musical grammar of Nikolai Diletskii]. Edited by S. V. Smolenskii. OLDP Izdaniia 128 ([St. Petersburg]: Tip. M. A. Aleksandrova, 1910.

Dmitrieva, R. P., comp. *Bibliografiia russkogo letopisaniia* [A bibliography of Russian chronicle writing]. Moscow: Akademiia nauk SSSR, 1962.

Dmytryshyn, Basil, ed. *Medieval Russia: A Source Book, 900–1700*. 2nd ed. Hinsdale, Ill.: Dryden, 1973.

Doklady i prigovory, sostoiavshiesia v Pravitel'stvuiushchem Senate v tsarstvovanie Petra Velikogo [Reports and comments made in the ruling Senate during the reign of Peter the Great]. 5 vols. St. Petersburg: Tip. Imp. Akademii nauk, 1887.

Dolskaya, Olga. "Choral Music in the Petrine Era." In *Russia in the Reign of Peter the Great: Old and New Perspectives*, ed. Anthony Cross, pt. 2, 173–85. Cambridge: Study Group on Eighteenth-Century Russia, 1998.

———, ed. *Vasilii Titov i russkoe barokko: Izbrannye khorovye proizvedeniia / Vasily Titov and the Russian Baroque: Selected Choral Works*. In Vladimir Morosan, ed., Pamiatniki russkoi dukhovnoi muzyki / Monuments of Russian Sacred Music, series 13, vol. 1. Madison, Conn.: Musica Russica, 1995.

Dolskaya-Ackerly, Olga. "The Early Kant in Seventeenth-Century Russian Music." Ph.D. diss., University of Kansas, 1983.

———. "Manuscript Collections of Seventeenth-century Russian Songbooks." *Australian Slavonic and East European Studies* 5, no. 1 (1991): 1–14.

———, ed. *Spiritual Songs in Seventeenth-century Russia*. Bausteine zur Slavischen Philologie und Kulturgeschichte Reihe B, Neue Folge Band 4. Cologne: Böhlau, 1996.

———. "Vasilii Titov and the 'Moscow' Baroque." *Journal of the Royal Musical Association* 118, no. 2 (1993): 203–22.

Dostál, Antonín, and Hans Rothe, eds. *Der altrussische Kondakar': Auf der Grundlage des Blagoveščenskij Nižegorodskij kondakar'*. Vol. 2 of Bausteine zur Geschichte der Literatur bei den Slawen 8. Giessen: Wilhelm Schmitz, 1976.

Drevniia Rossiiskiia Stikhotvoreniia, sobrannyia Kirsheiu Danilovym i vtorichno izdannyia, s pribavleniem 35 pesen i skazok, dosele neizvestnykh, i not dlia napeva [Old Russian poems, collected by Kirsha Danilov and published for the second time with an addition of 35 songs and tales hitherto unknown and with music for singing]. 2nd ed. Moscow, 1818.

Drevnosti Gerodotovoi Skifii. Sbornik [The antiquities of the Scythia of Herodotus. A collection]. 2 vols. St. Petersburg: n.p., 1866.

Drevnosti Rossiiskogo gosudarstva [Antiquities of the Russian state]. Drawings by F. Solntsev. Moscow: Tip. A. Semena, 1849–53. Reprint, A. N. Chirva, comp., and E. P. Chernukha, ed. Moscow: AO Kapital i Kul'tura, 1994.

Duichev, Ivan, ed. *Letopistsa na Konstantin Manasi. Fototipno izdanie na Vatikanskiia prepis na sredneb"lgarskiia prevod* [The Chronicle of Konstantin Manasses. A photo-facsimile edition of the Vatican manuscript in old Bulgarian]. Sofia: Izd-va na B"lgarskata Akademiia na naukite, 1963.

Dunning, Chester S. L. *Russia's First Civil War: The Time of Troubles and the Founding of the Romanov Dynasty*. University Park, Pa.: The Pennsylvania State University Press, 2001.

Duruy, Victor. *Histoire des Romains depuis les temps plus reculés jusqu'à l'invasion des barbares*. New and exp. ed. Paris: Hachette, 1879.

Emchenko, E. B., ed. *Stoglav: Issledovanie i tekst* [Stoglav: Analysis and text]. Moscow: Indrik, 2000.

Eremin, I. P. "Literaturnoe nasledie Kirilla Turovskogo" [The literary legacy of Kirill of Turov]. *TODRL* 11 (1955): 342–67; 12 (1956): 340–61; and 13 (1957): 409–26.

————, ed. *Simeon Polotskii: Izbrannye sochineniia* [Simeon Polotskii: Collected works]. Moscow: Akademiia nauk, 1953. Reprint, St. Petersburg: Nauka, 2004.

Estreicher, Karol. *Bibliografia polska*. 34 vols. 1872–1951. Reprint, Warsaw: Wydawnictwa artystyczne i filmowe, 1977.

Evarnitskii [Iavornytskyi], D. I. *Istoriia zaporozhskogo kazachestva* [History of the Zaporozhian Cossacks]. 3 vols. St. Petersburg, 1892. 2nd ed., Moscow, 1900. Reprint, *Istoriia zaporoz'kykh kozakiv* [A history of the Zaporozhian Cossacks]. Kiev: Nauk. dumka, 1990–91.

Evgen'eva, A. P., and B. N. Putilov, eds. *Drevnie rossiiskie stikhotvoreniia, sobrannye Kirsheiu Danilovym* [Old Russian poems, collected by Kirsha Danilov]. 2nd enl. ed. Moscow: Nauka, 1977.

Evgenii, Metropolitan [Evgenii Bolkhovitnikov]. "Svedenie o Kirike, predlagavshem voprosy Nifontu Novgorodskomu" [Information about Kirik, who posed questions to Nifont of Novgorod]. *Trudy i letopisi Obshchestva istorii i drevnostei rossiiskikh* [Works and annals of the Society of Russian History and Antiquities] 4 (1828).

Famintsyn, A. S. *Domra i srodnye ei muzykal'nye instrumenty russkogo naroda* [The *domra* and related musical instruments of the Russian people]. St. Petersburg: Tip. E. Arngol'da, 1891.

————. *Gusli—russkii narodnyi muzykal'nyi instrument* [The *gusli*, a Russian folk musical instrument]. St. Petersburg: OLDP, 1890.

————. *Skomorokhi na Rusi* [The *skomorokhi* in Rus']. St. Petersburg: Tip. E. Arngol'da, 1889. Reprint, St. Petersburg: Aleteiia, 1995.

Farrell, Dianne E. "Medieval Popular Humor in Russian Eighteenth-century *lubki*." *Slavic Review* 50, no. 3 (1991): 551–65.

Fennell, J. L. I. *The Correspondence between Prince A. M. Kurbsky and Tsar Ivan IV of Russia, 1564–1579*. Cambridge: Cambridge University Press, 1955.

————. "The *Slovo o polku Igoreve:* The Textological Triangle." *Oxford Slavonic Papers*, n.s., 1 (1968): 126–37.

Filaret, Bishop of Kharkov. "Zhitie prepodobnogo Feodosiia Pecherskogo v perevode na sovremennyi russkii iazyk Preosv. Filareta, Episkopa Khar'kovskogo" [The Life of the Reverend Feodosii Pecherskii, translated into modern Russian by the Rev. Filaret, Bishop of Kharkov], *Uchenye zapiski II-go otdeleniia Imp. Akademii nauk* [Scholarly notes of the second section of the Imperial Academy of Sciences] 2, fasc. 2 (1856): 129–92.

Filippov, T. I., and N. A. Rimskii-Korsakov, comp. *40 narodnykh pesen, sobrannykh T. I. Filippovym i garmonizovannykh N. A. Rimskim-Korsakovym* [40 folk songs, collected by T. I. Filippov and harmonized by N. A. Rimskii-Korsakov]. Moscow: P. Iurgenson, 1882.

Findeizen, N. F. "Evreiskie tsimbaly i tsimbalisty Lepianskie" [Hebrew *tsimbaly* and the *tsimbaly* players of Lepiansk]. *Muzykal'naia etnografiia* [Musical ethnography] (1926): 37–42.

————. "Petrovskie kanty" [Petrine *kanty*]. *Izvestiia Akad. nauk SSSR* [Proceedings of the Academy of Sciences of the USSR], 6th series, 7–8 (1927): 667–90.

Flier, Michael S. "Breaking the Code: The Image of the Tsar in the Muscovite Palm Sunday Ritual." In *Medieval Russian Culture*, ed. Michael S. Flier and Daniel Rowland, 2:213–42. Berkeley: University of California Press, 1994 [*California Slavic Studies*, vol. 19].

Folkmann, Josef. *Die gefürstete Linie des uralten und edlen Geschlechtes Kinsky*. Prague: K. André, 1861.

Franklin, Simon. *Sermons and Rhetoric of Kievan Rus'*. Harvard Library of Early Ukrainian Literature. English Translations 5 ([Cambridge, Mass.]: Harvard University Press, 1991.

Freeze, Gregory L., ed. *Russia: A History*. Oxford: Oxford University Press, 1997.

Frolov, S. V. "Iz istorii drevnerusskoi muzyki (Rannii spisok stikhov pokaiannykh)" [From the history of old Russian music (an early copy of the repentance verses)]. In *Kul'turnoe nasledie drevnei Rusi* [The cultural heritage of old Rus'], 162–71. Moscow: Nauka, 1976.

———. "K probleme zvukovysotnosti bespometnoi znamennoi notatsii" [On the problem of pitch in "un-reformed" neumatic notation]. In *Problemy istorii i teorii drevnerusskoi muzyki* [Problems in the history and theory of early Russian music], ed. A. S. Belonenko and M. V. Brazhnikov, 124–47. Leningrad: Muzyka, 1979.

Galitzin, E. M. *La Russie du XVIIe siècle dans ses rapports avec l'Europe occidentale: Récit du voyage de Pierre Potemkin*. Paris: Gide et J. Baudry, 1855.

Gardner, I. A [Johann]. *Bogosluzhebnoe penie russkoi pravoslavnoi tserkvi* [Liturgical singing of the Russian Orthodox Church]. 2 vols. Jordanville, N.Y.: Holy Trinity Russian Orthodox Monastery, 1978.

———. *Das Problem des altrussischen demestischen Kirchengesanges und seiner linienlosen Notation*. Slavistische Beiträge 25. Munich: Sagner, 1967.

———. *Russian Church Singing*. Vol. 1, *Orthodox Worship and Hymnography*. Vol. 2, *History from the Origins to the Mid-Seventeenth Century*. Translated by Vladimir Morosan. Crestwood, N.Y.: St. Vladimir's Seminary Press, 1980 and 2000.

Garkavi [Harkavi, Harkavy], A. Ia. *Skazaniia musul'manskikh pisatelei o slavianakh i russkikh s poloviny VII veka do kontsa X veka po R. Kh.* [The stories of Muslim writers about the Slavs and Russians from the second half of the 7th century to the end of the 10th century AD]. St. Petersburg: Tip. Imp. Akademii nauk, 1870. Reprint, Slavistic Printings and Reprintings 96. The Hague: Mouton, 1969.

Garrard, John G. *Mixail Culkov. An Introduction to His Prose and Verse*. The Hague: Mouton, 1970.

Gedeonov, S. A. *Variagi i Rus'* [The Varangians and Rus']. St. Petersburg: Tip. Imp. Akademii nauk, 1876.

Gertsman, E. V. *Vizantiiskoe muzykoznanie* [Byzantine musicology]. Leningrad: Muzyka, 1988.

Gil'ferding, A. F. "Onezhskie byliny" [*Byliny* from Onega]. *Sbornik Otd. Rus. iazyka i slov. Akademii nauk* [Papers of the Section for Russian Language and Literature of the Academy of Sciences] 59–61 (1894).

Glareanus, Henricus. *Dodecachordon*. Translated, transcribed, and with commentary by Clement A. Miller. n.p.: American Institute of Musicology, 1965.

Golikov, I. I., ed. *Dopolnenie k Deianiiam Petra Velikogo* [Addenda to the Acts of Peter the Great]. 18 vols. Moscow: Universitetskaia tip., 1790–97.

Golovatskii, Ia. *Dopolnenie k ocherku slaviano-russkoi bibliografii V. M. Undol'skogo* [Addendum to the essay on Slavonic-Russian bibliography by V. M. Undol'skii]. St. Petersburg: Imp. Akademii nauk, 1874.

Golubinskii, E. E. *Istoriia russkoi tserkvi* [History of the Russian Church]. 2 vols. Moscow: Universitetskaia tip., 1901.

Golubtsov, A. "Chinovnik Novgorodskogo Sofiiskogo sobora" [Book of Rites of the Novgorod Cathedral of St. Sophia]. *ChOIDR* 2 (1899), pt. 1: i–xx, 1–272.

Golyshenko, V. S., and V. F. Dubrovina, eds. *Kniga naritsaema Koz'ma Indikoplov* [The book called Koz'ma Indikoplov]. Moscow: Indrik, 1997.

Gordienko, E. A. *Novgorod v XVI veke i ego dukhovnaia zhizn'* [Novgorod in the 16th century and its spiritual life]. St. Petersburg: Bulanin, 2001.

Gorskii A. V., and K. I. Nevostruev. *Opisanie slavianskikh rukopisei Moskovskoi Sinodal'noi biblioteki* [Catalog of Slavic manuscripts in the Moscow Synodal Library]. 5 vols. Moscow: Sinodal'naia tip., 1855–1917. Reprint, Wiesbaden: Otto Harrassowitz, 1964.

Gosudarstvennaia Oruzheinaia palata [The State Armory]. Compiled by I. A. Bobrovnitskaia. Moscow: Sovetskii khudozhnik, 1988.

Gosudarstvennaia Tret'iakovskaia Galereia. Katalog sobraniia [State Tret'iakov Gallery. A catalog of the collection]. Vol. 1, *Drevnerusskoe iskusstvo X–nachala XV veka* [Early Russian art from the 10th to the beginning of the 15th century]. Moscow: Krasnaia ploshchad', 1995.

Gosudarstvennyi arkhitekturno-istoricheskii zapovednik [State architectural-historical monument]. Kiev: Mistetstvo, 1984.

Grabar, André. "Les Fresques des escaliers à Sainte-Sophie de Kiev et l'iconographie impériale Byzantine." *Seminarium Kondakovianum: Recueil d'études* 7 (1935): 103–17.

Grebeniuk, V. P., and O. A. Derzhavina. *Panegiricheskaia literatura petrovskogo vremeni* [Panegyrical literature of the Petrine era]. Moscow: Nauka, 1979.

Grigor'ev, A. D. *Arkhangel'skie byliny i istoricheskie pesni* [The Arkhangel'sk *byliny* and historical songs]. Vol. 1. Moscow: Imp. Akademii nauk, 1904.

Grimsted, Patricia Kennedy, ed. *Archives of Russia: A Directory and Bibliographic Guide to Holdings in Moscow and St. Petersburg.* 2 vols. Armonk, New York: M. E. Sharpe, 2000.

Gudziak, Borys. *Crisis and Reform: The Kyivan Metropolitanate, the Patriarchate of Constantinople, and the Genesis of the Union of Brest.* Cambridge, Mass.: Distributed by Harvard University Press for the Ukrainian Research Institute, Harvard University, 1998.

Günther, K. "Das Weimarer Bruchstück des ersten russischen Dramas 'Artaxerxovo dejstvo' (1672)." *Studien zur Geschichte der russischen Literatur des 18. Jahrhunderts* 3 (vol. 28 of Veröffentlichungen des Instituts für Slawistik): 120–78.

————. "Neue deutsche Quellen zum ersten russischen Theater." *Zeitschrift für Slawistic* 8, no. 5 (1963): 664–75.

Guseinova, Z. M. *'Izveshchenie' Aleksandra Mezentsa i teoriia muzyki XVII veka* ["Report" by Aleksandr Mezenets and music theory in the 17th century]. St. Petersburg: St. Petersburg Conservatory, 1995.

Gusev, P. L. "Novgorod XVI veka po izobrazheniiu na khutynskoi ikone: 'videnie ponomaria tarasiia'" [Novgorod in the sixteenth century according to the depiction in the icon The Vision of the Sexton Tarasii]. *Vestnik arkheologii i istorii* [Archaeological and historical herald] 13 (1900): 7–66.

Guthrie, Matthew. *Dissertations sur les antiquités de Russie.* St. Petersburg: Impr. du Corps Impérial des cadets nobles, 1795.

Halperin, Charles. "In the Eye of the Beholder: Two Views of Seventeenth-century Muscovy." *Russian History/Histoire Russe* 24, no. 4 (1997): 409–23.

Haney, Jack, and Eric Dahl, trans. *The Discourse on Igor's Campaign: A Translation of the "Slovo o polku Igoreve"* [Seattle]: n.p., 1989.

Heppell, Muriel, trans. *The Paterik of the Kievan Caves Monastery.* Harvard Library of Early Ukrainian Literature. English Translations 1. Cambridge, Mass.: Harvard University Press, 1989.

Herasymova-Persyds'ka, N. O. [Gerasimova-Persidskaia, N. A.] *Khorovyi kontsert na Ukraini v XVII-XVIII st.* [The choral *kontsert* in Ukraine in the 17th–18th centuries]. Kiev: Muzychna Ukraina, 1978.

————. *Materiali z istorii ukrains'koi muzyky: Partesnii kontsert* [Materials from the history of Ukrainian music: Polyphonic *kontsert*]. Kiev: Muzychna Ukraina, 1976.

————. *Ukrains'ki partesni motety pochatku XVIII stolittia z Iuhoslavs'kykh zibran'* [Ukrainian choral motets of the early 18th century from Yugoslav collections]. Kiev: Muzychna Ukraina, 1991.

Hilton, Alison. *Russian Folk Art.* Bloomington: Indiana University Press, 1995.

Hippisley, A. *The Poetic Style of Simeon Polotsky.* Birmingham Slavonic Monographs 16. Birmingham: Department of Russian Language and Literature, University of Birmingham, 1985.

[Horsey, Jerome]. *Russia at the close of the sixteenth century. Comprising the treatise "Of the Russe common wealth," by Dr. Giles Fletcher; and the travels of Sir Jerome Horsey, knt., now for the first time printed entire from his own manuscript.* Edited by Edward A. Bond. London: Printed for the Hakluyt Society, 1856.

[———.] *Zapiski o Moskovii XVI v. sera Dzheroma Gorseia* [Notes about Muscovy in the 16th century by Sir Jerome Horsey]. St. Petersburg: Suvorin, 1909.

Horvath-Peterson, Sandra. *Victor Duruy and French Education: Liberal Reform in the Second Empire.* Baton Rouge: Louisiana State University Press, 1984.

Hughes, Lindsey. *Peter the Great: A Biography.* New Haven: Yale University Press, 2002.

———. *Russia and the West, the Life of a Seventeenth-century Westernizer, Prince Vasily Vasilevich Golitsyn (1643–1714).* Newtonville, Mass.: Oriental Research Partners, 1984.

———. *Russia in the Age of Peter the Great.* New Haven: Yale University Press, 1998.

———. *Sophia, Regent of Russia, 1657–1704.* New Haven: Yale University Press, 1990.

Ianin, V. L. *Novgorodskie posadniki* [The Novgorodian *posadniki*]. 2nd rev. and exp. ed. Moscow: Iazyki slavianskoi kul'tury, 2003.

Igoshev, L. A. "Proiskhozhdenie grecheskogo rospeva (opyt analiza)" [The origin of Greek chant (an essay in analysis)]. *PKNO for 1992* (1993): 147–50.

Il'ichev, L. F., and E. S. Sanchez, eds. *Rossiia i Ispaniia: Dokumenty i materialy 1667–1917* [Russia and Spain: Documents and materials, 1667–1917]. 2 vols. Moscow: Mezhdunarodnye otnosheniia, 1991.

Imperatorskii Rossiiskii istoricheskii muzei. Ukazatel' pamiatnikov [The Imperial Russian Historical Museum. A guide to the monuments]. 2nd ed. Moscow: Tip. A. I. Mamontova, 1893.

Iosif, *Opis' rukopisei perenesennykh iz biblioteki Iosifova Monastyria v biblioteku Moskovskoi dukhovnoi akademii* [A listing of manuscripts transferred from the library of the Joseph [of Volokolamsk] Monastery to the library of the Moscow Divinity School]. Moscow: Universitetskaia tip., 1882.

Istomin, Karion. *Bukvar'* [Primer]. Commentary by V. I. Lukianenko and M. A. Alekseevna. Leningrad: Avrora, 1981.

Ivanits, Linda J. *Russian Folk Belief.* Armonk, N.Y.: M. E. Sharpe, 1992.

Ivchenko, L. V., comp. *Ukrains'kyi kant XVII–XVIII stolit'* [Ukrainian *kant* in the 17th–18th centuries]. Edited by N. O. Herasymova-Persyds'ka. Kiev: Muzychna Ukraina, 1990.

Jakobson, Roman, and Dean S. Worth, eds. and trans. *Sofonija's Tale of the Russian-Tatar Battle on the Kulikovo Field.* Slavistic Printings and Reprintings 51. The Hague: Mouton, 1963.

Jensen, Claudia R. "Music for the Tsar: A Preliminary Study of the Music of the Muscovite Court Theater." *Musical Quarterly* 79, no. 2 (1995): 368–401.

———. "Nikolai Diletskii's 'Grammatika' (Grammar) and the Musical Culture of Seventeenth-century Muscovy." Ph.D. diss., Princeton University, 1987.

———. "Orpheus in Muscovy: On the Early History of the Muscovite Court Theater." *Gimnologiia 4, Vizantiia i Vostochnaia Evropa: Liturgicheskie i muzykal'nye sviazi; k 80-letiiu doktora Milosha Velimirovicha / Hymnology 4, Byzantium and East Europe: Liturgical and Musical Links; in Honor of Miloš Velimirović* (2003): 281–300.

———. "A Theoretical Work of Late Seventeenth-century Muscovy: Nikolai Diletskii's *Grammatika* and the Earliest Circle of Fifths." *JAMS* 45 (1992): 305–31.

Jensen, Claudia R., and John Powell. "'A Mess of Russians left us but of late': Diplomatic Blunder, Literary Satire, and the Muscovite Ambassador's 1668 Visit to Paris Theaters." *Theatre Research International* 24 (1999): 131–44.

Kachenovskii, M. "Ob istochnikakh dlia russkoi istorii" [On sources for Russian history]. *Vestnik Evropy* [European herald], pt. 43, no. 3 (1809): 193–210; pt. 44, no. 5 (1809): 3–19; pt. 44, no. 6 (1809): 98–119; pt. 46, no. 15 (1809): 209–18.

[Kalachev, N.] *Arkhiv istoriko-iuridicheskikh svedenii, otnosiashchikhsia do Rossii* [Archive of historical-legal information relating to Russia]. Moscow: Tip. A. Semena, 1850.

———, ed. *Pistsovye knigi Moskovskogo gosudarstva.* Chast' 1, *Pistsovye knigi XVI veka* [Cadastres of the Muscovite state. Part 1, Cadastres of the sixteenth century]. St. Petersburg: Izd. Imp. Russkogo geograficheskogo obshchestva, 1872. 2nd ed., St. Petersburg: Tip. II-go otd. Sobstvennoi E. I. V. kantseliarii, 1877.

Kalaidovich, K., and P. Stroev. *Obstoiatel'noe opisanie slaviano-rossiiskikh rukopisei, khraniashchikhsia v Moskve v biblioteke . . . grafa Fedora Andreevicha Tolstogo* [Detailed catalog of Slavo-Russian manuscripts preserved in Moscow in the library . . . of Count Fedor Andreevich Tolstoi]. Moscow: V. Tip. Selivanovskogo, 1825.

Kalaidovich, K. F. "Ob uchenykh trudakh mitr. Kipriiana" [On the scholarly works of Metropolitan Kipriian]. *Vestnik Evropy* [European herald], pt. 72, nos. 23–24 (1813): 207–24.

Kalashnikov, I. T. "Zapiski irkutskogo zhitelia" [Notes of a resident of Irkutsk]. *Russkaia starina* [Russian antiquity] (July 1905): 187–251.

Kaliazina N. V., and G. N. Komelova. *Russkoe iskusstvo Petrovskoi epokhi* [Russian art of the Petrine era]. Leningrad: "Khudozhnik RSFSR," 1990.

Kaminskii, F. V. "Otryvki evangel'skikh chtenii XI v., imenuemye Kupriianovskimi (Novgorodskimi)" [Fragments of the gospel readings from the 11th century, called Kupriianov (Novgorodian)]. *Izvestiia II-go otd. Russk. Akademii nauk* [Proceedings of the Second Section of the Russian Academy of Sciences] 28 (1923): 273–320.

Kantemir, Antiokh Dmitrievich. *Sobranie stikhotvorenii* [A collection of poetic works]. Introduction by F. I. Priima. Leningrad: Sovetskii pisatel', 1956.

Karamzin, N. M. *Istoriia gosudarstva rossiiskogo* [History of the Russian state]. 5 vols. Moscow: Nauka, 1989–98.

Kargareteli, I. G. *Ocherk gruzinskoi narodnoi muzyki* [A study of Georgian folk music]. Tiflis: n.p., 1901.

Karinskii, N. M. *Khrestomatiia po drevne-tserkovno-slavianskomu i russkomu iazykam* [A reader in the Old Church Slavonic and Russian languages]. n.p.: Savinov, 1883 and 1889.

———. "Ostromirovo evangelie kak pamiatnik drevnerusskogo iazyka" [The Ostromir Gospel as a document of the old Russian language]. *Zhurnal Ministerstva narodnogo prosveshcheniia* [Journal of the Ministry of Public Enlightenment] 5 (1903): 94–110.

Karlinsky, Simon. *Russian Drama from Its Beginnings to the Age of Pushkin.* Berkeley: University of California Press, 1985.

Karpiak, Robert. "The Culture of the Keyboard in 18th-century Russia." *Continuo* (December 1998): 5–8.

———. "Researching Early Keyboards in Russia." *Continuo* (February 1996): 2–6.

Karpov, A. P. *Azbukovniki, ili alfavity inostrannykh rechei, po spiskam Solovetskoi biblioteki* [Azbukovniki or alphabets of foreign words, based on manuscripts in the Solovetskii Library]. Published as an appendix to *Pravoslavnyi sobesednik* [The Orthodox interlocutor] 1877. 2nd ed. Kazan: Tip. Imp. universiteta, 1878.

Kastal'skii, A. D. *Peshchnoe deistvo: Starinnyi tserkovnyi obriad* [The Play of the Furnace: An old church rite]. Moscow: P. Iurgenson, 1909.

Katalog tserkovnykh i dr. predmetov drevnosti, nakhodiashchikhsia v drevlekhranilishche Kostromskogo tserk.-ist. obshch. v pokoiakh Mikhaila Fedorovicha Romanova, chto v Ipat'evskom monastyre [Catalog of ecclesiastical and other ancient objects presently in the repository of the Kostroma Society for Church History in the chambers of [Tsar] Mikhail Fedorovich Romanova, in the Ipat'ev Monastery]. Kostroma, 1914.

Kazanskii, P. S. "O prizyve k bogosluzheniiu v vostochnoi tserkvi" [The summons to the divine service in the Eastern Church]. *Trudy I-go arkheologicheskogo s'ezda v Moskve, 1869 g.* [Report of the First Archaeological Congress in Moscow, 1869] (1871).

———. *Selo Novospasskoe, Dedenevo tozh i rodoslovnaia Golovinykh, vladel'tsev onogo* [The villages of Novospasskoe and Dedenevo and the genealogy of the Golovins who possess them]. Moscow: S. Selivanovskii, 1847.

Keenan, Edward L. *Josef Dobrovský and the Origins of the Igor Tale.* Cambridge, Mass.: Harvard University Press, 2004.

———. *The Kurbskii-Groznyi Apocrypha: The Seventeenth-century Genesis of the "Correspondence" attributed to Prince A. M. Kurbskii and Tsar Ivan IV.* Cambridge, Mass.: Harvard University Press, 1971.

Keldysh, Iu. V. *Istoriia russkoi muzyki* [History of Russian music]. Moscow: Muzgiz, 1948.

———. "Renessansnye tendentsii v russkoi muzyke XVI veka" [Renaissance traits in Russian music of the 16th century]. In *Teoreticheskie nabliudeniia nad istoriei muzyki* [Theoretical research in the history of music], 174–99. Moscow: Muzyka, 1978.

———. *Russkaia muzyka XVIII veka* [Russian music in the 18th century]. Moscow: Nauka, 1965.

Khalidi, Tarif. *Islamic Historiography: The Histories of Masudi.* Albany: State University of New York Press, 1975.

Kharlampovich, K. V. *Malorossiiskoe vliianie na velikorusskuiu tserkovnuiu zhizn'* [Ukrainian influence on Great Russian church life]. Vol. 1. Kazan, 1914. Reprint, Slavistic Printings and Reprintings, no. 119, The Hague: Mouton, 1968.

[Khodakovskii]. "Istoricheskaia sistema" [Historical system]. In *Russkii istoricheskii sbornik* [Russian historical collection], ed. M. Pogodin, vol. 1, bk. 3. Moscow: Universitetskaia tip., 1838.

Khoinovskii, I. A. *Kratkie arkheologicheskie svedeniia o predkakh slavian i Rusi i opis' drevnostei* [Brief archaeological testimonies about the ancestors of the Slavs and of Rus' and a description of the artifacts]. Kiev: Tip. Imp. universiteta, 1896.

Kholodov, E. G. "K istorii starinnogo russkogo teatra (neskol'ko utochnenii)" [Toward the history of the old Russian theater (some clarifications)]. *PKNO for 1981* (1983): 149–70.

Khristofor, monk. *Kliuch znamennoi* [A key to znamennaia notation]. Edited by M. V. Brazhnikov and G. Nikishov. PRMI 9. Moscow: Muzyka, 1983.

Khvol'son, D. A., ed. and trans. *Izvestiia o Khozarakh, Burtasakh, Bolgarakh, Mad'iarakh, Slavianakh i Russakh Abu-Ali Akhmeda Ben Omar Ibn-Dasta* [Reports about the Khazars, Burtas, Bulgarians, Hungarians, Slavs, and Rus' by Abu-Ali Ahmad Ben Omar Ibn-Dasta]. St. Petersburg: Tip. Imp. Akademii nauk, 1869.

Kindstrand, Jan Fredrik. *Anacharsis: The Legend and the Apophthegmata.* Uppsala: Distributed by Almqvist & Wiksell, 1981.

Kirpichnikov, A. "K voprosu o drevnerusskikh skomorokhakh" [On the question of the old Russian *skomorokhi*]. *Sbornik II-go otd. Imp. Akademii nauk* [Collection of the Second Section of the Imperial Academy of Sciences] 52, no. 5 (1891): 1–22.

Kniga glagolemaia Kozmy Indikoplova [The book called Kozma Indikoplov]. OLDP Izdaniia 86. St. Petersburg: Foto-Litografiia P. Golike, 1886.

Kniga Stepennaia tsarskago rodosloviia, soderzhashchaia istoriiu Rossiiskuiu s nachala onyia do vremen gosudaria tsaria i vel. kniazia Ioanna Vasil'evicha, sochinennaia trudami preosv. mitropolitov Kipriiana i Makariia, a napechatannaia pod smotreniem Kol. Sov. i Ak. nauk Chlena Gerarda Friderika Millera [The Book of Degrees of the Imperial genealogy, containing the history of Russia from its beginnings to the times of the Sovereign

Tsar and Great Prince Ivan Vasil'evich, compiled by the labors of the Most Reverend Metropolitans Kipriian and Makarii and printed under the supervision of the Collegiate Councilor and Member of the Academy of Sciences, Gerard Frederick Miller]. Moscow: Universitetskaia tip., 1755.

Koch, Ernst. "Die Sachsenkirche in Moskau." *Neues Archiv für Sächsische Geschichte und Altertumskunde* 32 (1911): 270–316.

Kolchin, B. A. "Gusli drevnego Novgoroda" [*Gusli* of old Novgorod]. In *Drevniaia Rus' i Slaviane* [Ancient Rus' and the Slavs], 358–66. Moscow: Nauka, 1978.

———. "Kollektsiia muzykal'nykh instrumentov drevnego Novgoroda" [A collection of musical instruments of old Novgorod]. *PKNO for 1978* (1979): 174–87.

Kolesov, V. V., and V. V. Rozhdestvenskaia, eds. *Domostroi* [The *Domostroi*]. St. Petersburg: Nauka, 2000.

K[olomiitsov], V. P. *V. V. Andreev i ego velikorusskii orkestr* [V. V. Andreev and his Great Russian orchestra]. St. Petersburg: Tip. A. S. Suvorova, 1909.

Kononenko, Natalie O. *Ukrainian Minstrels: And the Blind Shall Sing.* Armonk, N.Y.: M. E. Sharpe, 1998.

Konotop, A. V. "Drevneishii pamiatnik ukrainskogo notolineinogo pis'ma—Suprasl'skii irmologion 1598–1601 gg." [The oldest document of Ukrainian staff notation: The Irmologii from Suprasl' of ca. 1598–1601]. *PKNO for 1974* (1975): 285–93.

Korb, Johann Georg. *Diary of an Austrian Secretary of Legation at the Court of Czar Peter the Great.* Translated by Count Charles MacDonnell. London: Bradbury & Evans, 1863. Reprint, *Russia through European Eyes* 8 (New York: Da Capo, 1968).

———. *Dnevnik puteshestviia v Moskoviiu (1698 i 1699 gg.)* [Diary of a trip to Muscovy in 1698 and 1699]. Translated and with commentary by A. I. Malein. St. Petersburg: A. S. Suvorin, 1906.

———. *Tagebuch der Reise nach Russland.* Edited by Gerhard Korb, commentary by Edmund Leingärtner. Graz: Akademische Druck-u. Verlagsanstalt, 1968.

Korenevskii, P. I. "Arkheologicheskie raskopki v Kieve" [Archaeological excavations in Kiev]. *Istoricheskii vestnik* [Historical herald] 121 (1910): 980–84.

Korifei, ili kliuch literatury [Korifei, or the key to literature]. 11 vols. St. Petersburg: V Tip. Shnora, 1802–7.

Korsh, F. E., ed. *Slovo o polku Igoreve* [The lay of the Host of Igor]. St. Petersburg: Akademiia nauk, 1909.

Koschmieder, E., ed. *Die ältesten Novgoroder Hirmologien-Fragmente.* 3 vols. Munich: Verlag der Bayerischen Akademie der Wissenschaften, 1952–58.

Koshelev, V. V. *Skomorokhi: Annotirovannyi bibliograficheskii ukazatel' 1790–1994 gg.* [*Skomorokhi:* An annotated bibliographic guide, 1790–1994]. St. Petersburg: Liki Rossii, 1994.

Kostomarov, N. I. *Ocherk domashnei zhizni i nravov velikorusskogo naroda v XVI i XVII stoletiiakh* [An essay on home life and customs of the Great Russian people in the 16th and 17th centuries]. 3rd ed. St. Petersburg: M. Stasiulevich, 1887.

———. *Russkaia istoriia v zhizneopisaniiakh* [Russian history in biographies]. 4th ed. St. Petersburg: M. Stasiulevich, 1896.

Kotkov, S. I., ed. *Vygoleksinskii sbornik* [The Vygoleksinskii collection]. Moscow: Nauka, 1977.

Kotliarevskii, A. A. *O pogrebal'nykh obychaiakh iazycheskikh slavian* [On the funeral customs of the pagan Slavs]. Moscow: [Sinodal'naia tip.], 1868.

Kotoshikhin, Grigorii Karpovich. *O Rossii v tsarstvovanie Alekseia Mikhailovicha* [On Russia during the reign of Aleksei Mikhailovich]. Edited with commentary by Anne E. Pennington. Oxford: Clarendon; New York: Oxford University Press, 1980.

———. *O Rossii v tsarstvovanie Alekseia Mikhailovicha* [On Russia during the reign of Aleksei Mikhailovich]. In *Moskva i Evropa* [Moscow and Europe], ed. A. Liberman and S. Shokarev,

11–146. In the series Istoriia Rossii i doma Romanovykh v memuarakh sovremennikov XVII–XX vv. [A history of Russia and the house of the Romanovs in memoirs by contemporaries, 17th–20th centuries]. Moscow: Fond Sergeia Dubova, 2000.

Kovalevskii, A. P. *Kniga Akhmeda Ibn-Fadlana o ego puteshestvii na Volgu v 921–22 gg. Stat'i, perevody i kommentarii* [Ahmad Ibn-Fadlan's book about his trip on the Volga in 921–22. Articles, translations, and commentary]. Kharkov: Izd-vo Khar'kovskogo universiteta, 1956.

Kovtun, L. S. *Azbukovniki XVI–XVII vv.* [Alphabets of the 16th–17th centuries]. Leningrad: Nauka, 1989.

Kozlovskii, M. M. *Issledovanie o iazyke Ostromirova evangeliia* [A study of the language of the Ostromir Gospel]. St. Petersburg: Akademiia nauk, 1885.

Kriaras, Emmanouel [Κριαράς, Εμμανουήλ]. Λεξικό της Μεσαιωνικής Ελληνικής Δημώδους Γραμματείας, *1100–1669* [Lexicon of medieval Hellenic folk literature, 1100–1669], 14 vols. to date. Thessaloniki, 1969–.

Kruchinina, A. N., and B. A. Shindin. "Pervoe russkoe posobie po muzykal'noi kompozitsii" [First Russian handbook on musical composition]. *PKNO for 1978* (1979): 188–95.

Kulakovskii, L. V. *Pesn' o polku Igoreve* [The song of Igor]. Moscow: Sovetskii kompozitor, 1977.

Kulikowski, Mark. *A Bibliography of Slavic Mythology.* Columbus, Ohio: Slavica, 1989.

Kulish, P. O. *Zapiski o iuzhnoi Rusi* [Notes on southern Rus']. St. Petersburg: A. Iakobson, 1856. Reprint, Kiev: Izd-vo khudozhestvennoi literatury "DNIPRO," 1994.

Kuz'mina, V. D. *Devgenievo deianie. (Deianie prezhnikh vremen khrabrykh chelovek)* [The deeds of Devgenie (The deeds of brave men of former times)]. Moscow: Izd-vo AN SSSR, 1962.

Lahana, Martha Luby. "Novaia Nemetskaia Sloboda: Seventeenth-Century Moscow's Foreign Suburb." Ph.D. diss., University of North Carolina at Chapel Hill, 1983.

Laskovskii, V. P. *Putevoditel' po drevnemu Novgorodu* [Guide to old Novgorod]. Novgorod: Gubernskaia tip., 1910. 2nd rev. ed. Novgorod: Gubernskaia tip., 1913.

Latyshev, V. V. *Izvestiia drevnikh pisatelei grecheskikh i latinskikh o skifakh [skifii] i Kavkaze* [Reports of ancient Greek and Latin writers about the Scythians and the Caucasus]. St. Petersburg: Tip. Imp. Akademii nauk, 1893–1906. Published as an addendum to the *Zapiski Imperatorskogo Russkogo arkheologicheskogo obshchestva* [Notes of the Imperial Russian Archaeological Society] 1.

Lazarev, V. N. *Drevnerusskie mozaiki i freski XI–XV vv.* [Old Russian mosaics and frescoes, 11th–15th centuries]. Moscow: Iskusstvo, 1973.

———. *Novgorodskaia ikonopis' / Novgorodian Icon-Painting.* Moscow: Iskusstvo, 1969.

Lenhoff, Gail. "Beyond Three Seas: Afanasij Nikitin's Journey from Orthodoxy to Apostasy." *East European Quarterly* 13, no. 4 (1979): 431–47.

Lenrot, Elias. *Kalevala, finskii narodnyi epos* [*Kalevala*, the Finnish folk epic]. Translated by L. Bel'skii. 2nd ed. Moscow: Izd. M. i S. Sabashnikovykh, 1915.

Leonid, Archimandrite, ed. *Akty Iverskogo sviatoozerskogo monastyria (1582–1706)* [Acts of the Iverskii Sviatoozerskii Monastery, 1582–1706]. *RIB* 5. St. Petersburg: A. Transhel', 1878.

———. *Sistematicheskoe opisanie slaviano-rossiiskikh rukopisei sobraniia grafa A. S. Uvarova* [Systematic description of the Slavonic-Russian manuscripts in the collection of Count Uvarov]. 4 vols. Moscow: Tip. A. I. Mamontova, 1893–94.

———. "Stikhiry polozhennye na kriukovye noty. Tvorenie tsaria Ioanna despota Rossiiskogo" [*Stikhiry* set to *kriukovaia* notation, composed by Tsar Ivan, autocrat of Russia]. *Pamiatniki drevnei pis'mennosti* [Monuments of early writing]. St. Petersburg, 1886.

"Letopisets Pereiaslavlia Suzdal'skogo s predisloviem i opisaniem rukopisei: Letopisets russkikh tsarei" [The Pereiaslavl-Suzdal short chronicle, with a preface and a description of the manuscripts: The short chronicle of the Russian tsars]. *Vremennik Obshchestva istorii i drevnostei*

Rossiiskikh [Annals of the Imperial Society of Russian History and Antiquities] 9 (1851), pt. 2: i–c, 1–112.

Lewin, Paulina. "The Staging of Plays at the Kiev Mohyla Academy in the Seventeenth and Eighteenth Centuries." *Harvard Ukrainian Studies* 5, no. 3 (1981): 320–34.

Likhachev, D. S., ed. *Puteshestviia russkikh poslov XVI–XVII vv: Stateinye spiski* [Voyages of Russian ambassadors of the 16th–17th centuries: Diplomatic reports]. Moscow: Izd. Akademii nauk SSSR, 1954.

Likhachev, D. S., A. M. Panchenko, and N. V. Ponyrko. *Smekh v drevnei Rusi* [Laughter in early Rus']. Leningrad: Nauka, 1984.

Likhachev [Likhachov], D., V. Laurina, and V. Pushkariov [Pushkarev]. *Novgorod Icons 12th–17th Century.* Leningrad: Aurora, 1980.

[Likhachev, V.] "Stateinoi spisok posol'stva ... Vasil'ia Likhacheva vo Florentsiiu v 7167 (1659) g." [The diplomatic report of Vasilii Likhachev's embassy to Florence in 1659], 339–59. *Drevniaia rossiiskaia vivliofika* [Ancient Russian library] 4. Moscow: Tip. Kompanii tipograficheskoi, 1788.

Lineva, E. E. *Velikorusskie pesni v narodnoi garmonizatsii: Pesni novgorodskie* [Songs from Great Russia in folk harmonization: Songs from Novgorod]. St. Petersburg: Imp. Akademii nauk, 1909.

Lissa, Z. *Polsko-rosyjskie miscellanea muzyczne* [A Polish-Russian musical miscellany]. [Kraków]: Polskie wydawnictwo muzyczne, 1967.

Listopadov, A. M. "Narodnaia kazach'ia pesnia na Donu" [Cossack folk song in the Don area]. *Trudy muzykal'no-etnograficheskoi komissii* [Reports of the Musical-Ethnographic Commission] 1. Moscow: Tip. K. L. Men'shova, 1906.

Livanova, T. N. *Ocherki i materialy po istorii russkoi muzykal'noi kul'tury* [Studies and materials on the history of Russian musical culture]. 2 vols. Moscow: Iskusstvo, 1938.

Lohvyn, H. N. *Kiev's Hagia Sophia: State Architectural-Historical Monument.* Kiev: Mistetstvo, 1971.

Longworth, Philip. *Alexis: Tsar of All the Russias.* New York: Franklin Watts, 1984.

———. *The Cossacks.* New York: Holt, Rinehart and Winston, 1970.

Loparev, Kh. M. *Opisanie rukopisei Imperatorskogo Obshchestva liubitelei drevnei pis'mennosti* [Description of the manuscripts of the Imperial Society of Friends of Old Literature]. 3 vols. St. Petersburg: Tip. Imp. Akademii nauk, 1899.

Lopatin, N. M., and V. P. Prokunin, comps. *Sbornik russkikh narodnykh liricheskikh pesen* [A collection of Russian lyric folk songs]. Moscow: Tip. A. I. Mamontova, 1889.

Louria, Yvette. "The Comedy of Artaxerxes (1672)." *Bulletin of the New York Public Library* 72, no. 3 (1968): 139–210.

Lozovaia, M., main ed. *Gimnologiia: Materialy Mezhdunarodnoi nauchnoi konferentsii "Pamiati protoiereia Dimitriia Razumovskogo" (k 130-letiiu Moskovskoi konservatorii) 3–8 sentiabria 1996 / Hymnology: Papers of [the] Musicological Congress "Rev. Dimitry Razumovsky's ad memoriam" (on the occasion of the 130th Anniversary of the Moscow Conservatory) September 3–8, 1996.* 2 vols. Moscow: Kompozitor, 2000.

Luppov, S. P. "Prodazha v Moskve uchebnykh psaltyrei" [The sale in Moscow of educational psalters]. In *Knigotorgovoe i bibliotechnoe delo v Rossii v XVII–pervoi polovine XIX v.* [Bookselling and bibliographic affairs in Russia in the 17th–first half of the 19th centuries], ed. S. P. Luppov and N. B. Paramonova, 6–21. Leningrad: Biblioteka AN SSSR, 1981.

L'vov, N. A., and Ivan Prach. *Russkie narodnye pesni, sobrannye N. A. L'vovim. Napevy zapisal i garmonizoval Ivan Prach* [Russian folk songs, collected by N. A. L'vov, tunes written down and harmonized by Ivan Prach]. 4th ed. Edited by A. S. Suvorin. St. Petersburg: A. S. Suvorin, 1896.

Maikov, V. V. *Kniga pistsovaia po Novgorodu Velikomu kontsa XVI v.* [The cadastres of Great Novgorod from the end of the sixteenth century]. St. Petersburg: Tip. M. A. Aleksandrova, 1911.

———. "Poslanie k patriarkhu Germogenu o zloupotreblenii v tserkovnom penii 'khabuva'" [A letter to

Patriarch Germogen on the abuse of the *khabuva* in church singing]. In *Sergeiu Fedorovichu Platonovu ucheniki, druz'ia i pochitateli* [To Sergei Fedorovich Platonov from students, friends, and admirers], 415–31. St. Petersburg, 1911. Reprint, Düsseldorf: Brücken-Verlag and Vaduz, Liechtenstein: Europe-Printing, 1970.

Makarii, Archbishop of Don and Novocherkassk. *Arkheologicheskoe opisanie tserkovnykh drevnostei v Novgorode i ego okrestnostiakh* [Archaeological description of ecclesiastical antiquities in Novgorod and its environs]. Part 2. Moscow: V Tip. V. Got'e, 1860.

Maliaras, Nikos. *Die Orgel im byzantinischen Hofzeremoniell des 9. und 10. Jahrhunderts.* Miscellanea Byzantina Monacensia 33. Munich: Institut für Byzantinistik und Neugriechische Philologie der Universität, 1991.

Malinin, V. N. *Desiat' slov Zlatostruia XII veka* [Ten sermons of the *Zlatostrui* of the 12th century]. St. Petersburg: Imp. Akademii nauk, 1910.

Margeret, Jacques. *Un mousquetaire à Moscou: Mémoires sur la première révolution russe, 1604–1614.* Edited by Alexandre Bennigsen. Paris: La Découverte/Maspero, 1983.

———. *The Russian Empire and Grand Duchy of Muscovy: A 17th-Century French Account.* Translated by Chester S. L. Dunning. Pittsburgh: University of Pittsburgh Press, 1983.

Markov, A. V. "Materialy i issledovaniia po izucheniiu narodnoi pesni i muzyki" [Materials and investigations on the study of folk songs and music]. *Trudy muzykal'noi etnograficheskoi komissii* [Reports of the musical ethnographic commission] 1 (1906).

Markov, A. V., A. L. Maslov, and B. A. Bogoslovskii. *Materialy sobrannye v Arkhangel'skoi gubernii letom 1901 goda* [Materials collected in Arkhangel'sk province in the summer of 1901]. Moscow: Tip. K. L. Men'shova, 1905.

Maskiewicz, Samuel, and Bogusław Kazimierz Maskiewicz. *Pamiętniki Samuela i Bogusława Kazimierza Maskiewiczów* [The diaries of Samuel and Bogusław Kazimierz Maskiewicz]. Edited by A. Sajkowski. Wrocław: Zakład narodowy im. Ossolińskich, 1961.

Maslov, A. "Lira." *RMG* (1902).

Massa, Isaac. *A Short History of the Beginnings and Origins of These Present Wars in Moscow under the Reign of Various Sovereigns down to the Year 1610.* Translated and edited by G. Edward Orchard. Toronto: University of Toronto Press, 1982.

Massa, Isaak, and Petr Petrei. *O nachale voin i smut v Moskovii* [On the beginning of the wars and the Time of Troubles in Muscovy]. In the series Istoriia Rossii i doma Romanovykh v memuarakh sovremennikov XVII–XX vv. [A history of Russia and the house of the Romanovs in memoirs by contemporaries, 17th–20th centuries]. Moscow: Fond Sergeia Dubova, 1997.

Massie, Robert. *Peter the Great: His Life and World.* New York: Ballantine, 1980.

"Materialy dlia arkheologicheskogo slovaria" [Materials for an archaeological dictionary]. *Drevnosti* 2 (1870).

Mathiesen, Thomas J. *Apollo's Lyre.* Lincoln: University of Nebraska Press, 1999.

Mazon, André, and F. Cocron. *La comédie d'Artaxerxès (Artakserksovo deistvo) présentée en 1672 au Tsar Alexis par Gregorii le Pasteur.* Paris: Institut d'Études Slaves de l'Université de Paris, 1954.

Mel'gunov, Iu. N., comp. *Russkie pesni, neposredstvenno s golosov naroda zapisannye i s ob"iasneniiami izdannye Iu. N. Mel'gunovym* [Russian songs, written down directly from the voices of the people and published with commentaries by Iu. N. Mel'gunov]. Fasc. 1. Moscow: E. Lissner i Iu. Roman, 1879.

Mel'nikov, P. "Dorozhnye zametki" [Observations from on the road]. In *Polnoe sobranie sochinenii* [Complete collected works]. Vol. 12. St. Petersburg, 1898.

Mendel, H. *Musikalisches Conversations-Lexikon.* 11 vols. Berlin: Robert Oppenheim, 1870–79.

Metallov, V. M. *Ocherk istorii pravoslavnogo tserkovnogo penii v Rossii* [An essay on the history of Orthodox church singing in Russia]. Moscow: A. I. Snegireva, 1915.

———. *Osmoglasie znamennogo rospeva* [The octoechos of the *znamennyi* chant]. Moscow: Sinodal'naia tip., 1899.

———. *Russkaia simiografiia* [Russian sign notation]. Moscow: Izd. Mosk. arkheologicheskogo instituta, 1912. Translated as *Russische Semeiographie*. In Sagners slavistische Sammlung 7. Munich: O. Sagner, 1984.

———. "Sinodal'nye byvshie patriarshie pevchie" [The Synodal, formerly patriarchal, singers]. *RMG* 1898, nos. 10–12; 1901, nos. 17, 19–26; also published as a separate offprint.

Meyerberg, Augustin [Avgustin Meierberg]. *Al'bom Meierberga: Vidy i bytovye kartiny Rossii XVII veka* [Meyerberg's album: Views and scenes of daily life in Russia in the 17th century]. Edited by Friedrich Adelung. St. Petersburg: A. S. Suvorin, 1903.

———. *Puteshestvie v Moskoviiu barona Avgustina Meierberga* [A journey through Muscovy by Baron Augustin Meyerberg]. *Utverzhdenie dinastii* [The establishment of the dynasty]. Edited by A. Liberman and S. Shokarev, 43–184. In the series Istoriia Rossii i doma Romanovykh v memuarakh sovremennikov XVII–XX vv. [A history of Russia and the house of the Romanovs in memoirs by contemporaries, 17th–20th centuries]. Moscow: Fond Sergeia Dubova, 1997.

Mezenets, Aleksandr. *Azbuka znamennogo peniia (Izveshchenie o soglasneishikh pometakh) startsa Aleksandra Mezentsa (1668-go goda)* [Alphabet of *znamennoe* singing (Report about the most harmonious notational signs) by the monk Aleksandr Mezenets, 1668]. Edited by S. V. Smolenskii. Kazan: Tip. Imp. Universiteta i Tipo-litografiia N. Danilova, 1888.

Miege, Guy. *A Relation of Three Embassies from His Sacred Majestie Charles II, to the Great Duke of Muscovie, the King of Sweden, and the King of Denmark.* London: J. Starkey, 1669.

Mikulinskaia letopis', sostavlennaia po drevnim aktam, ot 1354 do 1678 goda [The Mikulin Chronicle, compiled according to ancient acts, 1354–1678]. Moscow: V Tip. V. Got'e, 1854.

Miller, A., and A. de Mortillet. "Sur un bandeau en or avec figures Scythes découvert dans un kourgan de la Russie Méridionale." *L'Homme préhistorique* 9 (1904).

Miquel, A. *La géographie humaine du monde musulman jusqu'au milieu du XI siècle.* Paris: Mouton, 1980.

Mishina, E. A. *Russkaia graviura na dereve XVII–XVIII vv. / Russian Woodcuts of the 17th–18th Centuries.* St. Petersburg: ARS and Dmitrii Bulanin, 1998.

Moore, Thomas, trans. *The Odes of Anacreon.* New York: Putnam's, 1903.

Mooser, Robert-Aloys. *L'opéra-comique français en Russie au XVIIIe siècle.* Geneva: R. Kister, 1954.

Mordvinov, A. "Vesna v Kurskoi gubernii" [Spring in Kursk province]. *Vsemirnaia illiustratsiia* [Illustrated world] 120 (1871).

Morosan, Vladimir. *Choral Performance in Pre-Revolutionary Russia.* Russian Music Studies 17. Ann Arbor: UMI Research Press, 1986.

———. "*Penie* and *Musikiia*: Aesthetic Changes in Russian Liturgical Singing during the Seventeenth Century." *St. Vladimir's Theological Quarterly* 23, nos. 3–4 (1979): 149–79.

———, ed. *Tysiacha let russkoi tserkovnoi muzyki / One Thousand Years of Russian Church Music.* Vol. 1 of Monuments of Russian Sacred Music series 1. Washington D.C.: Musica Russica, 1991.

Morozov, P. O. *Istoriia russkogo teatra do poloviny XVIII stoletiia* [History of the Russian theater to the middle of the 18th century]. St. Petersburg: Tip. V. Demakova, 1889.

Muller, Alexander V., trans. and ed. *The Spiritual Regulation of Peter the Great.* Seattle: University of Washington Press, 1972.

Muratova, Irina. "Debiut rossiiskogo muzykal'nogo: Beseda" [A Russian musical debut: A conversation]. By E. Pol'diaeva. *Muzykal'naia akademiia* [Musical academy] 2 (1992): 119–20.

Myers, Gregory, comp. *The Lavrsky Troitsky Kondakar.* Monumenta Slavico-Byzantina et Mediaevalia Europensia 4. Sofia: Heron, 1994.

"Nachalo stsenichnykh predstavlenii v XVII v. v Moskve" [The beginning of stage presentations in Moscow in the 17th century]. *Vsemirnaia illiustratsiia* [Illustrated world] 110–11 (1871).

Nasonov, A. N., ed. *Novgorodskaia pervaia letopis' starshego i mladshego izvodov* [The Novgorod I Chronicle in the earlier and later recensions]. Moscow: Izd-vo AN SSSR, 1950.

———, ed. *Pskovskie letopisi* [Pskov chronicles]. Vol. 1, Moscow: Izd. AN SSSR, 1941; Vol. 2, Moscow: Izd-vo AN SSSR, 1955.

Nazarenko, A. V., ed. *Nemetskie latinoiazychnye istochniki IX–XI vekov. Teksty, perevod, kommentarii* [German sources in Latin from the 9th–11th centuries. Texts, translation, commentary]. In Drevneishie istochniki po istorii Vostochnoi Evropy [The earliest sources for the history of Eastern Europe]. Moscow: Nauka, 1993.

Nikol'skii, A. I. *Opisanie rukopisei, khraniashchikhsia v arkhive Sviateishego pravitel'stvuiushchego sinoda* [Description of manuscripts in the archive of the Holy Ruling Synod]. St. Petersburg: Sinodal'naia tip., 1904.

Nikol'skii, K. T. *O sluzhbakh russkoi tserkvi, byvshikh v prezhnikh pechatnykh bogosluzhebnykh knigakh* [About the services of the Russian Church in early printed liturgical books]. St. Petersburg: V Tip. Tovarshchestva "Obshchestvennaia pol'za," 1885.

Nikol'skii, N. K., Kh. M. Loparev, V. I. Sreznevskii, A. A. Titov, et al. *Opisanie rukopisei Kirillo-Belozerskogo monastyria, sostavlennoe v kontse XV veka* [Description of manuscripts of the St. Cyril–Belozersk Monastery, compiled at the end of the fifteenth century]. Pamiatniki drevnei pis'mennosti [Monuments of early writing] 113. St. Petersburg: Sinodal'naia tip., 1897.

Nosov, I. *Khronika russkogo teatra* [Chronicle of the Russian theater]. Moscow: n.p., 1863. Supplement published by E. B. Barsov. Moscow: Izd. Imp. obshchestva istorii i drevnosti rossiiskikh, 1883.

Novgorodskie pistsovye knigi izdannye Arkheograficheskoi komissiei [Novgorod cadastres published by the Archaeographic Commission]. 6 vols. St. Petersburg: Tip. Bezobrazova, 1859–1910. Reprint, Slavistic Printings and Reprintings, no. 212, vols. 1–3. The Hague: Mouton, 1969.

Okenfuss, Max J. *The Discovery of Childhood in Russia: The Evidence of the Slavic Primer.* Newtonville, Mass.: Oriental Research Partners, 1980.

———. "Education in Russia in the first half of the eighteenth century." Ph.D. diss., Harvard University, 1970.

Okenfuss, Max J., trans. and ed. *The Travel Diary of Peter Tolstoi, A Muscovite in Early Modern Europe.* De Kalb: Northern Illinois University Press, 1987.

Okulich-Kazarin, N. F. *Sputnik po drevnemu Pskovu* [Guide to old Pskov]. Pskov: Izd. Pskovskogo arkheologicheskogo obshchestva, 1911.

Olearius, Adam. *Opisanie puteshestviia v Moskoviiu i cherez Moskoviiu v Persiiu i obratno* [Description of travels to Muscovy and through Muscovy to Persia and back]. Introduction, translation, notes, and index by A. M. Loviagin. St. Petersburg: A. S. Suvorin, 1906.

———. *Vermehrte Newe Beschreibung Der Muscowitischen vnd Persischen Reyse.* Edited by D. Lohmeier. Tübingen: Max Niemeyer Verlag, 1971.

Ol'shevskaia, L. A., and S. N. Travnikov, eds. *Puteshestvie stol'nika P. A. Tolstogo po Evrope 1697–1699* [The travels of *stol'nik* P. A. Tolstoi in Europe, 1697–99]. Moscow: Nauka, 1992.

Opisanie rukopisei kn. P. P. Viazemskogo [A description of the manuscripts of Prince P. P. Viazemskii]. Pamiatniki drevnei pis'mennosti i iskusstva [Monuments of early writing and art] 119. St. Petersburg: Tip. glavnogo upr. delov, 1902.

"Opisanie Sanktpeterburga i Kronshlota v 1710-m i 1711-m gg." [A Description of St. Petersburg and Kronshlot in 1710 and 1711]. *Russkaia starina* [Russian antiquity] (October 1882): 32–60; (November 1882): 293–320.

"Opyt russkogo prostonarodnogo slovotolkovateliia" [Essay in compiling a glossary of the Russian language of the simple folk]. *ChOIDR* 9 (1847): section 4.

Orlov, A. "Chashi gosudarevy" [Toasts to the tsar]. *ChOIDR* 4 (1913), pt. 2: 1–69.

Ovsiannikov, Iu. *Lubok. Russkie narodnye kartinki XVII–XVIII vv. / The Lubok. Russian Broadsides of the 17th–18th Centuries.* Moscow: Sovetskii khudozhnik, 1968.

Pal'chikov, A. E., ed. *Krest'ianskie pesni, zapisannye v sele Nikolaevke Menzelinskogo uezda Ufimskoi gubernii N. E. Pal'chikovym* [Peasant songs collected by N. E. Pal'chikov in the village of Nikolaevka in the Menzelin district of Ufa province]. St. Petersburg: A. E. Pal'chikov, 1888.

Panchenko, F. V., comp. *Pevcheskie rukopisi v sobranii biblioteki Rossiiskoi Akademii nauk* [Notated musical manuscripts in the collection of the library of the Russian Academy of Sciences]. St. Petersburg: Biblioteka Rossiiskoi Akademii nauk, 1994.

Papadopulo-Keramevs, K. I. "Proiskhozhdenie notnogo muzykal'nogo pis'ma u severnykh i iuzhnykh slavian po pamiatnikam drevnosti, preimushchestvenno vizantiiskim" [The origin of musical notation among the northern and southern Slavs according to documents from antiquity, primarily Byzantine]. *Vestnik arkheologii i istorii* [Archaeological and historical journal] 17 (1906): section 1.

Papadopoulos, George-Julius, and Claudia Jensen. "'A Confusion of Glory': Orthodox Visitors as Sources for Muscovite Musical Practice (late 16th–mid-17th century)." *Intersections: Canadian Journal of Music* 26, no. 1 (2005): 3–33.

Parfent'ev, N. P. "Aftografy vydaiushchegosia russkogo muzykal'nogo teoretika XVII v. Aleksandra Mezentsa (Stremoukhova)" [Autographs of the outstanding 17th-century Russian music theorist Aleksandr Mezenets (Stremoukhov)]. *PKNO for 1990* (1992): 173–85.

———. *Drevnerusskoe pevcheskoe iskusstvo v dukhovnoi kul'ture rossiiskogo gosudarstva XVI–XVII vv.* [The old Russian art of chanting in the religious culture of the Russian state in the 16th–17th centuries]. Sverdlovsk: Izd. Ural'skogo universiteta, 1991.

———. "O deiatel'nosti komissii po ispravleniiu drevnerusskikh pevcheskikh knig v XVII v." [On the work of the commission for the correction of old Russian singing books in the 17th century]. *AE for 1984* (1986): 128–39.

———. *Professional'nye muzykanty rossiiskogo gosudarstva XVI–XVII vekov* [Professional musicians of the Russian state in the 16th–17th centuries]. Cheliabinsk: Kniga, 1991.

Parfent'ev, N. P., and N. V. Parfent'eva. *Usol'skaia (Stroganovskaia) shkola v russkoi muzyke XVI–XVII vekov* [The Usol'e (Stroganov) school in Russian music in the 16th–17th centuries]. Cheliabinsk: Kniga, 1993.

Parfent'ev, N. P., and Z. M. Guseinova. *Aleksandr Mezenets i prochie, Izveshchenie . . . zhelaiushchim uchitsia peniiu, 1670 g.* [Aleksandr Mezenets and others, the "Report . . . for those who wish to learn singing," 1670]. Introduction, [facsimile] publication, translation of the documents, and historical study by N. P. Parfent'ev. Commentary and analysis of the documents and deciphering of the notation by Z. M. Guseinova. Cheliabinsk: Kniga, 1996.

Parfent'eva, N. V. *Tvorchestvo masterov drevnerusskogo pevcheskogo iskusstva XVI–XVII vv.* [Works of masters of old Russian singing, 16th–17th centuries]. Cheliabinsk, 1997.

Parsons, Charles H., comp. *Opera Composers and Their Works.* 4 vols. The Mellen Opera Reference Index. Lewiston, N.Y.: Edwin Mellen, 1986.

Paterik Kievskogo Pecherskogo monastyria [*Paterik* from the Kievan Caves Monastery]. St. Petersburg: [Izd. Imperatorskoi arkheograficheskoi komissii], 1911.

Patriarshaia, ili Nikonovskaia, letopis' [The Patriarchal or Nikonian chronicle]. St. Petersburg: Arkheograficheskaia komissiia, 1862.

Paul of Aleppo. *The Travels of Macarius, Patriarch of Antioch: Written by his attendant Archdeacon Paul of Aleppo.* Translated and edited by F. C. Balfour. 2 vols. London: Printed for the Oriental Translation Committee, 1829–36.

Pekarskii, P. P. *Nauka i literatura pri Petre Velikom* [Science and literature during the reign of Peter the Great]. 2 vols. St. Petersburg: V Tip. tovarshchestva "Obshchestvennaia pol'za," 1862.

———. *Opisanie slaviano-russkikh knig i tipografii, 1698–1725* [Catalog of Slavonic-Russian books and presses, 1698–1725]. St. Petersburg: V Tip. tovarshchestva "Obshchestvennaia pol'za," 1862.

Perepelitsyn, P. D. *Istoriia muzyki v Rossii* [History of music in Russia]. St. Petersburg: M. O. Vol'f, 1888.

Perepisnaia kniga goroda Moskvy 1638 goda [The Moscow census book of 1638]. Moscow: Tip. M. P. Shchepkina, 1881.

"Perepisnaia okladnaia kniga po Novugorodu Vot'skoi piatiny" [Census and tax register of Novgorod's Vot'ska county]. *Vremennik Imp. Obshchestva istorii i drevnostei Rossiiskikh* [Annals of the Moscow Society for Russian History and Antiquities] 11 (1851): materialy, 1–464.

Perepisnye knigi goroda Moskvy [Census records of the city of Moscow]. Moscow: Gorodskaia tip., 1886.

Peretts, V. N. *Istoriko-literaturnye issledovaniia i materialy* [Historical and literary studies and materials]. St. Petersburg: Tip. F. Vaisberga i P. Gershunina, 1900.

———. "Kukol'nyi teatr na Rusi" [Puppet theater in Rus']. *Ezhegodnik Imp. teatrov* [Annual of the Imperial Theaters]. 1894–95 season, appendix.

Perfecky, George A., trans. and ed. *The Hypatian Codex Part Two: The Galician-Volynian Chronicle.* Harvard Series in Ukrainian Studies 16, no. 2. Munich: Wilhelm Fink Verlag, 1973.

Perrie, Maureen. *Pretenders and Popular Monarchism in Early Modern Russia: The False Tsars of the Time of Troubles.* Cambridge: Cambridge University Press, 1995.

Perrot, Jean. *L'orgue de ses origines hellénistiques à la fin du XIIIe siècle.* Paris: A. et J. Picard, 1965. English translation, slightly abridged, as *The Organ from Its Invention to the End of the Thirteenth Century.* Translated by Norma Deane. New York: Oxford University Press, 1971.

Pervoe uchenie musikiiskikh soglasii [First lesson in musical concordances]. OLDP Izdaniia 6. St. Petersburg: Lit. A. Beggrova, 1877.

Petrejus, Petrus [Petr Petrei]. *Istoriia o velikom kniazhestve Moskovskom* [History of the great principality of Moscow]. *O nachale voin i smut v Moskovii* [On the beginning of the wars and the Time of Troubles in Muscovy]. Edited by A. Liberman and S. Shokarev, 151-464. In the series Istoriia Rossii i doma Romanovykh v memuarakh sovremennikov XVII–X vv. [A history of Russia and the house of the Romanovs in memoirs by contemporaries, 17th–20th centuries]. Moscow: Fond Sergeia Dubova, 1997.

———. *Reliatsiia Petra Petreia o Rossii nachala XVII v.* [Petrus Petrejus's *Relatio* on Russia at the beginning of the 17th century]. Edited by Iu. A. Limonov and V. I. Buganov. Moscow: AN SSSR, 1976.

Petrov, N. "Podlinnost' pouchenii Feodosiia Pecherskogo o pitii i chashakh troparnykh i o kazniakh bozhiikh" [The authenticity of the instructions of Feodosii Pecherskii about drinking and chanted toasts and about God's punishments]. *Izvestiia Otdeleniia russkogo iazyka i slovesnosti Imp. Akademii nauk* [Proceedings of the Department of Russian Language and Literature of the Imperial Academy of Sciences] 2, bk. 3 (1897).

Petrovskaia, I. F. *Istochnikovedenie istorii russkoi muzykal'noi kul'tury XVIII–nachala XX veka* [Source studies in the history of Russian musical culture, 18th–beginning of the 20th centuries], 2nd exp. ed. Moscow: Muzyka, 1989.

Petukhov, M. O. "Ivan Aleksandrov, odin iz poslednikh predstavitelei igry na torbane" [Ivan Aleksandrov, one of the last representatives of *torban* playing]. *Vsemirnaia illiustratsiia* [Illustrated world] 12 (1891).

———. *Narodnye muzykal'nye instrumenty Muzeia S.-Peterburgskoi konservatorii* [Folk musical instruments in the Museum of the St. Petersburg Conservatory]. St. Petersburg: Tip. Imp. Akademii nauk, 1884.

Pierling, P. *L'Italie et la Russie au XVI siècle.* Paris: E. Leroux, 1892.

"Pis'ma o Rossii v Ispaniiu Duka de Liriia, byvshego pervym Ispanskim poslannikom v Rossii pri imperatore Petre II i v nachale tsarstvovaniia Anny Ioannovny" [Letters about Russia to Spain by Duke de Liria, the first Spanish emissary in Russia during the reign of Emperor Peter II and the beginning of the reign of Anna Ioannovna]. In *Osmnadtsatyi vek* [Eighteenth century], 2:5–198; 3:27–132. Moscow: P. Bartenev, 1869.

Pistsovaia i perepisnaia knigi XVII veka po Nizhnemu Novgorodu [A cadastre and census record from the 17th century for the city of Nizhnii Novgorod]. *RIB* 17. St. Petersburg: Sinodal'naia tip., 1896.

Pistsovye knigi Riazanskogo kraia [Cadastres of the Riazan district]. Riazan: Tip. M. S. Orlova, 1898–1904.

Platonov, S. F. "Iz bytovoi istorii petrovskoi epokhi" [From the history of daily life in the Petrine era]. *Izvestiia Akademii nauk* 8 (1926).

———. *Moscow and the West.* Translated by J. L. Wieczynski. Hattiesburg, Miss.: Academic International, 1972.

Podobedova, O. I. *Miniatiury russkikh istoricheskikh rukopisei. K istorii russkogo litsevogo letopisaniia* [Miniatures in Russian historical manuscripts: Toward a history of Russian illuminated manuscript writing]. Moscow: Nauka, 1965.

Poe, Marshall. *Foreign Descriptions of Muscovy: An Analytic Bibliography of Primary and Secondary Sources.* Columbus, Ohio: Slavica, 1995.

Pogodin, M. P. *Drevniaia russkaia istoriia do mongol'skogo iga* [History of early Russia to the Mongol yoke]. Moscow: Sinodal'naia tip., 1871. Reprint, Slavistic Printings and Reprintings 256, no. 3. The Hague: Mouton, 1971.

Pokrovskii, A. A. *Drevnee pskovo-novgorodskoe pis'mennoe nasledie* [The written heritage of old Pskov and Novgorod]. Moscow: Sinodal'naia tip., 1916.

Poliński, A. *Dzieje muzyki polskiej w zarysie* [A history of Polish music in outline]. Lwów: H. Altenberg, 1907.

Popova, O. *Les miniatures russes du XIe au XVe siècle.* Leningrad: Aurora, 1975.

Porfir'eva, A. L. "Legenda o kapelle gertsoga golshtinskogo i podlinnaia istoriia pridvornogo orkestra v 1702–1728 gg." [The legend of the Duke of Holstein's cappella and the true history of the court orchestra, 1702–1728]. *PKNO for 1996* (1998): 168–85.

"Posol'stvo Tsaria i Velikogo Kniazia Petra Alekseevicha k rimskomu imperatoru Leopol'du v 1697–1698 godakh" [Tsar and Great Prince Peter Alekseevich's embassy to the Roman Emperor Leopold in 1697–98]. *Pamiatniki diplomaticheskikh snoshenii* [Monuments of diplomatic relations] 8 (1867): cols. 750–1416.

Potebnia, A. *K istorii zvukov russkogo iazyka* [On the history of the sounds of the Russian language]. Voronezh: V Tip. V. I. Isaeva, 1876.

Pouncy, Carolyn Johnston. *The* Domostroi: *Rules for Russian Households in the Time of Ivan the Terrible.* Ithaca, N.Y.: Cornell University Press, 1994.

Povetkin, V. I. "Drevnii novgorodskii odnostrunnyi muzykal'nyi instrument (K voprosu o drevnerusskom smyke)" [An old Novgorodian single-stringed musical instrument (On the question of the old Russian *smyk*)]. *PKNO for 1998* (1999): 180–86.

———. "Gudebnye sosudy drevnego Novgoroda" [Musical vessels of old Novgorod]. *PKNO for 1984* (1986): 155–67.

———. "Mir muzyki drevnikh novgorodtsev. Arkheologicheskie otkrytiia 2000 goda" [The musical world of the ancient Novgorodians. Archaeological discoveries in 2000]. *Proshloe Novgoroda i novgorodskoi zemli: Materialy nauchnoi konferentsii 2001–2002 gg.* [The past in Novgorod and the Novgorodian lands: Materials from a scientific conference, 2001–2002], pt. 1: 23–34. Novgorod: Novgorodskii gos. universitet imeni Iaroslava Mudrogo, 2002.

———. "Otkrytie treshchotok novgorodskikh" [The discovery of Novgorodian rattles]. *PKNO for 2000* (2001): 160–66.

———. "'Russkii' izobrazitel'nyi kanon na muzykal'nye instrumenty" [The "Russian" representational canon of musical instruments]. *PKNO for 1989* (1990): 136–59.

———. "V mire muzyke drevnego Novgoroda i Rusy. Arkheologicheskie otkrytiia 2000 g." [In the musical world of ancient Novgorod and Rusa: Archaeological discoveries in 2000]. *Novgorod i novgorodskaia zemlia: Istoriia i arkheologiia / Novgorod and [the] Novgorod Region: History and Archaeology* 15 (2001): 59–66.

Powell, John. *Music and Theatre in France, 1600–1680.* Oxford: Oxford University Press, 2000.

Pozhidaeva, G. A. "Formy izlozheniia demestvennogo mnogogolosiia" [The presentation of *demestvennyi* polyphony]. *AE* 1981 (1982): 123–33.

———. "Prostrannye raspevi drevnei Rusi XI–XVII vekov" [The long (or drawn-out) chants of early Russia of the 11th–17th centuries]. Moscow, 1999.

———. *Traditsii russkogo tserkovnogo penii. Vypusk I. Demestvennyi raspev XVI–XVIII vv.* [Traditions of Russian church singing. Part 1. *Demestvennyi* singing, 16th–18th centuries]. Moscow: Kompozitor, 1999.

———. "Vidy demestvennogo mnogogolosia" [Aspects of *demestvennyi* polyphony]. In *Russkaia khorovaia muzyka XVI–XVIII vekov* [Russian choral music of the 16th–18th centuries], 58–81. Moscow: Gos. muzykal'no-pedagogicheskii institut im. Gnesinykh, 1986.

"Pravilo Kiurilla mitropolita rus'skago" [The rule of Kirill, Russian metropolitan]. *Russkie dostopamiatnosti* [Russian monuments]. (Moscow, 1815), pt. 1: 104–18.

Preobrazhenskii, A. V. *Ocherk istorii tserkovnogo peniia v Rossii* [Essay on the history of church chant in Russia]. 2nd ed. St. Petersburg: n.p., 1910.

———. "O skhodstve russkogo muzykal'nogo pis'ma s grecheskim v pevcheskikh rukopisiakh XI–XII vv." [On the resemblance of the Russian notation to the Greek in musical manuscripts of the 11th–12th centuries]. *RMG* 16 (1909), nos. 8, 9, 10.

———. *Vopros o edinoglasnom penii v russkoi tserkvi XVII-go veka* [The question of monophonic singing in the Russian Church in the seventeenth century]. Pamiatniki drevnei pis'mennosti i iskusstva [Monuments of early writing and art] 155. [St. Petersburg]: OLDP, 1904.

Privalov, N. I. *Gudok, drevne-russkii muzykal'nyi instrument* [The *gudok,* an old Russian musical instrument]. St. Petersburg, 1904.

———. *Lira, russkii narodnyi muzykal'nyi instrument* [The *lira,* a Russian folk musical instrument]. St. Petersburg, 1905.

———. "Lozhki. Russkii narodnyi muzykal'nyi instrument" [Spoons, a Russian folk musical instrument]. *RMG* (1908), nos. 28–33, 36.

———. *Muzykal'nye dukhovye instrumenty russkogo naroda* [The musical wind instruments of the Russian people]. 2 vols. St. Petersburg: Tip. I. N. Skorokholova, 1906–8).

Prokhorov, V. A. *Khristianskie i russkie drevnosti* [Christian and Russian antiquities]. St. Petersburg, 1871.

Prokopovich, Feofan. *Sochineniia F. Prokopovicha* [Works of Feofan Prokopovich]. St. Petersburg, 1761.

Propp, V. Ja. *Russian Folk Lyrics.* Translated and edited by Roberta Reeder. Bloomington: Indiana University Press, 1993.

Protopopov, V. V. "Chetyrekhgolosnaia khorovaia kompozitsiia tsaria Alekseia Mikhailovicha" [A four-part choral composition by Tsar Aleksei Mikhailovich]. *PKNO for 1991* (1997): 107–10.

———. *Muzyka na Poltavskuiu pobedu* [Music for the victory at Poltava]. PRMI 2. Moscow: Muzyka, 1973.

———. "Muzyka petrovskogo vremeni o pobede pod Poltavoi" [Petrine-era music on the Poltava victory]. *SM* 12 (1971): 97–105.

————. "Notnaia biblioteka Stroganovykh v Sol'vychegodske (1627 g.)" [The music library of the Stroganovs in Sol'vychegodsk (1627)]. *PKNO for 1981* (1983): 182–86.

————. "Notnaia biblioteka tsaria Fedora Alekseevicha" [The music library of Tsar Fedor Alekseevich]. *PKNO for 1976* (1977): 119–33.

————. *Russkaia mysl' o muzyke v XVII veke* [Russian thought about music in the 17th century]. Moscow: Muzyka, 1989.

————. *Russkoe tserkovnoe penie: Opyt bibliograficheskogo ukazatelia ot serediny XVI veka po 1917 god* [Russian church singing: An essay in creating a bibliographic index from the mid-16th century to 1917]. Moscow: Muzyka, 2000.

Prussak, A. V. *Opisanie azbukovnikov, khraniashchikhsia v rukopisnom otdelenii Imperatorskoi publichnoi biblioteki* [Description of the *azbukovniki* in the Manuscript Division of the Imperial Public Library]. Pamiatniki drevnei pis'mennosti [Monuments of early writing] 186. St. Petersburg: M. A. Aleksandrov, 1915.

"Pskov i ego prigorody: Pistsovaia kniga po Pskovu i ego prigorodam XVI v." [Pskov and its suburbs: A cadastre from Pskov and its suburbs from the sixteenth century]. *Sbornik Moskovskogo Arkhiva Ministerstva iustitsii* [Collection of the Moscow Archive of the Ministry of Justice] 5 (1913); 6 (1914).

Pushkarev, Sergei G. *Dictionary of Russian Historical Terms from the 11th century to 1917.* New Haven: Yale University Press, 1970.

Putilov, B. N., ed. *Pesni, sobrannye P. N. Rybnikovym* [Songs collected by P. N. Rybnikov]. 3 vols. Petrozavodsk: Kareliia, 1989–91.

Pypin, A. N. *Istoriia russkoi literatury* [History of Russian literature]. 4 vols. St. Petersburg: M. M. Stasiulevich, 1898. 2nd exp. ed. St. Petersburg: M. M. Stasiulevich, 1902–3. Reprint, Slavistic Printings and Reprintings 92, nos. 1–4. The Hague: Mouton, 1968.

————. "Petr Velikii v narodnom predanii" [Peter the Great in folk legend]. *Vestnik Evropy* [European herald] (August 1897): 640–90.

————. "Puteshestviia za granitsu vremen Petra Velikogo" [Travels abroad in the time of Peter the Great] *Vestnik Evropy* [European herald] 9 (1897): 244–87; 10 (1897): 692–741.

Ramazanova, N. V. "'Skomorosh'e delo' v ocherkakh N. F. Findeizena po istorii muzyki v Rossii" ["*Skomorokh* activities" in N. F. Findeizen's works on the history of music in Russia]. In *Skomorokhi: Problemy i perspektivy izucheniia* [*Skomorokhi:* Scholarly problems and perspectives], ed. V. V. Koshelev, 41–50. St. Petersburg: Rossiiskii institut istorii iskusstv, 1994.

Razumovskii, D. V. "Gosudarevy pevchie d'iaki XVII veka" [The sovereign singers in the 17th century]. *Obshchestvo drevne-russkogo iskusstva* [Society for early Russian art] (1873): 153–81.

————. "O notnykh bezlineinykh rukopisiakh" [On notated staffless manuscripts]. *Chteniia v Moskovskom Obshchestve liubitelei dukhovnogo prosveshcheniia* [Readings of the Moscow Society of Friends of Religious Education] 1 (1863): 55–164.

————. *Patriarshie pevchie diaki i poddiaki i gosudarevy pevchie diaki* [The patriarchal singers (*diaki* and *poddiaki*) and the sovereign singers]. [St. Petersburg:] N. F. Findeizen, 1895.

————. *Tserkovnoe penie v Rossii* [Church singing in Russia]. Moscow: Tip. T. Ris, 1867.

————. "Tserkovnoe russkoe penie" [Russian church singing]. *Trudy I-go arkheologicheskogo s"ezda v Moskve, 1869 g.* [Report of the First Archaeological Congress in Moscow, 1869] (1871).

Razumovskii, D. V., I. A. Fortunov, and G. Karpov. *Krug tserkovnogo drevnego znamennogo peniia* [The cycle of the old *znamennoe* church singing]. St. Petersburg: Tip. V. S. Balasheva, 1884.

Reese, Gustave. *Music in the Middle Ages.* New York: Norton, 1940.

Reutenfels, Jacob [Iakov Reitenfel's]. *Skazaniia svetleishemu gertsogu toskanskomu Koz'me Tret'emu o Moskovii* [Reports on Muscovy to the honorable Duke of Tuscany, Cosimo III]. *Utverzhdenie dinastii* [The establishment of the dynasty]. Edited by A. Liberman and S. Shokarev, 231–406.

In the series Istoriia Rossii i doma Romanovykh v memuarakh sovremennikov XVII–XX vv.
[A history of Russia and the house of the Romanovs in memoirs by contemporaries, 17th–
20th centuries]. Moscow: Fond Sergeia Dubova, 1997. [Reprint of translation in *ChOIDR* 3
(1905) and 3 (1906).]

Riemann, Hugo. *Muzykal'nyi slovar'* [Music dictionary]. 3 vols. Moscow: P. Iurgenson, 1901–4.

[Rigel'man, A.] *Letopisnoe povestvovanie o Maloi Rossii i eia narode i kazakakh voobshche . . . Sobrano i
sostavleno chrez trudy inzhen., gen.-maiora i kavalera Aleksandra Rigel'mana, 1785–86* [Annals-
chronicle about Little Russia and its people and about Cossacks in general . . . collected
and compiled by the labors of engineer, general major, and cavalier Aleksandr Rigel'man,
1785–86]. Moscow: Universitetskaia tip., 1847. Also published in *ChOIDR* 5 (1846); 6–9 (1847);
6 (1848). Ukrainian edition issued as *Litopysna opovid' pro Malu Rosiiu*. Kiev: Lybid, 1994.

Rinhuber, Laurent. *Relation du voyage en Russie fait en 1684*. Berlin: A. Cohn, 1883.

Robinson, A. N. *Bor'ba idei v russkoi literature XVII veka* [The conflict of ideas in Russian literature in
the 17th century]. Moscow: Nauka, 1974.

———, ed. *Pervye p'esy russkogo teatra* [The first plays of the Russian theater]. Vol. 1 of *Ranniaia
russkaia dramaturgiia (XVII–pervaia polovina XVIII v.)* [Early Russian dramaturgy, 17th–first
half of the 18th century]. Edited by A. N. Robinson et al. Moscow: Nauka, 1972.

Rogov, A. I., comp. and ed. *Muzykal'naia estetika Rossii XI–XVIII vekov* [Musical aesthetics in Russia
in the 11th–18th centuries]. Moscow: Muzyka, 1973.

Roizman, L. I. "Iz istorii organnoi kul'tury v Rossii (vtoraia polovina XVII veka)" [On the history of
organ culture in Russia (second half of the 17th century)]. *Voprosy muzykoznaniia* [Questions
of musicology] 3 (1960): 565–97.

———. *Organ v istorii russkoi muzykal'noi kul'tury* [The organ in the history of Russian musical cul-
ture]. Moscow: Muzyka, 1979.

Rostovskii, Dimitrii. *Rozhdestvenskaia drama* [Christmas drama]. Edited by E. M. Levashev. Moscow:
Sovetskii kompozitor, 1989.

Rovinskii, D. A. *Podrobnyi slovar' russkikh gravirovannykh portretov* [A detailed dictionary of Russian
engraved portraits]. 4 vols. St. Petersburg, 1886–89.

———. *Russkie narodnye kartinki* [Russian folk drawings]. 5 vols. St. Petersburg: Tip. Imp. Akademii
nauk, 1881–93.

———. *Russkie narodnye kartinki, sobral i opisal D. Rovinskii* [Russian folk drawings, collected and
described by D. Rovinskii]. Edited by N. Sobko. 2 vols. St. Petersburg: Izd. P. Golike, 1900.

Rozov, N. N. "Muzykal'nye instrumenty i ansambli v miniatiurakh Khludovskoi (russkoi) psaltiri"
[Musical instruments and ensembles in the miniatures of the Khludov (Russian) Psalter]. In
Drevnerusskoe iskusstvo: Problemy i atributsii [Old Russian art: Problems and attributions],
91–105. Moscow: Nauka, 1977.

Rybakov, S. G. "Muzyka i pesni ural'skikh musul'man s ocherkom ikh byta" [Music and songs of the
Muslims from the Urals, with an essay concerning their daily life]. *Zapiski Imperatorskoi
Akademii nauk* series 8 [Notes of the Imperial Academy of Sciences], vol. 2, no. 2 (1897).

———. *Tserkovnyi zvon v Rossii* [Church bell ringing in Russia]. St. Petersburg: Tip. E. Evdokimova,
1896.

Rybnikov, P. N., ed. *Pesni, sobrannye P. N. Rybnikovym* [Songs collected by P. N. Rybnikov]. Moscow:
A. Semen, 1861.

Saitov, V. I., and B. L. Modzalevskii, comps. *Moskovskii nekropol'* [Moscow necropolis]. 3 vols. St.
Petersburg: Velikii kniaz, 1907–1908.

Sakharov, I. P. "Issledovaniia o russkom tserkovnom pesnopenii" [Studies of Russian church singing].
Zhurnal Ministerstva narodnogo prosveshcheniia 61 (February 1849): section 2, 147–96; (March
1849): 263–84.

————. *Pesni russkogo naroda* [Songs of the Russian people]. 5 vols. St. Petersburg, 1838.

Samokvasov, D. Ia. "Drevnie zemlianye nasypi i ikh znachenie dlia nauki" [Ancient earthen mounds and their scholarly significance]. *Drevniaia i novaia Rossiia* [Ancient and new Russia] 1, no. 3 (1876).

Sanchuk, G. E. ed., *Koz'ma Prazhskii, cheshskaia khronika* [Cosma of Prague, Czech chronicle]. Moscow: Izd-vo AN SSSR, 1962.

Sander, Elizabeth C. "Social Dancing in Russia at the End of the Petrine Era: Friedrich Wilhelm von Bergholz's *Tagebuch*, 1721–1725." Ph.D. diss., University of Western Ontario, 2002.

Saverkina, I. V., and Iu. N. Semenov. "Orkestr i khor A. D. Menshikova" [The orchestra and choir of A. D. Menshikov]. *PKNO for 1989* (1990): 160–66.

Savvaitov, P. I. *Opisanie starinnykh russkikh utvarei* [Description of old Russian utensils]. St. Petersburg: Akademiia nauk, 1865.

————. *Opisanie Vologodskogo kafedral'nogo sobora* [Description of the Cathedral Church in Vologda]. Moscow: Bakhmetev, 1863.

Saxo Grammaticus. *Danorum Regum Heroumque Historia*. Translated and edited by Eric Christiansen. BAR International series 118(i). Oxford: BAR, 1981.

Sazonova, L. I. "Teatral'naia programma XVII v., 'Aleksei chelovek bozhii'" [A theatrical playbill of the 17th century: *Aleksei, Man of God*]. *PKNO for 1978* (1979): 131–49.

Schidlovsky, Nicolas, ed. *Sticherarium paleoslavicum Petropolitanum: Codex Palaeoslavicus no. 34.7.6, Bibliothecae Academiae Scientiarum Rossicae*, Monumenta Musicae Byzantinae 12. Hauniae: C. A. Reitzel, 2000.

Schlafly, Daniel. "Filippo Balatri in Peter the Great's Russia." *Jahrbücher für Geschichte Osteuropas* (spring 1997): 181–98.

————. "A Muscovite *Boiarynia* Faces Peter the Great's Reforms: Dar'ia Golitsyna between Two Worlds." *Canadian-American Slavic Studies* 31, no. 3 (1997): 249–68.

Schuchardt, Karl. *Arkona, Rethra, Vineta. Ortsuntersuchungen und Ausgrabungen*. Berlin: H. Schoetz, 1926.

Sebastian of Felstin [Sebastian Felsztyna]. *Opusculum musices noviter congestum*. Kraków: Hieronim Vietor, 1534; facsimile edition in Monumenta musicae in Polonia, series D: Bibliotheca antiqua 4. Kraków: Polskie wydawnictwo muzyczne, 1976.

Seregina, N. S. "Otrazhenie istoricheskikh sobytii v stikhire o Temir-Aksake i v drugikh pesnopeniiakh vladimirskoi ikone i problema avtorstva Ivana Groznogo" [The reflection of historical events in the *stikhira* about Tamerlane and in other chants to the Vladimir icon and the problem of Ivan the Terrible's authorship]. *PKNO for 1985* (1987): 148–64.

————. "Pokaiannyi stikh 'Plach Adama o Rae' rospeva Kirila Gomulina" [The repentance verse "Adam's Lament for Paradise" in the version by Kiril Gomulin]. *PKNO for 1983* (1985): 258–62.

Shalina, I. A. "Pskovskie zvonnitsy i kolokol'ni XVI v." [Belfries and bell towers in Pskov in the 16th century]. *PKNO for 1997* (1998): 473–84.

Shambinago, S. K., ed. *Skazanie o Mamaevom poboishche* [The tale of Mamai's bloody battle]. Izdaniia OLDP, no. 125. [St. Petersburg]: Tip. M. A. Aleksandrova, 1907.

Shashkina, T. B. "Kolokola domongol'skoi Rusi po dannym arkheologii" [Bells in pre-Mongol Rus' according to archaeological data]. *PKNO for 1995* (1996): 477–83.

Shboul, A. *Al-Masudi and His World: A Muslim Humanist and His Interest in Non-Muslims*. London: Ithaca Press, 1979.

Shchegoleva, L. I. *Putiatina mineia (XI vek): 1–10 maia* [The Putiatina Mineia (11th century): 1–10 May]. Moscow: Territoriia, 2001.

Shchepkin, V. N. "Dva litsevykh sbornika Istoricheskogo muzeia" [Two illustrated manuscripts in the Historical Museum]. *Arkheologicheskie izvestiia i zametki* [Archaeological reports and notes] 4 (1897): 97–128.

Shchepkina, A. V. *Vospominaniia* [Reminiscences]. Sergiev Posad: Tip. I. I. Ivanova, 1915.

Shchepkina, M. V. *Miniatiury Khludovskoi Psaltyri* [Miniatures of the Khludov Psalter]. Moscow: Iskusstvo, 1977.

Shcherbatov, M. M. *Istoriia Rossiiskaia* [Russian history]. 1771. Reprint, I. P. Khrushchev and A. G. Voronov, eds. St. Petersburg: Izdanie kniazia B. S. Shcherbatova, 1901–3.

Sheffer, P. N., ed. *Sbornik Kirshi Danilova.* [The collection of Kirsha Danilov]. St. Petersburg: Tip. Imp. Akademii nauk, 1901.

Shein, P. V. *Belorusskie narodnye pesni* [Belorussian folk songs]. St. Petersburg: Tip. Maikova, 1874. Reprint, *Belaruskiia narodnyia pesni.* Minsk: Dziarzh. vyd-va BSSR, 1962.

———. *Materialy dlia izucheniia byta i iazyka russkogo naseleniia severo-zapadnogo kraia* [Materials for the study of the daily life and language of the Russian population of the north-western territory]. 3 vols. St. Petersburg: Tip. Imp. Akademii nauk, 1887.

Sheremetev, S. D. *Staraia Vozdvizhenka* [Old Vozdvizhenka Street]. St. Petersburg: Tip. M. M. Stasiulevicha, 1892.

Shindin, B. A. "Problema proiskhozhdeniia demestvennogo rospeva v otechestvennom muzykoznanii" [The problem of the origin of *demestvennyi* chant in our country's musicology]. In *Problemy istorii i teorii drevnerusskoi muzyki* [Problems in the history and theory of old Russian music], ed. A. S. Belonenko and M. V. Brazhnikov, 109–23. Leningrad: Muzyka, 1979.

Shindin, B. A., and I. V. Efimova. *Demestvennyi rospev. Monodiia i mnogogolosie* [*Demestvennyi* singing. Monody and polyphony]. Novosibirsk: Novosibirskaia gos. Konservatoriia im. M. I. Glinki, 1991.

Shirskii, V. "Ocherki drevnikh slaviano-russkikh slovarei" [Essays on old Slavonic-Russian dictionaries]. *Filologicheskie zapiski* [Philological notes] 1869, fasc. I and II.

Shletser, Avgust Ludovik [Schlözer]. *Nestor. Ruskiia Letopisi na drevle-slavenskom iazyke* [Nestor. Russian sources in old Slavonic]. Vol. 1. Translated by Dmitrii Iazykov. St. Petersburg: V Imperatorskoi tip., 1809.

Shliapkin, I. A. *Tsarevna Natal'ia Alekseevna i teatr ee vremeni* [Tsarevna Natal'ia Alekseevna and the theater of her time]. Pamiatniki drevnei pis'mennosti [Monuments of early writing] 128. St. Petersburg: V. Balashev, 1898.

Shtritter, I. [Johann Gotthelf von Stritter]. *Izvestiia vizantiiskikh istorikov* [Reports of Byzantine historians]. St. Petersburg: Tip. Imp. Akademii nauk, 1770. This is a translation by Vasilii Svetov of Stritter's *Byzantinae historiae scriptores.* Paris: Ex. Typ. Regia, 1648–1702.

Simoni, P. K. *Pamiatniki starinnogo russkogo iazyka i slovesnosti, XV–XVIII st.* [Sources of old Russian language and literature, 15th–18th centuries]. St. Petersburg: Akademiia nauk, 1922.

Simonov, R. A. *Kirik Novgorodets—uchenyi XII veka* [Kirik the Novgorodian—a twelfth-century scholar]. Moscow: Nauka, 1980.

Simson, P. F. *Istoriia Serpukhova* [History of Serpukhov]. Moscow: T. Ris, 1880. Reprint, Moscow: Arkheograficheskii tsentr, 1992.

———. *Opisanie rukopisei, prinadlezhashchikh P. F. Simsonu* [A description of manuscripts belonging to P. F. Simson]. Tver: Izd. Tverskoi uchenoi arkhivnoi komissii, 1902.

Smith, Gerald. "A. V. Pozdneev and the Russian 'Literary' Song." *Journal of European Studies* 5 (1975): 177–89.

Smolenskii, S. V. *Kratkoe opisanie drevnego (XII–XIII veka) znamennogo Irmologa, prinadlezhashchego Voskresenskomu, "Novyi Ierusalim" imenuemomu, monastyriu* [A brief description of the old notated Irmologii (of the twelfth-thirteenth century) belonging to the Resurrection Monastery, called New Jerusalem]. Kazan: Tip. Imp. universiteta, 1887.

———. "Neskol'ko novykh dannykh o tak naz. kondakarnom znameni" [Some new data about the so-called *kondakarnaia* notation]. *RMG* (1913), nos. 44–47, 49.

————. *Obzor istoricheskikh kontsertov Sinodal'nogo uchilishcha tserkovnogo peniia v 1895 g.* [A survey of historical concerts of church singing at the Synodal School in 1895]. Moscow: Sinodal'naia tip., 1895.

————. "O drevnerusskikh pevcheskikh notatsiiakh" [On old Russian chant notations]. *Pamiatniki drevnei pis'mennosti i iskusstva* [Monuments of early writing and art] 145 [St. Petersburg:] I. N. Skorokhodom, 1901.

————. "O sobranii russkikh drevne-pevcheskikh rukopisei v Moskovskom Sinodal'nom uchilishche tserkovnogo peniia" [On the collection of old Russian singing manuscripts at the Moscow Synodal School of Church Singing]. *RMG* (1899), nos. 3–14.

————. Review of V. M. Metallov, *Bogosluzhebnoe penie russkoi tserkvi* [Liturgical singing in the Russian Church]. *Otchet Akademii nauk* [Report of the Academy of Sciences] (1909).

————. "Znachenie XVII v. i ego 'kantov' i 'psal'mov' v oblasti sovremennogo tserkovnogo peniia t. n. 'prostogo napeva'" [The significance of the 17th century and its *kanty* and psalm settings in the realm of contemporary church singing of the so-called simple chant]. *Muzykal'naia starina* [Musical antiquity] 5 (1911).

Snegirev, I. M. *Russkie prostonarodnye prazdniki i suevernye obriady* [Russian folk festivals and super-stitious rituals]. Moscow: Universitetskaia tip., 1837.

Sobranie pisem tsaria Alekseia Mikhailovicha [Collection of letters of Tsar Aleksei Mikhailovich]. Moscow: Tip. V. Got'e, 1856.

Sokolov, D. P. *A Manual of the Orthodox Church's Divine Services.* Translated from Russian. 1899. Reprint, Jordanville, N.Y.: Holy Trinity Russian Orthodox Monastery, 1968.

Solov'ev, S. M. *Istoriia Rossii s drevneishikh vremen* [A history of Russia from the earliest times]. Vol. 5 of *Sochineniia* [Works]. Moscow: Mysl', 1990. English translation: S. M. Soloviev, *The First Romanov: Tsar Michael, 1613–1634.* Vol. 16 of *History of Russia.* Edited, translated, and with an introduction by G. Edward Orchard. Gulf Breeze, Fla.: Academic International, 1991.

Solov'ian, N. A. "Pesennyi sbornik V. Titova na teksty S. Polotskogo—kak vydaiushchiisia pamiatnik russkoi kamernoi vokal'noi muzyki vtoroi poloviny XVII veka" [V. Titov's song collection on texts by S. Polotskii—as an outstanding monument of Russian chamber vocal music in the second half of the 17th century]. Unpublished *diplomnaia rabota*, Moscow Conservatory, 1978.

Spafarii, Nikolai. *Esteticheskie traktaty* [Treatises on aesthetics]. Edited by O. A. Belobrova. Leningrad: Nauka, 1978.

Speranskii, M. "Devgenievo deianie. K istorii ego teksta v starinnoi russkoi pis'mennosti. Issledovanie i teksty" [The deeds of Devgenii. On the history of its text in old Russian writing. Investigation and texts]. *Sbornik Otd. russkogo iazyka i slovesnosti Ross. Akademii nauk* 99, no. 7 (1922).

Spitsyn, A. "Peshchnoe deistvo i khaldeiskaia peshch'" [The Play of the Furnace and the Chaldean fur-nace]. With an additional note by I. Shliapkin. *Zapiski Russkogo arkheologicheskogo obshchestva* [Notes of the Russian Archaeological Society] 12 (1901): 95–136, 201–9.

Sreznevskii, I. I. *Drevnie slavianskie pamiatniki iusovogo pis'ma* [Old Slavic monuments of uncial writ-ing]. St. Petersburg: Akademii nauk, 1868. Reprint, Nendeln, Liechtenstein: Kraus Reprint, 1966.

————. *Materialy dlia slovaria drevnerusskogo iazyka* [Materials for a dictionary of the old Russian language]. 3 vols. St. Petersburg: Tip. Imp. Akademii nauk, 1893–1903. Reprint, Moscow: Gos. izdatel'stvo inostrannykh i natsional'nykh slovarei, 1958.

————. *Sviatilishcha i obriady iazycheskogo bogosluzheniia drevnikh slavian, po svidetel'stvam sovremen-nym i predaniiam* [Sanctuaries and rituals of the pagan religious services of the ancient Slavs, according to contemporary testimonies and traditions]. Kharkov: Universitetskaia tip., 1846. Reprint, Madison: University of Wisconsin Library, 1980.

————, ed. *Zadonshchina velikogo kniazia gospodina Dmitriia Ivanovicha i brata ego Volodimira Andreevicha* [*Zadonshchina* of the Great Prince Lord Dmitrii Ivanovich and his brother, Vladimir Andreevich]. St. Petersburg, 1858. This is a separate offprint of the article appearing in *Izvestiia Imperatorskoi Akademii nauk* [Proceedings of the Imperial Academy of Sciences] 6 (1858): cols. 337–62; 7 (1858): cols. 96–100.

Stählin, Jakob von. "Nachrichten von der Musik in Russland." In *M. Johann Joseph Haigolds Beylagen zum neuveränderten Russland.* Riga: J. F. Hartknoch, 1769–70.

Starikova, L. M. "Dokumental'nye utochneniia k istorii teatra v Rossii petrovskogo vremeni" [Some documentary clarification on the history of the theater in Russia in the Petrine era]. *PKNO for 1997* (1998): 179–90.

————. "K istorii domashnikh krepostnykh teatrov i orkestrov v Rossii kontsa XVII–XVIII vv." [Toward a history of domestic serf theaters and orchestras in Russia at the end of the 17th and in the 18th century]. *PKNO for 1991* (1997): 53–65.

————. "Russkii teatr petrovskogo vremeni, komedial'naia khramina i domashnie komedii tsarevny Natal'i Alekseevny" [Russian theater of the Petrine era, the theatrical quarters ("comedy mansion") and the domestic theater of Tsarevna Natal'ia Alekseevna]. *PKNO for 1990* (1992): 137–56.

Stasov, V. V. "Katakomba s freskami, naidennaia v 1872 g. bliz Kerchi" [Catacomb with frescoes, discovered in 1872 near Kerch]. In *Sobranie sochinenii* [A collection of works]. Vol. 1. St. Petersburg: Tip. M. M. Stasiulevicha, 1894.

————, ed. *Miniatiury nekotorykh rukopisei vizantiiskikh, bolgarskikh, russkikh, dzhagataiskikh i persidskikh* [Miniatures in some Byzantine, Bulgarian, Russian, Chagatai, and Persian manuscripts]. [St. Petersburg]: Tip. I. N. Skorokhodova, 1902.

————. *Risunki k sochineniiam* [Illustrations to accompany the works]. St. Petersburg: Tip. A. Benke, 1894.

————. *Slavianskii i vostochnyi ornament* [Slavic and Oriental ornament]. St. Petersburg: Kartograficheskoe zavedenie A. A. Il'ina, 1887.

————. "Zametka o demestvennom i troestrochnom penii" [A note on the *demestvennoe* and tripartite chant]. *Sobranie sochinenii* [A collection of works]. Vol. 3 St. Petersburg: Tip. M. M. Stasiulevicha, 1894. Reprint edited by P. T. Shchipunov, *Izbrannye sochineniia* [Selected works], 1: 123–40. Moscow: Iskusstvo, 1952.

Stender-Petersen, A. *Die Varägersage als Quelle der Altrussischen Chronik.* Aarhus: Universitetsforlaget, 1934.

Stroev, P. *Opisanie rukopisei monastyrei Volokolamskogo, Novyi-Ierusalim . . .* [A description of manuscripts of the Volokolamsk [and] New Jerusalem monasteries . . .]. St. Petersburg: Tip. Stasiulevicha, [1891].

Strunk, Oliver, ed. *Source Readings in Music History: From Classical Antiquity through the Romantic Era.* New York: Norton, 1950.

Svetlov, V. "Pridvornyi balet v Rossii" [Court ballet in Russia]. *Ezhegodnik Imp. teatrov* [Annual of the Imperial Theaters]. 1901–2 season, supplement.

Swan, Alfred. *Russian Music and Its Sources in Chant and Folk Song.* London: J. Baker, 1973.

————. "The Znamenny Chant of the Russian Church." *Musical Quarterly* 26, no. 2 (1940): 232–42; no. 3 (1940): 365–80; no. 4 (1940): 529–45.

Sytova, A. *The Lubok: Russian Folk Pictures, 17th–19th Century.* Leningrad: Aurora, 1984.

Thibaut, J. B. "Etiud o vizantiiskoi muzyke" [Study of Byzantine music]. *Vizantiiskii vremennik* [Byzantine annals] 6, pt. 1 (1899): 1–12.

————. *Monuments de la notation ekphonétique et hagiopolite de l'église grecque.* St. Petersburg: Impr. Kügelgen, Glitsch & Cie, 1913. Reprint, Hildesheim: Georg Olms, 1976.

———. *Monuments de la notation ekphonétique et neumatique de l'église latine*. St. Petersburg: Impr. Kügelgen, Glitsch & Cie, 1912. Reprint, Hildesheim: Georg Olms, 1984.

Thietmar of Merseburg. *Dithmarus restitutus Chronicon*. Hanovere, 1707.

Thompson, M. W. *Novgorod the Great: Excavations at the Medieval City Directed by A. V. Artsikhovsky and B. A Kolchin*. New York: Praeger, 1967.

Tikhomirov, N. B. "Katalog russkikh i slavianskikh pergamennykh rukopisei XI–XII vekov, khrani-ashchikhsia v otdele rukopisei Gosudarstvennoi Biblioteki SSSR im. V. I. Lenina. Chast' II (XII vek)" [Catalog of Russian and Slavonic parchment manuscripts from the 11th–12th centuries in the Manuscript Division of the USSR State Lenin Library. Part 2 (12th century)]. *Zapiski otdela rukopisei* [Notes of the Manuscript Division] 27 (1965): 93–148.

Tikhonravov, N. S. *Russkie dramaticheskie proizvedeniia 1672–1725 godov* [Russian dramatic works, 1672–1725]. 2 vols. St. Petersburg: Izd. D. E. Kozhanchikova, 1874.

Timkovskii, R. "Poucheniia arkhiepiskopa Luki k bratii" [The sermons of Archbishop Luke to the bretheren]. *Russkie dostopamiatnosti* [Russian monuments]. (Moscow, 1815), pt. 1: 3–16.

Titov, A. A., ed. *Dozornye i perepisnye knigi drevnego goroda Rostova* [Overseers' records and census books of the old town of Rostov]. Moscow: M. N. Lavrov, 1880.

———. *Iaroslavskii uezd* [The Iaroslav district]. Moscow: I. A. Vakhrameev, 1884.

———, commentary. *Letopis' o rostovskikh arkhiereiakh* [The chronicle of Rostov church hierarchs]. OLDP Izdaniia 94. St. Petersburg: Tip. S. Dobrodeeva, 1890.

———. *Rostovskii uezd iaroslavskoi gubernii* [The Rostov district of Iaroslav province]. Moscow: Sinodal'naia tip., 1885.

Tolstoi, I., and N. P. Kondakov. *Russkie drevnosti v pamiatnikakh iskusstva* [Russian antiquities in monuments of art]. Vol. 4, *Khristianskie drevnosti Kryma, Kavkaza i Kieva* [Christian antiquities of the Crimea, the Caucasus, and Kiev]. St. Petersburg: Tip. Ministerstva putei soobshcheniia, 1891.

[Tolstoi, P. A.] "Puteshestvie stol'nika P. A. Tolstogo" [The journey of *stol'nik* P. A. Tolstoi]. *Russkii archiv* [Russian archive] no. 2 (1888): 161–204; no. 3: 321–68; no. 4: 505–52; no. 5: 5–62; no. 6: 113–56; no. 7: 225–264; no. 8: 369–400.

Totskaia, I. F., and A. M. Zaiaruznyi. "Muzykanty na freske 'Skomorokhi' v Sofii Kievskoi" [Musicians on the fresco "Skomorokhi" at St. Sophia in Kiev]. In *Drevnerusskoe iskusstvo. Khudozhestvennaia kul'tura X–pervoi poloviny XIII v.* [Old Russian art. Artistic culture from the tenth–first half of the thirteenth century], 143–55. Moscow: Nauka, 1988.

Tournefort, Joseph Pitton de. *Relation d'un voyage du Levant: fait par ordre du Roy: Contenant l'histoire ancienne et moderne de plusieurs isles de l'Archipel, de Constantinople, des côtes de la Mer Noire, de l'Armenie, de la Georgie, des frontières de Perse et de l'Asie Mineure . . .* Lyon: Anisson et Poseul, 1717.

———. *Relation d'un voyage du Levant fait par ordre du roy enrichie de descriptions et de figures d'un grand nombre de plantes rares, de divers animaux, et de plusieurs observations touchant l'histoire naturelle . . .* Paris: Imprimerie Royale, 1717.

Tschan, Francis J. *History of the Archbishops of Hamburg-Bremen*. New York: Columbia University Press, 1959.

Tzetzis, I. D. [Τζέτζης, Ι. Δ.]. Η Επινόησις της Παρασημαντικής των κατά τον Μεσαίωνα Λειτουργικών και Υμνολογικών Χειρογράφων των Ανατολικών Εκκλησιών [The invention of Byzantine musical notation in the medieval liturgical and hymnological manuscripts of the Eastern churches]. Athens: n.p., 1886.

Undol'skii, V. M. *Zamechaniia dlia istorii tserkovnogo peniia v Rossii* [Obervations on the history of church singing in Russia]. *ChOIDR* 3 (October 1846), pt. 1: 1–46 [and published as a separate offprint].

Undol'skii, V., ed. "Slovo o velikom kniaze Dmitrie Ivanoviche i o brate ego Vladimire Andreeviche
. . ." [The tale of Great Prince Dmitrii Ivanovich and of his brother, Vladimir Andreevich
. . .]. *Vremennik Moskovskogo obshchestva istorii i drevnostei rossiiskikh* [Annals of the Moscow
Society for Russian History and Antiquities] 14 (1852): materialy, 1–8.

Uspenskii, N. A. *Drevnerusskoe pevcheskoe iskusstvo* [Old Russian singing]. Moscow: Sovetskii kompozitor, 1971.

———. *Obraztsy drevnerusskogo pevcheskogo iskusstva* [Examples of the old Russian art of chanting].
Leningrad: Muzyka, 1971.

Uspenskij [Uspenskii], B. A. "Tsar and Pretender: *Samozvančestvo* or Royal Imposture in Russia as
a Cultural-Historical Phenomenon." In Ju. M. Lotman and B. A. Uspenskij, *The Semiotics of
Russian Culture,* ed. Ann Shukman, 259–92. *Michigan Slavic Contributions* 11 (1984).

Ustrialov, N. G. *Skazaniia sovremennikov o Dimitrie Samozvantse* [Contemporary reports about
Dimitrii the Pretender]. 2nd ed., pt. 1. St. Petersburg: Tip. Imp. rossiiskoi akademii, 1859.

Vagner, G. K. *Skul'ptura drevnei Rusi. XII vek. Vladimir. Bogoliubovo.* [The sculpture of ancient Rus'.
Twelfth century. Vladimir and Bogoliubovo]. Moscow: Iskusstvo, 1969.

Varentsov, V. *Sbornik pesen Samarskogo kraia* [Collection of songs from the Samara district]. St.
Petersburg: Izd. N. A. Serno-Solov'evicha v. tip. O. I. Baksta; 1862. Reprint, Samara: Obl.
tsentral'nogo narodnogo tvorchestva, 1994.

Vasenko, P. G. *"Kniga Stepennaia tsarskogo rodosloviia" i ee znachenie v drevnerusskoi istoricheskoi
pis'mennosti* [The *Book of Degrees* and its significance in old Russian historical writing]. St.
Petersburg: Tip. I. N. Skorokhodova, 1904.

Vasil'ev, V. N. *Starinnye feierverki v Rossii, XVII–pervaia chetvert' XVIII veka* [Early fireworks in
Russia, 17th–first quarter of the 18th century]. Leningrad: Izd-vo gos. Ermitazha, 1960.

Velimirović, Miloš. *Byzantine Elements in Early Slavic Chant.* Monumenta Musicae Byzantinae,
series Subsidia, vol. 4. Copenhagen: Munksgaard, 1960.

———. "The First Organ Builder in Russia." In *Literary and Musical Notes: A Festschrift for Wm. A.
Little,* 219–28. Bern: Peter Lang, 1995.

———. "Liturgical Drama in Byzantium and Russia." *Dumbarton Oaks Papers* 16 (1962): 351–85.

———. "The Present Status of Research in Slavic Chant." *Acta Musicologica* 44 (1972): 235–65.

———. "Der Stand der Forschung über kirchenslavische Musik." *Zeitschrift für slavische Philologie* 31
(1963): 145–69.

———. "Warsaw, Moscow and St. Petersburg." In *The Late Baroque Era: From the 1680s to 1740,* ed.
George J. Buelow, 435–65. London: Macmillan, 1993.

Verdeil, R. Palikarova. *La musique byzantine chez les Bulgares et les Russes (du IXe au XIVe siècle).*
Copenhagen: Munksgaard, 1953.

Veresai, O. M. *Kobzar' Ostap Veresai, ego muzyka i ispolniaemye im narodnye pesni* [*Kobza* player Ostap
Veresai, his music, and the folk songs he performed]. Kiev: n.p., 1874.

Vernadsky, George. *Ancient Russia.* Vol. 1 of George Vernadsky and Michael Karpovich, *A History of
Russia.* New Haven: Yale University Press, 1943.

Vershinskii, A., ed. "Mikulinskaia letopis'" [The Mikulin chronicle]. *Tverskaia starina* [Antiquities
of Tver] (February 1911): 46–53; (March 1911): 38–46; (April 1911): 35–45; (May 1911): 41–44;
(June 1911): 41–48; (July 1911): 34–41; (August 1911): 48–52; (September 1911): 25–29; (October–
November 1911): 27–34; (December 1911): 23–30; (January–February 1912): 63–67.

Vertkov, K. A., ed. *Atlas muzykal'nykh instrumentov narodov SSSR* [An atlas of musical instruments of
the peoples of the USSR]. Moscow: Gos. muzykal'noe izdatel'stvo, 1963. English translation
by Natasha Bushnell Yampolsky. 2nd rev. ed. Seattle: n.p. 1980.

———. *Russkie narodnye muzykal'nye instrumenty* [Russian folk musical instruments]. Leningrad:
Muzyka, 1975.

Veselovskii, A. N. "Razyskaniia v oblasti russkogo dukhovnogo stikha" [Investigations in the realm of the Russian spiritual verse]. *Zapiski Imperatorskoi Akademii nauk* [Notes of the Imperial Academy of Sciences] 45 (1883), prilozhenie 1.

Viktorov, A. E. *Opisanie zapisnykh knig i bumag starinnykh dvortsovykh prikazov, 1584–1725* [Description of expense books and papers of old court departments, 1584–1725]. Moscow: S. P. Arkhipov, 1877.

Villoteau, Guillaume André. "Description historique, technique et littéraire des instruments de musique des Orientaux." *Description de l'Egypte* 13 (1823).

Vlasova, Z. I. *Skomorokhi i fol'klor* [The *skomorokhi* and folklore]. St. Petersburg: Aleteiia, 2001.

Vogt, Albert, trans. and ed. *Constantin VII Porphyrogénète: Le Livre des cérémonies.* 2 vols. Paris: Société d'édition "Les Belles Lettres," 1935–39.

Volkov, N. V. *Statisticheskie svedeniia o sokhranivshikhsia drevnerusskikh knigakh XI–XIV vv. i ikh ukazatel'* [Statistical data about old Russian books preserved from the 11th –14th centuries and an index]. Pamiatniki drevnei pis'mennosti [Monuments of early writing] 123. St. Petersburg: Tip. I. N. Skorokhodova, 1897.

Voltiggi, Giuseppe. *Ricsoslovnik (vocabolario-Woerterbuch) illiricskoga, italianskoga i nimacskoga.* Vienna: U Pritesctenici Kurtzbecka, 1802.

Vostokov, A. Kh. *Filologicheskie nabliudeniia* [Philological observations]. St. Petersburg: Tip. Imp. Akademii nauk, 1865.

———. *Opisanie russkikh i slovenskikh rukopisei Rumiantsovskogo muzeuma* [Description of Russian and Slavonic manuscripts in the Rumiantsev Museum]. St. Petersburg: Tip. Imp. Akademii nauk, 1842.

———. *Slovar' tserkovno-slavianskogo iazyka* [Dictionary of Church Slavonic]. 2 vols. St. Petersburg: Izd. II-go otdeleniia Akademii nauk, 1858–61.

Voznesenskii, I. I. *Osmoglasnye rospevy trekh poslednikh vekov pravoslavnoi russkoi tserkvi* [The octoechal melodies of the three last centuries of the Russian Orthodox Church]. Kiev: Tip. S. V. Kul'zhenko, 1888. [There is an accompanying volume, *Obraztsy osmoglasiia rospevov kievskogo, bolgarskogo i grecheskogo s ob"iasneniem ikh tekhnicheskogo ustroistva, prilozheniia k sochineniiu "Osmoglasnye rospevy trekh poslednikh vekov pravoslavnoi russkoi tserkvi"* [Examples of octoechal Kievan, Bulgarian, and Greek melodies, with an explanation of their technical construction, appended to the work "The octoechal melodies of the three last centuries of the Russian Orthodox Church"]. Riga: Tip. Ernesta Platesa, 1893.]

———. *O tserkovnom penii pravoslavnoi greko-rossiiskoi tserkvi: Bol'shoi i malyi znamennyi rospev* [On the church singing of the Greek-Russian Orthodox Church: The great and lesser *znamennyi* chant]. Riga: Tip. G. T. Korchak-Novitskogo, 1889.

Vsevolodskii-Gerngross, V. N. *Istoriia russkogo dramaticheskogo teatra* [History of Russian dramatic theater]. 7 vols. Edited by E. G. Kholodov et al. Moscow: Iskusstvo, 1977.

Vysotskii, S. A. *Svetskie freski Sofiiskogo sobora v Kieve* [Secular frescoes in the Cathedral of St. Sophia in Kiev]. Kiev: AN Ukrainskoi SSR, 1989.

Vysotskii, S. A., and I. F. Totskaia. "Novoe o freske 'Skomorokhi' v Sofii Kievskoi" [New information about the fresco "Skomorokhi" at St. Sophia in Kiev]. In *Kul'tura i iskusstvo drevnei Rusi* [Culture and art in early Rus'], 50–57. Leningrad: Izdatel'stvo Leningradskogo universiteta, 1967.

Vzdornov, G. I. *Iskusstvo knigi v drevnei Rusi: Rukopisnaia kniga severo-vostochnoi Rusi XII–nachala XV vekov* [The art of the book in ancient Rus': The manuscript book in north-east Rus' in the 12th–beginning of the 15th centuries]. Moscow: Iskusstvo, 1980.

Waugh, Daniel C. "The Library of Aleksei Mikhailovich." *Forschungen zur osteuropäischen Geschichte* 38 (1986): 299–324.

——— [Uo, D. K.]. *Slavianskie rukopisi sobraniia F. A. Tolstogo* [The Slavic manuscripts in the collection of F. A. Tolstoi]. Leningrad: BAN SSSR, 1980.

Weaver, Robert Lamar, and Norma Wright Weaver. *A Chronology of Music in the Florentine Theater, 1590–1750.* Detroit Studies in Music Bibliography 38. Detroit: Information Coordinators, 1978.

Wegner, M. *Musikgeschichte in Bildern.* Vol. 2, no. 4. Leipzig: Deutscher Verlag für Musik, 1963.

Wellesz, Egon. *A History of Byzantine Music and Hymnography.* 2nd rev. and enl. ed. Oxford: Clarendon, 1961.

Wichmann, Burchard von, ed. *Sammlung bisher noch ungedruckter kleiner Schriften zur ältern Geschichte und Kenntniss des russischen Reichs.* Berlin: Bey Georg Reimer, 1820.

Williams, Edward V. *The Bells of Russia: History and Technology.* Princeton, N.J.: Princeton University Press, 1985.

Wortman, Richard. *Scenarios of Power: Myth and Ceremony in Russian Monarchy.* Vol. 1, *From Peter the Great to the Death of Nicholas I.* Princeton, N.J.: Princeton University Press, 1995.

Wright, F. A., trans. *The Works of Liudprand of Cremona.* New York: Dutton, 1930.

Wright, Thomas Temple. "The Presentation of Euripides in Old Comedy." Ph.D. diss., University of Virginia, 1988.

Zabelin, I. E. *Domashnii byt russkikh tsarei XVI i XVII stoletiiakh* [Domestic lives of the Russian tsars, 16th and 17th centuries]. Vol. 1 of *Domashnii byt russkogo naroda v XVI i XVII st.* [Domestic lives of the Russian people in the 16th and 17th centuries]. Moscow: Tip. Gracheva, 1872. Reprint (most recent), from several earlier editions, Moscow: Iazyki russkoi kul'tury, 2000.

———. *Istoriia goroda Moskvy* [History of the city of Moscow]. 2nd ed. Moscow: Kushnerev, 1905.

———. *Istoriia russkoi zhizni s drevneishikh vremen* [History of Russian life from the earliest times]. 2 vols. Moscow: Tip. Gracheva, 1876–79.

———. *Materialy dlia istorii, arkheologii i statistiki goroda Moskvy* [Sources for the history, archaeology, and statistics of the city of Moscow]. Moscow: Moskovskaia gorodskaia tip., 1884.

Zablotskii, M. P., comp. "Opis' moskovskoi meshchanskoi slobody" [Register of the Moscow meshchanskaia quarter]. *ChOIDR* 2 (1860), pt. 5: 1–20.

Zakrevs'kii, N. V. *Letopis' i opisanie goroda Kieva* [Annals and description of Kiev]. Moscow: Universitetskaia tip., 1858.

Zaozerskii, A. I. *Fel'dmarshal B. P. Sheremetev* [Field Marshal B. P. Sheremetev]. Moscow: Nauka, 1989.

Zapiski russkikh puteshestvennikov za granitsei [Notes of Russian travelers abroad]. In Kul'turnaia istoricheskaia biblioteka [Cultural historical library]. St. Petersburg, 1914.

Zenkovsky, Serge A., ed. and trans. *Medieval Russia's Epics, Chronicles, and Tales.* Rev. ed. New York: Dutton, 1974.

Zenkovsky, Serge A., and Betty Jean Zenkovsky, trans. *The Nikonian Chronicle.* 5 vols. Princeton, N.J.: Kingston Press, 1984–89.

Zguta, Russell. "*Byliny:* A Study of Their Value as Historical Sources." Ph.D. diss., Pennsylvania State University, 1967.

———. *Russian Minstrels: A History of the* Skomorokhi. ([Philadelphia]: University of Pennsylvania Press, 1978.

Zhikarev, S. P. *Zapiski Stepana Petrovicha Zhikhareva* [Memoirs of Stepan Petrovich Zhikarev]. Moscow: Izd. Russkogo arkhiva, 1890.

"Zhitie prepodobnogo ottsa nashego Fedosiia, igoumena Pecher'skogo" [The life of St. Fedosii, Father Superior of the Caves Monestary]. Commentary by A. Popov. *ChOIDR* 1 (1879): 1–10, 1–42.

Zimin, A. A. "Iz istorii sobraniia rukopisnykh knig Iosifo-Volokolamskogo monastyria" [From the history of the collection of manuscript books of the Joseph of Volokolamsk Monastery]. *Zapiski otdela rukopisei* [Notes of the Manuscript Division] 38 (1977): 15–29.

————. *Oprichnina Ivana Groznogo* [The *Oprichnina* of Ivan the Terrible]. Moscow: Mysl', 1964.

————. *Rossiia na poroge novogo vremeni* [Russia on the threshold of the modern age]. Moscow: Mysl', 1972.

Znamenskii, P. V. *Rukovodstvo k russkoi tserkovnoi istorii* [Manual for Russian church history]. Kazan: Universitetskaia tip., 1870.

Znayenko, Myroslava T. *The Gods of the Ancient Slavs: Tatishchev and the Beginnings of Slavic Mythology.* Columbus, Ohio: Slavica, 1980.

Zurcinski, J. "Die alte polnische Kirchen-componisten und deren Werke." *Kirchenmusikalisches Jahrbuch* (1900).

Zvereva, S. G. "O khore gosudarevykh pevchikh d'iakov v XVI v." [On the choir of the sovereign singers in the 16th century]. *PKNO for 1987* (1988): 125–130.

Index

References to figures and musical examples are italicized.

Abramychev, N.: *Sbornik russkikh narodnykh pesen* [Collection of Russian folk songs], *131–132*
Academic Bookstore (St. Petersburg), 285
Achermann, Christophor (musician associated with court theater), 251, 394–395n383
Adam of Bremen (historian), 19, 38, 312n60
Adamov, Matiusha (Matiushka, Matvei) (singer), 194, 259, 369n313
Adam's Lament, 205–211, *207–211*, 370n, 376n317. *See also* Church Chant, Types and Notations
Adrian (Patriarch), 401n398E
Afanas'ev (Afonas'ev), Gavrilka (singer), 194, 259, 369n313
Afanas'ev, Maksim (singer), 259
Aleksandropol, 9
Aleksandrovskaia sloboda, 104, 106–107, 195, 365n
Aleksei Mikhailovich (Tsar), 123, 212–213, 247–248, 388n; as composer, 248, 392n377; music at weddings, 248; and new singing styles, 231, 246. *See also* Theater at Court of Tsar Aleksei Mikhailovich
Aleksei Petrovich (tsarevich), 155, 246, 266, 390n372
Alfavit rechei inostrannykh [Alphabet of foreign words, Solovetskii collection], 143–144, 145–152t, 172. *See also* Alphabetic Glossaries
Alphabet (1654), 153–154, 171. *See also* Alphabetic Glossaries
Alphabetic Glossaries (*azbukovniki*), 137, 143–144, 182, 186, 350–351n222; *Alfavit rechei inostrannykh* [Alphabet of foreign words, Solovetskii collection], 143–144, 145–152t, 172; Alphabet (1654), 153–154, 171; *Azbukovnik* [Alphabet, publ. Sakharov], 143, 145–152t; definitions of musical terms compared, 144, 145–152t, *150*,

152–155; definitions of non-musical terms, 144, 153–155; *Kniga glagolemaia Alfavit* [A book called an alphabet], 143, 145–152t, 351n222A; *Leksykon slovenoros'kyi* [Slavonic-Russian lexicon, by Berynda], 143–144, 145–152t; *Se zhe pritochne rechesia* [How to say it correctly], 350n222; *Skazanie o neudob' poznavaemykh rechakh* [An explanation of difficult words], 143; *Slovesa ot grecheskago iazyka* [Words from the Greek language], 350n222; *Tolkovanie neudob' poznavaemym v pisanii rechem* [Interpretation of difficult words found in writings], 154–155, 350n222; *Tolkovanie o nerazumnykh slovesekh* [Interpretation of incomprehensible words], 350n222
Amazons, 3–4
Anacharsis, 3, 300n4, 300–301n5
Anacreon, 2
Anan'ev, Trofim (*gusli* player), 176–177, *176*
Anan'in, Ivan (singer), 259
Anastasia Romanovna (wife of Ivan IV), 195
Anastasius (Greek historian), 17
Andreev, Andrei (court keyboardist), 246
Andreev, Grigorii (singer), 259
Andreev, V. V., *166*, 172, 175, 180, 357n261
Anna (wife of Prince Vladimir, Kiev), 38, 64
Anna Ioannovna (Empress), 411n419B
Anna Petrovna (tsarevna), 278, 281, 405n
Anthony of Rome, Saint, 103–104
Apraksin, Fyodor Matveevich, 405n; musical ensembles associated with, 279
Arabic Travel Accounts: descriptions of musical instruments, 11–14, 43; by Ibn Dasta, 11, 12,

13–14, 303n18; by Ibn Fadlan, 10–11, 12, 13, 303nn18–19; by Al-Farabi, 313n64B; by Al-Masudi, 12, 18, 19, 21, 40, 43
Araja, Francesco, 399n392
Archaeological Sites: Aleksandropol, 9; Black Sea littoral, 4, 6–8, *7, 8,* 9, 301–302n13; Chernigov, 15–16, *15,* 43, 165, 299n, 305n; Chertomlytsk, 9, *10;* Kerch, 6, 8, *8, 9,* 299n; Kiev, 312–313n62 (*see also* Kiev); Nikopol, 299n; Novgorod, 331n, 361n278A (*see also* Novgorod); Panticapaeum catacomb, 4–6, *5;* Sakhnovka (Kiev province), *3, 3,* 300; Simferopol, 8, *9,* 16
Aristophanes, 2, 300n2
Arkona, 18–19, 306n26. *See also* Pagan Traditions: temples and sites of worship
Artamonov, Fyodor (*gusli* player), 177, 360n267
Askol'd (Prince), 33
Assemblies, 269, 277, 278, 412n422
Avvakum (archpriest), 382n353
Azbuki (lists of neumes), 73–74, *74–75,* 234, 320n, 334n. *See also* Church Chant, Types and Notations
Azbukovnik [Alphabet, publ. Sakharov], 143, 145–152t. *See also* Alphabetic Glossaries
Azbukovniki. See Alphabetic Glossaries

Babin, Semyon (singer), 107–108, 259
Balatri, Filippo (singer), 404n
Baryshevskii, Andrei (singer), 259
Basilian Monastic Order, 219
Baskakov, Petrushka (singer), 259
Bassewitz, Henning Friedrich von (Holstein diplomat), 280
Bavykin, Nikolai (singer, composer), 235, 241, 259
Beer (Behr), Martin: conflicting attribution to Bussow, 220, 373n
Beliaev, Stefan (singer, composer), 246, 259, 268

Beliai, Ivan (singer), 259
Bells, 332n; in archaeological excavations, 9–10, *10*, 12, *13*, 15,
302n15, 312–313n62; bell ringing and bell ringers, 100–101,
111, 218, 340n158; descriptions of, 99–100; foundrymen, 102, 104; in Khludov
Psalter, 302n15; in Novgorod,
99–104, 111, 337n143B, 338n149;
in Novgorodian *byliny*, 81; in
processions and ceremonies,
214–215, 217–218, 248, 275; repair
of, 103, *104*; terminology, 101,
214, 336–337n142C, 337nn143A–
143B. *See also Bila*
Belorussia. *See* Musical
Instruments: Belorussian
Berezhanskii, Pyotr (singer), 259
Berge, Gottfried (musician associated with court theater), 251,
394–395n383
Bergholz, F. W. von (diplomat),
267, 363n289, 405n, 412n424;
bandura and folk music, 185–
186, 278, 363n289, 413–414n426;
Holstein ensemble, 278–281,
413–414n426; military and signaling instruments, 410n413;
music at assemblies and weddings, 278–279, 412nn422–422A
Bersen' Beklemishev, Ivan, 192,
366–367n297A
Berynda, Pamva: *Leksykon
slovenoros'kyi* [Slavonic-
Russian lexicon], 143–144, 145–
152t, 154. *See also* Alphabetic
Glossaries
Besov, Tomilo (court keyboardist), 246
Bezborodyi, Markell (singer), 259
Bidloo, Nicholas (physician, head
of Surgical School), 270, 272–
273, 408–409n407A
Bila, 12, *13*, 101, *103*, 218, 304n22,
337–338n147. *See also* Bells
Black Sea Littoral, 4, 6–8, *7, 8*, 9,
301–302n13
Blagoveshchenskii Kondakar, 66,
67, 70–72, *72*, 326n109, 329n116.
See also Kondakari
Blumentrost, Laurentius (phy-
sician): and court theater,
395–396n385
Boethius, 66, 324n101
Bogdanov, Efim (singer), 259
Bogoglasnik, 219, 378n336

Bogoslovskii, B. A.: *Materialy
sobrannye v Arkhangel'skoi
gubernii* [Materials collected in
Arkhangel'sk province, with A.
V. Markov and A. L. Maslov],
89, *90*
Boieldieu, Adrien, 175, 357–358n263
Bomelius, Elisei (physician), 245,
390n368A
Boris Godunov (Tsar), 123;
descriptions of military instruments, 178, 179
Borzakovskii, Andrei (singer), 259
Borzakovskii, Iakov (singer), 259
Branten, Ianus (Janus) (musician
associated with court theater),
251, 395n384
Bremburgh, Quirinus (physician),
245, 390n369
Bunin, Leontii (engraver), 155
Burmistrov, Larion (Lavrentii), 259
Bussow, Conrad, 220, 369–
370n315B, 370n315C; and conflicting attribution to Beer,
373n
Bykovskii, Mikhail (singer), 260,
390n371
Byliny, Kievan: Diuk Stepanovich,
37, 312n59C; Dobrynia, 19, 51–53,
56, 83, 113, 335n125D; echoes of
Byzantine influence in, 36–37;
and *skomorokhi*, 52–53; *Slovo o
polku Igoreve* [Lay of the Host
of Igor], *see* Sources, Literary:
Slovo o polku Igoreve; Solovei
Budimirovich, 43, 52, 84; Vol'ga
Vseslav'evich, 51–52
Byliny, Novgorodian, 331–332n;
characteristics of, 79–80, 125;
comparison to Kievan, 79, 90–
91; Sadko, 79–80, 82–83, *89–90*,
115, 334n125C; and *skomorokhi*,
80, 83, 84–85, 125; Terent'ishche
the merchant, 80–82, 84–85,
90–93, *91–93*; Vas'ka Buslaev, 57,
80–82, 83, *86–88*, 94
Byliny, Songs: "A kak khvalittse
Sotko" [How Sadko boasts],
90; "Gostia Terent'ishcha"
[Terent'ishche the mer-
chant], *91*; "Sadko bogatoi
gost'" [Sadko the wealthy mer-
chant], *89*; "Sadkov korabl' stal
na more" [Sadko's ship put to
sea], *89*; "Terentii muzh" [The
man Terentii], *92–93*; "Vasil'ia
Buslaeva," *86–88*; "Zhil byl

Buslavei divenosto let" [Thus
lived Buslavei ninety years],
87–88
Byliny, Terms: *naigrysh*, 86;
peregudka, *91*;*starina*, 84, 86, 87,
91, 348n215
Byzantium: court traditions, 34–36;
influences on Muscovite culture, 192, 194; music in state
ceremonies, 34–36; musical
influences on Kievan Rus',
37; organs, 34–36, 310n, 311n53,
311n55A, 311–312n56; and St.
Sophia (Kiev), 37, 39–40, 310–
311n; singing, 35–36, 37; visit
of Olga, 34–36, 312n56A. *See
also* Church Chant, Byzantine,
Church Chant, Singers and
Ensembles

Capella, Martianus, 3–4, 301n5A
Carlisle Embassy. *See* Howard,
Charles, Earl of Carlisle
Carnival: in Venice, 269
Carols (*koliadki*), 28
Catherine I (Empress), 264, 283;
coronation music, 281, 282–283,
284, *297*, 414n426A; music asso-
ciated with, 279
Chashi. See Toasts
Chastushka, 91, 125
Cherkasskaia, Maria Iur'evna, 185,
279, 281, 285, 406n
Chernigov, 15–16, *15*, 43, 165, 299n,
305n
Chertomlytsk, 9, *10*
Chinovnik (St. Sophia,
Novgorod): bells and bell ring-
ing, 100–101, 217–218; liturgical
singing, 105, 199, 216–217, 221,
338n149A, 339n155, 379n340
Chinovniki (excluding St. Sophia,
Novgorod), 205, 215–216
Chronicles. *See* Sources, Russian
Chronicles
Chulkov, M. D.: *Sobranie raznykh
pesen* [A collection of vari-
ous songs, 1770–1774], 27–28,
308n47B
Church Chant, Byzantine, 37;
Byzantine musical sources, 60,
62, 63t; Byzantine singers in
Kiev, 38–39, 59, 313n62A; influ-
ence on Kievan practice, 37. *See
also* Church Chant, Singers
and Ensembles, Church
Chant, Types and Notations

Church Chant, Linguistic
Divisions, 66, 319–320n; copyists of *narechnoe penie*, 229,
246, 260, 261, 262, 263, 264,
266, 390n371 (*see also* Church
Chant, Linguistic Divisions:
new istinnorechie); *istinnorechie*,
66–67, *66, 68, 70; khomoniia*,
see Church Chant, Linguistic
Divisions: *razdel'norechie; new
istinnorechie*, 68, *68,* 229 (*see
also* Church Chant, Linguistic
Divisions: copyists of *narechnoe penie*); *razdel'norechie*,
67–68, *68,* 205, 227, 231–232,
325n106, 325n107

Church Chant, Singers and
Ensembles: abuses in singing, 68, 227, 231–233, 325n106,
382n353 (*see also* Evfrosin,
Loggin); bilingual sources and
practice, 69–70, *69,* 215, 328n112;
domestiki, 39, 59; Greek singers in Kiev, 38–39, 59, 313n62A;
Greek singers and hierarchs
in Muscovy, 215, 216, 220, 231,
248, 261, 263, 377–378n329A,
390n371; Greek singers in
Stepennaia kniga account, 59,
64–66, 323n96; instruction,
196, 227–229, *228,* 246, 248, 266,
390n371; in Kievan period, 59,
321n86G; monastic practices,
206, 213–214 (*see also* Toasts); in
Novgorod, 105, 106–108, 196–
199, 332–333n, 339n153, 339n154,
340n158; Old Believers, 67, 68,
70, 72, 219, 242, 282, 375n (*see
also* Old Believers); *pevchie
d'iaki*, 193–194, 214–215, 217,
221, 245–246, 248, 339n155A,
365n, 380n345, 390n370 (*see also
Pevchie d'iaki*); and Stroganov
family, 106–107, 199, 246, 260,
262, 332–333n, 339n154, 383n355;
Ukrainian singers in Muscovy,
216, 246, 259, 260, 261, 263, 264,
265, 266, 370n, 390n371 (*see
also individual names*). *See also
Mnogoletie*

Church Chant, Theorists and
Theory: Khristofor, "Kliuch
znamennoi" [A key to *znamennaia* notation], 374n;
Makar'evskii, Tikhon, 230, 262,
375n, 381nn347–348, 401n398E;
Martem'ian, Shestak, 262;

Mezenets, Aleksandr, 110,
229–230, 233, 263, 322–323n94,
374–375n, 380n346, 381n346A
(*see also* Mezenets, Aleksandr);
Octoechos and theoretical systems, 74–77, 76t, 265, 323n97,
330n121; *Pervoe uchenie musikiiskikh soglasii* [First lesson in
musical concordances], 230,
351n223, 401n398E; *pomety,
see* Church Chant, Theorists
and Theory: terminology;
Shaidur, Ivan, 108–109, *108,*
229, 230, 232, 265, 333n, 340n156;
soglasiia, see Church Chant,
Theorists and Theory: terminology; terminology, 108–
110, *108,* 230, 231, 340n155C;
trichords, *see* Church Chant,
Theorists and Theory:
terminology

Church Chant, Types and
Notations, 319–321n; Adam's
Lament, 205–211, *207–211,*
370n, 376n317 (*see also* Church
Chant, Types and Notations:
penitential and spiritual
verses); *ananeiki*, 69–70, 227,
328n111, 380n343; *azbuki* (lists
of neumes), 73–74, *74–75,* 234,
320n, 334n; Byzantine influence, 59–60, 69, *69, 70,* 75–76,
320–321n; *chashi, see* Toasts;
demestvennoe singing, 39, 105,
106, 213, 265, 371n; *demestvennoe* terminology, 213, 219,
313n62A, 333–334n, 378n335A;
dvoznamenniki, 374n; early
Kievan compositions, 328n110;
ekphonetic notation, 59–64,
61–62, 63t, 68, 321n88, 321–
322n89, 322nn90–91 (*see also*
Ekphonetic Notation); Kazan
notation, 199–201, *200,* 366n;
Kniga glagolemaia Kokizy
[Book called *Kokiza*], 199–201,
200, 366n, 369n314; *kondakarnaia* (kondakarian) notation, 69–72, 71t, *72,* 320–321n,
329–330n117, *329; kriukovaia*
notation, *see* Church Chant,
Types and Notations: *znamennaia* notation; lists of neumes,
see Church Chant, Types and
Notations: *azbuki;* liturgical
drama, *see* Liturgical Drama;
mnogoglasie, 68, 325n106 (*see*

also Church Chant, Singers
and Ensembles: abuses in
singing); Novgorod, 68, 79,
105–107, 107t, 111; penitential and spiritual verses, 205,
219 (*see also* Adam's Lament);
polyphonic settings, 105, 106,
110, 216–217, 227–228, 231, 263,
265, 371n; reforms, *see* Church
Chant, Theorists and Theory;
relationships among vari-
ants and dialects, 70–72, 71t,
329n116; *Stepennaia kniga*
account, 59, 64–66; *strochnoe* (part) singing, 105, 265 (*see
also* Church Chant, Types and
Notations: polyphonic settings); terminology, *see* Church
Chant, Theorists and Theory:
terminology; toasts (*chashi*), 19,
205, 210–213, 215, 370n, 377n320;
troestrochnoe (three-part) singing, 106, 231 (*see also* Church
Chant, Types and Notations:
polyphonic settings); variants
and dialects, 216–217, 262, 264,
371n, 374n; *znamennaia* notation, 70, 74, 106, *110,* 213. *See
also* Sources, Liturgical

Church Chant, Works, 328n110,
380n345; "Blagosloven esi,
gospodi" [Blessed art thou,
o Lord], 224; "Dnes' blago-
dat'" [Today the grace], 221;
"Gospodi vozzvakh tebe" [I
cried unto the Lord], 232; "I
iako vo tmakh agnets tuchen"
[The lamb in darkness],
379–380n342; "I potshchi-
sia na pomoshch'" [And harken to help us], 225, *225;* "Iako
shchedr gospod" [How gen-
erous is the Lord], 215; "Iazhe
obrete o peshchi khaldeistei"
[As we found ourselves in the
Chaldean furnace], 379n342;
"Imeiai prestol nebo" [With
heaven as the throne], 221;
"Izhe neizrechennago mudrostiiu sostavivshii" [In the
unspoken wisdom having cre-
ated], 213; "Kymi pokhvalenymi venetsy ouviazemo" [To
whom do we braid wreaths;
attrib. to Ivan IV], 195, *197–
199;* "Na pole molebne" [The
tyrant would place a furnace

on the place of prayer], 224, *225;* "Na reke vavilonstei" [By the waters of Babylon], 228; "O velikoe miloserdie" [O, Most merciful; attrib. to Ivan IV], 195; "Osanna v vyshnikh" [Hosanna in the highest], 221; "Plachiu i rydaiu egda v chiuvstvo priimu" [I cry and weep as I face the eternal flame], 210, 377n319A; "Prechistomu tvoemu obrazu pokloniaemsia blagii" [We bow before your most immaculate image], 215; "Predstatel'nitsa strashnaia i nepostydnaia" [The appearance terrifying and unashamed], 212, 213; "Sede Adam priamo raia" [Adam sat facing Paradise], 210, *210–211;* "Slavitsia Khristos bog nash" [We glorify Christ our Lord], 212; "Spasi blagovernago tsaria nashego Feodora" [Save our Orthodox Tsar Feodor], 213; "Spasi, Gospodi, liudi tvoia" [Save, O Lord, thy people], 212, 213, 215; "Velichit dusha moia, gospoda" [My soul doth magnify the Lord], 231; "Vladychitse, priimi" [Heavenly Mother, accept or take us], 212; "Voznesyisia na krest voleiu" (You have been raised onto the cross), 212, 213; works attributed to Ivan IV, 195–196, *197–199,* 365–366n, 368n309. *See also* Sources, Liturgical

Church Music, Western Polyphonic Styles: arrival of Ukrainian singers, 246, 259, 260, 261 (*see also* Church Chant, Singers and Ensembles); Diletskii, Nikolai, *see* Diletskii, Nikolai; *kanty, see* Kanty; Kievan square (staff) notation, 155, 246, 263, 370–371n, 374n, 410–411n415; *Kniga, glagolemaia Musikiia* [A book called music], 235; *kontserty, see* Church Music, Western Polyphonic Styles: *partesnoe penie;* Korenev, Ioann, *see* Korenev, Ioann; *Nauka vseia musikii* [The complete science of music], 235, 384n358B; *partesnoe penie,* 213, 227, 231, 235,

241–244, 246, 248, 257, 371n, 403n; *Pervoe uchenie musikiiskikh soglasii* [First lesson in musical concordances], 401n398E; *Sem' svobodnykh mudrostei* [Seven liberal arts], 351n223; singers and composers, 241–242, 259, 261, 264–265; Spafarii, Nikolai, *Skazanie o 7 svobodnykh mudrostiakh* [An explanation of the seven liberal arts], 153, 351n223; theory, 228–229, 234

Church Music, Western Polyphonic Styles, Works: "Blagoslovi dushe moia gospodi" [Praise the Lord, O my soul; Titov], 241, 384n360; "Glasom moim k gospodu vozzvakh" [I cried unto the Lord with my voice; Vinogradov], 241, 266; "Izhe zapovedi" [As commandments], 261; *Mnogoletie* settings, 235, 236, 241, 275, *289, 295,* 384n360; "Na primirenie Poltavskoi batalii" [On the peace at the Battle of Poltava; *kontsert*], 274; "Nebesa ubo dostoino da veselitsia" [Let heavens rejoice; Bavykin], 241

Cimmerian Bosphorus. *See* Black Sea Littoral

Constantine Kopronymos (Byzantine Emperor), 311–312n56

Constantine VII Porphyrogenitus (Byzantine Emperor), 34–36, 312n56A

Cosmas Indicopleustes. *See* Koz'ma Indikoplov

Danilov, Kirsha, 57, 135, 282, 318n83A, 332n, 349n216A; *Drevniia Rossiiskiia stikhotvoreniia* [Old Russian poems], *86–87, 89, 91,* 335nn132,135

Ibn Dasta, 11, 12, 13–14, 303n18. *See also* Arabic Travel Accounts

Deistva. See Liturgical Drama and Actions

Demestvennoe Singing. *See* Church Chant, Types and Notations

Denisov, Semyon (singer), 246, 260, 399–400n397

D'iakovskii (singer), 241, 260

Diletskii, Nikolai (theorist, com-

poser), 228, *228,* 230–231, 233–235, 236, 260, 375–376n; compositions by, 234, 403n; connection with Stroganov family, 199, 233, 260; other theorists and composers cited by, 230, 234, 261, 390n371, 401n398C; terminology used by, 234–235, 242, 381n347A, 384n358; versions and sources of treatise, 233–234, 260, 381n349A, 382n353A, 383–384n357. *See also* Church Music, Western Polyphonic Styles

Dimitrii Rostovskii (metropolitan of Rostov, playwright), 270–271, 404n

Dir (Prince), 33

Diuk Stepanovich. *See Byliny,* Kievan

Dmitrevskii, I. A. (actor), 392n378

Dmitrii (Greek singer), 260

Dmitrii (the Pretender), 186, 201–203; contemporary accounts of, 201–202, 369n314A; music at court of, 201–202; musical imagery in death of, 202, 369–370n315B

Dmitrii Donskoi (Grand Prince, Moscow), 44, 46, 47, 191

Dobrynia. *See Byliny,* Kievan

Domostroi, 19, 196, 366n

Ekphonetic notation, 321n88, 322n90; in Gospel (1519), 60, 63t; in Kupriianov leaflets, 59–64, *61,* 68, 322n91; neumes used in, 60–64, *61–62,* 63t; in Ostromir Gospel, 59–64, 68, 321–322n89, 322n90; relationship to Byzantine sources, 59–60, *62,* 63t, 322n90; relationship to later notations, 60. *See also* Church Chant, Types and Notations

Ekstsellentovannyi bas (*ekstsellentovanie;* ornamented bass line), 242–243, *244*

Elizabeth I, 192–193

Eve of St. John the Baptist (*Kupalo*), 21, 23, 114

Evfrosin: *Skazanie o razlichnykh eresekh* [An account of various heresies], 232, 260, 381–382n352. *See also* under Church Chant, Singers and Ensembles

Ibn Fadlan (traveler), 10–11, 12, 13, 303nn18–19. *See also* Arabic Travel Accounts

Falaleev, Dimitrii (singer), 260

Al-Farabi (philosopher), 313n64B. *See also* Arabic Travel Accounts

Les Faux Moscovites (play by Poisson), 393n380

Felstin, Sebastian de (theorist), 65–66, 324n101

Feodosii Pecherskii (Caves Monastery, Kiev), 39, 175, 179, 313nn62C-63, 316n73B; and church chant, 59; and toasts, 19, 210–212, 377n320. *See also* Toasts

Filippov, T. I.: *40 narodnykh pesen* [40 folk songs, with N. A. Rimskii-Korsakov], 28, *31,* 132–134, *133*

Findeizen, N. F., xii-xiv

Finland: *Kalevala,* 164, *164,* 175–176, 358n264, *359*

Fioravanti, Aristotle (architect), 192, 194, 364n, 368n304

Fireworks, 267

Fletcher, Giles (English traveler, writer), 226, 372n

Florence: in report of Likhachyov, 249

Folk Festivals and Celebrations: Eve of St. John the Baptist (*Kupalo*), 21, 23, 114; *Koliada,* 22, 308n43; *Maevki,* 301n5; *Rusaliia,* 23, 113, 114; *Semik,* 24, 352n228D (*see also* Woodcuts, *Semik*). *See also* Skomorokhi

Folk Songs. *See Podgoloski,* Song Collections and Singers, Songs

Foma and Eryoma (folk characters), 131–132, *131–132,* 158, *159*

Foreign Quarter (Moscow). *See* Moscow

Funeral Customs, 4–6, *5,* 8–9, 11, 12, 34

Fürst, Otto (Artemii) (director of public theater), 270, 271–272, 404–405n

Fyodor Alekseevich (Tsar), 236, 257, 266, 307n40, 385n361; music library of, 248, 392n377, 399–400n397

Fyodor Ivanovich (Tsar), 123, 192–193, 212

Gasenkrukh (Hasenkruch), Timofei (performer in court theater), 254

Gazette rimée (Paris), 250, 393n380

Gerasimov, Dmitrii (Muscovite diplomat), 194–195, 368n307A

Germogen (Patriarch), 231

Glareanus, Henricus (music theorist), 76

Glinka, Mikhail, 235

Godunov Psalter, 137–139, *138, 140,* 155, 226, 379n340. *See also* Psalters

Gogol, Nikolai, 174–175

Golitsyn Family, 387n, 393–394n381, 404n, 414n427

Golitsyn, Boris Alekseevich, 270, 403–404n

Golovin Family, 285, 412n423

Golovin, Fyodor Alekseevich (head of Foreign Office and theater), 272, 404–405n, 409n409

Golovkin, Gavriil Ivanovich, 406n; music at home of, 278, 412n422A

Golutvin, Vladimir (singer), 260

Golysh, Stefan (singer), 106–107, 197–199, 229, 260, 262

Gospels, *95,* 97, *99,* 113

Gosudarevye pevchie d'iaki. See Church Chant, Singers and Ensembles: *pevchie d'iaki*

Grabovskii, Il'ia (singer), 260

Greece (Classical): views of Scythians, 2

Greek Colonies (Black Sea littoral), 4, 299n; Panticapaeum, 4–6

Gregory, Johann (playwright), 251–252, 254, 256, 388–389n, 395–396n385

Grigor'ev, A.: *Arkhangel'skie byliny* [The Arkhangel'sk *byliny*], *87–88,* 90, *92–93, 125–131,* 348–349n216

Guarient, Ignatius Christophorus von (Imperial ambassador in Russia), 269–270, 273, 403–404n, 408n406

Guseinova, Z. M.: revised views of Mezenets, 374–375n

Gusli, 173, 175–178, 357–358n263, *359;* association with Biblical figures, 50, 53–54, 95, 99, 137–143, 155, 170, 175, 317n76B; association with Biblical figures (illustrations), *53, 96, 138, 140–142, 156;* association with *skomorokhi,* 50, 111, 113–115,

118–121, *120–121,* 123–124, 170, 175, 360–361n270C (*see also Skomorokhi*); in *byliny,* 51–53, 81–84, 85; late development and use, 358–360n266, 360n267; in Novgorodian sources, 94–95, *94–95,* 111, 176, 177; performers, 175, 176–177, *176,* 178, 360n267; terminology, 175, 357n261A (*see also* Musical Instruments, Terminology)

Guthrie, Matthew (ethnographer), 354n230; *gusli,* 175, *176;* percussion instruments, 180, *181;* stringed instruments, 170, *171,* 172, *172;* wind instruments, 164, *164,* 165–166, *166, 168*

Gutovskii, Simon (organist), 247, 254, 387n, 391n374A-374B, 391n376, 399n393

Helmhold (historian), 19

Hermannus Contractus (music theorist), 108, 340n155C

Herodotus, 3, 300–301n5

Hoelleman, Constantin (musician in Imperial retinue), 269

Holstein, Duke of. *See* Karl Friedrich, Duke of Holstein

Horns, 164, 308; hunting and ibex horns, 8, *9,* 15–16, *15,* 43; oliphants, 8, 15, 16, 307n35, 354n232

Horsey, Jerome (English representative in Muscovy), 192–193, 365n, 367n302

Howard, Charles, Earl of Carlisle (English ambassador to Muscovy), 250, 388n, 393n380B

Hübner, Johann (horn player, violinist), 273, 279, 281, 283, 284, 406n

Iaguzhinskii, Pavel Ivanovich, 405–406n, 412n422; musical ensembles associated with, 279, 280, 285

Iakovlev, Simeon (composer), 241, 260

Iaroslav the Wise (Prince, Kiev), 38

Iaroslavets, Vasilii (singer), 260

Icons. *See* Sources, Artistic and Iconographic

Igor Riurikovich (Prince, Kiev), 19, 20, 304n21

Ilarionov, Kondratii (deacon), 261, 380n346

Il'in, Iakushko (Iakov) (singer), 261, 390n371

Installation of a prelate. *See*
Liturgical Drama and Actions
Ioakim (Patriarch), 352n227
Ioasaf (metropolitan), 220
Ioasaf II (Patriarch), 220
Iona (metropolitan of Rostov), 124
Iosifov, Tit (singer), 261
Instruction (non-musical), 380n345
Irmologii, 73, *74–75*, 212, 264,
327n109, 339n152
Isaakii Pecherskii (Caves
Monastery, Kiev), 50
Istomin, Karion, 349n, 352n227;
Bukvar' [Alphabet], 155–157,
156–157, 164
Ivan III (the Great, Grand Prince,
Moscow), 105, 111, 368n306;
foreign contacts during reign
of, 191–192, 364n; marriage
to Sofia Paleologue, 192, 194,
364n
Ivan IV (the Terrible, Tsar),
103, 104, 172, 348–349n216;
Aleksandrovskaia sloboda, 104,
106–107, 195, 365n; compositions attributed to, 195–196,
197–199, 365–366n, 368n309;
musical inclinations of, 195, 196,
368n308B; and Novgorod, 104,
111, 116, 195, 331n; singers associated with, 106–107, 111, 196–
199, 217 (*see also* Church Chant,
Singers and Ensembles); and
skomorokhi, 123, 195 (*see also*
Skomorokhi)
Ivan V (co-Tsar with Peter),
385n361
Ivanov, Bogdan (singer), 261
Ivanov, Daniil, (singer), 261
Ivanov, Grigorii (singer), 261,
390n371
Ivanov, Pyotr (singer), 261, 390n371
Iverskii Monastery (Monastery
of the Iversk Mother of God),
180, 213–214

James Fitzjames, Duke de Liria,
284, 415n434
Job (Patriarch), 212
Johan Magnus (Danish prince),
195, 368n308B
John of Damascus, 75
Joseph (metropolitan), 123
Joseph (Patriarch), 234

Kalachnikov, Nikolai (composer),
241, 261, 400n

Kalevala, 164, *164*, 175–176, 358n264,
359
Kantemir, A. D., 363n289, 386n364
Kantemir, D. K., 185–186, 285,
363n289
Kanty and Psalm Settings, 371n,
402–403n; development of
form, 236, 242; fanfare styles
and *vivaty*, 242, 275; and penitential and spiritual verses, 205,
219; Petrine and Post-Petrine,
214, 219, 268, 275, 278, 282–283,
284; and theatrical presentations, 253, 254–255, *254*, 271; victory and celebratory, 274, 405n,
410n414; for victory at Nystadt,
274–275, 279, *288*, 413–414n426;
for victory at Poltava, 274, 405n,
410–411n415. *See also* Polotskii,
Simeon, Titov, Vasilii
Kanty and Psalm Settings, Works:
"Bog nam sila pribezhishche"
[God is our strength and ref-
uge], 237, *237*, 240, 386n363,
386; "Desnitsa tvoia gospodi"
[Thy right hand, Lord], *293–
294*; "Dnes' vozgreme truba
dobroglasna" [Today the sonorous trumpet thunders], 213;
"Dondezhe proidut liudie tvoi"
[Until your people pass], *295*;
"Gospodi, tebe sia az vsem
serdtsem" [O Lord, I shall
praise Thee with all my heart],
239, *239*; "I pokorim" [And we
shall vanquish], *292*; "Kant
na konchinu Petra" [*Kant* on
the death of Peter], *see* "V
slezakh Rossiia vsia pogruzhalas'"; "Khvalite boga v sviatykh
rabekh ego" [Praise God in
the sanctuary of His servants],
239, *239–240*; "Kirie eleison,"
290; "Mnogaia leta" [Many
years], *289*, *295*; "Napadet na
nia strakh" [Fear descends],
294; "Osanna," *291–292*;
"Pobeditel na tebe vospevaem"
[We sing to you, the victor],
294; "Poem [vsi] gospodevi"
[We all sing, Lord], *292–
293*; "Raduisia Rosko zemle"
[Rejoice Russian land], 274,
288; "Raduisia Rossie radosti
skazuiu" [Rejoice as I tell of
Russia's joy], 275; "Silne v zlobe
chto blazhishi" [Powerful

in evil why do you stray],
236, *237*; "Slavoiu i chestiiu"
[With glory and honor], *291*;
"Sotvorizh ftlineemu, gospodi" [Let us create for him, O
Lord], *290*; "Torzhestvennaia
paki vam otrada" [For
you a festive delight], *276*;
"Torzhestvui, likovstvui
Bellona preslavna" [Rejoice,
sing praises, Bellona glorious],
292; "Tsariu Rossiiskii voine
preslavnyi" [Russian Emperor,
in war all-glorious], 275; "V
slezakh Rossiia vsia pogruzhalas'" [Drowned in tears, Russia
wept], *297*, 282–283, 414n429;
"Velichit dusha moia gos-
poda vsekh boga" [My soul
doth magnify the Lord], 240;
"Veselisia Rossiia so otro-
kom preslavnym" [Rejoice,
Russia, with the all-glorious
child], 284; "Vivat," *289*, *291*,
294, *296*; "Vospoem pesn' novu"
[Let us sing a new song], 242,
243; "Vozdvigni nas lezhashchikh i spiashchikh" [Raise us
lying and sleeping], 242, *243*;
"Voznesu tia syi v nebesi" [I
shall praise Thee to the skies],
238, *238–239*; "Vsederzhiteliu
Khriste bozhii syne" [Almighty
Christ, Son of God], 242–243,
244
Karl Friedrich, Duke of Holstein
(ambassador), 278–281, 405n,
412n424, 413–414n426; serenade
for royal family, 279–281. *See
also* Bergholz, F. W. von
Karsakov, Ignatii (hieromonk,
music copyist), 261
Kelch, Christian (historian), 195,
368n308B
Kerch, 6, 8, *8, 9*, 299n
Keyboard Instruments (excluding
organs), 285; in Horsey, 192–
193, 365n, 367n302; sale of, 284,
414–415n433; terminology, 139,
246, 364n291A, 391n373, 406n,
406n398P. *See also* Musical
Instruments, Organs and
Organists
Kherugovskii, Grigorii (music
copyist), 246, 261, 399–400n397
Khludov Psalter, 46, *46*, 53–54, 154,
302n15. *See also* Psalters

Khorovod, 14, 21, 23; *khorovod* song, 28, 132–134, *133;* in St. Sophia fresco and revised interpretations of, 39, 310–311n
Khrisanf (singer), 261
Khristianin, Fyodor. *See* Kristianin, Fyodor
Khristofor (monk, theorist): "Kliuch znamennoi" [A key to *znamennaia* notation], 374n
Khrunov (balalaika player), 357n261
Kiev, 12–13, 38; Desiatinnaia Church (Church of the Tithe), 38, 39, 312–313n62; St. Elijah in the Podol district, 20, 304n21; St. Sophia, 36, 37, 38, 39–42, *41,* 310–311n; Vydubitskii Monastery, 38. *See also Byliny,* Kievan, Church Chant, Singers and Ensembles, Sources, Literary
Kiev Academy, 270, 404n
Kinsky, S. W. (Imperial ambassador), 406n; musical ensemble associated with, 279, 281
Kirik (singer, Novgorod), 105
Kirill (metropolitan), 113
Kniga glagolemaia Alfavit [A book called an alphabet], 143, 145–152t, 351n222A. *See also* Alphabetic Glossaries
Kniga glagolemaia Kokizy [Book called *Kokiza*], 199–201, *200,* 366n, 369n314
Kniga, glagolemaia Musikiia [A book called music], 235. *See also* Church Music, Western Polyphonic Styles
Köhlbel, M. (horn player), 410n412
Kokiznik, 199–201, *200,* 369n314
Kolenda, Ioann (Ian) (singer), 261, 390n371
Koliada, 22, 308n43
Koliadki (carols), 28
Kolpenskii (composer), 241, 261
Kondakari, 70, 105, 326n109, 338–339n152; Blagoveshchenskii Kondakar, 66, *67,* 70–72, *72,* 326n109, 329n116
Kondakov, N. P. (historian): and interpretation of St. Sophia fresco, 39–42, 310–311n
Koniukhovskii, Ivan (singer), 246, 261
Konovskii, Klim (singer), 262
Konstantinov, Fyodor (singer), 246, 262, 380n346, 399–400n397

Kontserty. See Church Music, Western Polyphonic Styles: *partesnoe penie*
Korb, Johann (diplomat in Russia), 269–270, 273, 403–404n; musical ensemble associated with, 269, 408n406
Korenev, Ioann (theorist), 232–233, 257, 262, 376n, 384n358A; and Nikolai Diletskii, 228, 230–231, 232–233, 235. *See also* Church Music, Western Polyphonic Styles
Korsakov, Grigorii (singer), 262
Korsh, F. E. (historian): and performance of *Slovo o polku Igoreve* [The lay of the host of Igor], 55, 57, 317n77A
Kostitsa, Ivashka (singer), 194, 262, 368n305
Kotliarevskii, A. A. (historian), 11, 303n18A
Kotoshikhin, Grigorii (Muscovite official), 169, 257, 350n
Koz'ma Indikoplov (Cosmas Indicopleustes), 50, 95, *96,* 137–139, *141–142,* 154, 168, 316–317n73F, 336n138. *See also* Minei: Makarii Chet'ia Mineia
Kral'tson, Ianus (musician associated with court theater), 251, 395n384
Kravchenko, Mikhail (*bandura* player), 185
Kreikenau, Maximilian (musician associated with court theater), 251, 395n384
Krest'ianin, Fyodor. See Kristianin, Fyodor
Kristianin (Krest'ianin, Khristianin), Fyodor (singer), 106–107, 196, 261, 339n154
Kriuk, Iurii (copyist), 262, 399–400n397
Krivopolenova, Maria (informant for Grigor'ev collection), *126,* *128–131*
Kunst, Johann (director of public theater), 270, 271–272, 404–405n, 409n409
Kupalo. See Eve of St. John the Baptist
Kupriianov Leaflets, 59–64, *61,* 68, 322n91. *See also* Ekphonetic Notation
Kurakin, B. I. (Russian traveler), 269, 270, 408n403

Kurbskii, Andrei, 123, 195, 346n210A
Kuz'min, Andrei (singer), 262

Ladoga, 119, *120,* 351n224A, 391n374
Lay of the Host of Igor. *See* Sources, Literary: *Slovo o polku Igoreve*
Lefort, General Franz Iakovlevich, 269, 272, 274, 408nn406–406A
Leksykon slovenoros'kyi [Slavonic-Russian lexicon, by Berynda], 143–144, 145–152t. *See also* Alphabetic Glossaries
Leo the Deacon (Byzantine historian), 23
Leont'ev, Ivan (composer), 241, 262
Leshkovskii, Aleksandr (singer), 262
Leutenberger, Johann (horn player), 279–280, 413n425A
Liapunov, Sergei (clerk), 272, 409n409
Likhachyov, Vasilii (Muscovite ambassador), 249, 387–388n, 392nn377A–377B
Linyova, E. (folk song collector), 86, 317n77A
de Liria, Duke. *See* James Fitzjames, Duke de Liria
Literary Sources. *See* Sources, Literary
Liturgical Books. *See* Sources, Liturgical *and under names of individual sources*
Liturgical Drama and Actions (*deistva*), 215, 219–221, 223, 227, 372–373n; Chaldeans in Play of the Furnace, 224–227, 372–373n, 379n341, 379–380n342; Palm Sunday Procession, 220–221, *222,* 372–373n; Play of the Furnace, 223–227, *223–225,* 253, 339n155, 372n, 378n337, 379n340, 379–380n342; possible role of *skomorokhi* in Play of the Furnace, 372–373n; Procession on the Ass, 220; training of singers for Play of the Furnace, 259, 379n341
Litvinov, Paisii (singer), 262
Liutprand (historian), 34–36, 40
Loggin (Login; Longin) (singer), 196, 217, 231, 232, 262. *See also* Church Chant, Singers and Ensembles
Lopatin, N. M.: *Sbornik russkikh narodnykh liricheskikh pesen*

[A collection of Russian lyric folk songs, with V. P. Prokunin], 26, *29–30*

Lubki. See Woodcut Illustrations

Luhn, Johann and Melhart (organists), 247, 387n, 391n374A

Luke (archbishop of Novgorod), 113

Lukoshko (Lukoshkov), Ivan (singer), 106–107, 229, 232, 234, 260, 262

L'vov, N. A.: *Russkie narodnye pesni* [*Sobranie russkikh narodnykh pesen* (A collection of Russian folk songs), with I. Prach], 24, *25*, 308n46

Macarius (Patriarch of Antioch), 214–215, 220

Maevki (folk festival), 301n5

Makar'evskii, Tikhon (chant theorist): "Kliuch" [The key], 230, 262, 375n, 381nn347–348, 401n398E. *See also* Church Chant, Types and Notations

Makarii (archbishop of Novgorod), 104

Makarii (metropolitan), 323n98

Makarii Chet'ia Mineia. *See* Minei

Maksim Grek, 366–367n297A

Maksimov, Potap (singer), 246, 262, 390n371A

Mamai (Cossack figure), 183–185, *184*

Marais. *See* Théâtre du Marais

Margeret, Jacques, 221, 373n

Maria Miloslavskaia (first wife of Aleksei Mikhailovich), 248, 250

Marina Mniszech (wife of Dmitrii the Pretender), 201–202

Markel (Bezborodyi) (singer), 106–107, 196–197

Markov, A. V.: *Materialy sobrannye v Arkhangel'skoi gubernii* [Materials collected in Arkhangel'sk province, with B. A. Bogoslovskii and A. L. Maslov], 89, *90*

Markus, Maximilian (musician associated with court theater), 251, 395n384

Martem'ian, Shestak: "Slovo o edinoglasii" [A commentary on monophonic chant], 262. *See also* Church Chant, Theorists and Theory

Maslenitsa (Shrovetide), 206, 352n228D, 397n386A, 397–

398n388; in woodcut illustrations, 158–159, *161,* 168, *169,* 170

Maslov, A. L.: *Materialy sobrannye v Arkhangel'skoi gubernii* [Materials collected in Arkhangel'sk province, with B. A. Bogoslovskii and A. V. Markov], 89, *90*

Masquerades, 281; music associated with, 281, 413–414n426

Massa, Isaac (traveler, merchant), 202, 369n314A, 369n314D, 369n315A

Al-Masudi (traveler), 12, 18, 19, 21, 40, 43. *See also* Arabic Travel Accounts

Maszkiewicz, Samuel (diplomat), 186, 221, 373n

Matveev, Artemon (head of Foreign Office), 388n; and theater, 250–251, 254, 257

Matveev, Iva (singer), 263

Maximus of Tyre, 3

Medvedev, Sil'vestr (poet, educator), 196

Melani, Jacopo: *Il ritorno d'Ulisse,* 249, 388n

Meletii (Greek singer), 263, 390n371, 399–400n397

Mel'gunov, I. N.: *Russkie pesni* [Russian songs], 28, *31*

Menshikov, Aleksandr Danilovich, 405n; musical ensembles associated with, 279

Mertz, Justus (resident of Foreign Quarter), 247, 391n374B, 396n385

Meyerberg, Augustin (diplomat), 221, *222,* 373–374n

Mezenets, Aleksandr, 110, 229–230, 233, 263, 381n346A; commissions for reforms, 229, 261, 263, 375n, 380n346; *Izveshchenie* [Report], 110, 229–230, 322–323n94; revised views of biography, 374–375n

Mielczewski, Marcin (composer), 234, 382–383n354, 401n398C

Mikhail (metropolitan of Kiev), 83

Mikhail (metropolitan of Rostov), 59, 64

Mikhail Fyodorovich (Tsar), 117, 119; instrumentalists at court of, 246–247; music at wedding of, 246, 247, 391n374

Mikhailov, Andrei (singer), 263

Mikhailov, Leontii (singer), 263

Mikhailov, Pavel (singer), 246, 263

Mikhailov, Savin (singer), 263

Mikhailov, Semyon (singer), 263

Military and Signaling Instruments, 168–170, 178–180, 355nn242,244, 410n413; foreign models, 46, *46,* 169, 179; in Guthrie, 164–165, *164–165;* in Istomin, 155–156, *156;* in medieval sources, 44–49, *45–46, 48,* 170; in Nikonian chronicle, 44, 164, 169, 179, 180, 361n270D; in Novgorod, 95–97, *97–99;* terminology, 355nn243,245, 360n270B, 367n303, 406n. *See also* Musical Instruments, Percussion Instruments

Miloslavskii Family, 387n, 393–394n381

Minei, 50, 68, 72–74, *73,* 163, 178, 315n73A, 328n109, 330n118; Makarii Chet'ia Mineia (includes Koz'ma Indikoplov), 95, *96,* 137–139, *142,* 336n138

Mnogoletie (polychronion), 36, 212–213, 215, 220, 379–380n342; in Greek, 70, 220, 226, 328n111 (*see also* Church Chant, Singers and Ensembles: bilingual sources and practice); polyphonic settings, 235, 236, 241, 275, *289, 295,* 384n360

Mogila (Mohyla), Pyotr (metropolitan of Kiev), 270, 404n

Molière, Jean Baptiste Poquelin, 250, 409n408

Mollinius, Gottfried (trumpeter), 273, 409–410n412

Monasteries: Trinity-St. Sergius, 206, 217, 231; St. Cyril-Belozersk, 205, 206, 217; Solovki, 267. *See also under individual cities*

Morin, Jean Baptiste, 279, 413n425, *413*

Moscow: Aleksandrovskaia sloboda, 104, 106–107, 195, 365n; Byzantine influence at court, 192, 194; Cathedral of the Dormition, 192, 194, 223, 283, 338n149A, 365n; Cathedral of the Presentation, 232, 382n352B; Chudov Monastery, 196, 264, 380n346; Convent of the Ascension, 202; development under Ivan III, 191–192, 194; Foreign Quarter, 245, 247, 250,

269, 273, 365n, 391n374B, 395–
396n385; Izmailovo, 269, 270,
273, 408n406; *Poteshnaia palata* (Hall of Entertainment),
171, 246–247, 316, 391n374;
Preobrazhenskoe selo (village near Moscow), 215, 251,
270, 272, 397n386; Rasstriginy
Palaty, 272, 369n314D; Slavo-
Greco-Latin Academy, 270,
276, 404n; Surgical School, 270,
272–273, 408–409n407A; Third
Rome theory, 192, 367n297A;
Zaikonospasskii Monastery, 257.
See also under individual rulers
Museums: Hermitage Museum
(artifacts discussed), 6–8, *7–8*,
301–302n13; Music History
Museum, 305n25
Musical Instruments (general),
349n; in Arabic travel accounts,
11–14; in archaeological excavations, *see* Archaeological Sites;
association with *skomorokhi*,
see *Skomorokhi*; Belorussian,
170, 187–188, *187–188*, 355n236;
at Byzantine court, 311n55A (*see
also* Byzantium); condemned
by Church, 97–99, 155, 170, 173,
188–189 (see also *Skomorokhi*,
Gusli); in court practice, 43,
169, 171, 179, 242, 248, 356n251;
definitions in alphabetic glossaries, 144, 145–152t, *150*, 152–
155; folk instruments (excluding *gusli*), 185–186, 278, 281,
411–412n421 (*see also* Musical
Instruments: Belorussian,
Ukrainian Instruments, *and
individual categories of instruments*); in Khludov Psalter, 46,
46, 53–54, 154, 302n15; mixed
ensembles in Biblical illustrations, 137–143, *138*, *140–142*,
155, *156*; mixed ensembles in
Petrine era, 269–270, 273–274,
277–281, *277*, 284, 408n406,
409–410nn412–413, 412n424 (*see
also* Bergholz, F. W. von); in
St. Sophia fresco and revised
interpretations, 39–42, *41*, 310–
311n; terminology, 313n62C-
63, 316n73B, 353nn228F-228G,
353n229, 354nn233A-233B,
354n234, 356n250, 360n270C.
See also Alphabetic Glossaries,
Gusli, Keyboard Instruments,

Military and Signaling
Instruments, Organs and
Organists, Percussion
Instruments, Stringed
Instruments, Theater at Court
of Aleksei Mikhailovich,
Ukrainian Instruments, Wind
Instruments
Mystery and School Plays, 270–271

Naigrysh, 86
Naritsyn, Pyotr (composer), 241,
263
Natalia Alekseevna (tsarevna), 273;
theater associated with, 270,
272, 389n, 404n
Natalia Naryshkina (second wife
of Aleksei Mikhailovich), 248,
250, 388n
Nauka vseia musikii [The com-
plete science of music], 235,
384n358B. *See also* Church
Music, Western Polyphonic
Styles
Nektar'ev, Ivan (singer), 263,
390n371
Nemetskaia sloboda (Foreign
Quarter). *See* Moscow: Foreign
Quarter
Nifont (bishop of Novgorod), 19,
39, 212, 313n62C
Nikiforov, Ivan (singer), 246, 263,
390n371B, 399–400n397
Nikitin, Afanasii, 179, 192, 193,
361n271, 367n303
Nikitin, Faddei (singer), 107, 263,
380n346
Nikitin, Ivan (singer), 263
Nikitin, Prokofii (singer), 263
Nikon (Patriarch), 214, 248, 370n;
and new singing styles, 213,
231, 382–383n354; and religious
pilgrimages, 213–214. *See also*
Church Chant, Singers and
Ensembles, Church Music,
Western Polyphonic Styles
Nikopol, 299n
Nizhegorodets, Andrei (singer),
263, 386n363
Nos, Grigorii (singer), 264,
380n346
Nos, Ivan (singer), 106–107, 196,
229, 264
Nosov, I. (historian): unreliability
of, 392n378
Notation. *See* Church Chant,
Types and Notations, Church

Music, Western Polyphonic
Styles
*Noveishii polnyi i vseobshchii pesen-
nik* [The latest complete and
general songbook, 1818], 27
Novgorod: archaeological excavations in, 331n, 361n278A; bells,
99–104, 111, 337n143B, 338n149;
byliny, see Byliny; characteristics of artistic life, 79–80,
90–91, 110–111; *gusli, see* Gusli;
incorporation into Muscovite
state, 79, 331n; origins and early
history, 16, 79, 331n; plays performed in, 270–271; resettlement of populace, 86, 104–105,
107, 111, 123, 195, 196 (*see also*
Ivan IV); singers and chant,
68, 79, 105–107, 107t, 111 (*see
also* Church Chant, Singers
and Ensembles, Church
Chant, Types and Notations);
skomorokhi, see Skomorokhi,
social and political structures,
79, 331n; trade and foreigners,
79, 84, 331n
Novgorod, Churches and
Monasteries: Antoniev
Monastery, 99, 105, 197,
213, 259; Cathedral of St.
Sophia, 83, 99–101, 102, 104,
105, 220 (*see also* Sources,
Liturgical, and Sources,
Artistic and Iconographic);
Cathedral of the Sign, 95–
96, *97*, 99; Cathedral of the
Transfiguration (Khutyn
Monastery), 96, *98;* Church of
Archangel Michael, 99–100,
106; Church of St. Dmitrii,
100; Church of St. Theodore
Stratilates, 100, 106; Church
of Sts. Boris and Gleb,
82–83, 100; Church of the
Transfiguration of the Savior
on the Nereditsa River, 100,
102; Icons, *see* Sources, Artistic
and Iconographic; Khutyn
Monastery, 96, *98,* 107, 259;
Mechinskaia Church, 100;
Monastery of St. Cyril, 81;
Monastery of St. George, 99,
100
Nydbailo family (*bandura* play-
ers), 185

Obikhodniki, 205

Octoechos. See Church Chant, Theorists and Theory

Oginskii, G., 273, 410n412

Old Believers, 159, 352–353n228E; and church singing, 67, 68, 70, 72, 219, 242, 282, 375n

Olearius, Adam (diplomat), 172, 247, 340n; destruction of instruments, 123–124, 188–189, 343n170, 387n; musical instruments, 159, 170, 177, 246, 346n198A; processions, 221, 226–227; skomorokhi, 119–121, 120–121, 172, 342n168, 351n224A, 391n374

Oleg (the Wise; Prince, Kiev), 33–34

Olga (widow of Prince Igor Riurikovich, Kiev): visit to Constantinople, 34–36, 312n56A

Opekalov (monastery), 108, 339n155B, 400n

Organs and Organists: Byzantium, 34–36, 310n, 311n53, 311n55A, 311–312n56; foreign models depicted in Russian sources, 95, 143, 155; Gutovskii, Simon, 247, 254, 387n, 391nn374A-374B, 391n376, 399n393; illustrated in manuscript and printed sources, 137–139, 140–143, 156, 157, 193; Kievan period, 43, 310–311n; Luhn, Johann and Melhart, 247, 387n, 391n374A; at Muscovite court, 192–193, 245, 246–247, 367n302, 387n; presence in Foreign Quarter, 391n374B; Proskurovskii (Proskurowski), Iurii, 247; in Russian travel accounts, 268; Salvatore, Giovanni (Ivan Spasitel'), 191, 192, 364–365n, 367n300; terminology, 139, 311n53, 311n55A, 313n62C, 313n63; Vasilevskii, Kazimir, 247, 254; Zaval'skii (Zawalski), Fyodor, 245, 247. See also Musical Instruments, Keyboard Instruments

Osipov, Mikhailo (singer), 246, 264, 390n371, 399–400n397

Ostromir Gospel, 59–64, 68, 321–322n89, 322n90. See also Ekphonetic Notation

Pagan Traditions: in Christian practice, 38; in chronicle

and literary accounts, 19–20, 58; gods and idols (excluding Perun), 17–20, 28, 37–38, 306n29, 307n30; music associated with, 18–20, 308n42; musical instruments associated with, 50; Perun, 18, 80, 83, 304n21; songs and singing associated with, 21–31, 42–43, 314n69 (see also Pagan Traditions, Songs); temples and sites of worship, 17–19, 20–21, 22, 23–24, 306n26; toasts, 19, 212. See also Skomorokhi

Pagan Traditions, Songs, 21–31, 42–43; "A my proso seiali [Ah, we have sown the millet], 14; "Ai, na gore" [Ai, on the mountain], 24–26, 25; "Ai, vo pole lipin'ka" [Ai, in the field [stands] a little linden tree], 24; "Gory" [Mountains] and variants, 26–28, 29–30; "Oi na gore" [Oi, on the mountain], 24–25, 25; "Oi, ty roshcha" [Oi, you tiny grove], 26, 26; "Pod lipoiu stol stoit" [Beneath the linden stands a table], 24; "Slava Bogu na nebe" [Glory to God in heaven], 28; "Slaven es', gei, slaven es'" [You are glorious, ah! you are glorious], 28; "Vstavshi rano, ia smotriu" [Having risen early, I look about me], 303–304n19; "Vzoidi, vzoidi, solntse" [Arise, arise, oh sun] and variants, 28, 30, 31; "Za rekoiu, za bystroiu" [Across the river, the rapid river]," 22–23

Paisius (Patriarch of Alexandria), 214–215, 220

Pal'chikov, N. E.: Krest'ianskie pesni [Peasant songs], 26–27, 134, 308n47

Pamfilii (abbot), 170

Panfilov, Grigorii (copyist), 264, 399–400n397

Panticapaeum Catacomb, 4–6, 5

Paraklitike, 322–323n94

Parfent'ev, N. P.: revised views of Mezenets, 374–375n

Paris: in report of Potyomkin, 250

Partesnoe penie. See Church Music, Western Polyphonic Styles: partesnoe penie

Pashkova, Katerina (informant for Grigor'ev collection), 125–127

Patriarchate: abolition of, 245, 276; establishment of in Muscovy, 212; singers associated with, 212, 260. See also Church Chant, Singers and Ensembles, Pevchie d'iaki (sovereign and patriarchal singers), and under individual names

Patriarshie pevchie d'iaki. See Church Chant, Singers and Ensembles, Pevchie d'iaki (sovereign and patriarchal singers)

Paul of Aleppo (cleric, traveler), 377–378n329A

Paulsen, Anna (head of theatrical troupe): and Aleksei Mikhailovich's theater, 250, 394n382

Pavlov, Roman (singer), 264, 390n371

Pecherskii, Aleksandr (monastic elder), 264, 380n346

Percussion Instruments (excluding military), 159–160, 161, 178–181, 180–181, 361n279A; association with skomorokhi, 178, 179, 360–361n270C; foreign models, 169, 179; terminology, 180, 313n62C, 360n270C. See also Musical Instruments

Peregudka, 91

Pereiaslavl: Cathedral of St. Nicholas, 196

Pervoe uchenie musikiiskikh soglasii [First lesson in musical concordances], 230, 351n223, 401n398E. See also Church Music, Western Polyphonic Styles

Peter I (the Great, Tsar, Emperor), 135, 203, 250, 356–357n258, 385nn361–362, 399n393; assemblies, 269, 277, 278, 412n422; and folk music, 171, 278, 281–282; musical tastes of, 267; persistence of pagan traditions, 24; and religious music, 213, 267–268; singers associated with, 246, 259, 260, 263–264, 268, 385n362; social reforms, 257, 270, 273, 276, 282; travels abroad, 267, 270, 403–404n. See also Kanty and Psalm Settings, Musical Instruments, Theater, Petrine and Post-Petrine

Peter II (Emperor), 283–284, 414n432

Petrejus (Petreius), Petrus (diplomat), 221, 373n

Pevchie d'iaki (sovereign and patriarchal singers), 339n155A, 400n; attached to various hierarchs, 215; in ceremonies and processions, 214–215, 221, 248, 391n375C; duties of, 194, 217, 245; establishment of, 193–194, 365n; organization of, 193, 194, 245–246, 390n370; repertory of in "Pokazaniia" [Testimonies], 259, 380n345. *See also* Church Chant, Singers and Ensembles, Liturgical Drama and Actions

Philips, Iacob (musician associated with court theater), 251, 394–395n383

Picart (engraver), 256, *256*, 397n386, 398n388A

Pikulinskii, Vasilii (singer), 264

Pimen (archbishop of Novgorod), 172, 195

Platenschleger, Friederich (musician associated with court theater), 251, 394–395n383

Plays. *See* Theater at Court of Tsar Aleksei Mikhailovich, Plays, Theater, Petrine and Post-Petrine, Plays

Pliasovye (dance) Songs, 25

Plutarch, 3

Podgoloski, 308n47. *See also* Folk Songs, Pal'chikov, N. E.

Poggenkampf, Hermina (actress in public theater), 272, 409n411

Poisson, Raymond (actor): *Les Faux Moscovites*, 393n380

"Pokazaniia" [Testimonies, by singer Anan'in], 259, 380n345. *See also* Church Chant, Singers and Ensembles, *Pevchie d'iaki*

Pokrovets, Pyotr (singer), 246, 264

Polianinov, Matvei (singer), 264

Pollux, Julius 2, 3

Polotskii, Simeon (poet, educator), 371n; Hymn to Saints (*Pesn' sviatym*), 241, 265–266, 385n361, 386n365; plays, 252–253, 254, 256–257, *256*, 398n388A, 398n389; Versified Psalter and musical settings, 219, 236–241, *236–239*, 265–266, 371–372n, 385nn361–362. *See also Kanty* and Psalm Settings, Titov, Vasilii

Polovtsians, 43, 47, 55, 58

Polychronion. See Mnogoletie

Polyphony. *See* Church Chant, Types and Notations, Church Music, Western Polyphonic Styles

Popovskii, Ivan (singer), 264

"Poslanie" to Patriarch Germogen, 231. *See also* Church Chant, Singers and Ensembles

Poteshnaia palata (Hall of Entertainment), 171, 316, 391n374; instrumentalists assigned to, 246–247.

Potyomkin, Pyotr (Muscovite ambassador), 250, 388n, 393n379A, 393n380

Pozharskii, D. M. (Prince), 117, 122

Prach, Ivan: *Russkie narodnye pesni* [*Sobranie russkikh narodnykh pesen* (A collection of Russian folk songs), with N. A. L'vov], 24, *25*, 308n46

Praskov'ia Fyodorovna (tsaritsa): theater associated with, 270

Preobrazhenskoe selo (near Moscow), 215, 251, 270, 272, 397n386

Privalov, N. I.: *Muzykal'nye dukhovye instrumenty* [Musical wind instruments], 167, *167*

Prokopovich, Feofan (rector of Kiev Academy, archbishop of Pskov), 283

Prokunin, V. P.: *Sbornik russkikh narodnykh liricheskikh pesen* [A collection of Russian lyric folk songs; with N. M. Lopatin], 26, *29–30*

Proskurovskii (Proskurowski), Iurii (organist), 247

Protopopov, Ivan (singer), 241–242, 264

Psalm Settings (polyphonic). *See* Kanty and Psalm Settings

Psalters, *94*, 107, 353n228F, 360n270C; Godunov Psalter, 137–139, *138, 140*, 155, 226, 379n340; Khludov Psalter, 46, *46*, 53–54, 154, 302n15

Pskov, 99, 105

Pyotr (metropolitan of Moscow), 195, *197–199*

Radilov (singer), 107, 199, 264, 339n155

Redrikov, Fyodor (composer), 235, 241, 264–265

Repskii, Vasilii (instrumentalist at court), 394n381

Reutenfels, Jacob (foreigner in Muscovy): and court theater, 255, 399n394

Rezvitskii, Iakov (composer), 265

Rigel'man, A. I. (historian), 182, 362–363n286

Rimskii-Korsakov, N. A., 24; *40 narodnykh pesen* [40 folk songs, with T. I. Filippov], 28, *31*, 132–134, *133; Russkie narodnye pesni* [Russian folk songs], 348n211, 358n265, *360*

Rinhuber, Laurentius (foreigner in Muscovy): and court theater, 254, 396–397n385, 397n386

Riurik (Prince, founder of ruling dynasty), 33

Riurik Rostislavich (Prince), 43

Rogov, Savva (singer), 106–107, 197, 199, 229, 264, 265

Rogov, Vasilii (singer), 106–107, 197, 199, 229, 265, 339n153

Roizman, Leonid: and presence of organs in Foreign Quarter, 391n374B

Romanov, Nikita Ivanovich, 257, 387n, 393–394n381

Rostov, 106, 124; chants performed in, 70; plays performed in, 270–271, 404n

Rostovskii, Dimitrii. *See* Dimitrii Rostovskii

Różycki, Stanisław (Jacek) (composer), 234, 382–383n354

Rummel (horn player), 279–280

Rusaliia, 23, 113, 114. *See also Skomorokhi*

Sadko. *See Byliny,* Novgorodian

St. Petersburg: Ekaterinhof, 280; founding of, 276; Summer Palace, 412n424; Winter Palace, 280, 283

Sakharov, I. P.: *Pesni russkogo naroda* [Songs of the Russian people], 27–28, 347n211

Sakhnovka (Kiev province), 3, *3*, 300

Sakketti, L. A. (music historian), 253, 399n391

Salvatore, Giovanni (Ivan Spasitel') (organist), 191, 192, 364–365n, 367n300

Savinov, Andrei (archpriest), 251

Saxo Grammaticus (historian), 19, 306nn26,26C

Schütz, Heinrich: and Muscovite theater, 255–256, 389n, 397n386

Scythian Culture and Artifacts:
Amazons, 3–4; Anacharsis, 3,
300n4, 300–301n5; Greek views
of, 2; musical instruments, 2–3,
3, 300n3; tribes, 2
Se zhe pritochne rechesia [How to
say it correctly], 350n222. *See
also* Alphabetic Glossaries
Sedoi, Osip (singer), 265
Seliverstov, Ivan (singer), 265,
390n371
Sem' svobodnykh mudrostei [Seven
liberal arts], 351n223. *See also*
Church Music, Western
Polyphonic Styles, Spafarii,
Nikolai
Semik: as folk tradition, 24,
352n228D; in woodcut illustrations, 158–159, *161*, 168, *169*, 170
Shaidur (Shaidurov), Ivan (music
theorist), 108–109, *108*, 229, 232,
265, 333n, 340n156; *Skazanie o
pometkakh* [A treatise on additional signs], 108, 230
Shein, P. V.: *Belorusskie narodnye
pesni* [Belorussian folk songs],
347n211; *Materialy* [Materials],
187–188, *188*
Sheremetev, B. P. (Russian trav-
eler abroad), 268, 407n400B,
409–410n412
Shibanov, Timofei (informant for
Grigor'ev collection), 87, *87–
88*, 91
Shila, Nikita (singer), 265
Shishkov, Gurii (singer), 265
Shrovetide (*Maslenitsa*), 158–159,
161, 206, 352n228D, 397n386,
397–398n388
Shuia, 23, 117
Shuiskii, I. I. (Prince), 117, 122
Sienknecht, Heinrich (oboist), 273
Sifov, Mikhail (singer), 235, 242,
265
Sil'vestr (archpriest, Novgorod),
196, 366n
Simeon Polotskii. *See* Polotskii,
Simeon
Simferopol, 8, *9*, 16
Simon (archbishop of Vologda and
Belozersk), 259
Simonov, Nikifor (singer), 265
Simonovskii, Timofei (singer), 265
Skazanie o Mamaevom poboishche
[The tale of Mamai's bloody
battle], 44, 46–47, *48*, 180,
315n73

*Skazanie o neudob' poznavaemykh
rechakh* [An explanation of
difficult words], 143. *See also*
Alphabetic Glossaries
*Skazanie o 7 svobodnykh mudros-
tiakh* [An explanation of the
seven liberal arts, Spafarii], 153,
351n223. *See also* Church Music,
Western Polyphonic Styles
Skomorokhi, 340–341n; banishment and dispersal of, 86,
98–99, 111, 117, 123, 124, 135, 195,
343n170; and bears, 114, 115,
116, 117, 119, 120–121, 123, 124,
346n198A; clothing worn by,
113, 114; condemnation and
prohibition of, 97–99, 113–
115, 121–124, 248, 348n214; in
Belorussian ensembles, 188;
in *byliny*, 52–53, 80, 83, 84–85,
125; depictions of, 95, *95*, 113,
119–121, *120–121*, 157–161, *158–
161*; folk festivals and celebrations, 113–114, 348n214; funerals,
114, 115; musical instruments
associated with, 50, 111, 113–
121, 123–124, 168, 170, 175, 360–
361n270C (*see also Skomorokhi:*
depictions of); in Olearius,
119–121, *120–121*, 123–124, 172,
342n168, 346n198A, 391n374;
origins of term, 341n159; possible roles in liturgical drama,
372–373n; puppets and theater,
114, 119, 120–121, *121*, 342nn167–
168; references in Muscovite
sources, 117–119, 121–124,
343n173, 346n204; references
in Novgorodian sources, 111,
115–116, 344–345n176, 345nn177–
179, 345nn186,188; references
in other sources, 113–114; in
St. Sophia fresco and revised
interpretations, 39–42, *41*, 310–
311n; songs, *see Skomorokhi,*
Songs Associated with; and
thievery, 122–123, *130–131*, 346–
348n211, 349n216A; in urban
settings, 117–119; and weddings,
114, 115, 342n169
Skomorokhi, Songs Associated
with, 91, *91–93*, 125–134, *125–134*,
135, 348n215; "A Erema zhil na
gorke" [Eryoma lived on a little hill], 131–132, *131–132*; "A kak
by kto zhe skomoroshechka da
podvez?" [Who would want

to give the *skomorokh* a lift?],
342n169; "A Kostriuk poskakivaet" [And Kostriuk keeps
on hopping], 348–349n216;
"Ai, matushka Likova" [Ai,
mother Likova], 347n211; "Akh,
Suzdal'tsy, Volodimertsy"
[Ah, you folks from Suzdal'
and from Vladimir], 347n211;
"Bychok" [Fish (or bullhead)],
134, *134*; "Dala lyn', dala lyn'!
Po iaichen'ku!" [Dala-lyn,
dala-lyn, an egg for each!],
348n211; "Gostia Terent'ishcha"
[Terent'ishche the merchant],
91; "Ishli-briali volochebniki"
[The dragging singers went
with a bang and a clatter],
347n211; "Kostriuk," 127, *128–
130*; "Nebylitsa" [An invented
tale], *125–126*; "Nebylitsa v litsiakh" [Invented tale], 125,
126; "Puteshestvie Vavily so
skomorokhami" [Vavilo's journey with the *skomorokhi*], 127,
128; "Terentii muzh" [The man
Terentii], *92–93*; "U vorot, vorot
batiushkinykh" [By the gates,
by my father's gates], 132–134,
133; "Usishcha grabiat bogatogo
krest'ianina" [Usishcha (and his
gang) rob the rich peasant], 127,
130–131; "Vdova i tri docheri"
[The widow and three daugh-
ters], 127, *126–127*; "Zaprech' zhe
by vorona konia" [Get a black
horse], 342n169
Slavo-Greco-Latin Academy
(Moscow), 270, 276, 404n
Slavs: described by Greek historians, 17; origins of, 16–17; music
associated with, 17; as musicians in Byzantium, 33
Slovesa ot grecheskago iazyka
[Words from the Greek lan-
guage], 350n222. *See also*
Alphabetic Glossaries
Slovo o polku Igoreve [The lay of
the host of Igor], 18, 44, 191,
309n; *gusli* in, 53, 170, 175, *176*;
as sung, 54–58
Sluzhebnik, 94
Smolenskii, Osip (*gusli* player), 177
Smolenskii, S. V. (music historian): and *Stepennaia kniga*,
65, 323n96. *See also Stepennaia
kniga*

Sofia Alekseevna (tsarevna), 236, *236*, 265, 385n362, 402n398L

Sofia Paleologue (wife of Ivan III), 192, 194

Solovei Budimirovich. *See Byliny, Kievan*

Song Collections and Singers, 305n; Abramychev, N., *Sbornik russkikh narodnykh pesen* [Collection of Russian folk songs], *131–132*; Chulkov, M. D., *Sobranie raznykh pesen* [A collection of various songs, 1770–1774], 27–28, 308n47B; Danilov, Kirsha, *Drevniia Rossiiskiia stikhotvoreniia* [Old Russian poems], *86–87, 89, 91*; Filippov, T. I., and Rimskii-Korsakov, N. A., *40 narodnykh pesen* [40 folk songs], 28,*31*, 132–134, *133*; Grigor'ev, A., *Arkhangel'skie byliny* [The Arkhangel'sk *byliny*], 87–88, 90, *92–93*, 125–131, 348–349n216; Krivopolenova, Maria (informant for Grigor'ev collection), *126, 128–131*; Lopatin, N. M., and V. P. Prokunin, *Sbornik russkikh narodnykh liricheskikh pesen* [A collection of Russian lyric folk songs], 26, *29–30*; L'vov, N. A., and I. Prach, *Russkie narodnye pesni* [*Sobranie russkikh narodnykh pesen* (A collection of Russian folk songs)], *24*, *25*, 308n46; Markov, A. V., A. L. Maslov, and B. A. Bogoslovskii, *Materialy sobrannye v Arkhangel'skoi gubernii* [Materials collected in Arkhangel'sk province], 89, *90*; Mel'gunov, I. N., *Russkie pesni* [Russian songs], 28,*31*; *Noveishii polnyi i vseobshchii pesennik* [The latest complete and general songbook, 1818], 27; Pal'chikov, N. E., *Krest'ianskie pesni* [Peasant songs], *26–27, 134*, 308n47; Pashkova, Katerina (informant for Grigor'ev collection), *125–127*; Privalov, N. I., *Muzykal'nye dukhovye instrumenty* [Musical wind instruments], 167, *167*; Rimskii-Korsakov, N. A., *Russkie narodnye pesni* [Russian folk songs], 348n211, 358n265,*360*; Sakharov, I. P., *Pesni russkogo naroda* [Songs of the Russian people], 27–28, 347n211; Shein, P. V., *Belorusskie narodnye pesni* [Belorussian folk songs], 347n211; Shein, P. V., *Materialy* [Materials], 187–188, *188*; Shibanov, Timofei (informant for Grigor'ev collection), 87, *87–88*, 91; Varentsov, V., *Sbornik pesen Samarskogo kraia* [Collection of songs from the Samara district], 342n169

Songs: "A Erema zhil na gorke" [Eryoma lived on a little hill], 131–132, *131–132*; "A kak by kto zhe skomoroshechka da podvez?" [Who would want to give the *skomorokh* a lift?], 342n169; "A kak khvalittse Sotko" [How Sadko boasts], *90*; "A Kostriuk poskakivaet" [And Kostriuk keeps on hopping], 348–349n216; "A my proso seiali" [Ah, we have sown the millet], 14; "Ai, matushka Likova" [Ai, mother Likova], 347n211; "Ai, na gore" [Ai, on the mountain], 24–26, *25*; "Ai, vo pole lipin'ka" [Ai, in the field [stands] a little linden tree], 24; "Akh pod vyshnei" [Ah, under the cherry tree], 357–358n263,*359*; "Akh, Suzdal'tsy, Volodimertsy" [Ah, you folks from Suzdal' and from Vladimir], 347n211; "Bychok" [Fish (or bullhead)], 134, *134*; "Byli u bats'ki tri syny" [The old man had three sons], 188, *188*; "Dala lyn', dala lyn'! Po iaichen'ku!" [Dala-lyn, dala-lyn, an egg for each!], 348n211; "Gory" [Mountains] and variants, 26–28, *29–30*; "Gostia Terent'ishcha" [Terent'ishche the merchant], *91*; "Hrai, hrai! Ot zakynu zaraz nohy azh za spynu" [Play, play, kick your legs behind your back], 181; "Ishli-briali volochebniki" [The dragging singers went with a bang and a clatter], 347n211; "Kostriuk," 127, *128–130*; "Nauchit' li te, Vaniusha" [Shall I teach thee, Vaniusha], 167, *167*; "Nebylitsa" [An invented tale], *125–126*; "Nebylitsa v litsiakh" [Invented tale], 125, *126*; "Oi bez dudy" [Oh, if there is no *duda*], 187–188; "Oi na gore" [Oi, on the mountain], 24–25, *25*; "Oi, ty roshcha" [Oi, you tiny grove], 26, *26*; "Po boru khodila" [As I was walking through the woods; or, As she was walking through the woods], 411–412n421; "Pod lipoiu stol stoit" [Beneath the linden stands a table], 24; "Puteshestvie Vavily so skomorokhami" [Vavilo's journey with the *skomorokhi*], 127, *128*; "Sadko bogatoi gost'" [Sadko the wealthy merchant], 89; "Sadkov korabl' stal na more" [Sadko's ship put to sea], 89; "Slava Bogu na nebe" [Glory to God in heaven], 28; "Slaven es', gei, slaven es'" [You are glorious, ah! you are glorious], 28; "Stopochki po stoliku" [The shot glasses on the table], 411–412n421; "Svetit mesiats" [The moon shines], 357n261,*358*; "Terentii muzh" [The man Terentii], *92–93*; "U vorot, vorot batiushkinykh" [By the gates, by my father's gates], 132–134, *133*; "Usishcha grabiat bogatogo krest'ianina" [Usishcha (and his gang) rob the rich peasant], 127, *130–131*; "Vasil'ia Buslaeva" [Vasily Buslaev], *86–88*; "Vdova i tri docheri" [The widow and three daughters], 127, *126–127*; "Vstavshi rano, ia smotriu" [Having risen early, I look about me], 303–304n19; "Vzoidi, vzoidi, solntse" [Arise, arise, oh sun] and variants, 28, 30,*31*; "Za rekoiu, za bystroiu" [Across the river, the rapid river], 22–23; "Zaprech' zhe by vorona konia" [Get a black horse], 342n169; "Zelena grusha v sadu shataetsia" [In the garden the green pear tree sways], 358n265,*360*; "Zhil byl Buslavei divenosto let" [Thus lived Buslavei ninety years], *87–88*

Sources, Artistic and Iconographic, 44; Gelatskii Monastery miniatures, 36; Icon of the Miraculous Intervention (Novgorod), 95–96, 97, *97*; Icon of the Vision of Sexton Tarasii (Novgorod), 96, *98*, 169; Khludov Psalter, *see* Sources, Liturgical; Manasses Chronicle, *see* Sources, Literary; St. Sophia (Kiev) fresco and interpretations, 36, 37, 39–42, *41*, 310–311n

Sources, Literary (excluding *byliny* and chronicles), 44; Andrei Iur'evich (*Life*), 50; Anthology of 1300, 113; Cosma of Prague, 115; *Devgenievo deianie* [The deeds of Devgenii], 175; *Domostroi*, 19, 196, 366n; Ephrem the Syrian, 163, 353n229; Feodosii Pecherskii (*Life*), 19, 39, 59, 175, 179, 210–212, 313n62C-63, 316n73B, 377n320; George (saint) (*Life*, in Trinity-St. Sergius Monastery source), 103, *103*; Gregory of Nazianzus, 163, 353n229, 353n229A; Grigorii (monk) (Sermons), 166; Kirill of Turov (Sermon), 50, 316n73E; *Kormchaia*, 307n32; Koz'ma Indikoplov (Cosmas Indicopleustes), 50, 95, *96*, 137–139, *141–142*, 154, 168, 316–317n73F, 336n138 (*see also* Minei: Makarii Chet'ia Mineia); Malalas chronicle, 114, 342n167, 354n233A; *Matitsa zlata* [Golden queen bee], 212, 377n321; Nestor Iskander, 361n270D; Nikitin, Afanasii, 179, 192, 193, 361n271, 367n303; Nomocanons, 163, 166, 353n228G, 356n247; Paisii collection, 19–20, 307n35, 353n229, 354n232, 360n270C; Paterik (Kievan Monastery of the Caves), 316n73B; St. Cyril-Belozersk Monastery collection, 205; *Skazanie o Mamaevom poboishche* [The tale of Mamai's bloody battle], 44, 46–47, *48*, 180, 315n73; *Slovo* [Discourse, sixteenth century], 353n229; *Slovo* [Discourse] of St. Gregory, 19–20; *Slovo*

Khristoliubtsa [The discourse of the lover of Christ], 19; *Slovo o polku Igoreve* [The lay of the host of Igor], 18, 44, 53, 54–58, 170, 175, 176, 191, 309n; *Stepennaia kniga* [The book of degrees], 59, 64–66, 83, 323nn96,98, 324n99; *Stoglav* (document), 114, 171, 201, 229, 325n106, 346n211 (*see also* Stoglav Council); Troitskii anthology, 19; *Tsarstvennaia kniga*, 103, *104*, 338n148; Viazemskii manuscript (no. 79, in Society for Old Literature collection), 348n214; Volokolamsk Monastery anthology, 59, 319n86D; *Voproshanie Kirika* [Kirik's inquiry], 19, 212, 307n32, 338n151; *Zadonshchina*, 50, 56–58, 163, 178, 191, 317n80, 353n229, 366nn296C,297; *Zlataia chep'* [The golden chain], 113–114; *Zlatostrui*, 166, 170

Sources, Liturgical, 68, 321n86H; Blagoveshchenskii Kondakar, 66, *67*, 70–72, *72*, 326n109, 329n116; Bogoglasnik, 219, 378n336; Chinovnik (St. Sophia, Novgorod), 100–101, 105, 199, 216–218, 221, 338n149A, 339n155, 379n340; Chinovniki (excluding St. Sophia, Novgorod), 205, 215–216; Godunov Psalter, 137–139, *138*, *140*, 155, 226, 379n340; Gospels, *95*, *97*, *99*, 113; Irmologii, 73, *74–75*, 212, 264, 327n109, 339n152; Khludov Psalter, 46, *46*, 53–54, 154, 302n15; Kokiznik, 199–201, *200*, 369n314; Kondakari, 70, 105, 326n109, 338–339n152; Kupriianov leaflets, 59–64, *61*, 68, 322n91 (*see also* Ekphonetic Notation); Makarii Chet'ia Mineia (includes Koz'ma Indikoplov), 95, *96*, 137–139, *142*, 336n138; Minei, 50, 68, 72–74, *73*, 163, 178, 315n73A, 328n109, 330n118; Obikhodniki, 205; Octoechos, 265 (*see also* Church Chant, Theorists and Theory); Ostromir Gospel, 59–64, 68, 321–322n89, 322n90 (*see also* Ekphonetic Notation); Paraklitike, 322–323n94;

Psalters, *94*, 107, 353n228F, 360n270C; Sluzhebnik, *94*; Stikhirari, 67, 69, 326–327n109, 339n152; Triodi, 66, *66*, 210, 327–328n109, 339n152, 377n319A, 402n398I

Sources, Russian Chronicles, 44–45, 305n, 311n; Gustinskaia, 19, 38; Hypatian, 44, 56, 58, 64, 329n115; interpretations of, 331–332n, 334n122D; language in, 56–59; Manasses, 44, *45*, 315n70; Nestor, 113; Nikonian, 34, 44, 81, 164, 169, 179, 180, 354n234, 361n270D; Novgorod I, 334n125A, 338n148B; Novgorod II, 83, 111, 117, 334n125C, 338n148C; Novgorod III, 82, 334n125A; Novgorod IV, 97, 163; pagan traditions in, 19–20, 33–34; Pereiaslavl-Suzdal Short Chronicle, 113, 341n162; Primary Chronicle (Laurentian text), 33, 39, 79, 83, 163, 179, 356n247; Pskov I, 82, 360n270C; Radziwill (Königsberg) Chronicle, 47, 49, *49*, 169; St. Sofia Annals, 169, 178, 179, 368n306; Sofiia I, 306n26C; Suzdal, 44, 170; Troitskaia, 178; Voskresenskaia, 58–59, 314n69C

Spafarii, Nikolai: *Skazanie o 7 svobodnykh mudrostiakh* [An explanation of the seven liberal arts], 153, 351n223

Spasitel', Ivan. *See* Salvatore, Giovanni

Splavskii, Ian, 272, 409n409

Staden, Nicolay von: role in Aleksei Mikhailovich's theater, 250–251, 254, 394n382

Stählin, Jacob von (academician), 177, 414n432

Starina, 84, 86, 87, 91, 348n215

Stasov, V. V. (historian): and *Stepennaia kniga*, 65–66

Stepanov, Melentii (court keyboardist), 246

Stepennaia kniga [The book of degrees], 83, 323n98, 324n99; and account of Byzantine singers, 59, 64–66, 323n96

Stikhirari, 67, 69, 326–327n109, 339n152

Stoglav (document), 114, 171, 201, 229, 325n106, 346n211

Stoglav Council, 123, 201, 325n106

Strabo, 3

Stringed Instruments, 55, 170–175, *171–174*, 356n251, 357n261, *358;* foreign models, 40–42, *42,* 54, *54,* 95, 139, 155, 157–158, *158–159,* 171–172, 181, 362n282, *362;* terminology, 119–120, 170, 171, 399n393; in woodcuts, 158–159, *159–161, 173. See also* Musical Instruments

Stroganov Family. *See* Church Chant, Singers and Ensembles

Stroganov, Grigorii Dmitrievich, 233–234, 279 (as Andreevich), 383n355, 405n

Surgical School (Moscow), 270, 272–273, 408–409n407A

Sviatopolk (Prince, Kiev), 50

Sviatoslav Iaroslavich (Prince, Chernigov), 50, 316n73B

Sviatoslav Igorevich (Prince, Kiev), 23, 44

Tacitus, 19

Tauride Straits, 3

Terent'ishche the Merchant. *See Byliny,* Novgorodian

Ternopol'skii, Fyodor (singer), 265, 390n371

Theater at Court of Aleksei Mikhailovich, 250–257, 388–389n, 397n386, 397–398n388, 398n389; Gregory, Johann, 251–252, 254, 256, 388–389n, 395–396n385; hiring of musicians for, 250–251, 394–395n383; Matveev, Artemon, 250–251, 254, 257; music in, 252–255, 389n; Polotskii, Simeon, 252–253, 254, 256–257, *256,* 398n388A, 398n389; Preobrazhenskoe selo, 251, 397n386; preparations for, 394n382, 397n386, 399n394; reports on foreign theatrical practice, 248–50, 387n, 393n379–379A, 393n380, 393n380B; Reutenfels, Jacob, 255

Theater at Court of Tsar Aleksei Mikhailovich, Music, 252–255, 389n; "Blagosloven esi gospodi" [Blessed art Thou, o Lord, in *King Nebuchadnezzar* and in liturgical drama], 253; "Chrez adamovo padenie" [Through Adam's fall, in *The Woeful*

Comedy of Adam and Eve], 252, 398–399n390A; "Kako vosplachiu, kako vozrydaiu" [How I weep, how I lament, attrib. to Esther in *The Play of Artaxerxes*], 253, *254,* 399n391; "O prognevannyi bozhe" [Oh, furious God, attrib. to Amarfal in *Judith*], 253–254, *255*

Theater at Court of Tsar Aleksei Mikhailovich, Plays: *Aleksei, bozhii chelovek* [Aleksei, man of God], 251, 389n, 397n387; *Artakserksovo deistvo* [The play of Artaxerxes], 251–253, *254,* 388–389n, 396n385, 397n386, 399n392; *Iudif'* [Judith], 251, 252, 253–254, *255,* 389n, 398n389; *Komediia pritchi o bludnom syne* [The comedy of the parable of the Prodigal Son], 252–253, 256–257, *256,* 397n386, 398n388A, 399n396; *Malaia komediia Baiazet i Tamerlan* [The little comedy of Bajazet and Tamerlane], 252; *Malaia prokhladnaia komediia ob Iosife* [The little pleasing comedy of Joseph], 252; *O Navukhodonosore tsare* [King Nebuchadnezzar], 252, 253; *Orfei i Evridika* [Orpheus and Euridice, attrib. to Schütz], 251, 255–256, 389n, 397n386; *Tovii mladshii* [Tobit the younger], 251; *Zhalostnaia komediia ob Adame i Eve* [The woeful comedy of Adam and Eve], 252

Theater, Petrine and Post-Petrine, 409n410; associated with Tsarevna Natalia Alekseevna, 270, 272, 389n, 404n; associated with Tsaritsa Praskov'ia Fyodorovna, 270; Bidloo, Nicholas, 270, 272–273, 408–409n407A; Dimitrii Rostovskii, 270–271, 404n; Fürst, Otto (Artemii), 270, 271–272, 404–405n; Golovin, Fyodor Alekseevich, 272, 404–405n, 409n409; Kiev Academy, 270, 404n; Kunst, Johann, 270, 271–272, 404–405n, 409n409; Liapunov, Sergei, 272, 409n409; Mogila (Mohyla), Pyotr, 270, 404n; mystery and

school plays, 270–271; performance venues, 270–273, 283, 409n409; Poggenkampf, Hermina, 272, 409n411; post-Petrine performances, 283–284; Preobrazhenskoe selo, 270, 272; Slavo-Greco-Latin Academy, 270, 276, 404n; Splavskii, Ian, 272, 409n409; Surgical School, 270, 272–273, 408–409n407A; Willich, Johanna von, 272

Theater, Petrine and Post-Petrine, Plays: *Bozhie unichizhitelei gordykh* [God's castigation of proud castigators, at Slavo-Greco-Latin Academy], 271, 409n408B; *Chestnyi izmennik* [The honest traitor, in Kunst and Fürst repertory], 271, 272; *Dafnis* [Daphne, St. Petersburg?], 271, 272, 404n; *Deistvie na strasti Khristovy* [Passion play, Dimitrii Rostovskii], 270; *Dragyia smeianyia* (*Les précieuses ridicules,* Molière), 271, 409n408; *Iosif, patriarkha* [Patriarch Joseph, at Kiev Academy], 271; *Komediia na uspenie bogoroditsy* [Play of the Dormition of the Virgin, Dimitrii Rostovskii], 404n; *Obmanutyi okhotnik* [*Le chasseur trompé,* The deluded hunter], 284; *Orfei v Adu* [Orpheus in Hades], 283, 414n432; *Le pédant scrupuleux* [*Sovetnyi shkolnyi master,* The counseling schoolmaster], 284; *Rozhdestvenskaia drama* [Christmas drama, Dimitrii Rostovskii], 270, 404n; *Strashnoe izobrazhenie* [The fearful representation, at Slavo-Greco-Latin Academy], 271; *Stsipio Afrikan* [Scipio Africanus, in Kunst and Fürst repertory], 271, 272, 404n; *Tsarstvo mira* [The kingdom of the world, at Slavo-Greco-Latin Academy], 271; *Uzhasnaia izmena* [The terrifying change, at Slavo-Greco-Latin Academy), 270–271; *Venets slavno* [A victorious crown, Dimitrii Rostovskii], 271, 409n408A; *Vladimir* (at Kiev Academy), 270, 272

Théâtre du Marais (Paris), 250
Theodosius (Byzantine Emperor), 311n56
Theophanes (Greek historian), 17
Theophilus (Byzantine Emperor), 35, 311n56
Theophylact (Theophylactus Simocatta), 13, 17, 305n22A
Thietmar of Merseburg (historian), 19, 38, 312n59D
Time of Troubles, 123, 227, 231
Timofeev, Stepan (singer), 265, 390n371
Titov, Vasilii (composer, singer), 219, 236, 235–241, 384n359; Hymn to Saints (*Pesn' sviatym*, Polotskii), 241, 385n361, 386n365; *Mnogoletie* settings, 235, 236, 241, 384n360; possible role in court theater, 254, 399n393A; sources and works, 263–264, 265–266, 384n360, 386n366, 402n398M; Versified Psalter (Polotskii), 236–241, *236–239*, 371–372n, 385nn361–362, 386n363
Third Rome Theory. *See* Moscow
Toasts (*chashi*): in pagan context, 19, 212; in Church tradition, 205, 210–213, 215, 370n, 377n320; in *Life* of Feodosii Pecherskii, 19, 210–212, 377n320
Tobol'sk, 114–115, 343n170
Tolbuzin, Semyon (diplomat), 192, 364n
Tolkovanie neudob' poznavaemym v pisanii rechem [Interpretation of difficult words found in writings], 154–155, 350n222. *See also* Alphabetic Glossaries
Tolkovanie o nerazumnykh slovesekh [Interpretation of incomprehensible words], 350n222. *See also* Alphabetic Glossaries
Tolstoi, Peter (Russian traveler), 268–269, 403n, 407nn401–402
Tragoedia Moscovitica, 201
Triodi, 66, *66*, 210, 327–328n109, 339n152, 377n319A, 402n398I
Trofimov, Ivan (singer), 266
Troianovskii, B. S. (balalaika player), 357n261, *358*
Trutovskii, Fyodor (*gusli* player), 175
Tsaryov, Mit'ka (Dmitrii) (singer), 194, 266, 369n313

Ufa province, 26
Ukhtomskii, Fedot (singer), 246, 266
Ukraine. *See* Church Chant, Singers and Ensembles, Church Music, Western Polyphonic Styles, Ukrainian Instruments, *and under individual names*
Ukrainian Instruments, 54, 58, 170, 182, 185; *bandura* and related types, 155, 180–186, *182–183*; *lira*, 158, *158*, 186–187, *186*, 363n291; Mamai (Cossack figure), 183–185, *184*; in Muscovy, 155, 185–186, 278, 281; music in Cossack society, 181, 182–185, *184*, 363n287. *See also* Musical Instruments
Usol'e, 106–107, 199, 234, 262, 332–333n, 339n154. *See also* Church Chant, Singers and Ensembles: Stroganov Family

Varangians, 33, 79
Varentsov, V.: *Sbornik pesen Samarskogo kraia* [Collection of songs from the Samara district], 342n169
Varsanofii (monk), 376n319
Vasil'ev, Aleksandr (singer), 266, 390n371
Vasil'ev, Mikhaila, 266
Vasilevskii, Kazimir (organist), 247, 254
Vasilii III (Grand Prince, Moscow), 103, 192, 194
Vasilii Shuiskii (Tsar), 202
Vas'ka Buslaev. *See Byliny*, Novgorodian
Venice: in Tolstoi's description, 268–269, 407nn401–402
Veresai, Ostap (*kobza* player), 182
Viazemskii, Nikifor (singer), 246, 266, 390n372
Vinogradov, Vasilii (singer), 241, 266
Vladimir (Prince, Kiev), 19, 33, 37, 38
Vladimir (city), 49; Cathedral of St. Dmitrii, 47, 368n304; Church of the Intercession on the Nerl River, 53, *53*, 317n76B
Vladimir Monomakh (Prince, Kiev), 39, 58, 313n63
Vodovozov, A. M. (*gusli* player), 178, 360n267

Vol'ga Vseslav'evich. *See Byliny*, Kievan
Vsevolod (Prince, Vladimir), 47, 49
Vsevolod Iur'evich (Prince, Suzdal), 79

Waldonn, Iohann (trumpeter associated with court theater), 251, 394–395n383
Warsaw: and report of theatrical production, 393n379
Weber, F. C. (diplomat), 356–357n258
Willich, Johanna von (actress in public theater), 272
Wind Instruments (excluding military), 157, *158*, 158–60, *161*, 163–164, 165–169, *166–169*; foreign models, 46, *46*, 139, *143*, 168, 179, 316n73B; terminology, 163, 165–167, 300n3A, 353n229A, 364n291A, 407n401. *See also* Musical Instruments
Woodcut Illustrations (*lubki*), 137, 157–161, *158–161*; "The Banquet of the Pious and the Profane," *160*, 167–168; "Bear and Goat Entertain Themselves" ("The Bear and the Goat"), 159, *161*, 180; Foma and Eryoma, 158, *159* (*see also* Foma and Eryoma); "The Jesters Savos'ka and Paramoshka," 158, *159*, 180; "The Little Old Man Plays the Little *Gudok*," *159;* "The Mice Bury the Cat," 159–160, 167–168, 173, *173*, 179, 282, 352–353n228E; "The Parable of the Wealthy and Wretched Lazarus," 158, *160;* "The Story of *Semik* and of *Maslenitsa*," 158–159, *161*, 168, 169, 170; Vavilo and Danilo, 158

Zadonshchina, 56–57, 178, 317n80, 366n296C, 366n297; Boian and gusli in, 50, 57–58, 163, 191, 353n229, 366n296C
Zagvoiskii, Iosif (singing teacher), 266
Zamarevich, Nikolai (composer), 234
Zarlino, Giuseppe (music theorist), 234
Zaval'skii (Zawalski), Fyodor (organist), 245, 247

Zimmer, Johann (musician in Imperial retinue), 269
Ziusk, Ivan (composer), 234

Zlatoustovskii, Bogdan (copyist), 246, 266, 399–400n397
Zubov, A. (engraver), 277, 277, 411n419A

Zvenigorod: Monastery of St. Savva, 229, 380n346
Zverintsev, Tret'iak (singer), 194, 266, 369n313

Author Biographies

Nikolai Findeizen (1868–1928) studied at the St. Petersburg Conservatory and committed his life to the study of music and music history. In 1894 he founded *The Russian Musical Gazette,* which was published until the revolutions of 1917. After the revolution he was president of the Commission for the Study of Folk Music set up by the Russian State Geographical Society and a member of the artistic council of the State Opera and State Ballet Theater. His crowning achievement was *Ocherki po istorii muzyki v Rossii s drevnei-shikh vremen do kontsa XVIII veka,* published by the State Publishing House in Moscow and Leningrad in 1928 and 1929 and translated here for the first time.

Samuel William Pring (1866–1954), whose home was the Isle of Wight, was an accountant, a student of natural history, and an amateur clarinetist who became fascinated with Russian music and taught himself to read Russian in order to translate works about Russian music into English. His translation of Findeizen's monumental work was commissioned by the American Council of Learned Societies before World War II but was never brought to publication.

Miloš Velimirović is Professor Emeritus of Music at the University of Virginia. His two-volume work *Byzantine Elements in Early Slavic Chant* was published in Copenhagen in 1960. He was editor of the Yale Collegium Musicum series, 1958–1973, and of *Studies in Eastern Chant* (4 volumes, Oxford, 1966–1979).

Claudia R. Jensen received an M.F.A. and a Ph.D. in Music History from Princeton University and studied at the Moscow State Conservatory, 1980–1981. She has published articles in *The Musical Quarterly* and *Journal of the American Musicological Society,* and received a fellowship from the National Endowment for the Humanities for her work on Muscovite music.

Malcolm Hamrick Brown is founding editor of the series Russian Music Studies at Indiana University Press. From the time he was a graduate exchange student at the Moscow Conservatory in 1962, he has been continuously involved in teaching, lecturing, writing, and publishing on Russian, Soviet, and post-Soviet music.

Daniel C. Waugh is Professor Emeritus of History, International Studies, and Slavic Languages and Literatures, University of Washington, Seattle. He is a specialist on the pre-modern history of Russia and Central Asia.